Politics in the Developing World

Politics in the Developing World

FIFTH EDITION

Edited by

Peter Burnell

Lise Rakner

Vicky Randall

OXFORD

UNIVERSITY PRESS

Great Clarendon Street, Oxford, OX2 6DP,
United Kingdom

Oxford University Press is a department of the University of Oxford.
It furthers the University's objective of excellence in research, scholarship,
and education by publishing worldwide. Oxford is a registered trade mark of
Oxford University Press in the UK and in certain other countries

Second edition 2008
Third edition 2011
Fourth edition 2014

Impression: 1

Published in the United States of America by Oxford University Press
198 Madison Avenue, New York, NY 10016, United States of America

British Library Cataloguing in Publication Data
Data available

Library of Congress Control Number: 2016960743

ISBN 978–0–19–873743–8

Printed in Great Britain by
Bell & Bain Ltd., Glasgow

Preface

This fifth edition of *Politics in the Developing World*, just like the previous editions, has benefited substantially from feedback by referees and readers. The editors wish to thank all those who offered comments and also Oxford University Press (OUP) for its decision to commission a fifth edition. We would also like to thank Jessica Smith (Birkbeck, University of London) for her really excellent work updating the bibliography, glossary, and appendix tables. Sarah Iles at OUP has been a tactful, but vigilant, publishing manager, keeping us on our toes and a pleasure to work with.

In terms of content, the fifth edition reflects a decision to slightly reduce the thematic coverage, so as to allow for twelve short country case studies. These case studies, organized around four key challenges facing developing countries, include a newly commissioned account of the Sudan (Liv Tønnessen), as well as a study of Syria (Reinoud Lenders, previously online). In the fifth edition, we also introduce a number of new authors either working alone (Robert Ahearne, writing on the global economy; Anna Persson, contributing a new chapter the state; Vicky Randall, presenting a new chapter on gender and politics in the developing world; Gyda Marås Sindre, writing on Indonesia) or in conjunction with existing authors.

All of the chapters retained from the fourth edition have been revised and updated to include recent global events and developments. Donald Trump's unanticipated election to the White House occurred when this volume was nearing publication, but while it seems bound to have significant consequences for such fields as environmental policy, democracy assistance and politics in the Middle East, it is much too soon to know quite what these will be. The edited chapters contain, among other things, fresh illustrative material and pedagogic content, which extend to new sample questions and guidance on further reading. Throughout, a conscious attempt has been made to emphasize gender issues more adequately, although doubtless there is scope to do even more in this regard. The overall composition of authors is both more international and closer to gender parity.

Finally, the Online Resource Centre contains new extra material that readers of the book are also urged to consult.

New to this Edition

- A brand new case study on Sudan has been added to this edition, increasing the coverage of the African continent.
- All chapters have been updated to increase coverage of the following pertinent themes: refugee movements; the so-called Islamic State; organized crime; the role of social media and social networks in political organization and mobilization; the launching of the United Nations' Sustainable Development Goals (replacing the Millennium Development Goals); and the impact of declining oil prices.
- The Syria case study (previously found online) has been updated and moved into the book.

Guided Tour of Textbook Features

We have developed a number of learning tools to help you to develop the essential knowledge and skills you need to study politics in the developing world. This guided tour shows you how to get the most out of your textbook.

Overviews

Each chapter opens with an overview outlining what you can expect to cover in the chapter.

22

Iraq
A Failing State?

Nadje Al-Ali and Nicola Pratt

Overview

This chapter explores whether Iraq is a failed state and how it arrived at that tion. It examines the period since the US-led invasion of Iraq in 2003, which the dictatorship of Saddam Hussein. It focuses on three areas: the reconstru

---

Overview

Sudan is 'Africa in microcosm', with multiple languages, religions, and ethnicities. The largest geographic nation-state in Africa, spanning nearly 1 million square miles, has had a complex and conflictual political history since its independence from British colonial rule in 1956. Formerly a single country, political conflict between the north and south spawned Africa's longest civil war, which culminated in a peace agreement in 2005 and the secession of South Sudan in 2011. A year after South Sudan's secession, new conflicts over oil erupted along disputed borders between the two states. A civil war erupted in Africa's newest nation South Sudan in 2013. Sudan has remained embroiled in conflict in the western province of Darfur since 2003.

The political and economic marginalization of the regions in the south, east, and west has been a constant feature in Sudan's political history, and has significantly contributed to the country's instability, underdevelopment, and human rights difficulties. Competition for economic resources (both oil and land), as well as ethnic, cultural, and religious divisions, are basic ingredients of Sudan's conflictual

---

Boxes

Throughout the book, boxes give you extra information on particular topics, define and explain key ideas, and challenge you to think about what you've learned.

BOX 4.4 WOMEN IN THE GLOBAL ECONOMY

In 2014, of the approximately 3 billion people in paid employment worldwide, 1.2 billion were women. Women are consistently overrepresented in the agricultural sector, especially in Asia and Africa, and a larger proportion of women are employed in the service sector. Only 18 per cent of the 1.2 billion women were employed in industry (compared to 26.6 per cent of men), indicative of the reality that women tend to be subject to more insecure employment. Wage inequality between men and women is a worldwide phenomenon, and in most countries, developed or developing, women can expect to earn 60–90 per

and especially in the Export-processing z encourage inward in manufacturing produ The factories are oft the poor conditions owing to low wages, Women remain disp (Braunstein 2006), b deemed more passi

---

Key points

Each main chapter section ends with key points that reinforce your understanding and act as a useful revision tool.

---

e ruling party, and pport and resources

tions often played r democratization ylen (1993), for ex- community-based ns and artisanal ventional political n were significant from which to mo- tratization in coun-

KEY POINTS

- Women's experience has been importantly shaped by politics and the state.
- Under colonial rule, policies and ideals of both colonial rulers and nationalist movements had ambiguous implications for women.
- Authoritarian rule in newly independent states offered women few opportunities for political participation. Women have since been extensively involved in movements for democratization, whilst post-conflict situations have more recently offered women

QUESTIONS

1. Why did Syria's uprising commence in a peripheral area of the country and no[t]
2. How, and to what extent, were features of the clan system in Syria instrumenta[l]
   authoritarian regime?
3. Why did the initial Syrian uprising escalate into a civil war and military insurgen[cy]
4. What counter-measures did the Syrian regime take to fight off the popular up[rising]
   to have contributed to the country's civil war?

Questions

End-of-chapter questions probe your understanding of each chapter and encourage you to think critically about the material you've just covered.

FURTHER READING

Basu, A. (ed.) (2010) *Women's Movements in the Global Era: The Power of Local Feminism[s]* overview of national women' movements across the world, written by women wh[o]
ticipants.

Cornwall, A., Harrison, E., and Whitehead, A. (eds) (2007) *Feminism in Developme[nt]* *Challenges* (London and New York: Zed Books) Thoughtful reflections on feminis[t] studies.

Rai, S. M. (2002) *Gender and the Political Economy of Development: From Nationalism* Helpful overview of the field of political economy from a gender perspective.

Further reading

Annotated recommendations for further reading at the end of each chapter identify the key literature in the field, helping you to develop your interest in particular topics.

WEB LINKS

http://africanarguments.org/category/making-sense-of-sudan/   An excellent we[bsite]
Sudanese politics.

https://www.crisisgroup.org/africa/horn-africa/sudan   The International Crisis G[roup]
https://www.theguardian.com/world/sudan   For updated news on Sudan (and S[outh]
https://www.hrw.org/africa/sudan   Human Rights Watch (HRW) on Sudan.
https://www.icc-cpi.int/darfur   The International Criminal Court (ICC) on Darf[ur]
https://www.irinnews.org/afrique/afrique-de-lest/sudan   Irin on Sudan.

Web links

Carefully selected lists of websites direct you to the sites of institutions and organizations that will help to develop your knowledge and understanding.

alternative politics Political activity that emerges 'from below', in the sense that it centrally involves or-dinary people, as opposed to political elites, and takes place outside of formal **politics** and established politi-cal channels, such as parties, elections, and parliamen-tary politics.

apartheid An Afrikaans word meaning 'separate-ness', in South Africa expressed as the official govern-ment policy of racial segregation between 1948 and 1989.

ascriptive identities Groupings to which people be-

Christian demo[cracy] precepts to elect[oral]

civic nationalism an autonomous s[tate]

civil regulation I[n] to a range of activi[ties] tors aimed at crea[ting] and obligation for

civil society A hi[gh] realm of voluntar[y]

Glossary terms

Key terms appear in bold on their first instance in each chapter and are defined in a glossary at the end of the book, allowing you to identify and define key terms and ideas as you learn, and acting as a useful prompt when it comes to revision.

Guided Tour of the Online Resource Centre

http://www.oxfordtextbooks.co.uk/orc/burnell5e/

The Online Resource Centre that accompanies this book provides you with ready-to-use learning materials. These resources are free of charge and have been created to take your learning further.

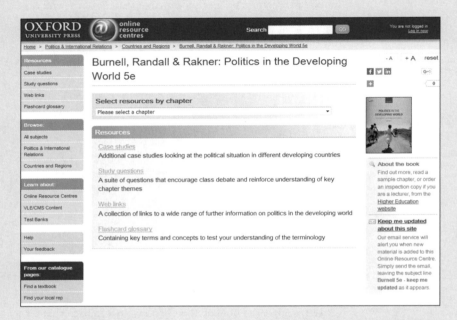

Case studies

Existing case studies on political parties, and on the politics of Zambia, have been updated. In addition, short exploratory 'think pieces' have been included to encourage you to consider the political situations in different developing countries.

Study questions

Additional questions are designed to support your understanding of each chapter and to encourage you to think critically about the material in the textbook.

Flashcard glossary

A series of interactive flashcards containing key terms allows you to test your knowledge of important concepts and ideas.

Web links

Carefully selected lists of websites direct you to the sites of institutions and organizations that will help develop your knowledge and understanding of politics in the developing world.

Brief Contents

Detailed Contents

List of Boxes

List of Figures

List of Tables

List of Abbreviations

9/11	11 September 2001 terrorist attacks on the United States
AAP	Aam Aadmi Party (India)
ADB	Asian Development Bank
AFRICOM	African Command (US)
AIDS	acquired immune deficiency syndrome
AIIB	Asia Infrastructure Investment Bank
AKP	Justice and Development Party (Turkey)
ALBA	Bolivarian Alliance of Latin America
AMAR	All Minorities at Risk project
AMOs	administered mass organizations (South Korea)
ANC	African National Congress (South Africa)
AOSIS	Alliance of Small Island States
APRM	African Peer Review Mechanism
ASEAN	Association of Southeast Asian Nations
Attac	*Association pour une Taxation des Transactions financières pour l'Aide aux Citoyens* [Association for the Taxation of Financial Transactions and Aid to Citizens]
Avaaz	Global civic organization promoting activism on issues such as climate change, human rights, animal rights, corruption, poverty, and conflict
BASIC	Brazil, South Africa, India, and China
BIS	Bank for International Settlements
BJP	Bharatiya Janata Party (India)
BRICs	rapidly developing emerging economies, comprising Brazil, Russia, India, and China
BRICS	BRICs plus South Africa
CACM	Central American Common Market
CAN	Andean Community
CAP	Common Agricultural Policy (EU)
CARICOM	Caribbean Community and Common Market
CBOs	community-based organizations
CCI	Contemporary Capabilities Index
CCP	Chinese Communist Party; Comparative Constitutions Project
CCTV	China Central Television
CDB	China Development Bank
CDSA	South American Defense Council
CEDAW	UN Convention on the Elimination of All Forms of Discrimination against Women
CGD	Center for Global Development
CIA	Central Intelligence Agency (US)
CIS	Commonwealth of Independent States
CIVETS	Colombia, Indonesia, Vietnam, Egypt, Turkey and South Africa
CNDM	National Council for Women's Rights (Brazil)
CNG	compressed natural gas
COMESA	Common Market for Eastern and Southern Africa
CPA	Coalition Provisional Authority (Iraq); comprehensive peace agreement (Sudan)
CPI	Corruption Perceptions Index
CPRC	Chronic Poverty Research Centre
CRG	Centre for Research on Globalization
CSOs	civil society organizations
CSR	corporate social responsibility
DAC	Development Assistance Committee (of the Organisation for Economic Co-operation and Development)
DfID	Department for International Development (UK)
DPD	*Dewan Perwakilan Rakyat* [Peoples Representative Council] (Indonesia)
DPRK	Democratic People's Republic of Korea
DRC	Democratic Republic of the Congo (formerly Zaire)
DSB	Dispute Settlement Body (WTO)
ECOSOC	Economic and Social Council (UN)
ECOWAS	Economic Community of West African States
EIAs	environmental impact assessments
EPB	Economic Planning Board (South Korea)
EPZs	export-processing zones
EU	European Union
FDI	foreign direct investment
FOCAC	Forum on China–Africa Cooperation
FOMWAN	Federation of Muslim Women's Associations in Nigeria
FPTP	first past the post
FRELIMO	Mozambican Liberation Front
FRG	*Frente Republicano Guatemalteco* [Guatemalan Republican Front]
FSA	Free Syrian Army
FSB	Financial Stability Board (BIS)
FSC	Forestry Stewardship Council
FTAs	free trade agreements

FTAA	Free Trade Area of the Americas		**ILO**	International Labour Organization
G2	China and the United States		**IMF**	International Monetary Fund
G7	Group of seven established industrial countries, comprising Canada, France, Germany, Italy, Japan, United Kingdom, and United States		**INDCs**	intended nationally determined contributions
			IPCC	Intergovernmental Panel on Climate Change
			IPU	Inter-Parliamentary Union
G8	Group of established industrial countries comprising G7 plus Russia (and EU representation)		**IS**	so-called Islamic State (otherwise known as ISIS, ISIL, or Daesh)
G20	Group of finance ministers and central bank governors of twenty leading industrialized and developing economies		**ISI**	import-substituting industrialization; Directorate of Inter-Services Intelligence (Pakistan)
G77	Group of seventy-seven least-developed countries		**ISIL**	*See* IS
			ISIS	*See* IS
GAM	Aceh Freedom Movement (Indonesia)		**ISNIE**	International Society for New Institutional Economics
GATT	General Agreement on Tariffs and Trade			
GCC	Gulf Cooperation Council		**ISO**	International Organization for Standardization
GCF	Green Climate Fund		**IT**	information technology
GDP	gross domestic product		**ITEC**	Indian Technical and Economic Cooperation
GEF	Global Environment Facility		**KPK**	Corruption Eradication Commission (Indonesia)
GHG	greenhouse gas			
GM	genetically modified		**KPU**	Independent Election Commission (Indonesia)
GNI	gross national income			
GNP	gross national product		**KWAU**	Korean Women's Associations United
Golkar	*Golongan Karya* [Functional Group] (Indonesia)		**LDCs**	least-developed countries
			LGBT	gay, lesbian, bisexual, trans, intersex, and queer
Hanura	People's Conscience Party (Indonesia)		**MAD**	mutually assured destruction
HCI	heavy and chemical industries		**MAR**	Minorities at Risk project
HDI	Human Development Index		**MAVINS**	Mexico, Australia, Vietnam, Indonesia, Nigeria, and South Africa
HIV	human immunodeficiency virus			
HRW	Human Rights Watch		**MDGs**	Millennium Development Goals (of the United Nations)
IAEA	International Atomic Energy Agency (UN)			
IBRD	International Bank for Reconstruction and Development (World Bank)		**MEND**	Movement for the Emancipation of the Delta (Nigeria)
IBSA	India, Brazil, South Africa		**MERCOSUR**	Southern Common Market (Latin America)
ICCPR	International Covenant on Civil and Political Rights 1966		**MINT**	Mexico, Indonesia, Nigeria, and Turkey
			MNCs	multinational corporations
ICESCR	International Covenant on Economic, Social and Cultural Rights 1966		**NAFTA**	North American Free Trade Agreement
			NAM	Non-Aligned Movement
ICG	International Crisis Group		**NATO**	North Atlantic Treaty Organization
ICJ	International Court of Justice		**NCP**	National Congress Party (Sudan)
ICNL	International Center for Non-Profit Law		**NDB**	New Development Bank
IDA	International Development Association		**NDD**	non-DAC donor
IDEA	International Institute for Democracy and Electoral Assistance		**NEPAD**	New Economic Partnership for Africa's Development (AU)
IDS	Institute of Development Studies (UK)		**NGO**	non-governmental organization
IFE	Federal Electoral Institute (Mexico)		**NICs**	newly industrialized countries (mainly East Asia)
IFI	international finance institution			
IGAD	Intergovernmental Authority on Development (Eastern Africa)		**NLD**	National League for Democracy (Myanmar)
			NPT	Non-Proliferation Treaty
IIED	International Institute for Environment and Development (UK)		**NRM**	National Resistance Movement (Uganda)
			OAS	Organization of American States
IISD	International Institute for Sustainable Development (Canada)		**OAU**	Organization of African Unity

ODA	official development assistance		SPM	Special Secretariat of Public Policies for Women (UN)
OECD	Organisation for Economic Co-operation and Development		TEPJF	Electoral Tribunal of the Judicial Power of the Federation (Mexico)
OHCHR	Office of the United Nations High Commissioner for Human Rights		TI	Transparency International
OPEC	Organization of the Petroleum Exporting Countries		TNCs	transnational corporations
			TTP	Tehrik-i-Taliban Pakistan
OSW	Office of the Status of Women (South Africa)		TWN	Third World Network
PAN	National Action Party (Mexico)		UK	United Kingdom
Partai Nasdem	Nasdem Party (Indonesia)		UN	United Nations
PD	Democratic Party (Indonesia)		UNAMI	United Nations Assistance Mission for Iraq
PDI	Indonesian Democratic Party		UNASUR	Union of South American Nations
PDI-P	Indonesia Democratic Party–Struggle		UNCAC	United Nation Convention against Corruption
PDP	People's Democratic Party (Nigeria)		UNCED	United Nations Conference on Environment and Development
PDPA	People's Democratic Party of Afghanistan			
PEGIDA	Patriotic Europeans against the Islamisation of the West		UNCTAD	United Nations Conference on Trade and Development
PES	payments for ecosystem services		UNDP	United Nations Development Programme
PKB	National Awakening Party (Indonesia)		UNEP	United Nations Environment Programme
PKI	Communist Party of Indonesia		UNFCCC	United Nations Framework Convention on Climate Change
PKS	Justice and Welfare Party (Indonesia)			
PML(Q)	Pakistan Muslim League (Quaid)		UNHCR	United Nations High Commissioner for Refugees
PPP	Pakistan People's Party; purchasing power parity		UNIFEM	United Nations Development Fund for Women
PR	proportional representation		UNITA	National Union for Total Independence of Angola
PRC	People's Republic of China			
PRD	Party of the Democratic Revolution (Mexico)		UNMOGIP	United Nations Military Observer Group in India and Pakistan
PRI	Institutional Revolutionary Party (Mexico)			
PRN	National Revolutionary Party (Mexico)		UNOCHA	United Nations Office for the Coordination of Humanitarian Affairs
R2P	Responsibility to Protect		UNSC	United Nations Security Council
RCTs	randomized control trials		UNU-WIDER	United Nations University's World Institute for Development Economics Research
REDD	reducing emissions from deforestation and forest degradation			
			URA	Uganda Revenue Authority
RENAMO	Mozambican National Resistance		URNG	*Unidad Revolucionaria Nacional Guatemalteca* [Guatemalan National Revolutionary Unity]
ROC	Republic of China			
ROK	Republic of Korea (South Korea)		US	United States
RUF	Revolutionary United Front (Sierra Leone)		USAID	United States Agency for International Development
SALs	structural adjustment loans			
SAPs	structural adjustment programmes		VAT	value added tax
SARS	South African Revenue Services		V-DEM	Varieties of Democracy project
SAVAK	Organization for Intelligence and National Security (Iran)		WAF	Women's Action Forum (Pakistan)
			WBCC	World Bank Control of Corruption
SBY	Susilo Bambang Yodhoyono		WEDO	Women's Environment and Development Organization
SCs	Scheduled Castes (India)			
SCO	Shanghai Cooperation Organization		WGI	World Governance Indicators
SDGs	Sustainable Development Goals		WHO	World Health Organization
SDRs	special drawing rights		WLUML	Women Living under Muslim Laws
SERNAM	*Servicio Nacional de la Mujer* [National Women's Service] (Chile)		WMDs	weapons of mass destruction
			WSF	World Social Forum
SIDA	Swedish International Development Agency		WSSD	World Summit on Sustainable Development
SMEs	small and medium-sized enterprises		WTO	World Trade Organization
SMUG	Sexual Minorities Uganda			

About the Contributors

Tony Addison is Chief Economist and Deputy Director of the United Nations University's World Institute for Development Economics Research (UNU-WIDER) in Helsinki, Finland.

Robert Ahearne is a senior lecturer in international development with the School of Social Sciences, University of East London, UK.

Nadje Al-Ali is Professor of Gender Studies and Director of the Gender Studies Centre, School of Oriental and African Studies, University of London, UK.

Leslie Elliott Armijo is Associate Professor, School for International Studies, Simon Fraser University, Canada, and Non-Resident Fellow at the Center for Latin American and Latino Studies (CLALS), American University, Washington, DC, US.

Jóhanna Birnir is Associate Professor in the Department of Government and Politics and Research Director of the Center of International Development and Conflict Management at the University of Maryland, College Park, MD, US.

Deborah Bräutigam is Professor of International Development and Comparative Politics, and Director of the International Development Program, Johns Hopkins University School of Advanced International Studies, Washington, DC, US.

Peter Burnell is Emeritus Professor in the Department of Politics and International Studies, University of Warwick, UK.

Yunnan Chen is a PhD student in international development at the Johns Hopkins University School of Advanced International Studies, Washington, DC, US.

James Chiriyankandath is Senior Research Fellow with the Institute of Commonwealth Studies, School of Advanced Study, University of London, UK.

Peter Ferdinand is Reader in the Department of Politics and International Studies, University of Warwick, UK.

Michael Freeman is Research Professor in the Department of Government and was formerly Deputy Director of the Human Rights Centre, University of Essex, UK.

Siri Gloppen is Professor in the Department of Comparative Politics, University of Bergen, and Senior Researcher at the Chr. Michelsen Institute, Bergen, Norway.

Jeff Haynes is Professor in the Department of Law, Governance, and International Relations, London Metropolitan University, UK.

Stephen Hobden is Reader in international politics in the School of Social Studies, University of East London, UK.

Reinoud Leenders is Reader in International Relations and Middle East Studies, King's College, London, UK.

Gyda Marås Sindre, is Marie Curie Fellow and Senior Research Associate, Peterhouse College, University of Cambridge, UK, and Researcher, Department of Comparative Politics, University of Bergen, Norway.

Emma Mawdsley is Fellow of Newnham College and a senior lecturer in the Department of Geography, University of Cambridge, UK.

Peter Newell is Professor of International Relations at the University of Sussex, UK.

Marina Ottaway is Senior Scholar, Middle East Program, The Woodrow Wilson Center, Washington, DC, US.

Jenny Pearce is Professorial Research Fellow, Latin America and Caribbean Centre, London School of Economics, and Visiting Professor, Edge Hill University, Ormskirk, UK.

Anna Persson is Assistant Professor, Department of Political Science and Quality of Governance Center, University of Gothenburg, Sweden.

Nicola Pratt is Associate Professor of International Politics of the Middle East in the Department of Politics and International Studies, University of Warwick, UK.

Lise Rakner is Professor in the Department of Comparative Politics, University of Bergen, and Senior Researcher at the Chr. Michelsen Institute, Bergen, Norway.

Vicky Randall is Emeritus Professor in the Department of Government, University of Essex, UK.

Ingrid Samset is Assistant Professor in Peace and Conflict Studies, Leiden University College, The Hague, The Netherlands.

James R. Scarritt is Emeritus Professor in the Department of Political Science and formerly Faculty Research Associate in the Institute of Behavioral Science at the University of Colorado, Boulder, CO, US.

Andreas Schedler is Professor of Political Science in the Department of Political Studies, Centro de Investigación y Docencia Económicas (CIDE), Mexico City, Mexico.

Rachel Sieder is a senior researcher, Centro de Investigación y Educación Superior en Antropología School of Advanced Study (CIESAS), Mexico City, and a senior lecturer in Latin American Politics at the Institute for the Study of the Americas, School of Advanced Study, University of London, UK.

Astri Suhrke is a senior researcher, Chr. Michelsen Institute, Bergen, Norway, and Fellow, Asia-Pacific College of Diplomacy, The Australian National University, Canberra.

David Taylor is Director of the Aga Khan University Institute for the Study of Muslim Civilisations and Senior Research Fellow, Institute of Commonwealth Studies, University of London, UK.

Liv Tønnessen is a senior researcher at the Chr. Michelsen Institute, Bergen, Norway.

Torunn Wimpelmann is a researcher at the Chr. Michelsen Institute, Bergen, Norway.

Stephen Wright is Professor of Political Science at Northern Arizona University, Flagstaff, AZ, US.

Introduction

Lise Rakner and Vicky Randall

The aim of this book is to explore the changing nature of **politics** in the **developing world** in the twenty-first century. It analyses central developments and debates, illustrated by current examples drawn from the global South, covering such issues as **institutions** and **governance**, but also the growing importance of **alternative politics** and **social movements**, security, and post-conflict state-crafting. The present edition builds on earlier editions, but brings the discussion up to date. It looks at the 'Arab uprisings', considered as social movements or from the perspectives of religion, **gender**, and democracy, offering new case studies of Syria and the Sudan. And it highlights the growing importance of South–South relations, with case studies of China, India, and Brazil.

Both 'politics' and the 'developing world' are concepts that require further elaboration, and which are discussed more fully next. By 'politics', we mean broadly activities associated with the process and

institutions of government, or the state, but in the context of wider power relations and struggles. By the 'developing world', we are primarily referring to those regions that were formerly colonized by Western powers, which have been late to industrialize and which sustain relatively high levels of poverty—that is, Africa, Asia, the Middle East, and Latin America, including the Caribbean.

In our analysis of politics in the developing world, the complex and changing nexus between state and society has centre stage. This is because it is the reciprocal interaction of state and society, and the influence that each one exerts on the other, that most accounts for the distinctive character of developing countries' politics. Needless to say, that influence varies in both degree and kind, over time, as between individual states and inside states. The book does not set out to present a case for saying that the state is now marginal for the political analysis of developing countries nor does it argue that we must 'bring the state back in'. On the contrary, it recognizes that issues concerning the state have been, are, and will remain central to the political analysis, notwithstanding important developments—political, financial, economic, technological, and even social, at the sub-state, regional, and especially global levels—that are reshaping the nature, size, role, and performance of individual states.

A book about politics in the developing world is not the same thing as a book about development per se, or about development studies. Indeed, the book does not have as its main objective an emphasis on the politics *of* development by which is meant the elucidation of different development theories. There are other books that have been designed for this purpose. Certainly, there has been a trend in the study of development to comprehend development in an increasingly holistic sense—one that emphasizes its multifaceted nature and the interconnectedness of the various parts, of which politics provides one very important element. And while the chapters of the book do explore key relationships between politics and society, and between politics and the economy, they do so without any mission to demonstrate that politics is in some sense the 'master science' that unlocks all other subjects. Instead, the consequences that development can have for politics in the developing countries are as much a part of the analysis in this book as the implications that the politics have for development. So, although the book's primary focus is politics rather than development, we hope that its contents will still be of interest to anyone who is involved in development studies more generally.

A word is also needed explaining the geographical coverage of the book. The boundaries of the developing world are neither uncontentious nor unchanging. We have already suggested which regions have tended historically to be associated with it. However, this book's coverage—and more especially its case studies—do not include all of the possible candidates, primarily for pragmatic reasons. Thus Cuba, Vietnam, and some other countries that at one time claimed to be socialist, even Marxist–Leninist, are just as much part of the developing world as are the many countries that now defer to capitalism and adopt political pluralism. But, notwithstanding the financial and economic traumas that hit the global system in 2008, such countries remain a small band. A few, such as Bolivia and Ecuador, are currently pioneering redistributive social and economic policies, but the forces of **globalization**

in the post-Soviet, post-cold-war world do seem to militate against a more widespread radical socialist transformation. Indeed, China, whose credentials to be considered part of the developing world are open to debate, shows no intention of reverting to communism as an organizing principle for political economy even though it remains a one-party communist state. However, because contemporary China's relations with developing countries are increasingly significant and the distinctive combination of China's own politics with its rapid economic development appears to some to be a model for others to follow, a chapter on China's relations with the developing world is included in this book.

There are other parts of the world, beyond the regions traditionally included, that might now be considered to fall into this 'developing world' category. Although no express reference is made in the book to those elements of the post-communist world, a handful of the new European and Central Asian states that formerly belonged to the 'Second World' have certain characteristics long associated with the developing world. Some of them have come to acquire developing country **status**, in as much as the Organisation for Economic Co-operation and Development's (OECD's) Development Assistance Committee (DAC) has made countries such as Albania and Armenia eligible for **official development assistance (ODA)**. By comparison, the post-communist world's more advanced members were styled 'countries in transition' and judged ineligible for such aid. Readers are free to apply the concepts and propositions in this book to an examination of all of these other countries if they wish, just as area specialists seeking insights into those countries will find here material that resonates for their own subject. After all, the growing interdependence of states, and the rise of trans-territorial and supranational issues, such as those embraced by what might be called the 'new security agenda', certainly do not respect all of the distinctions between categories of countries, let alone national borders. The geopolitical unit of analysis that is most relevant to understanding the issues can easily straddle different states only some of which possess all of the main traits conventionally associated with developing countries. Similarly, there are regions and localities inside the wealthiest countries ('the South in the North') that share certain 'Southern' or 'Third World' characteristics, relative economic and social deprivation being one such characteristic, which the global economic recession since 2009 brought into sharper relief.

From Third World to Developing World

The developing world has been variously referred to as the 'Third World', the 'South', and the 'less developed countries (LDCs)', among other titles. Some of the members are rightly deemed 'emerging economies', and there is a distinctive group—the so-called BRICs (Brazil, Russia, India, China—supplemented by South Africa since 2010 and now referred to as BRICS)—that current debate singles out as rising powers, the harbingers of a new emerging multipolarity or more fragmented world. For example, four of these countries—Brazil, South Africa, India, and China—played a key role alongside the United States in negotiating the Copenhagen Accord of the United Nations Climate Change Conference (December 2009), and the same countries, plus Argentina, Indonesia, Mexico, Saudi Arabia, South Korea, and Turkey, also formally belong to the G20 group of the world's leading economies, taking part in, for example, the succession of summit talks on tackling global economic crisis and promoting economic development, most recently held in Brisbane in 2014 and Istanbul in 2015.

In fact, the question of the meaningfulness of the Third World as an organizing concept has long been the subject of as much dispute as the term's precise definition or true origins. Successive rationales for marking out a distinct Third World associated this world with a stance of non-alignment towards the capitalist and communist superpowers, with post-colonial status, with dependence on Western capitalism, and with poverty and economic 'backwardness'. Together, this comprised a confusing melange of external, as well as internal, economic and political descriptors. Following the collapse of Soviet power, the disappearance of the 'Second World' served to hasten the decline of the 'Third World' as a category name. Here is not the place to revisit the history of the debates about a term that, by and large, have now been brought to a conclusion. An abundant literature exists (Wolf-Phillips 1979; Berger 1994; Randall 2004). In keeping with the general trend, then, we have preferred to use the term 'developing world' for this book. In so doing, we do not mean to imply that this term is entirely uncontroversial or unproblematic. Assuming a conventional understanding of 'development', there are many parts of the developing world in which such a process is little in evidence and some in which it might even seem to be in retreat. There are also those who question the validity of such conventional understandings of 'development'—who indeed see development itself as an ideological construct subservient to the interests of Western donors, the international aid 'industry', and suchlike. We recognize the force of many of these arguments. At any rate, whatever term is favoured, there has also been a growing appreciation of the very considerable diversity to be found among and within those countries traditionally seen to come under its umbrella, and the widening of differences in their role and stance towards major issues in world politics.

Notwithstanding what, in many instances, has been a shared colonial past, some of the differences have always been there, such as the enormous range in demographic and territorial size. At only the lower end of the scale, the distinction between 'small' and 'micro' states—which, in total, make up around 40 per cent of all developing countries and territories—is a topic for debate. In contrast, in a regional context, some of the larger developing countries now appear to be approaching almost superpower-like status, even while remaining vulnerable to major external shocks. Thus a country such as India, a nuclear power with a population that exceeds 1 billion people, has very strong claims to be admitted to the permanent membership of the United Nations Security Council (UNSC). Some people champion similar claims for Brazil and Nigeria, although the latter is less stable politically and its fortunes continue to rest heavily on a very narrow base of energy exports.

Similarly, the developing world has always been noted for considerable variety in terms of economic dynamism and technological progress, and recent decades have served only to make these contrasts more pronounced. Just as average incomes were in decline in many parts of Africa in the latter years of the twentieth century (although, in the second decade of the twenty-first century, there are real signs that this may be changing), so some of the so-called tiger economies in East Asia have become developed countries in all but name. South Korea is a member of the OECD and now a member of the DAC. Its inclusion as a case study in this book illustrates how far and how quickly countries can develop if political and other conditions are favourable. Yet in many parts of the developing world, including India, China, and large parts of Latin America, great inequalities persist alongside the growing prosperity of an emerging middle class and political elite. It may be significant that, when the World Economic Forum met in Davos in January 2013, hundreds of economic experts from around the globe agreed that the biggest challenge facing the world is the increasing income gap between rich and poor. It was noted not only that is there an income gap between individual countries, but also that many developing countries are currently experiencing dramatic income disparities between various groups.

Until the 1980s, despite the differences in size and economic performance, it was possible to argue that most countries in the developing world had in common certain domestic political traits. These included a tendency towards authoritarian rule, whether based on the military, a single ruling party or personal dictatorship, or severe instability and internal conflict, and endemic **corruption**. But, more recently, political differences that were already there have become much more pronounced—and nowhere more so than in the recognition that some states are failing, or are even close to collapse. We are increasingly aware of the wide disparities in state strength and of the significance (not least for development) of variations in the quality of governance. The role played by ethnic and religious identity in politics has also come more to the fore, with the misfortunes of Iraq since the fall of Saddam Hussein providing a vivid example. In contrast, in Latin America, ethno-nationalism and religious conflict have been relatively minor themes, which is not to say that they are absent: indigenous peoples have started to come out of the shadows. Examples of alternative politics and non-violent action by social movements are demanding increasing attention in this and some other parts of the developing world, whilst the complex chain of events originating in the 'Arab uprisings' continues to defy confident categorization and prediction.

In sum, we are increasingly conscious of change, complexity, and diversity in the developing world, and of significant disagreements that follow from differences such as those related to national power. Some common features among developing countries, such as the colonial experience, are now receding into history, which makes old manifestations of 'Third World solidarity', such as the Non-Aligned Movement (NAM), harder to keep alive in their original form. This means that the many differences within the developing world now appear in sharper relief even as new ways of constructing shared interests vis-à-vis the rich world and forging new South–South links among governments and non-governmental actors also proceed apace.

Politics as Independent or Dependent Variable?

Most people—still more so, politics students—will have some idea of what is intended by the term 'politics'. Generally, political scientists understand it to refer to activities surrounding the process and institutions of government or the state, and that is a focus that we share in this book. However, there is another tradition, which some describe as 'sociological', that tends to identify politics with power relationships and structures, including, but by no means confined to, the state. They include, for instance, relationships between socio-economic classes or other kinds of social group, and between genders. When studying politics in the developing world, we believe it to be particularly important to locate analysis of political processes in their narrower sense within the wider context of social relationships and conflicts. Here, one of the themes and puzzles is the relationship between the more formal aspects of political processes and institutions, which may, to some degree, have been imposed or modelled on Western prototypes, and their 'informal' aspects. The latter can be very resilient and may even be regarded as more authentic. The informal hierarchies of power between patrons and clients are a specific example that applies especially, although not exclusively, to the developing world.

Despite our insistence on the need to understand politics in the wider power context, this does not rule out what is sometimes referred to as the 'autonomy of the political'—that is, the ability of politics to have independent and significant effects of its own. Thus any account of politics in the developing world that goes beyond the merely descriptive can have one or both of two objectives: to make sense of the politics; and to disclose what else the politics itself helps us to understand better. Succinctly, politics can be treated as *explanandum* or *explanans*, and possibly as both.

For some decades, there was a large movement in political science to view politics as the dependent variable. Analysts sought to advance our understanding of politics and to gain some predictive potential in regard to future political developments by rooting it in some 'more fundamental' aspects of the human condition, sometimes called structural 'conditions'. This was nowhere more evident than in the tendency to argue that the kind of political **regime**—namely, the relationship between rulers and ruled, usually depicted somewhere along the continuum from a highly authoritarian to a more liberal democratic polity—is a product largely of economic circumstance. The level of economic achievement, the nature and pace of economic change, and the social consequences were all considered highly important. It was not only Marxists who subscribed to broadly this kind of view; there were also others who sought to explain politics, especially in some parts of the developing world, more as an outcome of certain cultural conditions. This invoked a matrix of social divisions much richer and potentially more confusing than a simple class-based analysis would allow. These and other inclinations that view politics as contingent are still very much in evidence in contemporary theorizing about politics in the developing world, as several of the chapters in Parts 1 and 2 of the book will show.

However, over recent decades in political science, the larger study of comparative politics and area studies too have increased the weight given to the idea of politics as an independent variable, claiming in principle that politics matters: not only is it affected, but it too can have effects. Mair (1996) characterized this as a shift from an emphasis on asking what causes political systems to emerge, to take shape, and possibly to persist towards questions about what outputs and outcomes result from the political processes, and how well various political institutions perform. Making sense of the politics now goes beyond only explaining it; it extends also to investigating the impact of politics and its consequences. That includes the way in which contemporary politics are affected by the political history of a country—a proposition that is sometimes given the label of **path dependence**, which, in its more narrow and most meaningful application, suggests that **institutional** choices tend to become self-reinforcing (see Pierson 2000).

This move to view the more autonomous side of politics coincides with the rise of new institutionalism in political studies. New institutionalism has been described in a seminal article by March and Olsen (1984: 747) as neither a theory nor a coherent critique of one, but instead 'simply an argument that the organisation of political life makes a difference'. The new institutionalism (explored more fully in Chapter 3) directs us to the study of political process and political design, but not simply as outcomes or in terms of their contextual 'conditions'. This is not a completely new mood. As March and Olsen (1984) rightly say, historically, political science has emphasized the ways in which political behaviour is embedded in an institutional structure of norms, rules, expectations, and traditions that constrain the free play of individual will. The implications of this approach, and of tracing what political forms and political choices mean for a large set of issues of public concern—environmental issues, for instance—are explored in Parts 3 and 4 of the book especially. In doing so, the chapters provide a bridge to studying the larger phenomenon of **human development**. Here, we take our cue from the United Nations Development Programme (UNDP), which said that its 2002 Human Development Report was 'first and foremost about the idea that politics is as important to successful development as economics' (UNDP 2002: v). The UNDP's understanding is that human development, an idea that has grown in acceptance across a broad spectrum of development studies, aims to promote not simply higher material consumption, but also the freedom, well-being, and dignity of people everywhere. Development, then, has a political goal, just as politics is integral to how we understand the meaning of development.

Global Trends

Notwithstanding the increasing differentiation within the developing world, it is a fact that, over the last few decades, there has also been a growing convergence. This is the result of the presence of a number of major interconnected trends, political and economic, domestic and international. But these trends, far from reconfirming the more old-fashioned notions of the Third World, are instead ensuring that some of the most striking similarities emerging in the developing world today have a very different character from the Third World of old. This point is well worth illustrating before moving on.

One such trend, entrenched towards the end of the last century, comprised pressures from within and without the societies to adopt the so-called **Washington consensus** of the Bretton Woods institutions—the International Monetary Fund (IMF) and World Bank—on economic policy and national economic management. These developments have been held responsible in part for a near-universal movement in the direction of **neoliberalism** and marketization. There has been a shift from public ownership and the direct control of economic life by the state towards acceptance and encouragement of for-profit enterprise and growing opportunities for non-governmental development organizations. Although proceeding at different paces in different places and experiencing widely varying degrees of success, the implications of such changes for politics generally and for the state specifically can be quite profound. Ultimately, the same might be true of the **post-Washington consensus**, which is now commonly said to have succeeded the earlier development and which appears to give a bit more priority to tackling poverty, as well as to highlighting the developmental importance of attaining **good governance**. How this trend may be further modified by the growing importance of the new non-DAC donors, especially China (see Part 8), it is too early to say.

If *economic* liberalization has been one prong of a growing convergence among developing countries, then pressures towards *political* liberalization and democratization have been a second and, according to some accounts, symbiotically related development. The amount of substantive change that has actually taken place and its permanence are both open to discussion. Indeed, after a time in the early 1990s when the third wave of democratization seemed to have unstoppable momentum and some observers talked about the 'end of history', far more cautious claims are now much in evidence. By 2016, the reality has become much more confused: authoritarian or semi-authoritarian persistence in some places sits alongside evidence of democratic reversal in yet others. While a number of the 'new democracies' are of questionable quality, the progress made by others has confounded the cynics. Yet, irrespective of how truly liberal (in the political sense) or even democratic most developing countries really are and of how many possess market economies that are truly vibrant, recognition of the importance of governance in whatever way we define it (the definitions are many, some of them so vague or all-encompassing as to be almost useless—see Chapter 15) is ubiquitous. All of these agendas have been driven strongly by developed-world institutions and, notwithstanding the varied responses and reactions, the developing world now looks a rather different place from the way in which the Third World was formerly understood.

Underpinning these and many other contemporary developments—such as the campaigns for gender equity, the salience of 'new security' issues, and international monitoring of **human rights**—there is the growing significance ascribed to globalization. Here, globalization is understood at a minimum as 'the process of increasing interconnectedness between societies such that events in one part of the world more and more have effects on peoples and societies far away' (Baylis and Smith 2001: 7). The influence may be direct and positive, or negative, or both. It can also work indirectly. And, of course, the developing countries are touched unevenly and in different ways, as is made clear in this book. In purely economic terms, some are largely bystanders: they may share few of the claimed benefits even while incurring accidental and unintended costs. Their continuing vulnerability to fluctuations in the world market for their commodities is illustrative. Globalization theorists tell us that the sites of power are becoming more dispersed and some say that power is leaking away from the state—more so in the case of many developing countries, which may be small or very poor, or have weak governance structures, than for big countries such as the United States, Japan, Russia, China, or even the other BRICS. This unevenness is an unwritten assumption in much of the international political economy literature on globalization, which, by its own admission, biases attention towards the economically more developed parts of the world (see, for example, Phillips 2005). It provides one more reason for arguing that treating the developing world as a distinct, but not separate, entity continues to make sense.

Thus while the old order summed up by 'First', 'Second', and 'Third' Worlds has disappeared and the international system appears to be edging towards a very uncertain future characterized by a greater dispersion of power compared to the cold war and its immediate aftermath, differences still exist between the developing world and its counterpart in the more affluent North. And if US foreign initiatives after the **terrorist** attacks of 11 September 2001 ('9/11'), especially in the Middle East, caused widespread resentment in developing regions triggered by perceptions of a new imperialism reminiscent of older struggles for liberation from colonial rule, then claims to developing world solidarity might be credited with some purchase even now. A shared sensitivity to incursions or infringements of their sovereignty still supplies a common cause, one that China quite expressly promotes, although, of course, unlike European Union (EU) member states, countries such as the United States are hardly keen to surrender **political autonomy** either. Perhaps the dividing lines are nowhere more evident than in the North–South alignment over how to respond to global climate change. Most of the developed world sees a reduction in global greenhouse gas emissions as the priority, but many developing countries—including India and, at least until recently, China—have seemed less convinced, and rather draw attention to the urgency of climate adaptation in developing countries and to the rich world's obligation both to cut emissions and to offer help. A new focus of mutual resentment and suspicion may be building over the issue of refugee and migrant flows. Always pressing, this has recently become still more acute, sharpened for those in the developed world by the unprecedented influx from Syria, Libya, Afghanistan, and beyond into Europe over the summer of 2015. The image of the lifeless body of the boy Aylan Kurdi on a Turkish beach became emblematic of the crisis, inspiring compassion and panic in equal measure in the developed world. And yet four-fifths of the world's refugees are hosted by developing countries themselves. Interests and issues like these share with identities a responsibility for how the different worlds are constructed, or construct themselves—sometimes expressly in opposition to one another.

Even so, we should be continually challenging ourselves to distinguish between, on the one side, what, how, and how far changes really are taking place in developing world politics and, on the other side, the changes in our understanding that owe most to the lens through which we study the subject. Here, history tells us that, for the most part, the lens tends to originate, or comes to be ground more finely, outside and not inside the developing world. This is an important point: registering major developing world contributions to the way in which developing world politics is understood by observers in the developed world is crucial, but, while far from impossible, is not an easy or straightforward task.

Organization of the Book

The book comprises eight parts, the last four of which (Parts 5–8) contain case studies that illustrate some of the key concepts and themes presented in the first parts of the book (Parts 1–4). Each part is introduced by its own brief survey of contents; these short introductions can be read alongside this opening chapter. Part 1, on analytical approaches and the global context, should be read first. The aim of this part is to provide an introduction to general theoretical approaches that offer different ways of making sense of the politics in the developing world. These simplifying devices enable us to bring some order to a great mass of facts. They are useful both for directing our inquiries and because they provide a lens or lenses through which to interpret the empirical information. They suggest explanations for what we find there. Ultimately, the point of theorizing is not simply to explain, but also to provide a gateway to prediction. And however tenuous social science's claims to be able to predict with any confidence may be, the book aims both to assess the present of developing countries in the light of the past and to identify the major political uncertainties facing them in the foreseeable future.

So it is entirely appropriate that, immediately following the analytical overview, there is a chapter on colonialism and post-coloniality—themes that still resonate in so many different ways. Special attention is then given to institutional perspectives, followed by the changing international context. The glib conviction that now, more than ever, all of humanity resides in 'one world' betokens a very real fact of growing interconnectedness and interdependence, albeit highly asymmetric. There is increasing global economic integration at its core, but important political and other expressions of globalization, including new patterns in relationships among developing countries and China, should not be ignored either. The different analytical approaches that these chapters offer should not be viewed as entirely mutually exclusive. Each can quite plausibly have something valuable to offer, even though the emphases may shift when applied to different country situations and historical epochs. Readers must form their own judgements about which particular theoretical propositions offer most insight into specific issues and problems, or the more general condition of politics in developing countries. It is not the book's aim to be prescriptive in this regard, other than to restate that, where possible, notable perspectives from the developing world should be reflected.

Parts 2 and 3 set out to illuminate the changing nature, role, and situation of the state in relation to key social variables within developing countries. The two parts are a mirror image of one another. Together, they explore both how the politics reflects or is affected by social context, and how states specifically have responded to the challenges posed by society and the social effects. Particular attention is given to what this means in terms of the changing use and distribution of political power among state institutions and other actors. Thus Part 2 introduces the themes of inequality, ethnopolitics and nationalism, religion, gender, **civil society**, and alternative politics and social movements, in that order. Part 3 proceeds to theorize the state, before going on to examine the distinctive features of states that are trying to escape violent conflict at home. This is followed by an examination of the conditions of democratization, and of the relations between democratization and development, and by a discussion of governance, in which emphasis is placed on how power is exercised and checked once a government is in office.

Part 4 identifies major policy issues that confront all developing countries to a greater or lesser degree. In general terms, the issues are not peculiar to the developing world, but they do have a special resonance and their own character there. And although the issues also belong to the larger discourse on development per se, Part 4 aims to uncover why and how they become expressly political. It compares different political responses, and their consequences both for politics and development. The issues range from economic development and the environment, to human rights and security. Some of these could just as well have been introduced in earlier chapters of the book. This is because the presentations in Part 4 do not concentrate purely on the *details* of policy, but rather, out of necessity, seek to locate the policies within the context of the policy *issues* as such. However, all of these more policy-oriented chapters are grouped together because they are representative of major challenges for society and for government. Of course, where readers prefer to relate material from a chapter in Part 4 more closely to the material that comes earlier in the book, then there is no need for them to follow the chapters in strict numerical order.

Parts 5–8 aim to illustrate in some depth, or by what is sometimes called 'thick description', principal themes raised in the earlier parts, so complementing the use there of examples drawn more widely from around the developing world. While space limitations mean that the case studies are not designed to cover all aspects of a country's politics, the cases have been selected both with an eye to their intrinsic interest and for the contrasts that they provide in relation to one or more of the larger themes introduced earlier. Also, attention has been given not simply to illustrating developing country problems and weaknesses, but also to highlighting cases that offer a more positive experience. A deliberate aim of the book is to show the developing world as a place of diversity and rapid transformations. All of the main geographical regions are represented in Parts 5–8, together with the supplements offered by the book's Online Resource Centre. Part 5 includes three case studies, of Pakistan, Indonesia, and Syria, highlighting the issue of **regime change**. In Part 6, focus shifts to the debates over state power, and over fragile and strong states, illustrated by the cases of Iraq, Mexico, and South Korea. Part 7 draws on the debates about development and human rights discussed in more detail in Part 4, illustrated by three case studies of Nigeria, Guatemala, and the Sudan, respectively. In the final section (Part 8), emphasis is put on the increasingly strong South–South relations. The new role of developing countries in international politics is illustrated through country case studies of Brazil, China, and India.

In total, the country studies once again highlight the great range of experience in the developing world. They also demonstrate the benefit to be gained from a detailed historical knowledge of the individual cases. But although the cases differ not least in respect of their relative success or failure regarding development in the widest sense and politics specifically, none of them offers a simple or straightforward picture. The case studies should be read in conjunction with the appropriate chapter(s) from the earlier parts and are not intended to be read in isolation.

The editors' view is that a final chapter headed 'Conclusions' is not needed. The chapters each contain their own summaries; such a large collected body of material is not easily reduced without making some arbitrary decisions—and, most importantly, readers should be encouraged to form their own conclusions. It is almost inevitable that readers will differ in terms of the themes, issues, and even the countries or regions about which they will most want to form conclusions. And it is in the nature of the subject that there is no single set of 'right' answers that the editors can distil. On the contrary, studying politics in the developing world is so fascinating precisely because it is such a rich field of inquiry and constantly gives rise to new rounds of challenging questions.

So we finish here by posing some overarching questions that readers might want to keep in mind as they read the chapters. These questions might be used to help to structure the sort of general debate that often takes place towards the end of courses or study programmes that this book aims to serve. In principle, the individual subject of each of the chapters and of each of the case studies merits further investigation.

But for courses occupying a very limited number of weeks, lectures or tutor presentations might concentrate only on material drawn from Parts 1–4, and the allotted preparatory student reading each week might include the relevant case study material.

- Is politics in the developing world so very different from politics elsewhere that understanding it requires a distinct theoretical framework?

- Is there a single theoretical framework adequate for the purpose of comprehending politics in all countries of the developing world, or should we call on some combination of different frameworks?

- Are the main political trends experienced by the developing world in recent decades summed up best by 'increasing diversity' or by 'growing convergence', and are these trends likely to continue in the future?

- What are the advantages of applying a gendered framework of analysis to the study of politics in developing countries, and does one particular gendered framework offer equivalent insights in all countries?

- In what political respects is the developing world truly developing and in what respects are significant parts of it *not* developing—or even travelling in the opposite direction?

- What grounds are there for being optimistic, or pessimistic, about the ability of states to resolve conflict and to manage change peacefully in the developing world?

- Are the role of the state and the nature of the public policy process fundamentally changing in the developing world, and if so, in what respects?

- What principal forces, domestic or global, are creating incentives and pressures for fundamental political change and what forces are resisting or obstructing such change?

- How should developing countries' policies concerning the major public issues of our time differ from the typical policies that we see widely adopted in developed countries?

- What lessons most relevant to other societies can be learned by studying politics in the developing world and to which countries, or groups of countries, are these lessons most relevant?

- Drawing on what you understand about politics in the developing world, should China be included among the countries that are studied as part of the developing world?

 WEB LINKS

http://www.crisisgroup.org   International Crisis Group is a non-governmental organization (NGO) that provides regular updates and reports on geopolitical issues.

http://www.eldis.org   Thousands of online documents, organizations, and messages convey information on development policy, practice, and research.

http://www.gdnet.org   The site of the Global Development Network, a worldwide network of research and policy institutes aiming to generate research at the local level in developing countries and to provide alternative perspectives to those originating in the more developed world.

http://www.ids.ac.uk/british-library-for-development-studies   The British Library for Development Studies claims to be Europe's largest research collection on social and economic change in developing countries.

http://www.lib.utexas.edu/maps/index.html   A collection of contemporary and historical maps is housed at the University of Texas at Austin.

http://www.undp.org   The UNDP is an organization advocating for change and facilitating exchange of knowledge about the developing world.

PART I
Approaches and Global Context

Politics in the **developing world** offers an enormously rich and fascinating canvas of material for investigation. If we are to make sense of what we find, we must approach the subject in a structured and orderly way, with a clear sense of purpose. That means having an adequate framework, or frameworks, of analysis comprising appropriate concepts lucidly defined, together with a set of coherent organizing propositions. Propositions are advanced to explain the political phenomena in terms of their relationships both with one another and with other variables—including the influencing factors and the factors that are themselves influenced by, and demonstrate the importance of, politics. This part of the book introduces analytical approaches to the study of politics in the developing world. It reviews the contribution that can be made by a particular focus on **institutions** and the analytical purchase that adopting such a focus entails. It also sets out to situate politics within both an historical and an international and increasingly globalizing environment, as befits the increase of interdependence ('one world') and supra-territoriality that appear so distinctive of modern times.

   This part has two aims. *First*, it aims to identify the most enlightening analytical approaches for an understanding of politics in the 'developing world'. Is this a sufficiently distinct entity to warrant its own theory, or can we usefully apply approaches that are current in 'mainstream' political science? It compares the main broad-gauge theoretical frameworks that, at different times, have been offered for just this very purpose. Have the theoretical approaches that were pioneered in the early years of decolonization and post-colonial rule now been overtaken and made redundant by the other, more recent, critical perspectives, such as those offered by post-modern and **post-structuralist** thinking, **orientalism**, and the like? Do some theories or perspectives work better for some cases than for others? It also considers the application of a specific approach, the 'new institutionalism', which is currently widely deployed in the discipline as a whole. How helpful is this approach and what adaptations need to be made?

The *second* aim is to show why and in what ways it is becoming increasingly difficult to understand, or even to describe, politics within developing countries without taking account of its distinctive context. The first aspect of this context to be examined is the influence of pre-colonial and colonial legacies. Upon differences in pre-colonial patterns of society and the structuring of authority were superimposed a variety of colonial **regime** types (for instance regarding the duration of colonial rule and the cultural background of the colonizers). How, and to what extent, have these diverse experiences shaped trajectories of the state and development in the developing world? To what extent do such legacies continue to be relevant to a proper understanding of politics in the contemporary developing world?

The second and essential contextual consideration is the role of factors in the contemporary international system. These latter inter-state and supra-state influences originate in economic, financial, diplomatic, cultural, and other forums. Many of these influences can penetrate state borders without having either express consent or tacit approval from government. They collaborate and collide with a variety of intra- and non-state actors, reaching far down to the sub-state and subnational levels. At the same time, developing countries also participate in, and seek to influence, regional networks and wider international organizations. The so-called BRICS (referring to Brazil, Russia, India, China, and South Africa) are a good example: even if the potential of this group of states to act as one in international affairs is not fully realized, recent changes on the international stage, plus the emergence of China and India as new development donors, suggest a paradigm shift in North–South, as well as South–South, relations. The nature of 'South–South' relations should be compared with 'North–South' relations before and since the end of the cold war. This part helps us to consider the developing world's place within the global system as a whole: how far are developing country politics conditioned by powerful constraints and pressures originating outside? Are those pressures and constraints, and their impact, in any sense comparable to 'neo-colonialism' or, indeed, the imperialism of old? Is power in the developing world now being ceded not so much to governments in the rich world as to a more diffuse, and less controllable, multilayered set of global commercial, financial, and economic forces and institutions? Or does their possession of valuable resources and growing presence enable at least some developing countries to be increasingly assertive in respect of their **political autonomy** and influence on world affairs? Readers are encouraged to consult relevant case studies—in particular, Chapters 28–30 in Part 8 on 'South–South Relations' and the changing landscape of international development cooperation—alongside the chapters in Part 1.

1

Changing Analytical Approaches to the Study of Politics in the Developing World

Vicky Randall

Chapter contents

Overview

Two contrasting broad approaches long dominated political analysis of developing countries. One was a politics of modernization that gave rise to political development theory, then to revised versions of that approach, which stressed the continuing, if changing, role of tradition and the need for strong government, respectively. Second was a Marxist-inspired approach that gave rise to dependency theory and, subsequently, to neo-Marxist analysis, which focused on the relative autonomy of the state. By the 1980s, both approaches were running out of steam, but were partially subsumed in globalization theory, which emphasized the ongoing process, accelerated by developments in communications and the end of the cold war, of global economic integration, and its cultural and political ramifications. In the absence of a systematic critique, an alternative to this mainstream perspective was provided in the literatures on orientalism and post-coloniality, and on post-development, and more generally from a post-structural perspective. Nowadays, the very concept of a developing world is increasingly hard to sustain and, with it, the possibility of identifying one distinct analytic approach, as opposed to middle-range theories and a particular focus on the role of institutions more widely evident in contemporary political studies. However, certain key themes and agendas provide some degree of coherence. Similarly, there is no distinctive set of methodological approaches, but rather the application of approaches more generally available in the social sciences.

Introduction

This chapter provides an introduction to the main broad analytical approaches or frameworks of interpretation that have been employed in studying **politics** in the **developing world**. The 'developing world' contains numerous highly diverse political systems. To varying degrees, its analysts have looked to theories or frameworks of analysis to provide appropriate concepts or containers of information, and to allow comparison and generalization across countries or regions. Some frameworks have been relatively modest or 'middle-range', but others have been much more ambitious. Moreover, despite aspirations to scientific objectivity and rigour, they have inevitably reflected the circumstances under which they were formulated—for instance political scientists' underlying values, domestic political pressures, and funding inducements, as well as perceived changes in the developing countries themselves. We all need to be aware of these approaches, and the surrounding debates, if we are to read the literature critically and form our own views.

We begin with 'the politics of **modernization**', emerging in the United States in the 1950s. This approach, including political development theory and its various 'revisions', operated from a mainstream, liberal, or (to its left critics) pro-capitalist perspective. The second and opposed approach, stemming from a critical, Marxist-inspired perspective, has taken the form, first, of **dependency theory**, and then of a more state-focused Marxist approach. More recently, the dominant, although by no means unchallenged, paradigm has been **globalization theory**, to some degree incorporating elements of both developmentalist and dependency perspectives. Globalization theory, however, has also served to problematize politics in the developing world as a coherent field, partly because it tends to undermine the premise of a distinct developing world. For this and other reasons, some have suggested that the field is currently in crisis. The latter part of this chapter considers how far a distinctive and coherent approach to politics in the developing world is still discernible in the present day, and also asks whether such an approach would be desirable.

'Politics' and the 'Developing World'

Before considering the three main approaches themselves, we need briefly to revisit the central notions of 'developing world' and 'politics'. As noted in the introduction to this part, the term 'developing world' has conventionally referred to the predominantly postcolonial regions of Africa, Asia, Latin America and the Caribbean, and the Middle East, perceived to be poorer, less economically advanced, and less 'modern' than the developed world. 'Developing world' is preferred to 'Third World', because the latter term carries some particular historical connotations that make it especially problematic.

But even when we use the less problematic 'developing world', there have always been questions about what exactly are the defining features that these countries have in common and which distinguish them from the 'developed world'. These questions have become yet more pressing as the differences within the 'developing world' have widened: does it make sense to discuss the World Bank's 'lower-income countries' or the United Nations' 'least developed countries' (LDCs) alongside 'upper middle-income countries' or the BRICS (Brazil, Russia, India, China, and South Africa)? Still more basically, some seek to question the assumptions underlying the notion of 'development': from what to what are such countries supposed to be developing, and from whose perspective?

Similarly, 'politics' is a highly contested notion. On one understanding, it is a kind of activity associated with the process of government and linked with the 'public' sphere; on another, it is about 'power' relations and struggles not necessarily confined to the process of government or restricted to the public domain. This volume takes the view that neither perspective on its own is sufficient—in general, but particularly in a developing world context. A further important question concerns the **autonomy of politics**: how far is politics, as a level or sphere of social life, determined by economic and/or social/cultural dimensions of society, and how far does it independently impact on those dimensions? Is the autonomy of politics itself variable? The different approaches to be considered all address this question, more or less explicitly, but arrive at very different conclusions.

KEY POINTS

- The expression 'developing world' is preferable to 'Third World', but the increasing diversity of the countries included still makes generalization problematic.

- Studying politics in developing countries means investigating both central government processes and power relations in society.

- A further important question concerns the relative autonomy of politics.

Modernization and Dependency Approaches

Most studies of politics in developing countries have been informed to some degree by one or other of three main dominant approaches: modernization theory; Marxism-inspired theory; and globalization theory. These approaches, or theoretical frameworks, themselves have not necessarily been directly or centrally concerned with politics; however, both modernization theory and dependency theory have helped at least to generate more specifically political approaches.

The politics of modernization

The emergence of the 'politics of modernization' approach reflected both changing international political circumstances and developments generally within social science, and specifically within political science. Out of the Second World War, a new world was born, in which, first, two superpowers—the United States and the Soviet Union—confronted one another, and second, a process of decolonization was set in train, leaving a succession of constitutionally independent states. Soon, the two powers were vying for influence in these states. Within the United States, social scientists—and increasingly political scientists—were encouraged to study them.

For this, the field of comparative politics at that time was ill-equipped; it concentrated on a narrow range of Western countries, was typically historical and legalistic in orientation, and was not systematically comparative at all. Responding to this new challenge, comparative politics drew on two developments in the social sciences: first, the 'behavioural revolution' encouraged a more 'scientific' approach that sought to build general social theories and test them empirically; second, especially in sociology, but also in economics, interest was growing in tracing and modelling processes of 'modernization'. Whilst modernization theory took different forms, its underlying assumption was that the process of modernization experienced in the West provided a valuable guide to what to expect in the developing world.

Political development theory

In this context, interest grew in elaborating a specific concept and theory of political development. The framework of analysis developed by Gabriel Almond was particularly influential. He developed a structural-functional approach to comparing politics in different countries and as a basis for his concept of political development, which distinguished a series of political functions and then examined their relationship with particular structures or **institutions** (see Box 1.1). There were four 'input' functions: political socialization (instilling attitudes towards the political system); political recruitment; and the 'articulation' and 'aggregation' of interests (demands). On the 'output' side, three functions were identified: rule-making; rule implementation; rule adjudication; and a more pervasive function of political communication.

Almond originally suggested that political development could be understood as the process through which these functions were increasingly associated with specialized structures—parties for interest aggregation, legislatures for rule-making, and so on—and with the emergence of modern styles of politics (achievement-based versus ascriptive, and so forth). Later, he identified five political system 'capabilities' (extractive, regulative, distributive, symbolic, and responsive), which were expected to grow as structures became more specialized and political styles more modern. These capabilities in turn would help the system to deal with four main problems (to which some writers later referred as 'crises')—of state-building (with the focus on state structures), **nation-building** (focusing on cultural integration), participation, and distribution.

Almond's approach has been extensively and justly criticized, although it must be said that political scientists continue to use many of the concepts he developed, such as state-building (see Chapter 12) and nation-building. Similar criticisms were made of other attempts to conceptualize political development, with the added observation that they were excessively diverse, demonstrating a lack of consensus on what political development actually was (Pye 1966).

Political development theory, in this form, was in decline by the late 1960s, not least because supporting

---

BOX 1.1 ALMOND'S FRAMEWORK FOR COMPARATIVE ANALYSIS

Political systems

Input functions (and typical associated structures)	Output functions (and typical associated structures)
Political socialization (family, schools, religious bodies, parties etc.)	Rule-making (legislatures)
Political recruitment (parties)	Rule implementation (bureaucracies)
Interest articulation (interest groups)	Rule adjudication (judicial system)
Interest aggregation (parties)	

↓ Political communication ↑

Political systems develop *five capabilities*:

- extractive (drawing material and human resources from an environment);
- regulative (exercising control over individual and group behaviour);
- distributive (allocation of different kinds of 'good' to social groups);
- symbolic (flow of effective symbols, for example flags, statues, ceremony); and
- responsive (responsiveness of inputs to outputs).

These help them to face *four kinds of problem*:

- state-building (need to build structures to penetrate society);
- nation-building (need to build culture of loyalty and commitment);
- participation (pressure from groups to participate in decision-making); and
- distribution (pressure for redistribution or welfare).

Source: Almond and Bingham Powell (1966)

---

funding was drying up. But it has not entirely disappeared; indeed, many of its characteristic themes resurfaced in the literature emerging from the 1980s concerning democratization and **governance** (see Chapters 14 and 15). Before leaving political development theory, though, two further developments should be noted.

Modernization revisionism

One strand of criticism of political development theory—**modernization revisionism**—centred on its oversimplified notions of tradition, modernity, and their interrelationship. Taking up arguments voiced by social anthropologists against modernization theory, some political scientists questioned what they perceived as an assumption that political modernization would eliminate 'traditional' elements of politics such as **caste** and ethnicity (the topic of religion was largely ignored until the 1980s—see Chapter 8). Instead, they suggested that aspects of political modernization could positively invigorate these traditional elements, albeit in a changed form, and also that these elements would invariably influence in some measure the form and pace of political change.

This perspective also drew attention to the ubiquity and role of **patron–client relationships**. In their 'traditional' form, local notables, typically landowners, acted

as patrons to their dependent clients, typically peasants, in relationships that were personalized, clearly unequal, but framed in terms of reciprocity and affection. With greater 'modernization', and extension of state and market into the 'periphery', a modified kind of relationship emerged between peasant/clients and local 'brokers' who could mediate their dealings with the centre. But at the centre, emerging, seemingly modern, political institutions—political parties and bureaucracies—also often operated on the basis of informal, but powerful, patron–client relationships, which moreover often linked into those at the periphery. Where such relationships pervaded government, scholars drew on sociologist Max Weber's typology of forms of rule (Weber 1970), to talk about **patrimonialism**, or **neo-patrimonialism**. This insight into the realities of **patronage** and **clientelism** was extremely valuable, and has continuing relevance (see Box 1.2; see also Chapters 6 and 10). Indeed, with the more recent emphasis on the role of political institutions, discussed further later in this chapter and in Chapter 3, there has been renewed interest in these relationships, as part of the wider question of the relationship between formal and informal processes within institutions. Despite further criticisms that have been made of modernization revisionism in its turn, this perspective has greatly enhanced our understanding of political processes in the developing world.

BOX 1.2 PATRON–CLIENT RELATIONS

An anthropological account of a traditional patron–client relationship between landlord and sharecropper:

A peasant might approach the landlord to ask a favour, perhaps a loan of money or help in some trouble with the law, or the landlord might offer his aid knowing of a problem. If the favour were granted or accepted, further favours were likely to be asked or offered at some later time. The peasant would reciprocate—at a time and in a context different from that of the acceptance of the favour in order to de-emphasize the material self-interest of the reciprocative action—by bringing the landlord especially choice offerings from the farm produce or by sending some members of the peasant family to perform services in the landlord's home, or refraining from cheating the landlord, or merely by speaking well of him in public and professing devotion to him.

(Silverman 1977: 296)

Patron–client relationships in Mexican party politics:

Given PRI [Mexico's Institutional Revolutionary Party] monopolization of public office, for much of the post-revolutionary period the most important actors in the competition for elected and appointed positions have been political *camarillas* within the ruling elite. *Camarillas* are vertical groupings of patron–client relationships, linked at the top of the pyramid to the incumbent president. These networks are assembled by individual politicians and bureaucrats over a long period of time and reflect the alliance-building skill and family connections of the patron at the apex.

(Craig and Cornelius 1995: 259–60)

Politics of order

Samuel Huntington (1971) launched a scathing attack on political development theory for its unrealistic optimism, suggesting that, rather than political development, it might be more relevant to talk about political decay. He criticized an assumption in political development theory that, in developing societies, economic growth would lead to social change conducive to liberal democracy. Instead, he argued that rapid economic growth from low initial levels could be profoundly destabilizing, generating excessive pressures on fragile political institutions. In this context, what mattered was not what form of government existed (whether democratic or communist), but the degree of government.

Critics accused this 'strong government', or **politics of order**, perspective of inherent conservatism and authoritarianism. But, at the time, Huntington's thesis also injected a welcome dose of **realism** into the discussion, as well as drew attention to the ability of political institutions not only to reflect economic and social development, but also themselves to make an active difference—that is, to the 'relative autonomy of the political'.

Huntington's ideas continue to influence our understanding of developing countries. Thus the theme of the importance of institutions re-emerged in the 1990s with the emphasis of institutions such as

the World Bank on 'governance' (as explored further in Chapter 3). His arguments about the relative timing of, and relationship between, democracy and development pinpointed what has remained a key debating point. For instance some experts have questioned the appropriateness of democratic governance for economic development in low-income countries, as in much of Africa, with the strong government perspective echoed by exponents of the 'developmentalist state' and even the China-based **Beijing consensus**, defined by Kurlantzik (2014) as entailing 'repressive politics and high-speed economic growth'. And, recently, Fukuyama (2011, 2014), with an explicit debt to Huntington, has revisited and sought to update, in two substantial volumes, the whole question of the origins and strength of political institutions.

Marxist-inspired approaches

The second main category of approaches to be examined stems from a broadly Marxist perspective. As such, it opposed the 'politics of modernization' school as reflecting bourgeois or capitalist interests, and stressed the determining role of processes of economic production and/or exchange and the social class relationships embedded in them. In fact, dependency theory, which emerged in the late 1960s, was primarily concerned to refute orthodox models of economic development and also modernization theory; its implications for politics, at least in the narrower governmental sense, were almost incidental, although its impact was considerable.

One main reason was that it drew attention to a serious shortcoming of all forms of political development theory: their near-total neglect of the international context and the implied assumption that politics in developing countries were shaped by purely domestic forces. Dependency theory originated in South America and reflected that continent's experience, but was quickly applied to other parts of the developing world. It has taken numerous forms, but will be briefly illustrated here through the arguments of a leading exponent, Gunder Frank (see also Chapter 5).

Frank (1969) maintained that the developing world had been increasingly incorporated into the capitalist world economy from the sixteenth century onwards. In fact, development of the developed world (known as the 'metropolis', or 'core') was premised upon **underdevelopment** of the developing world (known as 'satellite economies', or the 'periphery'); development and underdevelopment were two sides of the same coin. Despite formal political independence, former colonies remained essentially dependent because the metropolis was able to extract most of their economic surplus through various forms of monopoly. Even when such economies appeared to be developing, this was only dependent and distorted development. Frank argued that the only way in which a satellite economy could end this dependence was to drastically reduce ties with the metropolis; later, he recognized that even this was not really an option.

Whilst, for a time, dependency theory was extremely influential, it was also increasingly and justly criticized for the crude generalization and determinism of its economic analysis. Not all versions were quite as deterministic as Frank's. Wallerstein (1979), for instance, recognized a 'semi-periphery' of countries, such as the East Asian 'tigers', which, over time, had been able to improve their position within the overall 'world system' and, by their example, offered others on the periphery the hope of doing so too. By the 1980s, dependency theory was losing currency, although, ironically, the emerging 'debt crisis' of that same decade and imposition of structural adjustment requirements has seemed one of its best illustrations.

What did dependency theory have to say about politics in developing countries? Frank tended to minimize the independent effects of politics. He argued that both

the state and the national political elite in such countries were identified with the *comprador* economic class, which served as the local agent of metropolitan capital and consequently had a vested interest in the status quo. The only real possibility of change would be a revolution of those at the end of the chain of **exploitation**—the peasantry and urban poor—who had nothing to lose. Short of that, the different forms of politics, contests between political parties, and so forth, had little significance. Again, there were some variations in this position. Wallerstein had more to say about politics and a less reductionist view of the state, but still ultimately saw strong states as a feature of the developed world and reinforcing capitalist interests. In general, dependency theory shed little direct light on the political process as such within developing countries. Its real contributions were to insist on the intimate link between politics and economics, which had been largely neglected in the politics of modernization literature, and to demonstrate that the domestic politics of developing countries was incomprehensible without reference to their position within the world capitalist system.

Neo-Marxism rediscovers politics

Despite its Marxist associations, dependency theory had many neo-Marxist critics. They rejected its economic analysis, which, they argued, was based on falsely equating capitalism with the market, rather than seeing it as a system of production. They also cherished hopes that the socialist revolution that had failed to materialize in the West would begin in the developing world. Such hopes were raised by a 'third wave' of revolutionary developments from the late 1960s (following a first wave centred on China, and a second wave from the late 1950s including Cuba and Algeria), which included Communist victories in Vietnam, Cambodia, and Laos, revolution in Ethiopia, the overthrow of Portuguese **regimes** in Africa, and revolution in Nicaragua (Cammack 1997). For these reasons, neo-Marxists engaged in a much more detailed and rigorous analysis of social structure that was, in some sense, aimed at assessing the eligibility of different social categories—peasants, the lumpenproletariat (the urban poor who were not regular wage-earners), and so on—to inherit the role of revolutionary vanguard originally attributed to the industrial working class.

At the same time, there was a new interest in what Marxists typically referred to as the **post-colonial state**. Marx himself generally depicted the state as a simple instrument of class domination—in the famous words of the *Communist Manifesto* (1872, in Marx and Engels 2002): 'The executive of the modern state is but a committee for managing the common affairs of the whole bourgeoisie.' But his writings sometimes alluded to a second possibility, as in France during the second empire under Louis Napoléon, when the weakness or divisions of the bourgeoisie allowed an authoritarian state to emerge that was 'relatively autonomous' from any particular social class. This notion, as developed by neo-Marxists such as Antonio Gramsci (1891–1937) and, later, Nicos Poulantzas (1936–79) analysing capitalist states in the West, was later seized on to explore the relationship between the state and social classes in post-colonial societies. Hamza Alavi (1979), for instance, argued (with particular reference to Pakistan) that the post-colonial state enjoyed a high degree of autonomy. This was, first, because it had to mediate between no fewer than three ruling classes, but second, because it had inherited a colonial state apparatus that was 'overdeveloped' in relation to society because its original role was holding down a subject people (although others later questioned whether the post-colonial state in Africa could be described as overdeveloped).

KEY POINTS

- The 'politics of modernization' approach emerged in the 1950s, initially taking the form of political development theory.

- Political development theory was criticized by 'revisionists' for simplifying and underestimating the role of tradition, and by advocates of political order for excessive optimism.

- From the left, dependency theory criticized the modernization approach for ignoring former colonies' continuing economic, and thus political, dependence.

- Neo-Marxists criticized dependency theory's determinism, and explored the relative autonomy of politics and the state.

Globalization: Theories and Responses

By the early 1980s, and despite their diametrically opposed starting points, the lines of thought evolving out of early political development theory, on the one hand, and dependency theory, on the other, were converging around a re-appreciation of the independent importance of 'the political', and an interest in strong government and/or the state. But both of these lines of thought were also tending to run out of steam. Modernization-based approaches were particularly vulnerable to the charge of insufficient attention to the economic and international context. In the meantime, dependency theory was increasingly challenged by apparently successful cases such as the oil-producing Gulf states and the **newly industrializing countries (NICs)**, whilst the neo-Marxist focus on socialist revolution appeared increasingly anachronistic.

Reflecting these changes in the global environment, by the 1990s, a new 'macro' approach was emerging, globalization theory, which tended both to absorb and displace the previous two. (For a valuable early overview, see McGrew 1992.) Globalization theory focuses on a process of accelerated communication and economic integration that transcends national boundaries, and increasingly incorporates all parts of the world into a single social system. Globalization theory (see also Chapters 4 and 12) should more properly be referred to as 'globalization theor*ies*', since it has taken many different forms. As with the previous two approaches, it can also often seem closer to an ideology or policy strategy than a theoretical framework. Although the process of **globalization** is often seen as originating in the distant past, there is general agreement that it accelerated in particular from the 1970s, spurred by developments in transport and communications, and subsequently by the collapse of the Soviet bloc and end of the cold war.

Probably the most important dimension of this process—certainly the most analysed—is economic, with particular attention paid to developments in global trade, foreign direct investment (FDI), and finance (see Chapter 4). Associated with these economic trends, however, has been a significant cultural dimension of globalization that is increasing cultural awareness and interaction across national boundaries. Central to this process has been the remarkable development and expansion of information technology and the new electronic mass media, enormously extending the scope and immediacy of communication. The consequences of this process are undoubtedly complex and contentious. For globalization pessimists such as Sklair (1991: 41), the predominance of US-based media conglomerates has meant the diffusion of images and lifestyles that promote the 'culture-ideology of consumerism'. Powerful media industries have emerged in a number of developing countries such as India, Brazil, and Mexico. Thai soap operas are popular in China, Turkish soap operas in Saudi Arabia, and even Mexican telenovelas in Zambia! This has led commentators such as Pieterse (2015) to suggest that, especially with China's growing influence, we are witnessing the emergence of more genuinely 'hybrid' cultures. Yet it is questionable just how truly 'global', in the sense of multidirectional, cultural communications have become. By the same token, however, the perceived threat of cultural globalization has prompted complex counter-trends, including reassertion of local and national cultural identities (on religious identity, see Chapter 8).

Different forms of globalization theory have emphasized different aspects—economic, cultural, and so on. They differ in what they understand to be the prime moving mechanism of the globalization process: some see it as driven by the underlying logic of unfolding capitalism associated in particular with an aggressive **neoliberalism**, relentlessly expanding global markets—for instance in labour and capital—at the expense of national state institutions and boundaries; others, as primarily a consequence of developments in communications; others, as a combination of factors. Some accounts, echoing modernization theory, are essentially optimistic: they stress, for instance, the extent to which a globalizing economy, in which capital is increasingly mobile, hugely extends opportunities for investment and employment for those who are enterprising and adaptable. Others, echoing the mistrust and many of the arguments of dependency theory, have been more pessimistic; they have depicted an increasingly unfettered global capitalism, ruthlessly exploiting people and resources. Globalization theory has taken stronger forms—sometimes referred to as 'hyperglobalization'—and more cautious, moderate forms. The debate too has changed over time: Jones (2010: 12), in his overview of key globalization thinkers, traces an evolving dialogue involving emphatic statements, sceptical reactions, more cautious reformulations, and so forth, although he suggests that there is a growing consensus that 'globalization does amount to something "new"'.

Finally, globalization theory creates difficulties for the notion of a distinct developing world. Even if we talk about a 'developing world' rather than a 'Third World' and are careful about which countries we include or exclude, this still implies a distinct geographic entity. However, globalization theorists such as Berger have argued that if we want to retain the idea of a Third or developing world, this should be conceived of in sociological, rather than geographic, terms. The ongoing process of economic globalization means that economically based social classes are increasingly transnational or global in span. Thus dominant classes in the developing world are more oriented towards Western capitalist centres, where 'they have their bank accounts, maintain business links, own homes and send their children to school', than to their own countries (Berger 1994: 268). Meanwhile, countries in the developed world, not least the United States, each have their own underclass (or 'Third' or developing world), even if there are few signs that such underclasses are coming together at a global level.

Responses: 'Anti-globalization' and alternative critical perspectives

Whereas it was possible to see modernization theory and dependency approaches as, to some degree, internally coherent and radically opposed to one another, in the case of globalization theory, it ranges so widely that it tends to have encompassed key debates, including those derived from modernization and dependency outlooks, within its own parameters. So we have seen that globalization pessimists have emphasized 'negative' traits, including US cultural dominance, and growing global inequality. In this context, the 'anti-globalization movement', sometimes also referred to as the **global justice movement** (see Chapter 11), emerging from the late 1980s, has identified globalization largely in terms of the global spread of neoliberal ideology and corporate power. It has comprised a hugely heterogenous and changing network of groups, many based in the developing world, and of causes, such as environmentalism, the rights of the landless, fair trade, and ending exploitation of child labour.

Partly associated with this anti-globalization activism have been more sophisticated critiques of aspects of what is seen as mainstream thinking. Besides those directly engaging with the economic assumptions of globalization optimists, there have been those criticizing globalization ideology from a **gender** perspective (see Chapter 9). Alternatively, there have been attempts to 'deconstruct' implicit elements of globalization thinking. One such critique is associated with the notion of **orientalism**. In his influential book, first published in 1978, Edward Said wrote about the lens of 'orientalism' through which many Western scholars

BOX 1.3 THE DEVELOPMENT INDUSTRY IN LESOTHO

Lesotho is a small, landlocked country in southern Africa, with a population of around 1.3 million. Ferguson (1997) lists seventy-two international agencies, **non-governmental organizations (NGOs)** and quasi-governmental organizations operating in Lesotho, and notes that, in 1979, it received some US$64 million in **official development assistance (ODA)**.

What is this massive internationalist intervention, aimed at a country that surely does not appear to be of especially great economic or strategic importance? . . . Again and again development projects in Lesotho are launched, and again and again they

fail: but no matter how many times this happens there always seems to be someone ready to try again with yet another project. In the pages that follow, I will try to show . . . how outcomes that at first appear as mere 'side-effects' of an unsuccessful attempt to engineer an economic transformation become legible in another perspective as unintended yet instrumental elements in a resultant constellation that has the effect of expanding the exercise of a particular sort of state power while simultaneously exerting a powerful depoliticizing effect.

(Ferguson 1997: 7–21 passim)

---

have interpreted Asian and Middle Eastern societies in imperial times. This discourse, which tended to 'essentialize' such societies, rendering them as exotic and 'Other', could also be seen as instrumental to the political aims of the imperialist powers (although it was not confined to them, as demonstrated in Marx's account of the 'Asiatic' mode of production). Said's work is said to have inspired a broader movement of 'post-colonial studies'. Specifically, in India, it stimulated the emergence of 'subaltern studies', the original rationale of which was to rewrite India's colonial history from the standpoint of the oppressed, subaltern classes. (For a fuller discussion of these developments, see Chapter 2.) Although Said was primarily writing from a historical and cultural viewpoint, he subsequently argued that orientalist discourse was being revived in the post-cold-war context, and especially after 9/11, to help to justify US policy in the Middle East. Similarly Bayat (2015) invokes a 'neo-orientalism' evident in the current era of globalization, in which Muslims and Islam in particular are depicted as imminently threatening to Western values and security.

Another critique with great relevance to this volume is directed at the assumptions of development theory and the development 'industry', and referred to as 'post-development theory'. This entails a criticism of development as discourse. One influential exponent, who explicitly situates himself within the parameters of discourse theory, is Arturo Escobar (1995). Escobar, who incidentally acknowledges a debt to Said, suggests that whatever kind of development is advocated, whether capitalist or 'alternative', there is still the assumption that developing countries have to be made to change, which helps to rationalize continuing intervention of outside interests, experts, and

perspectives. Ferguson (1997) provides a good illustration, writing about external intervention in Lesotho, and drawing a contrast between the repeated 'failure' of development projects and the significance of their apparently unintentional political side-effects (see Box 1.3). It must be stressed that this line of argument has generated much counter-criticism, not least that 'development' is not only an elite preoccupation, but also an almost universal aspiration.

Globalization and politics

Although the voluminous literature on globalization, certainly to begin with, had relatively little directly to say about politics in the developing world, its implications are far-reaching. First, it suggests changes in the character of politics as a whole. While it would be premature to talk about a process of political globalization comparable with what has been claimed in the economic and cultural spheres, one can point towards a series of developments that incline that way. There is the increasing perceived urgency of a range of issues—such as global warming, refugee flows, **terrorism**—the origins of, and solutions to, which transcend national borders. Correspondingly, we have seen a proliferation of international regulatory organizations and governance regimes, such as the **international human rights regime**, discussed in Chapter 18, of NGOs, and of transnational **social movements**, including the so-called anti-globalization movement itself (see Chapters 10 and 11).

At the same time, globalization theory has emphasized ways in which the nation-state is losing autonomy. It is increasingly difficult for the individual state to control the flow of information across its borders or to protect its people from global security threats.

Likewise, globalizing trends have greatly reduced its economic options, for instance its ability to fend off the consequences of economic upheaval elsewhere, such as the 1997 East Asian financial crisis, or to successfully promote 'Keynesian' economic policies, to enhance welfare and protect employment, when these run counter to the logic of the global economy. With reduced autonomy, it is argued, comes reduction in the state's perceived competence and, accordingly, in its **legitimacy**. It comes under increasing pressure from within, as well as without, contributing to a process of 'hollowing out' the state. This increased vulnerability of the nation-state has particular relevance for poorer countries of the developing world. Clapham (2002: 785) suggests that, in such countries, 'the logic of incorporation into the modern global system . . . has undermined the state's coercive capabilities, weakened its legitimacy and subverted its capacity to manage the inevitable engagement with the global economy'.

Having said that, in recent years, there have been increasingly audible revisionist voices where the state's importance is concerned. Observers have, first, debated the significance of the 'new regionalism' evident from the 1980s, which Gamble and Payne (1996: 2) defined as 'a state-led or states-led project designed to recognize a particular regional space along defined economic and political lines'. By 2007, there were 380 regional trade associations notified to the World Trade Organization (WTO), including such South–South associations as the Southern Common Market (MERCOSUR) in South America, the Association of Southeast Asian Nations (ASEAN), and the Common Market for Eastern and Southern Africa (COMESA). The question was whether these were to be seen as stepping stones en route to global economic integration or as stumbling blocks and a form of resistance.

Second, critics of the globalization hypothesis have long argued that it greatly overstates the threat posed to the nation-state, pointing out, for example, that many states, including the East Asian NICs, have actively promoted and benefited from the process of economic globalization, and suggesting that states may be able to invoke or harness **nationalist** reaction to globalizing pressures as an alternative source of legitimacy, as in India. More recently, such debates have paid more systematic attention to the experience of developing countries. Mosley (2005) found that, in a number of the more developed countries in South America and where there was the political will, the state was better placed to resist these global pressures. Following

the 1997 financial crisis and during the most recent global financial crisis (2007–08), it has been noted that a number of emerging economies—notably, China and India, but also others, such as Malaysia and Indonesia—had retained sufficient protective regulation to withstand the worst economic consequences.

With renewed acknowledgement of the independent agency of the nation-state has come re-appreciation of the role of the state itself, for instance in development and security. If neoliberalism, with which globalization theory has been closely associated, tended to advocate a reduced role for the state in favour of the market, by the end of the 1990s there were already signs of reappraisal. The World Bank's 1997 report, *The State in a Changing World*, and the emerging so-called **post-Washington consensus** recognized the importance of an effective state to complement and support the activities of markets (Stiglitz 1998). In South America, many commentators have pointed to a 'return of the state' over the last decade, associated with a succession of left-leaning governments, as in Bolivia and Ecuador (Grugel and Riggirozzi 2012). So, as with modernization and dependency perspectives, over time, globalization approaches have been modified by increased awareness of the role and efficacy of the (nation-)state.

KEY POINTS

- Globalization theory, drawing on both modernization and dependency theory, emphasizes increasing global economic integration. It also implicitly calls into question the existence of a distinct developing world.

- Critical responses to globalization as neoliberal ideology have been associated with the 'anti-globalization movement', and have included arguments about orientalism and 'post-development' theory.

- Early globalization theory suggested the declining importance of the (nation-)state, although, more recently, revisionist arguments have qualified this position.

Current Approaches

A state of 'disarray'?

Both modernization-based approaches and Marxist-inspired approaches were found increasingly wanting by the 1980s. Although globalization theory incorporates significant elements of both, it too tends to undermine the rationale for studying politics in the developing world as a distinct field. Moreover, globalization theory reflects changes in the real world, including increasing differentiation amongst countries of the 'developing world', which pose further problems for meaningful generalization.

These developments within the field have coincided with a wider disillusionment with attempts at grand theory-building in the social sciences. One general school of thinking, originating in linguistics and philosophy, which contributed to and helped to articulate such misgivings, has been **post-structuralism**. The approach adopted by post-structuralists, discussed further later in this chapter, questioned the epistemological basis and claims of all of the great theoretical approaches, or 'meta-narratives', such as liberalism, Marxism, or indeed 'modernization'.

There has also been a steady growth of information about politics in different developing countries since the first attempts at generalization in the 1950s. Western governments—above all, the US government—have funded research and teaching, some of it under the rubric of 'area studies'. Professional associations of area specialists, conferences, and journals have proliferated. At the same time, political science expertise—concerning both the country in question and politics in developing countries more broadly—is expanding in a growing number of developing countries: not only in India, where authors such as Rajni Kothari have been challenging received thinking over many decades, but also, for instance, in Argentina, Brazil, Chile, Mexico, South Africa, South Korea, Taiwan, and Thailand. Admittedly, such indigenous authors often gravitate towards the relative comfort and security of American universities; Africa, for instance, has its own 'academic diaspora'. The ranks of these indigenous authors are swelling all the time, but include, for example: Guillermo O'Donnell, from Argentina, who devised the influential concept of **delegative democracy** (see Chapter 14); Arturo Escobar, from Colombia, associated (as we have seen) with the notion of 'post-development'; Doh Chull Shin, from South Korea, who has written on democracy, with special reference to that country's experience (see Chapter 24); and Claude Ake, from Nigeria (who died in 1996).

All of this has heightened awareness of the complexity and diversity of politics across this great tranche of the world's countries. Surveying all of these developments, one might well conclude that politics in the developing world no longer even has pretensions to being a coherent field of study; rather, as Manor (1991: 1) had already suggested more than twenty years ago, it is 'in disarray'.

Themes and agendas

If this remains to some extent true, the globalization background provides one element of commonality, whilst in the foreground one can also discern three, partly overlapping, themes or research issues that have tended to predominate and shape lines of more recent comparative inquiry, supplemented, or even challenged, in the last few years by a fourth.

The first is democratization (see Chapter 14). When the **third wave of democracy** broke in the mid-1970s, spreading through South America in the 1980s and much of tropical Africa in the 1990s, it served to confound the expectations of a generation of political scientists who had come to see political authoritarianism or decay as an intrinsic political feature of the developing world. The global reach of democratization extended not only as a consequence of pressures within developing countries, or of the collapse of the Soviet bloc and end of the cold war, but also through more deliberate interventions of Western governments and intergovernmental organizations. As Chapter 14 describes, these included attaching political conditions to forms of economic assistance, but also more direct international **democracy promotion** through financial and other forms of support to democracy projects. Linked to this drive, Western government and research foundation funding helped to generate a huge literature apparently covering every aspect of democratic transition, including analysis of the effectiveness of international **democracy assistance**.

Already in the 1990s, Diamond (1996) was asking whether democracy's third wave was over; increasingly, in the new millennium, the literature has come to focus on the limitations and failures of the democratizing process, and the survival or revival of authoritarianism in democratic guise. The arrival of the so-called Arab Spring in 2011 (see Chapters 11 and 14) encouraged a new surge of 'demo-optimism', with speculation that this could even herald a 'fourth wave'. Five years on, at time of writing, however, the brutal sequel in, for instance, Libya and Syria has largely put paid to such expectations (Masoud 2015).

The second theme is the relationship between politics and economic development or growth. An influential strand of thinking now sees **good governance**, and even democracy, as a prerequisite of economic growth. This represents an inversion of the early political development literature in which economic growth was generally assumed to be a condition of democracy (Leftwich 1993). We have already noted a reassessment of the importance of the state by bodies such as the World Bank, which opened its 1997 report, *The State in a Changing World*, by declaring that the state is central to economic and social development, not so much as a direct provider of growth, but rather as a partner, catalyst, and facilitator. The 2007–08 global financial crisis has reinforced this interest as observers debate which kinds of political arrangement have been associated with the most resilient economies. It has also led to an interest in the economic role played by **civil society** organizations (CSOs) and **social capital**. This theme, again, lacks a fully elaborated theoretical context, but owes something to the strong government variant of the politics of modernization. But again, like the democratization theme, it is clearly partly driven by concerns of Western governments and intergovernmental organizations.

A third prominent theme concerns peace, stability, and security versus conflict and risk (see Chapter 13). Again, this overlaps with the two previous themes: domestic conflict inhibits the emergence of political conditions conducive to economic growth, for instance, whilst many champions of democratization believe that democratic values and institutions provide the best guarantee both of domestic and of international security and order. The growing focus on causes and consequences of conflict and instability within developing countries is also, however, a result of the perception that such conflict has been on the increase since the end of the cold war. An additional impetus has been the perceived need to combat international terrorism, heightened in the wake of 9/11. In this context, there has been particular interest, on the one hand, in the pathology of 'failing' and 'failed', or collapsed, states, and on the other, in the 'politics of identity', especially ethnic and religious identity, in developing countries (see Chapters 7 and 8). Building on this theme, the most recent trend has been in analysis of the record and challenges of state-building in post-conflict societies (see Chapter 13).

These three themes do not amount to, or derive from, one coherent analytic framework, although they echo and incorporate elements of the earlier dominant paradigms, as well as globalization ideas. But they do overlap in the sense that democratization, economic performance, and the presence or absence of internal conflict either do, or are seen to, significantly affect one another. These themes also clearly relate to observable trends in the developing world, but also reflect the concerns, interests, and research-funding priorities of international agencies, Western governments, and, to a lesser extent, NGOs (see Chapter 10).

A fourth emerging theme, however, also requires mention: the implications of China's growing ascendancy. India is sometimes coupled with China in this context, but its rise is seen in more provisional and future terms. This China theme does not dovetail so neatly with the other three, although it is regularly discussed in relation to them. Increasingly, in the new century and especially since the global financial crisis, China has come to be seen as a key global player, not only as one of the five designated BRICS countries, but also potentially part of a G2 with the United States or even a global hegemon. Its rise has compounded the conceptual difficulties of defining and demarcating a developing world. China likes to present itself as a Third World or developing country (see Chapter 29), but some see in its relationship with other developing countries an element of North–South imperialism rather than South–South solidarity. The complexity of its internal relations also tend to undermine the North–South distinction; rather, China contains its own 'north' and 'south' (Eckl and Weber 2007).

Perhaps the most debated aspect of China's rise concerns the economic implications. By 2015, with a population of nearly 1.4 billion, it had become the world's second largest economy, largest exporter, and second largest importer of goods (see the discussion in Chapter 4). We have seen that this has raised big questions about China's impact on the (modified) neoliberal agenda associated with globalization and how far China offers an alternative development model, sometimes referred to as the 'Beijing Consensus' (Ramo 2004; Kurlantzik 2014); along with this growing economic influence, observers have anticipated more directly political effects. Questions have been asked about not only the prospects for democracy within China, but also the implications of China's rise for relatively fragile new democracies in East Asia (Kraft 2006; Diamond 2012). There have been concerns about the apparent lack of **conditionality** attached to Chinese foreign aid in Africa, which could undermine the good governance agenda of the Organisation for Economic Co-operation and Development's (OECD's) Development Assistance Committee (DAC) donors (Tan-Mullins et al. 2010).

KEY POINTS

- The decline of modernization- and Marxist-based approaches and the ascendancy of globalization theory have coincided with questioning of the need for grand theory in political studies.

- Expanding scholarship has increased awareness of the empirical complexity of the field.

- However, some coherence is provided by key themes of democratization, politics and economic development, conflict/post-conflict, and, increasingly, the role of China.

- Recent scholarship is marked by a preference for middle-range theory, with an emphasis on the role of political institutions.

Strategies and Methods of Analysis

We need to consider, finally, the strategies, categories, and more specific methods of analysis that have been typically deployed to analyse the politics of developing countries. As already noted, the tendency has been to apply those developed initially within 'mainstream' and Western political science. This is even more noticeable now that the notion of a distinct 'developing world' is increasingly problematized. An important contemporary illustration is the focus of much recent analysis of politics in developing countries on political institutions, which is part of a broader trend in political science from the 1980s (see Chapter 3).

The politics of individual developing countries is studied in the context of area or regional studies (for instance centred on Latin America, the Caribbean, or South Asia), or as part of cross-national and regional thematic inquiries (for instance into executive–legislative relations or **corruption**). There has also latterly been some tendency to emphasize the international or global dimension of politics, for example the increasing salience of the religious dimension of politics (see Chapter 8) in individual developing countries, especially those in sub-Saharan Africa. The implicit argument is that, in such countries, external determinants are so powerful that apparently domestic political processes are best understood through the prism of international political economy and international relations approaches.

Most commonly, studies of developing country politics fall into the broad category of comparative politics. Accordingly, we find a range of comparative

'strategies' deployed. First is the case study approach, in which the politics of a single country is explored in some depth. In theory, at least, such exploration should be informed by a research agenda reflecting a wider body of comparative research and should aim to test or generate propositions relating to that research. Case studies that simply celebrate the 'exceptionalism' of the country in question would not be considered proper social science, although, of course, even the idea of an 'exception' implies a broader pattern that is being deviated from. More middle-range comparative studies focus on particular questions; they may use a subset of cases (such as countries, local governments, parties) selected to illuminate the matter in question. In a methodological distinction going back to J. S. Mill (1888), cases in a 'most similar' design will be similar in a number of key respects, whilst differing in regard to the variable being explored. In a 'most different' design, they will differ in many key respects, but not as regards that variable. In-depth qualitative analysis, often involving a historical perspective, will aim to identify particular factors associated with the variable under review. A good example of such an approach is Bratton and van de Walle's (1997) study of *Democratic Experiments in Africa*. Alternatively, studies take a 'large *n*' of cases and use statistical methods to analyse comparative data. The availability of such data is steadily growing. They include, for instance, election results and survey data collected through instruments such as Latinobarometer and Afrobarometer, and the databases collected by Freedom House, Transparency International, and the Governance Matters project (see Chapter 15). Such an approach, increasingly favoured within mainstream political science and international relations, can yield valuable and counter-intuitive findings, but is, of course, heavily dependent on the availability of data that is reliable, valid, and appropriate. (For an excellent account of these issues, see Landman 2008.) Finally, recent studies, especially those concerned with assessing the impact of aid and **institutional** reform, have shown growing interest in employing quasi-experimental methods, seeking to reproduce some aspects of laboratory techniques (see, for instance, Grossman and Paler 2015).

In arriving at propositions to be explored, or even tested statistically, studies draw on existing studies and middle-range theorizing. Some, however, establish their own central propositions more systematically and deductively, building on the precepts of rational choice theory. This is an approach that takes as its primary unit of analysis the individual actor, who is presumed to make rational choices on the basis of self-interest. Within the framework of the 'new institutionalism', the focus is on the way in which institutional incentives and opportunities influence the individual's strategic calculations. As discussed further in Chapter 3, this approach has recently been very evident in work on constitutional and electoral systems design in new democracies.

The dominant assumption in the 'mainstream' comparative strategies and methods of analysis explored so far is that it is appropriate to apply them in contexts differing from those in which they first evolved. This is, in many ways, an attractive argument that emphasizes what is common and continuous in human experience—in contrast to those that point towards possibly unbridgeable cultural differences, as is said to be the case in forms of 'orientalism' discussed earlier. Nonetheless, there is a danger, unless these approaches are used sensitively, that aspects of politics in developing countries will be wrongly assumed or misinterpreted. For a long time, comparative political analysts have been urged to ensure that the concepts they use actually do 'travel'. For instance, doubts have been raised about the relevance of rational choice theory in contexts in which cultural values weigh heavily; indeed, the notion of rational choice itself could be seen as the product of a specific US social science culture.

The approaches discussed so far are also, to a large extent, empirical and positivist. But there is an alternative type of approach that focuses more centrally on issues of meaning (sometimes referred to as 'interpretavism') and thus incidentally potentially suffers less from problems of cultural imposition or misinterpretation. This comes in what might be called stronger and weaker forms, ranging from post-structuralism and discourse theory, to types of social constructivism. It also tends, although not inevitably, to be associated with more radical, or critical, accounts of politics.

Post-structural, or 'discourse', approaches question the very epistemological foundations of knowledge, including political science. Within the study of politics, the ideas of Michel Foucault (1926–84) have been especially influential. He understood political processes, institutions, and indeed 'subjects' (actors) to be constructed through dominant 'discourses', understood not simply as language and ideas, but also as the practices embodying them. A central concern of discourse theorists, then, has been to trace the originating historical practices (genealogy) of such discourses. We have seen, for example, how Said's critique of 'orientalism' and radical critiques of the discourse of development have drawn on post-structural methods of analysis.

Constructivism does not go so far, but still argues that central concepts such as 'power' or 'ethnicity' through which we organize our understanding are themselves 'socially constructed'. It makes use of notions such as **framing**, or the way in which political issues are constructed to reflect and favour different interests and agendas. It has been especially influential within the study of international relations. **Feminists** have, for instance, drawn upon it to critically deconstruct use of the notion of the 'empowerment' of women by development agencies (della Faille 2011). Within comparative politics, including the study of developing polities, it has been used to analyse the construction of political identities, for instance **ethnopolitical identity** (see Chapter 7). It has been especially prominent in analysis both concerning and stemming from the new social movements and their 'alternative' political projects (see Chapter 11).

KEY POINTS

- Politics in developing countries is generally studied using 'mainstream' political science comparative strategies and methods, although these may not always be appropriate or sensitively applied.
- Interpretivist approaches run less risk of misrepresentation, but tend to be used less frequently and more critically.

Conclusion

The dominant paradigms in the past, associated with modernization theory and dependency theory, were valuable to the extent that, by suggesting the importance of particular factors or relationships, they helped to generate debate; also, they encouraged political analysis and generalization beyond the particularities of individual country case studies. But, at the same time, they were overgeneralized, excessively influenced by Western ideological assumptions and agendas—whether 'bourgeois' or 'radical'—and Western historical experience, and based on inadequate knowledge and understanding of the developing world itself. They created, as Cammack and colleagues (1993: 3) phrased it, 'a problem of premature and excessive theorization'.

Over time, our knowledge of the developing world has grown, and with it, inevitably, our awareness of its diversity and complexity. Moreover, that developing world itself has become increasingly differentiated. Especially in the context of globalization theory, this greater recognition of diversity has called into question the coherence of the developing world as a geographic—and political—category. These developments have coincided with a tendency for political science to rein in its theoretical aspirations, focusing on 'middle-range' rather than grand theory. Post-structural thinking has also diminished the appeal of grand interpretative narratives.

Presently, then, whilst globalization theory continues to provide an implicit backdrop to much political analysis, the field of politics in the developing world has become less obviously coherent. However, it is possible to perceive an implicit agenda of inquiry, focusing on democracy or governance, development, conflict, and, increasingly, the implications of China's rise, which remains strongly influenced by Western interests and perspectives. At the same time, radical, critical perspectives persist. In addition to a continuing Marxist-inspired materialist critique can be found alternative critiques, some of them emanating from 'indigenous' sources, which seek to problematize the whole enterprise of 'Western' attempts to understand and influence politics in developing countries. For many of us, this may be a step too far, but we should by now recognize the need to proceed with all due caution and humility.

? QUESTIONS

1. What are the implications of globalization theory for both the character of politics in the developing world and the way in which it should be studied?

2. In what sense, and for what reasons, is the study of politics in the developing world currently in 'disarray'?

3. Do we need a distinct theoretical framework for analysing politics in the developing world?

4. In what ways is Said's critique of 'orientalism' relevant to the understanding of politics in developing countries?

5. To what extent have Huntington's arguments about the 'politics of order' continued to have relevance for the field of developing-world politics?

6. How might China's growing global influence reshape the study of politics in the developing world?

FURTHER READING

Berger, M. (ed.) (2004) 'After the Third World?', Special issue of *Third World Quarterly*, 25(1) Collection of articles that reflect upon the historical significance and contemporary relevance of the notion of a 'third world'.

Cammack, P. (1997) *Capitalism and Democracy in the Third World: The Doctrine for Political Development* (Leicester: Leicester University Press) Well-argued, critical reflection, from a left-wing perspective, upon 'mainstream' accounts of the political development literature.

Fukuyama, F. (2011) *The Origins of Political Order: From pre-Human Times to the French Revolution* (London: Profile Books) Broad comparative overview, explicitly building on Huntington's work, examining the origin of political institutions.

Fukuyama, F. (2014) *Political Order and Political Decay: From the Industrial Revolution to the Globalization of Democracy* (New York: Farrar, Straus & Giroux) Extends the analysis of the 2011 volume to the present day.

Hagopian, F. (2000) 'Political Development Revisited', *Comparative Political Studies*, 33(6/7): 880–911 Retrospective overview of political development thinking.

Higgott, R. A. (1983) *Political Development Theory* (London/Canberra: Croom-Helm) Account of the development and persistence of political development thinking.

Jones, A. (2010) *Globalization: Key Thinkers* (Cambridge: Polity) Accessible and up-to-date overview of the strands and development of globalization thinking.

Landman, T. (2008) *Issues and Methods in Comparative Politics*, 3rd edn (London: Routledge) Clear and engaging introduction to comparative analysis.

Manor, J. (ed.) (1991) *Rethinking Third-World Politics* (London: Longman) Collection of essays, some using post-structuralist concepts or approaches, seeking to go beyond old theoretical perspectives.

Randall, V., and Theobald, R. (1998) *Political Change and Underdevelopment: A Critical Introduction to Third-World Politics*, 2nd edn (London: Macmillan) Provides an account of theories and debates concerning politics in the developing world, from political development to globalization.

Said, E. (1995 [1978]) *Orientalism* (Harmondsworth: Penguin) Influential critique of 'orientalist' approaches to history and culture.

Smith, B. C. (2013) *Understanding Third-World Politics*, 4th edn (Basingstoke: Palgrave) Useful overview of themes in the study of the politics of the developing world.

 WEB LINKS

http://archive.is/faculty.hope.edu   Provides materials on the scope and methods of political science.

http://thebricspost.com   For material on the BRICS.

http://www.brookings.edu/sabout#research-programs/   Provides general updates on research on politics, development, and globalization.

http://www.theglobalist.com   On globalization.

http://www.ids.ac.uk/idsresearch/centre-for rising-powers-and global-development   For research on global development.

 For additional material and resources, please visit the Online Resource Centre at:
http://www.oxfordtextbooks.co.uk/orc/burnell5e/

2

Colonialism and Post-Colonial Development

James Chiriyankandath

Overview

The variety of states and societies found in the developing two-thirds of the world is reflected in their political diversity. The contemporary polities of the global South bear the imprint of the legacy of colonialism, but are also marked both by their pre-colonial heritage and their different post-colonial experiences. This chapter argues that while the historically proximate experience of colonialism has had a significant impact on post-colonial political development, attention to the pre-colonial past and to political agency after independence yield a more nuanced perspective on the varied politics found across the developing world. The different ways in which post-independence politicians reacted and adapted to—and were constrained by—the past legacies and present situations of their countries helped to determine the shape of the new polities.

Introduction: The Post-Colonial World

In the middle of the last century, the world was still dominated by mainly European empires. By 1921, 84 per cent of the earth had been colonized and there were as many as 168 colonies (Go 2003: 17). Although, by the 1960s, most were at least nominally independent, subsequent decades showed how much the spectre of colonization still loomed. While the varied history of **post-colonial states** illustrates the importance of their pre-colonial past, as well as of factors such as geography, geopolitics, and political agency, Hall (1996: 246, 253) points out that the fact that countries are not 'post-colonial' in the same way does not mean that they are not 'post-colonial': colonization 'refigured the terrain' everywhere. The concept of the post-colonial offers a point of entry for studying the differences between formerly colonial societies (Hoogvelt 1997: xv).

Whatever the varied reality of their present condition, their colonial background is still used to associate the contemporary states of the **developing world** with a pre-modern, traditional, backward past—the antithesis of the 'modern', post-imperial West (Slater 2004: 61–2). In this way, colonial perceptions linger on, sustained by the persisting imbalance in geopolitical power relations (North–South, West–non-West). One important result is the remarkable resilience of racialized discourse in the West when it comes to discussing issues such as migration and development, albeit one that shifted from being expressed in biological terms during the heyday of colonialism to being voiced in a sociocultural idiom in the wake of decolonization (Duffield 2006; see also Wallerstein 2003: 124–48).

It is to this reality that the rise of post-colonial theory, especially in the field of cultural studies, sought to draw attention. Influenced by post-modernist and **post-structuralist** perceptions, it was born of disillusionment with the failure of the Third World to, in the words of Frantz Fanon (1967: 255), start a new history and 'set afoot a new man'. Going beyond a temporal understanding of post-colonialism, post-colonial theory sought to analyse its cultural aftermath: the 'cultures, discourses and critiques that lie *beyond*, but remain clearly influenced by colonialism' (McEwan 2009: 17).

Colonialism was the obvious place to start explaining why political independence had not resulted in the emancipation for which people like Fanon, a black psychiatrist from the French Caribbean who devoted himself to the Algerian struggle for independence, yearned. The emancipatory project, belying the hope expressed by Fanon, had been fatally undermined by its 'imperial genealogy' (Cooper 2005: 25). While a number of political scientists, historians, and anthropologists (Crawford Young, Mahmood Mamdani, Bernard Cohn, and Nicholas Dirks among them) sought to analyse the lasting impact of colonialism on the colonized, much post-colonial theory has followed Edward Said's (1993, 1995 [1978]) seminal work on **orientalism** in focusing attention more on imperial intent than colonial consequence (for example Viswanathan 1990). That the

colonial past might be of great significance in determining the future of post-colonial states was recognized even as decolonization proceeded, although then it was adherents of what they saw as the imperial mission who were more inclined to do so. Margery Perham (1963: 18), colonial historian of British Africa, remarked: 'Our vanishing empire has left behind it a large heritage of history which is loaded with bequests good, bad and indifferent. This neither they [the critics of colonialism] nor we can easily discard.'

Thirty years later, the interest aroused by post-colonial theorists served to refocus attention on the nature of the colonial legacy. Birmingham (1995: 6–8), writing of post-colonial Africa, highlighted lasting geographical, financial, and cultural legacies: the remarkable persistence of colonial borders, trade and currency links (especially in the ex-French colonies), and the way in which 'the minds of many Africans continued to work on colonial assumptions'. Mayall and Payne (1991: 3–5), dealing with the 'Commonwealth Third World', suggested that the more durable legacies of the British Empire may have been its military and statist characteristics rather than ideologies such as **liberalism** and **nationalism**. It is also argued that direct British rule led to more successful development (Lange 2009), and that the reason why former British colonies may have fared better was the role of Christian Protestant missions and the autonomy that they enjoyed in relation to the colonial state (Woodberry 2004).

That the impact of colonialism has been transformative rather than transitory is now widely accepted. Half a century or more after their independence, developing countries still live with colonialism (Sharkey 2003: 141; Dirks 2004: 1; see Box 2.1). The way in which the 2011 partition of Sudan, Africa' largest state, after more than half a century of failed state-building did not resolve the deep crises afflicting that country showed that their roots lay in how the colonial Sudanese state had been created, and not only in racial and religious differences—most obviously, between the more Islamic and Arabized north and the south (Bassil 2013: 193–4). In concluding his comparative study of Spanish America, Mahoney (2010: 269) says: 'Colonialism usually brought countries to relative levels of development that have been remarkably enduring . . . the international hierarchy created from colonialism will not be easily rearranged.'

Despite the differences in formation and practice between the European colonial powers, it is argued that the phenomenon of colonialism is united to a large

BOX 2.1 COLONIZING THE MIND

How to come to terms with the survival of not only **institutional** forms (administrative, legal, educational, military, religious) and languages (English, French, Portuguese, Spanish, Dutch), but also the mentality bequeathed in part by the colonial heritage has been a preoccupation of Third World intellectuals. Some, like the Kenyan writer Ngũgĩ wa Thiong'o (1986), sought a resolution to the dilemma by abandoning the colonial language (English) to write in their native tongue—in Ngũgĩ's case, Gĩkũyũ. However, mentality is shaped by much more than only the language used, and Partha Chatterjee (1986) and Ramachandra Guha (1989) have noted nationalism's role in embedding colonialist historiography into Indian understandings of India, European history serving as a kind

of *metahistory* (Chakrabarty 2003) that relegated the people of the developing world to being 'perpetual consumers of modernity' (Chatterjee 1993: 5). When it came to defining state forms and political structures, Indian nationalist and post-independence leaders, 'coloured by the ideas and institutions of Western colonialism' (Jalal 1995: 11), preferred the familiar structures of the British Raj. Although no African or Asian state went to the extent of the founders of the Brazilian republic who, in 1889, adapted the motto of Auguste Comte, the nineteenth-century French positivist philosopher, in adding the words 'order and progress' to their flag, the post-Christian myth of modernity (Gray 2003: 103) certainly found many devotees across the developing world.

extent by its legacies (Dirks 2004: 2). Yet differences in the trajectories of post-colonial development matter and require explanation. One way of attempting to do so that has been gaining currency is **path dependence**, an idea borrowed from economics (see Chapter 3). This emphasizes the importance of choices made and the difficulties of changing a course once set. Yet, as we shall see, other factors also matter: geopolitical and strategic considerations, and political agency.

KEY POINTS

- **Politics** in developing countries are influenced by their pre-colonial heritage, and colonial and post-colonial experiences.
- Virtually all developing countries are, in some sense, post-colonial, although not necessarily in the same ways. Post-colonial theory seeks to examine the continuing impact that colonialism has on post-colonial development.
- The impact of colonialism was transformative, rather than transitory. As well as reshaping economic and political forms, it also changed the way in which people, especially the educated, came to see the world.
- 'Path dependence' emphasizes the importance of history in shaping choices for states and societies.

Pre-Colonial States and Societies

Among the best predictors of the resilience of post-colonial states is whether the societies they contain possess a significant pre-colonial experience of statehood (Clapham 2000: 9). From this perspective, it is instructive to consider the political map of the pre-colonial world.

Eighteenth-century Asia was dominated by states that included some of the world's largest empires (Ottoman Turkey, Safavid Iran, Mughal India, and Manchu China), with only sparsely populated Central Asia and the interior of the Arabian Peninsula occupied by nomadic pastoral societies. In contrast, prior to the sixteenth-century Spanish and Portuguese conquest, the Americas were largely inhabited by dispersed hunter-gatherer, fishing, and farming communities. The important exceptions were the Inca empire on the western seaboard of South America and, in Central America, the Aztec empire, a number of smaller kingdoms, and Mayan city-states. Before being overwhelmed in the nineteenth-century European **scramble for Africa**, more than two-thirds of the African continent was also occupied by non-state societies, with kingdoms and other state formations found only along its Arabized Mediterranean coast and scattered across more densely populated pockets south of the Sahara.

In the Americas, colonization by European settlers resulted in the creation of some twenty independent settler states in the century following the US Declaration of Independence in 1776, making America 'post-colonial' before some European colonial powers such as Germany, Italy, and Belgium had even become states, let alone acquired colonies (McEwan 2009: 51). In the 1900s, Australia and New Zealand also became self-governing British dominions. The post-colonial experience of the United States, Canada, Australia, and New Zealand is thus quite distinct from that of Asian and African states, while Latin American states are distinguished by the varying admixture of European and indigenous American elements in their social make-up. Recently, Latin American political leaders—especially those of, at least partly, non-European descent, such as Hugo Chávez in Venezuela (president from 1999 to 2013) and Evo Morales in Bolivia (president from 2006)—have sought to emphasize the latter, still visible in syncretic political, religious, and social practice. In Africa and Asia, European settlement was not a significant feature of colonization except for isolated instances such as French Algeria, the 'white' highlands of Kenya, and, most importantly, South Africa, where the white supremacist **apartheid** state was displaced only in 1994.

Pre-colonial Africa featured a variety of polities, among which were the city-states (for example Kano) and empire-states (such as Songhai, Ghana, Mali, Asante) of the west (Mazrui 1986: 272–3), as well as conquest states, such as that of the Zulus in the south, emerging in the period preceding European colonial rule. African scholars (for example Mazrui 1986: 273; Mamdani 1996: 40) have stressed the discontinuity between the pre- and post-colonial state, Mahmood Mamdani blaming, in particular, the deliberate colonial generalization of the conquest state and the administrative chieftainship as the basic modes of African rulership that were to serve as the template for their practice of **indirect rule** (see later in the chapter). The colonial rulers disregarded differences between societies and the restraints sometimes placed by tradition upon rulers. For instance, among the Akan of southern Ghana, the king (*Asantehene*) was chosen by a group of 'kingmakers' from among a number of candidates from a royal matrilineage and could be removed if deemed to have breached his oaths of office (Crook 2005: 1). In contrast, societies in northern Ghana had kings who ruled in a much more authoritarian manner, or had chiefs imposed by the British of a kind that did not previously exist. Basil Davidson (1992), in contrasting the achievements of Meiji Japan with the Asante state, argued that colonialism prevented the potential for the natural maturing of pre-colonial African institutions, but this is unconvincing given the continent's relative economic backwardness and the deeply rooted historical factors that gave rise to the logic of **extraversion** (see Box 2.2). Reinforced by its relative isolation, nineteenth-century Japan was a nation-state in being, 'Meiji political nationalism [creating] the modern Japanese nation on the basis of aristocratic (*samurai*) culture and its ethnic state' (Smith 1991: 105). There were hardly any pre-colonial nation-states in sub-Saharan Africa—although there might be a case for suggesting that Buganda in East Africa, what is now southern Uganda, was one (Green 2010)—an important reason why most African countries remain preoccupied by state formation rather than state consolidation (Hyden 2006: 70).

BOX 2.2 AFRICA'S GEOGRAPHY AND THE CONCEPT OF EXTRAVERSION

The history of Africa has been profoundly influenced by its geography. Clapham (2000: 5) described the bases for states in pre-colonial sub-Saharan Africa as 'peculiarly feeble', with the few relatively densely populated pockets creating a very discontinuous pattern of state formation across the vast continent. It is this historical geography that French political scientist Jean-François Bayart (1993: 21–2) had in mind when elaborating the concept of 'extraversion' to explain the politics of post-colonial Africa. He argued that the relatively weak development of its productive forces and its internal social struggles had combined to make political actors in Africa disposed to mobilize resources from their relationship with the external environment. The collaboration of African rulers in the transatlantic slave trade that resulted in the transportation between the sixteenth and nineteenth centuries of an estimated 13 million Africans—roughly one in ten of the population of West Africa from where most were taken to the Americas (Whatley 2015: 506)—was the most notorious aspect. Colonialism and its legacy served to emphasize the operation of the logic of extraversion, reinforcing a strong indigenous tendency to favour trade and commerce over manufacture (Chabal 2009: 117).

Pre-colonial Asia represented a considerable contrast to sub-Saharan Africa in being dominated by states, albeit diverse in size, depth, and durability. Indeed, the Mughal empire that flourished in India between the sixteenth and eighteenth centuries dwarfed its European counterparts in extent, population, and wealth, as did the Ming and, subsequently, Manchu empires in China and the Ottoman, and the Safavid empires to the west. Only in the Philippines did the establishment of Spanish dominion in the sixteenth century largely succeed in erasing the pre-colonial past from history (the country having the dubious distinction of being the only post-colonial state that bears the name of a colonial ruler, Philip II of Spain). In terms of prior state tradition, there is no gainsaying the antiquity of those in the rest of Asia. Yet, at first glance, the lineage of the post-colonial states of Asia too seems to owe far more to their immediate colonial predecessors than to their historic traditions.

There are a number of reasons for this. Perhaps most important are the obvious institutional, and more subtly influential ideological, legacies of colonialism, both of which appear more tangible despite the efforts to trace a pre-colonial ideological lineage, not least by nationalist leaders such as India's Jawaharlal

Nehru (1961). Typically, descriptions of post-colonial institutions *begin* with the colonial past. Four decades after the Indian parliament came into being, an account of its historical origins by its secretary-general devoted barely two unconvincing pages to the pre-colonial period, almost wholly focused on ancient India; the two millennia prior to the advent of British rule merited less than a sentence (Kashyap 1989: 1–3). While between one and two centuries of British dominion over the subcontinent may have left only a slight imprint on aspects of the everyday lives of many people, it was long enough, and the nature of the contrast stark enough, to have altered the context of government and politics fundamentally.

Anthropologists have been better at capturing this alteration than political historians or political scientists (Cohn 1996; Dirks 2001). Bernard Cohn (1996: 18) noted that while 'Europeans of the seventeenth century lived in a world of signs and correspondences . . . Indians lived in a world of substances'. His phrase captured a profound shift in how people first constituted, then transmitted, perceived, and interpreted, authority and social relations. In the mentality of government, the malleability and pliability afforded by 'substance' gave way to the unyielding notional rigour of scientific classification—the intention being to set rigid boundaries so as to control variety and difference. As Cohn (1996: 16) put it, the 'command of language' was paired with the 'language of command'. While this did not erase the legacy of the pre-colonial, it transformed it. How it did so is what we shall now consider in examining patterns of colonial rule.

KEY POINTS

- Varying patterns of state formation in pre-colonial Africa, Asia, the Americas, and Australasia influenced both the kind of colonization that they experienced and their post-colonial development.

- The post-colonial experience of areas that were the focus of European settlement is quite distinct from that of Asia and Africa. However, in Latin America, indigenous American influences are still perceptible.

- It has been argued that the geography and demography of Africa has had a significant influence in the persistent weakness of states, as reflected in Bayart's theory of extraversion.

- Even in Asia, where the pre-colonial era was dominated by state societies, the colonial state profoundly affected the development of politics and government.

Colonial Patterns

The era of European colonialism overseas was proclaimed in 1493, a year after Christopher Columbus's 'discovery' of America when Pope Alexander VI apportioned newly discovered non-Christian lands between the two main Catholic maritime powers of the day, Spain and Portugal. The greatest impact was felt in Central and South America, where the Spanish swiftly conquered the Aztec and Inca empires in the 1520s and 1530s, while the Portuguese focused on the coastline of much more sparsely populated Brazil. In under a century, the populations of the two great pre-colonial American empires declined by as much as 90 per cent to fewer than 2 million, decimated not so much by Spanish arms as by European-borne diseases such as smallpox, measles, yellow fever, and influenza (Mahoney 2010: 60, 68). The new Iberian empires were mercantilist until the eighteenth century, when they belatedly followed the British in undertaking liberal economic reforms, at the same time professionalizing and modernizing the absolutist state.

Over the next four-and-a-half centuries, the scope of European settlement and dominion expanded to cover the whole of the Americas, and much of South and South East Asia, Oceania (including Australia and New Zealand), Africa, and the Arab Middle East. Typically beginning with small coastal, generally commercial, enclaves, they subsequently expanded to cover the hinterland as conquest followed trade. The different periods in which regions were colonized by a number of European states (Spain and Portugal being followed by Holland, England, and France in the course of the sixteenth and seventeenth centuries, and by Belgium, Germany, and Italy in the nineteenth century) gave rise to a varied pattern of colonialism. The emergence of the United States (Hawaii, Cuba, Puerto Rico, Guam, and the Philippines) and Japan (Taiwan, Korea, and Manchuria) as overseas colonial powers by the end of the nineteenth century added to the variety, as did the peculiar situation of China.

After being defeated by Britain in the First Opium War of 1839–42, China suffered further military humiliation in the following decades (including at the hands of Japan in 1894–95), and had to acquiesce to leasing coastal territories to Britain, France, Germany, Russia, and Japan, and conceding territorial rights and consular jurisdiction to as many as nineteen, mainly European, countries (Feuerwerker 1983: 128–53). This 'treaty-port form of colonialism' (Maddison 2007: 167) survived until 1943. When the Communists established the new People's Republic in 1949, after more than a decade of war against, first, the invading Japanese, and then the Guomindang (Nationalist) government, Mao Zedong declared that the Chinese people had stood up, ending a period in which they had fallen behind 'due entirely to oppression and **exploitation** by foreign imperialism and domestic reactionary governments' (Mao 1977: 16–17).

Although their respective colonialisms expressed distinctive experiences of statehood, colonial powers also borrowed and learned from each other, by the early twentieth century perceiving themselves as being engaged in a common progressive endeavour of developing 'scientific colonialism' (Young 1998: 105). While the pattern varied, it is possible to discern certain common features across the colonial world. Referring to Michel Foucault's characterization of power as 'capillary', historian Frederick Cooper (2005: 49) argues that power in most colonial contexts was actually 'arterial'—that is, 'strong near the nodal points of colonial authority, less able to impose its discursive grid elsewhere'. This was in part because, as a number of writers put it, the colonial intent was to 'rule on the cheap' (Sharkey 2003: 122; Cooper 2005: 157). On the eve of its transfer from the brutally exploitative personal rule of King Leopold II to the Belgian state in 1908, the Congo Free State had only 1,238 European military and civilian officers covering more than 900,000 square miles (Young 1994: 107). In British India, the centrepiece of Britain's colonial empire, the entire European population in 1921 amounted to just 156,500 (or 0.06 per cent) out of a total of more than 250 million (Brown 1985: 95). The colonial state was coercive and extractive, yet thin, with local collaborators, especially those recognized as 'traditional' rulers, forming an indispensable element. Such a state also made the exercise of symbolic, as well as punitive, power very important. The routine British use of aircraft to both awe and bomb into submission rebellious Arab tribes in Iraq in the 1920s was an innovative case.

Until relatively late in their history, colonial states had a poor record of investment, with barely a tenth of total British overseas investment in the Victorian era going to the non-white colonies (Chibber 2005). Davis (2001: 311) notes that India recorded no increase in its per capita income in 190 years of British rule, with the colonial **regime** operating a policy of deliberate neglect when it came to development (Tomlinson 1993: 217). Lord Lugard (1965 [1922]: 617), the first governor-general of Nigeria and credited with introducing the policy of

indirect rule to British Africa, admitted that 'European brains, capital, and energy have not been, and never will be, expended in developing the resources of Africa from motives of pure philanthropy'. The fact was that the philanthropic element was not readily evident. The widespread consequence of cheap colonialism was uneven development and wide disparities between small, more-or-less Westernized elites and the rest (Dirks 2004: 15). In addition, the movement of labour between colonies to work in the plantation sector in particular introduced new social and economic divisions. In the course of the nineteenth and early twentieth centuries, hundreds of thousands of Indians, mainly indentured labourers, were transported to British colonies in the Caribbean, as well as to Burma, Ceylon, Malaya, Fiji, South Africa, Kenya, and Mauritius—a factor that contributed to ethnic political tensions in all of these territories after they became independent.

For colonial powers such as Britain and France, the paradox of their rule was that its survival depended on *failing* to fulfil the universal promise of their liberal state ideology. The **rule of law** in British India was necessarily despotic in that the rulers could not be held to account by those whom they governed, but only by their imperial masters in London. In the French colonies, the concept of assimilation (that is, ultimately making colonial subjects French) was never officially jettisoned, although by the 1920s it was obvious that the language of assimilation was merely the 'rhetoric of colonial benevolence' (Dirks 2004: 14). It could scarcely be otherwise since 'if the colonized . . . is found to be exactly the same . . . the colonizer is left with no argument for his supremacy' (McEwan 2009: 67). Under such circumstances, it was logical that the post-eighteenth-century European enlightenment discourse of rights should become translated into the language of liberation for the Western-educated colonized elite (Young 1994: 228).

A feature of colonial rule that was to have far-reaching consequences for the post-colonial world was what Nicholas Dirks (in his foreword to Cohn 1996: ix–xv; see also Dirks 2004: 1) described as a 'cultural project of control'—one that 'objectified' the colonized, and reconstructed and transformed their cultural forms through the development of a colonial system of knowledge that outlived decolonization. It was an approach that reified social, cultural, and linguistic differences, causing the colonial state to be described as an 'ethnographic state' (Dirks 2001). Yet while imperial anthropologists such as Herbert Risley, census commissioner and later Home Secretary in British India in the 1900s, helped to furnish 'a library of ethnicity, its shelves lined with tribal monographs' (Young 1994: 233), what colonial regimes generally did was adapt and develop pre-colonial differences and processes of identification rather than create them where none previously existed.

In India, the British rulers learned from the practices of their Mughal, Hindu, and Sikh predecessors in categorizing their Indian subjects, the novelty lying in their systematic method, modern 'scientific' techniques, and the scale on which they sought to enumerate and classify **castes**, tribes, and religions (Bayly 1999). The effect, as in Africa (Chabal 2009: 33), was to make the consciousness and instrumentalization of such group identities far more pervasive and politically potent. The creation of separate representation and electorates in the representative and elected bodies that were introduced from the 1900s on (Chiriyankandath 1992) also served to institutionalize these identities, making them less fluid than they had been. While such categorization may have initially had as its primary purpose making intelligible, and encompassing, an alien public sphere (Gilmartin 2003), it also proved useful in deploying divide-and-rule tactics against emergent anti-colonial nationalism. In the Indian case, the eventual outcome was the partition of the subcontinent in 1947, with the creation of Muslim Pakistan, and a post-independence politics in which such group identities remain of central significance (see Chapter 30). In Africa as well, a complex cartography of racial difference was introduced in place of the historical

ambiguity and relative indifference that had previously characterized regions such as Sudan, eventually producing a similar outcome (Bassil 2013: 100).

The colonial investment in emphasizing the traditional character of the colonized 'others' produced another of the peculiar paradoxes of colonialism: the civilizing colonizer's nostalgia for, in the words of the British imperial writer Rudyard Kipling (1987 [1890]: 183), 'the real native—not the hybrid, University-trained mule—[who] is as timid as a colt'. Yet deprecating the 'inauthentic' hybrid did not prevent colonial regimes from often favouring politically useful pre-colonial elites in imparting Western education, thereby creating a monocultural elite that created a nationalism in their own image; in more extreme cases, such as Pakistan and Sudan, this proved impossible to sustain in the multicultural context of the post-colonial state (Alavi 1988; Sharkey 2003). However, internalizing the colonial representation of them as the 'other' caused Asians and Africans to stress their 'dedicated' non-Western identities (Sen 2006: 102), ironically making the identities shaped under colonialism the force for decolonization (Dirks 2004: 30). Anti-colonial nationalists sought to distinguish between a material 'outer' masculine domain of economy, statecraft, science, and technology, in which they acknowledged the superiority of Western modernity, and a spiritual and cultural 'inner' feminine domain of language, religion, and family—the 'private essences of identity' (Young 1994: 275)—the distinctness of which had to be preserved (Chatterjee 1993: 6–9).

Despite overarching commonalities, there were important differences between colonies (see Box 2.3).

BOX 2.3 COLONIAL MUTATIONS OF THE MODERN STATE

Colonialism in Africa created mutations of the modern state. Among the ways in which this has been theorized is in terms of a 'gatekeeper' (Cooper 2002) or, from a different perspective, 'bifurcated' (Mamdani 1996) state. Unlike the nightwatchman state favoured by libertarians (Nozick 1974), the role of the colonial **gatekeeper state** was not to serve its inhabitants, but to control the intersection of the colony and the outside world, collecting and distributing the resources that control brought. However, while such a state was conceived as weak in terms of its social and cultural penetration, the same could not be said of the bifurcated colonial state. Seen as the prototype for the apartheid regime in South Africa, Mamdani (1996: 29) describes it as the outcome of the simultaneous operation of two different modes of dominion: a racially discriminatory direct rule, based on the exclusion of most, if

not all, natives from civil rights, in urban centres; and a method of indirect rule resting upon the institution of customary tribal authority that produced a system of **decentralized despotism** in the rural hinterland. The latter generally involved the conflation of a variety of forms of pre-colonial authority into one essentially monarchical, **patriarchal**, and authoritarian model (Mamdani 1996: 39) that was also territorially demarcated. Such an approach had the effect of disassociating power from authority in a way that subsequently came to pose a formidable challenge to post-colonial African rulers seeking to establish their **legitimacy** (Chabal 2009: 41). Elements of this model could be discerned in colonial practices outside Africa—most notably in the colonial search for, or creation of, a more authentically native aristocracy to enlist as subordinate collaborators.

While the British colonial state left behind an entrenched legacy of autocratic government in both India and Africa, in India this was tempered by nearly three decades of a widening measure of partly representative quasi-constitutional self-government at the provincial level, as well as a superior administration (the Indian Civil Service) that was nearly half Indian when independence came (Chandra et al. 1999: 18) and which maintained a tradition of political neutrality that ensured administrative continuity (Burra 2010). Although anti-democratic tendencies persisted in post-independence India (and, much more obviously, in Pakistan) (Jalal 1995), the contrast with the rapid breakdown of post-colonial constitutional government in Britain's erstwhile African colonies was striking.

From the outset of the establishment of colonial rule, the weak demographics that underpinned what Bayart (1993) calls the 'politics of extraversion' meant that the primary focus of colonial extraction in Africa was labour rather than land revenue, as in the much more densely populated Indian subcontinent (Young 1994: 273). From their relatively late inception, mainly in the late nineteenth century, the European colonial states in Africa relied heavily on the institution of various forms of forced and tributary labour. Although its most brutal manifestations, as in King Leopold II's Congo Free State, largely disappeared after the First World War, the practice survived well into the first half of the twentieth century. The colonial economics of sub-Saharan Africa resulted in either the absence of—or a much weaker—indigenous capitalist class, with Africans effectively excluded from all but petty trade in most regions (Tordoff 1997: 42; Hyden 2006: 46–7). European companies and immigrant Asian merchants dominated larger-scale economic activity, with African integration in the global economy mainly taking the form of cash-crop farming, especially in French and British West Africa, and labouring in diamond, gold, copper, bauxite, and other mines, particularly in central and southern Africa. These features, together with the relatively brief span (of between sixty and eighty years) of colonial rule across much of the continent, had the consequence that both the colonial state in Africa and indigenous political and economic forces were more weakly developed than in India, the colonial powers having not modernized society enough (Hyden 2006: 232).

Colonies have been described as 'underfunded and overextended laboratories of modernity' (Prakash 1999: 13). They were laboratories within which the subjects of the experiments proved unwilling to live. Through specific ideologies such as Gandhian nationalism in India, Négritude, pan-Africanism, and African socialism in sub-Saharan Africa, Arabism in the Arab Middle East, and varieties of nationalism influenced by pre-colonial Muslim identity across the Islamic world and Buddhism in South East Asia, the anti-colonial nationalism of the Western-educated elite succeeded in mobilizing a mass following. Yet while this evocation of what Chatterjee (1993) termed the 'inner domain' proved effective as an anti-colonial tool, colonialism left a material legacy in the institutions of state (the bureaucratic, judicial, and educational systems, the police, and the military), and entrenched patterns of trade and exchange (for example the French franc zone and the British sterling area in Africa). It also bequeathed ideologies exported from the West—nationalism itself, liberalism, and socialism—as well as global languages of power (English, French, Spanish, and Portuguese). The rest of this chapter describes how this polyglot legacy has served post-colonial states and societies.

KEY POINTS

- The era of European colonialism stretched over five centuries, during which different colonial powers emerged and patterns of colonialism changed.

- The colonial state was typically extractive in intent, and autocratic and coercive in form. A thin, cheap state, it relied on local collaborators to maintain its authority.

- Colonialism developed a system of knowledge that 'objectified' the colonized, one consequence being to harden and highlight ethnic and religious distinctions.

- Variations in colonial rule had repercussions for post-colonial development, as in the contrasting experience of decolonization in much of Africa and in India.

- Colonialism created mutations of the modern state. In Africa, this has been described variously in terms of a 'gatekeeper' or 'bifurcated' state.

Post-Colonial Development

In contrast to the drawn-out history of colonization, the tide of decolonization came in fast. Beginning in Asia, the Middle East, and North Africa in the decade after the Second World War, it covered most of sub-Saharan Africa within a few years of Ghana (formerly the British Gold Coast) becoming the first independent black African state in 1957; by 1980, it had taken in much of the rest of the erstwhile European colonial empire in the Caribbean, the Persian Gulf and South Arabia, and the Pacific. This rapid transformation was in part the outcome of geopolitical factors: the perceptible weakening of European power following the two world wars; and the emergence of the United States and the Soviet Union, each competing to win over anti-colonial nationalists to their respective camps, as the pivots of the post-war bipolar cold war world. However, it was increasing pressure from anti-colonial nationalism, inspired in part by Indian independence in 1947, and a desire on the part of the colonial powers to retain as much of the moral, cultural, and economic **soft power** of empire as possible that forced the pace of change (Midgley and Pichaud 2011: 33).

But how much change did decolonization bring? The passionate desire of anti-colonial idealists such as Fanon (1967: 252) not to imitate Europe starkly contrasted with the imperial paternalism of colonial officials such as Phillip Mitchell, British governor of Kenya, who could say as late as 1945 that, faced with 'the choice of remaining a savage or of adapting our civilisation, culture, religion and language, [the African] is doing the latter as fast as he can' (quoted in Cooper 2002: 73). The post-colonial reality belied both Mitchell's belief and Fanon's hope. Colonialism, by globalizing the European 'Westphalian' template of an international system constituted of sovereign nation-states, determined that the primary object of anti-colonial nationalism would be the transformation of colonies into independent nation-states within a system that bore the deep impress of the erstwhile colonizers. Despite seeking to assert their political and cultural autonomy, anti-colonialists demanding independence had little choice but to operate within this system, since it was the only one that was also imaginable to their rulers (Cooper 2003: 67).

It was a dynamic that helped to ensure that while pan-African and pan-Arab dreams remained unrealized, in British India Muslim insecurities recognized in colonial policy resulted in partition and the creation of Pakistan as a separate 'Muslim' nation-state. Although East Pakistan subsequently seceded to form Bangladesh in 1971, in Africa, apprehending the potential for incessant conflict, the Organisation of African Unity, founded in 1963, and its successor, the African Union, enshrined respect for inherited colonial borders in its 2000 Constitutive Act. Despite numerous secessionist movements and civil wars, this position was largely maintained (Bereketeab 2015), the only exceptions being recognition of the new states of Eritrea (which had been federated with Ethiopia in 1950) in 1993 and South Sudan (part of Sudan after independence in 1956) in 2011, both with the acquiescence of the states from which they separated. This maintenance of the post-colonial state system was helped by the way in which '[t]erritorial nationalism has become embedded in the quotidian subconscious of most Africans' (Young 2012: 332).

The new states faced the unprecedented challenge of fashioning 'a peculiarly *modern* form of statehood', modelled not on earlier, more basic, forms of the state, but on the elaborate modern Western state that had been developed over centuries (Clapham 2000: 6–7). They were also inhibited by the fact that the conditions in which power was generally transferred were far from optimal. Even though, in the majority of cases, independence was not accompanied or preceded by war or violence, it was marred by the hurried transfer of administrative responsibilities, belated and unsustainable political compromises, economic dependence, and largely untested legislatures and governments. In noting how colonialism fatefully structured political choices along regional and ethnic lines in Britain's most populous African territory, Nigeria, Nolutshungu (1991: 100) observed that the political systems of post-colonial societies 'carried . . . in their genes—the heritage of the colonialism that designed them, authoritarian in its day, but also, invariably, in its retreat, a champion of elitist and paternalist notions of democracy'. In Nigeria, the system quickly, and tragically, gave way to successive military coups in 1966, six years after independence, followed by a three-year civil war that claimed between 1 million and 3 million lives. By contrast, an instance of a creative African post-colonial response occurred in Tanzania, where the country's first leader, Julius Nyerere, used the language of *ujamaa* (Swahili, meaning 'familyhood') socialism to instil a political discourse of progress that sought to link local themes with global arguments about capitalism and modernity in engendering a sense of national unity and purpose (Hunter 2015).

Whether states achieved independence via a negotiated constitutional transition or a war of liberation did not appear to make much difference to the lasting influence of the colonial legacy. Certainly, in Africa, the trajectory of development of the minority of post-colonial states that were the outcome of armed struggle (Algeria and the ex-Portuguese colonies of Guinea-Bissau, Angola, and Mozambique, as well as Zimbabwe, Namibia, and Eritrea) showed much in common with that of their neighbours (Young 1998: 107). Although peaceful transfers of power may have assisted what Young (2012: 29) calls the inertial forces favouring the retention of colonial legal and bureaucratic legacies, the troubled post-independence histories of the liberated colonies demonstrated that it was not possible to remove the long shadow cast by the colonial past through struggle. In fact, the bitterness of the struggle itself seems, in some cases (Algeria, Angola, Mozambique), to have contributed to subsequent civil war. Being accepted as legitimate by its population was a major preoccupation for post-colonial states given the generally multi-ethnic and multi-religious character of most post-colonial states, and often—especially in Africa and the Middle East—the absence of a pre-colonial state tradition. Their colonial predecessors had demanded obedience, not consent, and been content with commanding fear rather than affection. While the legacy of anti-colonial nationalism was helpful, especially where, as in India, it encompassed decades of struggle and mass engagement, this plural context meant that the concept of development was particularly attractive to nationalist leaders pursuing popular acclaim and concerned with getting their publics to shake off habits

of disobedience to the colonial state institutions that they had inherited. Even in India, one of the main nationalist criticisms of British rule was that, having brought the gift of science, it was stunting India's growth and arresting her progress (Nehru 1942: 433–49; Nehru 1961: 508). A developmental ideology thus became central to the self-definition of the post-colonial state (Chatterjee 1993: 203): in 1945, Nehru (1961: 504), soon to become independent India's first prime minister, felt that 'planned development under a free national government would completely change the face of India within a few years'.

In Africa, the predilection on the part of post-colonial leaders to embrace the cause of development was strongly influenced by the late British and French colonial interest in ushering in a **developmental state**. A belated attempt to justify colonialism as it found itself under challenge—the shift from a primarily exploitative and preservationist colonialism to one that claimed to actively champion and invest in progress and development—did not save the colonial state (see Box 2.4). Indeed, Cooper (2002: 66) suggests that, in Africa, it was the lead that the British and French took in this shift that ensured that it was their empires that first started giving way as the changes introduced stimulated growing demands for self-government. The developmentalist authoritarianism subsequently pursued by their post-colonial successors also failed to secure their regimes. The successful military coup in Ghana in 1966 against President Kwame Nkrumah epitomized this failure: inheriting the economically

---

BOX 2.4 INGREDIENTS FOR POST-COLONIAL SUCCESS: EAST ASIA AND BOTSWANA

Despite lingering until the 1990s, developmentalist authoritarianism in Africa proved a dead end. Whereas, in East Asian states such as South Korea and Taiwan, both Japanese colonies in the first half of the twentieth century, it was credited with producing an economic miracle, post-colonial Africa was very different. It lacked the societal cohesion, state tradition, and cold war geopolitical significance of the East Asian states, as well as the peculiar legacy of state-led capitalist development left by a colonial power that was close both geographically and culturally. In this connection, it is noteworthy that Botswana, despite inheriting a 'colonial state not worth the name' and long serving as a labour reserve for the South African mining industry (Samatar 1999: 95), represented a rare African success story, recording average annual growth of over 6 per cent even in 1985–95, a decade during which most other African states recorded

negative growth (World Bank 1997: 214–15). While very different in other respects, Botswana benefited, like Korea and Taiwan, from an ethnically homogenous society with a cohesive dominant class and a purposeful leadership under the country's first president, Seretse Khama, also the hereditary chief of the Ngwato, the biggest *morafe* (nation) in the country. The colonial mediation of indigenous socio-political institutions and practices, and the post-colonial incorporation of indigenous authorities in the bureaucratic structures of the modern state through rational-legal means, were crucial elements in producing a strong state with a sustainable government (Gulbrandsen 2012), capable of building successful public development institutions (the Botswana Meat Commission and the Botswana Development Corporation), and of avoiding the rampant **corruption** and autocratic tendencies that disfigured post-colonial Africa.

interventionist and centralizing late colonial state in the Gold Coast, Nkrumah had assumed dictatorial powers, and had pursued a succession of wasteful and ill-planned projects aimed at transforming Ghana into an industrialized state.

In most of Africa, the patterns of post-colonial government that developed in the 1960s and 1970s traced their lineage to colonial forms: 'Africanised but ... still impervious, greedy and coercive' (Chabal 2009: 90). Mamdani's 'bifurcated' colonial state mutated into two types. In the majority of cases, conservative post-colonial decentralized despotisms were not really transformed by the reintroduction of multiparty systems in many countries in the 1990s (for example Kenya under President Daniel arap Moi in the 1990s). A minority turned into radical centralized despotisms in which local authority was dismantled without central government being democratized (for example Uganda in the first decade after Yoweri Museveni's National Resistance Movement took control in 1985).

Alternatively, Cooper's gatekeeper state in its post-colonial form, lacking its predecessors' external coercive capacity or financial resources, was left dependent on either the former colonial power or one of the main protagonists in the cold war: the United States, the Soviet Union, or, in a few cases, Communist China. This was perhaps most obvious in the Francophone states in West and Central Africa, most of which belonged to the *Communauté française d'Afrique* (French Community of Africa) and had their currencies pegged to the French franc (and, after 1999, the euro). Into the early twenty-first century, France continued to be an important source of economic aid. Often maintaining a long-standing military presence, she intervened militarily to prop up post-colonial rulers in several former French colonies. To a lesser extent, Britain played a similar role in countries such as Sierra Leone, intervening to end the civil war there in 2000–02. Political independence, by placing the resources of the 'gate' in local hands rather than changing the nature of the state, simply intensified the struggle for the gate. The beleaguered new gatekeepers, usually ethnically defined, were dependent on external agencies for international recognition and aid (Cooper 2002: 200), with the representatives of the international development industry playing a role in 'reproducing relations of power and authority between the West and the rest' reminiscent of colonial times (Kothari 2009: 170).

These trajectories of dependent political development can be interpreted in different ways. Some see them as basically an adaptation of the inherited Western colonial template of **modernization** as Eurocentric development and progress, albeit inflected locally through a continuing process of hybridization (Ahluwalia 2001: 67–71)—that is, the post-colonial state as a hybrid creature (Young 2012: 70). Others reject the extraneous nature of the post-colonial state. Bayart (1993: 265) suggests that what is negatively described in terms of 'tribalism' or 'instability' in Africa reflects the local appropriation of alien institutions. He evokes the image of a rhizome—a continuously growing underground stem constantly generating both shoots and roots—to explain the dynamic linkage of African societies to institutions of the post-colonial state (Bayart 1993: 220–1). However, these links can be viewed more critically as reflecting the emergence of a form of **clientelism** that, while drawing upon pre-colonial customary patrimonial relations between rulers and ruled, is more instrumentalist and unaccountable (Chabal 2009: 95).

Bayart's notion has the value of conceiving of the post-colonial as part of a historical continuum (the *longue durée*), but in doing so it risks underplaying the impact of colonialism. Bayart's 'rhizome' concept avoids the link between political regimes in post-colonial states and the **globalization** of capitalism that European colonialism did so much to bring about. From a Marxist perspective, there was no gainsaying that 'two-thirds of the world's people do not have liberal states because of the structure of the capitalist world-economy, which makes it impossible for them to have such regimes' (Wallerstein 2003: 164).

The European export of the idea of the monocultural nation-state left most post-colonial states with the dilemma of how to reconcile this with ethnically and religiously plural societies. Chatterjee (1993: 11) identifies this 'surrender to the old forms of the modern state' as the source of 'postcolonial misery'. Acceptance of the usefulness in governing of the authoritarian modes of exercising power bequeathed by colonialism was widespread and in some countries, such as Iraq, created under a British League of Nations mandate in 1921 and formally independent by 1932, the shallow foundations of colonial rule necessitated recourse to particularly high levels of violence, setting a pattern for post-colonial government that persisted (Dodge 2003: 157–71).

As in Africa, colonialism in South Asia left in its wake visions of society and polity that were distorted. Some outside observers have suggested that India owed its comparatively stable post-independence political and economic development to its 'relative immunity from western ideologies' (Gray 2003: 18), but this argument is hard to sustain. More to the point, perhaps are three kinds of ingredient that were more evident in the post-colonial Indian mix than, say, in Africa. First, in the realm of cultural politics, there ran a deep vein of the non- (if not pre-) modern. Gandhi tapped into this in developing the 'saintly' idiom of Indian politics (Morris-Jones 1987: 60), and the metaphor of the sanctified and patriarchal extended family has been described as one of the most important elements in the culture of Indian nationalism (Chakrabarty 2003: 71).

Second, the phenomenon of caste associated with Hinduism, while rendered less fluid, more regulated, and institutionalized under colonialism, gave to India a particularly encompassing, yet supple, resource in adapting colonial institutions (Rudolph and Rudolph 1967).

Third, there was the important role played by political agency—in this case, the Congress Party that had spearheaded the campaign for independence. Already more than sixty years old at independence, Congress, under the leadership of Nehru, reinforced India's liberal democratic institutional framework by accommodating not only the dominant classes, but also a variety of caste, religious, linguistic, and regional identities, both through the party and in the structures of government (Adeney and Wyatt 2004: 9–11).

In contrast, lacking in these ingredients, India's subcontinental neighbours, Pakistan and Sri Lanka, proved far less successful, both in sustaining stable constitutional government and in preventing civil war. While India experienced localized civil wars, these outbreaks were insulated and ultimately defused (in which respect, Kashmir, a bone of contention between India and Pakistan since independence, remained the exception). However, as the 'formal' democracy of the British Dominion of Ceylon (as it was until 1972) was displaced by the more brash and intolerant 'social' democracy of the Republic of Sri Lanka (Wickramasinghe 2006: 160), the island state witnessed a descent into decades of civil war between the Sinhala Buddhist majority and the minority Tamils. In contrast, although the 'democratization' of Indian democracy through the politicization of previously oppressed and marginalized lower castes and other peripheral groups (Yadav 1996) confronted the state in India with formidable challenges, its post-colonial institutions coped. The partition of the subcontinent, by removing roughly two-thirds of the Muslim population, might have made the issue of

state and **national identity** in India less problematic. Even so, it was because the post-colonial state in India transcended, in some measure, the colonial logic of divide and rule that it appeared better at digesting ethnic and religious plurality. Despite the recent political salience of Hindu chauvinism, it is still possible to conceive of Indian culture as 'constructed around the proliferation of differences' (Ghosh 2002: 250).

> ### KEY POINTS
>
> - In contrast to colonization, decolonization occurred apace and, twenty-five years after the Second World War, was largely achieved.
> - Colonies became nation-states despite the form being ill-suited to most post-colonial societies.
> - Development was prominent as a legitimizing motif for late colonialism and became central to the self-definition of its post-colonial successors, albeit often degenerating into unsuccessful developmentalist authoritarianism.
> - While the development record of many post-colonial states was disillusioning, a few registered success owing to history, geopolitical situation, and political agency.

Conclusion: The Colonial Legacy

As the tide of decolonization was reaching its peak, both the departing colonizers and the anti-colonial nationalists anticipating freedom were disposed to strike a positive note. Colonial historian Margery Perham (1963: 99) held, in 1961, that 'Britain on the whole was the most humane and considerate of modern colonial nations and did most to prepare her subjects for self-government'. As power was handed over by the last British governor of the Gold Coast, Kwame Nkrumah, Ghana's first leader, declared confidently: 'We have won independence and founded a modern state' (James 1977: 153). Yet, less than a decade later, on the eve of losing power, Nkrumah summed up his misgivings about the reality of independence in a book entitled *Neo-Colonialism*:

" The essence of neo-colonialism is that the State which is subject to it is, in theory, independent and has all the outward trappings of international sovereignty. In reality its economic system and thus its political policy is directed from outside. "

(Nkrumah 1965: ix)

In the 1990s, one international relations theorist coined the phrase 'quasi-states' to describe the majority of post-colonial states (Jackson 1990), while an analyst of African development saw imported statehood as the basic problem, asserting 'it is *because* it is not African that the African state is not a state' (Englebert 1997: 767).

In the early twenty-first century, there was a resurgence of interest in the West in the idea of a **liberal imperialism** as a solution to the continuing political and economic crisis that many post-colonial states, especially in Africa and the Middle East, faced (Cooper 2004; Ferguson 2004; Lal 2004). The United Nations' adoption in 2001 of an international Responsibility to Protect in the wake of the 1994 Rwanda **genocide** and the massacres in the civil wars in the former Yugoslavia in the 1990s enshrined this Kantian-inspired vision of humanitarian intervention by powerful liberal democratic states (Pourmokhtari 2013). Echoing earlier justifications for colonial rule, adherents of a revival of paternalist imperialism shared a sense of civilizational superiority, and disregard of the logic of domination and exploitation that underpinned European colonialism. This logic had also been apparent in the behaviour of the United States, the first post-colonial imperial power, towards native, African, and Hispanic Americans in extending its domain across North America in the course of the nineteenth century, and then in the Philippines, Latin America, and the Caribbean in the years following the Spanish–American War of 1898 (Slater 2004: 15, 44–53). Attributable to a 'geopolitical amnesia' engendered by imperial—and post-imperial—culture in the West (Slater 2004: 148), the renewed fascination with liberal imperialism was both a reflection of post-cold-war Anglo-American hubris and a legacy of colonialism's 'civilizing mission' (Watt 2011: 1–12). It was perceived in the Western-led occupations of Afghanistan (2001) and Iraq (2003), and other military interventions in post-colonial states. However, subtler and more widespread was the post-cold-war effort to globalize a hegemonic discourse of democratization and **governance** that arguably interpreted self-determination for post-colonial societies in terms of 'the "freedom" to embrace the rules, norms and principles of the emerging [informal imperial] (neo)liberal global order' (Ayers 2009: 21). For post-colonial states, sovereignty was proving double-edged: they were free to do what was expected of them (Williams and Young 2009: 105–6).

While virtually the entire developing world experienced colonialism, the experience differed from place to place, and this is reflected in the varied legacy (see Box 2.5). The settler and slave societies of post-colonial Latin America and the Caribbean present a contrast to Africa and Asia. For example, in the Caribbean, the private hierarchies of exploitation that underpinned slavery, and the subsequent drawn-out history of slave emancipation and struggle for political rights, helped the state structures, closely modelled on the British parliamentary system, to gain acceptance as autochthonous (Sutton 1991: 110).

In the African case, the patchiness of pre-colonial state traditions, and the relative brevity and 'thinness' of colonial rule, generally resulted in post-colonial states incapable of achieving the ambitions of nationalist leaders and the expectations of their peoples. By the end of the twentieth century, a large part of the colonial state legacy in many African countries had

BOX 2.5 ASSESSING THE COLONIAL LEGACY

In an ambitious effort to examine the legacy of colonialism comparatively, James Mahoney (2010: 3) studied the experience of fifteen mainland Latin American countries colonized by Spain, seeking to develop hypotheses that might explain variations in levels of colonialism—that is, the extent of settlement and institutional implantation—and post-colonial economic and social development. The study found that, under mercantilist colonialism, there was an inverse relationship between the levels of colonialism and post-colonial development. Peripheral or marginal colonial territories (Argentina, southern Brazil, Chile, Costa Rica, Uruguay) achieved higher levels of development, while erstwhile important colonial centres (Bolivia, northeast Brazil, Mexico, Peru), in which powerful coalitions of merchants and landowners blocked successful adaptation to an advancing capitalist world economy, fared less well. Significant in terms of social development was the fact that the people of the former were more European by descent, and their societies were thus not built around excluding a subordinated indigenous and African majority from social goods. The study also argued that, under a liberal colonizing power such as Britain, the intensity of colonialism was positively related to post-colonial development—the four British settler colonies (the United States, Canada, Australia, and New Zealand) and the city-states of Hong Kong and Singapore serving as prime examples (Mahoney 2010: 256).

been effaced by institutional decay (Young 1998: 116), making 'the explanatory power of the colonial legacy' less central (Young 2012: 339). What also needs to be reckoned is the legacy of the anti- and post-colonial movements in Africa. The characteristics of these responses to colonialism militated against a transition to multiparty democratic politics, leading instead to a personalization of politics (Hyden 2006: 48, 232).

This is not to negate the continuing historical significance of the colonial—and, indeed, pre-colonial—past. For instance, contrasting the former Belgian Congo with regions that possessed effective states before colonialism, such as the south of Uganda (Buganda) and Ghana (Asante), and northern Ethiopia, the latter have proved better able to survive phases of bad government (Clapham 2000: 9). Although the model of the nation-state has proven a burdensome legacy for contemporary Africa, the consequences of **state collapse** in Somalia, Liberia, Sierra Leone, Congo, and Libya in the 1990s, 2000s, and 2010s showed the high human cost exacted by its absence. In a world of states, vulnerable regions and their inhabitants are left dangerously exposed by state collapse. Although some (for example Clapham 2000) argue that societies might conceivably be able to function without states, it is difficult to foresee them being tolerated for long in the globalized world of states.

Historical differences reflected in institutional weakness may have compounded the crisis faced by the post-colonial state in Africa, but in Asia too the colonial legacy presented post-colonial states with their greatest challenges, especially in grappling with issues of political identity. The problem in countries such as Sri Lanka was that the concept of multiculturalism introduced by the British colonial rulers stressed the fragmentary nature of society (Wickramasinghe 2006: 13). By doing so, it left the post-colonial state with its composite identity particularly vulnerable to being torn apart by incompatible visions of the nation.

The condition of the post-colonial state today continues to be influenced by a combination of factors marked by its colonial past: history and geopolitical situation; location in the world economy; and the influence of Western powers, and international governmental and non-governmental institutions, latterly expressed through a globalized discourse and practice of democratization, governance, and the market.

? QUESTIONS

1. How can the contemporary politics of post-colonial states be related to their colonial past?
2. Can a history of *pre-colonial* statehood help to make *post-colonial* states more viable?
3. Can the world in the twenty-first century escape the imbalances in power, wealth, and knowledge wrought by colonialism?
4. How have the European languages introduced under colonial rule influenced the course of post-colonial development?
5. What factors are most useful in explaining the differing trajectories of political development in former colonies?
6. Can development ever be *post-colonial*?
7. Is it the case that the Westphalian international state system, quadrupled in size by decolonization, left many post-colonial states without substantial sovereignty?

FURTHER READING

Chatterjee, P. (1993) *The Nation and Its Fragments: Colonial and Postcolonial Histories* (Princeton, NJ: Princeton University Press) An insightful examination by a leading Indian political theorist of the impact of colonialism on the nationalist imagination in Asia and Africa.

Chiriyankandath, J. (1992) '"Democracy" under the Raj: Elections and Separate Representation in British India', *Journal of Commonwealth and Comparative Politics*, 30(1): 39–63 Shows how the British introduction of communal forms of political representation helped to shape the post-colonial politics of the Indian subcontinent.

Cooper, F. (2002) *Africa since 1940: The Past of the Present* (Cambridge: Cambridge University Press) Considers the post-colonial development of Africa from a historical perspective, with particular reference to the concept of the 'gate-keeper' state.

Dirks, N. (2004) 'Colonial and Postcolonial Histories: Comparative Reflections on the Legacies of Empire', UNDP Human Development Report Office Occasional Paper No. 2004/4, available online at **http://hdr.undp.org/sites/default/files/hdr2004_nicholas_dirks.pdf** Background paper for the United Nations Development Programme (UNDP) in which a historical anthropologist specializing in South Asia, Nicholas Dirks, considers the colonial legacy.

Hall, S. (1996) 'When Was "the Post-Colonial"? Thinking at the Limit', in I. Chambers and L. Carti (eds) *The post-Colonial Question: Common Skies, Divided Horizons* (London: Routledge), 242–60 A thoughtful exploration of the term 'post-colonial'.

Hyden, G. (2006) *African Politics in Comparative Perspective* (Cambridge: Cambridge University Press) A review of the development of post-colonial Africa.

Mahoney, J. (2010) *Colonialism and Postcolonial Development: Spanish America in Comparative Perspective* (Cambridge: Cambridge University Press) A wide-ranging empirical inquiry into the developmental legacies of colonialism in Latin America and beyond.

Pourmokhtari, N. (2013) 'A Post-colonial Critique of State Sovereignty in IR [International Relations]: The Contradictory Legacy of a "West-Centric" discipline', *Third World Quarterly*, 34(10): 1767–93 An insightful examination of how contemporary international relations is shaped by its 'Westphalian [Western] common sense'.

Young, C. (1994) *The African Colonial State in Comparative Perspective* (New Haven, CT: Yale University Press) Wide-ranging comparative study of the colonial state by a political scientist.

Young, C. (2012) *The Postcolonial State in Africa: Fifty Years of Independence, 1960–2010* (Madison, WI: University of Wisconsin Press) Young's reconsideration of the condition of the post-colonial African state.

WEB LINKS

http://www.au2002.gov.za Constitutive Act of the African Union, Lome, Togo, 11 July 2000.

https://scholarblogs.emory.edu/postcolonialstudies/ Blog on postcolonial studies maintained by the Department of Comparative Literature at Emory University, Atlanta, GA, which emphasizes literature and culture more than politics, but is still useful regarding the postcolonial situation.

http://www.lib.utexas.edu/maps/index.html University of Texas at Austin Perry-Castañeda Map Collection.

For additional material and resources, please visit the Online Resource Centre at:
http://www.oxfordtextbooks.co.uk/orc/burnell5e/

3

Institutional Perspectives

Lise Rakner and Vicky Randall

Overview

A crucial question facing developing countries today is why some states and localities are able to provide security, safe water, development, schools, and health services to their inhabitants, while others are not. Further, when are decision-making processes transparent and the leaders accountable to their citizens? The answers to these questions are often sought in political institutions, but in reality we know surprisingly little about how political and economic institutions induce policymakers to act in a certain way. We know even less about how social norms, or informal institutions, shape and interact with the formal rules. This chapter focuses on the role of institutions and how institutionalism is applied in the analysis of politics in the developing world. It presents central theoretical concepts and approaches helping us to understand institutional origins and change, and explores the interrelationship between formal and informal institutions.

Introduction

As noted in Chapter 1, a marked feature of the literature relating to **politics** in the **developing world** since the 1980s has been the centrality assigned to institutions. This 'new institutionalism', which

actually includes many different scholarly traditions, holds that institutions explain political outcomes, and may provide a solution to political and economic problems across nations. As this chapter will show, there is little agreement about precisely *how* political and economic institutions affect development, and which institutions are most important. In considering institutionalism as an approach, this chapter touches on the character of political institutions in developing countries, thereby anticipating chapters in Part 3 of this book that focus on political processes and the state. We begin by reflecting on the increasing popularity of institutionalism within analyses of politics in developing countries. We then discuss the theoretical underpinnings of 'new institutionalism', before looking more directly at its application to institutions in developing countries, both formal and informal. In a final section, we assess the appropriateness of institutionalist analyses in developing countries.

New Institutionalism and the Study of the Developing World

Institutions are frequently identified with organizations or formal structures and although, in practice, there is still much interest in organizations, today an institution is more often understood as a 'stable, recurring pattern of behaviour' (Goodin 1996: 22), or as defined by Nobel Laureate Douglass North (1990: 3), as 'the rules of the game in society, or, more formally, the humanly devised constraints that shape human interaction'. A main underlying theme in most definitions is that, in an institutionalized setting, human behaviour is considered to be more stable and predictable.

Institutionalism has always been a prominent approach in mainstream political science. In the early years, there was an emphasis on the historical and legal aspects of political institutions and on constitutions. The 'behavioural' revolution from the 1950s and, subsequently, the development of rational choice analysis entailed a reaction against this kind of institutionalism in favour of approaches that focused on the individual, broadly understood as an autonomous actor. Obviously, this did not mean that the study of institutions ceased, but it was not until the 1980s that the beginnings of a counter-revolution in political science was discernible, famously launched by March and Olsen (1984) as the 'new institutionalism'. The new institutionalism then emerged within 'mainstream' political science from the 1980s and, in its different guises, has become increasingly prevalent, leading to the claim 'we are all institutionalists now' (Pierson and Skocpol, cited

by March and Olsen 2006: 5). New institutionalism has also been increasingly applied in the analysis of politics in developing countries. While the new institutionalism has much in common with the 'old' and it has taken many different forms, it also manifests some important and novel features (Peters 2005; Lowndes 2010).

1. Institutions are no longer implicitly identified with organizational structures; instead, the focus of analysis has moved towards rules, and even norms.

2. Where the focus had originally been on formal institutions, there is now at least as great an interest in **informal institutions**.

3. The new institutionalism is more explicitly theoretical than the old institutionalism, which was more interested in processes of **institutional change**.

Institutionalism applied to the developing world

The growing application of the new institutionalism in analysis of the politics of developing countries is partly explicable in terms of more general developments in political science, together with the declining sense that developing countries need their own specialized analytic frameworks. The new emphasis in the scholarly literature also coincided with a shift in the policies of the international financial institutions toward the developing world from the late 1980s. During the 1970s and 1980s, major international organizations such as the World Bank played down the role of state institutions in terms of forging development in the South. Inspired by neoclassical economic analyses, the international financial institutions argued that a particular feature of the least-developed nations was corrupt and inefficient state institutions, and they encouraged a *reduced* role for the state. However, recognizing that the **Washington consensus** had neglected the need for appropriate institutional design for achieving development, in the 1990s the World Bank began actively to promote the role of institutions to protect property rights and contracts, and to encourage **civil society** and **good governance** (World Bank 1994; see also Chapters 10 and 15). Key in the new development scholarship and the policies of the multilateral institutions was the interest in institutions, and in how institutional practices could be built and nurtured to secure accountability in new and fragile democracies in the developing world. This focus on institutions has not waned over time; recently, it has been applied to issues of conflict and security by the World Bank (2011: 8), which notes that '[w]eak institutions are particularly important in explaining why violence repeats in different forms in the same countries or subnational regions'. Underscoring the role of institutions for development, in the United Nations' 2030 Agenda for Sustainable Development, Sustainable Development Goal (SDG) 16 is devoted to 'peace, justice and strong institutions'.

This (new) institutionalism is everywhere apparent in the study of politics in developing countries. It arises in numerous thematic contexts and across regions, for instance in studies of democratization in Latin America (Helmke and Levitsky 2006), in accounts of parliaments in Asia, and in relation to African politics (Posner 2005; Lindberg 2006). To assess its implications for studying politics in developing countries, we need now to consider more systematically the theoretical foundations and complications of the new institutionalism.

KEY POINTS

- Compared with old institutionalism, new institutionalism focuses less on organizational structures and more on rules and norms. It is more explicitly theoretical and interested in processes of change.

- Institutions are often defined as the rules of the game in society and the constraints that shape human interaction. In an institutionalized setting, behaviour is considered to be more stable and predictable.

- The application of the new institutionalism to developing countries is partly a consequence of the recognition that the 'Washington consensus' neglected the role of appropriately designed institutions for achieving developmental goals.

The Theoretical Underpinnings of Institutionalism: Three Kinds of Institutionalism

The premise of the new institutionalism is that 'institutions matter' and that, to quote Peters (2005: 155), 'scholars can achieve greater analytic leverage by

beginning with institutions rather than individuals'. However, the new institutionalism actually embraces several different approaches. In an influential article, Hall and Taylor (1996) identified three main forms: sociological, rational choice, and historical. Although many other candidates have emerged and Peters (2005) claimed to have found *seven* types, for present purposes it is helpful to review the main differences between these original three. The main differences between the different approaches are linked to the role of individual actors and their ability to change institutions, and, more generally, to how institutional change comes about.

Sociological institutionalism

Sociological institutionalism is also referred to as 'cultural', or 'normative', institutionalism. As its name implies, this perspective has been heavily influenced by a tradition in sociology concerned with how collective institutions establish forms of social control over individual action—but it also draws on the sociological study of organizations (Selznick 1948). March and Olsen (1984, 1989)—in some ways, the founding fathers of the new institutionalism—broadly fall into this category. Like other new institutionalists, they do not equate institutions with formal organizations; rather, they define an institution as 'a relatively enduring collection of rules and organized practices' (March and Olsen 2006: 5). Sociological institutionalists tend to stress the role of norms and values in constituting institutions, and in socializing individuals into conforming behaviour through what March and Olsen (2006: 7) term a 'logic of appropriateness'. By the same token, they tend to see individual preferences as shaped by the institutions within which they become embedded rather than arising exogenously. An example of the sociological institutionalism approach is Tsai's (2007) study of development in rural China, where she finds that social organizations embedded within the community foster better services, since their local ties give local authorities a reason to cooperate with them.

Rational choice institutionalism

Although the 'new institutionalism' can be understood as a reaction against what was seen as the extreme methodological individualism of behavioural and rational choice approaches, this form of institutionalism comes from within the rational choice perspective itself. It has been strongly influenced by developments in economics based on the assumption of an idealized free agent interacting in an idealized free market. Institutional analysis within economics has reacted against this by showing how collective action can be institutionally embodied, and can thereby shape and constrain individual choice. New institutionalism within economics is represented most prominently by Nobel Laureate Douglass North (1990), whose ideas have been extensively taken up in political science.

A key premise of rational choice institutionalist approaches in political science is that institutions represent rules, as well as incentives, that constrain and give direction to individual behaviour. Within this perspective, the fundamental principles of political action and human behaviour are the same across different political systems, institutional set-ups, and levels of development. Rational actors respond to institutional constraints in identical ways regardless of strategic position, and institutions emerge and persist because the actors—who cooperate voluntarily—see the value and benefits of their functions. Contrary to 'the logic of appropriateness' of sociological institutionalism, rational choice institutionalism considers actors to behave according to a 'logic of consequentiality': rules reflect the explicit intent and powers of individual actors. One of the first analysts to apply the rational choice perspective to the study of institutions in developing countries was Robert Bates, whose work generated huge interest amongst both scholars and policymakers (see Box 3.1).

Historical institutionalism

The third strand to be introduced, although possibly the first to emerge, is historical institutionalism. An early statement of its approach can be found in Thelen and Steinmo (1992). Historical institutionalism is not a unified intellectual enterprise: some scholars within this tradition, relying on quantitative approaches, treat history as the outcome of rational and purposeful behaviour; other, more qualitatively oriented, scholars emphasize the role of randomness and accidents. Historical institutionalism views institutions as the formal and informal procedures, routines, norms, and conventions embedded in the organizational structure of the polity. Institutions range from the rules of a constitutional order or the standard operating procedures of a bureaucracy to the conventions governing trade union behaviour or bank–firm relations (Hall and Taylor 1996: 6–7). What differentiates historical institutionalism from the two other strands is the emphasis on historical context. At its simplest, the historical institutionalist argument is that once a particular path is taken, it becomes increasingly difficult to alter it. This is so because the commitments that the institution comes to embody as a consequence will continue to shape its subsequent development through a process of **path dependence** (Pierson 2000). Path dependence analysis also includes the notion of critical junctures—that is, critical moments in history with lasting consequences (Thelen 2004). Dramatic historical moments, such as independence from a colonial power, may create new institutions and substantially change power resources of various groups in society. Collier and Collier's (1991) study of political developments in Latin America in the twentieth century illustrates a historical institutionalist approach. They focus on the response of states to the newly radicalized working class and organized labour movements that arose earlier in the century in the course of capitalist **modernization**.

BOX 3.1 ROBERT BATES ON THE RATIONALITY OF AFRICAN PEASANTS

Writing in contradiction of the interpretations prevailing at the time, in the mid-1970s, Bates' work on African agricultural policies adopted methodological individualism, emphasizing economic reasoning and choice. He criticized the cultural interpretations that were dominant within development studies at the time and argued that it was more fruitful to view the behaviour of African farmers as a result of choice made under institutional constraints, rather than to explain it in terms of tradition. Analysing the institutional origins of Kenyan agricultural institutions, Bates pointed towards the importance of special interests and large agents in explaining why it was rational for agricultural producers to pay the cost of political organizing in agricultural cooperatives. In addition to helping to counteract ethnocentric stereotypes depicting African peasants as 'backward', a major contribution of Bates' rational approach has been his contribution to applying a theoretical agenda to new empirical grounds. His *Markets and States in Tropical Africa: The Political Basis of Agricultural Policy* (Bates 1981) and *Beyond the Miracle of the Market: The Political Economy of Agrarian Development in Kenya* (Bates 1989) generated important theoretical and empirical debates that have influenced the scholarship on political and institutional development in sub-Saharan Africa.

They set forth a theory of sequences whereby (a) structured conditions led to (b) societal cleavages or crisis, which (c) again triggered a critical juncture, (d) so crystalizing a process of reactions and counter-reactions.

How do institutions emerge and change?

Institutions, although stable, are not eternal, but answers to the question of how institutions arise have varied considerably, and have often been vague and unsatisfactory. Goodin (1996) suggests that there are three main ways in which institutions come about—by accident, through a process of evolution, or intentionally—and that, in practice, any actual instance of institutional change will almost certainly involve a combination of these three elements. In practice, sociological institutionalists have tended to depict institutions as emerging out of their social context and often as embodying dominant social values. Deriving from this perspective, the important notion of 'political institutionalization' as a process has been widely taken up, either in reference to the regularization of political processes as a whole or more particularly in reference to political parties. On the other hand, rational choice institutionalists have been criticized for having an implicitly functional approach in which institutions are consciously designed by individuals to reduce **transaction costs** and increase efficiency.

More effort has been addressed to the connected question of how institutions change. Generally, the assumption is that changes are exogenous—that is, driven by outside pressures—but more recent research points towards a more complicated process in which external pressures or opportunities combine with the effects of internal dynamics and opportunism of 'institutional entrepreneurs' (Lowndes 2010). As Mahoney and Thelen (2010) remind us, it is important not to take compliance with institutions for granted: institutions will be contested; struggle over the meaning of an institution will be constant; and this struggle is a key source of institutional change.

KEY POINTS

- An institution is a stable, recurring pattern of behaviour, often referred to as 'the rules of the game'.
- The main strands of new institutionalism within political science are often referred to as 'historical', 'sociological', and 'rational choice' institutionalism.

- Institutions come about by accident, through a process of evolution, or intentionally—or in a combination of these three ways. Change is driven by the interaction of external pressures and internal dynamics.
- Institutions are contested, and the struggle over their meaning and value is a key source of institutional change.

Political Institutions in Developing Countries

Influenced by, and drawing on, these theoretical developments, political scientists have focused with renewed interest on a range of political institutions in developing countries. Examining institutions at the centre of government, they have considered executive and legislative institutions and their interrelationship. Long-standing arguments about the respective merits of presidential and parliamentary executive arrangements are now being rehearsed in a developing-world context (see Box 3.2). Related to this, generally, until recently, the assumption was that executive power in such countries, through both formal and informal means, dominated the legislature—where it existed—to such an extent that the latter institutions barely warranted independent study. Increasingly, scholars are taking legislatures seriously not only in established democracies such as India, or some Latin American countries, where it has been argued that 'legislatures play a vital role' (Huneeus et al. 2006: 422), but also in Africa (Barkan 2009).

Two further and overlapping subjects for extensive political analysis have been political parties and party systems, and electoral systems. Political parties are considered essential institutions for democracy's proper functioning (Sartori 1976). Scholars generally find that electoral rules and social cleavages provide law-like guidance in accounting for the establishment of stable parties in advanced democracies (Cox 1997). However, studies have produced inconsistent findings on the relative importance of such factors in developing countries (Basedau and Stroh 2008). Underlining our initial claim that we have scant knowledge of exactly *how* institutions induce policymakers to act in a certain way, social scientists have been unable to explain why stable parties have taken root in some developing countries and not others. In many developing nations, parties are weak, short-lived organizations. These parties are incapable of performing the

BOX 3.2 PARLIAMENTARY VERSUS PRESIDENTIAL SYSTEMS

In *presidential* systems, the president is head of government and state, popularly elected for a fixed term; in *parliamentary* systems, the prime minister or head of government is selected by the legislature and depends upon its support to continue in office. In between are various kinds of 'semi-presidential' system, such as when a directly elected president coexists with a prime minister dependent on parliamentary support. Although instances of all three types of governmental system can be found in the developing world, parliamentary systems cluster in South Asia (India, Bangladesh, and currently Pakistan) and the Caribbean, whilst presidential systems predominate in Africa (exceptions include Botswana, Mauritius, and South Africa, the 'president' of which is actually elected by the legislature) and especially Latin America.

In the context of democratic transition, a lively debate has arisen about the respective merits of presidential and parliamentary systems. Some political scientists have agreed with Linz (1990),

who famously warned against the 'perils of presidentialism', suggesting that parliamentary systems were preferable because they offered greater democratic stability. Others, such as Shugart and Carey (1992), have questioned whether presidential systems are in fact less stable, arguing that they provide greater democratic transparency and accountability. Cheibub (2007), on the other hand, while accepting that presidential democracies may be more unstable, concludes that this is less because of intrinsic flaws of presidential systems than because they tend to be associated with less favourable political contexts—notably, those in which the military plays a prominent political role. It is increasingly clear that the way in which these systems operate in practice is strongly shaped by contextual institutional factors, such as the degree of fragmentation of the party system and the prevalence or otherwise of informal neo-patrimonial relationships.

organizational tasks required for robust democracy despite acquiring greater experience with electoral competition (Rakner and van de Walle 2009). Randall and Svåsand (2002) consider the 'institutionalization' of political parties, distinguishing between 'internal' and 'external' aspects of the process. They conclude that, with notable exceptions, political parties in developing countries tend to be weakly institutionalized, but also warn against imposing expectations derived from an uncritical account of parties in the developed world. (For a fuller account, see the 'Political Parties' case study available on the Online Resource Centre.)

It is widely accepted that political parties, and especially party systems, are significantly affected by electoral systems. Beyond the familiar distinction between majority or 'first past the post' (FPTP) electoral systems, those embodying some form of proportional representation, and 'mixed systems', there are all manner of possible variations, with claimed consequences for the quality of representation, including women's presence in legislative bodies, on the one hand, and government stability and conflict resolution, on the other. In practice, partly as a legacy of colonial rule, FPTP systems predominate in Africa and Asia, although proportional representation largely prevails in Latin America. However, it is important, when estimating the consequences of electoral systems, especially in a developing-world context, to recognize that they do not exist in a vacuum, but interact with other

institutional features, such as whether the government is unitary or federal and the pattern of social divisions. Recent research in this area emphasizes the importance of resources and the personalized networks of **patron–client relations** that link politicians to voters, often through intermediaries (Stokes et al. 2013).

Designing political institutions

Given this focus on political institutions and belief in their independent consequences, there has been particular interest, both theoretical and practical, in **intentional institutional design**, or how institutions can be designed *ab initio* or modified to achieve particular desired ends. A major area for this kind of work is the design and critique of electoral systems, but its scope is far wider, including the design of systems of party regulation and of constitutions (see Box 3.3).

Whilst many political scientists, as well as multilateral agencies and national governments, have taken up such schemes enthusiastically, others remain more sceptical. Acknowledging that sometimes there is no option other than to create or engineer new institutions, Bastian and Luckham (2003) nonetheless caution against the risks of unintended consequences. It is also important to consider the political context in which such engineering is attempted: who is supporting it? Whose vested interests may it in fact promote and whose may suffer? In other words, what is the hidden political agenda?

BOX 3.3 DESIGNING CONSTITUTIONS

The process of making a new constitution can involve assemblies, executives, ordinary legislatures, or the public, and most utilize several actors in the constitution-making process. There is a trend towards including the population in the ratification process and earlier in the process. Based on data from the Comparative Constitutions Project (CCP), Ginsburg and colleagues (2009) find that processes that are either very long or very short tend to occur in non-democracies and can sometimes be unstable. Also, the size of the deliberative body may matter: too many may be problematic. Elster (1997) claims that constitutions produced in more democratic processes will be more democratic. The CCP shows that those constitutions in which public participation has been an integral part of the process on average yielded more rights and provided more opportunities for participation of citizens later on.

In general, however, it is very hard to establish what makes a constitution 'good' or 'bad'. A central idea is that constitutions should provide stability. Enduring constitutions are considered good because they may provide for a more stable environment for both investment and democratic stability (Ginsburg et al. 2009). Most constitutions do not last very long and 50 per cent of constitutions are dead within eighteen years. However, there are large regional disparities. Constitutions in Western Europe last, on average, three times longer than African or Latin American constitutions. Internal factors that are considered to ensure constitutional longevity are linked to the inclusiveness of the constitution's origins and the constitution's ability to adapt to changing conditions (Ginsburg et al. 2009). More specific constitutions will be able to anticipate potential problems in the future, and this specificity includes both attention to detail and the scope of events covered. An inclusive constitution will tend to be more democratic, and since more people will know of the constitutional provisions, it will provide a clear focal point for citizens and thus be more self-enforcing. This counts for both the drafting stage and the approval stage. Adaptable constitutions will be more able to resist shocks through either formal amendments or informal amendments that come from interpretative changes.

An example of a constitutional process that did not succeed in providing stability and democracy is Iraq's constitution. This is mainly owing to a lack of **legitimacy** and latent religious, ethnic, and economic tensions (Elkins et al. 2008: 34–5). The case of Iraq highlights some of the importance of extra-constitutional variables in explaining constitutional outcomes.

BOX 3.4 TRUTH COMMISSIONS

The 'first' truth commission was set up in Uganda in 1974, whilst Idi Amin was still firmly in power, to inquire into the 'disappearances of people'. Although hearings were public, the report was never published and the **regime's** infamous brutality persisted. As of 2015, truth commissions had been deployed in thirty-six different countries. The most recent was Tunisia's Truth and Dignity Commission established in 2014, with further commissions anticipated in Aceh, Colombia, and Sri Lanka.

Truth commissions have been defined as 'temporary bodies, usually with an official **status**, set up to investigate a past history of **human rights** violations that took place within a country during a specified period of time' (Chapman and Ball 2001: 2). Whilst potentially providing a 'third way' between prosecution (which would hardly be feasible given the scale of collective violence) and blanket amnesty, they have all faced innate difficulties, not least in gathering and processing the vast amount of potentially relevant data, and in squaring the search for 'truth' with reconciliation. 'Success' is, in any case, difficult to define and measure, although failure is relatively clear in the cases of commissions in Bolivia and in the Philippines, which broke up before their task was completed (Brahm 2007). In practice, however, the impact of truth commissions has varied enormously, affected by such factors as: how restrictive the terms of their original mandate have been, limitations of time, and resource limitations. Contrast the commission in Haiti, for example, with around US$1 million funding and seventy-five staff, with that of South Africa, with roughly US$28 million funding and, at its peak, more than 400 staff (Chapman and Ball 2001: 16–17).

Transplanting political institutions

Closely related to designing new political institutions is the option of transferring or transplanting institutions, or institutional models, from other countries. This could be said to have a long history in much of the developing world, with governing institutions modelled on those of departing colonial powers, as in the 'Westminster' model of government. But, post-independence, such experimental borrowing has persisted whether freely chosen by the sovereign government, or under pressure from donor countries or multilateral agencies. Recent examples include anti-**corruption** commissions or agencies (see Chapter 15), truth commissions (see Box 3.4), and women's national policy machinery (see Chapter 9). Generally, the direction of borrowing has been from developed to developing countries, but South–South exchanges are also increasingly in evidence, with truth commissions a case in point. The wisdom of such transplanting exercises is disputed. We have seen that the rational choice institutionalism assumes that the principles governing political behaviour are broadly similar whatever the regional or cultural context; others are more wary about the consequences of applying 'lessons' from one political context to another very different one. In practice, institutional transplanting may be, to some degree, an unavoidable aspect of policy innovation—but it could also be part of a strategy of cosmetic change and policy avoidance, or lead to unintended outcomes as 'implanted' formal institutions interact with existing informal rules and norms. Any assessment of 'success' needs to take such contextual factors into consideration.

KEY POINTS

- Political scientists and policymakers are increasingly interested in how formal political institutions shape political developments and outcomes in developing countries. This has led to an interest in intentionally designing, and transplanting, institutions.

- Scholars interested in measuring the effect of political institutions have, in particular, focused on political parties, party systems, and electoral systems.

- Estimating the consequences of institutional reform in a developing-world context, it is important to recognize that they do not exist in a vacuum, but interact with other institutional and contextual features.

Formal and Informal Institutions

The growing focus on the role of formal political institutions, including those that have been intentionally designed or transplanted, has been accompanied by a recognition, especially in relation to developing countries, that their performance can be highly variable, unpredictable, and often disappointing. Amongst the numerous explanations, a key contributory factor is the impact of informal institutions.

Chapter 1 of this book discusses the **modernization revisionism** that emerged in reaction to some of the cruder depictions in modernization theory of the relationship between tradition and modernity. Rather than expecting modernization to eliminate tradition, it was more realistic to recognize the persistence and reworking of tradition in new symbiotic forms with modernity. The present interest in informal institutions to some extent echoes that argument and examines some of the same kind of phenomena, especially forms of patron–client relationship that work in and through formal political institutions. However, informal institutions cannot simply be equated with tradition or culture; they are both less and more than this. Helmke and Levitsky (2006: 5) define informal institutions as 'socially shared rules, usually unwritten, that are created, communicated and enforced outside officially sanctioned channels'. Andrews (2013) uses the analogy of the iceberg to illustrate the relationship between formal and informal institutions. The tip of the iceberg represents the visible formal rules that are in play—that is, written laws, constitutions, freedom of association, etc.; the submerged part of the iceberg consists of all of the informal rules that shape social interactions, which rules are unwritten and seldom visible.

Informal institutions interact with formal political institutions in highly significant ways. In many cases, informal political institutions—such as political **clientelism**, corruption, the 'big man' syndrome, customary law—undermine the formally specified political rules, but in a few cases the working of formal political institutions can actually be facilitated by a set of informal rules and conventions. Specifically in the context of democratization, Helmke and Levitsky (2006) build on the initial analysis of Lauth (2000) to suggest four different possible kinds of interaction (see Table 3.1).

- As the name suggests, *competing* informal institutions compete with and subvert weak formal institutions, a very common occurrence in new democracies.

- *Substitutive* informal institutions share goals with, and take the place of, weak or non-functioning formal institutions.

- *Accommodative* informal institutions have divergent goals and values from formal institutions, but do not ultimately undermine them.

- In a *complementary* relationship, informal institutions are compatible with, and may actually reinforce, formal institutions.

Table 3.1 A typology of relationships between informal and formal institutions

Outcomes/effectiveness	Effective formal institutions	Ineffective formal institutions
Convergent	Complementary	Substitutive
Divergent	Accommodating	Competitive

Source: Gretchen Helmke and Steven Levitsky (eds) (2006) *Informal Institutions and Democracy: Lessons from Latin America* (Baltimore, MD: Johns Hopkins University Press), 14, Fig. 1.1. ©2006 Johns Hopkins University Press. Reprinted with permission of Johns Hopkins University Press.

Indeed, an important new insight emerging from the works of authors such as Helmke and Levitsky (2006) is that, in emerging democracies, informal institutions can actually have a positive effect on governance.

In the next section, we turn to discuss empirical examples and studies that illustrate the complex interactions between formal and informal institutions. The cases emphasize how informal institutions may undermine—or compete—with formal political institutions, as illustrated by the continued prevalence of neo-patrimonial rule in countries in sub-Saharan Africa. The example of campaign clientelism in Peru provides an illustration of how informal institution may substitute for non-existing organized parties. In the example of the electoral quota rule in India, we see that formal rules may change 'sticky' informal traditions and customary rule, thus providing an example of accommodating formal and informal institutions.

Formal and informal institutions in sub-Saharan Africa

The role of informality has been particularly marked in analyses of politics in sub-Saharan African countries, and new institutionalist perspectives have illuminated our understanding of African politics. They have demonstrated the continuing salience and impact of informal institutions, especially those associated with **neo-patrimonialism**. Most recently, however, they have also been associated with a new and cautious optimism that perhaps formal institutions, or the rules of the game, really are beginning to matter as well.

One classic neo-patrimonial account is Bratton and van de Walle's (1997) analysis of democratic transitions in Africa from the early 1990s (see Box 3.5). Situating themselves firmly in the 'new institutionalist' school, they pose the question of the extent to which

these apparent democratic transitions really constitute a turning point in African political development. They note areas of change, but also strong elements of continuity, such as the *de facto* persistence, despite ostensibly competitive elections, of traditional leaders and the old political elite. And they suggest that transition has not, in general, strengthened political institutions—by which they mean political parties, legislatures, and electoral institutions. Instead, they show how the operation of such formal democratic political institutions are *competing* with, and are being subverted by, the persistence of informal institutions associated with the preceding neo-patrimonial regimes.

Formal rules and presidential politics: Formality trumping informality?

This perception of African politics in which informal, neo-patrimonial institutions pervade and largely undermine formal institutions remains widespread, and

---

BOX 3.5 NEO-PATRIMONIALISM DEFINED

In neo-patrimonial regimes, the chief executive maintains authority through personal **patronage** rather than through ideology or law. Relationships of loyalty and dependence pervade a formal political and administrative system, and leaders occupy bureaucratic office less to perform public service than to acquire personal wealth and status. The distinction between private and public interests is deliberately blurred. The essence of neo-patrimonialism is the award by public officials of personal favours, both within the state (notably, public sector jobs) and in society (for instance licences, contracts, and projects). In return for material rewards, clients mobilize political supporters and refer all decisions upwards as a mark of deference to patrons (Bratton and van de Walle 1994: 458).

indeed largely appropriate. But research also points out that formal political institutions in Africa are beginning to affect the behaviour of political and economic elites, and that, as such, formal and informal institutions are becoming *complementary*. Posner and Young (2007: 126), reflecting on some recent trends in African presidential politics, conclude that '[t]he formal rules of the game are beginning to matter'. They note the increasing importance of elections: by 2000–08, 98 per cent of presidential elections were contested (although, even then, incumbent presidents were re-elected more than 85 per cent of the time). They also note that, since 1990, more than thirty-six African countries have adopted new constitutions, most of which do not permit a third presidential term. It is encouraging that no incumbent president has tried to get rid of the constitution altogether and that nine out of eighteen agreed to step down after two terms. The remaining nine sought to change the constitution: three failed—Chiluba in Zambia, Muluzi in Malawi, and Obasanjo in Nigeria—although six, including Nujoma of Namibia and Museveni of Uganda, succeeded. Posner and Young (2007) accept that the role of external pressures in modifying presidential behaviour should not be underestimated. Nonetheless, they find grounds for 'cautious optimism' in what appears to be the unwillingness of presidents to openly defy growing public support for contested presidential elections and presidential term limits. In this context, it is worth mentioning the military coup in Niger (February 2010), which was blamed on the president's successful referendum extending his term of office. This could be seen as a further encouraging sign, although the fact of military intervention in itself is less reassuring. In 2012, in Senegal, President Wade was permitted, despite mass protests, to stand for an unconstitutional third term, but then conceded defeat when he lost the election. However, recent trends suggest that the formal institutional rule of presidential term limits continues to be challenged by the competing informal institution of presidentialism. In Burundi, President Nkurunziza was elected for a third term in July 2015. In the February 2016 elections in Uganda, the National Resistance Movement (NRM) won more than 70 per cent of the vote. Many expect that the parliamentary majority will remove presidential age limits and allow President Museveni (now aged 71), who has been in power since 1986, to be re-elected in 2021.

Complementary formal and informal institutions: Courts and anti-corruption commissions

The argument that formal rules are beginning to matter has also been echoed in other institutional contexts. Suberu (2008) looks at the role of Nigeria's Supreme Court. He notes the widely held view that Western-style institutions such as courts are simply facades for neo-patrimonial rule, but he argues that 'the neo-patrimonial framework of such analysis often trivializes the significant recent advances towards democratization, liberalization and institutionalization of power in Africa' (Suberu 2008: 458). This neo-patrimonial interpretation might have been appropriate for the Supreme Court before 1999, but since the transition in that year from military to civilian rule, the Court has emerged as 'a prominent and independent adjudicator of intergovernmental disputes' (Suberu 2008: 451). Suberu (2008) demonstrates this by means of an analysis of all fifteen major intergovernmental disputes concerning central government and Nigeria's thirty-six state governments, from 1999 to 2007. Beyond establishing the Supreme Court's increasing independence and integrity, he also points towards the contributory role of two other institutions, the National Judicial Council and the Federal Judicial Service Commission, which, under the 1999 Constitution, helped to ensure that members of the Supreme Court have been recruited on the combined basis of seniority and merit (see also Chapter 25).

Lawson (2009) focuses on the issue of anti-corruption reform, comparing the achievements in this respect of Kenya's Anti-Corruption Commission with Nigeria's Economic and Financial Crimes Commission. (For further discussions of corruption, see Chapter 15.) She points towards the way in which earlier studies tended to emphasize how incumbent elites used anti-corruption campaigns to target their political enemies. Lawson (2009) does not deny this aspect of anti-corruption initiatives, but argues that a subtler analysis is needed. In Kenya's case, she found that the Anti-Corruption Commission was indeed sidelined; in the Nigerian case, the Commission had a degree of success. More generally, Lawson (2009) suggests that factors such as timing and 'unintended consequences' of reform can make a difference. If an anti-corruption clean-up following an election were to be too obviously targeted at the previous incumbents, this could alienate public support. In addition, those heading up the new organizations could, as appeared to happen in Nigeria, seek to assert their independence from the new political leaders by adhering to and implementing their formal organizational mandate.

Substituting for weak formal rules and organizations: The case of campaign clientelism in Peru

Moving from African case studies that suggest competing, but in some cases also complementary, relationships between formal and informal institutions, we now turn to a Latin American example that illustrates how, in Peruvian elections, informal institution of vote-buying or campaign clientelism may *substitute* for non-existent formal party organizations.

Why would indiscriminate distribution of goods be considered a rational campaign strategy? Many studies have tried to explain the persistence of clientelistic linkages and vote-buying from historical institutionalist perspectives and with rational choice reasoning, as well as with sociological institutionalist explanations with roots in modernization theory. But, so far, we have few satisfactory answers as to why politicians invest in clientelism during campaigns when they lack the appropriate organizational apparatus to guarantee a pay-off of these financial efforts. This puzzle is the starting point for Muñoz's (2014) analysis of electoral politics in Peru: why do politicians hand out money without any form of guarantee of a vote? Peru's political system since the turn of the millennium has been characterized as democracy without parties. In the absence of party organizations to mobilize voters and inform the party of the viability of their candidates, clientelism during campaigns provides important signals of the electoral viability of candidates. Muñoz (2014) shows that politicians routinely buy the participation of poor voters at campaign events. Turnout in large numbers again signals the electoral prospects of the candidates. In this perspective, the informal institution of clientelism may be considered information, which again underlines the indirect effects of electoral clientelism: campaign clientelism helps politicians to improvise political organization. Informal campaign finances can thereby be understood as a *substitutive informal institution*: in the absence of political party organization to mobilize voters and inform voters about the viability of the candidates, clientelism provides information at campaign events that help voters to make choices.

Formal institutions accommodating informal institutions: The case of electoral quotas in India

The next example is taken from India, and illustrates how formal and informal institutions may have divergent aims and goals, yet may *accommodate* one another. The Scheduled Castes (SCs or *Dalits*), India's former 'untouchables', have long been recognized as one of the most marginalized communities in the world. This large minority group, constituting about 16 per cent of the population of India, consists of **castes** that have traditionally been subjected to extreme social discrimination and **exploitation**. Nevertheless, because of an extensive electoral quota system that guarantees them a proportional presence in the national parliament and the state assemblies, this minority group has been guaranteed political representation in the national parliament. The quota system has been praised for empowering members of a deprived community, but it has also been criticized for bringing to power SC politicians who do not work for the interests of the SC community at large (Dunning and Nilekani 2013; Jensenius 2013).

The quota system came into effect in the 1950s. Since then, SC politicians have run for election under the banners of the main parties and have fought for similar causes as other politicians. Dalit politicians elected to reserved seats have therefore become embedded into the mainstream formal political institutions in much the same way as other politicians and they appear to see themselves as agents of their parties rather than of their group. By becoming mainstream and working within the formal political institutions, SC politicians have gradually become an integral part of India's ruling elite. As SC politicians have had the opportunity to gain political experience, several of them have become vocal and powerful politicians. Over time, they have honed their skills in mobilizing voters and gaining re-election; they have also come to acquire important positions of power, such as high-level cabinet positions. This seems to have resulted in a gradual reduction in the social bias against them, among elites and voters alike.

Although there is still significant discrimination against SC politicians in India, political experience, education, money, and power appear to be breaking down traditional caste hierarchies. Considering how strong the social stigma of being 'untouchable' has been throughout history, this gradual integration of SCs in circles of political power should be recognized as a significant achievement. The quotas for SCs have played an important role in empowering a new political elite among SCs—one that very gradually has gained respect and recognition. Although this new elite must battle caste-based discrimination on a daily basis, the intensity and type of discrimination have changed dramatically (Jensenius 2013).

Formal–informal institutional interrelations in the developing world

The case studies have illustrated a variety of national and thematic contexts in which the interrelationship of formal and informal institutions has increasingly been explored. Whilst the traditional assumption might be that informal institutions would tend to vitiate and compete with formal institutions of democracy and governance, the cases have shown a more varied and complex picture. In sub-Saharan Africa, where regimes have long been seen as quintessentially neo-patrimonial, with informal power relations competing with and subverting weak formal representative and administrative institutions, there may be signs that formal institutions are beginning to matter. In the case of Peru, we have seen how, in the absence of formal organizations, the informal institution of campaign clientelism may substitute for formal party organizations providing information about the viability of candidates. Finally, we have seen in the example of the electoral quota for Scheduled Castes in India that formal and informal institutions may have divergent goals, and that, while the informal institutions do not cease to matter, over time formal and informal formal institutions may accommodate one another and diminish patterns of discrimination that have persisted for centuries.

KEY POINTS

- Interest is growing in the interaction of formal with informal political institutions in developing countries.

- The case from sub-Saharan Africa illustrates the salience of neo-patrimonial politics and *competing* informal and formal institutions, but also offers examples of formal institutions beginning to shape the behaviour of political and economic elites, and thereby *complementing* informal practices.

- The case of campaign clientelism in Peru illustrates how informal institution may *substitute* non-existing formal institutions.

- The case of electoral quotas for India's Scheduled Castes shows that formal and informal institutions with divergent goals may *accommodate* one another, and that the formal institution may over time alter 'sticky' traditional norms and practices.

Conclusion: Institutionalism and the Developing World

The new institutionalism that now pervades mainstream political analysis represents a welcome reaction to the reductionism of earlier individual actor-based approaches. Whilst it takes different guises, all institutionalist approaches include in their analyses a focus upon both formal and informal rules, organizations, and procedures. Moreover, these different strands can be regarded as complementary (Goodin 1996). Although the new institutionalism has been criticized for internal ambiguities, and for inadequately engaging with questions of the origins of institutions and how institutions change, this is part of an ongoing dialogue in which such shortcomings are being addressed.

The new institutionalism is increasingly applied in analysis of politics in the developing world. We have seen that this partly reflects the new institutional emphasis of development economics, as purveyed by international bodies such as the World Bank. Sound, effective governance institutions are seen as a prerequisite of development. This raises the question of the extent to which the new institutionalism is an appropriate tool of analysis for developing countries. Actors and institutions engaged in promotion of good governance and sound institutions for development have turned to institutional analyses in search of tools for designing institutions that may achieve desired goals. But the question of intentional institutional design raises a number of critical questions: can institutional designs 'travel' from different political settings? What are the potential unintended consequences of creating new formal institutions in political contexts in which the informal institutions may not be accommodating the stated aims of the formal institutions designed?

Arguably, institutional analyses have tended to ignore the uneasy relationship between formal institutions designed with external assistance and deeply embedded local informal institutions. Remmer (1997: 50), emphasizing the fragility and constrained character of institutions in developing countries, argues that the new institutionalism, with its emphasis on domestic issues, has ignored the overwhelming importance of international actors and institutions for the developing world, as well as domestic economic constraints. She finds it ironic that new institutionalism places politicians and bureaucrats at the centre of analysis at a time when the activities, resources, and relative weight of the state are being reduced through processes of **privatization**, **globalization**, and the emphasis on civil society (see Chapters 10, 12, and 15).

Some writers go further in questioning whether an institutional emphasis is really illuminating. Sangmpan (2007: 201) maintains that 'empirical evidence reveals that outcomes in developing countries consistently defy institutions as explanation and prescription'. He wants to distinguish three aspects of political systems—politics, institutions, and the state—and argues that, in developing countries, it is what he calls 'society-rooted politics' that imprints, and even determines, the other two aspects. Sangmpan's conception of politics is avowedly 'sociological', referring to interests within society that compete for property, goods, services, values, and political power. His argument is that an institutional approach marginalizes such factors. Although Sangmpan directs his criticism against the new institutionalism and its application to developing countries,

he maintains that this new institutionalism, like the old institutionalism, tends to focus on formal institutions. We have argued in this chapter, however, that one of the great virtues of the new institutionalism has been its interest in informal institutions and their interaction with the formal sphere. Yet society-rooted politics is broader than anything typically connoted by informal institutions and, to that extent, critics of institutionalist analyses may be right to argue that the new institutionalism runs the risk of exaggerating the significance of institutions, as opposed to fundamental political interests and conflict.

In conclusion, the new institutionalism offers an exciting tool of analysis if used with sensitivity to context and without hegemonic claims to be the only proper approach to politics in developing countries. An important feature of the application of the new institutionalism to developing countries is that it offers important insights into why some formal institutional arrangements 'stick' and guide political actors behaviour, why, in some instances, formal institutions change because they do not serve the interest of the elites, and under what circumstances informal norms and practices simply render formal written constitutions irrelevant. Our case studies have demonstrated some of the productive ways in which this kind of analysis has been used.

? QUESTIONS

1. What explains the new emphasis on institutional analyses applied to the developing world?

2. Compare the sociological, historical, and rational choice institutionalist approaches to understanding institutional change.

3. How do institutions emerge and how do institutions change?

4. Discuss how a cultural and a rational choice approach may interpret traditional agrarian economies differently.

5. With particular reference to developing countries, how would you evaluate the 'success' of a (written) constitution?

6. What are the potential pitfalls and unintended consequences of designing institutions with external assistance in a developing country setting?

7. In accounting for politics in developing countries, should we pay more attention to informal than to formal institutions?

FURTHER READING

Andrews, M. (2013) *The Limits of Institutional Reforms in Developing Countries: Changing the Rules for Realistic Solutions* (Cambridge: Cambridge University Press) Explains why many institutional reforms in developing countries have had limited success and suggests ways of overcoming this.

Dunning, T., and Nilekani, J. (2013) 'Ethnic Quotas and Political Mobilization: Caste, Parties and Distribution in Indian Village Councils', *American Political Science Review*, 107(1): 35–56 A careful examination of the impact of ethnic quotas on political mobilization and the distribution of benefits in three Indian states.

Goodin, R. (1996) *The Theory of Institutional Design* (Cambridge: Cambridge University Press) A comprehensive review of major theoretical approaches to institutional design and change.

Helmke, G., and Levitsky, S. (eds) (2006) *Informal Institutions and Democracy: Lessons from Latin America* (Baltimore, MD: Johns Hopkins University Press) A valuable framework for analysing formal and informal institutional relations, with detailed case studies from Latin America.

Lowndes, V. (2010) 'The Institutionalist Approach', in D. S. Marsh and G. S. Stoker (eds) *Theory and Methods in Political Science*, 3rd edn (Basingstoke: Palgrave), 60–79 An excellent overview.

Mahoney, J., and Thelen, K. (2010) *Explaining Institutional Change: Ambiguity, Agency and Power* (Cambridge, Cambridge University Press) A central book addressing institutional change spanning the three institutionalist approaches.

March, J., and Olsen, J. P. (1989) *Rediscovering Institutions: The Organizational Basis of Politics* (New York: Free Press) A central text within new institutionalism.

Peters, G. D. (2005) *Institutional Theory in Political Science: The New Institutionalism*, 2nd edn (London: Continuum) A thoughtful and thorough overview.

Powell, B. J. (2000) *Elections as Instruments of Democracy: Majoritarian and Proportional Visions* (New Haven, CT: Yale University Press) A central text discussing key aspects of democratic institutional design.

Thelen, K., and Steinmo, S. (1992) *Structuring Politics: Historical Institutionalism in Comparative Analysis* (New York: Cambridge University Press) A key introduction to historical institutionalism.

WEB LINKS

http://www.cgdev.org/section/topics/internationalinstitutions   Center for Global Development (CGD).

http://comparativeconstitutionsproject.org/   Comparative Constitutions Project.

http://genderindex.org/   Social Institutions and Gender Index.

http://globalresearch.ca/   Centre for Research on Globalization (CRG).

http://www.isnie.org/   International Society for New Institutional Economics (ISNIE).

http://plato.stanford.edu/entries/social-institutions/   Social Institutions.

http://www.undp.org/content/undp/en/home/sdgoverview/post-2015-development-agenda/goal-16.html   UNDP, Sustainable Development Goal (SDG) 16, 'Peace, Justice and Strong Institutions'.

For additional material and resources, please visit the Online Resource Centre at:
http://www.oxfordtextbooks.co.uk/orc/burnell5e/

4

The Developing World in the Global Economy

Robert Ahearne

Chapter contents

Overview

This chapter outlines the ways in which developing countries operate in the contemporary global economy. This is a huge topic and this chapter therefore focuses on three key features of an increasingly globalized economy—trade, foreign direct investment (FDI), and financial flows—discussing the significance of each for the developing world. Overall, the past seventy years has seen an increase in global economic integration, a key feature of the complicated processes often described as globalization. In the recent past, a handful of 'emerging economies' (especially China) have begun to challenge the economic dominance of Europe and North America, while other less-developed countries have not experienced the same transformation.

Introduction: Trends in the Global Economy

For the purposes of this chapter, the term 'global economy' is understood as all economic transactions that occur across national borders: trade; financial flows (including international aid); and foreign direct investment (FDI). Many observers present increasing global economic integration in an extremely positive manner, further enhanced by the conclusion of the cold war. However, there is profound disagreement over the meaning of the concept of **globalization** and whether increased global integration has a positive effect on economic well-being in the **developing world** (see Box 4.1).

BOX 4.1 GLOBALIZATION

Globalization is a term much used in contemporary social sciences. There is no accepted definition and little agreement on how to measure this process of profound global change (Hirst et al. 2009); suffice it to say that it is a process of global change that has cultural, social, economic, and political dimensions. O'Brien and Williams (2013: 27) regard globalization as a process of deterritorialization, which 'involves the shrinking of time and space, as well as the creation of new sets of social relations and new centres of authority'. Yet, when discussed in relation to the developing world, most analysis focuses on whether globalization tends to worsen or reduce poverty, as demonstrated in the following extracts:

Globalization has been a force for higher growth and prosperity for most, especially for those in the bottom half of the world's population.

(Bhalla 2002: 11)

Globalization speeds up the economy magnifying the chasm between [rich and poor]. Both at home and abroad, the extremes of wealth and deprivation have become so great that the stability of the global system is threatened.

(Isaak 2005: xxi)

Such divergent views reflect huge contestation over both globalization and poverty. With regards to the latter, Isaak (2005) emphasizes relative poverty and the fact that the proportion of global wealth enjoyed by the richest (when compared to the poorest) has grown dramatically in recent times. Piketty (2014) argued that this is, at least in part, owing to the fact that multinational corporations (MNCs) are able to artificially shift profits from higher tax (developing) countries into tax havens, which are usually developed economies. This process of **transfer** **pricing** concentrates wealth in developed states and reduces tax receipts in developing countries, costing them around US$600 billion per annum (Crivelli et al. 2015). Further research has found that this practice has cost Zambia many billions in annual revenue from the copper industry (Hearson 2015). On the other hand, Bhalla (2002) asserts that the number of people living in absolute poverty, which the World Bank sets at an income of US$1.25 or lower per day, has fallen rapidly over the past thirty years.

While different measures of poverty are an important consideration for determining the role of globalization in the developing world, regional differences are also a crucial concern. China and India (to a lesser extent) have seen huge reductions in absolute poverty, but the differences are negligible across most of Africa over the same period. The more economically advanced countries in East Asia seem to have benefited from globalization, while many countries in Africa and Latin America—especially those that rely heavily on primary commodities—have not experienced the same benefits. Indeed, fluctuations in global commodity prices can significantly damage developing countries, with the recent collapse in oil prices devastating the economies of Venezuela and Angola, among others. This regional picture is further complicated when the situation within countries is also considered. One example comes from China, where people on the country's eastern edge have benefited from the country's recent rapid growth compared to the large rural population living on the western side. Globalization is therefore a multifaceted process that affects different countries and different social groups within countries differently. Rodrik (2011: 253) adds that a more 'sane globalization' would require economic transformations to fit more closely with the social demands of **human development**.

A major part of the emergence of this global economy has been the growth in the value of trade, with many writers arguing that past economic growth in the developed world is largely explained by deep involvement in an international trading system, feeding the view that 'free trade' is inherently beneficial (see Box 4.2).

The developing world increased its share of world manufacturing output from a mere 5 per cent in the early 1950s to close to 25 per cent by the end of the twentieth century—but this share is dominated by China, Brazil, South Korea, and Taiwan (Dicken 2003: 37). It could therefore be argued that few of the benefits from trade appear to have reached the large proportion of the global population who live in absolute poverty (1.4 billion people, or one in five of the human population) and largely outside of this handful of countries. In addition to this, trade is increasingly dominated by major MNCs, and intra-firm trade—that is, transnational movements of goods and services within MNCs—accounts for around a third of global trade (Holton 2014). This level of control calls into question the idea that trade is 'free' in a global economy based on equal competition. The potential benefits of joining the world economy must be positioned alongside the reality that many developing countries are less than keen to open their economies to 'free trade'.

Trade between different social groups has existed for as long as written records and has provided much of the motivation for global exploration. By the end of the nineteenth century, much of Asia, and most of Africa and the Caribbean, was ruled by a handful of European powers. Most of Latin America had achieved political independence by this time, having been colonized

BOX 4.2 FREE TRADE OR PROTECTIONISM?

The benefits of trade have long been discussed. Since the early mercantilist writings and policies of the sixteenth and seventeenth centuries, certain forms of economic protectionism have been in the spotlight. One of the most significant contributions to this literature came from Alexander Hamilton, the first US Secretary of the Treasury after independence in the late eighteenth century. He advocated for a combination of industrial subsidies, state infrastructure spending, and import tariffs and quotas—conditions he deemed necessary to create the manufacturing base that would allow the United States to 'catch up' with the more economically advanced countries of Western Europe (Payne and Phillips 2010). In turn, this would 'create and sustain wealth and power in order to preserve and protect national security and independence' (Balaam and Dillman 2014: 54). As with **realism** in political science, mercantilism seeks to counter foreign (economic) threats through purposive government policy. Concurrently, however, classical economic thinkers such as Adam Smith advocated for free trade, unencumbered by tariffs, quotas, or government subsidies. Building on this, David Ricardo argued that protectionism distorts the **comparative advantage** that all countries have in the efficient production of certain goods. The surpluses of these goods should then be traded freely.

An interesting platform for a discussion of free trade and protectionism is the recent transformation of the 'Asian tigers'—Taiwan, South Korea, Hong Kong, and Singapore—and latterly China from very poor, largely agricultural, economies into middle- and high-income industrialized countries. Economists who wish to promote free trade see these successes as a good model because of their apparent openness to global trade. While it is correct to suggest that trade barriers have been gradually reduced and export-led industrialization favoured, they were certainly used to protect industries in the early stages, echoing import-substituting industrialization (ISI) and the 'infant industry protection' advocated by Hamilton. Chang (2014) adds that the continuing influence of the mercantilist tradition is often overlooked, whilst acknowledging the significant influence of Ricardo's classical free trade theory, comparative advantage.

Most of these East Asian countries switched production over time to maintain their position of comparative advantage, initially producing textiles, before moving into mass-production items such as toys and then into more high-tech goods. For example, South Korea initially specialized in producing semi-conductors in the 1960s, a crucial part of electronic circuits, before moving onto cars, washing machines, and, more recently, televisions, computers, and smartphones (see Chapter 24). Samsung is a global leader in this area. These processes also emerged from a close relationship between industry and state, with the reinvestment of a certain percentage of company profits often mandatory. The state also used subsidies (another form of protectionism) and investment as a way of developing parts of the economy that were perceived to have the greatest potential or strategic value. However, this differed from ISI in that subsidies were maintained only in industries that proved successful and internationally competitive (Payne and Phillips 2010). This real history challenges the views set forth by free market proponents and demonstrates that replicating this success might be more difficult than they suggest.

earlier, yet colonial relations created and maintained a highly unequal trading system in which European powers exported manufactured goods to the colonies and imported the materials needed to make these goods (McMichael 2008: 31–42). For example, India had been a major garment producer for the British market until the start of the eighteenth century, when the colonial government in London implemented protectionist policies (tariffs and import quotas) to limit the import of garments. Britain continued to import Indian cotton and became a major manufacturer of textiles at huge cost to the industry in India. In other words, Britain prospered 'by manufacturing articles for sale abroad, which her customers paid for in raw materials and food' (Porter 1996: 4). Some argue that this global trading system has largely remained intact, with the economies of many former colonies dominated by primary commodities.

One way of imagining the international trading system is as a number of segments, with each comprising the colonial power and its colonies. The bulk of global trade at this time was between the colonial powers and their subject states, and to have an empire was seen as essential for the economic well-being of the colonizer. Standing outside of this economic system was the United States, which, in the early twentieth century, was becoming a significant source of global production. By 1945, it produced around 50 per cent of the total global output. Successive US administrations sought a larger role in the international economy, which would require breaking up the European empires to free up trade. At the outbreak of the Second World War, planners in the United States started to think about what the post-war economic and political order might look like. The fruits of this planning emerged in a document known as the 'Atlantic Charter', signed by President Roosevelt and Britain's Prime Minister Churchill in 1941. At the core of the Charter was a commitment to the end of empire and the creation of a more open world economy.

Despite initial resistance from the European powers, decolonization gradually occurred following the end of the Second World War. However, as a result of the cold war, a world economy segmented by the European colonies was replaced by a world economy divided between the superpowers, the United States and the Soviet Union, each with allies and client states. These systems resembled the preceding imperial systems in that the dominant states in the core of the world economy provided manufactured goods, whilst developing countries were major sources of raw materials. However, in seeking to maintain and enhance their spheres of influence, the governments in Moscow and Washington, DC, left open the possibility of client states benefiting from their enmity. For example, Tanzania was able to increase international aid flows throughout the 1970s by appealing both to Communist authorities (in the Soviet Union and China) and to the social democracies of Western Europe (Sweden, Norway, and Finland).

One major attempt to overcome this reliance on the export of raw materials was ISI. This policy sought to limit manufactured imports by producing them locally, thereby employing local labour, reducing unemployment, and allowing for the production of more affordable manufactured goods. Producing locally would reduce the reliance on imports and would promote the introduction of new technology. However, to allow local industries to develop without competition, tariffs were imposed on imports. This policy was attempted by many countries in Latin America soon after the Second World War and by others in the 1950s (including Ghana, India, and Egypt).

While ISI did produce some manufactured goods for developing countries, it failed to break the reliance on imports, since these could not be produced without machine tools, spare parts, and specialized knowledge, all of which had to be imported. Across Latin America, the industrial sector placed intense political pressure on governments to maintain high levels of subsidies and protectionism. This reduced the incentives for firms to manufacture efficiently and to become internationally competitive (Payne and Phillips 2010), while the domestic market in many developing countries was not large enough to reap economies of large-scale production. Import-substituting industrialization is generally regarded as a failure, to which other countries retaliated with tariffs of their own, yet it must be recognized that European and US industrialization occurred behind tariff walls. Moreover, the more recent industrialization of many East Asian

economies depended to varying degrees on this approach and used the early stages of ISI as an economic strategy (see Chapter 24 on South Korea). This differed from most other countries that implemented ISI in that, over time, the East Asian economies gradually exposed their industries to increased competition.

Trade has been a feature of human societies dating back thousands of years, yet there are two other features of economic activity, also associated with the term 'globalization', which have gained greater significance over recent decades. The first of these is foreign direct investment (FDI), which refers to the practice of MNCs locating production and marketing facilities in other countries. The total value of FDI has mushroomed in the last thirty-five years, although whether this has assisted or undermined the economic transformation of developing countries is open to discussion. Foreign direct investment is a relatively long-term form of investment in the global economy, yet a further development has been the buying and selling of currencies, and stocks and shares in local economies—primarily short-term financial flows. While FDI refers to investments such as buildings and machinery, and therefore takes some time to create, vast amounts of money in the financial system are moved simply at the press of a button, with the majority of the world's currency today in an electronic, rather than paper, form. Concerns have also been raised in light of some evidence that speculative financial flows can serve to destabilize the economies of all countries, whether poor or rich, developing or developed.

At the time of writing, more than halfway through the second decade of the twenty-first century, it is clear that a huge shift is taking place in the global system, with economic power shifting away from Europe and North America and towards Asia. At the forefront of this shift have been the economies of China and India, both of which enjoyed substantial growth rates for sustained periods from around the late 1980s onwards. The increasingly significant role of Asian states in the global economy augurs profound changes in the character of international relations, as emphasized by the impact of recent downturns. While the 2007–08 financial crisis had some impact on developing countries, many were insulated from the most damaging effects of this by their close relationships with emerging economies, and especially with China. On the other hand, the recent slowdown of the Chinese economy perhaps has more profound implications for the economies of other less-developed countries—as has already been shown from Venezuela to Sudan, and from Pakistan to Zambia.

of China, especially to the export of merchandise, indicates that the global economy is undergoing a profound change. Manufactured goods make up approximately 75 per cent of merchandise trade, with the amount of manufactured goods flowing from the developing world increasing substantially. In reality, however, this is from a small number of emerging economies, with the so-called BRICS countries—Brazil, Russia, India, China, South Africa (see Box 4.6)—accounting for a significant portion of global exports: 21.1 per cent (merchandise) and 13.3 per cent (services), respectively. The role that these states now play in the global economy calls into question the relevance of terms such as the 'developing world', especially since they are markedly different from other 'less-developed countries' that maintain a more traditional role of providing raw materials and agricultural products to the developed world.

Trade

Patterns of global trends

International trade generally grew throughout the nineteenth century and particularly in the period 1870–1914. However, imperial rivalries, conflict, and isolationism saw it steeply decline from 1914 to 1945. This period was blighted by two global conflicts, leading some to argue that increased international interdependence would reduce the likelihood of another conflict. The second half of the twentieth century saw a dramatic increase in world trade, by almost twenty times from 1950 to 2000, while over the same period production has only increased sixfold (Dicken 2011: 18). The 1950s and 1960s witnessed a rapid rise in trade as (a) the world recovered from the Second World War, and (b) many countries in Asia, Africa, and the Caribbean won their independence and began trading as separate states. In contrast, the rate of global trade growth slowed during the 1970s as the international economy contracted in the wake of large oil price rises. Trade grew again during the 1980s and through the 1990s, particularly in light of the introduction of neoliberal free trade policies that often forced developing countries to open up their economies to imports and foreign investment.

Another aspect worthy of note is the changing composition of international trade over the past sixty years or so. Table 4.1 shows that the developed world is still responsible for the bulk of global exports in merchandise and services, although the ever-increasing contribution

Free trade and developing countries

The relative prosperity of the developed world is linked by many economists to the rapid rise of global trade. The idea that unimpeded trade will benefit developing countries is a core principle of the neoliberal agenda, which derives from classical liberal economics and is expressed in what became known as the **Washington consensus**. This denotes the primacy of related ideas at the World Bank, the International Monetary Fund (IMF), and the US government, all based in Washington, DC (see Box 4.3). The package of measures associated with the neoliberal agenda comprises both national and international elements. At the national level, these policies fall into two main areas: the promotion of a more efficient use of labour; and the reduction of the role of the state in the economy. At the international level, policies that aim to remove hindrances to trade and to promote the inflow of FDI are encouraged. Tariffs and subsidies are opposed by free trade advocates, since they are seen to distort and undermine the potential gains derived from comparative advantage and do not allow domestic industries to be exposed to international competition. Free traders also advocate for currencies to float freely, rather than being managed by governments. In practice, this generally means devaluing the currency to make domestic production more competitive internationally, while increasing the cost of imports.

Prior to the 1980s, it was rather typical for developing countries to place considerable restrictions on the total level of investment in their economy and on

Table 4.1 Relative shares in global exports (2014)

	Merchandise (%)		Services (%)	
Developed world	**51.3**		**68.24**	
Germany		7.9		5.4
United States		8.5		14.1
Transition economies	**4**		**2.53**	
Russian Federation		2.6		1.3
Developing world	**44.7**		**29.23**	
Africa	2.9		2.1	
Nigeria		0.5		0.04
South Africa		0.5		0.3
Asia (excl. Japan)	35.9		23.6	
China		12.3		4.7
China (incl. Hong Kong and Macau)		15.1		7.8
India		1.7		3.1
Latin America (incl. Caribbean)	5.7		3.4	
Brazil		1.2		0.8
Mexico		2.1		0.4

Source: Adapted from UNCTAD (2015a: Tables 1.1 and 5.1)

BOX 4.3 THE BRETTON WOODS ORGANIZATIONS

Three organizations dominate international trade and finance: the World Bank; the International Monetary Fund (IMF); and the World Trade Organization (WTO). Collectively, these are known as the 'Bretton Woods organizations', because they originate from a conference held at a US holiday resort of that name in July 1944. The aim was to create international **institutions** that would prevent the reoccurrence of the Great Depression of the late 1920s and 1930s, and might reduce tariff competition, both seen as a contributory factors in the outbreak of the Second World War. All three organizations have had significant effects on developing countries.

The IMF was primarily established to help countries undergoing balance-of-payments crises (that is, where the value of imports have exceeded exports). Member countries experiencing a financial crisis are able to borrow money in tranches, but these are 'conditional' loans that require the government of the borrowing country to implement economic and political reforms dictated by the IMF.

The World Bank is a complex network of institutions and it makes more sense to talk of a 'World Bank group' rather than a specific organization. At the core is the International Bank for Reconstruction and Development (IBRD), which began by

making loans to aid the post-war reconstruction of Europe, but now specializes in loans to developing countries. However, even more relevant to developing countries is the International Development Association (IDA). The IDA provides loans and grants for programmes that aim to boost economic growth, reduce inequalities, and improve living conditions.

A controversial feature of both the IMF and the World Bank is the way in which decisions are made, since neither has a 'one member, one vote' system; instead, votes are allocated based on the amount that a country pays into the organizations, determined by the size of the economy. This has resulted in developed countries dominating decision-making, with the IMF perhaps the more striking example. For a vote to be carried at the IMF, an 85 per cent threshold needs to be met, but the fact that the United States provides more than 15 per cent of the funding means that it effectively has a veto. There have long been calls for a change to voting rights, but these grew louder after the 2007–08 global financial crisis; by 2010, developing economies were demanding increased representation. While change was finally implemented in December 2015 (after eventual agreement by the US Congress), which saw the Chinese vote share increase from 3.8 per cent to 6 per cent

(BBC News 2015), two institutions had been established as alternatives to the Bank and the Fund (see Box 4.6).

The WTO makes decisions by the process of 'one member, one vote'. The WTO was established only in 1995, but its forebear, the General Agreement on Tariffs and Trade (GATT), was discussed at Bretton Woods. The GATT was not a one-off agreement, but a number of consecutive 'rounds'—that is, meetings held with the principal aim of reducing tariff levels and cutting import quotas to promote international trade. During the Uruguay Round (the Latin American country held the GATT

in 1986), the decision was made to create the WTO as a more formal organization to oversee global trade and to adjudicate on disputes. This greatly expanded the role of the organization and its remit far beyond trade. The Doha Development Round of 2001 promised much for developing countries, with discussions focusing on the removal of agricultural subsidies in developed countries, which, it was argued, should also further open their markets to agricultural goods from the developing world. However, fifteen years later (at the time of writing), no substantive change has happened.

the areas of the economy in which foreign investment was allowed. However, free market policies argue that there should be no discrimination against foreign investment and that any barriers to investment should be removed. This can be mapped onto the past fifty years or so in Tanzania, which transformed from a country that had very tight controls on foreign investment and high rates of corporate tax under an ostensibly socialist Tanzanian government (1962–85) to become one of the most ardent followers of the newly dominant neoliberal agenda from the mid-1980s onward (Pitcher and Askew 2006). This was marked by the **privatization** of formerly nationalized industries, reduced investment in public services, the removal of food subsidies, and a far more liberal trading **regime** that saw a dramatic increase in the flow of goods, services, and capital, out of and (mostly) into the country.

Since the 1990s, the Washington consensus has come under sustained criticism. This is partly because the evidence of successful implementation of the prescribed policies is patchy and in light of major criticism of the ways in which the 1997 Asian financial crisis was handled by the IMF (see, in particular, Stiglitz 2002). Subsequently, a revised set of policies dubbed the **post-Washington consensus** have emerged, particularly popular at the World Bank. The focus on market mechanisms and 'getting the prices right' remains, yet the state is seen to have an important role to play in terms of overseeing the financial system and in providing support for education and infrastructure projects. Some have argued that the economic transformation of many East Asian states demonstrates that free market policies can contribute to rapid economic growth. However, it could equally be argued that protectionism, at least at the early stages of industrialization, is of equal or greater importance. This poses a number of difficult questions: why have other developing countries been unable to replicate this success? Why has the

enormous growth in international trade not resulted in a wider distribution of the fruits of that trade, as the theory of comparative advantage would suggest? Why have some parts of the developing world barely participated at all in the growth of world merchandise trade?

Africa's share of world merchandise trade was 5 per cent in 1980, but is (at time of writing) just 2.9 per cent. Similarly, the contribution of developing countries of the Americas has remained static at just under 6 per cent (UNCTAD 2015a). Critics of the neoliberal agenda argue that much of the developing world is disadvantaged in the global economy when compared to more developed countries. Furthermore, some rightly question the extent to which the 'Asian tigers' have followed free market policies, and while rapid economic growth in China and India has, at least in part, built on economic liberalization through the 1980s (China) and 1990s (India), this has swallowed up a high percentage of FDI that might have been invested elsewhere. It could be argued that elements of the neoliberal model have benefited some emerging economies at the cost of other, poorer, less-developed countries. It is again necessary to challenge the idea of a homogeneous 'developing world'.

The role(s) of developing countries in global trade

As discussed earlier, the primary function of many formerly colonized (developing) countries remains to provide raw materials and markets for manufactured goods. The first problem with this situation is that commodity prices tend not to keep pace with those of manufactured goods in the long term (known as the 'declining terms of trade'), meaning that increased exports of commodities are needed simply to maintain the same level of manufactured imports. The second is that primary commodities, such as coffee and cocoa, are liable to very large price fluctuations, which make future revenues difficult to predict. These two factors place many developing countries in a structurally weak and precarious position within the global economy. These risks were mitigated by consistently increasing prices for most of the twenty-first century, yet 2015 saw primary commodities lose nearly a third of their purchasing power relative to manufactures (IMF 2016). In particular, the collapse in oil prices has adversely affected the economies of Nigeria and especially Venezuela (among others), while falling prices are a risk to each of the forty-five (of fifty-four) African countries that derive more than 60 per cent of their merchandising exports from primary products (UNCTAD 2015b: 15).

The risks of commodity dependence are abundantly clear when we consider the history of Zambia. Booming world copper prices transformed Zambia into a middle-income country within a decade of independence (in 1964), yet rapidly falling prices, coupled with an overreliance on copper, saw government revenues decimated and the economy collapse in the early 1980s. Increased global demand for copper, especially from China, has seen prices rise in line with other commodities in the twenty-first century, and copper now accounts for 40 per cent of Zambian gross domestic product (GDP) and 74 per cent of export revenues (UNCTAD 2015b: 53). However, the recent slowdown in Chinese manufacturing and economic growth, coupled with continued dependence on the commodity, bring the risks of a repeated copper crisis into view.

A similar lack of economic diversification is a problem for a great many commodity-dependent developing countries (UNCTAD 2015b: 15) and serves to demonstrate the danger of relying solely on comparative advantage. Payne and Phillips (2010) thoughtfully remind us that if the Japanese government had accepted the theory of comparative advantage in the 1960s, rather than taking a more interventionist approach and subsidizing certain industries, Sony and Toyota would not have been formed. The country would have built on the inbuilt advantage in textile manufacturing, rather than moving towards technology and automobiles.

A further problem that developing countries confront is that of protectionism in developed countries. For example, the Common Agricultural Policy (CAP) of the European Union uses high tariffs to protect farmers from having to compete with the imports of certain agricultural products, whilst also providing huge subsidies. Around 38 per cent of the EU budget is spent on CAP (European Commission 2015), with a similar percentage (38 per cent) of the world's agricultural exports coming from the European Union (WTO 2015). Similarly, albeit in the United States, massive government subsidies paid to cotton farmers effectively close a major export market to producers such as Egypt. Other non-tariffs barriers also exist, and these include import quotas, safety requirements, and very stringent environmental or labour standards (see Chapter 17). For example, a number of Caribbean banana-producing countries and Ghanaian tomato growers alike have been unable to export into the EU market owing to stringent quality control protocols. These represent a clear example of a non-tariff barrier.

This whole area has been described as the **new protectionism** because governments have sought to defend domestic industries, while espousing commitments to lower trade tariffs as part of international agreements. Contrary to what is advocated by the governments of developed countries, the richest countries have tariff barriers far higher than those in the rest of the world and provide huge agricultural subsidies that make it harder for developing countries to compete. It has been estimated that developing countries lose US$1,000 billion each year from protectionist measures by industrialized countries (O'Brien and Williams 2013: 113), while the huge costs of tax avoidance burden developing countries still further (as discussed next in relation to FDI). It is, however, again crucial to distinguish between emerging economies, such as India, China, and Brazil, which have used WTO rules to protect their economies (Holton 2014; Shaffer et al. 2015), and other, less powerful, developing nations (less-developed countries), whose experience of the WTO framework has been as an institution dominated by wealthy countries that act in a self-interested manner.

KEY POINTS

- Since 1945, there have been massive increases in the levels of international trade.
- Despite some exceptions, many countries in the developing world have not benefited greatly, with the proportion of the world's exports from Africa and Latin America in decline.
- Although the theory of comparative advantage suggests that all countries should benefit from participation in trading, the 'gains from trade' do not seem to be shared equally.

Foreign Direct Investment and Financial Flows

Foreign direct investment

The theory of comparative advantage suggests that a country should specialize in those goods that it can produce more cheaply. One area in which the developing world has a distinct economic advantage is in labour costs. Throughout most of the developing world, and even though labour costs are rising in emerging economies, it is cheaper to employ workers than in developed economies. It would therefore seem logical for companies from the developed world to relocate production from those economies in which labour costs are high to those in which such costs are lower. For some companies, the employment of female workers has been particularly attractive (see Box 4.4).

Improvements to transportation and communications have made it far easier for companies to set up production facilities in different parts of the world. O'Brien and Williams (2013: 134) define FDI as 'investment made outside the home country of the investing company in which control over the resources transferred remains with the investor'. In other words, a key feature of FDI is that production will be directed by a corporation based outside of the territory in which the investment is made. One of the aims of much recent policy promoted by the World Bank and IMF has been to encourage governments in the developing world to promote inwards investment, for example by reducing taxation levels, setting up tax free zones, and removing controls on capital flows. However, there has been much debate about the extent to which investment by multinational corporations (MNCs) benefits the host economies, with accusations that they use their size to extract inordinate benefits (see Box 4.5). This is an area of much controversy and it is better to look at the actions of individual MNCs in different countries rather than to draw general conclusions.

There is a considerable amount of data on the levels of FDI and one of the features of this activity is that it fluctuates on a year-by-year basis. Levels of FDI dropped off quite considerably following the **terrorist** attacks on the World Trade Center in New York in 2001 ('9/11'), and while they increased again until the 2007–08 financial crisis, when they took a dip, they continued to increase until 2014–15, when they again fell. Tables 4.2 and 4.3 present data taken from statistics compiled by the United Nations Conference on Trade and Development (UNCTAD). From these tables, a few general observations can be derived, as follows.

- Levels of FDI have risen considerably over the past thirty-five years, with the figures for 2014 nearly thirty times higher than those of 1980. Most of this expansion, however, occurred between 1980 and 2000, and concerns over sluggish global growth rates saw annual FDI inflows fall by 16 per cent in 2014.

BOX 4.4 WOMEN IN THE GLOBAL ECONOMY

In 2014, of the approximately 3 billion people in paid employment worldwide, 1.2 billion were women. Women are consistently overrepresented in the agricultural sector, especially in Asia and Africa, and a larger proportion of women are employed in the service sector. Only 18 per cent of the 1.2 billion women were employed in industry (compared to 26.6 per cent of men), indicative of the reality that women tend to be subject to more insecure employment. Wage inequality between men and women is a worldwide phenomenon, and in most countries, developed or developing, women can expect to earn 60–90 per cent of their male counterparts' pay, and even lower proportions in parts of the Middle East and North Africa (WEF 2015).

One issue of particular relevance here has been the employment of women in **export-processing zones (EPZs)** and especially in the garment industry in developing countries. Export-processing zones have been set up by governments to encourage inward investment by foreign companies manufacturing products such as electronics, toys, and clothes. The factories are often described as 'sweatshops' because of the poor conditions for workers, and attract investment owing to low wages, non-unionized workers, and tax breaks. Women remain disproportionately represented therein (Braunstein 2006), based on the curious logic that they are deemed more passive and less likely to engage in labour struggles, more prepared to accept low wages, and more inclined to accept insecure work. They are also seen to be more nimble-fingered and amenable to training (Elson and Pearson 1981).

BOX 4.5 ADVANTAGES AND DISADVANTAGES OF FOREIGN DIRECT INVESTMENT

Advocates of FDI argue that MNCs:

- *introduce additional resources* Most significantly, they introduce the capital that is often lacking in developing countries, but they also bring with them the technology, managerial expertise, and foreign market access.

- *increase tax revenue* They may pay local taxes and do pay workers, who then pay income tax.

- *increase efficiency* They may introduce competition into the local economy, by providing links to the global economy, thereby encouraging more efficient production.

- *improve the balance of payments* They improve the balance of payments by producing local goods that previously had been imported and producing goods for export.

Critics, meanwhile, suggest that MNCs:

- *do not introduce advanced technology* Most MNC production primarily involves assembly of high-tech parts produced elsewhere.

- *do little for the local economy* They can drive local firms out of business using unfair competitive practices. Furthermore, many declare profits elsewhere, so as to pay tax in countries with low tax regimes (usually in the developed world).

- *worsen the balance of payments* Imported machinery and spare parts, and payments to the parent company, can have a negative impact on the balance of payments.

- *can damage the political system* Because MNCs are so large and powerful, and have a large impact on a small economy, they are able to extract concessions from governments by threatening to withdraw their facilities, or through bribery and **corruption**.

- Developing economies accounted for only 17 per cent of FDI in 1990, but they have received the majority since 2012, accounting for 55 per cent of the global total in 2014. Nevertheless, this is very concentrated, with ten countries absorbing more than 70 per cent of FDI directed to the developing world. China and Hong Kong combined account for more than a third.

- The relative proportion of FDI flowing into Africa remains very low, questioning the widespread 'Africa rising' narrative within mainstream media. While economic growth rates have been impressive across the continent, FDI inflows are concentrated on resource extraction—an inherently unstable industry—rather than manufacturing (Ferguson 2006).

Financial flows

Trade and FDI are the more visible aspects of the global economy, yet, in numerical terms, they are dwarfed by the movements of money through the world's foreign exchanges. World merchandise trade is worth around US$19 trillion per year (UNCTAD 2015a: Table 1.1),

---

Table 4.2 Foreign direct investment inflows by region, 1990–2014

Region	1990		2000		2010		2014	
	Total (US$bn)	% of total	Total (US$bn)	% of total	Total (US$bn)	% of total	Total (US$bn)	% of total
World	204.9		1,363.2		1,328.1		1,228.3	
Developed world	170.2	83.0	1,125.2	83.0	673.1	51.0	498.8	41.0
Developing world	34.6	17.0	232.2	17.0	579.9	44.0	681.4	55.0
Africa	2.8	1.4	9.6	0.7	44.1	3.3	53.9	4.4
Latin America and the Caribbean	8.5	4.1	79.6	5.8	131.7	9.9	159.4	13.0
Asia	22.9	11.8	142.7	10.5	401.9	30.3	465.3	37.9

Source: UNCTAD (2015a: annex tables)

Table 4.3 Top ten recipients of FDI in the developing world, 2014

Country	Total (US$bn)	% of total
China	128.5	18.9
Hong Kong, China	103.3	15.2
Singapore	67.5	9.9
Brazil	62.5	9.2
India	34.4	5.0
Chile	22.9	3.4
Mexico	22.8	3.4
Indonesia	22.6	3.3
Colombia	16.1	2.4
Thailand	12.6	1.8

Source: UNCTAD (2015a: annex tables)

which is equivalent to around six days of trading on the world's money markets (XE 2016). Many such transactions are speculative, with global financial flows comprising two main elements. The first of these is simply the buying and selling of money, with some such transactions related to trade and investment. For example, if a British company were to want to purchase goods from Nigeria, it would first need to purchase Nigerian naira to pay the supplier. However, much of the activity on the global currency markets could be more closely equated to gambling, with many of world's major currencies free-floating since the 1980s. In other words, governments have allowed the value of the currency to be largely dictated by the sentiments of the market, allowing investors such as George Soros to make large fortunes simply by buying currencies that they anticipate will go up in value or selling those that they expect will fall.

A second feature of global financial flows is investment in the stock markets of other countries, usually described as 'portfolio investment'. Whereas FDI generally involves the construction of factories and offices, and the purchase of machinery, portfolio investment does not give the investor any control or ownership of the bricks and mortar of the company concerned. Investors therefore have more freedom and can simply sell their holdings of shares in overseas territories almost instantaneously. This buying and selling of shares often takes the pattern of a herd, and certain countries or regions quickly become very

popular or unpopular, with large numbers of shares bought or sold. As with the buying and selling of currencies, this can lead to stock market booms and crashes, the aim of the insightful (or lucky) investor being to 'buy cheap and sell dear'. The rapid outflow of what is described as 'hot' money often has little to do with the underlying economic stability of the countries concerned, but can often serve to destabilize the economies. This has been the subject of considerable criticism, especially when it has taken place in the developing world.

During the late 1980s and early 1990s, many countries in the developing world were encouraged to open their economies to these kinds of financial flow, not least by the Bretton Woods institutions (see Box 4.3). Financial liberalization involves removing restrictions on the buying and selling of the country's currency, and on the movements of capital flowing in and out of the country, with such policies adopted by many countries in Latin America, East Asia, Africa and Eastern Europe, and the former Soviet Union (Stiglitz 2002). For many analysts, it is not a coincidence that these regions were afflicted by severe financial disruption soon after. Examples are the Mexican peso crisis of 1994–95, the Brazilian crisis, Russia's rouble crisis of 1998, and a financial crisis in Argentina that rumbled on for more than three years and saw off five presidents in ten days at its height in 2001. Perhaps the most famous financial crisis of the 1990s, however, was that which swept through East Asia in 1997, the causes of which are much contested.

East Asian countries had been very successful at following export-led models of development, and had enjoyed high levels of domestic saving and low inflation—seemingly a perfect combination for continued growth. Rapid financial liberalization in the 1990s led to a vast inflow of speculative investment based on the perceived profitability of the region. This speculative boom was followed by a blip, which saw capital flowing out of the region, yet Sachs (1998) argues that most East Asian countries maintained 'sound economic fundamentals'. Nevertheless, grave warnings from the IMF about the economic future of the region deepened the sense of panic' and were akin to 'screaming fire in the theatre . . . instead of dousing the flames' (Sachs 1998: 19). The outflow of speculative capital became more rapid, leading to bankruptcies in South Korea and Thailand. Both countries, along with others, saw their economies contract significantly. Analyses from the World Bank and IMF now suggest that the problem was initially too much government involvement in the economy, which shielded high debt ratios and hid corruption, followed by financial liberalization that was too rapid. However, it is worth noting that Malaysia was able to ride out the storm effectively by imposing very strict capital controls, stemming the outflow of capital through extremely punitive sanctions. While such measures were discouraged by the Bretton Woods institutions, since it was assumed that they would limit future investment, this risk has been proven to be unfounded.

KEY POINTS

- Foreign direct investment is a major part of global financial flows, dominated by a handful of developed and emerging economies. Less-developed countries are decreasingly significant in this area.

- There is considerable debate over the costs and benefits of FDI for developing countries.

- Two major components of the global economy are (a) the buying and selling of currencies and stocks and shares in local economies, and (b) the rapid movement of capital across borders.

- Both of these can cause serious economic disruptions, as financial liberalization in some developing countries has shown.

The Developing World Today

Many commentators claim that the global economic crisis that has persisted since 2007 is the most serious economic disruption since the Great Depression of the 1920s and 1930s. In 2009, global gross national product (GNP)—that is, the aggregate level of output across all economies—dropped for the first time since the Second World War. While there has since been something of a rebound, rates of growth in developed countries have generally remained sluggish or have fallen, prompting fears of a prolonged economic downturn (ILO 2013: 1). This had a substantial global effect and, according to the WTO, the rate of growth in global trade was 5.5 per cent in 2007, down from 8.5 per cent in 2006, while trade actually declined by 11 per cent in 2009 (Deshpande and Nurse 2012: 3). This is increasingly significant as more developing countries become integrated into the world economy and rely on exports to contribute substantially to GDP. Singapore, for example, saw a 30 per cent drop in exports in the fourth quarter of 2008. The loss of export income was compounded by a reduction in financial flows into developing countries.

In spite of all of this, however, developing countries tended not to suffer as much as developed countries in the wake of the 2007–08 financial crisis. Moreover, it can be argued that they have become increasingly important actors in global economic management, with a handful of prominent developing countries recently launching institutions to rival the World Bank and IMF (see Box 4.6). While the crisis saw aid budgets reduced and remittances fall (at least in the short term), two key areas of finance for developing countries, the fact that commodity prices returned to their pre-crisis levels more rapidly than expected supported the economies of many resource-dependent states. These price increases were largely the result of continued demand from Asia, especially from China and India, and it is the robustness of these economies that has insulated many less-developed countries from the worst effects of the global financial crisis. This is principally so since the emerging economies have become increasingly significant trade and investment partners for less-developed countries—a trend that is likely to continue.

Countries in the developing world are affected by multiple factors that can reduce their economic well-being. These include the loss of export possibilities, fluctuating commodity prices, and cuts to FDI. While the 2007–08 global financial crisis did not quite have

BOX 4.6 THE BRICS COUNTRIES, THE NEW DEVELOPMENT BANK, AND THE ASIAN INFRASTRUCTURE INVESTMENT BANK

BRICS countries

Economic liberalization at the end of the cold war led to the creation of an integrated global economy. This brought formerly Communist countries such as Russia and China to prominence as global economic actors, along with Brazil and India as populous and regionally powerful developing countries. This new formulation somewhat undermines the simplistic developed/developing world dichotomy, a challenge that is further taken up by Goldman Sachs economist Jim O'Neill. He designated this group as distinct from other developing countries, with South Africa added as the fifth BRICS country in 2010. This distinction from other developing countries is based on the fact that each of these countries is a key actor in regional and global affairs, with a large and rapidly growing economy. Estimates suggest that the BRICS will continue to increase their contribution to global GDP, which is already 20 per cent, and that, by 2050, the original four members will rank in the top six, with China (first), India (third), Brazil (fifth), and Russia (sixth) (BBC News 2014b). While Brazil is embroiled in a massive corruption scandal at the time of writing (March 2016) and economic growth figures might have been exaggerated by the Chinese authorities, the increased influence of this group has been clarified with the establishment of the New Development Bank (NDB).

The New Development Bank

The NDB—formerly known as the 'BRICS Development Bank'—was established as a new multilateral lender in 2015. The Bank claims not to be a rival to traditional organizations such as the World Bank and IMF, NDB President Kundapur Vaman Kamath asserting in July 2015 that its 'objective is not to challenge the existing system as it is but to improve and complement the system in our own way'. However, the Bank emerged as a result of the Bretton Woods institutions' failure to rebalance voting rights expeditiously (see Box 4.3)—a situation that the BRICS countries had previously criticized. Eventual agreement to rebalance voting rights at the IMF in 2015 came too late.

The NDB is to lend to developing countries to help to finance infrastructure projects, funded at first by US$50 billion—$10 billion from each of the five founding members. This is expected to double in the coming years, with the bulk coming from China.

The Asian Infrastructure Investment Bank

The creation of the Asian Infrastructure Investment Bank (AIIB) marks another major change in the global economic landscape. Much like the NDB, it is an infrastructure bank and is expected to lend between US$10 billion and $15 billion per year. So far, China has invested around $30 billion of the $100 billion total capital stock in the AIIB. The Bank will co-finance projects in Asia with other multilateral groups, such as the Asian Development Bank (ADB), in what Chinese Premier Li Keqiang describes as the most dynamic region for global growth. The AIIB insists that it will not demand the free market (neoliberal) reforms advocated by the Bretton Woods institutions, and has an internal department focused on compliance and integrity that will report directly to its board.

It is generally assumed that both the NDB and the AIIB will lend money to developing countries without the conditions that are attached to loans from the World Bank or the IMF. Moreover, these institutions have been set up in opposition to a global financial order that is dominated by US interests and is not, therefore, seen to adequately address the needs of developing countries. Whether or not these two new multilateral lenders will better serve developing countries can be judged only in time, but, by not insisting on liberalization, it does seem clear that the AIIB and the NDB are likely to receive less criticism from developing countries. Moreover, the establishment of these banks adds weight to claims that the global economy is being rebalanced. This view is strengthened by the fact that Australia, Germany, Italy, the Philippines, South Korea, and the United Kingdom have all agreed to join the AIIB, despite of opposition from Washington, DC.

Sources: BBC News (2015); Wong (2016)

---

the adverse economic impact that was anticipated and developing countries generally recovered better from the crisis than their contemporaries in the developed world, there are still clear risks. For example, a significant downturn in the Chinese economy shows no signs of abating in 2016, and this has the potential to destabilize the global economy and to do great damage to developing countries. The latter is a further concern, since this downturn has seen a reduction in the demand for the primary commodities upon which many developing countries rely for government revenues and economic stability. Chinese economic problems and falling commodity prices represent a dual threat to developing countries, and may increase the numbers living in absolute poverty around the world, throwing into reverse recent modest reductions in the numbers. It may even have more of a nefarious and lasting impact than the 2007–08 crisis.

- In 2007, the global economy entered a period of considerable instability, although emerging economies generally rode out the crisis more effectively than developed countries. The recent downturn in China might damage developing countries more.

- Two new international financial institutions might be proven to offer loans to developing countries with more favourable terms.

- Some developing countries are particularly susceptible to fluctuating commodity prices, and were damaged by the economic downturn and the slowdown in global trade.

Conclusion

The level of world trade has increased hugely since 1945, as has prosperity in the developed world. With the emergence of a single global economy since around 1990, these processes have accelerated. For most analysts, these two features are closely linked. Yet the benefits of greater engagement in the global economy do not appear to have been obtained by the poorest countries. Why, in an era of a global economy and neoliberal policies, does the gap between the richest and the poorest appear to be widening? A free market analysis might suggest that there are still too many blockages to the free movement of investment and goods. Poorer countries have undermined their own prospects of development by working against the market. A second position maintains that greater engagement is potentially beneficial, but that, because developing countries are behind the developed world in terms of industrialization, reforms to the global economy are required. A more radical position would argue that the global economic system entrenches inequality between the richest parts of the world and the poorest—a neo-colonial relationship.

For the past twenty years, the free market philosophy has dominated development policy, and while many developing countries have followed neoliberal prescriptions, they still face protectionist measures imposed in the developed world. The reasons for the disparity of wealth in the global economy will be disputed indefinitely and, for the foreseeable future, developing countries will have to make their way within a global capitalist environment. The operation of global markets has the potential to generate enormous wealth, as well as the capacity to exploit the most vulnerable. The governments of smaller and poorer developing countries face the difficult task of trying to minimize the negative impacts of global capitalism, while attracting potential benefits for their populations. Economic crises make this task even more difficult. However, the rise of China and other BRICS countries outlines the possibilities for developing countries within a globalized economy.

China has not, however, played by the globalization 'handbook' and participates in the global economy on its own terms, largely mimicking the behaviour of developed countries. Indeed, China and emerging economies have started to set their own rules, and are creating organizations such as the NDB and the AIIB (see Box 4.6) to rival their counterparts that were established at Bretton Woods. As such, it is necessary to reiterate that a major distinction needs to be drawn between less-developed countries and emerging economies. Meanwhile, governments of the developed world also confront a challenge: to resolve the contradiction of promoting free trade as a solution for the developing world, while maintaining protectionism at home. This is a contradiction that is difficult to justify; until it is resolved, it would appear that the global economy operates largely in the interests of the rich and powerful, and counter the interests of those in the poorest and least influential parts of the world.

QUESTIONS

1. Has globalization been a positive or negative force for developing countries?
2. Who benefits most from the global trading system?
3. Should developing countries be wary of foreign direct investment?
4. What was the Asian financial crisis? What are the lessons for developing countries?

5. What is protectionism? What is the impact on developing countries?

6. Based on the lessons from this chapter, what impact do you think that instability in Chinese markets will have on poorer developing countries?

 FURTHER READING

Balaam, D. N., and Dillman, B. (2014) *Introduction to International Political Economy*, 6th edn (London: Routledge)   Useful introduction to international political economy, and the important influence that historical ideas and theories have on contemporary debates.

Chang, H.-J. (2014) *Economics: A Users Guide* (London: Penguin)   A useful and accessible introduction to economics that does not prioritize one approach over another.

Dicken, P. (2011) *Global Shift: Mapping the Changing Contours of the World Economy*, 6th edn (London: Sage)   Clear overview of the emergence of a global economy, with good sections on the newly industrializing countries.

O'Brien, R., and Williams, M. (2016) *Global Political Economy: Evolution and Dynamics*, 5th edn (Basingstoke: Palgrave Macmillan)   Good discussion of the development of the global economy and key contemporary issues in international political economy.

Scholte, J. A. (2005) *Globalization: A Critical Introduction*, 2nd edn (Basingstoke: Palgrave)   A superb discussion of the subject and associated literature.

Todaro, M., and Smith, S. (2014) *Economic Development*, 12th edn (Harlow: Pearson)   Regularly revised and updated, contains excellent chapters on the role of developing countries in the global economy and on theories of trade.

Van Marrewijk, C. (2002) *International Trade and the World Economy* (Oxford: Oxford University Press)   Excellent introduction to theories of trade and investment in the global economy.

 WEB LINKS

http://www.cato.org/research/international-economics-development   The Cato Institute ('individual liberty, free markets, and peace') is a Washington, DC-based non-profit public policy research foundation committed to free markets and free trade.

http://www.oxfam.org   The site of the non-governmental organization (NGO) Oxfam (UK), containing many of its reports on trade and protectionism.

http://www.twnside.org.sg   The Third World Network (TWN) page on trade issues provides research critical of current global economic policies.

http://www.unctad.org   The site of the United Nations Conference on Trade and Development (UNCTAD) contains voluminous data on trade and investment, and reports on the global economy.

http://www.undp.org   The United Nations Development Programme (UNDP) focuses on development issues and produces an annual Human Development Report.

 For additional material and resources, please visit the Online Resource Centre at:
http://www.oxfordtextbooks.co.uk/orc/burnell5e/

5

The Developing World in International Politics

Stephen Hobden

Chapter contents

Overview

The previous chapter examined the role of the developing world in the global economy. In this chapter, the emphasis changes to the role of the developing world in international politics. International relations, as a discipline, has traditionally overlooked the significance of the developing world in global politics. The chapter opens by discussing the reasons for this and why such an oversight is lamentable. It then looks at the position of the developing world throughout the large structural changes that have occurred in the international system since 1945: the cold war; the post-cold-war world; and the emerging multipolar world, in which China is anticipated to return to the centre of international politics.

Introduction: International Relations and the Developing World

The **developing world** has been 'on the periphery' of the study or discipline of international relations (Thomas and Wilkin 2004). The discipline has primarily been concerned with relations between the great (or super-)powers. Although perhaps understandable, this focus is deeply problematic. First, it has meant that at least four-fifths of the global population were excluded as a subject of study; second, it overlooks the central role played by developing countries as actors in international **politics**, and as sites of confrontation and competition. It fails to acknowledge that while, during the cold war, there was a 'long peace' in Europe, many parts of the developing world were deeply mired in violent conflict, in which the superpowers were frequently involved. Superpower rivalry was played out in a way that was far from 'cold', fuelling **proxy wars**, for instance in southern Africa and Central America. Moreover, it overlooks and underestimates fundamental changes to the international system: the dissolution of the European empires; and the increasing power of a number of countries—in particular, the 'rise' of China.

The focus on the superpowers may reflect a deeper problem. Quite simply, traditional international relations theory lacks the tools with which to understand the developing world. For traditional international relations, the state is the key actor and guarantor of the 'good life' for its citizens. States operate in a situation of 'anarchy' in which all have equal sovereignty and must, in the final instance, be liable for their own self-defence. Within the confines of the state, there is order and hierarchy, while outside is characterized by unregulated disorder. From the perspective of the developing world, this world view may make little sense. The state, rather than being the guarantor of the 'good life', has frequently been a major threat to individual well-being. Many developing countries have been governed at some time or another by military **regimes**, which have targeted sections of the society for repression. The states of Latin America have, by and large, lived at peace with each other since the 1930s, but regimes in virtually every country in the region have committed major **human rights** violations. The anarchy has been on the inside, rather than the outside. Furthermore, the state, rather than being the key actor, has had to compete with numerous other powerful actors, such as **warlords**, guerrilla groups, **terrorist** organizations, and drug cartels, which in some places appear to threaten its very existence. At the same time as domestic politics in the developing world perspective can be viewed as disordered, the external world appears to be more hierarchical, with the most powerful states determining the fates of the less powerful. Sovereignty—that is, the right of states to govern within their own territory without external interference, a fundamental tenet of the Charter of the United Nations—has been breached many times since 1945 (see Dickson 1997: ch. 1; Neuman 1998: 2–12).

KEY POINTS

- The discipline of international relations has tended to focus on the role of the great (or super-) powers.
- This focus has ignored the vast proportion of the global population, and the key role that the developing world has played in the global politics of the cold war and post-cold-war periods.

North–South Relations during the Cold War

The cold war

The term 'cold war' refers to the period of confrontation between the United States and the former Soviet Union between 1945 and 1990. The international system during this time is often described as 'bipolar', meaning that there were two superpowers, although the now obsolete notion of a 'Third World' is also closely linked to this period. This term is derived from a perceived tripartite division of the world:

- a 'First World', comprising the United States and its allies;
- a 'Second World' comprising the Soviet Union and Eastern Europe; and
- a 'Third World' comprising the rest—that is, the newly decolonized countries of Asia and Africa, and the countries of Latin America, most of which had gained their independence at the start of the nineteenth century.

This was a ridiculous oversimplification, although the ideological and strategic conflict played out between the superpowers certainly had a major impact on most Third World countries. This conflict took a variety of forms. There were cases of direct military intervention by the superpowers, such as the United States in Vietnam and the Soviet Union in Afghanistan. There were many examples of indirect intervention using either the 'carrot' of aid or the 'sticks' of sanctions or the threat of the withdrawal of aid. There was also the use of proxy fighting forces to avoid direct intervention. Examples here include US funding of the Mujahidin to challenge the Soviet Union in Afghanistan and the use of the Cuban army to support leftist governments in southern Africa.

Once both superpowers had access to nuclear weapons, any direct confrontation would have been, in the terminology of the time, MAD—that is, 'mutually assured destruction'. However, a history of the cold war is incomplete without a consideration of how superpower competition was conducted in the developing world. A range of interests underpinned the superpowers' policies towards the developing world. For both, there were security issues, both had trading concerns, and for both there were ideological issues that related to their views of themselves as nations. These different interests played out differently at different times.

The cold war was a time of great upheaval for the developing world. In the period immediately after the Second World War, most of it was still under colonial control. By the end of the cold war, it was mostly independent. This wave of decolonization was accompanied by an international conflict between the two superpowers, fought over and in developing countries. For their governments, it meant choosing to align with one superpower or the other. This pressure provoked the creation of the Non-Aligned Movement (NAM) in 1961—a collection of states that claimed to reject both superpowers, although in reality most states (Cuba, for example) were aligned with one or other. The NAM has survived the end of the cold war and its 120 members continue to meet on a triannual basis.

The existence of two competing superpowers meant that a choice existed for developing countries. Many countries were courted by both sides, with rival offers of financial and economic aid. For some, the possibility existed of switching allegiances (or at least of threatening to switch). Egypt in the early 1970s changed its alignment from the Soviet Union to the United States, becoming one of the largest recipients of aid. The cold war provided these countries with at least an option between two superpowers with two ideologies concerning the operation of social and economic systems, and the goals and modalities of development (see Halliday 1989; Allison and Williams 1990; Merrill 1994; Westad 2005).

The United Nations

The United Nations was created during the latter part of the Second World War as an organization the key role of which was the maintenance of international peace and security. Although most would argue that the United Nations has been singularly unsuccessful in this respect, it has played a significant role in a number of others. In addition to its security remit, the Charter of the organization also commits its members to cooperation on economic and development issues, and these have had a number of implications for developing countries. In this development sphere (or the 'other United Nations'), the organization can perhaps claim the largest area of success (see Box 5.1). Furthermore, the organization had an in-built predisposition towards decolonization. Charter signatories with responsibilities for non-self-governing territories (in other words, colonies) committed 'to develop self-government, to take due account of the political aspirations of the peoples, and to assist

BOX 5.1 THE UNITED NATIONS' ACHIEVEMENTS IN DEVELOPMENT

The United Nations has been involved in development issues in a number of ways, including:

- as an information source, with experts in economics, agriculture, and industrial development;

- offering direct assistance in emergency situations;

- the creation of regional organizations to address the particular problems of specific areas, for example the Economic Commission for Asia and the Far East;

- specific development responsibilities of UN agencies, for example the UN Development Programme (UNDP) and the UN High Commissioner for Refugees (UNHCR);

- numerous resolutions in the UN General Assembly related to development issues; and

- a series of 'development decades', intended to keep issues such as global inequality on the agenda.

The United Nations can point to a number of areas of success, including that:

- life expectancy globally has increased;

- child mortality rates for under-5s have decreased; and

- immunization levels have improved, as have access to primary health facilities, the availability of clean water, and literacy levels.

Another achievement that can be directly attributed to a UN agency is the eradication of smallpox, coordinated by the World Health Organization (WHO).

BOX 5.2 THE UNITED NATIONS AND DECOLONIZATION

The end of the European empires is one of the most significant developments of the last century. The oversight of this process is perhaps one of the United Nations' greatest achievements. The notion of self-determination is at the core of the Charter, articulated in Article 1(2) and repeated in Article 55. Furthermore, a pledge to develop self-government in non-self-governing territories (a euphemism for colonies) is made in Article 73.

In the immediate aftermath of the Second World War, a small number of countries became independent, for example India gained independence from Britain in 1947. The first move of newly independent countries was to take up a seat in the UN General Assembly as a mark of sovereignty and independence. The newly independent states were critical of the continuation of empire and the General Assembly became the main forum in which calls for decolonization were voiced. By 1960, there were sufficient members to allow the passing of Resolution 1514, which condemned the continuation of colonialism. In the 1960s, several African states became independent and further resolutions were passed calling for colonialism to be eradicated.

The United Nations also acted in a very practical way to smooth the process of decolonization. The withdrawal of colonial powers from territories was seldom straightforward, frequently leaving civil strife and disastrous levels of **underdevelopment**. The United Nations was often drawn into such situations, as

peacekeeper and provider of essential services. With the withdrawal of the British from India, massive unrest broke out between the Hindu and Muslim populations of India, and the newly created state of Pakistan. There was huge loss of life and displacement of population. The UN Security Council voted to send an observer group to monitor the situation in the hope that an outside group might calm the situation. The United Nations Military Observer Group in India and Pakistan (UNMOGIP) was created in 1949 to patrol the border area in Kashmir. It remains in place today.

Decolonization also transformed the organization itself. There were fifty-one original members in 1945, and the United States and the West in general had a built-in majority in the General Assembly. By 1960 (when Resolution 1514 was passed), the situation had changed dramatically—to 100 members, of whom sixty-six were from the developing world, including forty-six from Africa and Asia. By this point, the General Assembly was supporting the position adopted by the United States in around half of all votes taken. By 1980, more than half of the United Nations consisted of non-founder members, which had not been sovereign states in 1945. Their loyalty to a US-dominated world order was low, and the vast majority of the votes in the Assembly were against the US position and in support of the Soviet Union. As a result, the General Assembly became the forum for issues that were a priority for the developing world.

them in the progressive development of their free political institutions' (UN Charter, Article 73.B). As discussed in Box 5.2, the United Nations played a key role in the process of decolonization, and in turn the character of the organization was transformed.

KEY POINTS

- During the cold war, the superpowers intervened in the developing world in a variety of different ways.

- The superpowers were motivated by a variety of interests, including military security, trade, and ideology, the significance of which differed over time and location.

- The cold war brought instability for many developing countries. However, in a world in which neutrality from the global struggle was difficult, there was a choice of ideology and model of development.

- A key feature of the cold war period was the dissolution of virtually all of the European colonies. The United Nations was a key actor in, and was itself transformed by, this process.

North–South Relations after the Cold War

A new world order?

The end of the cold war in the late 1980s was greeted with optimism. The United States emerged as the 'winner' of the contest, and appeared to enjoy an unassailable position in terms of economic, military, and political power. Some argued, however, that this dominant position (or unipolarity) might be short-lived (see Krauthammer 1991). How would the remaining superpower employ that considerable power and what would be the implications for the developing world? The father-and-son presidencies of George H. W. Bush (1989–93) and George W. Bush (2001–09) appeared to demonstrate very different visions of what came to be called the 'new world order'.

In a 1991 speech, US President George H. W. Bush spoke of a new world order that would be 'an historic period of cooperation . . . an era in which the nations of the world, East and West, North and South, can prosper and live in harmony' (quoted in Acharya 1999: 84). In the early 1990s, there was a sense that a new form of global cooperation could solve many of the world's problems. For many in the developed world, this sense of peace and well-being was enhanced by a prolonged economic boom through much of the 1990s.

For developing countries, too, there were reasons to be optimistic. The cold war had been a cause of instability, and its end promised greater peace and stability. Accompanying the end of the forty-year superpower conflict, a number of regional conflicts were also resolved—particularly in southern Africa (Mozambique, Namibia, and temporarily in Angola) and Central America (Nicaragua and El Salvador). A new spirit of cooperation in the UN Security Council enabled that organization to become more active in conflict resolution. The United Nations achieved notable successes in Namibia, El Salvador, and Cambodia. It authorized an international military response to Iraq's invasion of Kuwait in 1990. Furthermore, a number of corrupt regimes that had been supported by one side or the other were replaced by democratic governments. There was much talk of a 'peace dividend' and considerable reductions in arms spending, which could be funnelled towards development projects. At the Millennium Summit, a special meeting of the UN General Assembly, ambitious commitments were made by the member states to reverse global poverty. Also, the prospect of a truly global economy appeared to promise more extensive trading links, with the hope of generating greater wealth.

Such developments did indeed suggest that the world had reached the 'end of history', as claimed by Francis Fukuyama (1989) (see Box 5.3). There were indications, however, that this view might be optimistic. A UN-sponsored intervention in Somalia resulted in humiliating withdrawal following the killing of eighteen US soldiers. In 1994, the global community looked the other way while **genocide** occurred in Rwanda. A more sombre account of post-cold-war international relations was provided by Samuel Huntington (1993), who predicted that the cold war would be replaced by a **clash of civilizations** (see Box 5.3). The terrorist

BOX 5.3 THE 'END OF HISTORY' OR A 'CLASH OF CIVILIZATIONS'?

With the end of the cold war and the emergence of the United States as the dominant world power, two accounts of international politics made a crossover from the academic arena into the wider policy and media arenas. Both had implications for North–South relations. In 1989, Francis Fukuyama published a much-discussed article in which he speculated whether, with the demise of the Soviet Union as an ideological and military threat to the United States, the human race had reached the end of history:

The triumph of the West, of the Western *idea* is evident first of all in the total exhaustion of viable systematic alternatives to Western liberalism. What we might be witnessing is not just the end of the Cold War, or the passing of a particular period of post-war history, but the end of history as such: that is the end of mankind's ideological evolution and the universalisation of Western liberal democracy as the final form of human government. The vast bulk of the Third World remains very much mired in history and will be a terrain of conflict for many years to come, but large scale conflict must involve large states still caught in the grip of history, and they are what appear to be passing from the scene.
(Fukuyama 1989: 4, emphasis original)

Fukuyama's was essentially an optimistic liberal account. The global future was liberal democracy. Crucially, because conflict between democratic states was unlikely (the so-called democratic peace theory), the future prospect was for a more peaceful world.

A different view was offered by Samuel Huntington in an equally famous article, published in 1993. Rather than the world having reached the end of history, when conflict over the best form of social organization was over, Huntington argued that there were real differences at a civilizational level that would, in the future, lead to conflict:

The fundamental source of conflict in this new world will not be primarily ideological or primarily economic. The great divisions among humankind and the dominating source of conflict will be cultural. Nation states will remain the most powerful actors in world affairs, but the principal conflicts of global politics will occur between nations and groups of different civilizations. The clash of civilizations will dominate global politics. The fault lines between civilizations will be the battle lines of the future.
(Huntington 1993: 22)

This more pessimistic, **realist**-influenced view of global politics suggests that the future will be dominated by conflict between the developed and the developing world, although primarily divided by civilization.

This gloomier sentiment has been echoed by Andrew Bacevitch (2011), perhaps marking an end to the vision that Fukuyama popularized at the end of the cold war. Writing in the *Washington Post*, Bacevitch (2011) argued that:

[T]he beliefs to which the end of the Cold War gave rise— liberal democracy triumphant, globalization as the next big thing and American dominion affirmed by a new way of war—have all come to rest in that unmarked grave reserved for failed ideas.

BOX 5.4 US PRESIDENT GEORGE W. BUSH, 9/11, AND THE 'WAR ON TERROR'

There has been much discussion about whether the administration of George W. Bush, the attacks of 11 September 2001, and the subsequent **war on terror** marked a distinct turning point in US foreign policy. Two aspects of the Bush administration policy looked particularly important. First, the United States appeared more prepared to act unilaterally, and to be openly hostile to global organizations and commitments. Before 9/11, the Bush administration had signalled that it would withdraw from the Kyoto Agreement, which the previous Clinton administration had been involved in negotiating. Following 9/11, the invasions of both Afghanistan and Iraq occurred without a UN Security Council mandate. The invasion of Iraq occurred after an attempt to get UN authorization had been blocked in the Security Council.

This led to a second perceived area of major change: the so-called Bush doctrine. Under this doctrine, the United States claimed a right to intervene in other countries not only to *prevent* an imminent threat of attack on the United States, but also to *pre-empt* such a threat from emerging. According to the September 2002 US National Security Strategy:

For centuries, international law has recognized that nations need not suffer an attack before they can lawfully take action to defend themselves against forces that present an imminent danger of attack . . . We must adapt the concept of imminent threat to the capabilities of today's adversaries . . . The United States has long maintained the option of pre-emptive actions to counter a sufficient threat to our national security . . . To *forestall* or prevent such hostile attacks by our adversaries, the United States will, if necessary, act pre-emptively.

(White House 2002, emphasis added)

The presidential letter accompanying the Strategy document (White House 2002) puts the point more directly: 'As a matter of common sense and self-defence, America will act against such emerging threats before they are fully formed.'

These two developments appear of particular concern to countries of the developing world. International organizations and international law provide some measure of protection for the weak against the strong. By distancing itself from such arrangements, the US government indicated that it was not prepared to be constrained by international commitments. Likewise, the claimed right to intervene in countries solely on the basis that a threat to US security *may emerge* is open to abuse.

However, did foreign policy under the Bush administration change dramatically? Although it played a central role in the creation of much of the current international architecture, the United States has always had vacillating relations with international organizations. Relations with the United Nations have been uneasy since the General Assembly became dominated by countries from the developing world following decolonization. They were particularly difficult during the Reagan era, when the United States fell into serious financial arrears. Furthermore, the United States has displayed a consistent pattern of intervention in countries of the developing world, during and after the cold war. In the immediate aftermath of the cold war, the United States invaded Panama (during the presidency of George W. H. Bush)—a country that could hardly be considered a threat to US security. The most distinctive feature of US foreign policy during the George W. Bush presidency was perhaps the readiness of policymakers to be explicit about the rationale of foreign policy (Slater 2004: 190).

---

attacks on the United States in 2001 ('9/11') appeared to confirm this gloomy prognosis and the euphoria of the immediate post-cold-war period was replaced by a 'global melancholy' (Halliday 2002: 214). The prospects for developing countries started to look less promising. While the end of the cold war did provide greater stability in some areas, there has been greater instability in other regions. Afghanistan, for example, has been in a constant state of upheaval, and the Democratic Republic of Congo descended into chaos, with its neighbouring countries intervening on opposing sides.

With the election of George W. Bush, concerns started to surface about how the United States would use its position as the only superpower. The unipolar era of cooperation appeared to transform into one

in which 'cooperation' would be very much on the terms and in the interests of the dominant power. In the aftermath of 9/11, the US government declared its willingness to act unilaterally and pre-emptively to further its national security interests, and the invasion of Iraq in 2003 occurred without the clear support of the UN Security Council (see Box 5.4).

The two Obama administrations: Change and continuity in US foreign policy

With the inauguration of Barak Obama in January 2009, there were signs of a change of tone in relations between the United States and the rest of the world. The campaign slogan of 'Change we can believe in' prompted the view that this would extend to foreign policy. In the early phase of the Obama presidency, there appeared to be significant attempts to re-forge the relationship with the Muslim world. Indications included the 'Cairo' speech in June 2009 and hints that pressure would be put on Israel to negotiate with the Palestinians. On the basis of this change in approach, Obama was awarded the Nobel Peace Prize in 2009—an award that many commentators thought was premature, to say the least.

Hopes for a radical change in the direction of US foreign policy were disappointed during Obama's first term. While relations between the US administration and the Israeli government were tense, there was no progress on an Israeli–Palestinian peace process and no indication that the US government would be prepared to use its considerable financial leverage to pressurize Israel to negotiate. The US military completed a withdrawal from Iraq in 2011, ending a conflict that Obama had consistently criticized. However, in Afghanistan, while an end was brought to active patrolling, counter-insurgency troops remain in the country as part of the North Atlantic Treaty Organization (NATO) mission 'Resolute Support'. There has also been considerable criticism of the continuation of drone attacks against targets in several countries (see Box 5.5). Generally seen as a stain on the reputation of the United States internationally, the detention camp at Guantanamo Bay, Cuba, remains active despite Obama's promise to close it within the first year of his presidency.

A more sympathetic assessment of the Obama presidency would point to the spectrum of problems that the president faced in 2009, particularly with regard to the US economy. These limited the time and resources that President Obama was able to devote to an international agenda. To an extent, these problems reflect the declining international position of the United States and the transition to something beyond the post-cold-war period. The United States remains militarily dominant, but in relative terms its economic power is weakening, along with its political and ideological capabilities.

The decline of US power is perhaps most evident in the ongoing conflicts in the Middle East. While there were hopes that following the so-called Arab Spring—a series of democratic uprisings that originated in Tunisia in 2011—would bring peace to the region, the opposite seems to be the case. In Libya, long-serving dictator Muammar Gaddafi was overthrown. However, a botched NATO intervention (primarily pushed by the United Kingdom and France) failed to provide the basis for the emergence of a stable political situation. In Syria, a similar push for democracy resulted in prolonged civil war, with the UNHCR reporting nearly 5 million refugees fleeing the conflict (see Chapter 21). An already-difficult situation has been made more complex by the emergence of the so-called Islamic State (IS, otherwise known as ISIS, ISIL, or Daesh), an organization that has taken advantage of the regional chaos in the wake of the 2003 invasion of Iraq. The involvement of the military forces of Russia and some NATO countries (although supporting opposing sides) has done little to stabilize the situation. The Syrian crisis has had ramifications beyond the borders of the country. In addition to concerns about a military confrontation between Russia and the

BOX 5.5 THE RISE OF THE DRONES

One of the more startling developments in North–South conflict is the use of drones for the purpose of carrying out lethal attacks. Drones are unmanned aerial vehicles, originally intended to carry out surveillance activities. While the possibility of arming drones had been considered earlier, it was not until after the 9/11 attacks on the United States that the first armed use was made in Afghanistan to kill a senior Al Qaeda figure. While their use pre-dates his term of office, their deployment has risen rapidly during the time in office of Barak Obama. A total of forty-nine drone attacks were launched against targets in Pakistan during the George W. Bush administration; this figure was exceeded during Obama's first term in office and rose to a peak of 122 attacks in 2011. Drones have been used to carry out lethal attacks in Iraq, Afghanistan, Pakistan, Yemen, Libya,

and Somalia. Armed drones mark a notable change in the practice of conflict, because they require no risk in human terms to the side deploying them. Recent figures suggest that fatalities as a result of drone attacks between 2004 and 2014 total between 2, 400 and 3,900 for Pakistan alone.

Questions have been raised about whether it is legal to use lethal force in this way in countries with which the United States is not at war, such as Pakistan. Under international law, states can use military force against another state only in self-defence or at the direction of the UN Security Council. The argument of the US government has been that the drones have been used as self-defence against targets such as Al Qaeda leaders.

Sources: Kaag and Kreps (2014); Bureau of Investigative Journalism (n.d.)

West, the large numbers of refugees attempting to enter Europe sparked a crisis for the European Union. Furthermore European capitals have become the targets for IS terrorist attacks—in Paris in November 2015 and Brussels in March 2016.

As Obama's presidency drew towards an end, some high-profile foreign policy successes indicated that whilst his domestic policies might be stymied by Republican majorities in Congress, the president was prepared to take risks. In December 2014, an announcement was made in Havana and Washington, DC, that full diplomatic ties between the United States and Cuba would be re-established. This reversed a policy that had been in place for fifty years. In March 2016, Obama made the first visit to Cuba by a US president since 1928. Whilst this rapprochement allows US citizens to visit Cuba freely, it does not bring an end to the trade embargo—something that requires the approval of Congress and is unlikely in the short term. In July 2015, agreement was finally reached with Iran to restrict its nuclear programme.

The global picture for developing countries during the period of US dominance was mixed. Some states benefited from a greater stability, while for many global citizens the end of the cold war has meant greater instability. The post-cold-war boom of the 1990s also offered increased possibilities for more countries to participate in the global economy. However, the demise of the Soviet Union removed an option of choice: there was now one global economy and one system—capitalism—and the costs of defaulting from this system became higher. The option of playing one superpower off against the other no longer existed and hence the room for manoeuvre was reduced (Mesbahi 1994; Swatuck and Shaw 1994; Fawcett and Sayigh 1999; Halliday 2002).

KEY POINTS

- At the end of the cold war, the United States appeared to be in an unchallengeable position. This had implications for the developing world.

- A post-cold-war peace dividend has failed to appear for the developing world. Although some areas experienced greater stability, many have not. Fears increased regarding the deployment of US power, especially under George W. Bush.

- The period of US predominance in international affairs now appears to be drawing to an end.

All Change? The Developing World in the 'Chinese Century'

The changing structure of the international system

Since 1945, the international system has experienced three major structural changes. Thus far, we have discussed decolonization and the end of the cold war, which resulted in a (short) period of US pre-eminence. This section assesses the third transformation, currently under way and perhaps the most significant of all. Its most prominent feature is the rapid economic development of China. (See Box 5.6 for a discussion of some views on the implications of China's rise and see also Chapter 29.)

While China's economic development is breathtaking, it should not blind us to developments in other parts of the world (particularly India and Brazil), and the appearance of a new grouping of economically dynamic countries. These have been described by Parag Khanna (2009) as the 'second world' (not to be confused with the Communist 'Second World' of the cold war). He argues that the countries of this second world are crucial to understanding developments in international politics, noting that 'the second world shapes the global order as much as the superpowers do' (Khanna 2009: x). While, for Khanna, China is both part of the 'second' world and one of three competing empires (together with the United States and the European Union), another formulation has been to group it with Brazil, Russia, and India as the BRICs—and, since 2010, when South Africa was included, the BRICS.

The BRICSs are seen by some analysts as a rival grouping to Western-based organizations such as the Group of Eight (G8), and a challenge to Western domination in organizations such as the World Trade Organization (WTO), International Monetary Fund (IMF), and World Bank. In particular, the creation of the New Development Bank (NDB) can be seen as an alternative source of financing for developing countries. The NDB has the purpose of providing loans to the BRICS countries, as well as to other developing economies. In contrast to the Bretton Woods **institutions**, voting in the NDB is on a 'one member, one vote' basis (as opposed to size of economy, which favours Western economies), with no member having veto power. The basis for much discussion of the BRICS countries was a report produced by the accounting firm Goldman

BOX 5.6 THE END OF THE WESTERN WORLD?

Traditional accounts of the modern world have tended to depict the European example both as somehow exceptional and a model for the rest of the world. Europe and North America have been the dominant powers for the last 200 years. However, developments in the writing of world history (Frank 1998; Hobson 2004) suggest that this was something of an exception and that, for most of recorded history, the East has been the leading power in economic, scientific, military, and political terms. Furthermore, the rapid growth of China's economy leads some to argue that the brief period of Western/ North American domination is drawing to a close. But what does the rise of China mean for international relations?

Is it the end of the Western world?

In his provocatively entitled *When China Rules the World*, Martin Jacques (2012: ch. 11) argues not only that China is likely to become the dominant power internationally, but also that it will provide a very different model of society and development from that which the West has promoted. By contrast, John Ikenberry (2011) has argued that it will not be in China's interests to challenge the foundations of the Western liberal order (see also Chapter 29).

Does it mean that conflict is inevitable?

For realist writers, power transitions—that is, instances in which one hegemonic power is challenged by another—rarely occur without conflict. China's rise and the United States' apparent decline indicate that such a power transition is occurring, and is unlikely to happen peaceably. Hence Mearsheimer (2010: 382) warns that:

China's rise . . . is likely to lead to an intense security competition between China and the United States, with considerable potential for war. Moreover, most of China's neighbors, to include India, Japan, Singapore, South Korea, Russia, Vietnam—and Australia—will join with the United States to contain China's power. To put it bluntly: China cannot rise peacefully.

Nonetheless, Chinese President Hu Jintao (2003–13) stated in his report to the Eighteenth Congress of the Chinese Communist Party that 'China will unswervingly follow the path of peaceful development and firmly pursue an independent foreign policy of peace'.

Sachs, entitled *Dreaming with BRICS: The Path to 2050* (Wilson and Purushothaman 2003). Its startling conclusion was that, by 2050, the BRICS' combined gross domestic product (GDP) would exceed that of the current six largest economies (the United States, Japan, Germany, the United Kingdom, France, and Italy). While some of the report's underlying assumption may be questionable (pessimism about growth rates in the current largest economies; over-optimism regarding growth prospects of the newly emerging economies), it does indicate that even if the comparative growth rates for the BRICS are less than expected, major changes can be expected in the global architecture that could have enormous implications for all global actors—and especially developing countries (see Box 5.7). The economic crisis that has engulfed much of developed economies since 2007 (as discussed in Chapter 4) has hastened these trends. By 2014, China was well established as the world's largest economy, with Brazil, India, and Russia all in the top ten largest economies.

Implications for the developing world

Significant changes are occurring to the structure of the international system. A particular feature is the coming to prominence of large countries that would previously have been considered as developing (especially Brazil, China, and India)—potentially a truly revolutionary change. This section examines some of the possible implications for the developing world (see Chapters 28–30 on Brazil, China, and India).

China's reach

China, according to one Chinese government official, is 'all over Africa' (cited in Large 2008). A striking impact of China's economic rise is the extent to which its influence is being exerted over regions formerly within the European and North American spheres of influence. This may offer benefits to many developing countries, but also comes with potential risks. This has been particularly marked over areas of Africa. Rising commodity prices during the early years of the twenty-first century are often connected to China's enormous demand for raw materials (Johnson and Blas 2009). China has become a major trading partner with a number of African countries and also a major aid donor.

The significance of this growing relationship between China and the continent of Africa was demonstrated when China held a November 2006 summit in

BOX 5.7 THE BRICS: WILL THEY DOMINATE THE TWENTY-FIRST CENTURY?

The term 'BRICs', used to designate Brazil, Russia, India, and China, was coined by Goldman Sachs economist Jim O'Neill (2001). He highlighted the *combined potential of non-Western powers* controlling a quarter of the world's land mass and accounting for more than 40 per cent of its population. Since 2008, this label has gone from being an economic label to a political reality, with the BRICs members holding regular summit meetings to discuss a range of economic and political issues. In 2010, South Africa was invited to join the grouping, after which the acronym became 'BRICS'. Russia hosted the seventh summit meeting of the group in July 2013. These countries are seen not only as economic challengers to the current core economies, but also as representing a distinct set of interests, possibly at odds with the present dominant powers.

Without disputing the economic and political impact of these countries in the developing world, the view that the BRICS constitute a coherent bloc is disputed. First, their economies are radically different: Brazil and Russia's prime connection to the global economy is dependent on the export of raw materials; China's, on assembled manufactured goods; India's, largely on

services. Second, they have radically different political systems: India and Brazil are fully functioning and lively democracies; South Africa is a functioning democracy, although dominated by one party; Russia is a quasi-democratic authoritarian state; China is a one-party state. Furthermore, China has not always had the most peaceable relations with Russia or India. Finally, the current economic crisis in Russia, and the political and economic turmoil in Brazil, suggest that the international role of these major economies—at least in the short term—may be less significant than size and potential would suggest.

The formulation of the terms BRICs and BRICS has led financial analysts to dream up a number of alternatives, such as CIVETS (Colombia, Indonesia, Vietnam, Egypt, Turkey, and South Africa), MAVINS (Mexico, Australia, Vietnam, Indonesia, Nigeria, and South Africa) and MINT (Mexico, Indonesia, Nigeria, and Turkey). These groupings, however, reflect the concerns of analysts looking to make investments in rapidly growing economies. At the time of writing, none of these subsequent groupings reproduce the potential political challenge of the BRICS countries.

Beijing, attended by representatives from more than fifty African countries, at which a range of trade investment and aid proposals were announced. Another major feature of this growing influence has been a 'no strings attached' basis for trading and aid relations: China has been prepared to enter into friendly relations with countries considered to be pariah states by European and North American countries. For example, China has received considerable criticism for its relations with Sudan, a significant source of oil for the Chinese economy.

While China has provided a ready market for many of Africa's exports, it has done little to alter the composition of those exports. This has led to fears that the neo-colonial relations with the West might be being reproduced, albeit with a different power. Former South African President Thabo Mbeki warned about the possible unequal relationship between African countries and China: 'China cannot just come here and dig for raw materials and then go away and sell us manufactured goods' (cited in Alden 2007: 120). Despite these potential fears, China has been able to expand its contacts with African countries, prompting fears in North America and Europe that it may become the dominant power on the continent.

There are also indications of the growing influence of China in Latin America, a traditional site of US hegemony (Roett and Paz 2008).

Increased North–South conflict

The emergence of competing centres of power in the international system, and in particular the alternative development and political model offered by China, has reintroduced the possibility of choice of alliances for developing countries. There is some evidence that this increased range of possibilities has prompted developing countries to be more prepared to challenge the dominance of Europe and the United States in international financial institutions. A key example of this is the breakdown by 2008 of the Doha Round of WTO trade agreements. Developing countries in a variety of coalitions blocked discussions of a range of issues of interest to the United States and Europe, pending progress helpful to their agricultural exports. Hurrell and Narlikar (2006) provide a detailed account of the possible contours of future North–South confrontation.

The return of bipolarity

The discussion of the cold war earlier in this chapter indicated that, while there was peace in Europe, the conflict between the superpowers was very far from 'cold' in the developing world, with a range of interventions through Asia, Africa, and Latin America. One possibility of the end of the unipolar moment and the appearance of China as a possible second polar power is the return of great power confrontation and action along the lines that were evident during the cold war. Some US writers have already indicated their concerns about increased Chinese influence in Africa (see Campbell 2008) and growing links with Latin America. A direct military confrontation between China and the United States would be, as in the cold war, 'MAD', but this does not exclude the possibility of their rivalry again being played out in military form in the developing world.

Regional integration

The overlap between the international economy and international politics is also found in the attempts of developing countries to pursue policies of regional integration. Regionalism emerged as a separate strategy with a first wave in the 1960s, but that had run its course by the early 1970s and a second wave of, or a 'new', regionalism in the 1990s. The prime aim of the first wave of regionalism was to increase the size of the market for locally produced manufactures. Regional blocs were also thought potentially to increase negotiating power in international organizations. One of the features of the first wave of regional organizations, such as the Caribbean Community and Common Market

(CARICOM, established in 1973), was the attempt to implement a high level of political control over production, so that decisions about the siting of industrial production were supposed to be made at a regional level. The idea was that, by sharing out industrial production, the benefits from economies of scale could be maximized. This proved to be both politically and economically unviable. The first wave of regionalism foundered when the required degree of political cooperation and coordination failed to materialize. The maintenance of high tariffs once again resulted in inefficient industries, unable to compete internationally. Weak transport and other infrastructural links also played a part.

By the mid-1970s, many of the first wave of regional organizations were moribund in all but name. However, in the 1990s, a 'new' regionalism emerged, inspired by the European Union. These organizations adopted a much larger free market agenda, without the political baggage associated with the first wave. Some formerly dormant organizations, such as the Central American Common Market (CACM), were revitalized and other new groups emerged, such as Mercosur—the Common Market of the Southern cone, in South America (see Box 5.8), and the Bolivarian Alliance for the Peoples of Our America (ALBA), which has developed its own trading currency, the sucre. In Asia, the members of the Association of Southeast Asian Nations (ASEAN) are in the process of creating a free trade area. The aim of these organizations has been to promote interregional trade through the lowering of internal tariffs, without

BOX 5.8 A PROFILE OF MERCOSUR, THE COMMON MARKET OF THE SOUTH

The origins of Mercosur date back to 1985, when Presidents Raúl Alfonsín of Argentina and José Sarney of Brazil agreed an 'Argentina–Brazil Integration and Economics Cooperation Program'. Mercosur itself came into existence in 1991, comprising Argentina, Brazil, Uruguay, and Paraguay. Venezuela became a full member in July 2012 and Bolivia, in July 2015. Chile (since 1996), Colombia (since 2004), Ecuador (since 2004), and Peru (since 2003) are associate members, which means that they can enter trade agreements with member states, but remain outside the **institutional** mechanisms of the organization.

The stated aims of the organization are to increase the free movement of goods, capital, services, and peoples amongst member states, with the possible introduction of a common currency being considered. As an intergovernmental organization, Mercosur is often compared to the European Union and is one of the most developed regional trade

agreements in the developing world in institutional terms. In terms of area, it is four times the size of the European Union, with a population of 250 million people. The economic activity of Mercosur comprises more than three-quarters of that on the South American continent.

While, in relation to previous attempts at regional integration, Mercosur could be counted a success, it has not been without problems. Venezuela's incorporation into the organization has proved controversial, occurring as it did during a period when Paraguay was temporarily suspended. Deepening of integration—in particular, a move towards a full customs union—has been delayed by the economic storms that have swept the continent—especially Argentina's financial and economic collapse in 2001. Movement towards further integration has stalled over the last five years, in particular because of the more protectionist policies favoured by Argentina and Venezuela.

On the international stage, Mercosur has clashed with the United States over the possibility of creating a Free Trade Area of the Americas (FTAA). While, in principle, all countries in Latin America seek to be part of the FTAA, disputes have concerned both the nature of the agreement and the process of its creation. Mercosur members—in particular, Brazil—have sought to counter what is regarded as a neoliberal agenda implicit in the agreement. Furthermore, they have encouraged the countries to negotiate as a bloc, rather than as individual states, which has increased the continent's bargaining power related to the United States. The failure to agree an FTAA in many ways parallels the collapse of the Doha Round of the WTO: the issues—in particular, rich-country farm subsidies—were similar and Brazil played a key role in both.

Sources: Carranza (2004); BBC News (2012); *The Economist* (2013)

ambitious attempts at controlling the economic diversification of the countries involved.

In some ways, this can be seen as a reaction to the impacts of **globalization**. As a way of protecting their economies from the pressures of the global economic market, countries in different parts of the world have joined together to form regional blocs. However, in some ways, the 'new regionalism' can be viewed as a means of accelerating the speed of globalization. The aim of the old regionalism was to erect *external* barriers to protect domestic production; the aim of the new regionalism is to *reduce* internal barriers to trade as a means of promoting trade within the region (Payne 2004: 16–17).

Nuclear proliferation

A further area of change in relations between North and South is with regard to nuclear weapons and their proliferation. In 2009, there were eight known nuclear weapons states: the United States; the United Kingdom; France; China; Israel; India; Pakistan; and North Korea. At the start of the twenty-first century, there are fears that the non-proliferation regime is breaking down and that more states will be drawn into developing nuclear weapons, as a form of defence both against their neighbours and against a perceived threat from a unilateralist superpower.

Central to limiting the spread of nuclear weapons has been the Non-Proliferation Treaty (NPT), which came into force in 1970. In essence, the NPT sought to limit the spread of nuclear weapons technology and to push for disarmament (or at least a reduction in the numbers of nuclear weapons), while allowing non-nuclear states to develop nuclear energy under international supervision. Implicit in the Treaty was an agreement between nuclear and non-nuclear states: the nuclear states would move towards disarmament; the non-nuclear states would not attempt to develop, or obtain, the technology. With the exception of North Korea, it could be argued that the Treaty has 'worked' in the sense that, as far as we know, no other signatory has obtained nuclear weapons. India, Pakistan, and Israel have never been signatories. North Korea was a signatory, but announced its withdrawal from the Treaty in 2003. The Islamic Republic of Iran has been considered as providing a serious challenge to the non-proliferation regime. However the 'Joint Comprehensive Plan of Action', agreed in July 2015, between Iran and the permanent members of the Security Council, plus Germany and the European Union, appeared to provide safeguards that Iran will not proceed with the development of nuclear weapons.

Since the attacks on the United States on 11 September 2001, the issue of non-proliferation has become entwined with the 'war on terror'. The concern—given that the attacks indicated the organizational ability and murderous intent of non-state actors—has been that nuclear materials might be obtained by groups planning such attacks. This became part of the motivation for the 2003 attack on Iraq and the enormous international pressure currently being placed on Iran.

KEY POINTS

- The structure of international politics is again in flux, with a (relatively) declining United States confronting a resurgent China, plus a group of 'second world' countries enjoying rapid economic growth and enhanced international influence. This affects the developing world in several ways.

- In particular, China has emerged as a major alternate source of influence, trade, aid, and investment. This may result in a return to confrontation in the developing world between the United States and China.

- Regionalism has increased significantly, with regional blocs perceived as a possible source of confrontation between North and South.

- The nuclear non-proliferation regime appears to be under strain, with Iran a current focus of concern. (See the Online Resource Centre for a case study.)

Conclusion

The notion of a 'Third World' was primarily a construction of the cold war. As the conflict drew to an end, increasing diversity between regions, based on divergent rates of economic growth and competition between countries for the supposed fruits of globalization, has eroded the perception of shared interests that underlay earlier groupings, such as the Non-Aligned Movement (NAM). Regional groupings are now tending to replace specific Third World organizations. The increasing economic power and confidence to act on a global stage displayed by countries such as India and especially China indicate the major changes that are occurring in the international system. The implications for all actors in the international system are enormous. While it may not be the end of the 'Western world', the 200-year period in which Europe and North America have been dominant appears to be drawing to a close, with a multipolar and culturally plural world replacing Western dominance.

The central argument of this chapter has been that countries in the developing world have had, and continue to have, a major impact on international relations. Through the various permutations (bipolar, unipolar, multipolar) that have constituted the international system, the countries of the developing world have consistently played a significant role in international relations—as sources and sites of conflict, and as challengers to the existing political and economic order. Part of this contribution has come through the form of international organizations, such as the NAM. The diversity of patterns of development now means that organizations claiming to represent all less-developed countries are unlikely to be effective. The new drive towards regionalism offers an alternative forum and possibilities of exerting greater influence in negotiations with the developed world. The emergence of a global economy also offers immediate advantages to some. Where capital is more mobile, developing countries can exploit their advantage as sites of low-wage production. Countries in which there are high educational standards are particularly likely to be able to gain from this. For example, India has been particularly successful in attracting jobs in the information technology and call centre sectors. India, Brazil, and China are all regional superpowers, able to exert their influence internationally. In due course, the first two might gain more formal institutional recognition in the UN Security Council if that body is reshaped. The emergence of what has been described as a 'global **civil society**' offers additional possibilities. **Neoliberalism** is under attack from some quarters in the developed world, as the anti-globalization movement has demonstrated. And there are increasing avenues for the development of transborder and supra-territorial alliances between the peoples of the North and South.

The character of the global system remains unsettled following the end of the cold war. The election of Donald Trump as US president in November 2016 suggests that the period of instability in international relations may be persistent. But the situation of the majority of the world's population who reside in the developing world should become a more central area of study for those who seek to comprehend international processes.

? QUESTIONS

1. To what extent does the failure of international relations scholars to engage with North–South relations reflect an ideological bias in the discipline?

2. Assess the ways in which the situation of developing countries in the international system has changed since 1945.

3. To what extent did the process of decolonization impact the practice of international relations?

4. Have we reached the 'end of history' or is there a 'clash of civilizations'?

5. What are the implications for the Western liberal order of the emergence of the BRICS countries?

6. In what ways have the policies of the United States towards the developing world changed during the Obama administrations?

7. Assess the significance of regional trading organizations. Is the world breaking up into trading blocs?

FURTHER READING

Coker, C. (2014) *The Improbable War: China, the United States and the Logic of Great Power Conflict* (Oxford: Oxford University Press) A very readable discussion of the possibilities of great power conflict.

Duffield, M. (2014) *Global Governance and the New Wars: The Merging of Development and Security* (London: Zed Books) A new edition of Mark Duffield's classic analysis of the position of the developing world in the contemporary world order.

Fenby, J. (2014) *Will China Dominate the 21st Century* (Cambridge: Polity) Offers a sceptical view of China's rise.

Jacques, M. (2012) *When China Rules the World: The End of the Western World and the Birth of a New Global Order* (London: Allen Lane) Excellent study of China's rise and its implications for the international system.

Payne, A. (2005) *The Global Politics of Unequal Development* (Basingstoke: Palgrave) Superb discussion of issues of development and underdevelopment from a new political economy (NPE) perspective.

Slater, D. (2004) *Geopolitics and the Postcolonial: Rethinking North–South Relations* (Oxford: Blackwell) Outstanding overview of approaches to thinking about North–South relations, influenced by post-colonial and post-structuralist approaches.

Westad, O. A. (2005) *The Global Cold War: Third World Interventions and the Making of Our Times* (Cambridge: Cambridge University Press) Recent account of the cold war, focusing on the key role played by the developing world and the implications for contemporary international relations.

Wilkinson, R. (2014) *What's Wrong with the WTO—and How to Fix it* (Cambridge: Polity) Clear discussion of the ways in which the World Trade Organization (WTO) entrenches the position of the richest countries in the world and how the Organization might be reformed.

 WEB LINKS

http://www.brics.utoronto.ca   The BRICS Information Centre, run by the University of Toronto, containing a wealth of information on developments within the BRICS.

http://www.economist.com/topics/mercosur   News on the Mercosur region from *The Economist*.

http://www.iaea.org/newscenter/focus/iaeairan/index.shtml   International Atomic Energy Agency (IAEA) page, detailing negotiations with Iran relating to the Non-Proliferation Treaty.

http://www.imf.org   Official site provides details of role of the International Monetary Fund (IMF).

http://www.twn.my   The Third World Network (TWN) website contains information on economics, environment, and other issues, from a development perspective.

http://www.un.org   Official site provides overview of the organization and workings of the United Nations.

http://www.worldbank.org   Official site provides complete overview of the operation of the World Bank Group.

http://www.wto.org   Overview of the history, purpose, and working of the World Trade Organization (WTO).

 For additional material and resources, please visit the Online Resource Centre at:
http://www.oxfordtextbooks.co.uk/orc/burnell5e/

PART 2
Society and State

In Part 2, we introduce the social and cultural aspects of developing countries within which their **politics** are embedded, and which are so central to understanding political behaviour. The part has two main aims. The *first* is to indicate: the great diversity of social structure found in the **developing world** and in countries individually; the variety in terms of religious, ethnic, and other identities; and the divisions to which these features, together with **gender** and economically based inequalities, give rise. In contemporary social science, **civil society** also ranks very high as both a constituent feature and determining influence upon politics; that too can vary widely in practice. The role played by **social movements** and **alternative politics** is also gaining in recognition.

The *second* aim is to show the political significance of these complex social contexts and diverse forms of social and political organization, and how problematic they can be for political management. They pose challenges, as well as opportunities, for the **institutional** arrangements centred on the state—in some cases, expressly demanding political solutions outside of, and alternative to, the conventional mechanisms and processes of the state. The contents of this part thus set the scene for the investigation in Part 3 of how developing world states have responded to the many internal and external demands on them, and to their transformation in recent decades. So, for instance, societal features introduced in Part 2 can help to explain tendencies towards **state collapse**, and the pressures to engage in political liberalization and democratization, as well as the forces resisting those agendas.

The illustrative material included in Part 2 is drawn widely from around the developing world. By comparison, case studies of individual countries selected to illustrate specific themes can be found in Parts 5–8. For example, tendencies towards social fragmentation and political disintegration in developing countries are revisited in Chapters 22 and 23 on Iraq and Mexico, respectively. The political ramifications of extreme inequality are illustrated in Chapter 26, with the case of Guatemala. This choice of countries illustrates the multiplicity of social, as well as economic and political, challenges that can be present during attempts at post-conflict reconstruction. It also shows how easy it is to oversimplify the consequences of diversity for political unity, especially when set against a background of rapid change from more authoritarian and less inclusive forms of political rule to governing arrangements that resemble more closely Western-style liberal democracy (as in Indonesia—see Chapter 20).

Readers are encouraged to study the introductions to Parts 5–7, and to consult the relevant case studies, when reading the chapters in Part 2.

6

Inequality

Jenny Pearce

Overview

Two inequality-related questions have dominated development debates for decades: does growth inevitably lead to inequality? And if so, does it matter, as long as poverty declines? The debates around these questions began in the 1950s, with Simon Kuznets' 'inverted-U hypothesis', which posited that relative inequality increases, but only temporarily, in the early stages of economic development, improving once countries reach middle-income levels. Ultimately, initial inequality precipitated by economic growth does not prevent poverty reduction, although it might delay it. However, by the 2000s, while global poverty *and* inequalities between nations had declined overall (although the gap between the very richest and very poorest nations continued to grow), inequality within many countries increased and prompted some to announce the 'end of the "Inverted-U" ' (Palma 2011: 87). According to *The Economist*, 'more than two-thirds of the world's people live in countries where income disparities have risen since 1980 often to a startling degree' (Beddoes 2012: 13). The pattern that is of particular concern is the way in which the income share of the richest 1 per cent has risen not only in the United States, but also in the rising economic powers, such as China and India. The combination of this extreme concentration of wealth, and the character and impact of the 2007–08 global financial crisis, gave rise to a new question: does inequality in fact hinder growth? The publication of Thomas Piketty's (2014) study of capital, growth, and inequality gave this question an extraordinary impetus. Based on data going back to the eighteenth century and including twenty countries, Piketty demonstrated that, without intervention, the private rate of return on capital outstrips the rate of growth of income and output. Wealth accumulated in the past grows more rapidly than output and wages, with dangerous consequences for democracy, as well as growth. Politics and state policy play an important role in aiding or abetting this dynamic. Modern tax systems and tax reform, in particular, might be more important to developing countries, suggest Alvarado and Piketty (2010: 96), than service delivery, market-friendly economic institutions, more effective poverty reduction programmes, or trade and market liberalization.

Introduction

This chapter briefly reviews the key conceptual debates on inequality until the end of the Second World War and the birth of the field of 'development'. It will then explore how inequality thinking impacted on the **developing world** during and after the cold war. An implicit post-war consensus emerged in the industrialized world in the 1950s that government had a responsibility to address inequalities. The cold war played its role in the debate. Western financial **institutions** sought to demonstrate that capitalist economics could address poverty and growth more effectively than socialist egalitarianism. By the mid-1970s, however, the distribution of income was deteriorating in many 'Third World' countries, as they were then known, and the debate on poverty and inequality intensified. A new paradigm of market **liberalism** and state retreat arose in the 1980s, underpinned by the rising interest in monetarist and neoclassical economics. These posed a serious theoretical and practical challenge to redistributive theories of justice. Concern with income inequality as a goal of development policy declined. Pro-poor growth became the core theme of development rather than the impact of growth on income distribution. This was reinforced by the post-cold-war so-called **Washington consensus** around **neoliberalism**; the Millennium Development Goals (MDGs) reflected the ascendency of this perspective.

However, the debate on inequality remained lively, nourished by new theoretical contributions outside of economics. The collapse of universalizing social theory, for instance, resulted in an unprecedented uncovering of differential life experiences throughout societies all around the world, which has favoured new thinking on social stratification dynamics. The cultural dimensions of inequality were exposed, while recognition of human differences suggested that the 'equality of man' is not necessarily the best foundation for egalitarian theory. In its 2001 *World Development Report*, the World Bank acknowledged that 'high initial inequality' did reduce the poverty impact of a given rate of growth (similar to Kuznets' arguments), and that there may even be circumstances in which addressing asset inequality can enhance economic efficiency and benefit growth. It also recognized that **gender** inequalities have a particularly negative impact on economic growth, as well as poverty reduction. Interventions in the market can, it argued in a challenge to prevailing orthodoxies, aid poverty eradication amongst such socially disadvantaged groups as indigenous peoples, and certain **castes** and tribes. In 2005–06, both the World Bank and the United Nations Development Programme (UNDP) produced annual development reports dedicated to the themes of equity and inequality. These debates received a new boost following the economic crisis of 2008. If Kuznets had gone on to argue that growth would ultimately reduce both poverty and inequality, economic patterns of the late twentieth century were not only questioning this in the developing world, but also in the developed world. Thomas Piketty (2014) argued on the basis of an impressive amount of data that it was progressive income and estate taxation, introduced in response to the Great Depression and the world wars, which ensured that capital concentration did not regain the high levels of the first part of the twentieth century. However, as market liberals who advocated low taxation and welfare cutbacks gained power, unchecked inequality of wealth on a global scale grew from the 1980s and had become so extreme by the first decade of the twenty-first century that Piketty (2014: 572) argued that a decrease in economic growth was likely to be permanent.

As some developing countries began to overtake the developed world in rates of economic growth, but manifested high rates of within-country inequality, the debate around inequality took on new intensity. This time, the debate is as much about the rich as the poor. While there are ongoing discussions about whether or how inequality matters to development, a growing number of voices even in the mainstream have begun to agree that inequality does indeed matter not only to growth, but also to political community and to **governance**. At the grass roots, inequality became a source of **social movement** activity in the global North, particularly in the wake of the 2007–08 global financial crisis (see Chapter 11). In the global South, middle-income countries of Latin America and mineral-rich Southern Africa remain by far the most unequal regions of the world (Palma 2011), while, by 2007, China had the joint highest inequality in Asia (Knight 2014). By the second decade of the second millennium, new approaches to conceptualizing and measuring inequality over time generated a raft of new questions about **globalization**, inequality, and their effects on life chances and choices of an imagined global citizenry (cf. Milanovic 2012a). Thomas Piketty's 2014 book shook the world with its evidence that not only had Kutznets' optimism that inequality, as well as poverty, would decline through growth proven unfounded in the developing world, but also the developed world was showing that his famous curve had 'doubled back' on itself, with falling inequality during the first half of the twentieth century resulting from fiscal measures in a period of crisis, followed by increased inequality since the 1980s. The **international community** appeared to accept some of the arguments. Goal Ten of the seventeen **Sustainable Development Goals (SDGs)**, which replaced the MDGs in 2015, is to 'reduce inequality within and among countries'.

Key Conceptual Debates

The importance that we attach to the issue of inequality is rooted in some fundamental questions of political philosophy, and shifting values and norms. There is much disagreement about the meaning of 'inequality' and whether it matters, and conversely about whether equality is a legitimate aspiration, and if so, how it is to be achieved.

Over the past two centuries or more, these questions have been discussed repeatedly. During this period, there was a 'steady erosion in the **legitimacy** accorded to social inequality . . . for students of social stratification, this . . . is perhaps the most important feature of the nineteenth and twentieth centuries' (Béteille 1969: 366). However, by the end of the twentieth century, the pursuit of greater social and economic equality had become increasingly discredited; such concepts as 'social exclusion' and 'pro-poor growth' gained ground. The poor became 'targets' of anti-poverty programmes. Traditional leftist concerns about distribution and **exploitation** were abandoned. At the same time, interest grew in human diversity. Identity and culture, and their relationship with equality, led to what Fraser (1997) calls a shift from the '**politics** of redistribution' towards the 'politics of recognition'. Such a shift appeared to imply an abandonment—or at least weakening—of the idea of economic equality in favour of more robust mechanisms for ensuring political equality. But does equality of civil and political rights compensate for, or even work in the context of, social and economic inequalities? The twist in the second decade of the millennium has been the return of income inequality to mainstream debate. The trigger has been the process of concentration of income amongst the very rich, highlighted by the 2007–08 global economic crisis. This section traces the ebbs and flows of these conceptual debates.

Ontological equality and equality of outcome

The idea that men are born equal emerged in the eighteenth century as a philosophical challenge to the prevailing assumption that social stratification was a result of natural differences of rank between individuals. The ancient Greeks had built the *polis* on that assumption and equality existed only in the political realm. However, their belief in political equality irrespective of social or economic **status** remains an abiding reference point for many (despite the notorious exclusion of women, slaves, and foreigners). Rousseau (1755), in his *Discourse on Inequality*, began his investigation into inequality by assuming instead the equality of man in a pre-social original state of nature—an assumption of **ontological equality**. In the course of the eighteenth century, the idea that men are equal, rather than unequal, by nature took hold, with powerful political and intellectual consequences. But it inevitably led to the question: what, therefore, are the origins of *in*equality? Rousseau's answer is usually summed up as 'private property'. Those who came to see private property as a social evil emphasized the need for society to promote **equality of outcome** despite individual human differences. Karl Marx made equality of outcome the central tenet of his vision of the good society.

For Marx, writing in 1845–46, inequality had its origins in the division of labour, as well as private property. It is the former that 'implies the possibility, nay the fact that intellectual and material activity—enjoyment and labour, production and consumption—devolve on different individuals'; with the division of labour comes the question of distribution and 'indeed the *unequal* distribution, both quantitative and qualitative, of labour and its products, hence property, the nucleus, the first form of which lies in the family, where wife and children are the slaves of the husband' (Marx 1970: 52). Capitalism is the most advanced system of labour division yet, in which the capitalist class owes its wealth to its exploitation of another class with only its labour to sell. Marx not only places this unequal relationship to the means of production at the heart of his class analysis of history, but also his emphasis on exploitation indicates that such inequality between classes is unjust, which became a very influential argument for socialist—and often **nationalist**—movements of the nineteenth and twentieth centuries.

Marxist thinking tapped into deeply felt injustices at the popular level. For some, largely pre-industrial, developing societies, Marxist ideas appealed to the desire to retain some of the primitive communal forms of equality that persisted in agrarian societies and to restrain the differentiating process that comes with socio-economic change. Much Third World sociology in the post-war years was an effort to clarify its distinct forms of class composition and social inequality, and the relationship between class formation and development. A particularly vibrant debate concerned the analytical categories for exploring relationships between the developed and underdeveloped worlds. Could one nation exploit another? Gunder Frank (1971) powerfully argued that it could and traced the history of **underdevelopment** from 'core' to 'periphery'. He was criticized by others who claimed that he saw feudalism and capitalism only in terms of market exchange, not in Marx's true sense of relations to production and class exploitation. The ideas of **unequal exchange** and dependency would nevertheless provide one of the most important frameworks for understanding inequalities between countries in the North and the South in the early post-war decades.

Differentiating inequalities: Class, status, and power

Max Weber, writing early in the twentieth century, provided a more differentiated categorization than Marx. He argued that social divisions and the distribution of power that they convey encompass a range of non-economic, as well as economic, determinants. In addition to the class stratifications that emerge out of a person's relationship to the market, there is status—a quality of social honour or a lack of it, which is mainly conditioned as well as expressed through a specific style of life. A status group can be closed ('status by descent') or it can be open.

Weber's understanding of the distinctiveness of status groups was particularly helpful for those wishing to understand social differentiations in situations in which market transactions were fairly simple and class formation limited. He also observed, however, that technological advances and economic transformation threaten stratification by status, and will push the class situation further into the foreground.

In terms of the developing world, Weber was able to draw into the picture the forms of social stratification that Marxists have often found particularly difficult to explain, such as caste and tribe, and the distinctions between them. Caste, Weber argued for example, belonged to the 'closed status group', in which status distinctions are guaranteed not only by conventions and laws, but also by rituals, such as stigmatizing any contact between lower and higher castes through religious acts of purification. He explored the complexity of the **Hindu caste system** in India in some detail, seeking to explain its relationship to economic change and its 'elasticity', and hence its survival in the face of the logic of labour demands in the modern economy.

The nature of these traditional relationships and the impact of processes of economic change are particularly significant for an understanding of social divisions in the developing world. Systems of 'inherited inequality', such as those based on descent, lineage, and kinship, have persisted in many parts of the developing world. Anthropologists have long studied the lineage and kinship stratifications of indigenous populations. For example, Sahlins (cited in Béteille 1969: 239), who studied kinship in Polynesia in the 1950s, referred to 'a graduated series of different degrees of stratification'. He distinguished between stratified and egalitarian societies, and implied that ranking processes emerge in all human societies, but noted that they vary a great deal in terms of ranking criteria and how far they formally sanction social inequality (see Box 6.1). This is why writers such as Béteille (1969) have emphasized the values and norms that underpin social inequality or its qualitative dimensions. It has often been assumed that ranking on the basis of the hereditary principle will disappear with the process of economic development, and that industrialization will overcome the differentials associated with traditional and agrarian societies. The persistence of caste in India, where status is determined by birth and legitimized by religio-cultural belief, questions that assumption. In modern India, caste and class intersect in particularly complex ways, creating a potent and enduring source of social, economic, and political inequality.

But across the developing world even where 'closed status group' systems such as caste do not exist, kinship and ethnic group identity have been the basis of stratified, as well as segmented, forms of social differentiation. Ethnic coexistences have become the source of ethnically based stratifications at various points in history. Pre-colonial conquests, colonialism, and post-colonial political mobilization have all played a critical role in privileging some ethnic groups over others, and usually for some political, as well as economic, gain. As market economies expanded, so some ethnic groups were in a more privileged position than others to take advantage of opportunities. In this context, the debate about whether emerging stratifications are derived from market positioning, or from the logic of capital and its search for exploitable labour, or from **ethnic identity** per se has been particularly protracted. Thus relationship to production is a source of inequality, but not the only source of social differentiation. When class and status, and economic and social power all coincide, however, one of the most potent sources of inequality is created with the capacity to perpetuate itself through the generations.

The politics of inequality

One means by which inequality perpetuates itself is through the political system that develops around it. Unequal societies, no matter what the source of inequality, generate differential means of influencing political processes. This is true at all levels, from micro to macro, and in traditional, as well as more 'modern', development contexts. That means that power and powerlessness emerge out of inequality, and create the source for recycling it. As societies undergo transitions from more traditional to 'modern' economies, traditional power structures and ways of exercising power have often adapted to changing social conditions, so that they survived more or less intact, or persisted in new, but recognizable, forms. As the idea of political contestation (if not modern democracy) began to take root in the developing world, it frequently

BOX 6.1 BÉTEILLE ON INEQUALITY

Béteille (1969: 365) points out that the sanctioning of social inequality has taken place on very distinct grounds often legitimized by religious systems that paradoxically and simultaneously contain messages of equality. In the United States, commitment to the equality of man was a strong feature of cultural values and political ideals—even though, for many years, black people were denied the vote and were evidently not treated as equals by the dominant white population. Most societies have denied, and many still deny, women formal, as well as informal, social, economic, and political equality.

did so in contexts in which political and economic power were already tightly meshed. The 'delivery' of the political support of a dependent rural population to particular leaders and interests quickly became the norm. Such practices were then adapted to urban contexts, where the rapid growth of cities without adequate services or employment gave brokerage power to individuals with access to elites and decision-makers. **Clientelism** and **patronage** networks emerged throughout the developing world, creating vertical links to tie the poor to political power structures through favours granted in return for support. Such networks reflect differentials in power and income, and act as obstacles to independent political action and democratization, further entrenching the pre-existing structures of inequality. More than this, the relationships between dominated and dominant create internalized feelings of humiliation that have a lasting impact on generations of poor people (Scheper-Hughes 1992), and can often be overcome only through political mobilization.

KEY POINTS

- The ancient Greeks believed in the equal right to participate politically irrespective of social and economic inequalities.

- Both Rousseau and the French Revolution challenged assumptions that inequality was natural or divinely sanctioned; a good society should be dedicated to overcoming inequality.

- Marx believed that inequality derived from the division of labour, as well as private property, and advocated equality of outcome.

- Weber's notions of status and honour, derived from non-economic, as well as economic, determinants, assisted understanding of social stratification in the developing world.

- Social stratifications have exclusionary political consequences; clientelism and patronage are ways in which political brokers have used inequality to build a power base amongst the poorest.

The Politics and Economics of Inequality in Developing Countries: The Cold War and Its Aftermath

In the twentieth century, the discussion around the relative weight to be accorded to equality as a goal in **human development** was intense and conflictive. In

the mid-twentieth century, Tawney (1952: 106) made a case against the assumption that inequalities in industrial societies were simply the outcome of individual effort or failures. He argued that *opportunities* to rise were only one side of the picture and appealed for measures (such as progressive taxation and trade union rights) that would ensure that society actively aimed at 'eliminating such inequalities as have their source, not in individual differences, but in its own organization' (Tawney 1952: 57).

It was agreed that governments had some responsibility to pursue strategies of greater equality, although there was less agreement on what they were, and on the relationship between equality strategies and social justice theories. John Rawls (1971: 62), in his influential *Theory of Justice*, proposed that '[a]ll social values—liberty and opportunity, income and wealth and the bases of self-respect—are to be distributed equally unless an unequal distribution of any, or all, of these values is to everyone's advantage'. In other words, inequalities (benefits to those with greater talents, training, etc.) can be justified only if they are to the benefit of the least advantaged, and attached to offices and positions open to all under conditions of equality of opportunity.

During the cold war, these debates in the industrialized world impacted on policies towards the developing world, while in the developing world itself political movements emerged with equality as their stated goal and occasionally became governments. Huge controversies surrounded the efforts to put that goal into practice.

Equality as a political and moral goal

Moral and political arguments for an equitable model of economic development found concrete expression in a number of experiments that spanned the post-war decades, such as the model of socialism that followed the 1959 revolution in Cuba, the 1967 Arusha declaration and *Ujamaa* (Swahili meaning 'community-hood') socialism of Nyerere's government in Tanzania, and the Chilean road to socialism of Salvador Allende between 1970 and 1973. These experiments went further than economic egalitarianism; they were also about new forms of political participation and how to address the impact of economic inequality on political decision-making. They encountered hostility from Western governments opposed to non-capitalist paths to development.

Cuba and Allende's Chile faced attempts at destabilization from the United States in their pursuit of more egalitarian development. Tanzania, one of the most heavily aided countries, found its strategy of self-reliance and equality extremely difficult to combine with growth and development.

Measuring inequality

The inequality question in development was partly about moral and political arguments at this time, but it was also partly about the facts and how to measure them. Income distribution measurement is by no means straightforward. Unreliable data, choices over the best unit of measurement (individuals or households), the timescale of measurement, and the definition of income itself, which, given the high level of informal and unregistered earnings, is particularly problematic in developing countries, all represent significant problems.

The most frequently used approaches to measurement are the Lorenz curve and the **Gini coefficient**.

- The Lorenz curve, named after the American statistician Lorenz who developed it in 1905, uses a vertical axis (percentage of income earned) and horizontal axis (percentage of the population earning that income). The greater the bow of the curve, the larger the degree of inequality.

- The Gini coefficient, named after the Italian statistician who created it in 1912, uses areas of the Lorenz curve; it is the ratio of the area between the line of equality and the Lorenz curve to the total area under the line of equality. It offers an aggregate measure of inequality between 0 (perfect equality) and 1 (perfect inequality). The Gini coefficient for countries with highly unequal income distribution tends to lie between 0.50 and 0.70.

Structuralist and non-structuralist approaches to inequality

A great many qualitative, but empirically based, studies tried to identify the causes of income inequality and some examined its consequences. A division arose between structuralists and non-structuralists. The former emphasized the impact on income inequality of such factors as historically unequal landownership patterns and social structures that excluded people

on such bases as caste, race, sex, or religion. The concentration of physical and financial capital, as well as land, in the hands of small elites enabled them to buy access to educational opportunity and to control an ever greater proportion of national product. The consequences of this unequal distribution included malnutrition, poor housing, and little or no education for the majority, resulting in low levels of productivity. In contrast, the argument was made that a redistribution of income would increase production by boosting the consumption, and hence the health and productivity, of the poor.

Non-structuralists countered that inequality was the logical (some would say inevitable) outcome of economic growth. The apparent increase in inequality during the early stages of development is because development does not start at the same time in all parts of the economy. Growth in a poor, underdeveloped country will always raise some people's income before others—notably, those living where the growth is first located, for instance in urban rather than rural areas. Shifts in a country's structure of production will inevitably create inequalities between those engaged in agriculture compared to those in new, more highly remunerated industries. The non-structuralists argued that these inequalities would not necessarily result in absolute impoverishment, but only a relative decline in income of the poorest. The argument that the poor would see their living standards rise through economic growth, even though their relative share of income might not, gained ground in the 1980s.

However, in the 1970s, even the president of the World Bank, Robert MacNamara, was forced to admit that, despite a decade of unprecedented increase in the gross national product (GNP) of the developing countries, the poorest segments of their population had received relatively little benefit. Policies aimed primarily at accelerating economic growth in most developing countries had benefited, at most, the upper 40 per cent of the population.

Equality questioned

By the 1980s, support for the idea that reducing inequality is a task of government eroded in the Anglo-American world especially and in the international institutions that it influenced. The global economic recession that followed the 1973 oil shocks had resulted in a shift from Keynesian policies of demand management and welfare-oriented state interventions to monetarism, which cuts public expenditure on welfare and prioritizes investment and profitability. Monetarists, as they were called, denounced the coercive and bureaucratic state needed, they argued, to pursue egalitarian goals. Bauer (1981) also maintained that promotion of economic equality and the alleviation of poverty are distinct, and often conflicting, goals, and that to make the rich poorer does not make the poor richer.

The broad trend in thinking away from government regulation and intervention in markets for any purpose, including social justice, gathered pace in the 1980s. The argument against Kuznets that inequality had no inevitable consequences for poverty was boosted by the publication of several time-series studies showing that income inequality does not, in any case, change much over time, concluding that economic growth must reduce poverty to some extent. The pattern of overall distribution of goods in society now seemed less important than individual well-being and freedom to pursue private interests in the marketplace. These arguments paved the way for market liberalization, which was expected to reduce poverty through growth. It was followed by emphasis on political liberalization and governance reform, aimed at enhancing the **institutional** framework for growth and poverty reduction. Inequality was no longer considered a major issue for development (see Chapters 14 and 15).

KEY POINTS

- From the 1960s, egalitarian thinking influenced several policy experiments in developing countries, but most ran into difficulties.
- Measurement of inequality became an important field of study, whilst structuralists and non-structuralists debated the relationship between inequality and the 'political' economy.
- From the 1970s, as agreement grew that economic **modernization** was not benefiting the poor, international development policies focused on raising their living standards, but without radical redistribution.
- In the 1980s, priority shifted to market-driven growth and new arguments claimed that economic growth benefited the poor.

Inequalities in the Age of Globalization

The arguments around the inequality effects of market liberalization and the globalization of the economy over the three decades or more since the end of the cold war began to gather pace amongst economists at the turn of the new millennium, and particularly in the wake of the 2007–08 global financial crisis. A new global landscape developed over these decades, in which a range of developing countries began to outstrip the developed world in economic growth, at the same time as levels of inequality within them grew apace.

However, the first range of critiques came not from economists, but from sociologists, political theorists, and philosopher economists (Amartya Sen and Martha Nussbaum, for example). They began to question income as the main measure of inequality. The World Bank began to listen, and its 2001 World Development Report was much more nuanced than its 1990 report. Meanwhile, economists began to sharpen their own measurement tools and definitions of inequality. By the second decade of the new millennium, a rich new set of insights was emerging on the nature of inequalities in the age of globalization.

Inequality and human diversity

Interest waned in ideas of equality in the post-cold-war world and even in efforts such as those of Rawls (1971) to reach a shared 'theory of justice'. However, explorations into the relationship between human diversity and inequality generated new thinking on how substantial freedoms for all could be realized and thresholds of real opportunities established below which no human being should be allowed to fall. This was a period during which violent conflict in the world seemed to reflect what has been called 'horizontal inequalities' between cultural and religious groups, and between geographical regions of the same country (Stewart 2008). The impact of armed conflict on poverty became a central concern of the international community and, amongst other factors, drove institutions to embrace some of the new thinking.

Amartya Sen (1992), in *Inequality Re-examined*, offered one of the most sophisticated efforts to address the relationship between human diversity and equality. It has been particularly influential in development studies, refocusing attention away from income to human capabilities—a shift that can be followed in the evolution of the UNDP's annual human development reports (see Box 6.2). Sen is less interested in equality, as such, than in the question: 'Equality of what?' His thinking is heavily influenced by Rawls, but he has gone beyond Rawls' emphasis on the *means* of freedom to the **extents of freedom**, meaning the capabilities or freedom to achieve whatever functionings an individual happens to value.

The logic of Sen's argument is based on the assumption of human diversity. Equality claims must come to terms with this fundamental empirical fact, because there are times when equal consideration for all may demand unequal treatment in favour of the disadvantaged. Indeed, because we are diverse in our personal qualities, such as age, gender, talents, proneness to illnesses, and physical abilities, as well as in our external circumstances, such as material assets, social backgrounds, and environmental circumstances, insistence on egalitarianism in one field may imply rejecting it in another. Disadvantage is itself diverse. Moreover, disadvantage is not about only consumption of resources. Our capabilities to achieve whatever we value do not ultimately depend on income, but on all of the physical and social characteristics that make us what we are. Substantial inequalities in well-being and freedom can, given our variable needs and disparate personal and social circumstances, result directly from an equal distribution of incomes.

Inequalities, power, and politics

The emphasis on the diversity of inequalities led to a focus on the way in which politics and power impact on inequalities, and vice versa. Anne Phillips (1999) argued that political inequality cannot be addressed without addressing economic inequality. Disparities between rich and poor impede recognition of equal human worth. Political equality assumes equal worth, as well as equal access to political influence: When the World Bank acknowledged, in its 2001 World Development Report, that social discrimination can have economic effects that will undermine efforts at pro-poor growth, it advocated making 'public spending pro-poor', recognizing that this would encounter political resistance (see Chapter 16):

> Governments face important political issues in redistributing public spending to support asset accumulation by poor people. With finer targeting, public funds may in principle reach more poor people. But such targeting may lack political support from powerful groups that may lose out. Hence the importance of building pro-poor coalitions.

(World Bank 2001: 82)

While political liberalization in the post-cold-war decade opened up some new political spaces for participation, these were often filled by self-appointed allies of the poor, such as **non-governmental organizations** (**NGOs**). These organizations could at least advocate policies that might equalize the playing field politically and/or economically. Collective action remained another means by which the disadvantaged might make their voice heard and social movements proliferated in the developing world in this period (see Chapter 11). Such movements saw struggles in terms of rights and **entitlements**, and challenged the mainstream thinking that the poor are a 'target group' for policies, which ultimately maintains the division between 'rich' and 'poor'. Political leaders often emerged to mobilize the poor on grounds of class and ethnic exclusion, such as Hugo Chávez in Venezuela and Evo Morales in Bolivia. However, whereas in India the space for such movements remained relatively open, in China it did

BOX 6.2 THE HUMAN DEVELOPMENT INDEX

The UNDP's annual human development reports contain a range of indices that try to take into account non-income measures of development, and enable us to view the performance of a country in terms of both growth and freedoms. The best known is the Human Development Index (HDI), which incorporates data for human longevity and educational attainment, as well as material living standards. Comparing countries by their place in the HDI produces a very different picture from a rank that is based on the Gini coefficient alone. For example, Chile and Guatemala have a comparable level of inequality measured by the Gini coefficient that is very high. But, in human development terms, Chile easily qualifies among the top fifty countries (high human development), whereas Guatemala is in the middle of the medium human development range, many countries below Chile.

not—and these countries were both contributing to growth and poverty reduction in the new millennium, but also to rising inequalities.

Gradually, the policy debate on inequality moved beyond income inequality to explore the relationship between social and political inequalities, and economic inequalities, and between all of these and poverty and development. This renewed mainstream interest in inequality and its relationship to development is reflected in the 2005 and 2006 reports of the UNDP and World Bank, respectively, which were devoted to inequality (UNDP 2005) and equity (World Bank 2006). The reports go well beyond income inequality in their understanding of the relationship between inequality and development—a trend that has been led by the discussion on gender inequality. The impact of inequalities in race and ethnicity, as well as gender, began to be analysed. Brazil, for instance, revealed a large discrepancy in income inequality between population groups based on skin colour. In 2005, some 33 per cent of Afro-Brazilians lived in poor households whose incomes were below 50 per cent of the median income of the country, compared to 14 per cent of whites falling into this group (Gradín 2009). Similarly, in South Africa, where income inequality had risen in the post-**apartheid** years, as measured by a Gini coefficient that went from 0.64 in 1995 to 0.69 in 2005, it is the inequality between black African and white people that continues to drive overall inequality, although there is evidence of growing inequality also amongst black Africans.

Economic and political inequalities have been created around human differences, and embedded over time in structured social relationships. The mainstream financial and development institutions came to acknowledge that this impacts on democracy, governance, and the quality of institutions. This recognition took place at the same time as neoliberal economics remained unchallenged. The global financial crisis of 2007–08, however, led to new questions about the relationship between neoliberal globalization and inequality, and the debate returned to income inequality.

The economists return to inequality

New statistical evidence portrayed a stark picture of the extent of income inequality in the first decade of the new millennium. Latin America and sub-Saharan Africa stood out. The Gini coefficient for sub-Saharan Africa was 0.72 and for Latin America, 0.57, compared

to 0.52 for East Asia, 0.43 for Central and Eastern Europe and the Commonwealth of Independent States (CIS), 0.37 for the high-income Organisation for Economic Co-operation and Development (OECD) countries, and 0.33 for South Asia (UNDP 2005: 55). Countries with high income inequality, it began to be argued, required much higher rates of growth for poverty reduction than those with lower inequality (Ravallion 2001). Ravallion (2005) went on to question other assumptions of the previous decade, for instance that absolute poverty in terms of income is the overriding issue in poor countries and that only economic growth can reduce it. Economic growth did not reduce inequality in countries where it was historically high.

The Latin America case is particularly interesting in terms of these debates. Inequality in the region began to decline significantly in the majority of countries in the course of the 2000s and, by around 2010, the Gini coefficient was 0.488 (Lustig et al. 2013: 3). The impact on poverty reduction was significant: an estimated 38 million people came out of extreme poverty (Lustig et al. 2013: 4). Interestingly, analyses of this trend found no link between the decline in inequality and economic growth; rather, two factors stood out. On the one hand, the expansion of basic education reduced the so-called skills premium and led to relatively strong growth in labour income for workers at the bottom of the income distribution; on the other hand, growth was affected by government transfers to the poor. Latin America became a leader in conditional cash transfers. While inequality in Brazil remained high, for instance, it declined, as measured by the Gini coefficient, from 0.607 in 1990 to 0.537 in 2009 (Lopez-Calva 2012: 5). The cash transfer system (*Bolsa Familiar*) to poor families in exchange for ensuring educational and health investments in their children played a significant role. Nevertheless, Latin America remains one of the most unequal region of the world. The quality of education is low for the poorest, so that the equalizing effect of the decline in the 'skills premium' may not be sustained. Working-age women, youth, indigenous peoples, afro-descendants, and rural citizens remain excluded from labour markets and social safety nets. Most significantly, given that the only way in which to reduce inequality further must include progressive public spending, levels of taxation—particularly income taxes—remain low, and are resisted by the region's ultra-rich and politically powerful elites (Lopez-Calva and Lustig 2010: 18–19).

Brazil and Mexico, along with China, India, Russia, and South Africa, all became emerging economic powers in the 1990s and 2000s. The rise in inequality in most of these powers began to generate new debates. An important contribution from World Bank economist Branco Milanovic (2012a) has been to clarify terminology. He has pointed out that there are three potential measures of inequality. The first is in terms of mean incomes across all nations, without taking population size into account; a second conceptualization does take population into account. In both cases, the calculation is based on country averages: the first income measure shows a rise in inequality between nations during the years of neoliberal globalization; the second, which brings in the per capita averages, shows a decline, or greater convergence. China and India contribute a great deal to the latter finding, given their large populations. For much of the 1990s, China alone accounted for greater convergence, with its rapid rise in per capita incomes, until Indian economic growth added its statistical weight (Milanovic 2012a). In other words, as poorer and larger countries have caught up with richer countries, they have pushed global income inequality down, albeit only slightly.

However, a third conceptualization of inequality takes as its unit of measurement individuals, rather than countries, and their actual income. The data is based on household surveys of incomes or consumption, which are not available everywhere and are not always reliable. The first available such surveys in China were in 1982, for example. Some of the countries that do not have reliable surveys (Afghanistan, Sudan, Congo, Somalia, Eritrea) are amongst the poorest in the world (Milanovic 2012a: 10). The calculation also has to be adjusted using the purchasing power parity (PPP) dollar measure, which takes account of 'cheaper' living costs in some countries. Milanovic (2012a) shows that global inequality is higher when measured in a way in which every citizen counts, and increased between the late 1980s and 2005.

This third approach highlights what is happening to income disparities within countries rather than between countries. A divergence emerges between countries rather than the greater convergence on the measure of average per capita gross domestic product (GDP). The most consistent increase in inequality took place in China, the Gini coefficient of which climbed from about 0.30 in the early 1980s to about 0.45 in 2005 (Olinto and Saavendra 2012: 2), and which, by 2014, was almost 0.50 (Knight 2014). In terms of global patterns of within-nation inequality, there were now far more OECD countries in which inequality had increased rather than decreased—notably, Finland, Germany, New Zealand, Sweden, the United Kingdom, and the United States (Olinto and Saavendra 2012: 3).

One of the social trends in Brazil and other rising economies has been the emergence of a middle class. The figures of Milanovic (2012a) show that while the bottom third of the global income distribution have made gains over the last decades, the exception is the poorest 5 per cent of these. At the top of the pyramid, on the other hand, the highest 1 per cent—and, to a lesser degree, the top 5 per cent—have gained significantly. It is now also acknowledged that the very rich tend not to fill in household surveys, so that their share of income is often underestimated. The global financial crisis of 2007–08 highlighted the extraordinary rewards that could accrue to the super-rich, including the financial class of the developed world widely felt to be responsible for the crisis. Now, however, parts of the developing world also boast their own class of global billionaires.

KEY POINTS

- New awareness of social and cultural diversity increased the complexities of the inequality issue, and encouraged a focus on 'recognition' of difference, as well as 'redistribution' of income.
- Sen argued that policies need to recognize that people are diverse in their disadvantages and advantages, and the UNDP introduced new measures to estimate non-income aspects of inequality.
- Inequality is a source of contentious politics in the developing world, which can be positive in the case of self-empowering social movements, but can also be negative, polarizing, and potentially violent.
- By the new millennium, economists returned to the inequality debate, with new measurement tools for income inequality.
- Neoliberal globalization generated growth that decreased poverty overall and led to a rising middle class in a range of countries mostly from the global South, which became motors of global economic change.
- As these poorer and larger countries caught up with richer ones in terms of GDP, the global income gap between nations reduced.

- However, inequalities within countries grew significantly, particularly in some of the emerging economic powers, but also in the global North. Latin America and Southern Africa continued to be the most unequal regions of the world, despite a decline in inequality in the former.
- Mainstream economists came to accept that inequality matters to growth and financial stability.

Conclusion: Inequality Matters— Toward 'Shared Prosperity'?

The conceptual waters of the inequality debate have ebbed and flowed since the eighteenth century, with ontological equality challenged by the end of the twentieth century by the idea of equality based on human diversity. Sen has advanced on Tawney's vision of the 'largest possible measure of equality of environment', to the multiple environments that must be tailored to the capability enhancements of a diverse humanity. However, humankind is a long way from constructing the new social, political, and economic arrangements that would enable inequalities to be addressed in the multiple 'spaces' in which they appear. Equality practice has foundered on the power at the global, national, community, and family levels that protects embedded inequalities, and which allow some people to exploit, marginalize, and deprive others of a full life. In turn, inequality impacts on the political system, limiting participation of poor and discriminated people, and hence the possibilities of prioritizing the search for new solutions that might truly enhance the life chances of all.

By the second decade of the new millennium, the negative impacts of inequality had come to concern the international community once again. The assumption that market liberalism would reduce inequality had not been borne out, although numbers in absolute poverty had declined as new economic powers emerged amongst highly populated and poor countries of the developing world. A new middle class had come into being across the globe, but a significant proportion of people remained with a negligible share of their nation's income, while a very few had become a super-rich class of global billionaires, many from emerging economies of the global South.

A series of best-selling books by serious economists shook up the debate on inequality in the course of the second decade of the second millennium. Branco

Milanovic's (2011) essays on income distribution, economics Nobel Prize winner Joseph Stiglitz's (2012, 2015) books on global inequality and its remedies, Thomas Piketty's (2014) influential study of inequality and the logics of capital, and Anthony Atkinson's (2015) policy-oriented study on global inequality have transformed the debate on inequality within and between nations. The case that income inequality has increased significantly over recent decades has been made: it increased by 11 per cent in developing countries between 1990 and 2010, and the UNDP (2013: 3) cites 75 per cent of the population in those countries as living, by the second decade of the new millennium, in societies in which income is more unequally distributed than it was in the 1990s. The UNDP has recognized that inequality of outcome and inequality of opportunities cannot be treated separately. As outcomes become more unequal, opportunities to live fulfilling lives shrink for those who are born into relatively disadvantaged households (UNDP 2013).

The World Bank has changed its own discourse. In 2013, it began to incorporate the goal of 'shared prosperity' alongside its ongoing concern to reduce poverty. This concept appears in the work of Kuznets in the 1950s and that of Robert S. McNamara, World Bank president during the 1970s. This echo from the pre-neoliberal epoch when redistribution was on the policy agenda is in itself interesting. The World Bank has now taken up the task of raising the average *income growth* in *absolute terms* of what it calls the 'B40', or the bottom 40 per cent in income terms in the world, and is highlighting the non-income dimensions of poverty and the importance of equity and equality (Cruz et.al. 2015: 27). Shared prosperity, it argues, requires well-being to be shared across individuals over time, and attention to be paid to access to education, health, nutrition, and essential infrastructure, as well as an enhanced voice of all segments of society in the economic, social, and political spheres. Goal Ten of the SDGs agreed in 2015 focuses on tackling inequality, and acknowledges that inequality is potentially a threat to long-term social and economic development. While inequality is of central concern to these global institutions, however, at the national level, the political power of elites to block a more progressive annual tax on capital—which Piketty (2014: 572) has argued is the only way in which to interrupt an 'endless inegalitarian spiral'—remains a serious obstacle. For Piketty, the only way of overcoming this is through a high level of international cooperation and regional political integration. The greatest challenge of the twenty-first century may well be the extent to which an agreement can be forged capable of generating the political will to challenge those who continue to argue that a free market and light taxation is the only way in which to foster growth and reduce poverty, irrespective of the societal and other effects of unequal distribution.

? QUESTIONS

1. Is inequality unjust?

2. Discuss the persistence of caste inequalities in India since India has become an emerging economic power.

3. To what extent should the state address the question of inequality, as well as poverty, in its development strategies?

4. How does gender inequality impact on economic growth?

5. How has the World Bank's understanding of inequality shifted since 1990?

6. Compare the inequality impact of the approaches to development and growth of either Brazil and India, or India and China.

7. Why do Latin America and Southern Africa remain the most unequal regions of the world?

8. Evaluate the obstacles to the implementation of Goal Ten of the SDGs.

FURTHER READING

Atkinson, A. (2015) *Inequality: What Can be Done?* (Cambridge, MA, and London: Harvard University Press) Presents a comprehensive set of policies that may shift the distribution of income in developed countries.

Béteille, A. (ed.) (1969) *Social Inequality* (Harmondsworth: Penguin) A good set of conceptual and anthropological essays on social inequalities that still merits reading.

Gradín, C. (2009) 'Why is Poverty so High among Afro-Brazilians? A Decomposition Analysis of the Racial Poverty Gap', *Journal of Development Studies*, 45 (19): 1426–52 A useful attempt to understand the differential poverty levels between whites and blacks in Brazil.

Knight, J. (2014) 'Inequality in China', *The World Bank Research Observer*, 29 (1): 1–19 Good overview of the inequality debate in China after economic reforms.

Kuznets, S. (1955) 'Economic Growth and Income Inequality', *American Economic Review*, 45: 1–28 An important benchmark study on the relationship between inequality and development.

Lustig, N., Lopez-Calva, L., and Ortiz-Juarez, E. (2013) 'Deconstructing the Decline in Inequality in Latin America', World Bank Policy Research Working Paper No. 6552, available online at http://documents.worldbank.org/curated/en/792491468047055310/Deconstructing-the-decline-in-inequality-in-Latin-America Detailed analysis of why inequality declined in Latin America in the 2000s

Milanovic, B. (2011) *The Haves and the Have Nots* (New York: Basic Books) A history of global inequality.

Milanovic, B. (2012) 'Introduction', in B. Milanovic (ed.) *Globalization and Inequality* (Cheltenham: Edward Elgar), ix–xxiii A helpful introduction to what is one of the best collections of contemporary debates on inequality.

Olinto, P., and Saavedra, J. (2012) 'An Overview of Global Inequality Trends', *Inequality in Focus*, 1 (1): 1–4 Useful short discussion of global inequality in the second decade of the second millennium.

Palma, J. G. (2011) 'Homogenous Middles vs Heterogenous Tails, and the End of the "Inverted-U": It's All about the Share of the Rich', *Development and Change Forum*, 42 (1): 87–153 Provocative discussion on contemporary inequality.

Phillips, A. (1999) *Which Equalities Matter?* (Cambridge: Polity Press) Good discussion on the relationship between political and economic equality.

Piketty, T. (2014) *Capital in the Twenty-First Century* (Cambridge, MA, and London: Harvard University Press) The book that got the world discussing inequality.

Ravallion, M. (2005) 'Inequality is Bad for the Poor', World Bank Policy Research Working Paper No. 3677, available online at https://openknowledge.worldbank.org/handle/10986/8625 This background paper to the 2006 *World Development Report on Equity and Development* puts forward the arguments for bringing the issue of inequality back into development debates, with useful sections on China and India.

Rawls, J. (1971) *A Theory of Justice* (Oxford: Oxford University Press) A very influential contribution to the political philosophy of inequality.

Stewart, F. (ed.) (2008) *Horizontal Inequalities and Conflict: Understanding Group Violence in Multi-Ethnic Societies* (Basingstoke: Palgrave Macmillan) An important exploration of how inequalities around ethnic, religious, and subnational identities relate to armed conflict.

Tawney, R. H. (1952) *Inequality* (London: Allen and Unwin) A classic essay on inequality that challenges the notion that equality of opportunity is a sufficient approach to the question.

United Nations Development Programme (UNDP) (2013) *Humanity Divided: Confronting Inequality in Developing Countries* (New York: UNDPC) A very useful overview of how inequality has come to occupy a central place in UNDP thinking.

WEB LINKS

http://ucatlas.ucsc.edu   The University of California, Santa Cruz, Atlas of Global Inequality includes downloadable maps and graphics.

http://www.undp.org   The site of the United Nations Human Development Programme (UNDP) contains links to its annual Human Development Report.

http://www.wider.unu.edu/   Includes access to the United Nations University–World Institute for Development Economics Research (UNU-WIDER) database on world income inequality.

For additional material and resources, please visit the Online Resource Centre at:
http://www.oxfordtextbooks.co.uk/orc/burnell5e/

7

Ethnopolitics and Nationalism

James R. Scarritt and Jóhanna K Birnir

Chapter contents

Overview

From Indonesia to Ukraine, and Guatemala to Sudan, ethnic groups participate in civil conflict more than any other types of dissident group, putting the understanding of how ethnic identity contributes to war and the amelioration of ethnic conflicts at the top of the policy agenda. This chapter stresses the significance of both differences among ethnic, ethnopolitical, and national identities, and different types of relationship among groups having these identities in countries of the developing world. Ethnic identities are constructed and reconstructed over time, and some, but not all, are politicized. Specific processes for construction and politicization, and their variations across countries, are discussed. National identities in the developing world, which are inherently political, vary in strength as well as the degree to which they are civic, multi-ethnic or multicultural, or ethnic, and the chapter explains these variations. Both types of identity have been strongly influenced by European colonialism. Both types interact variously with group morphology, group advantages and disadvantages, organizations, institutions, mobilization and state response histories, and international influence. Based on such interactions, ethnopolitical groups engage in conflict, competition, and cooperation with one another and the state in different countries and at different points in time. Different interaction patterns are explored. Since national identities are relatively weak in many developing countries, while subnational ethnopolitical identities and groups are often stronger, developing states more or less successfully engage in a variety of nation-building activities; the chapter describes these activities, and explains their degree of success in the current era of electoral democracy, globalization, and the war on terror.

Introduction

Defining ethnicity and **nationalism** in ways that are uncontroversial is probably an impossible task. Yet these are vitally important topics in the **politics** of the **developing world**, affecting and affected by the other social and economic cleavages and characteristics discussed in this volume, the nature of the state and its degree of democratization, and policies for economic development and **human rights** protection. Baldly stated, a reasonably strong sense of civic or multi-ethnic nationalism and interactions among politicized ethnic groups based primarily on cooperation and institutionalized competition, rather than on conflict, tend to moderate economic and religious cleavages, strengthen **civil society**, and enhance state-building, democratization, economic development, and the provision of human rights. Although these generalizations are tendencies rather than universal relationships, these relationships leave no doubt about the vital importance of ethnicity and nationalism.

Rather than dwell on controversies about the definition of ethnicity and nationalism, this chapter assumes that:

- they are different and only sometimes closely related;
- both are socially constructed identities (Abdelal et al. 2009; Chandra 2012) that are subject to change in interaction with group morphology, group advantage or disadvantage, political organizations and **institutional** rules, mobilization histories, and international influences; and
- ethnicity is politicized in only some cases, but nationalism has an inherent political component.

The discussion thus begins with the construction and politicization of **ethnic identities**—in other words, the construction of ethnic and **ethnopolitical identities**—and then turns to the construction of a variety of nationalist identities. The next section deals with the conflictual, competitive, and cooperative interactions of groups based on these identities with one another and with states, while the penultimate section deals with states' efforts to mould these interactions in ways that enhance the **legitimacy** of state-based nations and their support from various groups.

The Construction and Politicization of Ethnic Identities

Ethnic identities are constructed when some people self-consciously distinguish themselves from others based on perceived common descent, frequently combined with shared cultural attributes, such as values, norms, goals, beliefs, and language (Chandra 2012). There is thus a wide variety in the specific contents of these identities even within a single country, to say nothing of across the countries of the developing world. Actual commonalities of language, a broader culture, or a common line of descent are often, but not always, included in ethnic identities. In spite of this wide variety in specific content, the common characteristics of these identities are sufficient to separate them clearly from other identities and to justify generalizing broadly about them (Horowitz 1985: 51–64; Eriksen 1993: 10–12; Gurr 2000: 3–5; Fearon 2006; Chandra 2012). Religious identities can be attributes of ethnic identities, but, as discussed in Chapter 8, it is sometimes useful to separate them (McCauley 2014).

Many, but not all, ethnic identities are politicized or, as Chandra and Wilkinson (2008: 523–6; see also Chandra 2012) put it, 'activated in politics'. This distinction is obviously very important for the analysis of the role of ethnicity in politics in the developing world and elsewhere (Birnir et al. 2015, 2016). Ethnopolitical identities are those ethnic identities that have been politicized. This term deliberately emphasizes the interactive causal significance of the ethnic and political components of these identities in their formation, continuing mobilization, and interaction with concrete organizations, institutional rules, and international influences (Gurr 2000: 5–8; Wimmer 2002; Mozaffar et al. 2003: 382–3). There is much debate about the relative strength of each component of ethnic identities, with a majority of recent analysts giving predominance to the political. But their relative strength, as well as the specific form of their interaction, may vary across ethnicities or countries and over time. Young (2001: 176) suggests that the political component is more important in Africa than in Eurasia. In Latin America, in contrast, perceived and real language and racial differences have long divided populations; the politicization of the indigenous people and of people of African descent is more recent, though this varies between countries (Van Cott 2005). The fact that ethnopolitical identities are activated through the processes discussed and thus change over time does not, however, mean that they are not often held with deep emotional intensity. They are constructed through a variety of interactions between leaders and masses in which everyone's rational calculations are structured by their existing values, norms, and identities.

With very few exceptions, European colonialism in the developing world played a crucial role in the construction of ethnic identities, and an even more crucial role in their politicization and organization into ethnopolitical groups. But the timing of colonial rule, the European powers involved and the specific policies that affected ethnic identities varied sharply between Latin America and the Caribbean, on the one hand, and Asia, the Middle East, North Africa, and sub-Saharan Africa, on the other, and to a lesser extent among and within the latter areas. The Spanish and Portuguese colonized virtually all of Latin America and much of the Caribbean from the sixteenth century until the first quarter of the nineteenth century. They brought in large numbers of settlers from their own countries and other European countries, and it was the Creoles—the American-born descendants of these settlers (Young 1976: 84; Anderson 1991: 47)—who seized power from the decaying colonial empires at the time of independence. In many of these countries, they were outnumbered by indigenous Indians alone, or (as in Brazil) in combination with imported African slaves, although extensive intermarriage created intermediate groups of people, many of whom adopted Creole identities. European or Creole, mixed race or Mestizo, Indian and African ethnopolitical identities developed over the following decades, roughly in that order. The increasing strength of national pan-indigenous identities across multiple tribes and as disadvantaged minorities has been one of the primary changes in the landscape of ethnopolitical identities in recent decades. Increasing understanding that the indigenous and disadvantaged Mestizos share some political interests is another (Madrid 2012). British and French colonialism in the Caribbean began slightly later, and the British held on to their colonies until the end of the Second World War. Descendants of former slaves from Africa are the overwhelming majority of the population in most of these countries. However, those countries with substantial East Indian populations are deeply divided in terms of ethnopolitical identities.

English, French, Dutch, and Spanish/American colonialism in South and South East Asia occurred somewhat later, beginning as early as the sixteenth century in the Philippines and as late as the late nineteenth century in Indochina, and lasting until after the Second World War. Very few permanent European settlers were brought in, although Chinese and Indian settlers were brought into some South East Asian countries. A core pre-colonial ethnic identity existed in many, but not all, Asian colonies, and was usually reinforced and given increased political significance by colonial rule. Myanmar is a clear example of this pattern. But minority ethnic identities within or outside the core were recognized and also politicized, especially by the British. Minority identities were strengthened in the process of resistance to the colonial reinforcement of the core identity. The two largest Asian colonies—British India and Dutch Indonesia—and a few others were amalgamations of a vast array of ethnic identities without a single dominant core. The British politicized these multiple identities more intensively and intentionally (through granting limited **political autonomy** to indigenous princely states) than the Dutch did, but the latter's classification of customary law zones constructed and politicized the ethnicity of their residents (Young 1994: 270). Post-independence politics including institutional changes (Bertrand 2008) and ethnic conflict (Taylor 2009b), in countries with amalgamation of groups have, at various times, intensified groups' politicization, which is also reinforced by international support for some disadvantaged minorities.

English, French, Belgian, and Portuguese colonialism in sub-Saharan Africa occurred much later, not really penetrating the subcontinent beyond a few coastal areas, the Portuguese-influenced Kongo Kingdom (most of which is now in Angola), and areas of European settlement in South Africa until the 1880s. Colonial rulers' reliance on local agents to cope with the dilemma of maintaining control at low cost encouraged these agents to differentiate their groups from those not so privileged by colonial authority, either by recombining and redefining existing markers of ethnicity, or by accentuating previously minor group differences. Colonial rulers' creation of administrative units to secure additional economies in the cost of **governance** incorporated culturally disparate groups within single administrative units or separated culturally similar groups into separate units.

At independence, therefore, sub-Saharan African countries inherited a distinctive **ethnic morphology** (the form and structure of groups) with three defining features:

- very few ethnopolitical groups comprise an outright majority in a country, although some comprise a large plurality;
- limited cultural differences among groups in most countries; and
- the territorial concentration of many ethnic groups that facilitates their construction as cohesive units for collective political action.

These three features have combined with the accommodation by post-colonial **regimes** of instrumental ('pork barrel') ethnopolitical demands to foster *communal contention* as the typical pattern of political interactions in which ethnopolitical groups serve as cost-effective resources for organizing political competition. Communal contention discourages political entrepreneurs from exaggerating cultural differences among groups, and encourages them instead to maintain strong group and coexisting subgroup identities that are sustained by their ability to access the state, and to secure valued goods and services for their followers (Mozaffar et al. 2003: 382–3).

In sub-Saharan Africa, construction of *ethnopolitical* groups occurred through organized group mobilization, articulation of grievances by leaders claiming to speak for a group, participation in collective action or conflict with other groups or the state, being subjected to state violence, encapsulation within or domination of an officially designated administrative unit, occupying a disproportionate number of high positions in the bureaucracy or the military, controlling disproportionate socio-economic resources, forming or joining an ethnic or multi-ethnic political party (Mozaffar et al. 2003: 383), or in response to changing institutional incentives over time (Posner 2005).

French and British colonialism came to North Africa with the French occupation of Algeria in 1830—fifty years before neighbouring Morocco and Tunisia—and the British occupation of Aden in 1839. The presence of numerous French settlers in Algeria, who campaigned to incorporate the colony permanently into France, was eventually a major force in politicizing Algerian and regional (Maghreb) Arab identity. Colonial rule by the same European powers came to the Asian Middle East the latest of all regions—at the end

of the First World War, in which the Ottoman Empire (the former colonial power in most of this region) was defeated—and lasted less than thirty years. Ottoman rule was assimilative, rather than alien, but it was more interventionist and integrative than previous localized rulers, and thus stimulated Arab nationalism within its territories, especially in its waning years. Post-independence interventionist states continued this process, as did the conflict surrounding the arrival of large numbers of European Jews in Palestine before and after the founding of Israel in 1948. Other Arab countries have had few European settlers. Thus the construction and politicization of Arab as the dominant ethnopolitical identity in the entire bi-continental region was a long process in which European colonialism played a more limited role than in other regions (Young 1976: 373–427). Apart from the Kurds of Iran, Iraq, and Turkey, whose identity was politicized primarily in the twentieth century, and Berber speakers in western North Africa, the main lines of division are religious. The Western powers have been seen as opposed to the emergence of a transnational Arab identity and not only with respect to Palestine. This opposition has been a powerful politicizing force.

KEY POINTS

- Ethnic identities are constructed from multiple underlying ethnic markers, some of which are emphasized and then are often politicized to become ethnopolitical.

- The ethnic and political components of ethnopolitical identities are both important, but their relative importance varies among groups, countries, and regions.

- Many ethnopolitical (politically relevant ethnic) identities in the developing world were constructed during the colonial period, but most are continuously modified by post-independence politics.

- Differences among regions of the developing world in the timing of colonialism, the policies of the major colonial powers, and the presence of European settlers significantly affected the construction of ethnopolitical identities.

Varieties of Nationalism in the Developing World

National identities are inherently political, emphasizing the autonomy and unity of the nation as an actual or potential political unit (Hutchinson and Smith 1994: 4–5). They can be broadly characterized as civic, multi-ethnic and multicultural, ethnonational, or a combination of these types (Eriksen 1993: 118–20; Croucher 2003: 3–5; Scarritt and Mozaffar 2003). Civic national identities involve unity among citizens of an autonomous state. The only cultural uniformity that is demanded is commitment to the existence of the nation, and to its political institutional norms and values. **Ethno-national identities** define the nation in ethnic terms, attaining unity through the merger of ethnic and national identities, and demand autonomy for ethnic nations. Multi-ethnic/**multicultural national identities** define the nation in terms of several ethnic identities that are united by, or nested within, citizenship and political interaction in an autonomous state, while often excluding other ethnic identities. They differ from **civic nationalism** in accepting the legitimacy and political utility of ethnopolitical identities, as long as they do not undermine national unity. Very few national identities in the developing world are purely civic, but a substantial majority of them contain civic or multi-ethnic aspects, so that they do not identify the nation with a single ethnic group. Consequently, there is an ongoing tension between the ethnic, multi-ethnic, and civic aspects of these identities in their interaction with group advantages and disadvantages, concrete organizations, institutional rules, and international influences.

Since nationalism is a constructed identity, the significant variations in the specific nature of nations in the developing world are not surprising. The boundaries of the vast majority of developing states were determined by colonial rulers, and the varieties of nationalism are products of the interaction between the states that rule within these boundaries and the morphology of ethnopolitical identities, the tactics of ethnopolitical groups, and the presence of alternative identities within the same boundaries, as discussed in the next section of this chapter: 'The normative model of the contemporary polity calls for the coincidence of nation and state' (Young 1976: 70). States attempt to create national identities that are co-extensive with their boundaries and the constituent ethnopolitical groups support or oppose these identities. National identities are still being constructed and this process is more advanced in some regions of the developing world than in others. But only in a very few developing countries are national identities

accepted as a matter of course and constantly reinforced by popular culture—as these identities are in most developed countries (Billig 1995). Thus nationalism in every country develops in relation to nationalism in all other countries, but especially in relation to nationalism in neighbouring countries and to the strong nationalism of the former colonial powers, including the United States. It is impossible to specify exactly the number of nations or potential nations in the developing world, but if one includes every state and every ethnopolitical identity that engenders an ethno-nationalist movement, there are probably several hundred.

Latin American states are former colonial administrative units: 'The first century of independent life saw the gradual transformation of what began primarily as the territorial heirs to colonial administrative divisions into nation-states' (Young 1976: 85). These countries officially pursue civic nationalism, but until the late twentieth century this was actually a cover for Creole assimilationist ethno-nationalism. Since the awakening of indigenous and/or African ethnopolitical identities in most countries, there has been a struggle by these groups to redefine national identity in more multi-ethnic/multicultural terms. Because of Creole elite resistance, the outcome of this struggle is very much in doubt. Civic and ethnic nationalism tend to merge in racially homogeneous Caribbean countries, but civic national identities are much weaker and ethno-national ones much stronger in countries, such as Trinidad and Guyana, with significant East Indian populations.

Nationalism in Asian countries containing politicized ethnic cores has tended to be ethno-nationalism focused on these cores and thus is often rejected by members of non-core cultural groups, who advocate civic or multi-ethnic nationalism or desire secession. As discussed in the next section, this can lead to violent conflict over the definition of the nation. In substantially different ways, multi-ethnic India and Indonesia constructed relatively strong multi-ethnic/multicultural national identities during the struggle for independence and the first decades of post-colonial rule. In India, the multiplicity of types of ethnic identity and the integrating force of the multi-ethnic and nationalist Congress Party facilitated the emergence of a **multi-ethnic national identity**, while the adoption of a lingua franca developed through trade as the national language did the same for Indonesia. These multi-ethnic national identities have weakened

substantially in recent decades, as discussed in the following section and in Chapter 20 on Indonesia. The
role of religion in weakening these identities is discussed in Chapter 8.

Sub-Saharan Africa is where multi-ethnic nationalism is most common, although ethno-nationalism
is by no means absent there. The predominance of
ethnopolitical cleavages, their complex multilevel
morphology, the absence of large cultural differences in most African countries (in contrast to the
multi-ethnic/multicultural societies of Asia, Latin
America, and the Caribbean) except those divided by
religion, and the politics of communal contention
combine to produce multi-ethnic national identities
that most effectively integrate national and ethnopolitical identities in this context. The presence of
substantial numbers of foreign Africans in the presently or formerly wealthier African countries helps
to solidify the multi-ethnic national identities that
exclude them, but include all ethnic groups comprising primarily citizens. It should be noted that these
identities are emerging, rather than fully formed,
and that they mitigate, rather than eliminate, ethnopolitical conflict. A minority of African societies are
deeply divided and thus torn by conflicts about national identity. That small cultural differences do not
always eliminate such conflict is amply illustrated by
Rwanda and Burundi, which can be called culturally
homogeneous because the pre-colonial Tutsi con-
querors adopted the culture of the conquered Hutu,
but colonial policies and post-independence political competition have created violent, deeply divided
societies.

In the Middle East and North Africa, the national
identities of states with colonially (Ottoman or
European) created boundaries compete with: the
transnational Arab nationalism, the primary competitor in the middle decades of the twentieth century; transnational Islamist identities (see Chapter
8), a primary competitor today; transnational non-
Arab identities (Berber in Algeria and Morocco,
and Kurdish in Iran, Iraq, and Turkey); and Sunni–
Shi'a ethno-religious identities. Consequently, these
national state identities are probably among the
weakest in the developing world. The high level of
violence among ethnopolitical groups in Iraq that
has followed the American military intervention (see
Chapter 22) demonstrates the weakness of efforts to
construct civic or multi-ethnic national identities in
that country.

KEY POINTS

• National identities are inherently political.
• National identities can be ethno-national, multi-ethnic/multicultural, and civic in varying degrees.
• Most national identities in the developing world were constructed during the colonial period, but some have been modified by post-independence politics.
• Differences among regions and countries of the developing world in the morphology of ethnopolitical identities, the tactics of ethnopolitical groups, the policies of the major colonial powers and post-independence states, and the presence of alternative identities significantly affected the construction of national identities.

Ethnopolitics in Multi-Ethnic and Deeply Divided Societies

Ethnopolitical morphology

The discussion of the construction of ethnopolitical and national identities in various regions of the developing world has revealed that the morphology of ethnopolitical groups varies greatly among the developing countries (see Box 7.1). Borrowing from Young (1976: 95–7), it is possible to specify at least five patterns of ethnopolitical morphology:

1. homogeneous societies, such as Korea, Lesotho, and Haiti;

2. societies with a single clearly dominant group, numerically and socially, and minorities, such as Algeria, Myanmar, and Nicaragua;

3. bipolar, or deeply divided, societies, such as Burundi, Guyana, Rwanda, and Sri Lanka;

4. multipolar societies, divided primarily on a single dimension, with no dominant groups, such as many sub-Saharan African countries; and

5. societies with a multiplicity of cultures, with more than one dimension of differentiation, such as India and Indonesia.

Another approach to comparing ethnopolitical morphologies is to develop an index of fractionalization or fragmentation for each country. To do this, one must first specify all of the ethnic or ethnopolitical groups that exist in each country of the developing world because of past construction processes.

BOX 7.1 ETHNOPOLITICS AND NATIONALISM IN GUATEMALA AND NIGERIA

The generalizations that we make in this chapter are useful in explaining events and trends in the following two countries.

Guatemala

Ethnic war has ramifications that often reverberate for decades after the war. Guatemalans continue to have some of the lowest regard for democratic norms in the region. This attitude is likely influenced by the fact that army officers who led the ethnic civil war in the 1980s still figure prominently in Guatemalan politics. This includes General José Efraín Ríos Montt, who assumed the presidency for a year in a coup in 1982, during one of the bloodiest phases of the war. After return to elections in 1986 and a peace accord in 1996, Ríos Montt unsuccessfully contested the presidency in 2003, but was elected to Congress in 2007 and gained immunity from prosecution for war crimes. After his term and immunity ran out, General Ríos Montt was found guilty by a Guatemalan court in 2013 of **genocide** and

crimes against humanity, but Guatemala's Constitutional Court later overturned the conviction (see https://hrdag.org/guatemala/). His retrial began in 2015, but was delayed again in 2016 (see Chapter 26).

Nigeria

Nigeria takes pride in having the largest population and the greatest economic output of any African country. Yet its multipolar society has experienced many years of violent conflict based on religious differences between Christianity and Islam, great economic inequality and enormous **corruption**, ethnopolitically based competition for power leading to civil war, repression of groups who resist oil drilling, and ethnopolitically motivated military coups. The intensity of these conflicts has decreased in recent years as a result of relatively free and fair elections, but Nigerian democracy and human rights remain fragile (see Chapter 25).

Fearon (2003) and Birnir and colleagues' (2015, 2016) All Minorities at Risk (AMAR) project have attempted to do this; Scarritt and Mozaffar (1999) have attempted to do it for Africa. Gurr and his associates in the Minorities at Risk (MAR) project (Gurr 1993, 2000; MAR 2009), and Wimmer and colleagues (2009) too, have attempted to specify a narrower list of politically relevant groups or groups 'at risk', respectively. These authors have different definitions of relevant ethnic groups. It is nevertheless

useful to examine these efforts to specify groups, as in Table 7.1, to get an idea of the very large number of them and to show that two regions are ranked in the same order in the three global data sets in terms of the number of groups specified: first, sub-Saharan Africa; and second, Asia.

Fearon's data, for example, presents a comparison of countries and regions in terms of fractionalization, which varies in his scale between 0 (homogeneous) and 1 (totally fragmented). This data, summarized in

Table 7.1 Numbers of ethnopolitical groups in the developing world

Region	Fearon (2003)	Scarritt and Mozaffar (1999)	Socially relevant groups over 1 per cent (AMAR): Gurr (1993, 2000); MAR (2009); Birnir et al. (2015)	Politically relevant groups: Wimmer et al. (2009)
Latin America–Caribbean	84		83	54
Asia	108		254	119
Sub-Saharan Africa	351	382	458	215
Middle East–North Africa	70		122	83
Total	**613**	**382**	**917**	**471**

Note: Countries with patterns (4) and (5), and those with pattern (2) in which the minorities do not cohere (a substantial majority of societies in that pattern at most points in time), can be called 'multi-ethnic societies'.

Table 7.2 Ethnic fractionalization in the developing world

Region	Average	Range	% of countries with majority group
Latin America–Caribbean	0.41	0.743–0.095	78
Asia	0.44	1.00–0.002	78
Sub-Saharan Africa	0.71	0.953–0.180	28
Middle East–North Africa	0.45	0.780–0.039	84

Table 7.2, shows that, within the developing world, the average level of ethnic fractionalization is lowest in Latin America–Caribbean, slightly higher in Asia and the Middle East–North Africa, and much higher in sub-Saharan Africa (Fearon 2003: 204, 209, 215–19). The range of countries in terms of fragmentation is greatest in Asia—almost as great in sub-Saharan Africa—and less in the other two regions. Finally, the percentage of countries in which the largest group comprises the majority of the population is only 28 per cent in sub-Saharan Africa, and between 78 per cent and 84 per cent in the other three regions. Thirty African countries (70 per cent of the total) have fragmentation scores above 0.7, while only four Asian countries (including the two largest ones, India and Indonesia), three Middle Eastern countries, and one Latin American country have scores this high. Fearon's data thus supports the conclusion that most African countries are far more fragmented than most countries in other regions.

Other relevant aspects of ethnopolitical morphology are geographic concentration, the extent of cultural differences among groups, and the presence of ethnic groups that have not been explicitly politicized, as described earlier. Available data indicates that ethnopolitical groups in sub-Saharan Africa tend to be the most geographically concentrated and tend to have the smallest cultural differences, and that there are more ethnic groups that have not been politicized there than in other regions of the developing world (Gurr 1993: 344–51; Fearon 2003: 211–14; Scarritt and Mozaffar 2003: 9–10).

Collective action and interaction

These different ethnopolitical morphologies interact with group advantage or disadvantage, political organizations and institutional rules, mobilization and state response histories, and international influences in causing different types of collective action by ethnopolitical groups and different types of interaction among them or with the state. Human agents who are rational within their belief and normative frameworks carry out these processes enabled and constrained by social structures (Mozaffar 1995; Gurr 2000: 65–95; Mozaffar et al. 2003: 380–2, 385–7). Ethnopolitical interactions cannot be fully explained without taking all of these factors and their interactions into account; the following presentation is organized factor by factor, but incorporates interactions among factors into the discussion of each one.

Group advantage or disadvantage can be economic, political, or cultural, or any combination of these forms. Crucial political organizations include various civilian state agencies, the military and police, political parties, and interest associations that are not ethnically based. Some are more institutionalized. Institutional rules can be broadly categorized as democratic, transitional, or autocratic (Gurr 2000: 154). Rules about the formation and control of ethnopolitical associations and the conduct of elections are of special importance. Group collective action and state responses have historical patterns that vary in violence and intensity in different countries of the developing world, although these patterns are more firmly established in some countries. These patterns are, of course, subject to change, but they have self-perpetuating qualities that resist change unless the forces supporting it are sufficient to overcome them. Finally, although ethnopolitics is primarily internal to states, it is significantly influenced by several aspects of **globalization**, diffusion, and contagion among identical or similar groups across state boundaries, and external political and material support.

Interaction within groups and between them and the state can be categorized as cooperative,

BOX 7.2 TWO CONCEPTIONS OF THE CAUSES OF ETHNOPOLITICAL CONFLICT

An adequate theory of ethnic conflict should be able to explain both elite and mass behaviour. Such a theory should also provide an explanation for the passionate, symbolic, and apprehensive aspects of ethnic conflict. Group entitlement, conceived as a joint function of comparative worth and legitimacy, does this—it explains why the followers follow, accounts for the intensity of group reactions, even to modest stimuli, and clarifies the otherwise mysterious quest for public signs of group status.

(Horowitz 1985: 226)

The motivations at the heart of ethnopolitics are assumed to be a mix of grievance, sentiment, solidarity, ambition, and calculation. It is simplistic to argue that one kind of motivation is primary and others subsidiary. Ethnopolitical protest and rebellion are consequences of complex interactions among collective experience, normative commitments, contention for power, and strategic assessments about how best to promote individual and collective interests.

(Gurr 2000: 66)

competitive, or conflictual. The boundaries among these three types of collective interaction are by no means perfectly clear, and a given action by a group or the state may involve any two or all three types vis-à-vis various targets. The relative importance of these interactions nevertheless provides a very useful way of comparing ethnopolitics in the countries of the developing world. As illustrated in Box 7.2, the literature on ethnopolitics there (Young 1976; Horowitz 1985; Gurr 1993, 2000) emphasizes the complex causation of conflict involving some degree of violence and, to a lesser extent, competition. Greater emphasis on competition than violence and on cooperation are necessary for a balanced understanding of ethnopolitics. To highlight this point, it is useful to separate—within the discussion of each factor and its interactions with others—the explanation of cooperation, institutionalized competition, and peaceful protest from the explanation of conflict and non-institutionalized competition.

Cooperation and institutionalized competition among ethnopolitical groups and states in the developing world do not get much attention in the global media, yet they occur with great frequency and have significant consequences. They are substantially greater in frequency and consequences than conflict is in many countries, although they often coexist with conflict (involving the same or other groups). Peaceful protest attracts more media attention. It is not institutionalized, but is more properly seen as competition rather than conflict, although it is easy for such protest to turn violent and thus become conflictual through the actions of the protesters or the authorities (usually the police). This is one reason why the boundaries between cooperation and competition, and between competition and conflict, are often difficult to draw. On the other hand, conflict in the forms of violent

protest, rebellion, and repression, as well as its almost indistinguishable cousin, non-institutionalized violent competition, get a great deal of attention from global media (and scholars); they are 'newsworthy'. The consequences of such conflict can indeed be horrific, but this is not always the case, and the media's view of ethnopolitical conflict as prevalent in most developing countries is distorted and vastly overstated, because only about a third of all socially relevant ethnic groups ever engage in conflict (Birnir et al. 2016).

Ethnopolitical morphology and types of ethnopolitical interaction

Cooperation, institutionalized competition, and peaceful protest, aspects of the politics of communal contention, are more frequent and consequential in multi-ethnic than in deeply divided societies, although they are not limited to the former type. The impossibility of majority support for the regime (important even for autocratic regimes) in the absence of such cooperation in the former type of society, and the tendency towards the mutual fears and hopes of ethno-nationalist 'winner takes all' politics among both groups in the latter type of society, account for this difference. Small cultural differences and the presence of non-politicized groups facilitate cooperation. Conflict and non-institutionalized violent competition are more frequent in deeply divided societies, although they are not limited to them and deep ethnic divisions sometimes are the consequence, as well as the cause, of conflict. The reasons for this are the inverse of those for the greater significance of cooperation in multi-ethnic society, which also experience their share of conflict. Organizations such as political parties and the military tend strongly to be arenas of conflict in deeply divided societies (Horowitz 1985: 291–525).

But, within each type of society, other factors account for substantial differences in cooperation, competition, and conflict.

Group advantages and disadvantages, and types of ethnopolitical interaction

Cooperation is easier the smaller the advantages or disadvantages of different groups. Advantages or disadvantages can be economic, political, or cultural, and can be the result of discrimination in either state policies or well-established social structures, or of more accidental factors such as regional differences in resource endowments. Disadvantages that are seen as caused by discrimination in state policies make cooperation especially difficult (Gurr 1993: 34–60; Gurr 2000: 105–32), but disadvantages caused by social structural discrimination and not counteracted by state policies also hinder it (Wilkinson 2004; Cederman et al. 2013). Since many groups in most countries of the developing world have advantages or disadvantages caused by discrimination (as described later in the chapter), ethnopolitical cooperation and the reduction of discrimination through state policies tend to go together.

Conflict is more likely to occur the greater the advantages or disadvantages of different groups, especially if these advantages or disadvantages are seen to result from discrimination in state policies. Horowitz (1985: 32) indicates that 'virtually all ranked systems of ethnic relations [in which class and ethnicity coincide] are in a state of rapid transition or of increasing coercion by the superordinate group to avert change'. According to the weighted AMAR sample of socially relevant ethnic groups (Birnir et al. 2016), over half of minority groups have experienced one or more forms of discrimination, with well over 40 per cent experiencing economic discrimination. Within the developing world, economic discrimination is proportionally most common in Latin America and the Caribbean (where indigenous peoples are subject to severe discrimination of all types), with nearly all minorities experiencing some economic discrimination. This is followed by Asia, where about 60 per cent of groups have experienced economic discrimination. In the Middle East and North Africa, the number is around 50 per cent, and sub-Saharan Africa follows, with around 38 per cent of groups having experienced economic discrimination. Political discrimination is equally prevalent in the developing world. This form

of discrimination is also greatest in Latin America and the Caribbean, where all included political minorities have experienced discrimination at some point. Asia comes second, with 70 per cent of groups discriminated against politically, the Middle East and North Africa, and sub-Saharan Africa, follow, with 45 and 39 per cent, respectively. Finally, cultural discrimination is less frequent, with a third of all groups having experienced it, most commonly in Latin America and Asia, less so in sub-Saharan Africa, and least in the Middle East. These forms of discrimination are highly correlated with group disadvantages (Gurr 2000: 105–27) and propensity for rebellion against the state (Birnir et al. 2016).

Organizations, institutional rules, and types of ethnopolitical interaction

Political cooperation among ethnopolitical groups occurs primarily within the previously listed political organizations, operating with more or less firmly institutionalized rules. Institutional differences are probably the most important factor in explaining cooperation in such organizations. Cooperation requires a relatively high degree of institutionalization of the organizations within which it occurs, although it is impossible to specify the required level exactly. Democratic **institutions**, particularly strong ones (highly institutionalized), promote cooperation, are the primary basis of institutionalized competition, and allow—and in some ways, encourage—relatively peaceful protest. Institutional rules providing relatively unrestricted freedom for group activities are crucial for both institutionalized competition and peaceful protest. Not surprisingly, the MAR data demonstrates the greater use of peaceful protest and less ethnopolitical conflict in democratic countries, and—perhaps more surprisingly—in transitional countries in the developing world as well (Gurr 2000).

In multi-ethnic societies, political parties contesting democratic elections need multi-ethnic support to win, unless one group constitutes a majority of the population or is close enough that a non-proportional electoral system can give that group control of a majority of seats in the legislature. But, even in the latter cases, democratic institutions encourage inter-ethnic cooperation more than autocratic institutions do. Multi-ethnic parties predominate in sub-Saharan Africa and are found in a number of countries in other regions of the developing world. Indeed, several multi-ethnic democratic countries have instituted special rules to encourage multi-ethnic parties (Reilly 2006). The debate continues about which institutions—including proportional representation or 'first past the post' (FPTP)—are more likely to promote cooperation in multi-ethnic parties (Horowitz 2014). The influence of such electoral institutions is perhaps outweighed by other factors. Horowitz (1985: 291–440) has analysed the ways in which ethnic parties, the support for which comes overwhelmingly from a single ethnopolitical group, enhance conflict in deeply divided societies by unreservedly pursuing the interests of that group and failing to form stable majority coalitions.

Conflict and non-institutionalized violent competition occur within and among the organizations where cooperation occurs (Horowitz 1985: 291–525), but more frequently occur outside formal organizations in the forms of violent protest, armed rebellion, and state repression varying from restrictions on civil and political liberties, through conventional policing, to genocide. Conflict has been most violent in deeply divided societies, when groups are severely disadvantaged by multiple forms of discrimination, and under weak autocratic institutions. In the MAR data, violent rebellion between 1985 and 1998 had a mean annual magnitude in autocracies that was two-and-a-half times that in new democracies; rebellion in transitional regimes was much closer to the level in new democracies. Partial or failed transitions in the developing world tend to increase protest, but decrease rebellion (Gurr 2000: 151–63). The data shows that, in part, democratization decreases conflict by decreasing discrimination (Gurr 2000: 163–77). Thus, while the institutional instability engendered by democratization can increase ethnopolitical conflict, as Snyder (2000) suggests, this is not its most common effect, at least beyond the transition period.

Mobilization, state response, and types of ethnopolitical interaction

Ethnopolitical identity construction and ethnopolitical group mobilization are closely related processes that tend to occur together over time. Mobilization of ethnic associations is part of the politicization of ethnic identities, which often leads to ethnopolitical mobilization through political parties. Thus much ethnopolitical mobilization has a history going back

to the colonial period in the developing world. Since independence, such mobilization has been most intense and violent in societies with reinforcing ethnic and other types of cleavage (Selway 2011) and/or where ethnic groups are geographically concentrated (Toft 2003), when groups are severely disadvantaged by multiple forms of discrimination (Wimmer 2002; Birnir 2007; Wucherpfennig et al. 2012), under weak or semi-democratic institutions (Lake and Rothchild 1996; Fearon and Laitin 2003), and in the presence of international conflict spillover (Salehyan 2007; Forsberg 2008), including political and material support for or against mobilization. Conversely, it has been least intense and most peaceful in highly multi-ethnic societies, when few or no groups are severely disadvantaged by any form of discrimination, under strong democratic institutions, and in the absence of international political and material support. The longer a specific pattern of mobilization occurs, the more likely it is to be self-perpetuating unless changed deliberately by powerful actors. It is very difficult to change a primarily conflictual pattern of collective interaction into a primarily cooperative pattern, or vice versa, and somewhat difficult to institutionalize un-institutionalized competition or to change violent protest into peaceful protest.

The tendency for patterns of mobilization to be self-perpetuating is reinforced by state repression of a pattern of mobilization or the absence of such repression. Not surprisingly, the more intense and violent the mobilization, the more severe the repression. In the MAR (and AMAR) data, repression varies from conventional policing to genocide (the extermination of an ethnic group) and **politicide** (the extermination of political enemies). Between 1955 and 1995, extensive ethnopolitical repression occurred in all areas of the developing world. It involved the largest portion of groups in Asia and Latin America and the Caribbean, but the highest number of repressed groups is in sub-Saharan Africa. Some argue that repression is far more likely to intensify violent mobilization than to stop it. Harff (2003: 66), for example, found that genocide or politicide is most likely to occur or to be repeated after political upheaval in autocracies based on the support of advantaged minorities with exclusionary ideologies. State response to peaceful protest, most common in democratic states, has often been to grant only a small proportion of the protesters' demands, but not to engage in repression. This response has typically led to the continuation of peaceful protest. The effectiveness of state repression in stemming dissident violence is still hotly debated (Davenport 2007).

International influences and types of ethnopolitical interaction

International influences have fostered both ethnopolitical cooperation and ethnopolitical conflict. Scholars have given some attention to the direct diffusion or indirect contagion of ethnopolitical conflicts across national borders (Saideman and Ayres 2000; Salehyan 2007) through the presence of the same or closely related groups on both sides of the border. Much less attention has been paid to the diffusion of ethnopolitical cooperation, which is more difficult to study. But as democracy has been diffused to much of the developing world since the end of the cold war, it is possible to argue that ethnopolitical cooperation and institutionalized electoral competition have often been diffused with it.

During the cold war, the superpowers and former colonial powers frequently gave material, political, and/or military support to parties in ethnopolitical conflict in the developing world. This was done to further the objectives of the powers giving aid, but it undoubtedly substantially exacerbated such conflict in a number of countries, including Afghanistan, Angola, Ethiopia, Guatemala, and Nicaragua. It is argued in the next section that international intervention in ethnopolitical conflicts has been less self-interested since the end of the cold war, but the combination of the persistence of some degree of self-interest and lack of adequate information about the consequences of specific forms of intervention mean that political and/or material support can still have conflict-enhancing effects. French intervention in Rwanda in favour of the existing government (and thus of its followers who were bent on genocide) before and during the genocide of 1994, and increased Sunni–Shiʿa–Kurd conflict in Iraq after the Anglo-American invasion are cases in point. Regional powers within the developing world have also supported parties to ethnopolitical conflict in their regions out of self-interest, which formerly included rewards from their cold war patrons. Finally, regional and international organizations—governmental and especially non-governmental—have struggled to resolve a number of ethnopolitical conflicts, with consequences that have varied from success to exacerbating the conflict, but it appears that some of these organizations are becoming more successful.

Globalization has stimulated ethnopolitical mobilization and **terrorism** (Juergensmeyer 2003) as tools in ethnopolitical conflict, but it has also strengthened international norms of democratization, human rights, and non-discrimination. International norms now favour ethnopolitical cooperation, institutionalized competition, and the peaceful resolution of ethnopolitical conflicts to a greater extent than ever before. However, this may be changing in light of terrorism and Anglo-American and European reactions to it, as discussed in the next section. Globalization of communications has provided new tools for constructing ethnopolitical groups, as well as nations. But, as Billig (1995: 128–43) argues, global culture cannot serve as the primary basis of resistance to economic globalization, because it is less banal than the cultures of the developed nations, which support such globalization.

> ### KEY POINTS
>
> - Ethnopolitical morphology takes a variety of forms in the countries of the developing world, ranging from highly multi-ethnic to deeply divided and homogeneous.
>
> - Interaction among ethnopolitical groups, and between them and states, involves a mixture of cooperation, competition, and conflict.
>
> - Cooperative interactions are most easily achieved in multi-ethnic societies that have small group advantages and disadvantages, democracy based on relatively institutionalized multi-ethnic parties, a historical pattern of non-violent ethnopolitical mobilization and minimal repression of it, and international influences that support 'managed heterogeneity' rather than one side of ethnopolitical conflicts.
>
> - Cooperation is possible when some of these conditions are absent.

The State and Nation-Building in the Developing World

Nationalism was relatively weak or absent in most developing states at independence; indeed, 'The initial "nation-building" ethos [in Africa] proposed to resolve the ethnic question by confining it to the private realm' (Young 2001: 174). Civic nationalism was asserted ideologically in spite of its empirical weakness. But authoritarian 'banishment of ethnicity from political assertion merely drove it underground' (Young 2001: 176), while rulers continued to make ethnopolitical calculations in appointments to high political positions and the placement of development projects. Many essentially similar histories of failed efforts to extinguish ethnopolitical identities and movements, and either to create civic nationalism by fiat or to assimilate minorities into the core ethno-national identity by force, are found in other regions of the developing world. Forced assimilation to ethno-nationalism has had the more severe consequences; in deeply divided societies with long histories of ethnopolitical mobilization, especially those characterized by great group differences, and external material and political support for one side or the other, it has usually led to extremely violent conflict.

Owing in part to the desire to reduce the negative effects of economic globalization and the support received from international norms and the globalization of communications, there has been a shift in some developing states from these unsuccessful policies of trying to impose civic nationalism by fiat or majority ethno-national identities by force towards accepting multi-ethnic/multicultural national identities as a viable compromise. As Sen (2006) points out (see Box 7.3), there is a substantial difference between state policies promoting rational multiculturalism and policies promoting plural monoculturalism. In the former, national identity is based on a freely chosen blend of diversity and commonality among interacting ethnic groups; in the latter, full diversity is enforced by isolated groups and national identity is based on a 'federation' of group identities. The shift to rational

BOX 7.3 SEN'S DEFINITIONS OF TYPES OF MULTICULTURALISM

- *Plural monoculturalism* values the diversity of existing cultures for itself and makes the nation a federation of isolated cultures.

- *Reason-based multiculturalism* focuses on the freedom of reasoning and decision-making, and celebrates cultural diversity among interacting groups, to the extent that it is as freely chosen as possible by the persons involved and makes the nation truly multicultural.

Source: Sen (2006: 150–60)

multiculturalism/multi-ethnicity has been easier in multi-ethnic societies than in societies with a single dominant group or deeply divided societies, but such national identities are potentially viable in all of these societies (Snyder 2000: 33). They tend to make state and nation mutually reinforcing; 'the persistence of states, however challenged or changed by globalization they may be, offers a partial explanation for the continuation of nationhood as a salient form of belonging' (Croucher 2003: 14). Immigration compels states to clarify and reinforce national boundaries; responses to terrorism have the same effect; 'Nationhood, then, continues to be a functional, familiar, and legitimate mechanism for belonging' (Croucher 2003: 16). The aspirations of stateless peoples to national states prove its value.

Gurr (2000: 195–211, 275–7) argues that the number and severity of ethnopolitical conflicts have declined since the end of the cold war, 'because of domestic and international conflict-mitigating doctrines and practices' (Gurr 2000: 277–8). But Gurr (2000: 223–60) also acknowledges that some ethnopolitical groups are still at risk of being involved in future violent conflicts, because they maintain the interaction patterns with other groups and states that have led to violent conflict in the past. Indeed, Sambanis (2001) argues that the purported decline in ethno-nationalist conflict since the end of the cold war is not substantiated in the literature at large. Possibly adjudicating this debate, Birnir and colleagues (2016) argue more recently that ethnic heterogeneity is in and of itself not a correlate of war. They suggest that only about a third of all socially relevant ethnic groups ever engage in conflict, which is far fewer than previously thought. At the same time, where a civil war begins, Denny and Walter (2014) argue that it is more likely to be initiated by an ethnic group than any other type of group.

The United States, an important player in this international regime, moved back to self-interest and interventionism under the Bush administration, although the Obama administration reversed this trend slightly. The consequences of this change for national identities are uncertain. As mentioned already, Iraqi national identity was weakened, rather than strengthened, by the Anglo-American invasion (see Chapter 22), and the same can be said even more emphatically for national identity in Afghanistan. Terrorists tend to promote transnational identities. On the other hand, national identities have probably been strengthened in countries such as Venezuela and Bolivia, where elected leaders have defied US pressures and, in Bolivia, represented the indigenous. It is far too soon to declare the demise of ethnopolitical conflict, exclusionary ethno-nationalism, or their exacerbation through foreign intervention and terrorism.

KEY POINTS

- Many states of the developing world have attempted to suppress ethnopolitical identities and conflicts by declaring civic nationalism by fiat or assimilating minorities into their core ethno-national identity by force, but more are now accepting multi-ethnic national identities as a viable compromise.

- National identities in the developing world, usually based on existing states, continue to be viable in the era of globalization and offer a basis for resisting the negative effects of economic globalization.

- Ethnic diversity in and of itself is not a sufficient cause of war, but where civil war breaks out, it tends to be initiated by an ethnic group.

Conclusion

Ethnopolitical and national identities are different, although both are socially constructed and thus change over time. The pattern of ethnopolitical identities (the ethnopolitical morphology) within countries involves the number and relative size of groups, their geographic concentration, and their degree of cultural differences, and varies from deeply divided to highly multi-ethnic. National identities are civic, multi-ethnic, or ethno-national. Collective action by ethnopolitical groups, and cooperative, competitive, and conflictual interactions among them and with states, are influenced by the interaction of ethnopolitical morphology, group advantages and disadvantages, political organizations and institutional rules, mobilization and state response histories, and international influences. Cooperative interactions are most easily achieved in multi-ethnic societies that have small group advantages and disadvantages, democracy based on relatively institutionalized multi-ethnic parties, a historical pattern of non-violent ethnopolitical mobilization and minimal repression of it, and international influences that support 'managed heterogeneity' rather than one side of ethnopolitical conflicts. These interactions, in turn, tend to promote **nation-building** through multi-ethnic/multicultural nationalism. There is evidence of a shift in this direction in some countries of the developing world, but conflictual interactions and failures of nation-building still occur all too frequently.

? QUESTIONS

1. If ethnopolitical and national identities are constructed, and thus can change, why do they not change more frequently and rapidly?

2. What are the major types of national identity and how different are they?

3. If the amount of violent ethnopolitical conflict has declined in the developing world as a whole, why is such conflict still so strong in some countries?

4. What are the effects of globalization and foreign intervention on national identities in the developing world?

5. What are the effects of policies of plural monoculturalism and reason-based multiculturalism (as defined by Sen) on different types of national identity?

6. What are the major differences in ethnopolitics and nationalism among the four regions of the developing world?

7. How are ethnic identities activated and does activation necessarily lead to ethnic conflict?

8. What types of ethnic diversity lend themselves best to inter-ethnic cooperation and what types are more problematic?

 **FURTHER READING**

Chandra, K. (ed.) (2012) *Constructivist Theories of Ethnic Politics* (Oxford: Oxford University Press) Presents a new definition of ethnic identities that relates attributes to categories, and a new model for analysing how these identities are politically activated and changed. Relations of ethnicity to electoral politics, patronage, riots, and state disintegration and reconstruction are discussed.

Eriksen, T. H. (1993) *Ethnicity and Nationalism: Anthropological Perspectives* (London: Pluto Press) Presents an anthropological perspective on ethnicity, identity, ethnic relations, nationalism, and relations between states and ethnic minorities.

Birnir, J., Wilkenfeld, J., Fearon, J., Laitin, D., Gurr, T., Saideman, S., Brancati, D., Pate, A., and Hultquist, A. (2015) 'Socially Relevant Ethnic Groups, Ethnic Structure and AMAR', *Journal of Peace Research*, 52(1): 110–15 Assesses the difficulty in constructing lists of ethnic groups and proposes one solution, the All Minorities at Risk (AMAR) sample frame, the objective of which is to construct a flexible list of ethnic groups that researchers may adjust to fit their research needs.

Forsberg, E., Birnir, J., and Davenport, C. (Forthcoming) 'State of the Field of Ethnic Politics and Conflict: Introduction', *Ethnopolitics* The article introduces the journal issue that contains a collection of essays assessing the state of the field, and suggesting future directions by fourteen leading authorities on ethnicity and conflict.

Gurr, T. R. (2000) *Peoples versus States: Minorities at Risk in the New Century* (Washington, DC: US Institute of Peace Press) The second book from the Minorities at Risk (MAR) project identifies communal groups at risk, and analyses forms of risk, group grievances, group mobilization, group protest and rebellion, and the resolution of group conflicts, along with the role of democracy and the risk of future ethnic violence. It includes a number of illustrative sketches from the developing world.

Horowitz, D. L. (1985) *Ethnic Groups in Conflict* (Berkeley, CA: University of California Press) Presents a definition of ethnicity and a theory of ethnic conflict among unranked groups derived primarily from social psychology. Also discusses the roles of political parties and the military in ethnic conflict, and strategies for its resolution, and emphasizes deeply divided societies in South East and South Asia, Africa, and the Caribbean.

Hutchinson, J., and Smith, A. D. (eds) (1994) *Nationalism* (Oxford: Oxford University Press) A very comprehensive reader that includes selections from classic works on the definition of nationalism, theories of nationalism, nationalism in the developing world, and the effects of trends in the international system on nationalism.

Young, C. (1976) *The Politics of Cultural Pluralism* (Madison, WI: University of Wisconsin Press) Discusses cultural pluralism, identities, the state, nationalism, and cultural mobilization in Africa, the Arab world, Asia, and Latin America, illustrated with comparative case studies from these regions.

 WEB LINKS

http://www.icr.ethz.ch/data/growup/epr-eth   The website for the data introduced by Wimmer and colleagues (2009), cited in Table 7.1.

http://www.mar.umd.edu/   The website of the Minorities at Risk (MAR) project, covering almost 300 politically active ethnic groups coded on approximately 1,000 variables. Qualitative assessments of every group's risk are included.

 For additional material and resources, please visit the Online Resource Centre at:
http://www.oxfordtextbooks.co.uk/orc/burnell5e/

8

Religion

Jeff Haynes

Chapter contents

Overview

Recent decades have seen widespread involvement of religion in politics, especially, but not exclusively, in parts of the developing world. Today, religion is central to much political turbulence in much of the developing world. This chapter, examining the relationship between religion and politics, is structured as follows. First, the concept of religion is defined, and its contemporary political and social salience in many developing countries is emphasized. Second, the chapter examines how religion interacts with politics in the developing world, not least because it is often associated with religious competition and conflict. Third, we look at how 'religion'—especially identifiable religious institutions and organizations—interacts with the state in the developing world, because of the importance of these relationships for the wider issue of religion and politics. Fourth, we examine how religion is involved in democratization in the developing world, with special focus on the 'Arab uprising' and its aftermath. Fifth, the chapter considers the differing impacts of the so-called Islamic State and Pope Francis on the relationship between religion and politics in the developing world.

Introduction

'Religion and **politics**' is everywhere. Newspapers, television news broadcasts, blogs, and other sources of information incessantly feature stories and commentary about how and why religion and politics interact. Often, the focus is on the competition and conflict that derive from this relationship, especially in the **developing world**. For example, a recent recurring theme is the issue of the role of religion in conflicts between militant 'religious actors' and the state, for example in Nigeria (Boko Haram), Somalia (al-Shabaab) and Iraq/Syria (the so-called Islamic State). In these countries, Islamist militants seek to change both domestic and international power configurations.

There is no obvious reason why **political Islam** cannot compete for power democratically. Events in the 'Arab uprisings' from 2011—which included initial electoral victories for Islamists in both Egypt and Tunisia—provide evidence of this contention. Generally, 'political Islam' refers to diverse political movements that are, however, all animated by an ideological belief in the desirability of an 'Islamic state'—that is, an ideal polity with often diverse characteristics that, at various times, has included elements of many other political movements, while simultaneously adapting the religious views of Islamism. In various Muslim-majority countries in recent years, including the Palestinian territories, Iraq, Turkey, Pakistan, and Egypt and Tunisia, Islamists have gained power either alone (Hamas in the Palestinian territories, and the Justice and Development Party, or AKP, in Turkey) or as part of a ruling coalition (Iraq, Egypt, and Tunisia). In these cases, we see Islamists to an extent being willing to play by the democratic rules of the game.

Elsewhere in the developing world, Islamists are also politically active, although not necessarily democratically orientated. For example, in Africa, Nigeria is increasingly polarized politically between Muslim and Christian forces, with the phenomenon of Boko Haram the most recent manifestation of an apparently intransigent Islamist militancy, fragmented Somalia has continuing conflict centrally involving various Islamists, including al-Shabaab, Sudan's instability continues following the country's long-running civil war between Muslims and non-Muslims, and in Iraq and Syria, the so-called Islamic State has both territorial control and the attention of Western governments. In these cases, Islamists have eschewed the ballot box and sought power via violence and conflict.

It is not only Islamists who pursue political goals related to religion. In officially secular India, a growth in militant Hinduism was highlighted by, but not confined to, the Babri Masjid mosque incident at Ayodhya in 1992, which was instrumental in transforming the country's political landscape. This mosque, according to militant Hindus, was built on the birthplace of the Hindu god of war, Rama. As long ago as 1950, the mosque was closed down by the Indian government because militant Hindus wanted to build a Hindu temple there. Since then, Hindu militants, whose primary political organization is the Bharatiya Janata Party (BJP), have grown to political prominence. From 1996 to mid-2004, the BJP was the dominant party in three ruling coalitions. Since then, the BJP has competed electorally and is back in power at the national level as the party with overall majority, having won 282 of 543 seats in the 2014 parliamentary elections.

On the other hand, religion can significantly contribute to political and social stability, for example in the way in which the Roman Catholic Church was a leading player in the turn to democracy in Latin America in the 1980s and 1990s. In that region, however, the rise of a strand of Protestantism known as Pentecostalism has served to challenge the Catholic Church's historical hegemony.

KEY POINTS

- The last four decades have seen widespread involvement of religion in politics, especially in many countries in the developing world.
- Several religious traditions have experienced increased political involvement.
- Religion and democracy do not always seem compatible, although religious actors have at times, and in specific contexts, contributed to democratization.

Religion and Politics

Before proceeding, it is necessary to define 'religion'. In this chapter, religion has two analytically distinct, yet related, meanings.

- In a *spiritual* sense, religion pertains in three ways to models of social and individual behaviour that help believers to organize their everyday lives.

- It is to do with the idea of *transcendence*—that is, it relates to supernatural realities.
- It is concerned with *sacredness*—that is, a system of language and practice that organizes the world in terms of what is deemed holy.
- It refers to *ultimacy*—it relates people to the ultimate conditions of existence.

- In another, *material*, sense, religious beliefs can motivate individuals and groups to act in pursuit of social or political goals. Very few—if any—religious groups have an *absolute* lack of concern for at least *some* social and political issues. Consequently, religion can be 'a mobiliser of masses, a controller of mass action . . . an excuse for repression [or] an ideological basis for dissent' (Calvert and Calvert 2001: 140). In many countries, religion remains an important source of basic value orientations; this may have social and/ or political connotations.

We saw in Chapter 7 that religion is one of the bases for **ethnic identity**. For instance, in India, Sikh ethnic identity has been defined largely in terms of adherence to a common religion. It could seem, then, that ethnicity is the overarching concept and religious identification is one subtype. However, there are situations in which people sharing a single religion are divided by ethnicity, such as in Pakistan, where people share a common Islamic faith, but are ethnically divided on the basis of region and language. Moreover, appeals to religion often seek to transcend particular local or ethnic identities in the name of a supposedly universal ideal. It is wisest, therefore, to see ethnicity and religion as terms the potential meaning and content of which overlap, but remain distinct.

An American commentator, George Weigel, claims that there is an '**unsecularization** of the world'—that is, a global religious revitalization (quoted in Huntington 1993: 26). This is manifested in a global resurgence of religious ideas and **social movements** not confined to one faith or only to poor, developing countries. This unexpected development can be explained in various ways. No simple, clear-cut reason or single theoretical explanation covers all of the cases; yet the widespread emergence of religious actors with overtly social or political goals is often linked to **modernization**—that is, the prolonged period of historically unprecedented, diverse, massive change, characterized by urbanization, industrialization, and abrupt technological developments that people around the world have experienced in recent times. Modernization is said not only to have undermined traditional value systems, but also to have allocated opportunities—both within and between countries—in highly unequal ways. This has led many people to feel both disorientated and troubled, and as a result some, at least, (re)turn to religion for solace and comfort. In doing so, they seek a new or renewed sense of identity—something to give their lives greater meaning and purpose.

A second, although linked, explanation for apparent religious resurgence moves away from the specific impact of modernization to point to a more generalized 'atmosphere of crisis'. A key factor is said to be widespread popular disillusion with the abilities of secular state leaders to direct their socio-economic polities so that people generally benefit. Such disappointment can then feed into perceptions that these leaders hold power illegitimately—a sense bolstered when leaders resort to political oppression. Adding to the sense of crisis is widespread popular belief that society's traditional morals and values are being seriously undermined, not least by the corrosive effects of **globalization**, Westernization, and secularization—that is, the reduction in influence, or even withdrawal, of religion from the public realm. These circumstances are said to provide a fertile milieu for many people's 'return' to religion.

This suggests that the influence of religion will not be seen 'only' in relation to personal and social issues. Commentators have additionally pointed to *political* effects of the 'return of religion', whereby, in many developing countries, highly politicized religious groups, **institutions**, and movements have emerged—or adopted a higher profile—in recent years. Such actors are found in many different faiths and sects, and what they have in common is a desire to change domestic—and, in some cases, international—arrangements, so as to (re)instate religion as a central societal and political influence. They adopt a variety of tactics to achieve their goals. Some actors confine themselves to the realm of legitimate political protest, seeking reform or change via the ballot box; others resort to violence and terror to pursue their objectives.

Other explanations are offered for what is widely seen as a global religious revival and revitalization, but some commentators suggest that, in the developing world, there is not a religious resurgence per se; rather, political religion is simply more visible—largely as a consequence of the global communications revolution. In other words, religion is not a novel political actor so much as a stubbornly persistent one. For Smith (1990: 34), 'what has changed in the present situation . . . is mainly the growing awareness of [global manifestations of political religion] by the Western world, and the perception that they might be related to our interests'. This makes the recent trends only the latest manifestation of *cyclical* religious activity, made more highly visible (and, to many, alarming) by advances in communications technology and availability. In short, globalization is a multifaceted process of change, universally affecting states, local communities, and individuals. Religions are not exempted from its influence; as a result, like other social agents, they participate in, and are affected by, globalization. Academic discussions of religion and globalization often highlight trends towards cultural pluralism as a result of globalization, examining how various religions respond (Haynes 2007). Some believers react 'positively', accepting or even endorsing pluralism, including some Christian ecumenical movements. Others emphasize more inter-religious differences, sometimes confronting non-believers in attempts to preserve their particular values from being eroded by globalization.

But they are not necessarily *sui generis*. In the developing world, various religious traditions—for example Hinduism, Buddhism, and Islam—all experienced periods of pronounced political activity in the first half of the twentieth century in what were then mostly colonized countries. In the 1920s and the 1930s, religion was frequently used in the service of anti-colonial **nationalism**, and was a major facet of emerging **national identity** in opposition to alien rule (see Haynes 1996: 55–6). For example, in various Muslim countries, such as Algeria, Egypt, and Indonesia, Islamic consciousness was the defining ideology of nationalist movements. In 1947, immediately after the Second World War, Pakistan was founded as a Muslim state, religiously and culturally distinct from India, which was 80 per cent Hindu. A decade later, Buddhism was politically important, inter alia, in Burma, Sri Lanka, and Vietnam. Later, in the 1960s in Latin America, both **Christian democracy**—the application of Christian precepts to politics—and **liberation theology**—a radical ideology using Christianity as the basis of a demand for greater socio-economic justice for the poor—were politically consequential. More recently, and in such diverse countries as Iran, the United States, and Nicaragua, religion (re)appeared as an important political actor. Religious actors became skilled

at using the media to spread their political messages (Tarrow 1998: 115). Whereas political religion is often depicted as in opposition to the status quo, current manifestations of political religion appear to stress continuity rather than change.

An example in this regard is Boko Haram, an Islamist religious sect active in northern Nigeria (Walker 2012). Since 2009, Boko Haram has violently targeted Nigeria's police, rival Muslim clerics, politicians, and **public institutions**. It is said to be leading an armed revolt against several targets, including governmental **corruption**, abusive security forces, strife between the disaffected Muslim north and Christian south, and widening regional economic disparity in an oil-rich, yet impoverished, country. It may be that Boko Haram's actions go beyond narrowly religious issues to include socio-economic concerns that Nigeria's government has shown little capacity to resolve in the country's disaffected Muslim north, a region of deep poverty and limited opportunities for improvement. In August 2011, Boko Haram's bombing of a United Nations building in the capital, Abuja, and claims that it has ties with Al Qaeda led to new Western fears about its growth and influence.

Boko Haram colloquially translates into 'Western education is a sin', which may be a name assigned by the government. The group calls itself *Jama'atul Alhul Sunnah Lidda'wati wal jihad*, which translates as 'people committed to the propagation of the Prophet's teachings and jihad'. In July 2009, Boko Haram members refused to follow a motorcycle helmet law, leading to heavy-handed police tactics that set off an armed uprising in the northern state of Bauchi and spread into the states of Borno, Yobe, and Kano. The incident was suppressed by the army and left more than 800 dead. It also led to the execution of Yusuf, the sect's founder and 'spiritual leader', as well as the deaths of his father-in-law and other sect members, which **human rights** advocates consider to be extrajudicial killings. In the aftermath of the 2009 unrest, an Islamist insurrection under a splintered leadership emerged. At that time, Boko Haram began to carry out a number of suicide bombings and assassinations from Maiduguri to Abuja, staged an ambitious prison break-in in Bauchi, freeing more than 700 inmates, in 2010, and since 2011 has regularly attacked Christian churches in northern Nigeria (Walker 2012). (For further information on Boko Haram, see Chapter 25.)

In the Middle East and North Africa, the last few decades have seen the region emerge as a global focal point of increased political involvement of religious actors both within countries and internationally. Across the region, religious minorities are being squeezed and their security compromised. While Islamism (sometimes referred to pejoratively as 'Islamic fundamentalism') has attracted much attention in this context, we can also observe increasingly serious sectarian division and conflict across much of the region, especially in Syria, Iraq, and Yemen. The situation was exacerbated by the Arab uprisings and their aftermath, when state weakness or breakdown, combined with the impact of politically assertive religious actors, saw increasing pressure on religious minorities to convert to the dominant religious tradition or, failing that, to flee for their lives.

Religious actors such as the so-called Islamic State thrive on sectarian division. Given the widespread diminution of state capacity in the Middle East and North Africa following the Arab uprisings, and the linked expansion of aggressive Sunni entities (notably, the so-called Islamic State), it seems highly likely that the short and medium terms will feature many sectarian conflicts in the region, which will cause significant friction and, in some cases, result in out-and-out conflict between warring sectarian groups. Tensions between Shi'ite Iran and the Sunni Gulf Cooperation Council (GCC) are likely to remain high in the next few years—not least because each is seen to support one sect of Islam only. However, not all Shi'a movements will necessarily be pro-Iranian and not every Salafi or Wahhabist Sunni movement kowtows to Saudi Arabia. Indeed, there are significant Shi'ite minorities in GCC countries, as well as a growing (Sunni) Salafi movement in Iran. Sectarian tensions also reflect socio-economic disparities and are likely to escalate if governments do not address these fundamental issues. For example, Bahrain and Saudi Arabia, where economic inequality between Sunni and Shi'a is greatest, are more likely to see tensions rise than other countries in the region. Globalization, represented by influential satellite television channels and social media, will play a growing—perhaps pivotal—role in spreading anti-government rhetoric and sectarian mistrust. In addition, over the next twenty years, we are likely to see growing tensions *within* Sunni and Shi'ite communities. Sunni Islam is particularly likely to become increasingly factionalized. As Salafist groups grow in prominence around the world, a backlash may emerge from moderate Sunnis. Correspondingly, Shi'ite Islam contains a number of internal divisions.

KEY POINTS

- Religion has spiritual, material, and, in some cases, political aspects.
- Religion played an important political role in many developing countries during the last years of colonialism.
- Patchy modernization and/or a more generalized 'atmosphere of crisis' are said to underpin religious resurgence.
- It is often claimed that there is a near-global religious revival, but globalization may simply be rendering religion in politics more visible.
- The rise of the so-called Islamic State is linked to political instability following the Arab uprisings.

Religion and the State

The relationship of religion to politics in the developing world centrally informs the importance of state–church relations—that is, the interactions in a country between the state and the leading religious organization(s). A major difficulty in trying to survey existing church–state relations in the developing world is that the very concept of *church* reflects a somewhat parochial Anglo-American standpoint with most relevance to Western Christian traditions.

Extending the question of church–state relations to non-Christian and developing world contexts necessitates some preliminary conceptual clarifications—not least because the very idea of a prevailing state–church dichotomy is culture-bound (see Box 8.1). *Church* is a Christian institution, while the modern understanding of *state* is deeply rooted in the post-Reformation European political experience. Overloaded with Western cultural history, these two concepts cannot easily be translated into non-Christian terminologies. Some religions—for example Hinduism—have no ecclesiastical structure at all. Consequently, there *cannot* be a clerical challenge to India's secular state comparable to that of Buddhist monks in parts of South East Asia or of *mullahs* in Iran. However, political parties and movements energized by religious notions—such as Hinduism and Sikhism—have great political importance in contemporary India. Within the developing world, only in Latin America is it pertinent to speak of church–state relations along the lines of the European model. This is because of the historical dominance in the region of the Roman Catholic Church

BOX 8.1 RELIGION, NATIONALISM, AND IDENTITY

What is the relationship between religion and nationalism? The first point is that nationalism is a source of identity for many people in the developing world. Many identities are based on shared values, beliefs, or concerns that not only include religion, but also can extend to ethnicity, nationality, culture, and political ideologies (Gopin 2000, 2005). This does not imply that such expressions of identity are necessarily monolithic entities—because, in fact, *everyone's* self-conception is a unique combination of various identities that can include, but are not limited to, community, religion, ethnicity, nationalism, **gender**,

class, and family. Their relative importance and compatibility will differ at various times and circumstances. For example, race and religion are important sources of identity in some societies, while in others political ideologies and nationalism are judged to be of more significance. In short, both individual and collective senses of identity are socially constructed from a number of available traits and experiences, all of which are subject to interpretation. People *choose* their history and ancestry, and as a result can *create*, as much as *discover*, differences from others (Gopin 2000; Malek 2013).

and the creation of European-style states in the early nineteenth century.

The differences between Christian conceptions of state and church, and those of other world religions, are well illustrated by reference to Islam. In the Muslim tradition, *mosque* is not church. The closest Islamic approximation to 'state', *dawla*, means, conceptually, either a ruler's dynasty or his administration. (Only with the specific proviso of *church* as generic concept for 'moral community', *priest* for 'custodians of the sacred law', and *state* for 'political community' is it appropriate to use these concepts in Islamic and other non-Christian contexts.) On the theological level, the command–obedience nexus that constitutes the Islamic definition of authority is not demarcated by conceptual categories of religion and politics. Life as a physical reality is an expression of divine will and authority (*qudrah*). There is no validity in separating the matters of piety from those of the polity; both are divinely ordained. Yet although both religious and political authorities are legitimated Islamically, they

invariably constitute two independent social institutions. They do, however, regularly interact with each other. In sum, there is a variety of church–state relations in the contemporary world (see Box 8.2). Note, however, that this typology is not exhaustive, but instead identifies common arrangements.

In the *confessional* church–state relationship, ecclesiastical authority is pre-eminent over secular power. A dominant religion—Islam in the countries in Box 8.2—seeks to shape the world according to its leadership's interpretations of God's plan for humankind. However, confessional states are rare in the early twenty-first century. One of the most consistent effects of secularization is to separate religious and secular power almost—but not quite—regardless of the religion or type of political system. However, as events in Saudi Arabia after the country's creation in 1932, in Iran since the 1978–79 Islamic revolution, and in Sudan and Afghanistan from the 1980s indicate, several Muslim countries have sought to build confessional polities.

BOX 8.2 A TYPOLOGY OF CHURCH–STATE RELATIONS

Confessional	'Generally religious'	Established faith	Liberal secular	Marxist secular
Iran, Saudi Arabia, Sudan, Afghanistan (under the Taliban, 1996–2001), the so-called Islamic State (parts of Iraq/Syria, 2014–)	Indonesia, United States	England, Norway (until 2014)	Netherlands, Turkey, India, Ghana	China, Albania (until 1991), Russia (until 1991), North Korea

Because of Islam's pivotal role, the overthrow of the Shah of Iran in 1979 was one of the most spectacular political upheavals of recent times. (See the Online Resource Centre for a commentary on the issue of religion and politics in Iran.) The Shah's **regime** was not a shaky monarchy, but a powerful centralized autocratic state, possessing a strong and feared security service (SAVAK), and an apparently loyal and cohesive officer corps. Unlike earlier revolutions in other Muslim countries, such as Egypt, Iraq, Syria, and Libya, Iran's was not a revolution from above, but one with massive popular support and participation. The forces that overthrew the Shah came from all of the urban social classes, Iran's different nationalities, and ideologically varying political parties and movements. Nevertheless, when an Islamic Republic was eventually declared, the outcome of the revolutionary process was a clerical, authoritarian regime. In these events, the *ulama* (or Muslim clerics)—who adhere, like the bulk of Iran's Muslims, to the Shi'a tradition—played a central role. Organized in and by the Islamic Republican Party, they came to power, established an Islamic constitution, and dominated the post-revolutionary institutions.

Alongside the confessional states such as Iran or the so-called Islamic State (Iraq/Syria) there are the 'generally religious' states, such as the United States and Indonesia. These are guided by religious beliefs in general, but are not tied to any specific religious tradition. Both the United States and Indonesia have a belief in God as one of the bases on which the nation should be built. In Indonesia, under General Suharto (1965–98), such a belief formed one of the five pillars of the state ideology, *Pancasila*. This position is very similar to the notion of 'civil religion' in the United States. However, whereas the generally religious policy of religion in Indonesia is an official policy, civil religion in the United States is not formally recognized.

Then there are countries that have an officially established faith, but which are also socially highly secular, of which Norway (until 2014) and England are examples. Over time, the voices of the established churches in public policy issues have generally become increasingly marginal.

Next, and frequently encountered in the modern era, the liberal secular model encapsulates the notion of secular power holding sway over religion, with detachment and separation between church and state. Here, the state may try to use religion for its own ends, to 'legitimate political rule and to sanctify economic

oppression and the given system' of social stratification (Casanova 1994: 49). Secularization policies are widely pursued as a means of national integration in post-colonial multi-religious states, such as India. It is worth noting, however, that the concept of secularism is not necessarily straightforward. For example, Hindu critics of India's religiously 'neutral' Constitution contend that it is not neutral, but rather privileges India's religious minorities, including Muslims, Sikhs, and Christians.

In the liberal secular model, no religion is given official predominance. In fact, in vigorously modernizing countries such as India and post-Ottoman Turkey, state policies of modernization were expected to lead—inevitably—to a high degree of secularization; hence their constitutions are neutral towards religion. But things turned out differently: in recent years, democratization and secularization have worked at cross-purposes. Increasing participation in the political arena has drawn in new social forces in India—religious Hindus, Sikhs, and Muslims, who, in demanding greater formal recognition of their religions by the state, have been responsible for making religion a central issue in contemporary politics. In Turkey, the accession to power of the AKP in 2002—claiming to be the party of the poor and the alienated—suggests that even when secularization is pursued with great determination over a long period (in Turkey's case, for eighty years), there is still no certainty that, for important constituencies, the socio-political appeal of religion will wither. Indeed, the AKP, which does not call itself an 'Islamic' party, yet has some Islamist characteristics and credentials, achieved a landslide victory in the 2007, 2011, and 2015 elections, which underlined its wide and continuing appeal in Turkey.

Finally, there is the category of Marxist secular states. Before the overthrow of communism in 1989–90, Eastern Europe contained anti-religious polities in which religion was stifled by the state. Most Marxist regimes were less hard-line than Enver Hoxha's Albania—where religion was 'abolished'—but religion was typically permitted to exist only as the private concern of the individual. This constituted a kind of promise that the authorities would respect the people's religious faith and practice—as long as it remained behind closed doors. Skeletal religious organizations were, however, allowed to exist—but only so that the state could use them for purposes of social control. They were reduced to liturgical institutions, with no task other than the holding of divine services.

Numbers of permitted places of worship were greatly reduced.

Paradoxically, however, even the most strident and prolonged Marxist anti-religion campaigns failed to secularize societies. The pivotal role of the Christian churches in the democratic openings in Eastern Europe and non-Marxist Latin America in the 1980s and 1990s, and the contemporary revival of Islam in some of the formerly communist Central Asian countries, indicate that popular religiosity has retained immense social importance. But we should not take it for granted that Marxist, 'anti-religion' states are of only historical interest. For example, the government of China—home to more than a billion people—has presided over a continuing campaign to 'teach atheism to Tibetan Buddhists'. This was necessary, the Chinese government argued, to enable Tibetans to 'break free of the bewitchment' of religion.

In sum, none of the various models of church–state relations has been permanently able to resolve the tension between religion and the secular world. The chief manifestation of this tension in recent times is the desire of many religious organizations not to allow the state to sideline them as—almost everywhere—increasingly secularized states seek to intervene ever deeper into social life.

KEY POINTS

- 'Church' is a concept that derives from Christianity and may have little relevance in other religious settings.
- There are various relationships between church and state in the developing world.
- States often seek to secularize their societies, to the dismay of religious actors.
- No model of church–state relations has been able to permanently resolve tensions between the religious and the secular world.

Religion and Democratization in the Developing World

The question of how religious actors might affect democratization is controversial. Some scholars stress the importance of what they call **political culture** in explaining success or failure of democratization (Huntington 1991; Linz and Stepan 1996;

Stepan 2000). During the **third wave of democracy** (spanning the mid-1970s to the early 2000s), much attention was paid to the role of religion in democratization (Huntington 1991). For example, in Poland, the Roman Catholic Church played a key role in undermining the communist regime and helping to establish a post-communist, democratically accountable regime (Weigel 2005, 2007). This had a wider political effect beyond Poland, extending from Central and Eastern Europe to Latin America, sub-Saharan Africa, and parts of Asia. There was also the rise of the religious right in the United States from the late 1970s, and its subsequent impact on the electoral fortunes of both Republican and Democratic parties. Add to this the widespread growth of Islamist movements across the fifty or more countries that comprise the Muslim world, with significant ramifications for electoral outcomes in various countries, including Algeria, Egypt, Morocco, and Tunisia, electoral successes for the BJP in India, and substantial political influence over time for various 'Jewish fundamentalist' political parties in Israel and an Islamist party (Hamas) in the Palestinian territories, and we can see clear and sustained evidence of religion's recent democratic importance in many parts of the developing world.

Juan Linz and Alfred Stepan (1996), academics based in the United States, argue that religion is *not* generally a key explanatory factor explaining democratization outcomes in the developing world and elsewhere. In relation to Muslim countries, the late Fred Halliday (2005) argued that apparent barriers to democracy are primarily linked to certain shared social and political features. These include, in many cases, long histories of authoritarian rule and weak civil societies, and although some of those features tend to be legitimized in terms of 'Islamic doctrine', there is in fact nothing specifically 'Islamic' about them. On the other hand, for Huntington (1993, 1996a), religions have a crucial impact on democratization. He claimed that Christianity has a strong propensity to be supportive of democracy, while other religions, such as Islam, Buddhism, and Confucianism, do not.

But, in fact, religious traditions are not necessarily connected to specific political preferences. For example, we have noted that some assert that Christianity has close connections to democracy. However, the fastest growing strand of Christianity in parts of the developing world—notably, Latin America—is Pentecostalism. The doctrine behind Pentecostalism fits neatly into a neoliberal market globalism, which is known as the 'prosperity gospel'. This draws on various Christian scriptures that proclaim God's wish generally to bless humanity. In the world view of the prosperity doctrine, this centres on the idea that God's blessings take the form of material wealth and that, to achieve this goal, Pentecostalists and others believing in the prosperity gospel must 'bless' others—that is, literally give their money away, typically to a church—so that God can them bless them. In other words, Christians who give generously will get generous rewards in return. The point is that this fast-growing strand of Christianity tends implicitly to downplay the redemptive power of politics to change people's lives by focusing on the give-and-take relationship inherent in the prosperity gospel.

In terms of the relationship of religion and political change in the developing world, three key points can be made. First, religious traditions have core elements that are *more* or *less* conducive to democratization and democracy. Second, religious traditions may be *multivocal*—but, at any moment, there may be dominant voices more or less receptive to, and encouraging of, democratization. Third, religious actors rarely, if ever, *determine* democratization outcomes. However, they may, in various ways and with a range of outcomes, be of significance for democratization. This may especially be the case in countries that have a long tradition of secularization.

Religion, democratization, and the 'Arab uprisings'

The issue of religion's relationship to political change and democratization is central to the phenomenon of the 'Arab uprisings', perhaps the most significant and complex political development currently affecting the Arab countries of the Middle East and North Africa (see Chapter 14). In particular, both Tunisia and Egypt were significantly politically affected by the events of the Arab uprisings. Both saw Islamist parties take a leading role in the post-uprising political arrangements. Each country had a different outcome politically: Egypt had a military coup following a brief period of Muslim Brotherhood rule; Tunisia managed to weather the political tensions well, with democracy continuing. The political situation in Egypt since the military takeover in the summer of 2013 is particularly volatile. For both Islamists and secularists, this involves confronting questions of how practically to accommodate demands of faith, and at the same time

accept and develop democratic pluralism—a *sine qua non* for successful democratization. Both Tunisia and Egypt saw new and inexperienced governments coming to power, and having to face immediate and very difficult issues to try to resolve economic questions, including youth unemployment, the proximate cause of their political uprisings in the first place.

Today, both Egypt and Tunisia are in a changed political place, yet the contours and outcomes of their new political regimes are not necessarily firm or certain. Michael Wahid Hanna (2012), a US-based commentator, argues that, in Egypt, the electoral triumph of the Islamist Muslim Brotherhood has led to what he calls an 'ambush' style of decision-making. This is characterized by a fundamental lack of consensus and consultation, the antithesis of democratic politics and an unlikely starting point for further or fundamental democratization. However, things are not improved democratically by the actions of Abdul Fattah al-Sisi, former head of Egypt's armed forces, who came to prominence as a member of the Supreme Council of the Armed Forces, which governed after the fall of President Hosni Mubarak in 2013. He resigned from the military on 26 March 2014 to run for president, won the election, and then led a crackdown on certain opposition forces, including the Muslim Brotherhood.

Hanna's assessment vis-à-vis Egypt is similar to what observers noted in relation to Tunisia following the country's political upheavals. *Ennahda*, an Islamist party, was also said to govern via a 'no consensus, no consultation' approach. As in Egypt, this was a politically dangerous strategy that made development of democratic norms and values difficult to achieve. Critics also contended that this suggested a real danger of a new post-Arab-uprising period of authoritarianism, this time led by Tunisia's political Islamists. However, in February 2015, the secularist *Nidaa Tounes* party won eighty-five of the parliament seats, followed by *Ennahda* with sixty-nine seats. Both parties now rule in a coalition government, although *Nidaa Tounes* is the leading party. At the time of writing (late 2016), democracy endures in Tunisia.

To explain the different approaches to governing and democracy in Egypt and Tunisia, it is relevant to note that many among the current Islamists were, for decades, jailed or forced underground or into exile by *ancien régimes*. Certainly, the Islamists' rise to power was both swift and unexpected, while jail, harassment, or exile are not necessarily conducive environments in which to develop a democratic approach to politics. Yet the speed of their ascent to power was also their Achilles' heel, because it offered appropriate conditions for secularist actors to gain to power via the ballot box.

Religion in International Politics after 9/11

So far, we have been concerned primarily with the domestic interaction of religion and politics within developing countries. However, no survey of the issue can legitimately ignore the international dimensions of the issue, including relations between the West and Islamists, which were highlighted following impact of the **terrorist** events of 11 September 2001 (known as '9/11') and, most recently, the 13 November 2015 attacks on Paris and similar attacks in Brussels in April 2016.

Prior to the eighteenth century, and the formation and development of the international state system, religion was the key ideology that stimulated conflict between social groups. Following the Peace of Westphalia in 1648 and the consequent development of centralized states, however, religion took a back seat as an organizing ideology at the international level. As already noted, it was not until the Iranian Revolution of 1978–79 that religion resumed a significant political role. Ten years later, in 1989, the cold war came to an end. During the 1990s, there were 110 major conflicts—that is, conflicts involving more than 1,000 fatalities each. Only seven were inter-state wars, while 103 were civil wars. Of the latter, over 70 per cent are classified as communal wars—that is, wars among

ethnic and other national groups, with religion very often playing an important part.

Western Europe, including the United Kingdom, is characterized by both religious **privatization** and secularization. ('Religious privatization' arises when religious belief becomes primarily a personal matter and does not impinge significantly or consistently upon public political and social issues.) In contrast, over half of all US citizens claim to attend regular religious, mostly Christian, services. Moreover, eight words are juxtaposed—'In God We Trust' and the 'United States of America'—on all US currency, both coins and notes.

The issue of what role religion should play there was sharpened by the arguments of US academic Samuel Huntington (1996a) in his **clash of civilizations** hypothesis. Huntington's key argument is that, following the end of the cold war, future international conflicts are increasingly likely to be along cultural fault lines. Now, he suggests, new rivalries are most important—notably, between the (Christian) 'West' and the (mostly Muslim, mostly Arab) 'East'. In short, the core of Huntington's argument is that, in the post-cold-war era, the 'Christian', democratic West finds itself in conflict with radical Islam ('Islamic fundamentalism'), a global anti-Western political movement said to be aiming for fundamental changes to the political order. Another influential US scholar, Francis Fukuyama (1992: 236), argued that what he called 'Islamic fundamentalism' was the antithesis of Western **liberalism**, with 'more than superficial resemblance to European fascism'.

Critics of such arguments maintain that although many radical Islamist movements and political parties would not classify themselves as liberal democratic, we cannot assume that this necessarily implies that such actors are willing to engage in violent conduct, including terrorism, to pursue their aims. The 9/11 atrocities in the United States—as well as the Bali and Kenya terrorist incidents that followed—appear to have been carried out by a shadowy transnational terrorist group, Al Qaeda. However, it is by no means clear that most 'ordinary' Muslim men and women support either its goals or its violent methods.

It is also important to see the struggle in the Islamic world of groups such as Al Qaeda and the so-called Islamic State as directed against their own rulers, as well as the West. Since the beginning of Islam in the seventh century, Muslim critics of the status quo have periodically emerged to oppose what they perceive as unjust rule. Important contemporary Islamists—including, arguably, Osama bin Laden, the late leader of Al Qaeda assassinated by US covert action in May 2011—seek to portray themselves as the 'just' involved in struggle against 'unjust', 'anti-religious' rulers and their allies. Bin Laden's key goal was said to be the creation of a pan-Islamic state to revive the glories of the Ottoman caliphate that collapsed after the First World War. Al Qaeda certainly opposes Western interpretations of democracy, in which sovereignty resides with the people, because it is seen as a system that negates God's own sovereignty. Finally, it is suggested that Western support for so-called un-Islamic rulers in the form, for example, of French support for a military junta in Algeria in the 1990s and US support for Saudi Arabia's allegedly unpopular rulers led some radical Islamist groups to target the West.

In recent times, the earlier leader of jihad—Al Qaeda—has been superseded by the so-called Islamic State. The group is today's key global purveyor of religious terrorism. Following the collapse of **governance** in several countries in the Middle East, especially the previously strong states of Syria and Iraq, the group became a key regional disseminator of religious terrorism. Its appeal seems to be wide-ranging, even global. For example, over the last few years, around 700 British (Sunni) Muslims left the United Kingdom to join the so-called Islamic State. This marks a considerable change in the focus of Islamist terrorism from Al-Qaeda-style plots to cause mass casualties to smaller plots, possibly by people acting alone. It also highlights the centrality of Sunni–Shi'a rivalry in many Middle Eastern countries.

While Al Qaeda and the so-called Islamic State are different phenomena, their rise is attributable to the same cause. We can see the failure of state-sponsored modernization as a key explanation. Contemporary Islamist resurgence is argued to be a vehicle for popular disillusion with many governments in the Muslim world, which have failed to achieve what they promised—both developmentally and politically—since independence from colonial rule. In addition, existing communitarian structures have been confronted by state power that apparently seeks to destroy and replace them with the idea of a national (increasingly secularized) citizenry. Thus the widespread Islamic awakening can be seen in relation to its *domestic* capacity to oppose what are perceived as oppressive states: 'It is primarily in **civil society** that one sees Islam at work' (Coulon 1983: 49). The point is that this

domestic response does not necessarily translate into a wider Muslim threat to *global* order.

The issue of Islam in international relations was given additional focus at the April 2009 Durban Review Conference, the official name of the 2009 UN World Conference against Racism. The aim of the Conference was to review implementation of the Declaration and Programme of Action from the 2001 World Conference against Racism, Racial Discrimination, Xenophobia and Related Intolerance. Many Western countries boycotted the Conference, fearing that it would be used by some Muslim countries, such as Iran and Saudi Arabia, to promote anti-Semitism, laws against blasphemy (seen as contrary to key principles of free speech), and attacks against Western countries for alleged racism and intolerance, but without mentioning such problems in the developing world. Such fears were given credence by a speech from then Iranian President Mahmoud Ahmadinejad, who used the opportunity to attack Israel and to accuse the West of using the European Holocaust as a 'pretext' for aggression against Palestinians. His speech polarized opinion among his audience, with delegates from the European Union leaving the conference room, while a number of the remaining delegates applauded him.

In addition to Ahmadinejad's provocative utterances, the Catholic Church saw the election of new pope, which is always a controversial issue. Following his election in March 2013, Pope Francis quickly developed a high international profile, with much to say about the plight of a religious minority, Christians in the Middle East, United States–Cuba relations, and Israel–Palestine affairs. As conditions worsened for Christians and other minorities following the Arab uprisings and the associated empowerment of the so-called Islamic State in Syria and Iraq, Pope Francis responded with both public statements and dramatic gestures to challenge political leaders and enlist ecumenical allies for besieged Christians. During a visit to Turkey in 2014, he joined Patriarch Bartholomew I, leader of Orthodox Christianity, in pleading for religious freedom and protection for Christians in their homelands. Francis also wrote an open letter addressed to Christians in the Middle East that both highlighted their plight and encouraged them to try to deal with often worsening political, social, and economic conditions with fortitude. Francis highlighted the great importance of dialogue and inter-religious unity and noted that:

> ❝The more difficult the situation, the more interreligious dialogue becomes necessary. There is no other way. Dialogue, grounded in an attitude of openness, in truth and love, is also the best antidote to the temptation to religious fundamentalism, which is a threat for followers of every religion.❞

(Pope Francis 2014)

Direct diplomacy emerged as key feature of Pope Francis's papacy during the first few years. As one observer noted, while 'the Vatican has long practiced a methodical, discreet brand of diplomacy', Pope Francis sought to emphasize and re-establish 'a vision of diplomatic boldness, a willingness to take risks and insert the Vatican into diplomatic disputes, especially where it can act as an independent broker' (*New York Times* 2014) Francis's approach was exemplified in the key role he played in helping to resolve one of the most long-running of international disputes: poor and tension-filled relations between the governments of the United States and Cuba. Pop Francis sent letters to both President Obama and President Castro, inviting rapprochement. In addition, he took a leading role when he set up a secret meeting between the two countries at the Vatican that facilitated diplomatic openings and eventually, in 2015, the increasing normalization of relations between the two countries.

Finally, Pope Francis also made an attempt to reconcile relations between Palestine and Israel. In June 2014, the Vatican hosted President Shimon Peres of Israel and President Mahmoud Abbas of Palestine to pray together and discuss peace. This gathering, termed a 'prayer summit', featured Jewish, Christian, and Muslim prayers emphasizing common humanity and forgiveness. The meetings gained extensive news coverage, but no breakthrough. It highlighted the extraordinary level of energy that the 78-year-old pope brought to his international activities, while at the same time underlining yet again the vast differences that remain between Israel and the Palestinians, and their continuing lack of ability to resolve their decades-old dispute.

KEY POINTS

- Religion plays a central role in international politics.
- Most Islamic critics of the status quo see their own governments as the main cause of political and developmental failures.
- The terrorist attack of 9/11 is sometimes said to provide evidence of an emerging 'civilizational' clash between Christianity and Islam, but the majority of Muslims were appalled by these and related terrorist acts.

Conclusion

The last forty years have seen much involvement of religion in politics. A serious new threat to world order, some claim, now emanates from Islamist militancy, with 9/11 and subsequent attacks on Western 'targets', including the Madrid railway bombings of March 2004, the July 2005 London bombs, and the multiple Paris attacks of November 2015 and Brussels in 2016, among the most egregious examples. Following Samuel Huntington's hypothesis in the early 1990s that the world was about to undergo a period of civilizational conflict, these attacks suggest to many people that he was indeed correct, and that the world is now embroiled in a conflict based on divisions caused by fundamentally incompatible beliefs and values between the West and militant Islamists, which may amount to a serious threat to global order and the stability of international relations.

Globally, the recent political impact of religion falls into two, not necessarily mutually exclusive, categories. First, if the mass of the people are not especially religious—as is the case in many Western countries—then religious actors tend to be politically marginal. However, in many developing countries, most people are already religious believers. Unsuccessful attempts by many political leaders to modernize their countries have often led to responses from various religious actors. Religion frequently serves to focus and coordinate opposition, especially—but not exclusively—among the poor and ethnic minorities. Religion is often well placed to benefit from a societal backlash against the perceived malign effects of modernization. In particular, various religious actors have sought support from ordinary people by addressing certain crucial issues. These include the perceived decline in public and private morality, and the insecurities of life—the result of an undependable market in which, it is argued, greed and luck appear as effective as work and rational choice. Such concerns sometimes feed into a direct involvement of religion in democratization, although outcomes in this regard are variable, as the example of the Arab uprisings indicates.

And what of the future? If the issues and concerns that have helped to stimulate what some see as 'a return to religion'—including socio-political and economic upheavals, patchy modernization, increasing encroachment of the state upon religion's terrain—continue (and there is no reason to suppose that they will not), then it seems highly likely that religion's political role will continue to be significant in many parts of the developing world. This will partly reflect the onward march of secularization in many countries and regions, linked to the spread of globalization—which no doubt will be resisted by religious leaders and their followers, with varying degrees of success. For this reason, it would be very unwise to neglect religion in analyses of contemporary politics in the developing world.

? QUESTIONS

1.   What are the characteristics of religious resurgence in the developing world and how are they important politically?

2.   What is the relationship of religion and democratization in the developing world?

3.   Why does India, a constitutionally secular country, have a 'Hindu nationalist' government controlled by the Bharatiya Janata Party (BJP)?

4.   Are modernization and secularization the same thing?

5.   Does underdevelopment in the developing world increase the significance of religious actors or undermine them?

6.   Fifteen years after 11 September 2001 ('9/11'), is there a clash of civilizations as envisaged by Samuel Huntington?

7.   Why did 'Islamist' governments in Tunisia and Egypt rule for only short periods of time after the Arab uprisings?

FURTHER READING

Flanagan, S. (2010) *For the Love of God: NGOs and Religious Identity in a Violent World* (West Hartford, CT: Kumarian Press) The book examines the ways in which history and religious identity influence faith-based organizations in Lebanon, Sri Lanka, and Bosnia Herzegovina, and finds that they often reinforce, rather than transcend, schisms found in the larger society.

Fox, J. (2015) *Political Secularism, Religion and the State* (Cambridge: Cambridge University Press) Fox provides a nuanced analysis of the political competition between 'religionists' and secularists.

Freeman, D. (2012) *Pentecostalism and Development: Churches, NGOs and Social Change in Africa* (Basingstoke: Palgrave Macmillan) This book explains why, and shows how, Pentecostalism informs local-level development processes in sub-Saharan Africa.

Haynes, J. (2013) *Introduction to Religion and International Relations*, 2nd edn (Harlow: Pearson Education) A survey of how international relations is affected by religious global resurgence.

Huntington, S. P. (1996) *The Clash of Civilizations* (New York: Simon and Schuster) Articulates the hypothesis that the world is poised to enter an era of 'civilizational clashes'.

Kubicek, P. (2015) *Political Islam and Democracy in the Muslim World* (Boulder, CO, and London: Lynne Rienner) Kubicek investigates the extent to which 'Islamism' is a shared characteristic of Islamist political actors who gain power via the ballot box in recognizably democratic elections.

Roy, O. (2010) *Holy Ignorance: When Religion and Culture Part Ways* (London: Hurst) The secularization of society was supposed to free people from religion, yet individuals are converting en masse to radical expressions of faith, including Protestant evangelicalism, Islamic Salafism, and Haredi Judaism.

Woodhead, L., Partridge, C., and Kawanami, H. (eds) (2013) *Religions in the Modern World*, 3rd edn (London: Routledge) A very useful survey of the contemporary position of religion.

WEB LINKS

http://www.archive.org/details/iraq_911   A collection of archive video footage and films relating to the 11 September 2001 ('9/11') terrorist attacks against the World Trade Center and Pentagon.

http://www.csmonitor.com/   *The Christian Science Monitor* is a useful source of material on many aspects of religious politics, including in the developing world. It does not have a Christian bias in its coverage.

http://www.uga.edu/islam/   Offers Islam and Islamic studies resources.

http://as.vanderbilt.edu/religiousstudies/   Site of the Center for the Study of Religion and Culture at Vanderbilt University, Nashville, TN.

https://w2.vatican.va/content/francesco/en/letters/2014/documents/papa-francesco_20141221_lettera-cristiani-medio-oriente.html   Pope Francis's 'Letter to the Christians in the Middle East'.

For additional material and resources, please visit the Online Resource Centre at:
http://www.oxfordtextbooks.co.uk/orc/burnell5e/

9

Women and Gender

Vicky Randall

Chapter contents

Overview

Gender inequality is a key feature of politics in the developing as in the developed world. Feminism, both as a movement and as a lens, has helped to shape our awareness and response to these issues, although its perception as 'Western' has posed particular difficulties in a developing world context. This chapter begins by examining the social context and 'construction' of gender. It also looks at ways in which the state and politics more broadly have shaped women's experience. Subsequent sections look at the women's movement, with case studies based in Brazil, Pakistan, and South Korea, women's political representation, and women's policy issues. Whilst any discussion must emphasize the diversity of women's experience and whilst the way in which factors combine in creating opportunities for, or challenges to, greater gender equality is inevitably complex, some patterns do emerge, including the importance—at least in the longer run—of pressure 'from below', from women's movement activists themselves.

Introduction

Women comprise roughly half the world's population. Historically, their subordination to men (**patriarchy**) has been a near-universal fact, and any adequate account of contemporary **politics** needs to address **gender** inequality and the surrounding political struggles. This remains as true of the developed, as of the developing, worlds, the latter being the focus of this chapter. Within the **developing world**, the picture is complex. It is true that there have been gains in female political representation: in mid-2015, at the very apex of national power, there were more elected women rulers (see Table 9.1) than ever before, including the presidents of Argentina, Brazil, Chile, and South Korea; by October 2016, two of these, Kirchner and Roussef, had been replaced by men, but Taiwan had gained its first woman president, Tsai Ing-wen. There have been areas of policy gain, for example girls' education, while (formally, at least) notions of gender equality and women's rights have become more solidly entrenched. At the same time, major trends such as pro-market-driven welfare cutbacks, the resurgence of religious fundamentalism, and the surge in violent conflicts in Africa and the Middle East, and their spillover effects, have brought with them new forms of jeopardy.

Scholarly interest in women's distinctive experience of politics and policy has been strongly influenced by the emergence of second-wave **feminism** in the United States and Western Europe from the late 1960s. This has helped to provide the perspective(s) through which this experience is analysed, in terms of both its language, including the transition from sex to gender, and the questions asked. In the developing world, the perceived Western provenance of feminist ideas has, however, sometimes created problems. Feminism, as a perspective, has also struggled to do justice to the actual diversity of women's identities and experiences. This chapter will first consider women in their wider social and political settings. The following section will focus on the development and impact of feminism and women's movements. The two subsequent sections will examine women's political participation and representation, and policy for women, respectively.

Women in Society

The relationship between women, or gender, and political processes—everywhere, but perhaps especially in the developing world—is deeply embedded in wider social (including cultural and economic) processes. In fact, as feminists have pointed out, this is one area in which the boundaries between politics and society can seem particularly hazy and arbitrary. Before looking at more conventionally political issues of political representation, then, we need to consider women in social context and the social constitution of gender identity.

Table 9.1 Women elected political leaders in the developing world, 2015

Country	Title	Name	Year
Argentina	President	Cristina Fernandez de Kirchner	Since 2007
Bangladesh	Prime minister	Sheikh Hasina Wajed	Since 2009
Brazil	President	Dilma Roussef	Since 2010
Chile	President	Michelle Bachelet	Since 2014 (Previously 2006–10)
Jamaica	Prime minister	Portia Simpson-Miller	Since 2012
Liberia	President	Ellen Johnson Sirleaf	Since 2006
South Korea	President	Park Geun-Hye	Since 2013
Trinidad and Tobago	Prime minister	Kamla Persad-Bissessar	Since 2010

If inequality between men and women has been such a near-universal and persistent feature of social life, one major cause of this seeming intractability concerns the nature of male–female relationships and the fact that a key dimension is founded in intimacy—that is, in the family and the 'private', or domestic, sphere. This has created practical, logistical obstacles to women organizing on their own behalf, as well as psychological barriers. It has also legitimized state inaction. Feminists themselves have had to campaign to bring issues such as domestic violence or reproductive rights into the public domain.

Women and gender

While earlier analysts, including feminists, were happy to talk about men and women, or sexes, later feminists came to reject these terms as conservative, or 'essentialist', tending to depict women as sharing a distinctive, and to some degree biologically determined, nature. Instead, these later feminists advocated the language of male and female 'gender', to highlight the extent to which male–female differences are 'socially constructed', and thus also historically and culturally variable, rather than innate and constant (Beckwith 2005). The distinction also draws attention to the interdependence and power relations between male and female genders. By now, the language of gender prevails in social science and development policy alike—even if, in practice, it is often used rather unreflectively, simply to mean 'women'. In turn, this language has been criticized: some have seen its incorporation into government-speak and policy as a way of blunting, or deradicalizing, the feminist message (Sardenberg 2007). There may, in fact, be situations in which a simple focus on women is most politically effective.

The social construction of gender

An emphasis on gender potentially draws attention to the ways in which assumptions about gender identity, and thus women's experience, vary markedly from context to context, shaped by cultural and economic—as well as political—circumstances. Cultural influences take many forms, including through the content of mass media entertainment for instance, but a key source has been religion. Traditionally, organized religion has tended to prescribe highly differentiated gender roles; more recent processes of

secularization have been partial in their impact, on occasion going into reverse. So, for instance, despite the inroads of Pentecostalism, Latin America is still predominantly Catholic; whilst the Roman Catholic Church's proscription of birth control is increasingly disregarded, abortion remains illegal in most circumstances throughout the region, with the exception of Uruguay. In Muslim-majority countries (primarily in the Middle East and North Africa, but also including Indonesia, Malaysia, and Pakistan), women's role and rights are strongly influenced by **Sharia** law (see Chapter 8). In certain countries where Sharia is fully incorporated into state law, such as Saudi Arabia and (from the 1980s) Pakistan, this has entailed severe restrictions, famously including the ban on women driving in Saudi Arabia (see Chapter 11).

In conjunction with such cultural factors, the nature of the local economy also powerfully affects women's resources and opportunities. Clearly, both the relative wealth of the country and the degree of social inequalities will have an important bearing. But the kind of economy can also be relevant: Ross (2008), for example, argues that, contrary to received opinion, it is not the prevalence of Islam, but the economics of oil that has hindered progress to greater gender equality in the Middle East—specifically, the extent to which the process of oil production is associated with lower rates of women's employment. The developing world is also affected by global economic trends. A substantial feminist literature has explored the gender impact of neoliberal economics, for instance looking at women's role in the **export processing zones (EPZs)** that proliferated through the 1990s and which, by 2003, could be found in 116 countries, in which women have formed the majority of workers (Rai 2002), and more recently at the gender-differentiated effects of the 2007–08 global financial crisis.

Women and diversity

As the previous section illustrates, a focus on gender also underlines the diversity of women's identities and interests. Within feminist thinking, it has long been recognized that women are differentiated and potentially divided above all, perhaps, by social class, but also by such dimensions as ethnicity and religion. This is true even regarding the seemingly quintessentially female issue of giving birth. Vincent (2004: 73), for instance, notes: 'It is genuinely impossible to find any substantive common ground in the way in which middle-class white South African women and rural African women experience childbirth.' In recent years, a sizeable literature has emerged around this notion of other identities or axes of disadvantage, cross-cutting with gender—often referred to as 'intersectionality'— and its implications, for example, for experiences of exclusion or discrimination and for policy.

KEY POINTS

- Women's relationship to politics cannot be understood outside its social context.
- In recent years, the language of 'gender' has largely supplanted that of 'sex' differences.
- The social construction of gender has important cultural and economic dimensions.
- There is increasing recognition of the diversity of gender identity.

The State, Politics, and Women

If women's experiences, opportunities, and consciousness have been largely shaped by cultural and economic forces, they also been more directly affected by the nature of politics and the state. This can be illustrated by a brief chronological survey. Whilst views differ as to women's **status** in most pre-colonial societies, in many cases colonial rule brought new forms of exclusion and reinforced others. In parts of Africa, colonial officials helped to restrict women's access to land by first, in a projection of Victorian-era gender stereotypes, identifying men as farmers, but their women folk as dependants, and second reinforcing, through codification, the customary marriage laws that already gave male elders authority over women. In India, the new land settlements, beginning with the 1793 Permanent Settlement Act, which led to the increasing commercialization of agriculture, again had the effect of restricting women's agricultural role by sequestering common land and excluding women from cash-crop production (Rai 2002).

At the same time, colonizers often sought justification for their actions in terms of their 'civilizing mission', through which they would bring enlightenment to 'traditional' indigenous societies (see Chapter 2). In this discourse, the treatment of women frequently played an emblematic role. Hence British rulers in India criticized such practices as child marriage and polygamy. Most famously, they outlawed the practice of *sati*, or widow-burning, in 1829—although, given prevalent colonial attitudes towards women at the time, it is doubtful how far this was actually motivated by revulsion against its barbarity (Mani 1987). In some cases, colonial rule in its latter stages also entailed expanded educational opportunities for some, generally elite, women.

The rise of **nationalist** movements in opposition to colonial rule was similarly ambiguous for women. Such movements offered them many new roles and opportunities; indeed, women's movements have often originated in anti-colonial or nationalist mobilization (Jayawardena 1986). At the same time, although nationalist ideologies historically and regionally have varied widely, as Yuval-Davies (1997: 2) writes, a central and recurrent understanding has been that 'it is women . . . who reproduce nations, biologically, culturally, symbolically'. In such nationalist constructions, elements of women's emancipation might be promoted as evidence of the movement's modernizing, progressive character. Thus, after Kemal Ataturk had led the Turkish National Movement to victory against the Western allies and established the Republic of Turkey on the ruins of the Ottoman Empire, the Turkish Civil Code adopted in 1926 abolished polygyny, and gave husbands and wives equal rights in divorce and child custody; by 1934, women were enfranchised and had the right to be elected (Kandiyoti 1991).

But, sometimes simultaneously, in seeking to embody and preserve an authentic indigenous identity different nationalist projects also fostered much more conservative conceptions of women's place in society. Even India's relatively forward-looking nationalist movement, Chatterjee (1989) argues, in seeking to negotiate its relationship with modernity and the West, tended to distinguish between an outer, practical, material world of science and reform and an inner, more spiritual home (*ghar*), the sphere of true Indian consciousness. In this conception, '[t]he home in its essence must remain unaffected by the profane activities of the material world—and woman is its representation' (Chatterjee 1989: 624). Besides these cultural expectations, women could face constraints and pressures as biological reproducers of the nation, for example where nationalist policy demands rapid population growth, as in Brazil under military rule, or where concerns about the 'purity' (Israel) or quality (Singapore) of the population discriminate against groups seen as less desirable (Yuval-Davis 1997).

In newly independent states, varying nationalist ideologies continued to construct and confine women's roles and citizenship significantly. They generally shared a commitment to 'development', although understood in very different ways, whether through a Marxist or more liberal capitalist lens, again with gender implications. But there was also a widespread tendency for authoritarian forms of government, whether single-party or military, to emerge over time (see Chapter 14). Military governments, as in Nigeria, by their very nature repressed popular participation, but in addition their formal political structures were almost exclusively male, leaving women marginalized (Rai 2002). In Chile, under Pinochet, the *Centros de Madres,* which had begun to acquire some autonomy, was 'completely subverted to the needs of the state . . . and (P)olitical participation was discouraged as unfeminine' (Safa 1990: 359–60). There was clearly more scope for participation within single-party **regimes**, but on severely circumscribed terms. In such regimes in Africa, women's autonomous organizing was typically suppressed, with participation often channelled through the women's wing of the ruling party, and largely focused on mobilizing support and resources for the regime (Tripp et al. 2009).

Women and women's associations often played a key role in the movements for democratization that emerged from the 1980s. Waylen (1993), for example, describes the growth of community-based activities—such as soup kitchens and artisanal workshops—located outside conventional political **institutions** and in which women were significant players, which provided an arena from which to mobilize in the early stages of democratization in countries such as Brazil, Chile, and Peru. Closely related were women's campaigns to find their 'disappeared' menfolk—most famously, Argentina's Mothers of the Plaza de Mayo. Processes of democratization, in turn, could provide a political environment much more favourable to women's political participation and the women's movement. This included new or reinstated representative institutions, a democratic discourse that, influenced by international norms and inducements, increasingly stipulated women's political presence, and, to varying degrees, a chance to participate in the accompanying process of constitutional reform. In sum, processes of democratization helped once more to change, and in many respects improve, the **political opportunity structure** (see Chapter 11).

Post-conflict societies, often in the wake of brutal and bitter internal wars, in which internationally supported efforts to rebuild the state are under way have similarly offered opportunities for change, but also severe challenges. These challenges persist even though, more recently, international agencies and donors have emphasized the need to address gender equality issues, as embodied in Resolution 1325 of the United Nations Security Council, passed in 2000. Discussing the cases of Afghanistan and Iraq, Kandiyoti (2007: 504) describes how the new state institutions have possessed 'juridical sovereignty but little de facto power', to assert against the reality of powerful and conservative communal forces. In Timor-Leste, which in 1999 gained its independence from Indonesia after a bitter decade-long struggle, a particular barrier has been the continuing political and military dominance of the (male) leaders of the former resistance organizations, with their expectation that women resume their temporarily disrupted 'traditional' and politically marginalized roles (Niner 2011).

KEY POINTS

- Women's experience has been importantly shaped by politics and the state.
- Under colonial rule, policies and ideals of both colonial rulers and nationalist movements had ambiguous implications for women.
- Authoritarian rule in newly independent states offered women few opportunities for political participation. Women have since been extensively involved in movements for democratization, whilst post-conflict situations have more recently offered women opportunities, but also severe challenges.

Women's Movements and Feminism

Feminism has a long history; in the United States and Western Europe, it enjoyed a major resurgence from the 1960s that in turn fed into politics, policy, and academic analysis. It has taken very different forms and any attempt at definition is likely to be contested. However, most contemporary understandings see it as a doctrine that advances gender equality and promotes women's rights.

Defined in this way, in the colonial era, there clearly were already feminist voices in the regions to which we refer as the 'developing world', such as those of

Adelaide Casely-Hayford, Sierra Leone's mixed-race 'Victorian feminist' (Cromwell 1986), Bertha Lutz (1894–1976), who campaigned for women's right to vote (granted in 1931) and founded the Brazilian Federation for Women's Progress in 1922; and Huda Sharaawi, founder of the Egyptian Feminist Union in 1923. In the context of the emergence of the 'new **social movements**' discussed in Chapter 11, there was a resurgence of women's activism from the 1970s and especially the 1980s across a swathe of developing countries, but its characterization as 'feminist' became more problematic. In much of Africa, Latin America, India, and Pakistan, for instance, feminism tended to be seen as a primarily Western or foreign, and thus politically suspect ideology, although this probably underestimated the role of indigenous and regional sources. Many women activists themselves shared this view, but in addition recognized a need to avoid a term that could delegitimize their activities.

Accordingly, many activists, and those who study them, have preferred to talk about 'women's movements'. Tripp and colleagues (2009: 14), in their survey of women's movements in Africa, define these as movements or organizations that 'have named women as the primary constituency which they are mobilizing', and the central goals of which are 'the improvement of women's economic standing, political representation, cultural status and legal rights'.

The history and character of women's movements varies enormously, reflecting in part their very different social and political contexts, but common themes are also apparent. Before directly considering these similarities, it is instructive to look at three examples: the movements in Brazil, Pakistan, and South Korea—all countries that feature in the case studies section of this volume.

The women's movement in Brazil

Soon after the turn of the millennium, Mala Htun (2002: 733) wrote that 'Brazil has Latin America's largest, most vibrant and most diverse women's movement'. The women's movement that emerged there during the 1970s has sometimes been described as engaging in a 'dual militancy', mobilizing against both patriarchy and the combination of military rule and capitalism (Maluf 2011). Under the succession of military regimes from the mid-1960s, while conventional political participation was severely restricted, community movements in response to economic hardship and

threats to family survival 'brought hundreds of thousands of poor and working-class women into local political struggles' (Alvarez 1990: 43). At the same time, increasing numbers of middle-class women were entering higher education, many of whom went on to become leading cadres of the feminist movement (Alvarez 1990). There is no doubt that political exiles returning from Europe and the United States in the late 1970s had a significant impact both in transmitting feminist ideology and in encouraging autonomous women's organization, but there is still disagreement concerning their contribution's importance for the Brazilian women's movement.

A high tide of mobilization was achieved in 1979, with the First Brazilian Women's Conference, held in Rio, stimulated by the prospect of the genuine opening up of the party system. In 1984, following demands of the women's movement, a federal National Council for Women's Rights (CNDM) was established, under the Ministry of Justice, including representatives of the women's movement, political parties, and government, with corresponding councils at state and municipal level. The CNDM in turn was very successful in getting its demands incorporated in Brazil's new constitution in 1988, including provisions for equal rights in marriage, the expansion of paid maternity leave, access to family planning, and rural women's **entitlement** to co-ownership of land. The CNDM later languished, under the less sympathetic President Collor, but following further lobbying by the women's movement and the UN Women's Conference in Beijing (see later), it was revived in 2003 as the Special Secretariat of Public Policies for Women (SPM). The SPM was located within the President's Office, by newly elected President Lula da Silva of the Brazilian Workers' Party, thereby ushering in a new era of 'participatory state feminism' (Sardenberg and Costa 2010: 258). The women's movement also helped to secure the (voluntary) adoption of party **gender quotas** in 1995, although women's presence in the judiciary and representative political bodies—excluding the presidency, of course—remains surprisingly low.

As in other parts of Latin America, the notion of feminism has been problematic for Brazilian women activists. Back in the 1970s, many avoided it, whilst, it is alleged, other left-wing activists sought to project their own strand as the only legitimate feminism. The women's movement has always been extremely diverse and, from its peak of unity in the late 1970s, has tended to fracture. As part of this process, Maluf (2011) describes the growth of networks of thematically linked women's organizations, such as Catholic Women for the Right to Choice. In Brazil's polarized society, social class differences also remain divisive—a tendency reinforced, according to many, by the steady 'NGO-ization' (that is, involvement of **non-governmental organizations**) and professionalization of the movement (Lebon 2013).

The women's movement in Pakistan

Pakistan's women's movement has been strongly shaped by its relationship with Islam, on the one hand, and a frequently repressive state, on the other. Women's organizations in the early years of independence had tended to focus on welfare and education issues; although Pakistan had been established as a non-theocratic Muslim state, in practice Islam came to play a crucial role in the construction of Pakistani nationhood (Shaheed 2010). Even so, there were some promising developments, including a broadening of women's rights in marriage, employment, and family planning in the constitution adopted in 1973. The movement's transformation in the 1980s was not so much an attempt to expand women's rights and opportunities as a reaction to losing them. General Zia-ul-Haq, who declared martial law in 1977, proceeded to pursue a programme of Islamization in which women were the 'linchpin' (Khan 1999). The alarming case in 1981 of a man and woman accused under the *zina* section of the 1979 Hudood laws, which criminalized all consensual sex outside marriage, was the 'spark igniting activism' (Shaheed 2007: 98). The Women's Resource Centre (*Shirkat Gah*), founded in 1975, called a meeting that led to the formation of the Women's Action Forum (WAF), to protest against the severe sentences meted out (death by stoning for the man, who was married, and 100 lashes of the whip for the woman). Subsequently, the WAF, which was inevitably largely made up of employed, middle-class, urban women, tended to focus on legislative change, campaigning on the issue of violence against women and, with the ending of martial law and re-emergence of party competition, for women's political representation. Partly as a result of pressure from the WAF and other women's organizations, gender quotas were adopted in local government elections (33 per cent) in 2000, and in provincial and national assembly elections in 2002.

Since Zia's death in 1988, successive regimes (see Chapter 19) have provided a somewhat varying political and cultural environment for women's activism—the prime ministerial terms of Benazir Bhutto (1988–90 and 1993–96) and presidency of Pervez Musharraf (2001–08) were relatively benign—but no overall dramatic improvement. A central issue for the movement has been its relationship with Islam. Inevitably simplifying—and recognizing that 'relatively few women in Pakistan self-identify as feminists' (Shaheed 2007: 94)—there are two broad approaches for feminists in Muslim countries: secular feminists, although Muslim, emphasize legal and women's or **human rights** arguments; Islamic feminists draw their arguments from religious sources, challenging patriarchal interpretations of key Islamic texts (Badran 2002). Although the WAF initially framed its demands through an Islamic discourse, in 1991 it declared itself secular. Whilst defenders of this stance stress the need to offer an alternative to the dominant Islamic discourse (Zia 2009), critics have suggested that it risks alienating other women's groups and the mass of poorer, rural women, and that a human rights framework presupposes the state as an effective and liberal agent of change, when in fact the state may be 'the, or one of the, main adversaries' (Shaheed 2007: 115).

By the late 1990s, WAF activism was suffering from burnout and internal divisions. At the same time, and especially in the wake of 9/11 and the so-called **war on terror**, women's organizations have increasingly adopted, or reverted to, an Islamic framework. As in Brazil, the movement has also experienced a process of NGO-ization, with women's organizations becoming steadily more 'donor-dependent' and even 'donor-driven'. This could be seen as a form of deradicalization, although Shaheed (2007: 106) suggests that this trend 'helped to sustain the movement in ways that were not possible on the strength of purely voluntary activism'.

The women's movement in South Korea

South Korea's women's movement is seen as one of the most successful in the region in terms of achieving favourable legislation. But it has to contend with the legacies of an authoritarian state, on the one hand, and a weak grass-roots base, on the other. Originating in the 1900s, the movement really gained strength only in the 1980s. Women's employment rates and educational levels had been rapidly rising through the 1970s, but, prior to democratization, women's organizations had tended to be administered mass organizations (AMOs), controlled and used by the state (Moon 2002). The new women's organizations were initially closely tied to the broader People's Movement, identified with the struggle for democracy and working class interests. In 1987, twenty-one of these more autonomous women's organizations came together to form the Korean Women's Associations United (KWAU), one immediate trigger being the revelations of Kwon Insook, a female student who disguised herself as a worker whilst supporting the labour movement and was sexually assaulted by the police. But it was not until the early 1990s that KWAU established greater independence from the People's Movement, with the slogan 'Together Yet Separate', and more fully embraced its identity as an autonomous feminist umbrella organization (Shin 2008).

Initially, women's organizations focused on women's working conditions; Korea's Equal Employment Opportunity Act was passed in 1987. They also took up the issue of sexual violence and campaigned against Korea's distinctive patrilineal family head (*hoju*) system, finally abolished in 2004 (Lee and Chin 2007). In particular, by the mid-1990s, KWAU, which had earlier been campaigning against the government, was working with state institutions and political parties as, with democratization and international influences such as the 1995 Beijing Women's Conference, these became more sympathetic. In 2003, a Ministry of Gender Equality was established; in 2004, political parties were obliged to adopt a form of gender quotas in selecting their candidates for national assembly elections.

Despite these undoubted achievements, there are fears that with greater institutionalization, the movement's radicalism, or progressive character (*jinbo*), has diminished. Increasingly, '[s]ocial activists have become bureaucrats and the division between government and social movements has become blurred' (Kim and Kim 2011: 392). In 2005, the Ministry of Gender Equality became the Ministry of Gender Equality and the Family (its title seems to have changed back and forth several times). The influence of the former women's AMOs, with their larger memberships, tended to grow at the expense of KWAU and family policy took a more conservative direction, reflecting fears about 'families in crisis' and a falling birth rate.

Common trends: Global and domestic institutionalization

These three profiles illustrate the greatly varying experiences of women's movements in developing countries, in terms of the main battles that they are having to fight and the resources at their disposal. In contrast to Brazil and Korea, for instance, Shaaheed (2007: 89) notes poignantly that, in Pakistan, there are few university contexts or journals in which feminists can discuss the deeper issues of feminism; such debate as there is tends to be 'confined to drawing rooms' or conducted 'on the run, between urgent campaigns, protests and picket lines'. There are nonetheless common themes. One already noted is the difficulty raised by the Western connotations of 'feminism', reported in all three countries; another is movement fragmentation or, more positively, diversity. This has probably gone furthest in Brazil, with the growth of issue networks and, at the same time, new vigorous movements around black, lesbian, and transgender identities (Maluf 2011).

Most strikingly, all three movements have been affected—albeit in different forms—by the related processes of global and domestic institutionalization. Going back at least to the first UN Women's Conference in Mexico City in 1975 (see Table 9.2), the international women's movement has had some success in embedding its concerns in the policies and institutions of international bodies—notably, the United Nations. One key development has been the adoption, in 1979, of the Convention on the Elimination of All Forms of Discrimination against Women (CEDAW), ratified to date by 189 states (although not including the United States and, in more than fifty cases, with significant reservations). Another has been the exhortation to national governments to set up 'national women's machinery' to monitor and improve women's status, first in the Forward-Looking Strategies for the Advancement of Women adopted after the 1985 Women's Conference and then as part of the Platform for Action adopted at the 1995 Beijing Women's Conference, which also advocated gender **mainstreaming** across all government institutions, rather than concentration in a bespoke unit (which is discussed later in the chapter).

These international developments have been one influence behind the parallel institutionalizing trend within national women's movements—that is, a tendency for formerly autonomous, or independent, women's organizations to become increasingly

Table 9.2 Milestones in international organization and policy for women

Year	Development
1975	First UN World Conference on Women in Mexico City
1979	Adoption of CEDAW by UN Assembly
1980	Second UN World Conference on Women in Copenhagen
1985	Third UN World Conference on Women in Nairobi Adoption of Forward-Looking Strategies for the Advancement of Women
1994	Adoption of Inter-American Convention on the Prevention, Punishment and Eradication of Violence against Women
1995	Fourth UN World Conference on Women in Beijing Adoption of Beijing Declaration and Platform for Action
2000	Adoption of UN Security Council Resolution 1325 on women and peace and security Third Millennium Development Goal (MDG) to promote gender equality and empower women
2003	Adoption of African Union's (Maputo) Protocol on the Rights of Women in Africa
2010	UN Women established
2012	World Development Report on Gender Equality and Development

integrated into and/or dependent upon the state or international donor bodies. To some extent, this is an inevitable process in social movements (see Chapter 11) as their initial momentum falters, activists suffer from burnout, and so forth. It also offers new resources and sources of authority. But it also often means that leading women activists are absorbed into the new institutions, thereby weakening the autonomous movement. Given their dependence on the state or donor bodies, these women have less control over the agenda and the way in which issues are framed, raising the strong possibility of deradicalization.

KEY POINTS

- In the developing world, feminist ideas go back to the colonial era, although the label 'feminist' has often been problematic.
- A comparison of the cases of Brazil, Pakistan, and South Korea indicates the variety of women's movement experiences in terms of resources and key sites of struggle.
- Common patterns nonetheless include internal diversity, the context of global feminist institutions, and the trend towards increasing absorption into women's state machinery and NGOs.

Political Representation and Participation

We have seen that women in the developing world have played a significant role in national movements, community and 'new' social movements, and more directly in democratizing movements directed against authoritarian regimes. With the emergence, in many developing countries, of more genuinely independent political parties and democratic representative institutions (see Chapter 14), interest grew in increasing women's participation and representation in the formal political sphere. This new focus was not without tension for women's movements, with many deeply mistrustful of political parties and the state, but it echoed a trend in feminist activism in established democracies. There was also growing international encouragement, especially following the 1995 Beijing Women's Conference, and increasing support from **democracy assistance** programmes.

In pursuing the goal of increased female political representation, women activists have used a range of arguments. It is urged on grounds of fairness. There have also been claims about the particular qualities that women could contribute to public politics. In many Latin American and African countries, this has been framed in terms of women's maternal nature—the language of the 'supermadre' or, as uncompromisingly expressed in the slogan of one Botswana women's organization, 'Vote [for] a woman! Suckle the Nation!' (Tripp et al. 2009: 26). Women have also been presented as less tainted by political machination—that is, as less corrupt. Finally, and importantly, it is claimed that, given their common, if historically determined, experiences, only women can properly represent other women's distinctive interests. As a coda to this, activists have taken up the thesis of 'critical mass', maintaining that, to be effective and extend beyond mere 'tokenism', women's representation needs to reach a certain level, often specified as around 30 per cent (which was actually adopted as a target by the 1995 Beijing Conference).

In fact, many of these arguments have been latterly queried, not least by feminist scholars themselves. For example, the suggestion that women politicians are necessarily less corrupt has been criticized both as essentialist and unwarranted by the evidence (Goetz 2007). Rather than a critical mass, some have argued that the vital need is for 'critical actors' (Childs and Krook 2009). In any case, those seeking to increase women's representation have looked to other, more practical, means.

Political parties are often vital 'gatekeepers': some women have benefited from the sponsorship of individual party leaders, while Htun (2004) describes how, in Latin America in the 1980s and 1990s, the parties' women's sections, formerly largely channels for mobilization, became more active in supporting women candidates, citing the example of Mexico's National Action Party (PAN) National Secretariat for the Political Promotion of Women during its 1997 and 2000 elections. Studies in Western countries have long noted that leftist parties tend to be more supportive—a tendency also evident in Latin America, although with little relevance in Africa or much of Asia.

Studies in the West have similarly stressed the role of electoral systems, with party-list forms of proportional representation seen as especially conducive, but this again seems less relevant in sub-Saharan Africa (Krook 2010). However, a factor that seems relevant almost everywhere is the adoption of gender quota systems, the subject by now of an extensive cross-national literature. Gender quotas were first adopted in Norway in the 1970s and then taken up in a series of Western European countries. Subsequently, their use has spread almost worldwide, especially following their endorsement by the 1995 Beijing Women's Conference. By 2014, they had been adopted in 118 countries (International IDEA 2014). Whereas originally, in European countries, their adoption tended to be gradual and voluntary, in the developing world, typically, they have been 'fast-tracked' by governments (Dahlerup and Friedenvall 2005).

Gender quotas have taken many different forms. They may be adopted by individual political parties, either voluntarily or at the state's behest; alternatively, they may take the form of reserved seats in the legislature. There is much debate concerning which of these forms is most effective in terms both of increasing the numbers of women elected and of increasing the likelihood of women-friendly legislation. Clearly, gender quotas should not be regarded as a panacea. There are a number of cases, for example in Uganda under Museweni (Muriaas and Wang 2012), in which effectively authoritarian regimes have adopted and manipulated them to increase their own apparent democratic **legitimacy**. Yet even then their adoption can provide women with a valuable opportunity.

Rates of representation

Partly as a consequence of these measures, overall rates of women's representation in the legislatures, and also provincial and local assemblies, in developing countries have risen remarkably. In fact, by 2014, those in the national parliaments of Rwanda (64 per cent) and Bolivia (53 per cent) had overtaken those in Sweden (44 per cent) (see Table 9.3). However, as Table 9.3 makes clear, levels of representation differ markedly. Adoption of gender quotas is certainly a factor, especially in conjunction with being in a post-conflict context, as in Rwanda, South Africa, and Mozambique.

Clearly, women are less well represented in executive positions, although even here there has been gradual improvement. As noted at the start of this chapter, by 2015, the political leaders of eight developing countries were women. According to the Inter-Parliamentary Union (IPU 2015), by January 2015, worldwide only 17.7 per cent of government ministers were women—a 3.5 per cent increase on 2005. Only one developing country featured in the five among which women ministers reached over 30 per cent: Cabo Verde, off the coast of West Africa. At the same time, five of the eight countries with no women ministers were in the developing world: Brunei, Pakistan, Saudi Arabia, Tonga, and Vanuatu. Women ministers'

Table 9.3 Women's political representation (selected countries)

Rank	Country	% of women in national parliament (lower or single house)	Year	Year of adoption of gender quotas	Form
1	Rwanda	64	2013	2003	Reserved seats
2	Bolivia	53	2014	1997	Legislated party quotas
5	Sweden	44	2014	1980s	Voluntary quotas in some parties
7	South Africa	42	2014	1995	Quotas in the ANC (party)
12	Mozambique	40	2014	1994	Quotas in FRELIMO (party)
18 =	Mexico	37	2015	1996	Legislated party quotas
36	Sudan	36	2015	2008	Reserved seats
38	United Kingdom	29	2015	1997	Voluntary quotas in Labour Party
45	Iraq	27	2014	2005	Legislated party quotas
57	China	24	2013	1973	Reserved seats
68	Pakistan	21	2013	1973	Reserved seats
75	United States	19	2014	–	–
85	Indonesia	17	2014	–	–
88	South Korea	16	2012	2004	Legislated party quotas
99	Guatemala	13	2011	–	Voluntary party quotas
105	Syria	12	2012	–	–
107	India	12	2014	–	–
116	Brazil	10	2014	1997	Legislated party quotas
132	Nigeria	6	2015	–	–

portfolios globally tended to remain concentrated in social areas (welfare, health, education), but with a gradual increase in other areas of responsibility, such as economic or legal affairs.

Consequences of women's descriptive representation

Feminist scholars have been particularly interested in the relationship between women's **descriptive representation**—that is, the extent to which their numbers in elected political office mirror their share (around 50 per cent) of the population at large—and their **substantive representation**—that is, the promotion of

their interests. There is no automatic reason for assuming that women representatives will either wish or be able to pursue women's interests. Context is clearly relevant; larger numbers—the critical mass argument—may, in the right circumstances, make it more likely. The most sophisticated argument for the 'politics of presence' has been developed by Phillips (1995), combining the ideas that some experiences are distinctively gendered and that, since issues may be clarified in the very process of representation and deliberation, women need to be present in that process.

But this raises the further issue of what we mean by women's interests both in general and in a developing world context. A major difficulty already noted is the diversity of women's status, resources, and experience; many issues—class, religion, ethnicity—appear to cut across their shared identities as women. In practice, the notion of women's interests has been strongly influenced by feminist thinking. One influential distinction advanced by Molyneux (1985), reflecting on the case of Nicaragua, is between practical and strategic women's interests. She suggests that practical interests are 'given inductively', arising from 'the concrete conditions of women's positioning within the gender division of labour' and 'are usually a response to an immediate perceived need' (Molyneux 1985: 233). Especially amongst poorer women, they are likely to focus on issues of family welfare and public provision. Strategic interests are identified deductively in terms of what is necessary to overcome women's subordination and these correspond most closely to a feminist agenda, including such issues as reproductive rights, freedom from male violence, and political gender equality.

It remains very hard to say whether increased descriptive representation for women brings greater substantive representation—that is, not only more favourable legislation and policy, but also improved policy implementation and outcomes. It is very difficult to separate out the effect of rates of female representation from other relevant factors and there is little systematic cross-national evidence from developing countries to go by. Research has indicated that women deputies in both Argentina and Honduras are more likely than men to prioritize women's rights, as well as issues concerning the family and children. In sub-Saharan Africa, with increased women's parliamentary representation, it has become much easier to get women's issues, such as land rights, **HIV/AIDS**, and domestic violence, onto the public political agenda, although this is less the case in Mozambique. Devlin and Elgie (2008) consider the case of Rwanda, where the rate of female parliamentary representation has risen swiftly to the world's highest in 2013, at 64 per cent. A substantial body of legislative reforms has accompanied this rise, although Devlin and Elgie (2008) note that the bulk of this was already in place before the surge in women's representation in 2003 from 26 to 49 per cent; between 2003 and 2008, the major achievement was the 2006 Law on the Prevention, Protection and Punishment of Any Gender-based Violence, which provides a legal definition for the rape of an adult women and makes polygamy illegal. Women deputies played a major part in getting this through.

KEY POINTS

- Activists, governments and scholars have increasingly emphasized women's political participation and representation.

- This has been justified on a range of grounds, whilst specific mechanisms—parties, electoral systems, and especially gender quotas—have been seen as particularly conducive.

- Rates of women's political representation have accordingly risen, although the impact on women's 'substantive' representation is difficult to ascertain.

Women and Policy

This final section looks more directly at the factors affecting policy related to women. As we have seen (in Table 9.2), a significant influence on the development of policy has been the internationalization and institutionalization of women's movement objectives. In addition to the conferences and measures—notably, CEDAW—already described, the United Nations has established its own **women's policy machinery**, the latest incarnation of which is UN Women, established in 2010. At the same time, there have been important regional developments, including the adoption in 1994 of the Inter-American Convention on the Prevention, Punishment and Eradication of Violence against Women, and the adoption by the African Union (formerly the Organization of African Unity, or OAU) in 2003 of the Protocol to the African Charter on Human and Peoples' Rights on the Rights of Women in Africa, usually referred to as the 'Maputo Protocol'. By 2013, thirty-six out of fifty-four African countries had signed up to the Protocol.

Against this background, a succession of states has incorporated commitments to gender equality in their constitutions. By 2011, this included over 80 per cent of countries worldwide (Cassola et al. 2014). Despite all of the difficulties surrounding implementation, such constitutional provisions are arguably important not only in symbolic terms, but also as a basis both for new legislation and for challenging existing laws that appear to be in contravention. When we come to consider the reality of policy and policymaking in developing countries, however, it is necessary to distinguish between different areas and types of policy. We also need to reflect on aspects of the process—the

institutional context and the strategies employed, including how an issue is framed—all within the wider context of political opportunities and resistance.

Policy areas and types

As with the notion of 'women's interests', the defining and itemizing of women's issues or policy is slippery and controversial. Waylen (2007) distinguishes between 'gender-neutral' issues that significantly affect both women and men, although perhaps in different ways, such as poverty or the environment, and those that particularly impact on women or on relations between men and women. But within those primarily affecting women, one could add that policies may have different implications for different subgroups of women.

In practice, discussion of women's issues has largely focused on a number of specific areas (some of which overlap): education; health and reproductive rights; employment, income, and resources; rights in marriage; freedom from sexual violence and **exploitation**; and—of growing concern as we have seen, partly as a perceived means of approaching the others—political rights. The priority attached to different areas and policies favoured within them are clearly influenced by the discourse and more material inducements of international agencies, but the actual issues that come to the fore at any given time will vary with the local context, as the case studies of Brazil, Pakistan, and South Korea have already illustrated.

The policy process

The way in which these issues are taken up is in part a function of the political opportunity structure, as discussed earlier. We have seen that certain conjunctures, for example during the process of democratic transition or in the aftermath of violent internal conflict when new constitutional arrangements are being put in place, present particular opportunities for constitutional innovation. Similarly, democratic discourse provides a legitimizing context for the introduction of women's representative claims. The converse is that the situation may include (many) elements that deter or constrict promotion of women's issues or gender equality—such as fundamentalist religious institutions and beliefs, and strongly patriarchal customary law.

Those seeking to advance gender equality will have different available strategies to choose from. One important aspect of this process is the way in which the issue is 'framed' (see Chapter 11). Issues are initially framed so

as to appeal to the shared understanding of the communities being mobilized, but, as they are taken up within the policy process, there will be a tendency for them to be reframed in ways more compatible with dominant interests and ideology. As but one example, we can consider Heo's (2010) discussion of how the women's movement in South Korea successfully campaigned to bring the issue of domestic violence, long regarded as a purely private matter, onto the public political agenda. Since dominant Confucian values prioritized the family, placing greater value on its survival than on the interests, or rights, of its individual members, the women's movement framed the issue in terms of 'the preservation of the family'—a theme with strong cultural resonance and to which the media quickly responded. This approach was ultimately successful in that it resulted in the 1997 Act against Domestic Violence, but it also represented a concession to more conservative ways of thinking and may have contributed in the longer term to the movement's deradicalization.

One increasingly influential way of **framing** women's issues is in the language of rights. This has always been an aspect of liberal feminist thinking. In a post-Soviet and, to an extent, post-socialist world, especially following the 1993 Vienna Human Rights Conference (see Chapter 18), the human rights approach has also become a central element of leftist ideology. Accordingly, in addition to demanding 'women's rights', feminists launched the slogan 'Women's rights are human rights', implicitly placing women's claims within the mainstream human rights agenda. This language of rights has been promoted by the United Nations' women's conferences and adopted by many women's NGOs. At the same time, its emphasis on the rights of the individual resonates with neoliberal thinking. It can therefore seem like a very powerful rhetorical tool; however, some have suggested its limitations in a developing world context (Grewal 1999). It can seem more relevant to elite, than to poorer, women; it can lack local legitimacy and can clash with understandings of what is private. At the same time, rights claims tend to look to the state as the means of redress, when the state itself may be the source of, or at least complicit in, injustice. More practically, rights claims imply a focus on the judiciary, and the need for suitably trained and sympathetic legal actors, including judges, all of which may be unrealistic.

As this reference to the judiciary reminds us, the policy process also entails different institutional arenas through which policy is determined and implemented. An important development, against the background of the 1985 and 1995 UN Women's Conference pro-gramme, has been the nearly worldwide adoption of national women's policy machinery. This machinery has varied widely in the forms it has taken, from a mere 'desk' to a government ministry, in its location, for instance in the president's office or as a bureau within a broader ministry, and in the resources it has enjoyed. We have seen that in both Brazil (in the form first of the CNDM, then the SPM) and South Korea (the Ministry of Gender Equality), these agencies have played a significant policymaking role. Waylen (2007) has also highlighted the contributions of Servicio Nacional de la Mujer (SERNAM) in Chile and of the Office of the Status of Women (OSW) in South Africa.

In practice, the situation has been very fluid. Women's machinery can lose the confidence of their key constituency, can suffer from cuts in staff and other resources, and can find their fortunes dependent on particular political leaders, as was said to be the case of Argentina's Consejo Nacional de la Mujer under President Menem in the 1990s. There have also been extensive debates concerning the most effective way of advancing women's interests within government. By the 1990s, the view was gaining ground that, rather than concentrate policymaking for women in one, possibly ghettoized, institutional location and in particular policies, it was better to promote 'gender mainstreaming', thereby ensuring, in the words of the 1995 Beijing Platform for Action (paragraph 189), 'a gender perspective in all policies and programmes'. To the extent that this approach has been adopted, however, new concerns have emerged that ordinary government actors will fail to identify with the gender equality agenda and will simply go through the 'box-ticking' formalities.

Besides this 'state feminism' route, women's policy agendas have been pursued, as already described, through the route of elections and legislation, and also, where this is an option, through the law courts. Particular types of policy may require the cooperation of specific government agents for their effective implementation. For instance, the enforcement of laws against domestic violence devolves on the (predominantly male) police, who may themselves be indifferent or unsympathetic. Both in India and in many Latin American countries, a recent response has been to set up all-women police stations; by 2010, there were 475 in Brazil.

Overall, the likelihood of success in pursuing a women's policy agenda will depend on a complex interplay of factors, including the nature of the issue, as we have seen. Two examples among many would be girls' access to education (see Box 9.1) and women's right to choose (abortion) (see Box 9.2). An effective state, provided that its support can be enlisted, is likely to be important, as is the way in which the issue is framed. But most accounts agree that an essential, if not sufficient, ingredient is sustained bottom-up pressure from the 'grass roots' women's movement.

BOX 9.1 POLICY FOR WOMEN: GIRLS' EDUCATION

Education has been a key issue for feminism, going back to Mary Wollstonecraft, if not earlier. Article 10 of CEDAW commits member states to establishing women and girls' equal education rights with men. Eliminating gender disparity in primary and secondary enrolment rates has also been a Millennium Development Goal (MDG 3.A). In the 2030 Agenda for Sustainable Development adopted by the United Nations in 2015, Sustainable Development Goal (SDG) 4 aims to ensure inclusive and equitable quality education for all, whereas SDG 5 concerns gender equality and empowerment of all women and girls. By the 1990s, girls' combined enrolment rates in primary and secondary education had risen to 87 per cent in Latin America and 83 per cent in East Asia. Here, feminist concerns are more likely to focus on the content, than on participation rates. However, average enrolment rates still remain much lower in South Asia and Africa. Female enrolment is especially low, even at primary level, in Pakistan and Afghanistan.

In many parts of the developing world, governments have recognized girls' education as emblematic of a modernizing country and a response to women's changing economic roles; it has not been particularly controversial. In the poorer countries, such as Bangladesh, from the 1990s at least, the World Bank has offered significant funding in partnership with local NGOs. In contrast, girls'—and boys'—education has elsewhere been severely disrupted by civil war; in southern Sudan, in 2010, only 2 per cent of girls were completing primary school, the majority dropping out because of early marriages, or to take on domestic chores or contribute to family income (Holmarsdotir et al. 2011). Girls' education has also been regarded with suspicion within more conservative Islamic societies and actively opposed by Islamic militants, as highlighted by successive poison gas and acid attacks on schoolgirls in Afghanistan, and the shooting of Malala Yousafzai in Pakistan in 2012.

BOX 9.2 POLICY FOR WOMEN: ABORTION—WOMEN'S RIGHT TO CHOOSE

Although in some ways the definitive issue for radical feminism, a woman's right to choose whether or not to have an abortion has paradoxically been an extremely divisive issue for women themselves. Arguments about the need to decriminalize and provide easy access to safe abortion have come up against doctrines asserting the sanctity of all human life. Powerful forces opposed to liberalization have included the US government from the 1970s, the Vatican, and, to varying degrees, the governments of Muslim majority nations. This was apparent, for example, in the deliberations of the world population conferences in Mexico City in 1984 and in Cairo in 1994. International agencies such as the World Health Organization (WHO) and the World Bank have been cautious in approaching the issue, and it is not directly addressed in CEDAW.

In practice, liberalization has gone furthest in Communist countries—China, Cuba, and more recently Vietnam. India and South Korea have also had relatively liberal laws for several decades. Within the Muslim world, Turkey and Tunisia, and periodically Iran, have been exceptional in allowing

non-therapeutic abortions (that is, not only when the mother's life is endangered). Within Latin America, where the Roman Catholic Church remains a major influence, apart from Cuba, only Uruguay (since 2012) has offered access to safe abortions. In countries in which the law has been liberalized, issues remain for feminists about the cost and quality of actual provision. In China and India, additionally, there are concerns about parents' use of sex-selective abortions to ensure that they have boy children.

In these circumstances, women's groups campaigning for abortion reform have faced severe challenges. Blofield (2008) suggests that it is as much a class, as a gender, issue; richer women can usually access private abortion provision, which is safe, if illegal, whilst for poor women, illegal abortions are much riskier. Women therefore need to mobilize across the class divide. In addition, they may find allies within the medical profession and sections of the legal profession; where this is relevant, they may also fare better in the presence of strong left-wing political parties.

KEY POINTS

- With increasing promotion of women's movement objectives through global women's machinery, more than four-fifths of states now include a commitment to gender equality in their constitutions.

- When considering the chance of promoting specific policy issues, account must be taken of the political opportunity structure, the type of issue, and the way it is 'framed', as illustrated by the contrasting examples of girls' school education and abortion policy.

Conclusion

Patriarchal values and practices have been a legacy of earlier times worldwide. Within developing countries, they have been distinctively shaped by such factors as colonial norms and extremes of inequality and poverty. Over the last half-century at least, attitudes have been slowly changing, in part associated with women's political mobilization. This has been reflected in the thinking of international institutions, which have in turn encouraged policies to promote greater gender equality. Individual developing nations have nonetheless presented very varying contexts within which to pursue this agenda. As we have seen, there has been considerable progress in such areas as women's political representation and girls' access to education, but much slower advance in others, particularly regarding contentious issues such as abortion law reform. The factors affecting policymaking and outcomes in these different areas are numerous, complex, and liable to vary according to the kind of issue concerned, but one constant necessary, if not sufficient, condition appears to be pressure from below from an active women's movement.

? QUESTIONS

1. With specific reference to the developing world, consider how far the idea of the 'social construction of gender' enhances our understanding of women's experience.

2. Compare and contrast the women's movement in Brazil, Pakistan, or South Korea with that in one of the other nine case study countries in this volume. (You will need to do some independent research to answer this question.)

3.   Assess the contribution of gender quotas to women's descriptive and substantive representation in the developing world.

4.   Under what circumstances have women's national machineries in developing countries been most effective in pursuing a gender equality agenda?

5.   Do women have a distinctive contribution to make to public political life in the developing world?

6.   To what extent have feminist causes in the developing world benefited from being framed in the language of human rights?

7.   Do women share identical policy interests? Discuss ways in which one might analyse women's interests in terms of ethnicity, race, class, or other factors.

8.   Do women in the legislature expand the policy agenda and address gender inequalities? Why—or why not?

 FURTHER READING

Basu, A. (ed.) (2010) *Women's Movements in the Global Era: The Power of Local Feminisms*, (Boulder, CO: Westview) Updated overview of national women' movements across the world, written by women who have themselves been active participants.

Cornwall, A., Harrison, E., and Whitehead, A. (eds) (2007) *Feminism in Development: Contradictions, Contestations and Challenges* (London and New York: Zed Books) Thoughtful reflections on feminist issues in the field of development studies.

Rai, S. M. (2002) *Gender and the Political Economy of Development: From Nationalism to Globalization* (Cambridge: Polity) Helpful overview of the field of political economy from a gender perspective.

Tripp, A. M, Casimiro, I., Kwesiga, J., and Mungwa, M. (2009) *African Women's Movements: Changing Political Landscapes* (Cambridge: Cambridge University Press) Excellent overview of women's movements in Africa.

Waylen, G. (2007) *Engendering Transitions: Women's Mobilization, Institutions and Gender Outcomes* (Oxford: Oxford University Press) Authoritative analysis of women's contribution to, and the implications for women of, democratic and economic transitions in Latin America, South Africa, and Eastern Europe.

Yuval-Davis, N. (1997) *Gender and Nation* (London: Sage) Influential exploration of the gender implications of nationalism.

 WEB LINKS

http://www.amnesty.org   Amnesty International, with a global campaign to stop violence against women.

http://www.awid.org   Association for Women's Rights in Development (English, Spanish, French).

http:/www.bridge.ids.ac.uk/   Development-Gender, Brighton Institute of Development Studies, University of Sussex, offers 'cutting-edge' packs on trade, migration, citizenship, participation, and other issues.

http://www.globalfundforwomen.org   Global Fund for Women (English, Spanish, French, Portuguese, Arabic).

http://www.ipu.org   The Inter-Parliamentary Union (IPU) is an up-to-date source for women's political representation in national representative institutions.

http://libarts.wsu.edu/polisci/rngs   Research Network on Gender Politics and the State.

http://www.sewa.org   Self-Employed Women's Association, India.

http://www.un.org/womenwatch   United Nations gateway on women's advancement and empowerment.

http://www.un.org/womenwatch/daw   United Nations Division for the Advancement of Women.

http://www.undp.org/women/   The United Nations Development Programme (UNDP) Women's Empowerment home page.

http://www.unifem.org   United Nations Development Fund for Women (UNIFEM).

http://www.wedo.org   Women's Environment and Development Organization (WEDO).

http://www.who.int/gender/en/   World Health Organization (WHO) Department of Gender, Women, and Health.

http://www.wluml.org   Women Living under Muslim Laws (WLUML).

http://www.womensenews.org   A website and source of daily news about women.

http://www.worldbank.org/gender   World Bank Gender home page.

 For additional material and resources, please visit the Online Resource Centre at:
http://www.oxfordtextbooks.co.uk/orc/burnell5e/

10

Civil Society

Marina Ottaway

Overview

The expression civil society has metamorphosed during the 1990s from a relatively obscure concept familiar mostly to scholars of Marxism to become a mainstream term freely used by social science analysts in general, and by practitioners in the international assistance field specifically. Several factors contributed to these developments. First, there was growing interest in the United States and many European countries in promoting democracy abroad at that time. The demise of the Soviet Union and the Eastern European communist regimes triggered a wave of more or less successful democratic transitions further afield, where regimes formerly influenced by the Soviet model, and often by the Soviet government, struggled to transform themselves into something both more acceptable to their populations and less anachronistic internationally. This wave of political transformations provided an opportunity for the industrialized democracies to actively promote the spread of political systems similar to their own. As international actors devised democracy promotion strategies, they focused much effort on promoting citizen participation and activism—what quickly came to be known as a vibrant civil society.

Another factor was the changes taking place in the established democracies themselves. Many organizations of what used to be called broadly 'the left', inspired by socialist or social democratic ideals of socio-economic equity and justice, were replaced by newer groups, whose concept of justice extended beyond the traditional concerns of socialist parties and labour movements. They embraced a broad array of causes such as environmental protection and sustainability, opposition to globalization, and protection of gay rights (see Chapter 11). The old left was rooted above all in political parties and labour unions; the new activists were organized in smaller, non-governmental organizations (NGOs), often loosely tied in broad networks that saw themselves as the embodiment of a mobilized civil society.

Disenchantment with the performance of state institutions was an additional factor, as political leaders made concerted efforts to narrow the functions of government, and to enlarge the spheres of the private and non-profit sectors. At the same time, the corruption and inefficiency of many developing countries' governments prompted international development agencies to rethink the assumption that development required state intervention. As a result, they sought ways in which to bypass governments and implement some development projects and programmes through NGOs.

Needless to say, the popularization of the concept of civil society has led to a blurring of its meaning. It has also led to a blurring of its political connotations: a greater role for civil society is now extolled by conservatives, liberals, and radicals alike as a crucial component of political, and even economic, reform. Analysts of different persuasions do not agree about which organizations should be considered part of civil society and which should not, but they all agree that civil society is a good thing.

Introduction: Defining 'Civil Society'

Defining **civil society** is difficult because the term is laden with theoretical assumptions, unsolved problems, and value judgements. According to Hegel's (1942 [1821]) oft-cited, but ultimately unsatisfactory, definition in his *Philosophy of Right*, civil society comprises the realm of organizations that lie between the family, at one extreme, and the state, at the other. While superficially clear and logical, this definition generates a lot of conceptual confusion and some political booby traps. The result is that very few scholars, and virtually no practitioners of **democracy promotion**, now accept such a broad definition in practice, even if they may cite it.

Intellectual conundrums

The definition is clear on one point: civil society is not the whole society, the entire web of social **institutions** and relations, but only one part of it. The problem is how to define that part with any degree of precision. Citing the realm of voluntary associations between the family and the state does not provide sufficient clarification. Three problems deserve special attention in terms of:

- distinguishing organizations that are truly voluntary from those that are not;

- determining whether all voluntary organizations between the family and the state deserve to be considered civil; and

- determining whether there is a conceptual difference between civil society and political society, as some argue, or whether this is a distinction with little analytical value that has gained currency for reasons of political expediency.

The concept of 'voluntary association' contains ambiguities, particularly when applied to the less formal organizations that constituted civil society in the past and which remain important in the **developing world**. According to definitions that stress civil societies' voluntary character, a civil society group is a formally constituted association of which individuals become members as part of a completely free choice. A club, for example, is undoubtedly a voluntary association; the family is not, because membership in it is not chosen. There is, however, a grey area of groups in which membership is not formally compulsory, but neither is it completely a matter of free choice. Religious associations offer one example. Very often, people are born into a church or another type of religious association by virtue of having been born in a family, and inertia explains continued membership; in other cases, membership in a religious group is a truly voluntary choice.

Similarly, people are born members of a clan, tribe, or ethnic group, but membership in an organization that claims to represent that group is a political choice made voluntarily and deliberately by some, but by no means all, members of that particular group. South Africa provides a telling example of how membership in an ethnic group can be an accident of birth or a voluntary decision to join a group. In the early 1990s, at a time of intense fighting between the supporters of Inkatha, a political party with a Zulu **nationalist** agenda, and other black South Africans, ethnic Zulus who did not support the party and its agenda referred to Inkatha supporters, but not to themselves, as Zulus.

The ambiguities even extend to organizations that appear at first sight to be clearly voluntary, such as political parties. In the early twentieth century, many Europeans were born as members of social democratic parties, figuratively, because of their families' allegiances, or even literally, being delivered by 'midwives' paid by the party as a service to their members. Membership was voluntary in that anybody could stop paying dues and quit the party, but, for many, membership became part of an identity acquired at birth. A contemporary example of this phenomenon is offered by Sudan, where major religious brotherhoods, into which people are born when families belong, have formed political parties to which adherence is equally automatic, although not compulsory.

Another common problem in determining whether an association is voluntary arises in relation to ruling political parties and the mass organizations that they control. Membership in the party or mass organization is rarely compulsory, but the absence of membership has negative consequences and many are forced to join. One of the difficult tasks faced by the United States as the occupying power in Iraq in 2003 was to distinguish between committed members of the Ba'th Party, who were part of the defunct **regime** of Saddam Hussein, and those who had joined so that they could keep their jobs.

A second thorny problem in determining the boundaries of civil society is ideological in nature, hinging on the interpretation of the word 'civil', which can mean both 'relating to citizens or the general public' and 'civilized'. The expansive definition of civil society as comprising all voluntary associations between family and state is based on the first meaning. For many, this is an unacceptable approach, because it combines in one category, for example **human rights** groups and **terrorist** organizations. In practice, the term 'civil society' is almost invariably used to denote organizations that share certain positive, 'civil' values. But there is no consensus on that point. During the 1980s, Scandinavian countries considered the organizations fighting **apartheid** in South Africa to be 'civil' and provided support. The United States defined them as terrorist organizations and refused to help; Nelson Mandela, the much-acclaimed first president of post-apartheid South Africa, was once considered a terrorist by the United States. Many liberals or radicals have no problem accepting labour unions as organizations of civil society, but are often reluctant to see a federation of employers in the same light.

Another controversial issue influenced by political and policy consideration is whether it is valid to draw a distinction between civil and political society. Those who defend the distinction, first made by Gramsci (1929–35, in his *Prison Notebooks*), admit that both civil society and political society play a political role and seek to influence policy decisions. But the political role of civil society is indirect: civil society groups do not aspire to control the government and exercise power, but see their role as that of influencing policies in the public interest; political society organizations—essentially, political parties—want to control the government. A corollary of this view is that the civil society is virtuously dedicated to giving citizens a voice, while political society is power-hungry, self-interested, and considerably less virtuous. A second corollary is that international agencies seeking to promote democracy can and should provide assistance to civil society organizations; supporting political society, which aspires to power and thus is partisan by definition, would be morally questionable and could also represent unjustifiable interference in the domestic **politics** of another country.

The distinction between civil and political society has theoretical justification. Its usefulness, however, is scant, because most civil society organizations are, overtly or covertly, more partisan and political than they claim to be. It is true that there are organizations of civil society that act purely as pressure or advocacy groups and have no intention of contesting public office—but civil society activists are often close to specific political parties, and many move freely between civil society organizations and parties. Furthermore, many political parties, including some in power, set up organizations of civil society in an attempt to capture some of the assistance that is available only to civil society organizations.

Examples of the blurring of the lines between political and civil organizations exist in most countries,
although more pronouncedly in some than in others.
Civil society organizations may be pushed into close alliance with political parties by government repression.
Many **non-governmental organizations (NGOs)** in
Zimbabwe, for example, developed during the 1990s
as bona fide, non-partisan civil society organizations
lobbying for improved human rights, constitutional
reform, better legal services for the poor, and a variety of similar causes. As the government turned increasingly repressive, violating laws and human rights
principles to stay in power, civil society organizations
increasingly became part of the political opposition.
Formally organized NGOs operating at the national
level are particularly likely to become politicized when
confronted by a repressive regime. Less formal, local
groups, sometimes referred to as 'community-based
organizations' (CBOs), rarely become openly political. These CBOs are usually concerned about local-
level development and welfare issues, focusing on
service delivery or simply self-help.

Politics and expediency

The abstract problems of how to define 'civil society'
remain a source of debate among academics, but in
the meantime civil society is being defined in practice by the policies of bilateral and multilateral aid
agencies, by the governments of countries receiving
democracy assistance, and by civil society organizations themselves.

Bilateral and multilateral international aid organizations define the boundaries of civil society when
they decide which organizations are eligible for assistance under democracy promotion programmes or
which should be consulted in the preparation of an
assistance strategy. This definition is based on a mixture of political considerations and administrative
requirements. The major political requirement is that
such organizations focus their activities either on civic
education or advocacy for human rights and democratic reform. Civic education programmes, particularly common in countries in the early stages of
political transition, seek to convey the basic meaning
of democracy, as well as to teach about the political
and **institutional** mechanisms of democratic systems.
In its more sophisticated, advanced form, civic education is also training for political activism: citizens are
encouraged to scrutinize the action of politicians, to

lobby them to enact reforms, and to hold them accountable by voting them out of office. Advocacy organizations that attract international support focus on
human rights, women's rights, legal reform, judicial
reform, and, occasionally, environmental sustainability. To be part of civil society thus means to belong to
one of these types of organization.

The aid agencies' definition of civil society is further narrowed by their administrative requirements.
The groups must be organized in a formal way because donors cannot provide support for an organization that is not registered in some way, does not have
a name and address, or cannot be audited. Informal
networks or vaguely organized civic movements may
play an important part in a society or a democratic
transition, but they do not meet donors' needs and
few foreign funders will provide support for them
on even an exceptional basis. For example, during
the apartheid era in South Africa, some Scandinavian
countries exceptionally agreed to provide assistance
to informal organizations affiliated to the African National Congress (ANC). For practical reasons, donors
also prefer to deal with organizations that speak, literally and figuratively, the same language.

As a result, the donors' civil society is an entity very
different either from the society at large or from civil society as the realm of voluntary organizations between
the family and the state. The term 'civil society' as used,
and financed, by the international aid agencies refers
to 'a very narrow set of organizations: professionalized
NGOs dedicated to advocacy or civic education work
on public interest issues directly relating to democratization, such as election monitoring, voter education,
governmental transparency and political and civil rights
in general' (Ottaway and Carothers 2000: 11).

Direct funding of civil society is not the only way
in which international assistance agencies support
that society. The influence of NGOs is strengthened
by the requirement, under which many agencies now
operate, that they consult with local civil society in
implementing a wide variety of development and democracy aid programmes. The World Bank has such
civil society requirements and many bilateral agencies
also hold wide consultations. In practice, many of the
groups so contacted are the same organizations that
the assistance agencies helped to set up or fund in the
first place—the ones that they know and which are capable of sending representatives to meetings.

The governments of countries that are recipients of
democracy assistance also try to shape the definition

of civil society by imposing registration requirements, which are sometimes very strict and used to prevent the formation of antagonistic organizations. Many also try to limit access to donor funding to only some categories of organization or to prevent it outright. Some international agencies are willing to circumvent such regulations and provide funding covertly; others are more anxious not to antagonize the government.

Civil society activists have also played a very important part in determining which organizations are recognized as part of civil society. Transnational networks of NGOs, usually led by the better funded groups of the industrialized countries, have been particularly influential here. For example, some networks successfully pressed the United Nations to accept their presence at international meetings; the World Bank agreed to undertake re-evaluations of some of its practices, particularly lending for the construction of dams, and to consult with the NGO sector before reaching decisions on certain issues. And, in the early 2000s, oil companies in Chad were required to pay royalties into specially controlled funds in which they were administered under strict controls with the participation of civil society organizations (a requirement that was, however, rescinded by parliament in December 2005). These examples are counterbalanced by more numerous examples in which the militancy of transnational civil society networks has failed to earn them recognition as rightful participants.

KEY POINTS

- The widespread agreement about the importance of civil society is accompanied by a great deal of controversy about what civil society is, not only among theorists, but also among practitioners.
- The term has been given a concrete meaning by the policies of international assistance agencies and, to a lesser extent, by the efforts of civil society organizations.
- Many governments in developing countries use a very restrictive definition of civil society, which includes organizations delivering health services, for example, but not human rights organizations.

Traditional and Modern Civil Society

It is common for donors to bemoan the weakness, or even the absence, of civil society in countries in which they try to promote democracy. This concern

has spurred governments of industrialized countries, as well as international NGOs and private foundations, to launch an array of civil society assistance programmes to strengthen what is invariably referred to as a 'fledgling' civil society. In many instances, even after years of effort, donors express concern about the slow progress of civil society development and its continuing need for support (see Box 10.1). Paradoxically, in the countries in which civil society is deemed at its weakest, for example in war-torn African countries, the population relies for survival on civil society networks that go well beyond the family, and which reveal a high degree of sophistication and organization. One of the problems faced by countries undergoing political upheaval is that some civil society networks quickly establish themselves in major fields of economic activity and even within parts of the government. The criminalization of the state that has been witnessed in **failing states** in West and Central Africa is the result of the disparity between the power of civil society organizations and that of a duly constituted government and administrative structure.

These considerations point towards the need to put the discussion of civil society in a broader perspective. Following the current use of the term, the discussion so far has dwelt on 'modern' civil society—that is, the part of civil society organized into formal, professionalized NGOs typical of industrialized societies today. But in all countries, including the industrialized ones, there is another civil society: 'traditional society'. This society is organized more informally, often through networks

BOX 10.1 POPPY GROWERS AND THE AFGHAN STATE

Poppy cultivation for heroin production has become the most important economic activity in Afghanistan since the overthrow of the Taliban in 2001. In 2006, an estimated 2.9 million farmers, or 12.6 per cent of the population, grew poppies. During this time, poppy growers could obtain production loans from illegal organizations controlling the illicit trade, but farmers growing legal crops could not obtain loans through government banks or extension services. Poppy cultivation generated more than US$3 billion in revenue in 2006, while the government could generate only about US$300 million in custom and tax revenue, and foreign assistance brought the country's total budget to only US$600 million.

rather than formally structured organizations, and often following patterns that existed in earlier times.

Traditional forms of civil society exist in most countries, particularly when the state is weak. Organizations that are traditional in form do not necessarily perform only traditional roles; on the contrary, they grow in new directions in response to contemporary needs and requirements. West African Sufi brotherhoods such as the Mourides are ancient, but when they establish control over the wholesale rice trade in Senegal, or set up mechanisms to help members to emigrate to the United States and find jobs there, they are performing definitely non-traditional functions in response to new challenges.

Modern and **traditional civil society** stand in inverse relation to each other. In countries in which the state is strong, traditional civil society is weak and **modern civil society** is strong. If the state is weak, so is modern civil society, but traditional civil society is strong (Migdal 1988). This explains the paradox outlined earlier: in countries in the throes of a difficult, state-weakening transition, citizens rely on civil society networks in many aspects of their lives even as donors bemoan the weakness of civil society. The lack of understanding or appreciation for the role of traditional civil society organizations can have significant negative consequences: donors seek to form and support 'modern' organizations while neglecting existing traditional ones that are already providing services and could become even more effective with some support. Micro-finance projects, for example, do not usually build on the rotating credit associations on which many people already rely.

Traditional civil society

Organizations of civil society have taken a great variety of forms traditionally, from the very informal to the highly structured. Loosely structured, but culturally sanctioned, mechanisms for swapping labour and joining efforts in the performance of large collective tasks exist in all societies, as do more structured mechanisms, for example the rotating credit associations that exist, under different names, almost everywhere (see Box 10.2).

Compared to modern ones, traditional civil society organizations were less specialized and formal. They were extremely unlikely to have full-time organizers and certainly not offices. Even in industrial countries, the professionalization of civil society—hence its separation from the society at large—is a recent phenomenon. When Alexis de Tocqueville visited the United States in the first half of the nineteenth century and wrote *Democracy in America* (published in two volumes, in 1835 and 1840), he was struck by the American propensity to form intermediate associations in the pursuit of a wide range of interests and projects; he was looking at loosely structured, ad hoc groups, not at formal organizations with professional staffs.

Modern civil society, defined as a set of NGOs, has clear boundaries that separate it from the family and indeed from the rest of society, as well as from the state. The expression 'members of civil society' refers to a rather small number of people who belong to, and very often work for, such NGOs, not to all citizens. Traditional civil society has no such clear boundaries, but fades into the larger society at one extreme and

BOX 10.2 FROM ROTATING CREDIT ASSOCIATIONS TO MICRO-CREDIT

Rotating credit associations exist in all countries and provide loans, usually small, to people who do not have access to, or who do not trust, banks. Members of such associations pay a small fee to the association every week and every week one of the members, in turn, receives the entire amount. Women use such credit associations to capitalize small businesses such as a food stand or the raising of chickens, to pay school fees, or to finance a celebration. Shoeshine boys in Addis Ababa use the system to cover the costs of a can of polish or a new brush.

The modern, formal variant of the rotating credit association is **micro-credit**. The Grameen Bank in Bangladesh pioneered the idea. The bank grants small loans to clients—predominantly women—who cannot offer collateral and thus cannot obtain loans from a normal commercial bank. Repayment of the loan is ensured by a group of guarantors, who are not entitled to receive loans themselves until the original borrower has repaid his or her loan. The idea has been replicated widely across the world. The founder of the Grameen Bank, Muhammad Yunus, was awarded the Nobel Peace Prize in 2006 for his pioneering work on micro-credit. More recent studies, however, have called into question whether micro-credit truly lifts most borrowers, particularly women, out of poverty or, like rotating credit associations, is simply a survival mechanism.

non-state forms of political authority on the other. In non-state societies, **governance** was an extension of the overall social organization, not the activity of specialized institutions.

The blurring of the lines between the society at large, more organized associations within it, and political authority is not completely a thing of the past, but can reappear in extreme situations of **state collapse**, as in Somalia (see Box 10.3).

Traditional civil society performed important economic activities that today are considered to be the responsibility of state authority. For example, long-distance trade was once organized and carried out through private civil society networks that extended over long distances. States took over much of the responsibility for protecting trade routes and otherwise making large-scale economic activity more feasible. In places where the state has collapsed or is severely weakened, civil society is again taking on some of those functions. This has been the case in the Democratic Republic of the Congo (formerly Zaire) since at least the 1980s, for example.

Traditional civil society and the state in the contemporary world

Some traditional forms of civil society exist even in the industrialized countries and they pose no problem. On the contrary, they contribute to the reservoir of what Putnam (1993) calls **social capital**. When traditional forms of civil society grow very strong as a result of the weakness or total collapse of the state, however,

they can become highly problematic. Traditional civil society in the contemporary world is both indispensable and dangerous. Where the state is incapable, it can help people to survive and maintain a semblance of normal life under very difficult conditions. But, in the absence of a strong state, civil society networks can also turn into criminal organizations—a source of power and domination for an oligarchy—and prevent the rebuilding of the state and the introduction of democratic forms of governance (Migdal 1988: 24–41). In extreme cases, as in Libya after the overthrow of the Qaddafi regime, organizations that started as a result of citizens' efforts to overthrow a dictator have turned into armed militias that are a threat to citizens and prevent the unification of the country under a single government.

The benign side of the reappearance of traditional civil society is apparent every day in countries in which government is unable to perform functions expected of a modern state. The government cannot fund schools for all children and civil society responds by setting up alternative schools. (This also happens in some industrialized countries: the Charter School movement in the United States is a civil society response to the failure of many urban public school systems.) The formal economy cannot provide jobs for everybody and civil society develops an informal sector that provides the livelihood of the majority of the population. State collapse forces banks to close and civil society responds by setting up informal systems. In the Arab world, the *hawala* system moves money rapidly and efficiently across continents and into remote villages.

But the line between beneficial and predatory forms of civil society can be thin. In Iraq and Syria, the so-called Islamic State, which has imposed its rule on regions that the governments of the two countries no longer control, is now taxing money transfers through the *hawala* system. Hence the informal system that helps people to survive is contributing to the finances of the terrorist organization that makes their lives miserable in the first place.

There is also a much more malignant side to the reappearance of traditional civil society, because it can further undermine the failed state institutions for which it is trying to compensate. During the transition from apartheid in South Africa, a weakened government lost its capacity to enforce the laws that kept peddlers away from the business district of Johannesburg. Informal sector businesses took over the sidewalks, to

---

BOX 10.3 ISLAMIC COURTS IN SOMALIA

In the power vacuum created by the collapse of the Somali state, and the failure of the United States and the United Nations to secure an agreement among warring clans and **warlords**, clan elders and ad hoc organizations tried to provide order and structure. Among these organizations were the Islamic courts, which sought to impose order and administer justice on the basis of a strict interpretation of **Sharia** law. First appearing in the early 1990s, these courts slowly organized into a Union of Islamic Courts. By 2006, the Islamic courts were well armed and competing for control over the country with an official, but powerless, government, which had emerged from negotiations backed by the **international community**.

the benefit of the people who were trying to make a living by selling vegetables and braiding hair on the street. But the informal marketplace also became the territory of criminal gangs, legitimate businesses were driven out, and the once-thriving business district became a 'no go' area.

And parts of the civil society that flourish because of the absence of the state may be hostile to efforts to revive it. The trading networks that form in war-ravaged countries respond to a need, but they can also become profitable organizations that resist the efforts of the new, stronger government to revive institutions. Vigilante groups, such as those that operate in many parts of Nigeria, are a civil society response to insecurity—but they tend to turn into criminal organizations that end up by preying on those they were supposed to defend.

> ## KEY POINTS
>
> - Traditional forms of civil society exist in all countries, but they do not necessarily perform traditional functions.
> - When the state is weak, traditional civil society tends to be strong.
> - Traditional forms of civil society help to alleviate certain problems created by the weakness of the state, but they can also prevent the strengthening of the state.

The Modern State and Civil Society as a Specialized Entity

The rise of civil society as an entity separate from the broader society and from the state is part of an overall process of specialization that has affected all social and political institutions, particularly in the latter part of the twentieth century. This specialization of functions has been accompanied by a formalization of the organizations that discharge those functions.

In developing countries as well new, specialized and professional organizations have proliferated, often as a result of the availability of funding by foreign donors who believe that such organizations can generate social capital, represent interests and demands, and provide services. Unfortunately, this is not always the case.

Consider first the widely held expectation that civil society organizations would generate social capital. This concept was first set forth by Putnam (1993) in

a study of regional government in Italy, as an explanation of why the same institutions functioned differently in the north and south of the country. He observed that the inhabitants of the northern region shared a civic culture rooted in earlier experiences with self-government and sustained over the centuries by a rich associational life. These attitudes constituted the social capital that determined the way in which people viewed government and related to its institutions. This social capital was scarce in the southern regions, which had both a different historical experience and a dearth of associational life.

It is open to question to what extent the more specialized civil society organizations of today, with their professional staffs and narrow focuses, generate social capital. The problem is particularly acute in developing countries, where many NGOs have small memberships, focus on a narrow range of issues, and are highly dependent on foreign governments or international NGOs. Their contribution to social capital is highly questionable, particularly when compared to the social capital generated by more traditional social institutions (see Box 10.4). Such traditional institutions also teach values and attitudes, but not necessarily those extolled by Putnam (1993) as necessary for democracy. They may include, for example, extremely negative views of other ethnic or religious groups, deep distrust of all strangers, or demeaning attitudes towards women. The fact that the content of this social capital is different and may be contrary to democratic values does not alter the fact that it is deeply embedded in social relations, however, and not

> ## BOX 10.4 THE CONUNDRUM OF ISLAMIC CHARITIES
>
> Since alms-giving (zakat) is one of the five pillars of Islam, Muslim countries have extensive webs of Islamic charitable organizations. Islamist movements and political parties have built on this charitable tradition to reach out to the population, providing educational and health services, while spreading their religious and political message. Islamist movements, in other words, build on the social capital of Muslim societies. This creates a conundrum for liberal democracy advocates in Muslim countries and their Western supporters: social capital favours Islamist organizations, while liberal organizations struggle to put down roots outside intellectual circles.

easily erased, particularly by professional NGOs with weak social roots.

Specialized civil society organizations do not represent society as a whole in any country. This is not a problem in well-established democracies, where the problem of representation is solved by the existence of elected officials, freely chosen by the voters to represent their various interests. Organizations of civil society are simply one among many types of organized interest group that put pressure on the elected officials to adopt the policies they favour. Professional NGOs are numerous and hold a variety of conflicting positions, as already stated, and compete for influence with a lot of other groups, including paid lobbies; thus they cannot advance a credible claim to represent the interests and the will of the entire population.

But, in many developing countries, representative institutions are often weak, and elections fall short of being free and fair; as a result, civil society organizations may more credibly claim to represent voiceless citizens. Indeed, civil society organizations do broaden the range of interests that are expressed—yet they do so in a lopsided way that favours groups with the capacity to organize and to access resources, even if their ideas are not widely held. Civil society organizations also have a degree of credibility when they claim to speak for unrepresented constituencies in international institutions, which are designed to represent states, but provide no formal channels through which popular demands can be expressed. Because lack of popular representation is a real problem in many developing countries and in international organizations, NGOs' claims that they 'give voice to the voiceless' have won a degree of acceptance in recent years and have even gained them a place at the table in many policy discussions.

The issue of whether NGOs should be consulted despite their lack of representativity remains highly controversial and is unlikely to be resolved soon. As long as countries do not have truly democratic institutions, the voice of NGOs adds an element of pluralism to the political system and the distortions created by this imperfect form of representation may be an acceptable price for such a broadening of the political process. On the other hand, there is an element of risk in mandatory consultations with organizations that are not representative and, above all, not accountable to the people in whose name they claim to speak.

The third function performed by modern, professional civil society organizations is the provision of goods and services to the population. Many voluntary organizations provide a wide range of assistance—from the very basic, survival-oriented food distribution or provision of emergency shelter, to the funding of research on rare diseases or the formation of support groups for people facing an almost infinite variety of problems. In this field, too, there are considerable differences between the importance of this civil society in industrial and less-developed countries, as well as in the issues raised by the existence of these organizations. On the one hand, these civil society organizations are much more numerous, better organized, and more capable in the industrialized countries. In developing countries, they are usually highly dependent on external funding, and very often find themselves in a subordinate position to the more affluent international NGOs that can access, with greater ease, money from rich countries and international organizations.

On the other hand, professional NGOs delivering goods and services often have a more important role in developing countries compared to that of richer counterparts in the industrialized West. In the poorest countries, for example, the help provided by NGOs is the main form of assistance available to the population; in the richer countries, NGOs supplement, rather than replace, the safety net provided by the government. This gives the foreign organizations that provide the funding for activities in developing countries a role that is often more important than that of the government. In extreme cases, the imbalance between the capacity of a developing country's government and that of the foreign and domestic NGOs operating there becomes a form of brain drain, attracting the most qualified people and hollowing out already-struggling government agencies (see Box 10.5).

BOX 10.5 THE DANGER OF INTERNATIONAL CIVIL SOCIETY

The policy of donors funding two civil services—the government bureaucracy at an average wage of [US]$50 per month and a parallel bureaucracy of their own at [US]$500 per month—draws talented people out of government in the short term and fundamentally undermines the creation of a sustainable state in the medium to long term.

(Ashraf Ghani, Governor of the Bank for the Islamic State of Afghanistan, speaking to World Bank Governors, 3 October 2004)

Civil Society and the State in the Developing World

Relations between state and civil society, in both its traditional and modern forms, are quite complex in the developing world, more so than in industrial countries. Political systems are undergoing change in many countries, some states are still consolidating or conversely are on the verge of failure, modern civil society is a recent construct, and traditional forms of civil society are still making adaptations to a changed social and political environment. As a result, relations between state and civil society are in flux. In consolidated democracies, the relationship is more stable and thus more predictable.

Civil society organizations relate to state institutions and officials in one of three different ways: they ignore them and try to avoid their control; they oppose them and work for their replacement; or they seek to influence their policies. The pattern of avoidance is most often found in countries in which the state is incapable of delivering services or other **public goods**. Civil society organizations give up on the state and seek to provide essential public goods on their own. Some of these activities are benign, for example the organization of alternative self-help schools for children neglected by the public system. Others are quite problematic: for example, in countries in which the police force is incapable of ensuring a minimum of security for citizens, vigilante groups emerge to fill the void, but sometimes degenerate into protection rackets or become predatory. The organizations of civil society that flourish in the space left by a failing state are unregistered and unlicensed—often illegal. In terms of structures, they thus fall into the category of traditional civil society, although the functions that they

perform are a response to contemporary problems created by state collapse and/or political repression.

When the state is capable of performing its functions, but the government is repressive and unresponsive, civil society organizations are more likely to take an antagonistic position. Some civil society organizations that take on an opposition role are simply fronts for political parties, deliberately set up to circumvent donors' rules against funding political organizations. As mentioned earlier, in some countries, civil society organizations have strong party links; in others, civil society organizations turn into opposition groups after trying to influence the government and discovering that they cannot do so. The example from Zimbabwe cited earlier illustrates this point very well. Organizations that see themselves as guardians of universal principles—human rights organizations, for example—are particularly likely to turn antagonistic when the government continues to violate those principles. Civil society groups that oppose the government can be organized as professional NGOs, or along less formal lines as broad **social movements** or loosely structured networks. Such a broad, loosely structured alliance of hundreds of small local organizations, or 'civics', formed in South Africa during the 1980s. The existence of this elusive hydra was crucial in convincing the apartheid regime that peace could not be restored by repressive measures and that a political solution was necessary.

Finally, the relationship of civil society to state and government can be a cooperative one. This is the ideal promoted by democratization programmes. There are various forms of cooperation. Civil society organizations, which possess a degree of expertise in their specialized area, lobby the government to promote specific policy reforms and may even provide the government with the technical help to implement the reforms, such as by helping to write legislation. Women's organizations, which are not usually seen as particularly threatening by governments, although they may antagonize conservative social forces, are adept at this advocacy role. For example, they helped to craft legislation in Uganda that expanded land ownership rights for women, as well as a new divorce law more favourable to women in Egypt.

Another form of cooperation between government and civil society is found when the government contracts out the delivery of services to non-profit NGOs. This is rarer in developing countries than in Europe, because it requires strong governments, capable of establishing a regulatory framework and providing supervision, and strong civil society organizations, capable of delivering complex services. The existence of a weak government on one side and strong international NGOs, often backed by large amounts of foreign money, gives rise to the common complaint that, in such conditions, international NGOs *de facto* make policy, further weakening the government and undermining its capacity.

The relationship between state and civil society in developing countries is rarely an easy one. This explains why many governments see civil society organizations as dangerous enemies to be tightly controlled. In democratic countries, setting up and registering an NGO is an easy process, and regulations aim above all at preventing abuse of tax-exempt **status** or the misuse of donations. By contrast, in many developing countries, NGOs are subject to complicated regulations aimed at suppressing groups that aspire to an advocacy role, instead of merely dispensing charity.

Efforts by international donors to promote democracy by funding NGOs, particularly those fighting for human rights, have created a backlash in many countries, with governments coming to see such organizations as thinly disguised tools used to undermine their authority or even to promote 'velvet revolutions' (see Box 10.6). One important example of such backlash followed the forced resignation of Serbian President Slobodan Milosevic in October 2000, when crowds protesting a flawed presidential election took to the streets and almost burned down the parliament building. The protest was organized largely by an organization called Otpor, which had received funding and some training by the United States and other donors. While the role of foreign donors in this episode was probably exaggerated by funders seeking to take credit for the overthrow of a dictator, it increased suspicion in semi-authoritarian countries about foreign funding of NGOs other than charitable organizations. Laws forbidding such funding became increasingly common thereafter.

KEY POINTS

- When the state is repressive, civil society organizations are usually antagonistic to it.
- When the state is weak and incapable of delivering services, civil society organizations seek to ignore the state and avoid its control, rather than to press for reforms.
- When the state is strong and civil society organizations are well developed, relations tend to be cooperative and constructive.
- Authoritarian and semi-authoritarian states have become increasingly suspicious of civil society organizations.

Civil Society and Democratization

The rapid transformation of the term 'civil society' from an obscure concept known to a few scholars to one that finds its place in all discussions of political transformation is a result of the rapid spread of democracy assistance initiatives that followed the end of the cold war. However, by the end of the 1990s, it was clear that many so-called democratic transitions had led at best to the formation of semi-authoritarian regimes rather than democratic ones (Ottaway 2003). Furthermore, the reform process was losing momentum almost everywhere (Diamond 1996). Nevertheless, democracy promotion abroad remained on the political agenda of most industrial democracies. The 'Arab uprisings' that began in 2011 in Tunisia, Egypt, Yemen, Libya, and Syria provided new incentives for democracy promotion, although hopes for democratic change were eventually dashed everywhere except Tunisia.

The concept of civil society became an important part of all discussions of democratization for reasons grounded to some extent in theory—as discussed

BOX 10.6 THE BACKLASH AGAINST NGO FUNDING

Reports from the United Nations document the negative trends concerning foreign funding of NGOs. In 2012–13, Egypt, Russia, Sudan, Azerbaijan, Turkmenistan, the British Virgin Islands, and Tajikistan enacted legislation further tightening rules concerning such funding, while Bangladesh, Israel, Kirgiztan, India, Malaysia, and Pakistan discussed such laws. Another report for 2014–15 flagged India, Ethiopia, Russia, and Azerbaijan as countries that had approved restrictive legislation. Many other countries already had restrictive laws on foreign funding.

Sources: Report of the Special Rapporteur on the rights to freedom of peaceful assembly and association, UN Doc. A/HRC/23/29 (April 2013); Report of the Special Rapporteur on the rights to freedom of peaceful assembly and association, UN Doc. A/HRC/29/25 (April 2015)

earlier—and to a larger extent in pragmatism. To provide democracy assistance, aid agencies had to break down the abstract idea of democracy into concrete component parts that could be supported with limited amounts of aid. Civil society was such a component—and a particularly attractive one. Developing civil society meant promoting government by the people and for the people. And when civil society was defined as a narrow set of professional NGOs, it was also an entity to which assistance could be easily provided.

Non-governmental organizations are easy to establish and cheap to fund; small grants go a long way. Professional NGOs were also a new type of association in many countries. Without roots in the traditional civil society and the culture of their countries, and highly dependent on outside funding, professional NGOs were easy to train and influence to conform to the funders' concept of what civil society should do. With donor support, NGOs multiplied rapidly in all regions of the world, displaying remarkably similar characteristics. This made the aid agencies' job of supporting civil society easier. It also raised the question of whether these organizations were truly addressing the specific challenges of democratization in their countries.

Although an important component of democracy promotion, assistance to organizations of civil society is not without problems. We have seen earlier how such assistance has created a backlash in many countries, which are now trying to curb the flow of funds. But even among those who support democratization and believe in the importance of civil society in such progress, concerns have arisen that international assistance has created dependent organizations and distorted the meaning of civil society.

Many studies of the donor-assisted civil society have reached the conclusion that pro-democracy NGOs tend to be quite isolated from the society at large. For instance, this was a nearly unanimous conclusion of the contributors to *Funding Virtue* (Ottaway and Carothers 2000), with the only exception being two experts on the Philippines, where the growth of civil society was an indigenous process that owed much less to foreign assistance. This suggests that donor support is an important contributor to the isolation of civil society organizations. Many professional NGOs have small or no membership. They are often exclusively urban organizations with little reach in the countryside; only the best organized are able to extend their reach through networks of less formal CBOs. Exchanges (often called 'networking') among the NGOs from different countries provide an opportunity for organizations to discuss their problems and to learn from each other, but they also contribute to creating a special international NGO world, the inhabitants of which talk to each other more easily than they do to their compatriots. These observations do not call into question the genuine commitment of many NGO leaders to democracy, human rights, or other causes. They do call into question, however, the capacity of these so-called organizations of civil society to influence their societies.

Democracy NGOs have other problems worth mentioning briefly. One is the opportunism that exists in the NGO world alongside genuine commitment: when assistance is available, setting up an NGO can simply be a way of making a living. **Corruption** also exists in the NGO world, which is unsurprising in view of its very rapid growth (see Chapter 15). And many, as mentioned earlier, become partisan organizations affiliated with political parties. These problems are tangible, but also inevitable, to some extent and not particularly worrisome, unless they are extremely widespread. They are simply part of the inevitable imperfection of the real world.

What is more worrisome is whether the growth of a small professional civil society actually contributes to democratization, and whether the attention lavished on these organizations has led to the neglect of organizational forms that might have greater popular appeal and greater outreach within the population. Democracy promoters recognize the weakness of the NGOs that they support and they equate it with the weakness of civil society. And yet, in many of the countries in which the organizations officially designated as civil society are weakest, for example in many war-torn African countries, informal civil society organizations have proven very resilient in trying to address the most severe difficulties created by state collapse. In their search for a society that is civil by their definition and assistable in terms of its formal characteristics, aid providers may have marginalized groups with a proven record of effectiveness.

Arab countries, with their contrast between a vast Islamic civil society and their struggling official civil society, illustrate the problem particularly well. In Egypt, the world of Islamic civil society was large and multifaceted. It included charitable groups, organizations that provided free-of-charge medical services that the state has stopped delivering, organizations that offered some educational opportunities for students underserved by failing public schools, and groups that provided textbooks for university students who could not afford them. Foreign funders shunned these organizations, suspecting that they also had political goals that did not satisfy the principles of liberal democracy. After a military coup in July 2013 that put an end to the government of the Muslim Brotherhood, the new government sought to eliminate all Islamic NGOs to weaken Islamists politically, but in doing so left many poor Egyptians without access to much-needed services.

This Islamic civil society was well rooted in the society at large. Even organizations that were by no means traditional, but represented a contemporary and (from a religious point of view) aberrant response to contemporary problems, could cast themselves as part of a well-established tradition. They were certainly better rooted in the society than the modern, professional, pro-democracy NGOs favoured by donors. But the new donors' civil society espoused the values of liberal democracy, while the more traditional Islamic civil society was, at best, ambiguous on this point. In the end, neither an isolated modern civil society nor a well-rooted Islamic one can be considered good vehicles for democratic transformation.

An additional issue concerning the role of civil society in democratization has arisen in the context of the Arab uprisings (see Chapters 11 and 14). The issue is that of the impact of large-scale participation by unorganized citizens on democratization and deserves more discussion than it has received so far, because this form of mass civil society participation can have an extremely positive impact, but also has a darker side.

In Tunisia and Egypt, civil society participation in the form of sustained mass demonstrations over a period of weeks brought down two extremely well-entrenched authoritarian regimes with remarkably little bloodshed. These uprisings represented civil society involvement at its best, showing the determination of ordinary citizens to reclaim their rights from repressive regimes and the strength that ordinary people can muster with a minimum of organization, relying largely on social media and word of mouth.

Fast-forward a few years and the darker side of mobilized civil society is also becoming apparent, particularly in Egypt, where the transition has failed. First, mass demonstrations changed subtly from the actions of citizens taking responsibility for their own future to become partisan affairs arranged by rival political organizations to whip up support for their own goals outside the formal political process. Not much seems wrong with these partisan demonstrations, until we reflect on the fact that the **exploitation** of large crowds by political parties outside a legal political process was one of the means used by fascist and Nazi parties in gaining, and then holding on to, power. In June 2013 in Egypt, the military helped organize mass demonstrations similar to those that had taken place spontaneously earlier, and used them as justification for intervening and deposing the elected government. The lessons of history is clear: mass civil society participation can be a positive means of forcing change on unmovable authoritarian regimes, but it can never become a means to govern a country democratically. In the long run, participation has to be filtered through institutions and legal processes, although in the short run and in specific historical circumstances, direct mass participation can open the way to democratic transformation. The problem is to understand when direct participation starts to transform from a positive phenomenon into the beginning of a new and dangerous authoritarianism.

KEY POINTS

- The difference between traditional organizations well rooted in the society, relatively close to the population, but not necessarily democratic or official, and the civil society recognized by international democracy promoters may be starker in the Muslim world than elsewhere at this time, but is found in all parts of the developing world.

- Democracy requires a large, active, democratically oriented civil society, but what is found in most countries is a bifurcated situation: an official civil society—small, democratic, but essentially elitist; and a less formal, traditional civil society—large, popular, well rooted, but of dubious democratic credentials.

- How to combine the democratic commitment of the former to the popular roots and outreach of the other is a major conundrum for democratization.

Conclusion

The chapter started with an acknowledgement of the ambiguity of the concept of civil society and of its lack of definitional clarity. It ends on the same note, but with a normative addendum. Not only is the concept of civil society an imprecise, ambiguous one, but it must also be accepted as such. The more strictly the concept is defined, the less it helps us to understand how people come together voluntarily to address problems that they cannot solve as individuals and which the state cannot, or does not want to, solve for them.

It is, of course, possible to narrow down the definition closely. This is what the international development agencies do all of the time when they select which organizations to support on the basis of the civility of their goals and the adequacy of their organizational structures. But what is gained in terms of clarity is lost in terms of the understanding of the society. First, the narrow definition loses sight of the many ways in which people in any society organize themselves to pursue their interests and satisfy their needs. It may reduce the effectiveness of any outside intervention, by focusing attention on groups that may be quite marginal to the society, but which happen to appear all-important to aid agencies. Second, a definition that separates a democratic, virtuous civil society, acting in the public interest, from a non-democratic, uncivil one, selfishly promoting narrow interests, is more normative than analytical. The idea of the common good and the public interest obfuscate the reality that all societies are made up of groups with different and often conflicting interests, and that all groups are equally part of the society, whether their goals conform to a specific idea of civility or not.

In conclusion, despite the caveat expressed at the outset, from an analytical point of view we need to accept that we cannot do better than accept that civil society comprises the entire realm of voluntary associations between the family and the state. It is a vast and complex realm. Voluntary associations take many different forms, ranging from small, informal self-help groups and ad hoc committees with narrow goals, to large, professional, and bureaucratic organizations with large budgets. In developing countries, civil society organizations perform a wide range of functions. At one extreme, there are narrowly focused groups that seek, for example, to provide support for **HIV/ AIDS** orphans in a community or to raise money to improve the track that connects a village to the nearest highway. At the other, there are organizations tied into transnational networks with goals such as changing the World Bank's outlook on the construction of dams or delivering humanitarian assistance to populations in need. Many voluntary associations in developing countries try to provide services that the state is unable to deliver. Others form to help citizens to resist pressure from predatory governments. Organizations that citizens develop voluntarily are not always 'civil' in the normative sense of the word. The realm of civil society comprises organizations that promote human rights and vigilante groups that prey on the people whom they are supposed to protect. While it is tempting to narrow the definition of civil society to organizations with commendable goals, this is not helpful. If we want to understand how people come together to defend their interests or to pursue their goals, we need to accept the diversity, the complexity, and, in many cases, the flaws of the associational realm that has become known as 'civil society'.

? QUESTIONS

1. Boundaries between civil and political society, clear in theory, often become blurred in practice. Is this a problem?

2. How can traditional forms of civil society persist in modern states, and what benefits and drawbacks do they offer to politics and development?

3. Should we be concerned about the potential negative repercussions of an empowered civil society for a weak state?

4. Can civil society organizations make up for weakness of political parties?

5. Is the development of a modern civil society sector a precondition or, conversely, an inevitable effect of democratization?

6. Should Western non-governmental organizations (NGOs) try to strengthen modern civil society groups in the developing world? If so, how can they do this without putting their legitimacy at risk?

7. Mass participation by relatively unorganized citizens opened the way to democratic transformation in Tunisia and Egypt, but it facilitated the rise of fascism and Nazism in Europe. When is mass participation positive and when is it dangerous?

FURTHER READING

Edwards, M. (2009) *Civil Society* (Cambridge: Polity Press) Updated version of the original 2004 edition, dwelling mostly on the practice, rather than the theory, of civil society. Addresses the recent challenges from persistent oppressive regimes and developments in the economic market.

Florini, A. M. (ed.) (2000) *The Third Force: The Rise of Transnational Civil Society* (Washington, DC: Carnegie Endowment for International Peace) Case studies of the role of transnational networks of civil society, including the global anti-corruption movement, human rights movement, organizations for democracy and against dam-building, and for environmental sustainability.

Hann, C., and Dunn, E. (eds) (1996) *Civil Society: Challenging Western Models* (New York: Routledge) A critical account that argues for a broader perspective on civil society.

Kaldor, M., Selchow, S., and Moore, H. (eds) (2012) *Global Civil Society 2012: Ten Years of Critical Reflection* (London: Palgrave) Reflections from the authors of ten yearbooks on civil society.

Kasfir, N. (ed.) (1998) *Civil Society and Democracy in Africa* (London: Frank Cass) A critical view of conventional Western attitudes towards civil society in Africa.

Nelson, J. (1979) *Access to Power: Politics and the Urban Poor in Developing Nations* (Princeton, NJ: Princeton University Press) A wide-ranging empirical assessment of political participation by the urban poor in many developing countries, which downplays their revolutionary potential.

Ottaway, M., and Carothers, T. (eds) (2000) *Funding Virtue: Civil Society Aid and Democracy Promotion* (Washington, DC: Carnegie Endowment for International Peace) A critical examination of civil society aid, drawing on cases in Africa, Asia, the Middle East, and Latin America.

Ottaway, M., and Chung, T. (1999) 'Debating Democracy Assistance: Toward a New Paradigm', *Journal of Democracy*, 10 (4): 99–113 A cautious view of international 'democracy assistance' to civil society, and to elections and parties too.

Putnam, R. (1993) *Making Democracy Work: Civic Traditions in Modern Italy* (Princeton, NJ: Princeton University Press) A seminal work on social capital.

Wickham, C. R. (2002) *Mobilizing Islam: Religion, Activism, and Political Change in Egypt* (New York: Columbia University Press) A highly acclaimed analysis of the role of cultural identity, political economy, mobilization, and organization in political Islam in Egypt.

WEB LINKS

http://business.un.org/en   Links to the ways in which the United Nations system works 'in partnership' with civil society on issues of global concern.

http://www.grameen-info.org   The website of the Grameen Bank Organization, including articles about micro-credit by its founder Muhammad Yunus.

http://icnl.org/   The International Center for Non-Profit Law monitors conditions under which civil society organizations operate in a large number of countries.

http://www.ids.ac.uk/ids/   The site of the Civil Society and Governance Research project at the Institute of Development Studies, University of Sussex, funded by the Ford Foundation, which examines the interplay of civil society and governments in twenty-two countries.

http://www.imf.org/external/np/exr/cs/eng/index.asp   The International Monetary Fund's *Civil Society* newsletter provides regularly updated information on the IMF's collaborative efforts with civil society groups around the world.

http://www.lse.ac.uk/collections/CCS   The Centre for Civil Society at the London School of Economics is 'a leading, international organisation for research, analysis, debate and learning about civil society'.

http://www.un.org/en/civilsociety/index.shtml/   The United Nations Civil Society site explains the different ways in which the United Nations interacts with and promotes the development of civil society.

 For additional material and resources, please visit the Online Resource Centre at:
http://www.oxfordtextbooks.co.uk/orc/burnell5e/

11

Social Movements and Alternative Politics

Siri Gloppen

Overview

Clarifying the concepts alternative politics and social movements, the chapter shows how different forms of social movements have emerged and been influential during different periods, and introduces the main theoretical perspectives about why this is so and how we should understand this phenomenon. Turning to past and present social movements and alternative politics in the developing world, it distinguishes between three categories: movements concerned with democracy and governance; movements concerned with identity politics; and movements concerned with social justice. Current examples of each type show how they operate, and their strengths and challenges. They also show that the categories are by no means mutually exclusive and that each movement may include a number of different concerns. Turning to the increasing globalization of social movements, we discuss how this affects, and is affected by, social movements in the developing world. The last part of the chapter asks what makes social movements successful and shows how this is answered in the literature.

Introduction

Throughout the **developing world**—and beyond—new forms of political participation challenge and transform established political **institutions**. Authoritarian rulers and democratically elected leaders alike are facing **social movements** and civic uprisings, as well as a range of strategies that aim to influence **governance** from below and to strengthen the accountability of ruling elites. Demonstrations for **regime change** in Cairo's Tahrir Square, anti-**corruption** movements in India, Buddhist **nationalists**' campaigns in Myanmar, the fight for recognition and rights for gay, lesbian, bisexual, trans, intersex and queer (LGBT) people in Uganda, and Andean indigenous peoples' struggle for constitutions respecting the rights of Mother Earth are very different forms of activism, yet share important commonalities. Rather than aiming for political office, these movements seek to alter the way in which the political system itself operates—sometimes by using parts of it (for example the courts) as instruments for change. In contrast to militant revolutionary movements, they aim to change the system in (predominantly) non-violent ways. They are often loosely organized, without clear leadership or organizational structures, which some see as a value in itself. And they increasingly rely on new information technology to mobilize and generate pressure, locally and globally. This chapter aims to show how social movements in the developing world and 'bottom-up' **alternative politics**, supported by new technology and globalized networks, can deepen democracy—but it also exposes the challenges inherent to sustaining such movements over time.

Social Movements and Alternative Politics

'Alternative politics' describes the burgeoning field of political activity that emerges 'from below', in the sense that it centrally involves ordinary people, as opposed to political elites, and takes place outside of formal politics and established political channels, such as parties, elections, and parliamentary politics. This includes one-off protests and riots, Facebook campaigns, and flash mobs, as well as long-term social movements pursuing social justice and political change.

A social movement can be defined as a loosely organized, but sustained, collective campaign in support of a social goal—typically for or against a change in society's structure or values—that (mainly) acts outside **institutional** and conventional channels. While going beyond a single riot or protest, social movements mainly employ such non-conventional ways of participating in order to influence authorities to grant their demands. They may engage in conventional lobbying or challenge authorities in court, but social movements are essentially about collective action. The degree of organization may vary from loosely organized movements to well-defined and clear hierarchies, but even in organized movements participants are defined by their common ideology or goal rather than formal membership. Thus they cannot be equated with formal organizations such as unions or **non-governmental organizations** (**NGOs**). However, unions and NGOs often participate in and organize movements—and social movements may develop into political parties, NGOs, or other formal organizations. Social movements (along with among other NGOs, the media, churches, and universities) form part of **civil society**, which is commonly understood as the 'third' sector of society—a sphere of interaction and communication distinct from the state and political society (government institutions; political parties), on the one hand, and the market (for-profit firms), on the other (see also Chapter 10). Jean Cohen and Andrew Arato (1994), building on the ideas of the German sociologist Jürgen Habermas, argue that civil society has a dual role vis-à-vis the state and the market that is crucial to develop and uphold democracy. On the one hand, civil society provides the cultural and social basis for the functioning of the political and economic spheres of society; at the same time, civil society enables individuals and groups to develop and advance interest and ideas that challenge and provide a corrective to the logic of the market and political society. Social movements are central to the latter function in that they often pursue radical goals and ideals challenging the status quo. The authority that they challenge may be the regime itself, as in the 'Arab uprisings', or cultural norms, for example related to **gender** or race (Goodwin and Jasper 2003; Snow et al. 2004; Amenta et al. 2010). A process that illustrates this ambiguous function of civil society as simultaneously supportive and critical of the status quo is the process of formulating the United Nations **Sustainable Development Goals** (**SDGs**). The predecessors of the SDGs, the Millennium Development Goals (MDGs) were adopted in a manner criticized for being top-down and unresponsive to societies' norms and needs. In response, an unprecedented public participation process was set in motion to engage civil society in deliberations on the new SDGs. This provided alterative, critical perspectives, but also served useful 'system purposes' by providing publicity and broader **legitimacy**.

Charles Tilly saw the early growth of social movements as a result of broad economic and political changes in the nineteenth century, including the spread of parliamentary politics, capitalist market economies, and the growth of the proletariat. Early social movements include the British abolitionist movement, and the labour and socialist movements of the late nineteenth century, which led to the formation of communist and social democratic parties and organizations, and nationalist liberation movements in the colonized territories. Typical of 'old social movements' is their focus on issues of economic and social justice.

In the 1960s and 1970s, so-called new social movements erupted, including the civil rights movement, the women and gay liberation movements, the environmental movement, anti-(Vietnam) war movements, the student movement, and general cultural revolt. These movements were seen as 'new' in orientation, organization, and style. While 'old' social movements typically recruited from the working class, focused on economic issues and labour conflict, directed their attention towards the state, and aimed for economic redistribution to benefit particular groups, the 'new' movements expressed universalist concerns, often in the name of morality and universal rights. 'New' movements were generally composed of people who shared a concern for social issues rather than a material interest. And the ideological orientation was more towards identity and lifestyle concerns. Their repertoire of action was, to a greater extent, outside institutionalized politics; it was diverse, on the streets, and made use of symbols. They orientated themselves more toward civil society than the state, and depended on mass media and new information technology to get their message out. To avoid being deradicalized and co-opted—what Michels (1962) famously termed 'the iron law of oligarchy'—many of these movements have sought to avoid highly organized structures and bureaucratic organizations (Pichardo 1997; Nash 2010).

In reality, the differences between the 'old' and 'new' movements are less clear. Already in the eighteenth and nineteenth centuries, unconventional direct action was prevalent among social movements. And contemporary social movements range from highly organized and hierarchical women's groups, to the loosely organized Occupy Wall Street protests of 2011–12. They regularly interact with governments and some movements have transformed into political parties. Non-materialist movements in which the role of identity was essential have existed from the early nineteenth century (**feminist**, nationalist), while contemporary movements such as Occupy and other anti-austerity movements have an 'old', materialist focus on economic justice and redistribution (Calhoun 1993; Pichardo 1997). Emphasis in the social movement literature has been on 'progressive' movements (pro democracy, social justice, tolerance, and equality). Yet, in recent years, the most marked trend is arguably the rise in more conservative or reactionary social movements, both in the global North and in the developing world. Prominent examples are the Tea Party movement and anti-abortion groups in the United States, right-wing **populist** groups such as Patriotic Europeans against the Islamisation of the West (PEGIDA) in Europe, and a plethora of Islamist, Christian, Buddhist, and Hindu fundamentalist movements across the world.

KEY POINTS

- 'Alternative politics' is political activity 'from below', outside of formal political channels, such as protests, riots, Facebook campaigns, and social movements.

- 'Social movements' are loosely organized, but sustained, collective campaigns in support of a social goal that (mainly) acts through alternative politics.

- 'Old social movements' typically focus on redistribution, and economic and social justice; 'new social movements', on non-material issues, values, and identity—but in practice the distinction is blurred.

The Origins of Social Movements

Why do social movement arise? Explanations have shifted. In the nineteenth and early twentieth centuries, social movements were frequently dismissed as primitive actions by the irrational 'crowd'. 'Collective behaviour' theories were influential until the 1960s. Based on a pluralist conception of politics, in which all relevant interests could and should be expressed in the political marketplace, collective behaviour theorists saw no need or role for movements acting outside of conventional politics. Social movement participation was explained by social strain, leading to psychological stress, and pushing individuals into acting not to attain a specific goal or outcome, but merely to manage psychological tensions (McAdam 1982).

With the many social movements of the 1960s and 1970s (civil rights, peace, and women's emancipation, among others), scholars increasingly recognized that those engaging in alternative politics were acting rationally. Influenced by the works of Mancur Olson (1965) and others, 'resource mobilization' theories focused on movement participants' active and rational choices to participate. In their famous article 'Resource Mobilization and Social Movements: A Partial Theory', McCarthy and Zald (1977) introduced the notion of the social movement organization steering the movement, aggregating resources and operating like a firm competing for support within a social movement 'industry'. Within a movement, there may be many different organizations, each offering a different direction. These theories take as a given that, at any time, there are a sufficient number of discontented people in society and that what matters is the resources available to the various organizations; the more resources they acquire, the more mobilization they are able to produce (McCarthy and Zald 1977).

Later, scholars recognized the importance of the political environment for social movements, using the concept of the **political opportunity structure** to explain why mobilization occurs in some situations and not in others (McAdam 1982; Kitschelt 1986; Kriesi et al. 1995). The core idea is that, to understand why and how social movements mobilize, attention should be focused not (only) on the social movements themselves and their resources, but (also) on their environment, and the barriers and opportunities that they face in reaching their aims. Some see the political opportunity structure narrowly in terms of possibilities for accessing state power (Kitschelt 1986); others employ a dynamic conception of political opportunities, including alliance structures and which party is in power (Kriesi et al. 1995). Yet others use a broader concept of opportunity structure that goes beyond the political to include the shifting legal and social environment facing social movements shaping their opportunities and resources for successful mobilization. The focus on changes in the environment of social movements helps to explain fluctuations in mobilization within a

country and why protest waves occur suddenly. Sidney Tarrow (1998: 142) also underscores the cumulative and interactive nature of social mobilization: how the successful mobilization of one group may lead others to mobilize, creating a protest wave or 'phase of heightened conflict across the social system'. In these periods of very high social movement activity, early mobilizers open opportunities for others by making authority (appear) vulnerable to protest. Protest thus spreads to different parts of society, involving new actors. This requires a response from the state either through concessions or harsher repressions. Cycles of contention may sometimes lead to revolutions, but this is in no way certain. The consequences of such cycles are, however, generally larger than those of individual movements.

Another key concept used in explaining social movement mobilization is **framing**. Framing processes give meaning to the actions of a movement, drawing on shared cultural understandings. This is important in mobilizing supporters, forming common identities, and garnering support, as well as for *de*mobilizing antagonists (Benford and Snow 1988). Contemporary political theories of social movements often integrate framing, resource mobilization, and political opportunity structure perspectives. Careful framing identifies opportunities that may spur mobilization. And by perceiving the political structure more in terms of opportunities than constraints and in terms of mobilizing resources, social movements may in fact create new opportunities, in which case the framing becomes a self-fulfilling prophecy (McAdam et al. 1996; Benford and Snow 2000).

KEY POINTS

- Early 'collective behaviour' theories explained mobilization as expression of grievances and deprivation.
- 'Resource mobilization' theories focused on people's active, rational choices to participate and the organization's own ability to mobilize resources.
- 'Political opportunity structure' theories focus on barriers and resources in the environment to explain why mobilization occurs.
- 'Framing' gives meaning to movement actions, and is important in mobilizing supporters and forming common identities.
- Scholars often combine resource mobilization, political opportunity structure, and framing perspectives.

Social Movements and Alternative Politics in the Developing World

The scholarly literature has predominantly focused on social movements in Europe and the Americas, but there is also a long history of social movements and social movement research in the developing world. Of immense historical importance is the rise of strong national liberation movements during colonial rule in Latin America, Asia, and Africa, which played crucial roles in struggles for national independence and, in many cases, turned into political parties, profoundly shaping the **post-colonial state**. The remainder of the chapter focuses on some significant contemporary social movements in the developing world. These fall into three categories:

- movements focusing on *democratization* (aiming to change the regime or the nature of the state, continuing the tradition of the anti-colonial struggle);

- movements with a focus on *identity politics* (religious identity, indigenous rights, gender equality); and

- movements aiming to organize the disadvantaged in a struggle for *social justice* and the redistribution of resources, locally and globally.

Social Movements and Democratization

Among the most spectacular social movements in the developing world in the past decade were those demanding regime change in North Africa and the Middle East in early 2011—often referred to as the 'Arab uprisings' or the 'Arab Spring'.

The Arab Spring: From Tunisia to Egypt and beyond

On 17 December 2010, a 26-year-old street vendor lit himself on fire in the Tunisian town of Sidi Bouzid. His fruit cart had been confiscated and, when his attempt to complain to the town governor proved futile, Mohamed Bouazizi chose self-immolation as his ultimate act of protest.

Tensions had been rising in Tunisia under the authoritarian rule of President Ben Ali. The secular and Western-oriented regime pushed market-based economic development and women's rights, but brutally repressed civil society. An all-pervasive security apparatus silenced dissenting voices. Political opponents, independent journalists, secular activists, and Islamists faced harassment, torture, and imprisonment. Tunisians also faced rising food prices, unemployment, and corruption in public administration. In this context, Bouazizi's suicide became a symbol of political despair and economic dislocation, triggering a wave of protests (Freedom House 2012).

Within hours, hundreds of people assembled to protest against police abuse and economic hardship. The events were recorded on mobile phones and posted on the Internet. The television network Al Jazeera broadcast them back to Tunisia, where the national media ignored the protests. Facilitated by mobile phones, international satellite television channels, online blogs, and social media such as Facebook and Twitter, protesters in Sidi Bouzid managed to get news out, sparking demonstrations throughout Tunisia. Some protests turned violent and were met with severe police repression and curfews. Dozens of people were killed. Still the rioting continued to escalate and spread, evolving into a popular uprising directly challenging the regime.

The president's promise not to seek re-election in 2014 did not prevent new large-scale demonstration. Hundreds of thousands joined and, crucially, the military sided with the people in what Western media dubbed the 'Jasmine Revolution'. On 14 January, Ben Ali dissolved the government and fled the country. In October 2011, Tunisia held its first free elections since independence to choose a constitutional assembly. The provisional constitution was adopted two months later, and, in January 2014, the new Tunisian constitution. Parliamentary and presidential elections followed in October and November 2014, returning secularist Beji Caid Essebsi as the new president.

A cross-section of the Tunisian society—civil society groups, trade unions, lawyers, teachers, leftists, **human rights** groups, Islamists, and opposition parties—participated in the revolution. And young Tunisians were key actors, with the use of communication technologies and the Internet widely credited as central to the successful mobilization and coordination, leading some to call it a 'Facebook revolution' (Howard and Hussain 2013).

The Tunisian revolt proved an emotional spark in the region. Popular protests spread like wildfire from one Arab country to another: on 7 January 2011, protests broke out in Algeria; on 12 January, in Lebanon; on 14 January, in Jordan; on 17 January, in Mauritania and Sudan; by 25 January, a revolution was under way in Egypt. In Yemen, a major demonstration was held on 27 January; on 14 February, in Bahrain. On 15 February, thousands of Libyans protested. The rioting reached Kuwait on 18 February, Morocco on 20 February, Iraq on 25 February, Western Sahara on 26 February, Saudi Arabia on 11 March, and then Syria on 18 March (MacQueen 2013).

In Egypt, popular discontent had long brewed under the authoritarian regime of President Hosni Mubarak. In the early 1990s, deteriorating living conditions and lack of a political outlet fuelled an Islamist insurgency, which was brutally repressed. In December 2004, Kifaya (meaning 'Enough'), an informal movement encompassing a broad spectrum of secular and Islamist activists, held the first-ever demonstration calling for President Mubarak to step down. Protests continued in 2005, but were met with a heavy-handed response (Beinin and Vairel 2011).

The Egyptian government, seeking to expand access to the Internet as an engine of economic growth, did not engage in substantial Internet censorship, relying instead on intimidation, detentions, and online surveillance to silence dissenting voices (Freedom House 2012). Despite these efforts, Egyptians continued to discuss issues of common concern on social media. In 2008, a Facebook group expressing solidarity with protesting workers attracted 70,000 followers and eventually coalesced into a political movement known as the 'April 6 Youth Movement'.

In June 2010, 28-year-old web activist Khaled Said was beaten to death by Egyptian police officers. Said's brother posted a photograph of the disfigured corpse online, sparking widespread demonstrations. Egyptian Google executive Wael Ghonim's Facebook page, 'We are all Khaled Said', was joined by hundreds of thousands in Egypt and globally. This contributed—together with the April 6 Youth Movement and bloggers such as Asmaa Mahfouz—towards mobilizing people for protests to bring down Mubarak's regime (Beinin and Vairel 2011).

On 25 January 2011, the 'Day of Revolt', organizers used mobile phones and landlines to disseminate information about the location and time of the demonstration. Tens of thousands of protesters—members of the Muslim Brotherhood, Salafists, Christians, secularists, intellectuals, and trade unionists—came together in Cairo's Tahrir Square and cities across the country. The regime shut down the Internet, deployed police, and hired thugs to assault protesters. Security forces detained a number of activists, bloggers, and Facebook group administrators—but the protests continued and grew.

On 28 January, Mubarak made a televised speech promising to dissolve the government. In the following week, he first announced that he would remain in office to ensure a peaceful transition and then promised to transfer powers to the vice president, but the demonstrations continued to escalate.

On 11 February 2011, millions took to the streets demanding an end to Mubarak's thirty-year rule. After eighteen days of nationwide protests, in which around 800 Egyptians were killed and thousands injured, the president stepped down. The Supreme Council of the Armed Forces took over, promising an orderly transition to civilian rule. Nationwide celebrations followed, but the transitional period proved long and troubled. Only in June 2012 did Mohamed Morsi of the Muslim Brotherhood's Freedom and Justice Party become Egypt's first elected president. A year later, after ongoing public protests, the Egyptian army chief removed President Morsi from power and suspended the constitution. Many of the social groups that had ousted Mubarak (Liberals, Christians, etc.) had now turned against the Muslim Brotherhood. Elections were held in May 2014, with the Freedom and Justice Party banned from participating by the Egyptian Supreme Court, and General Abdel Fattah el-Sisi received 97 per cent of the vote.

The Sisi government has been preoccupied with security concerns. The Muslim Brotherhood is outlawed; more than 100 people have been killed and 40,000 are reportedly jailed in a crackdown on dissent (BBC News 2016). Five years after the revolution, many of the activists who spearheaded the protests are in prison or have fled the country; others restrict their activities to social media. President Morsi was put on trial on several charges and was sentenced to death on 16 May 2015 (but has not been executed).

During 2011, the Arab uprisings forced rulers to step down in Tunisia, Egypt, Libya, and Yemen. Five years on, the revolutions remain incomplete or have been reversed, with the tragic and continuing civil war in Syria as the grimmest reminder that the 'Arab Spring' has turned to 'Arab Winter' in much of the region. The exception is Tunisia: while shaken by **terrorist** attacks and not yet a consolidated democracy, important strides have been made there, including competitive elections and a progressive constitution. One reason for the relative success is a strong civil society, which has managed to keep the democratization process on track (Moghadam 2013). Since 2013, the Tunisian National Dialogue Quartet—consisting of two unions, a human rights organization, and a lawyers' association—has worked to provide a road map for stability, for which it was awarded the 2015 Nobel Peace Prize.

The Arab uprisings of 2011 demonstrate the power of framing. When Bouazizi set himself on fire in Tunisia, activists succeeded in framing this as an act of sacrifice for the suffering of the nation, turning it into a powerful mobilization tool in a situation ripe with discontent. This, in turn, broke the dominant frame wherein democratic change was seen as impossible in the Arab world, unleashing mobilization elsewhere in the region.

It also demonstrated how conditions for social mobilization have radically changed as a result of new communication and information technology, thus altering the political opportunity structure of activists. Manuel Castells (2012), in his book *Networks of Outrage and Hope: Social Movements in the Internet Age*, shows how new technology not only altered the speed of the process, but also the structure of mobilization, under which networks made formal organization redundant and succeeded in bringing diverse groups together in forceful action. The question is whether the network character and lack of formal organization is also part of the reason why the movement for change so quickly fragmented once the regimes fell. The aftermath also shows how difficult it is to sustain a movement for change, with protest cycles giving rise to unpredictable outcomes.

Women played an important role in the Arab uprisings. The role of women is also pronounced in other social movements demanding political change in the developing world, as illustrated by the Women of Liberia Mass Action for Peace (see Box 11.1). Here, political changes were pursued and achieved by a movement composed by women, using strategies that underscored women's agency and social power. It thus served two goals: political change towards a more peaceful and democratic Liberia; and the empowerment of women.

Alternative politics to further democratization in the developing world is not always about regime change. We also see efforts to deepen democracy and to improve the functioning of existing systems.

BOX 11.1 LIBERIA: THE WOMEN OF LIBERIA MASS ACTION FOR PEACE

In 1989, civil war erupted in Liberia. Forces led by Charles Taylor launched a guerrilla insurgency against the country's military regime. The conflict escalated as a result of fractionalization among rebel groups and the intervention of foreign powers. More than 150,000 lives were lost before the warring factions signed a peace agreement in 1995 and agreed to hold elections. Taylor won and assumed presidency in 1997, but the peace was flawed. In 1999, civil war broke out again. By 2003, anti-Taylor rebels controlled two-thirds of Liberia, more than 200,000 had died in the conflict, and one in three Liberians had been forced to leave their homes. Opposition and government soldiers alike looted villages, raped women, and recruited children to fight.

Social worker Leymah Gbowee decided to bring women from her church together to pray for peace. They recruited hundreds of Christian and Muslim women, and formed the Women in Peacebuilding Network to secure peace through the collective action of women across ethnic and religious divides. Using the radio to spread the word, Gbowee called upon women to gather at a fish market in the capital Monrovia, past which President Taylor's motorcade drove every day. In April 2003, the Women of Liberia Mass Action for Peace staged their first public protest. Dressed in white and carrying banners, thousands of women danced and sang for peace. They rallied at the fish market for months and declared a sex strike—denying sex to their men until they stopped the violence.

The women forced a meeting with President Taylor and made him promise to attend peace talks. A delegation of women applied pressure on the factions during the process and staged a sit-in, blocking all doors and windows to prevent delegates from leaving the peace talks without a resolution. In August 2003, an agreement was reached.

Liberian women became a political force, contributing greatly to the end of the civil war and to the democratic elections in 2005. Their grass-roots campaign led to the election of President Ellen Johnson Sirleaf, the first woman elected as head of state in Africa (Fuest 2009; Gbowee and Mithers 2011).

172   Siri Gloppen

India: The India against Corruption Movement

With a population of 1.3 billion, India is the world's largest democracy. Except for a brief authoritarian interlude in 1975–77, she has maintained her democratic institutions since gaining independence from British colonial rule in 1947. India's democratic success runs counter to theories suggesting that democracy is unlikely to survive in poor countries with high levels of social diversity. But while India's democracy has been remarkably stable in terms of peaceful transfers of power through elections, it is flawed by government inefficiency and corruption. Corruption is omnipresent, ranging from the bribes that ordinary citizens pay to get a complaint recorded at the local police station to high-profile corruption scandals surrounding government contracts. This has made many Indians cynical about the workings of their democracy (Kohli and Singh 2013).

In 2011, following a string of major corruption scandals, anti-corruption activists began to coalesce into a new national movement, which gained momentum across the country and galvanized public attention, through the use of social media and protests by high-profile Bollywood stars. The primary goal was to convince the government to institute an independent ombudsman to investigate and prosecute corruption cases. Parliament had proposed the creation of such an institution in the draft Lokpal Bill of 2010, but the activists found it to be ineffective and drafted their own version, the Jan Lokpal Bill (Ganguly 2012).

In April 2011, controversial veteran activist Anna Hazare began a hunger strike to induce parliament to include civil society in the drafting of the Lokpal Bill. The 74-year-old's 'fast to death' campaign attracted enormous media attention, triggering demonstrations of solidarity across India. Global campaigning organization Avaaz promoted the anti-corruption movement on its website and, in 36 hours, 500,000 people had signed the petition to support the campaign. *The Times of India* called Avaaz a key player (see Box 11.2).

Four days into the fasting, the government agreed to create a joint committee of state and civil society to draft an effective Bill. But, as the government and the anti-corruption movement continued to disagree over the content, Hazare repeatedly embarked on new hunger strikes. The Lokpal Bill was passed by parliament in 2013.

The 2011 anti-corruption movement tapped into public anger over corruption and managed to bring

BOX 11.2 AVAAZ

Avaaz is a global online movement aiming to 'close the gap between the world we have and the world most people everywhere want'. The movement was founded in 2007, as a tool for activists globally. Through email, Internet petitions, and lobbying, Avaaz draws attention to various causes, reaching decision-makers worldwide. With 43 million members in 194 countries, it has a large base of potential donors and funders for projects that the community decides to promote.

Sources: Kavada (2012); Avaaz (2016)

together strands of the Indian middle class rarely gathering around the same cause. Towards the end of 2011, however, the protests slowed; in 2012, the India against Corruption movement split. Arwind Kejriwal formed the Aam Aadmi Party (AAP) to make the struggle more effective by taking it to the political arena (Ganguly 2012). The AAP contested the 2013 Delhi elections, winning 30 per cent of the votes. In 2015, the AAP won sixty-seven out of seventy seats and, at time of writing (October 2016), heads the Delhi government.

The Arab uprisings and India's anti-corruption movement are testaments to how social media is changing conditions for social mobilization, and how local activists are able to use technology to gain exposure and force by linking to global networks. But they also illustrate the transient nature of global public attention and how difficult it is to sustain pressure without a more solid organizational structure.

KEY POINTS

- The revolutions dubbed the 'Arab uprisings' or 'Arab Spring' demonstrated the power of effective framing and social media in mobilizing diverse groups—but also the vulnerability of weakly institutionalized movements once the common enemy is gone.

- The Women of Liberia Mass Action for Peace successfully mobilized women's own resources—for peace and development, but also for identity-building.

- India's anti-corruption movement gained force by using social media and linking with global online activist networks (Avaaz), but struggled to sustain attention, with parts of it becoming a political party.

Social Movements and Identity Politics

Social movements organizing around issues of identity and recognition, values, and world-views have proliferated since the 1960s. The developing world has seen mobilization for gender equality and sexual rights—including in places where the opportunity structure seems closed. In highly homophobic contexts, where same-sex intimacy is stigmatized, criminalized, and subject to harsh penalties, LGBT people fight for their rights. Amidst efforts to introduce the death penalty for homosexuality, Sexual Minorities Uganda (SMUG) employs a wide repertoire of strategies and arenas to advance its cause, ranging from 'everyday resistance' and Internet activism to using the courts to fight for LGBT rights (see Box 11.3).

Equally significant is the counter-mobilization against equality for LGBT people. This often forms part of a broader mobilization for 'public morality' or 'family values' that also denounces other sexual and reproductive rights—particularly abortion. Religious actors are central in the counter-movements, with evangelical churches linked to the United States the most active drivers of populist conservative mobilization in many African and Latin-American countries. Similar mobilization is found within the Catholic and Anglican churches. The strategies resemble that of the LGBT movement—with the addition of church gatherings as active mobilization arenas. Also here we see dense global support structures, as illustrated by the case of Scott Lively discussed in Box 11.3.

The religious 'morality movements' can be seen as part of a larger category of identity-based, religious social movements on the rise in the developing world, rejecting 'Western' liberal values. Some—most notably, radical Islamist movements such as Al Qaeda, the so-called Islamic State, and Boko Haram—spread terror though their widespread use of violence; others are more moderate and welfare-oriented, such as the Muslim Brotherhood. In Asia, nationalist Hindu and Buddhist movements are also on the rise, as in Myanmar (see Box 11.4).

Indigenous people, particularly in Latin America, have formed social movements to demand recognition for their identity, their rights to land and resources, their cultural autonomy, and public recognition of their legal norms. They challenge dominant conceptions of development and value, and prevailing

---

BOX 11.3 SEXUAL MINORITIES UGANDA AND THE 'KILL THE GAYS' BILL

Sexual Minorities Uganda (SMUG) was founded in 2004 as an umbrella organization for the nascent LGBT groups in the country. Increased visibility and advocacy for the human rights of LGBT people met with resistance, most aggressively from evangelical churches. In 2009, a Bill was tabled before parliament, proposing the death penalty for homosexual acts. Same-sex intimacy ('carnal knowledge against the order of nature') was made illegal under the British colonial rule and, like many former colonies, Uganda kept the provision, but rarely enforced it. The new Bill proposed harsher sentences, broadened the definition of homosexuality, criminalized advocacy for LGBT rights—and triggered enforcement of the existing law. Homophobic populism and social sanctions spiralled.

SMUG mobilized against the proposed law and the increasing vilification of homosexuals through a range of strategies. When, in 2010, the Rolling Stones newspaper published '100 Pictures of Uganda's Top Homos' under the heading 'Hang them', SMUG activists took the paper to court—and won. They successfully mobilized internationally, using LGBT activist networks, diplomatic channels, and Internet forums such as Avaaz and Section 76. The killing of prominent SMUG activist David Kato in January 2011 increased global attention to the cause. SMUG activists have also engaged in strategies of 'everyday resistance' and identity-building, including a gay bar in Kampala, an annual Beach Pride, a Gala and Equality Award, a magazine, and the online platform Kuchu Times. They have also sought alliances nationally, linking their cause to broader struggles for human rights and democratic constitutionalism.

Domestically, the international attention seemed to create a backlash. The Anti-Homosexuality Bill was enormously popular. While international pressure and threats of sanctions resulted in the capital punishment clause being dropped, the substance of the Bill was passed into law in December 2013. A network of Ugandan human rights organizations, including SMUG, took the matter to the Constitutional Court, which ruled the law unconstitutional. With the help of the Centre for Constitutional Rights, SMUG has also laid charges in a US court against Scott Lively, who was central in the drafting the Anti-Homosexuality Bill. The US-based activist is charged with crimes against humanity for stirring up hatred against LGBT people in Uganda.

BOX 11.4 BUDDHIST NATIONALISM IN MYANMAR

'The Face of Buddhist Terror', the cover story of *Time* magazine, 20 June 2013, featuring a picture of Wirathu, the leader of Myanmar's 969 Movement, triggered strong reactions. Globally, it brought attention to the anti-Muslim campaigns organized by Buddhist monks, to their ultra-nationalist rhetoric, and to the violence committed against the Rohingya Muslims. Locally, in Myanmar (also known as 'Burma'), the *Time* story rallied large crowds in support of Wirathu; government officials came to his defence and banned the *Time* issue.

The ties between political Buddhism and the state in Myanmar are ambiguous. When Wirathu started his Buddhist nationalist campaigns in 2001, he drew inspiration from the writings of Kyaw Lwin, a former government official mandated with repairing ties with the monasteries after the crackdown on monks in the 1988 democratic uprising. Wirathu was, however, jailed for fuelling anti-Muslim hatred in 2003. Since his release in 2011, political Buddhism has been on the rise, first with the 969 Movement and then, from 2014 onwards, the Organization for the Protection of Race and Religion (*Ma Ba Tha*). This period has been marked by strong anti-Muslim rhetoric, and riots that have killed hundreds of stateless Rohingyas and displaced hundreds of thousands, many of whom have tried to flee the country by boat. The nationalists have appealed for boycott of

Muslim businesses and lobbying for new legislation targeting the Muslim minority. Four such laws were passed in 2015, restricting interfaith marriages, introducing strict family planning, and outlawing polygamy.

The militant monks and their movement receive respect and support not only from the quasi-civilian government, which held power until the 2015 elections, but also from within the new governing party, Aung San Sun Kyi's National League for Democracy (NLD). The NLD did not field any Muslim candidates in the 2015 elections and Aung San herself has refrained from criticizing the Buddhist nationalists or the violence against the Rohyinga (although, in her first address to the United Nations in September 2016, she pledged to back an advisory commission on the conflict led by Kofi Annan). The widespread support stems in part from a culture of deep religious respect for the monks, but is also seen to reflect a 'siege mentality' whereby Buddhism is perceived to be under threat. While 90 per cent of the population in Myanmar are Buddhist and Muslims constitute only a 4 per cent minority, fears are fuelled by the rise of Islam globally and in the region. Similar movements, with close links, are on the rise also in the nearby predominantly Buddhists states of Thailand and Sri Lanka.

political and social establishments. In the next section, we look more closely at two cases: Bolivia and Brazil.

Bolivia: Indigenous mobilization and the Law of the Rights of Mother Earth

Two-thirds of Bolivians consider themselves to be of indigenous descent—the highest proportion of any Latin American country. Yet wealthy urban elites, mostly descendants of Spanish colonialists, dominate political, economic, and cultural life. In the 1990s, Bolivia's long-excluded indigenous population mobilized.

A broad-based movement of indigenous people, peasants, and workers calling for nationalization of gas resources and a new constitution led to the 2005 presidential election victory of former cocoa farmer Evo Morales. They pushed for transformation of the country's legal framework towards greater recognition of indigenous rights, beliefs, and legal norms. The 1999 constitution defines Bolivia as a pluri-national state, according more rights to the indigenous

majority. It gives greater local autonomy, enshrines government control over key resources, and reflects a deep ecological concern (Boyd 2012).

Bolivia suffers serious environmental problems associated with mining, soil erosion from overgrazing and poor cultivation methods, deforestation, melting glaciers, loss of biodiversity, and water pollution. This has sparked mobilization among indigenous groups who see not only threats to their livelihood, but also deep violations of the sacred in nature. In 2010, the Bolivian legislature passed one of the most radical environmental laws ever created: the Law of the Rights of Mother Earth.

The law was originally developed by Pacto de Unidad, an alliance of grass-roots organizations, drawing on the indigenous view of the *Pachamama* (meaning 'Mother Earth') as a sacred home on which humans intimately depend. The Law gives legal personhood to the natural system with comprehensive rights—to life, biodiversity, freedom from genetic modification, and restoration from the effects of human activity—that the state, individuals, and organizations are obliged to respect. An ombudsman is authorized to oversee implementation of the law and those infringing on the integrity of Mother Earth can be brought to court.

The law is ground-breaking, but five years later it remains in question whether it can prompt real change in a situation in which industries such as mining contribute a large portion of Bolivia's gross domestic product (GDP). Still, the law continues to be a rallying point and is a testament to the new importance of indigenous movements in Bolivia, after 500 years of political and economic marginalization.

The developments in Bolivia link to indigenous rights and climate justice movements in Latin America and globally. Disappointed by the outcomes of the 2009 UN Climate Change Conference in Copenhagen, an alternative conference was held in Cochabamba, Bolivia, in April 2010. Around 30,000 people attended the event, and conference topics included a Universal Declaration on the Rights of Mother Earth and the establishment of a climate justice tribunal.

Here, alternative and institutional politics intertwine as social movements engage in a range of alliances and strategies, including in party politics. Local and global processes connect, with local activists drawing strength from international allies. Different causes also intertwine. Indigenous activism and ecological movements link non-material issues of identity, values, and world views with material demands, as emerges clearly in the case of the Belo Monte Dam in Brazil (see Box 11.5).

The fight against the Belo Monte Dam has much in common with struggles in other parts of the world where invasive infrastructure projects affect indigenous land and destroy the livelihoods of poor people. Indian social 'movements' fight against the Narmada Dam and other mega-projects displacing large numbers of people have also attracted international attention (Nilsen and Motta 2011). Again, 'new' social movement issues of indigenous identity, ecology, and alternative development intertwine with 'old' attention to social justice and economic redistribution. And we find in them a similar mix of traditional social movement strategies (protests, demonstrations), the use of formal channels (litigation), and international alliances. Several transnational activist networks and NGOs have indigenous activism related to dam and river projects as their focus.

Material concerns and social injustice is important both for movements aiming for political change and for identity-based movements, but there are also contemporary social movements for which such 'old' concerns are the core concern and demand, to which we now turn.

BOX 11.5 BRAZIL: INDIGENOUS PROTESTS AGAINST THE BELO MONTE DAM

In the 1970s, Brazil's military dictatorship planned to build gigantic hydroelectric dams on the Xingu River in the Amazon to provide electricity for power-intensive industries, but shelved the plans after controversies over the location of dams on indigenous land. In 1989, Brazil's civilian government revitalized the proposal, but local Kayapó Indians successfully mobilized international allies, the media, celebrities, and foreign governments in an effort to stop the construction.

The government went back to the drawing board. To deal with soaring energy demands, plans were made to build more than sixty large dams in the Amazon Basin—among them, Belo Monte, the third largest dam in the world. Affecting a smaller area than previous proposals, the plan was presented as ecologically and politically sound. Still, it would dramatically divert the flow of the Xingu River, create drought, and destroy vast areas of pristine rainforest.

Realizing that the dam would force thousands of their tribe members to relocate, local social movements united. They organized non-violent protests and the Brazilian indigenous peoples of the Amazon released an Indian Declaration against Belo Monte (2010). Nevertheless, the government gave the construction the go-ahead.

The licensing processes have been mired in court battles. Both in 2012 and 2013, courts ordered work on the dam suspended, but were ultimately overturned; in November 2015, Belo Monte was granted an operational licence despite failing to meet requirement for protecting affected indigenous communities. Indigenous groups living in the Amazon fear that this will create a precedent for future destruction of rivers, and that they will lose both the means to sustain their livelihoods and their ancestral history. Helped by social media and websites such as Facebook and Twitter, their struggle continues to receive considerable international attention.

Social Movements and Social Justice

That social movements in the global South have material resources and social justice as central concerns is no surprise in a situation marked by widespread poverty, and vast social and economic inequalities, both internally in developing countries and globally. South Africa is one of the most unequal countries in the world, with a century-long tradition of social movements and activism.

South Africa: The shack dwellers' movement (*Abahlali baseMjondolo*)

When Nelson Mandela was elected president of South Africa in 1994, it marked the end of nearly fifty years of **apartheid**. A new constitution promised to protect the human rights of all South Africans—including their social and economic rights—in a situation in which the rights of the majority black population were severely curtailed, residential areas segregated, and political power (and valuable land) reserved for the white minority.

The African National Congress (ANC) won the elections in a landslide, promising redistribution of land to black South Africans. But, once in power, it adopted a range of neoliberal policies that did not benefit the country's poorest and only a small fraction of the land was redistributed. The gap between rich and poor has widened.

It is estimated that one in ten South Africans live in shack settlements. Living conditions are often abysmal, with poor housing infrastructure, and lack of electricity and water supply, as well as overcrowding. The Kennedy Road settlement in Durban is among the most notorious. In 2005, the local government promised settlers a nearby plot for housing, but then sold the land to a local industrialist. Outraged by the betrayal, thousands of shack dwellers took to the streets, physically blocking the plot. This sparked one of the most prominent social movements in post-apartheid South Africa—*Abahlali baseMjondolo* (meaning 'shack dwellers')—which has mobilized tens of thousands of members in more than sixty settlements. Their key demand is that the social value of urban land should take priority over its commercial value. Through methods ranging from street protests to election boycotts and litigation, Abahlali campaigns for quality housing and basic services to shack settlements, and for the expropriation of private land for public purpose (Mitlin and Mogaladi 2013).

The South African police violently repressed the shack dwellers' movement in the mid-2000s, but this declined after the repression was reported in the media and drew international condemnation. By using online and mobile tools to spread word of their successes, upcoming events, and ongoing efforts, Abahlali has built links with similar movements and garnered international support.

In October 2009, Abahlali won a major legal victory when the controversial Slums Act of 2007 was declared unconstitutional (Mitlin and Mogaladi 2013). The provincial government passed the Act to legalize the eviction of shack dwellers and to eradicate slums, allowing for mass evictions without the provision of suitable alternative accommodation. The South African Constitutional Court found the law to be in conflict with the constitution and struck it down.

Abahlali focuses on social justice concerns at the local level: the lack of material conditions for a decent life and broken promises to deliver basic services. It provides a structure to which people in the community can turn in emergencies and which can help to pressure local authorities on a daily basis. But it also addresses the laws, policies, and ideologies that underpin the system. Abahlali is organized around open mass assemblies and elected community-level committees. Rallies, workshops, and youth camps are held to mobilize and educate members, and a secretariat is elected at annual general meetings. It also engages formal government institutions, such as courts, and it has links to formal organizations locally and globally—links that help to secure both attention and resources.

The new globalization of social movements

Abahlali, like many of the other movements discussed in this chapter, is part of a profound process of social movement **globalization**. Social movements in the developing world connect with activists and organizations elsewhere, and use this to mobilize attention and resources. Social movement networks and exchanges across borders are not new. The anti-slavery movement, the women's suffrage movement of the nineteenth century, and the international labour movement were not confined within national borders. But the possibilities for cross-border exchanges between activists have increased enormously with the explosion of new media technologies (Nash 2010). Movements actively use the international level to affect national change. Margaret Keck and Kathryn Sikkink (1998) argue that, by using transnational activist networks, movements can achieve a boomerang effect in which their claim is reflected back at the national government, through court rulings, public naming and shaming, or the movement acquiring material resource.

There is also a globalization of the focus of attention, with a stronger attention to global justice and the global processes producing global poverty and inequality, and unsustainable development. This is evident both in organizations such as Attac (see Box 11.6) and events such as the World Social Forums, bringing together the **global justice movement**, consisting of diverse movements and organizations sharing a critical perspective on the nature of economic globalization, and dominant models of development. Central actors include *Via Campesina* (meaning 'Family Farmers' International'), Christian movements advocating international debt relief (Jubilee 2000), and environmentalists concerned with climate change, as well as youth and student groups, trade unions, peace groups, and development-focused think tanks. Conservative movements are also mobilizing transnationally, through international networks and church structures, or directly supporting similar groups in developing countries, as in the case of Scott Lively's involvement in the anti-gay movement in Uganda (Kaoma 2009; Bob 2012) (see Box 11.3).

BOX 11.6 ATTAC

The Association for the Taxation of Financial Transactions and Aid to Citizens (*Association pour une taxation des transactions financières pour l'aide aux citoyens*, or Attac) is a global organization that originally fought to introduce taxes on foreign exchange transactions (a 'Tobin tax'). Since its formation in France in 1998, the organization has spread worldwide to more than forty countries and works on a range of issues. Its major focus is the regulation of financial markets, the closure of tax havens, and fair trade. Although politically independent, Attac is associated with the causes of the international left.

Source: Stockemer (2011)

Social movements in the developing world are important in this process, but critics argue that rather than bringing out critical voices from the global South, they have become mainly a vehicle for NGOs and intellectuals from the North. More generally, it is important to ask whether local activists in the developing world always benefit from their global ties. Perhaps it is the other way around: perhaps they risk having their struggle hijacked by transnational activists in search of a cause. This brings us back to the question of what it is that makes a social movement successful.

KEY POINTS

- Social justice is a major concern for social movements in the developing world.
- Abahlali mobilizes South African shack dwellers to push government authorities to change living conditions for the worst off, enlisting international support.
- Attac and the World Social Forums illustrate the increasing globalization, in both scope and focus, of social movement mobilization.

What Makes Social Movements Successful?

A central question, both for analysts of social movements and for the actors themselves, is what makes some social movements succeed and others fail. This is a complicated question. Even to decide what counts as 'success' can be difficult and must be viewed in light of the various aims pursued. The explicit concern of a social movement is usually some form of external change (in the regime, public policy, or society), but movements may also aim to shape the identities of their members through mobilization and to make them (indigenous people, women, gay people, shack dwellers) see themselves as rights-holders owed equal concern and respect.

Theoretically, we can distinguish between degrees of success in terms of *material effects* (such as public spending, the introduction of new advantages), *political effects* (being accepted as someone representing legitimate interests, who should be at the table when decisions are made), and *symbolic effects*—that is, 'less tangible, such as new ways to refer to a group' (Amenta et al. 2010: 290; see also Rodríguez-Garavito 2010).

The transformations that social movements seek are often long-term processes that present additional methodological challenges with regard to identifying their impact and success. This has led scholars to focus on intermediate 'outputs', 'outcomes', or 'impact', rather than ultimate 'success', and to distinguish between low-level benefits (short-term, easily revoked), mid-level advantages (institutionalized, recurring, often more substantial), and high-level successes (such as voting rights for particular groups that are substantial and hard to revoke) (Amenta and Young 1999).

The literature seeking to explain why some movements succeed emphasizes different factors. Some focus on internal aspects of movements, including the degree of disruption that they are able to cause, threatening the interests of elites, gaining media attention, and thereby promoting the movement's message. However, by being too disruptive, a movement may alienate moderate supporters or fractionalize, providing opportunity for states to bargain selectively with parts of the movement, thereby reducing its mobilizing potential.

Social movements often struggle to maintain mobilization and pressure over time. This has led to a long-standing debate in the literature on whether it is good for social movements to institutionalize (Della Porta and Diani 2006). In their influential book on *Poor People's Movements*, Piven and Cloward (1977) argued that poor people have limited chances of getting their voices heard through regular channels of interest aggregation such as elections or interest groups. Their only chance is to disrupt elites and to threaten their

privileges through unconventional means, such as demonstrations or sit-ins. If movements institutionalize (cooperating and regularly interacting with the state), it can lead to co-option, the movement can lose its power to disrupt and its solidarity, and the leaders may prioritize the sustainability of the organization and demand less radical change.

Others argue that conventional tactics complement alternative politics, and that the relationship between state and the movement may combine cooperation and conflict. Research shows that people participating in protest activities are also more likely than others to participate in conventional politics such as voting (Goldstone 2003). Movement members may become 'institution activists' and contribute to producing policies that further the goals of the movement (Suh 2011). Social movement organizations may oscillate between protest activities and regular participation, and links between social movements and conventional politics are in practice often close.

How movements protest—that is, their tactical repertoire—also matters for success. Novel and surprising tactics makes success more likely, because they are prone to spur interest among potential supporters and the media, and authorities may not know how to respond. Shorter and Tilly (1974) argue that strikes were much more successful during the 1830s, when they were novel, than during the 1960s, when they were considered a routine part of protest. Employing a varied tactical repertoire may increase the size of the movement, getting more people into the streets. Size is theoretically linked to success in at least three ways: it attracts more attention from media; it signals stronger opposition to politicians who fear that it may hurt them electorally if they do not respond to the movement; and it increases movements' disruptive powers (Morris 1993).

If success were all about the movement itself, one could establish thresholds of participation or disruption above which success would be guaranteed. However, even big and innovative movements fail. This led authors to pay attention to the political environment or opportunity structure (McAdam 1982; Kitschelt 1986; Giugni 2004), and the interactions between the movements and their environment—known as a 'political mediation approach' (Amenta et al. 2010). Here, social movement success is seen to depend both on internal aspects of movements, what they are and do (resources, agency, strategic choices), and on external factors (barriers, potential allies)—and, most crucially, on the fit between the two or, in other words, how well suited the strategies of the movement are to the social and political environment in which they operate.

Conclusion

Alternative politics in the developing world is a diverse field, spanning Internet activism, disruptive mass demonstrations, and highly institutionalized social movements. Some movements seek to change the nature of the political regime; others focus on social injustice, or demand respect for their group identity, norms, and world view. Often, the aims combine and mix: the Women of Liberia Mass Action for Peace is also about women's rights and about livelihoods; Abahlali seeks social justice for shack dwellers, but its struggle is also about slum dwellers' identity and broad social transformation; and the indigenous peoples of Latin America struggle for respect for their culture and norms, but also for material rights to land and resources, and for constitutional change.

Social movements in the developing world are increasingly global, in terms of scope, mode of operation, and focus. New technology links them to activists elsewhere, and enables effective mobilization of support locally and globally. This offers enormous potential. Social media enables effective mobilization across diverse groups with few resources, spectacularly demonstrated by the Arab Spring revolutions, and global networks may generate instant pressure. The challenge is to convert this into sustained pressure.

QUESTIONS

1. What is meant by 'old' and 'new' social movements? How does this distinction relate to social movements in today's developing world?

2. Why are some social movements more successful than others?

3. What does it mean to say that social movements are 'globalized'?

4. What has social media meant for alternative politics in the developing world?

5. Using social movement theory, how would you explain the Arab uprisings and their subsequent demise?

6. Is institutionalization inevitable for movements in the long run?

FURTHER READING

Amenta, E., Caren, N., Chiarello, E., and Su, Y. (2010) 'The Political Consequences of Social Movements', *Annual Review of Sociology*, 36: 287–307 Gives a good overview of the consequences of social movements, and when and how they succeed.

Della Porta, D., and Diani, M. (2006) *Social Movements: An Introduction* (Malden: Blackwell) A thorough introduction to social movement research.

Dobson, W. J. (2012) *The Dictator's Learning Curve: Inside the Global Battle for Democracy* (New York: Doubleday) An intriguing book, written by renowned journalist William Dobson, about how movements learn from each other in the battle for democracy.

Nilsen, A. G., and Motta, S. C. (2011) *Social Movements in the Global South: Dispossession, Development, and Resistance* (London: Palgrave) Shows how contemporary popular struggles and social movements in Africa, South Asia, Latin America, and the Middle East politicize development in an age of neoliberal hegemony.

Stokke, K., and Törnquist, O. (2013) *Democratization in the Global South: The Importance of Transformative Politics* (Basingstoke: Palgrave Macmillan) The book looks to Nordic social democracy for insights into how democracy can be deepened in the Global South and made to serve the interests of working people without sacrificing economic growth.

 WEB LINKS

http://www.abahlali.org   Website of *Abahlali baseMjondolo*, the Shack Dwellers' Movement in South Africa.

http://amazonwatch.org   Website of Amazon Watch, a non-profit organization aiming to protect the rainforest and advance the rights of indigenous peoples in the Amazon Basin, which contains information about legal struggles and cases of social mobilization.

http://www.americanscientist.org/blog/pub/timeline-of-the-controversial-belo-monte-megadam-in-brazil   Website of the *American Scientist* magazine, providing a significant source of information about the controversy relating to the development of the Belo Monte Dam in Brazil.

http://www.dearmandela.com   The film *Dear Mandela* (2011) follows three young activists in the Shack Dwellers' Movement in South Africa.

http://www.theguardian.com/world/interactive/2011/mar/22/middle-east-protest-interactive-timeline   This timeline was a significant source for the events of the Arab Spring.

http://www.internationalrivers.org   Website of International Rivers, an organization working to halt destructive river infrastructure projects in the global South, address the legacies of existing projects, and improve development policies and practices.

http://messagefrompandora.org/   The film *A Message from Pandora* (2010) documents the battle to stop the construction of the Belo Monte dam in the Brazilian Amazon.

http://nvdatabase.swarthmore.edu/   The Global Nonviolent Action Database provides information about hundreds of cases of non-violent action.

http://www.praythedevilbacktohell.com   The documentary film *Pray the Devil back to Hell* (2008) tells the story of Women of Liberia Mass Action for Peace.

https://sexualminoritiesuganda.com   Website of Sexual Minorities Uganda, an umbrella organization for gay, lesbian, bisexual, transgender, and intersex (LGBT) people that has been central in the struggle against state-sponsored homophobia in Uganda and the region.

 For additional material and resources, please visit the Online Resource Centre at:
http://www.oxfordtextbooks.co.uk/orc/burnell5e/

PART 3
State and Society

The heading of Part 3 reverses the order of the two terms contained in the previous part, to signify that Part 3 focuses chiefly on the **institutions** of state and their importance to society. In **politics**, institutions matter. The state is not merely one among many political institutions, but has historically been the pre-eminent focus of attention. In the modern world, under the impact of rapid social, economic, technological, and other changes taking place at the global, regional, and sub-state levels, the exact nature, role, and significance of the state are continually evolving. Questions related to states' capacity, and how power is exercised and checked through mechanisms of accountability, are key concerns of our chapters on **governance** and democracy.

This part has two main aims. The *first* is to explore the idea of the state in a **developing world** context and how, if at all, it differs from the state in more developed countries. Among other things, this must involve some reference to past history. Can one framework accommodate all of the varieties of state formation? And what is most distinctive about the politics of countries characterized by endemic violent conflict or trying to emerge from **state failure**?

The *second* aim is to show how the governance capabilities of states and even more so the kind of political **regime**—the relationship between the institutions of government and society—have become a major focus for political inquiry. In at least some developing countries, there have been significant changes in the last few decades. This part is essential for enabling us to address important questions about how far the state in the developing world can be held responsible for addressing (or failing to address) fundamental developmental issues—and for determining whether it is equipped to resolve issues, including those affecting the economy, welfare, the environment, and **human rights**. For instance, what is the relationship between democracy, or democratization, and development? Is there a specific sequence in which these must arise? And how is power exercised and checked once a government is in office?

While Part 3 ranges over these issues, the more detailed policy matters that are bound up with them will comprise the substance of Part 4—which is best consulted after or alongside the material in Part 3. The illustrations in Part 3 are widely drawn from around the developing world. By comparison, case studies of countries selected to illustrate specific issues and themes can be found in Parts 5–8. For example, while Chapter 22 includes a case study of post-Saddam Iraq, Chapter 19 on Pakistan and Chapter 20 on Indonesia offer contrasting trajectories of political regime transformation. Readers are encouraged to consult the relevant case studies alongside the chapters in Part 3. In addition, for more extended discussion of the concept and debates about democratization and the contribution that party politics specifically makes to politics in developing countries, readers are recommended to visit the Online Resource Centre, where there is a comparative examination of the role of political parties specially written by Vicky Randall.

12

The Modern State
Characteristics, Capabilities, and Consequences

Anna Persson

Chapter contents

Overview

The aim of this chapter is to disentangle the concept of the modern state, in a developing world context. What characteristics and capabilities define the modern state, and to what extent can the state be seen as an autonomous actor with the potential to influence development outcomes? How can the evolution of the modern state be understood, and what consequences do different patterns of state formation have for how states further consolidate and develop? In particular, this chapter is devoted to the further exploration of what differentiates the 'weak' state found in the majority of developing countries from the 'strong' state typically found in the industrialized parts of the world. What characterizes these two types of states, what capabilities do they possess, and what consequences do they bring in terms of development?

Introduction: The State and Development

Whereas the state was for a long time in the shadows as a potential driver of development, since the 1980s the scenario has changed dramatically. For social scientists, the state was effectively brought (back) to centre stage as an (at least partly) autonomous actor with the potential to influence political, social, and economic outcomes by means of the seminal work *Bringing the State Back in*, edited by Peter B. Evans and colleagues (1985). The state soon gained further recognition as an important actor in development among social scientists, as well as among the wider public, when the 1993 Nobel Prize in Economics was granted to Douglass C. North for his research on how state **institutions**—particularly property rights—play a fundamental role in shaping the development paths of nations (North 1990). From this onset, a large literature has continued to explore the role played by the state—through its institutions and patterned relationships with societal groups—in the process of development (Migdal 1988; Evans 1995; Fukuyama 2011; Acemoglu and Robinson 2012).

Until the mid-1990s, international donors (by which is commonly meant governments providing development assistance in addition to the international finance institutions) tended to share this view of the state as something to be rolled back. But, in the past two decades, the idea of the state as a potential promoter of development has also gained resonance among policymakers (Leftwich 2000). The shift in ideas is effectively revealed in the World Bank's influential 1997 World Development Report, in which the leading international financial institution takes a clear stance against rolling back the state, arguing that development requires an effective state, one that plays a catalytic, facilitating role, encouraging and complementing the activities of private businesses and individuals (World Bank 1997: iii). In line with this acknowledgement, international donors today extensively promote and fund reforms aimed at enhancing and improving the capacities and **institutional** structures of states, principally under the conceptual umbrella of the '**good governance** agenda' (Andrews 2008) (see Chapter 15).

In short, the last couple of decades have witnessed a radical upswing of the idea of the state as a central actor in development. Scholars and policymakers still differ in how they view the state in terms of its potential to actively and directly influence development

outcomes, yet very few contemporary analysts would dispute the argument that the pure *existence* of a state—however predatory and kleptocratic—is absolutely essential for development to occur. In other words, there is general agreement with Thomas Hobbes' (2008 [1651]) argument that anarchy inevitably leads to a 'war of all against all', within the framework of which the life of man is 'solitary, poor, nasty, brutish, and short', as well as with Mancur Olson's (1993: 568) conviction that '[I]n a world of roving banditry there is little or no incentive for anyone to produce or accumulate anything ...'. Within this perspective, **weak states** are commonly seen as a threat to the world's population, causing the violation of basic rights to life and security, and failing to provide food, water, infrastructure, health, and education. Moreover, weak states risk falling prey to, and spawn, a host of transnational security threats, including **terrorism**, organized crime, infectious diseases, environmental degradation, and civil conflicts (Rotberg 2004a).

KEY POINTS

- While the state was for a long time in the shadows as a potential driver of development, the state is now at centre stage for scholars and policymakers alike.
- Scholars and policymakers differ regarding how active a role they attribute to the state in the process of development, but agree that anarchy is the worst-case scenario.
- State weakness is commonly argued to be a threat not only to national populations, but also to the global community.

Conceptualizing the Modern State

The modern state has been defined in many different ways, but two different conceptualizations are commonplace: the state as a *physical organism*; and the state as an *idea*.

Although these two strands of conceptualizations are interconnected—especially since very few scholars and policymakers would challenge the argument that the modern state can be understood, at least in part, in terms of its organizational and institutional expression—how the state is conceptualized still has important implications for which states are deemed weak as opposed to strong. Moreover, differences in how the state is conceptualized will lead to different views as regards the state's autonomy and potential to play a more active role in the development process through 'institutional engineering', and subsequently to potentially radically different approaches to state-building and reconstruction—with tangible real-life consequences for many people.

The state as a physical organism

Conceptualizations of the state as a physical organism are linked to German sociologist Max Weber's (1948 [1919]: 78, emphasis original) definition of the state as 'a human community that (successfully) claims the *monopoly of the legitimate use of physical force* within a given territory'. To this definition, Weber added the understanding of the modern state as being distinguished from traditional systems of rule, such as ancient city-states, feudal states, and pre-modern, early modern, absolutist, and princely states, also in terms of the source of authority. More specifically, whereas the rulers of non-modern systems of rule tend to gain their authority on the basis of tradition or charisma within the framework of a so-called patrimonial system of rule, in which there is no clear separation between the private and the public spheres, and in which all power flows directly from the leader; the main source of authority in the modern state would be what Weber (1978: 54) calls 'rational-legal authority', in which an impersonal and impartial bureaucratic logic governed by law and reason is the defining characteristic of legitimate authority.

In short, for Weber, as well as for scholars and policymakers in the so-called neo-Weberian, or 'institutionalist', tradition, at the most fundamental level, six characteristics capture the essence of the modern state: (a) a differentiated set of institutions and personnel, embodying (b) centrality, in the sense that political relations radiate outwards from a centre to cover (c) a territorially demarcated area, over which the state exercises (d) a monopoly of authoritative binding rule-making, guided by (e) rational-legal principles, and backed up by (f) a monopoly of the means of physical violence (Weber 1978; Mann 1984).

In line with this understanding, scholars in the neo-Weberian tradition typically evaluate state strength with reference to what Michael Mann (1984: 113) calls **despotic power**—that is, 'the range of actions that state elites can undertake without routine negotiation with **civil society** groups'. For example, Francis Fukuyama (2004: 7) conceptualizes the strong versus weak state on the basis of variation in 'the ability to plan

and execute policies and to enforce laws cleanly and transparently'. Like Weber's (1978: 55) assertion that it is not possible to define the state in terms of goals, Fukuyama carefully distinguishes state strength from the scope of the state. But many scholars in the Weberian tradition argue that, along with the provision of security, the capacity to tax and provide **public goods** are indeed defining features of the modern state (Evans 1995; see also Chapter 15). For example, Douglass North (1981) and Margaret Levi (1988) argue that the capacity to tax is a cornerstone of the modern state, while Robert Bates (2008: 5) holds that a political order forms a state when rulers—that is, 'specialists in violence':

> ... choose to employ the means of coercion to protect the creation of wealth rather than to prey upon it and when private citizens choose to set weapons aside and to devote their time instead to the production of wealth and the enjoyment of leisure.

The state as an autonomous actor

By understanding the state in organizational and institutional terms, scholars and policymakers in the neo-Weberian tradition tend to view the modern state as an autonomous actor, with the potential to formulate and pursue goals that are not simply reflective of the demands or interests of social groups, classes, or society (Skocpol 1985: 9). As such, they explicitly challenge the Marxist and pluralist theories of the state that dominated the social sciences until the 1980s, whereby the state is understood predominantly as a neutral arena in which different interest groups, ranging from class interests to ethnic groups, freely assert and advance their own goals and missions (even though neo-Marxists have sometimes conceded that the state could be 'relatively autonomous') (Levi 2006).

By emphasizing the autonomous power of states, the neo-Weberian school of thought is intimately linked to the assumptions inherent in institutional theory (see Chapter 3). Within this perspective, depending on the character of the institutions provided by a particular state —that is, the 'rules of the game'—and depending on the degree to which a particular state has the capacity to effectively enforce these 'rules of the game', at least in part through a monopoly of violence, the incentives and opportunities for public goods provision will vary considerably, leading to radically different development outcomes (North 1990; Acemoglu and Robinson 2012). For example, in their much acclaimed work, Acemoglu and Robinson

(2012) argue that variation in development across the former colonies is explained by the existence—or, respectively, absence—of extractive versus inclusive political institutions. *Extractive* institutions—that is, institutions designed to extract rents and maintain power on behalf of the 'few'—fail to create the incentives needed for people to save, invest, and innovate. *Inclusive* institutions—that is, institutions designed to benefit the larger population—instead serve to promote development.

The state as an idea

In contrast with theories that conceptualize the state as a physical organism, other theories define the modern state as helping to constitute the core identities of its subjects. According to this perspective, the modern state is not only a physical entity, but also an 'ensemble of affective orientations, images, and expectations imprinted in the minds of its subjects', as formalized by the means of territorial sovereignty and the institution of citizenship, and as further anchored in society through flags, anthems, currencies, military parades, and embassies (Young 1994: 33).

Within this perspective, the state is more an idea held in common by a group of people than a physical organism. Scholars adhering to this view therefore evaluate state strength not so much on the basis of the state's despotic power, but rather on the basis of its social reach. In particular, a strong state is a state that is able to penetrate its territory institutionally and mobilize the population, much in line with Michael Mann's (1984) notion of **infrastructural power**—that is, the institutional capacity of the state to exercise control and implement policy choices within the territory it claims to govern. As effectively captured by Joel Migdal (1988: 32):

> Social control is the currency over which organizations in an environment of conflict battle one another. With high levels of social control, states can mobilize their populations, skimming surpluses effectively from society, and gaining tremendous strength in facing external foes. Internally, state personnel can gain autonomy from other social groups in determining their own preferences for what the rules of society should be; they can build complex, coordinated bureaus to carry out those preferences; and they can monopolize coercive means in the society to ensure that other groups do not stand in the way of enforcing state rules.

Following from this, Migdal (1988) argues that increasing levels of social control—and thus state strength—are reflected in a scale of three indicators: compliance, participation, and legitimation. Whereas *compliance* refers to the strength of the state to gain conformance to its demands by the population, often with the use of the most basic of sanctions—that is, force, *participation* refers to the strength of the state to organize the population for specialized tasks in the institutional components of the state organization and, as such, denotes some voluntary component. Finally, the most potent factor accounting for the strength of the state—that is, *legitimation*—refers to 'an acceptance, even approbation, of the state's rules of the game, its social control, as true and right' (Migdal 1988: 33). In short, according to this perspective, whereas state institutions are certainly an important aspect of the state, it is in the realm of ideas and sentiment that the fate of states is primarily determined. Without a widespread and deeply rooted idea of the state among the population, the state institutions themselves have difficulty surviving (Holsti 1996).

By emphasizing statehood in terms of a state's social reach, scholars within the 'state-in-society approach' tend to view the state not as autonomous, as scholars adhering to a conceptualization of the state as a physical organism (Migdal 2001); instead, scholars within the state-in-society approach emphasize how, empirically, state strength is often a function of the varied forms in which state–society relations are interwoven. As such, they tend to leave the question about state autonomy open for empirical investigation as they explore how the character of state–society relations shape the state's ability to promote development. For example, Peter Evans (1995) has shown that what differentiates the **developmental state** (that is, a state that has not only presided over industrial transformation, but also can be argued to have played an active role in promoting it) from the 'kleptocratic state' (that is, a state which extracts at the expense of society, undercutting development) is that developmental states have **embedded autonomy**. Developmental states as such combine a Weberian legal-rational bureaucracy with being 'embedded in a concrete set of social ties that binds the state to society and provides institutionalized channels for the continual negotiation and re-negotiation of goals and policies' (Evans 1995: 12). Joel Migdal (1988: 5), on the other hand, asserts that 'the failure of states to have people in even the most remote villages behave as state leaders want ultimately affects the very coherence and character of the states themselves'.

Both conceptualizations of the state commonly found in the literature emphasize territorial control by the use of force as a basic criterion for modern statehood. Yet while conceptualizations of the state as a physical entity emphasize institutional quality and the capacity to tax and provide public goods as key indicators of state strength, conceptualizations of the state as an idea evaluate state strength also in terms of the ability to gain social control, particularly in the form of **legitimacy**. The two accounts also differ in the sense that, whereas, in conceptualizations of the state as a physical entity, the state is modelled as an autonomous actor, conceptualizations of the state as an idea treat the state as socially embedded.

KEY POINTS

- Definitions of the state vary in terms of conceptualization of the state as a physical organism or as an idea.

- How the state is conceptualized leads to different views of what constitutes a strong and a weak state.

- Conceptualizations of the state as a physical entity understand the state as an autonomous actor, whereas conceptualizations of the state as an idea see the state as 'socially embedded'.

Statehood in the Contemporary World

The emergence of the modern state is commonly dated from the sixteenth and seventeenth centuries. The Peace of Westphalia of 1648, which ended the Thirty Years' War and codified solutions to the problems of political order that the war revealed, is generally understood as a critical moment in the development of the modern state. Even though some scholars would question the significance attributed to this particular event, it is commonly understood as the point at which the modern state triumphed as *the* solution to the problem of political order, which then further consolidated and proliferated throughout the eighteenth, nineteenth, and twentieth centuries (Milliken and Krause 2002). Today, few analysts would counter the argument that the modern state—backed up by international norms of sovereignty, as codified in the Montevideo Convention on Rights and Duties of States, signed in

Montevideo, Uruguay on 26 December 1933, and as put into effect by mutual recognition—constitutes the main player in the international arena.

The triumph of the modern state is not least evident in the increased number of internationally recognized, sovereign political entities—that is, what Jackson and Rosberg (1982) would refer to as 'juridical', or *de jure*, states—from fifty-five at the beginning of the last century to 193 today. The last state to claim independence was South Sudan in 2011. Yet another significant number of potential states, including Somaliland, Kosovo, and Palestine, still await their 'ticket of general admission to the international arena' (Fowler and Bunck 1995: 12), in the form of recognition as sovereign political entities—not least since such recognition brings with it a large number of benefits (see Box 12.1).

However, whereas an increasing number of states subscribe to the legitimating doctrine of national sovereignty and claim to derive state power from, as well as exercise it for, a nation, these states vary significantly in terms of how closely they fit the two conceptualizations of the state outlined in the previous section—that is, they vary in terms of state strength, or what Jackson and Rosberg (1982) would call 'empirical', or *de facto*, statehood. In the contemporary world, we find, on the one hand, states that have the capacity to extract huge amounts of taxes, to adopt highly functional policies to avoid human tragedies such as mass starvation and civil war, and to protect their borders from external, as well as internal, threats. On the other

BOX 12.1 THE BENEFITS OF INTERNATIONAL LEGAL SOVEREIGNTY

- Recognized states can more easily, and under formalized conditions, enter into treaties with each other.

- International legal sovereignty offers the possibility for rulers to secure external financial, political, and military support through membership in international organizations, including the United Nations (UN), the International Monetary Fund (IMF), and the World Bank.

- Recognition provides a state—and, by implication, its rulers—with a more secure **status** in the courts of other states, as well as immunity for diplomatic representatives.

- Since recognition as a state is a universally understood construct, any ruler who enjoys this **entitlement** is likely to be more successful in terms of strengthening his or her position vis-à-vis the national population.

hand, there are a large number of sovereign states that do not have the capacity to do any of these things—states that are faced with prolonged and bloody civil strife, a weak state bureaucracy, dysfunctional policies, and low levels of public goods provision. There are even states that stand on the edge of **state collapse**—Iraq, Afghanistan, Syria, Libya, Liberia, Somalia, Sierra Leone, Burundi, and the Democratic Republic of Congo being some of the most recent examples of such a development. In fact, because of the international norm of sovereignty—and the resulting maintenance of territorial borders of even the weakest states—states today are more varied in their capacities and capabilities than ever before (Englebert 2000).

Overall, the largest variation in empirical statehood—as indicated by the number of internal conflicts, the level of (quasi-)voluntary compliance with state policies, the level of **corruption**, and the capacity to collect taxes and to provide public goods—is found between the industrialized and the developing (particularly the previously colonized) parts of the world, the **developing world** being home to comparatively weaker states. In fact, many states in the developing world do not qualify as states even in line with the most basic empirical criterion for statehood, because they lack the ability to control their designated territory even by the use of force. Since the end of the cold war, the world has witnessed an explosion in the number of intra-state conflicts, the majority taking part in the developing world (Jackson and Rosberg 1982). In sub-Saharan Africa, which is home to the majority of internal conflicts, this has been the case in Angola, Chad, Ethiopia, Nigeria, Sudan, Uganda, Somalia, Sierra Leone, Liberia, the Democratic Republic of Congo, and Côte d'Ivoire. However, largely owing to norms of international sovereignty, in only two instances have these conflicts led to *de facto* state collapse in terms of territorial disintegration: in 1993, Eritrea seceded from Ethiopia; and in 2011, South Sudan seceded from Sudan (Englebert and Hummel 2005). Although Somaliland has *de facto* seceded from collapsed Somalia since 1991, it has yet to be recognized by any other state. In Latin America, Peru, Guatemala, El Salvador, and Nicaragua have all recently experienced, or are now experiencing, prolonged civil wars, with the writ of the state being absent from large parts of the countries. In Mexico (see Chapter 23) and Colombia, drug cartels are in control of large segments of the population, as well as of important functions of the state. The same goes for Pakistan, Afghanistan, Iraq,

Libya, and Syria, where the central state has only diminutive control of some of the tribal areas, where **warlords**, guerilla groups, and/or drug cartels are increasingly taking control. At the time of writing, the world is witnessing one of the most tragic state developments in contemporary times, as the repressive Syrian central state—under the lead of President Bashar al-Assad—is crumbling and increasingly losing control to various violent factions of society, as well as to external forces, including the so-called Islamic State, with tremendous human suffering and mass flight as the result (see Chapter 21).

Although it is not fair to describe all states in the developing world as failed or failing in the sense that disorder, lack of control, and violence are widespread and rampant, still typical for many states in these parts of the world is that they have not been able to successfully mobilize their populations on any broader basis (Migdal 1988). Thus, while they may be in possession of despotic power, they (and especially former colonies) often lack infrastructural power, particularly in the form of legitimacy. In many parts of the developing world, tribal and ethnic-based authorities still constitute alternative sources of loyalty that indirectly or directly challenge the loyalty felt against, as well as the ambitions of, the central state. The existence of alternative sources of loyalty is reflected in that many former colonies, particularly in sub-Saharan Africa, operate according to a logic of 'it's our turn to eat' (Wrong 2009), with conflicting interests competing for power and state resources (see Chapter 3).

Even in the absence of competing loyalties, the inability of the state in many developing countries to mobilize the population on a broader basis and the resulting fragmented social control of the central state has serious repercussions for the management and operation of state affairs. In the absence of an organized demand for public goods, the impetus for elites to provide such goods is likely to be low (Persson and Sjöstedt 2012). Moreover, if the political elites were indeed to be incentivized to provide public goods, without the capacity to command loyalty they would be unlikely to be able to do so. This is because, quite in line with the conviction that the costs of maintaining a particular order are inversely related to the legitimacy of that order, in the face of limited social control many states in the developing world suffer high costs in their aim to collect the taxes necessary to provide public goods (Levi 1988).

In the absence of the resources needed to supply programmatic goods, the only alternative that remains for many former colonies is to supply goods on a much narrower basis in return for bribes. The spread of this type of corrupt exchange in the developing world is reflected in different indices of corruption and the extent to which the state operates in line with norms of impartiality (or, in the words of Weber, rational-legal principles), including Transparency International's Corruption Perception Index. In fact, in the more extreme cases of lack of social control—that is, in countries in which the ruling elites not only lack the capacity to command loyalty, but also face competing sources of loyalty and have a comparatively fragile power base—corrupt exchanges and kleptocratic rule can even be understood in terms of '**politics** of survival', because they often constitute the only means—along with repression and violence—by which elites can hold on to power (Migdal 2001).

In short, compared to the typical state in the industrialized world, states in the developing world are comparatively weak. This comparative weakness is effectively reflected in that the survival and welfare of the residents of many of these countries depend on international organizations, **non-governmental organizations** (**NGOs**), and other voluntary groups (Englebert 2009).

Yet, despite the generally bleak picture of state characteristics in the developing world, a small group of strong states must be acknowledged. Described more generally as 'developmental states' (Leftwich 1995), some countries—especially in East and South East Asia, such as South Korea (see Chapter 24), Taiwan, Singapore, Malaysia, China (see Chapter 29), Thailand, and Vietnam—have comparatively been very successful in promoting growth, reducing poverty, and enhancing overall welfare, even if many of these states remain authoritarian. Outside East and South East Asia, Chile, Botswana, Mauritius, and, more recently, Rwanda, are often described in terms of developmental states or 'development success stories' (Acemoglu et al. 2003).

These developmental states have taken both democratic and non-democratic forms (compare Botswana and China), and pursued both formally socialist and capitalist paths (compare China and Singapore). What these developmental states have in common, other than an outstanding development record, is that they are all institutionally strong states. They have concentrated sufficient power, autonomy, capacity, and (sometimes) accountability at the centre to ensure the successful achievement of their development goals (Leftwich 1995). Moreover, they are in possession of enough infrastructural power to mobilize the

population on a comparatively broad basis, if often through coercion.

The success story of Botswana is particularly interesting. To begin with, Botswana was worse off in terms of development and state capacity, including administrative capacity, tax capacity, and public goods provision, at independence than any other ex-British territory in Africa (Acemoglu and Robinson 2012). Yet, within a few years of independence, Botswana managed to turn these meagre prospects on their head. Botswana has moreover challenged the so-called **resource curse** (Ross 1999). This refers to states sometimes described as **rentier states**, in which a major part of state revenues are derived from taxes (hence 'rents') on companies involved in the extraction of some valuable natural resources, such as oil, diamonds (as in the case of Botswana), or copper. It is argued that three consequences for the state and its development capacity may flow from this dependence on resource rents. First, it undermines the prospects for accountable government by reducing the state's need for financial support by the population. Second, as has occurred in Sierra Leone, Nigeria, and Angola, the presence of such resources can fuel intense conflict between groups determined to control the trade or the state to capture the rents, which further weakens, and sometimes even destroys, the central power and authority of an already-weak **post-colonial state**. Third, natural-resource dependence has a direct negative effect on the developmental capacity of states, particularly through the so-called Dutch disease, which refers to a presumed negative causal relationship between growth in one economic sector (for example natural resources) and a decline in other sectors (for example agriculture) (Ross 1999; Leftwich 2014).

KEY POINTS

- The modern state today is generally perceived as *the* solution to the problem of world order.

- Juridical statehood does not necessarily coincide with empirical statehood.

- The contemporary developing world is home to the great majority of weak states.

- Some states in the developing world, including South Korea, Singapore, Taiwan, China, Botswana, Chile, and Rwanda, have managed comparatively well in terms of economic growth and welfare enhancement. These states are often referred to as 'developmental states'.

The Evolution of the Modern State: Variations on a Theme

What explains the general weakness of states in the developing world as compared to states in the contemporary industrialized world? And what explains variation *across* developing countries? While many different accounts have been put forward to explain existing variation in empirical statehood, the varying processes through which the state evolved are often argued to have played the most fundamental role in shaping the variation in outcomes.

State formation in the contemporary industrialized world

Our knowledge of the state-building process in the contemporary industrialized world is derived from a stylized reading of the triumph of the modern state in Western Europe. Conceptually, the emergence of the modern state can be told in at least two different ways—through the lenses of either predatory theory or social contract theory (see Box 12.2). However, contemporary scholars agree that, empirically, the emergence of the modern state in the industrialized world is best understood through the lenses of predatory theory as states in Western Europe typically predated nations.

The modern state in the contemporary industrialized world is typically understood to have emerged and evolved endogenously in the course of external warfare, **nationalism**, and industrialization. At the centre stage for this account is Charles Tilly's (1975: 42) assertion that 'war made the state, and the

state made war'. According to Tilly, the emergence of the modern state can be understood as an unintentional process by which coercive and self-seeking entrepreneurs seeking to consolidate their hold on power acted as the equivalent of protection rackets. These entrepreneurs offered often minimal security in return for extraction, thus unleashing a long process that contributed to the development of the modern state (Tilly 1975; Levi 1981). Since waging war was (and still is) expensive, for states to flourish they needed both resources of men and money within their jurisdiction *and* the capacity to extract them. These needs served to trigger developments in at least three directions, which together led to the emergence of what we today typically refer to as the 'modern state'.

To begin with, it triggered the development of the state apparatus required to extract the resources necessary to fuel these ambitions—that is, a bureaucracy big, organized, and powerful enough to conscribe and tax in an effective and sustainable manner (see Chapter 15).

Second, warfare contributed significantly to the nationalistic discourse that is so intimately linked with the modern state through territorial sovereignty, citizenship, flags, and national anthems, as well as through a history of ethnic cleansing, **genocide**, and the reordering of territorial borders (Mann 1990). This is because it is the fraternity of the nation—derived mainly from the common set of symbols and cognitions shared by the people belonging to it—that ultimately makes it possible for so many millions of people to pay the taxes to, or even willingly die for, the ambitions of the state (Anderson 1983).

BOX 12.2 TWO THEORETICAL ACCOUNTS OF MODERN STATE FORMATION

Two basic theories explain the origins of formalized political power, social contract theory, and predatory theory. Social contract theory, building on the work particularly of Thomas Hobbes, John Locke, and Jean-Jacques Rousseau, understands state formation as a voluntary process whereby individuals with common interests surrender their unlimited freedoms—and unlimited insecurities—to live within a civil order that guarantee security and order, and which, because of the voluntary element characterizing the process, enjoys a certain legitimacy (Olson 1993; Milliken and Krause 2002).

Within predatory theory, peaceful political orders are not assumed to emerge by voluntary agreement; instead, since '[w]hatever the ruler's ends, wealth and power are necessary to achieve them' (Levi 1981: 438), states are theorized to arise as a result of rational self-interest among those who can organize the greatest capacity for violence (Olson 1993). Because the ruler's interests tend to conflict with those of others, the ruler will need to give something in return for the continued support of the ruled (such as protection, property rights, and public goods). This, in turn, leads to the further consolidation of the modern state.

Finally, as the resources required to fund successful state-making and state-maintaining grew, success tended to fall to the most resourceful states (which also tended to be the states in which capitalism was most fully developed). As a result, war-making encouraged rulers to promote productive behaviour among the population (Olson 1993). This in turn set in motion the 'great transformation' from agrarian to industrial societies, which, in an attempt to facilitate and reap the fruits of industrialization, further served as an impetus for rulers to encourage the development of the institutional and regulatory frameworks associated with the modern state (see Box 12.3). In addition, as the industrial sector grew, so did the size and bargaining power of organized labour and, with this, the demands for redistribution (Marshall 1965). As a result, the twentieth century witnessed a transformation in the disposition of public expenditures in the contemporary industrialized world, with growing spending on public goods.

The modern state in the contemporary industrialized world was born out of interstate war, industrialization, and the successful mobilization of national populations. In particular, in a context of no recognition of international legal sovereignty—that is, in an era guided by the norm of 'the survival of the fittest'—state formation was an *endogenous* process, shaped by 'blood and iron' (cf. Bismarck's speech given in 1862 about the unification of the German territories). States that did not, through force or negotiation, manage to acquire the tools of political influence through the mobilization of human and material resources for state action not only fell apart, but also vanished from the map, leaving only comparatively strong states to posterity. At the most cynical level, it has even been argued that the dynamics of interstate war served as a 'filter' by eliminating weak or non-viable political arrangements (Herbst 2003: 166). This statement is supported by the fact that while, in late fifteenth-century Europe, there were some 500 independent political units, by 1900 this number had shrunk to about twenty-five (Tilly 1975).

State formation in the contemporary developing world

The story of state formation in the contemporary developing world is very different from the story of

BOX 12.3 THREE MODELS OF STATE-DRIVEN DEVELOPMENT

Three broad strategies of state-directed development have typically been used by today's leading industrial economies, as follows (Leftwich 2014).

- The Anglo-American and Western European model involves the state ensuring four prime conditions for the promotion of private, market-driven growth, as argued by Douglass C. North (1990):
  - securing property rights;
  - establishing a fair and efficient judicial system;
  - setting out an open and understood system of rules and regulations; and
  - facilitating market entry and functioning.
- The Soviet model of top-down industrialization involves pervasive state ownership, control, and management of the economy.
- The East Asian model of the developmental state involves a close symbiosis between the state and the private sector, and has sometimes been called 'managed capitalism' or 'governing the market'.

the emergence of the modern state in the contemporary industrialized world. In particular, it differs in the sense that the state was typically not shaped endogenously in the course of external warfare, nationalism, and industrialization, but was the result of a process whereby state structures were externally imposed by the colonizing powers. With few exceptions, the state in the developing world is not historically embedded into domestic relations of power and domination, but is rather an exogenous, artificial institution, superimposed over pre-existing political structures and inherited by domestic elites at independence (Englebert 2000). In Asia, the exceptions include China, South Korea, Japan, and Thailand, where some communities can be traced back to prior local (absolutist, monarchical, and imperial) systems and institutions of centralized rule, as in Egypt and Ethiopia in the case of Africa. In Latin America, the main pre-colonial political institutions, especially the great, centralized tribute-extracting empires of the Aztecs (Mexico) and the Incas (Peru), were extinguished by the Spanish conquest from the early sixteenth century, although cultural legacies remain even today.

The most dramatic illustration of the external shaping of geographical boundaries and institutional structures is what is commonly referred to as the **scramble for Africa**. This was the process whereby Africa was divided up between the colonizing powers in an almost cartographic manner. Whereas boundaries in pre-colonial Africa were fluid—so-called frontiers (Herbst 2000)—and based on people, rather than territorially defined, as a result of the external imposition of territorial boundaries being drawn at the 1884–85 Berlin Conference, even today some 44 per cent of the territorial borders in Africa remain straight lines (Herbst 2000).

Since Europe's transfer of its own state system to Africa, as in many places in the developing world, was not accompanied by any prior calculation to make statehood coincide with nationhood, states in the contemporary developing world were, in general, extremely diverse upon independence (Englebert 2002). Moreover, in the absence of the unifying and filtering effects of external warfare, national mobilization has been difficult to achieve. As Clifford Geertz (1973: 261) wrote upon observing the lack of integration of the states of the developing world, 'we have not just competing loyalties, but competing loyalties of the same general order'. This is particularly true in former British colonies—as well as, to some extent, in former Spanish colonies—as a result of the extensive use of so-called **indirect rule** by the colonizing powers.

Indirect rule meant that the colonizers depended on local-level 'bosses', 'big men', or oligarchs, some of whom derived their power originally from their traditional positions (such as the *caciques* of Latin America and the sometimes artificially created 'headmen' or 'chiefs' in colonial Africa) to exercise control, as well as to collect taxes. By granting powers to tribal authorities and strongmen, as well as creating new ones, such policies effectively helped to perpetuate and, in some cases, even to create the kind of tribal and ethnic consciousness that is commonly seen as seriously militating against successful state-building (Englebert 2000). In fact, by creating the building blocks for internal conflict in terms of politically mobilized ethnic, tribal, and religious cleavages, indirect rule in many ways functioned to reduce the prospects for national consciousness for years ahead. This is especially the case since the dynamics of internal warfare—the type of conflict most prevalent in younger states—have proven to differ radically from the dynamics of external warfare that contributed the most

to state-building in Western Europe: rather than 'making' states, internal conflicts seem to 'break' states.

In addition to having long-lasting, negative effects on patterns of national mobilization, the exogenous process of colonial state formation typically implied that there was no parallel process of industrialization and development accompanying the process. Neither did imperial rule lead to a transformation of state institutions in favour of professionalism and impartiality in the manner of the emerging modern states of Western Europe. This is because the project of colonial rule was, almost without exception, undertaken for the benefit of the colonizing countries. As such, the primary objective was the effective extraction of taxes and raw materials at the cheapest administrative cost, and public investments needed to be justified by their contribution to the interests of the colonial power. To the extent that the institutions of colonial rule can be termed 'colonial states' (Young 1994), they were thus essentially what Acemoglu and Robinson (2012) would call **extractive states**, designed to extract incomes and wealth from one subset of society (the masses) to benefit a different subset (the governing elite).

When the former colonies achieved independence, they typically inherited these extractive institutions that coerced the masses to produce wealth for dictators and the elite, retarding the prospects for successful development. In particular, the extractive purposes of the colonial powers played a fundamental role in shaping the types of state and state institution found in the majority of developing countries even today. Most notably, the bargaining with local brokers under indirect rule led to the establishment of complex, reciprocal networks of political influence and **patronage** in and around the institutions of the state, imposing serious constraints on its capacity and autonomy (Kohli 2004). As a result, general access to state-provided public goods has been severely limited throughout the independence period in the majority of former colonies (Banerjee and Somanathan 2007). In addition, indirect rule created a political setting in which patterns of patronage and **patron–client relationships** became pervasive in the post-colonial world, frustrating the emergence and consolidation of an impartial and professional bureaucracy. In large part a result of policies of indirect rule, many citizens and political leaders alike came to conceive of the post-colonial states not so much as the outcome of a social contract, an instrument of collective action based on common ideological convictions or a shared **national identity**, but rather as an 'alien' institution to be appropriated (Englebert 2000).

In sum, diverging stories of state formation in the contemporary industrialized and developing world show that, on the one hand, in the contemporary industrialized world, the state typically evolved endogenously in the course of external warfare, nationalism, and industrialism. The state in the contemporary developing world, on the other hand, was rather an exogenous construction. These different processes of state formation resulted in considerable variation in the level of 'empirical statehood' between the contemporary industrialized world and the contemporary developing world, with the majority of 'strong states' being situated in the contemporary industrialized world and the majority of 'weak states' being situated in the contemporary developing world.

However, not all states in the developing world are weak and there are examples of comparatively strong states also among post-colonial states, such as Botswana, Rwanda, Mauritius, Chile, South Korea, Malaysia, and Taiwan. Political will and high-quality leadership—such as the leadership of the first independent leader of Botswana, Seretse Khama—are often used to explain these success stories (Rotberg 2004b). But it may be argued that patterns of state formation also vary *across* the developing world—and that the resulting variation in the constellation of social, economic, and political forces explains the comparative success of Botswana, as well as of the other development success stories (Persson and Sjöstedt 2012).

For example, the application of indirect rule varied across the former British colonies, and developmental states such as Malaysia, Singapore, Mauritius, and Botswana were not subject to (as) substantive indirect rule as many other former colonies (Lange 2004). In Latin America, the comparative developmental success of countries such as Argentina, Uruguay, and Costa Rica, as compared to countries such as Mexico and Peru, has been attributed to variation in the degree to which the Spanish colonizers installed state institutions for the coordination of a mercantilist economy aimed at the extraction of precious metals and the **exploitation** of indigenous labour. To their advantage in terms of development today, such institutions were not present in the (during colonial times) backwater regions of modern Argentina, Uruguay, and Costa Rica (Mahoney and vom Hau 2005). Yet other aspects of colonial state formation that varied considerably across the former colonies and which have influenced development in the post-colonial period include the degree of artificialness of inherited borders (Englebert 2002), colonial patterns of slave trade (Nunn 2008), and the degree to which extractive (as opposed to inclusive) institutions were established (Acemoglu and Robinson 2012).

KEY POINTS

- The different ways in which the state emerged and evolved in the contemporary industrialized versus the developing world is key to understanding the variation in empirical statehood that we see between these two 'worlds' today.

- The story of the evolution of the modern state in the contemporary industrialized world is typically told through the lenses of state formation in Western Europe.

- In the contemporary industrialized world, the modern state evolved *endogenously*, in the course of external warfare, nationalism, and industrialization.

- In the contemporary developing world, state structures were typically imposed *exogenously* by the colonizing powers.

- Cross-country variation in state strength *within* the developing world is commonly attributed to variation in patterns of colonial state formation.

Opportunities and Strategies for Change

It is estimated that 85 per cent of the world's population today live in weak states and a major problem confronting the contemporary world is how to build strong states where they do not exist. The problem of building strong states has been described as the problem of 'getting to Denmark' after the title of a paper written by two social scientists at the World Bank, Lant Pritchett and Michael Woolcock (2004). The term 'getting to Denmark' refers to the fact that Denmark is perceived as a role model in terms of the quality of its institutions and standard of living.

Depending on what conceptualization of the state one relies on, the characterization of the problem of getting to Denmark—as well as the solution to this problem—will vary. In particular, whereas scholars and policymakers who rely on a conceptualization of the state as an autonomous organization and institution would argue that it is indeed possible to conduct state-building operations from the outside without entering into the contested social sphere, scholars and policymakers who rely on a conceptualization of the state as a socially embedded idea will argue that state-building from the outside will not lead to the expected outcome in terms of development unless the new institutions are firmly anchored in society, through shared expectations and beliefs.

Much in line with Evans and colleagues' (1985) call to 'bring the state back in', the overwhelming majority of scholars and policymakers of today understand the state primarily in organizational and institutional terms, and would argue that state-building is indeed possible to conduct from 'the outside'. As Francis Fukuyama (2006: 2) firmly states, 'the underlying problems caused by failed states or weak governance can only be solved through long-term efforts by outside powers to rebuild indigenous state institutions'.

In line with this reasoning, under the umbrella of the good governance agenda, international donors have promoted a variety of reforms aimed at strengthening the organizational and institutional capacity of states, and subsequently to set the stage for successful development (Pritchett and Woolcock 2004; see also Chapter 15 for a longer discussion).

However, although the vast majority of developing countries have been encouraged, even forced, to adopt the organizational and institutional features of industrialized and better governed states, these reforms have rarely led to the expected outcomes. In quite a few instances, it even seems as though organizational and institutional reforms have contributed to make an already bad situation worse. As forcefully argued by Pritchett and Woolcock (2004: 193), ' "[s]imply mimicking" . . . the organizational forms of a particular "Denmark" has in fact been a root cause of deep problems encountered by developing countries'.

How can we understand this outcome? Scholars adhering to a conceptualization of the state as a socially embedded idea offer a potential answer to this question. These scholars typically agree that organizational and institutional reforms in the form of constitutions, laws, regulations, and bills of rights adapted from successful polities are indeed necessary conditions for successful state-building and development. However, they argue that the outcomes of such

reforms will vary depending on the character of underlying social contracts (Persson and Sjöstedt 2012). Unless there is a shared social contract between the citizens and the state upon which the citizens collectively and (quasi-)voluntarily agree—that is, unless the state is widely perceived as a legitimate instrument of collective action, expected to provide public goods (Levi 1988)—institutions transplanted from industrialized to developing countries are unlikely to have the expected positive effect on development.

According to this perspective, changing beliefs and expectations among the national populations of developing countries is the way forward in transforming an ineffective government to an effective government. Yet how such a revolutionary, endogenous change in **informal institutions** can be achieved has so far attracted surprisingly little attention among scholars (Levi 2006; Persson and Sjöstedt 2012; Persson et al. 2013). An influential literature holds that the developing world, particularly Africa, has a 'secessionist deficit' (Englebert and Hummel 2005). According to this perspective, the splitting of states and redrawing of maps—and presumed subsequent 're-imagining of the nation' (cf. Anderson 1983)—would offer the best solution to the problem of state weakness and its consequences. This approach has, however, been criticized in particular because secessionism has been too rare in the developing world to assess whether it actually helps. Furthermore, in an era of **globalization**, secessionism risks spilling over to other countries and destabilizing whole regions (Collier and Hoeffler 2006). The question of how a strong state can be established where it does not exist thus remains largely unsolved, providing a major challenge for future research.

KEY POINTS

- Depending on how the state is conceptualized, different solutions to the problem of how to strengthen states and achieve positive development outcomes are put forward.
- Conceptualizations of the state as an autonomous organization and institution imply that state-building is possible from 'the outside'.
- Conceptualizations that emphasize the social foundations of states imply that institutional reform from 'the outside' will not deliver the expected development results unless they are accompanied by a change in the beliefs and expectations of national populations.

Conclusion

Virtually all human societies were once organized tribally. Yet over time—in the course of an endogenous, conflict-ridden process of force and negotiation—most countries in the contemporary industrialized world developed new political institutions, which included a central state that can keep the peace, uniform laws that apply to all citizens, accountable government, and public goods provision in return for taxes. However, while citizens of industrialized countries tend to take these institutions largely for granted, they are absent or unable to perform in many of today's developing countries—often with disastrous consequences for the rest of the world (Fukuyama 2011).

Nonetheless, despite the overall weakness of the majority of states, as indicated by widespread internal conflict, corruption, an inability to collect taxes, and the overall failure to deliver even the most basic public goods, until today—even in an era of globalization—the nation-state remains *the* solution to the problems of political order, as codified in the Montevideo Convention on Rights and Duties of States, and as backed up by international norms of legal sovereignty.

With the continued importance of the nation-state in a globalized world, the aim of this chapter has been to disentangle the concept of the modern state. It has identified two main sets of conceptualizations of the state: one that views the state primarily in organizational and institutional terms, and thus as an autonomous actor with the potential to actively influence development outcomes; and one that views the state as a socially embedded idea, constrained by its relations to society. The chapter has explored the characteristics and capabilities of states as they play out empirically in the developing versus industrialized worlds, focusing on how variation in so-called empirical statehood can be traced back to patterns of state formation and evolution. The chapter has shown that the evolution of the modern state in Western Europe—through external warfare, nationalism, and industrialization—set the standard for what we today refer to as 'the modern state'. Finally, the chapter discussed different views on how a 'weak' state can be transformed into a 'strong' one. Whereas scholars and policymakers who adhere to a view of the state primarily as an autonomous organization and institution see state-building from 'the outside' as a possible way forward, scholars adhering to a view of the state also as a socially embedded idea argue that, unless institutional and organizational reforms are firmly anchored in societal beliefs and expectations, they are not likely to have the expected effects. This latter approach has, so far, proven most valid empirically, with a large number of failed state-building efforts from 'the outside'. As long as the nation-state remains *the* solution to the problem of political order, the key challenge that lies ahead for any scholar or policymaker concerned with development remains how reform can be promoted *endogenously* to benefit those billions of people, including 'the bottom billion', to whom Paul Collier (2006) refers in his much-acclaimed book with the same title, who suffer from poverty and despair resulting from state weakness.

? QUESTIONS

1. In what ways do the two main conceptualizations found in the literature on the state differ?
2. In what ways can the differences in empirical statehood between the contemporary industrialized world and the contemporary developing world be seen as the outcome of varying patterns of state formation?
3. Would the relaxation of the norm of international legal sovereignty be a possible solution to the problem of state weakness?
4. What would an alternative to the modern state as *the* solution to the problems of world order look like?
5. In what ways, if any, has the largely external origin of many states in the developing world influenced their form and function?
6. To what extent did the different colonial economic institutions influence the character and capacity of the colonial and post-colonial states?
7. How may globalization pose a threat to state sovereignty in the developing world?

FURTHER READING

Acemoglu, D., and Robinson, J. (2012) *Why Nations Fail: The Origins of Power, Prosperity, and Poverty* (New York: Crown Business) A broad account of the institutional origins of state failure.

Englebert, P. (2002) *State Legitimacy and Development in Africa* (Boulder, CO, and London: Lynne Rienner) This account explains the causes and conditions of state failure in Africa from the perspective that what is lacking in Africa is a state that is firmly anchored in society.

Fukuyama, F. (2011) *The Origins of Political Order: From Prehuman Times to the French Revolution* (New York: Farrar, Straus & Giroux) An in-depth account of the origins of state failure.

Migdal, J. (1988) *Strong Societies and Weak States* (Princeton, NJ: Princeton University Press) The book that set the agenda for much of the research being conducted within the framework of the 'state in society' approach.

North, D. C., Wallis, J. J., and Weingast, B. (2009) *Violence and Social Orders: A Conceptual Framework for Interpreting Recorded Human History* (New York: Cambridge University Press) One of the finest accounts of the problems facing states in the developing world, and how institutional theory can be employed to explain development success and failure.

 WEB LINKS

http://www2.ids.ac.uk/futurestate/   Work and publications of the Centre for the Future State, at the Institute of Development Studies, University of Sussex, which promotes research on how public authority can be strengthened and reconstituted to meet the challenges of the twenty-first century.

http://www.qog.pol.gu.se/   Website of the Quality of Government Institute, offering a wide range of publications and data on the causes, consequences, and nature of impartial, uncorrupted, and competent government institutions.

http://www.transparency.org/   Website of Transparency International, offering information on global corruption, plus the widely used Corruption Perception Index.

http://www.worldbank.org/   Website of the World Bank, offering information and data on different aspects of state weakness and failure, including a large number of policy documents.

 For additional material and resources, please visit the Online Resource Centre at:
http://www.oxfordtextbooks.co.uk/orc/burnell5e/

13

Violent Conflict and Intervention

Astri Suhrke, Torunn Wimpelmann,
and Ingrid Samset

Chapter contents

Overview

This chapter examines patterns of violent conflict in the developing world since the onset of decolonization. It discusses shifts in how scholars and policymakers have understood such conflicts, and how these understandings have informed dynamics of foreign interventions and the international peacebuilding regime that developed in the 1990s. We then turn to new forces that shaped conflict during the first decades of this century.

Introduction: Decolonization and Its Aftermath

In retrospect, it seems remarkable how few of the 100-plus transfers of authority associated with decolonization in Africa and Asia were violent. The transition from colonial rule to independence often took the form of negotiations to widen political participation that enabled colonial rulers to disengage formally, yet retain some influence.

In some cases, however, the transition was violent. A key variable was the willingness of the colonial power to leave, which in turn was influenced by the colonial political economy. The existence of plantation economies with a sizable number of white settlers seemed to predispose the transition towards a violent outcome, as evident in South East Asia, Southern Africa, and Kenya—possibly because plantations are immobile property that is difficult to divide or transfer (Zolberg et al. 1989). Plantation economy by itself was not a necessary condition, however, as the long war over Algeria's independence from France demonstrated. India was another exception, where decolonization entailed an extremely violent partition (see Chapter 2). The colonial power's willingness to withdraw was also shaped by political change in the metropole: while Portugal's authoritarian **regime** waged wars against the liberation movements in its African colonies, the country's own democratic revolution in 1974 led to negotiations for independence in Angola, Guinea-Bissau, and Mozambique.

In Africa and in Indochina, some wars over decolonization were transformed almost seamlessly into continued wars. In several other post-colonial countries, peace was fragile and punctured by renewed strife. Broadly speaking, conflicts arose in relation to identity **politics** within the state, sometimes involving separatist demands, and from revolutionary struggles to capture the state and reshape the social order.

Conflicts related to ethnicity or 'identity politics' followed several patterns (see Chapter 7). Polities with 'ranked' or 'hierarchical' ethnic systems, in which distinctions between ethnic groups coincided with those between the ruler and the ruled, appeared particularly fragile (Horowitz 1985; Wucherpfennig et al. 2012). Violence directed against ethnic minorities occurred as part of state formation and **nation-building** policies in a number of newly independent states—a phenomenon known from European history as well. In Uganda, for instance, in 1972 President Idi Amin forcibly expelled the country's Indian minority, a move that enabled him to seize the assets of a prosperous trading group and, perhaps more importantly, harness an African **national identity** as a source of **legitimacy** for his rule. Other post-colonial conflicts pitted ethnic groups in the geographic periphery against the centre over autonomy or separatist demands. While expressed in ethnic terms, secessionist conflicts also reflected concurrent economic and political grievances or ambitions, for example Sri Lanka's civil war from 1983 to 2009 and Biafra's quest for independence from Nigeria in the 1960s.

The solid consensus among post-colonial governments against redrawing colonial boundaries ensured, however, that very few secessionist struggles succeeded. In other cases, independence struggles developed into conflicts over the political and socio-economic order, pitting rebels or revolutionary movements against existing elites, as in Southern Africa and Indochina. In Latin America, where decolonization had taken place in the nineteenth century, struggles over the political and socio-economic order followed different trajectories. In Central America, protests against deep-seated inequalities developed into revolutionary movements that gathered momentum in the 1970s and 1980s to challenge the landed oligarchy and its grip on the state. In South America, the military seized power in a wave of coups: by 1977, the armed forces governed in every state except for Colombia and Venezuela. Their shared rationale was to quell perceived national security threats from leftist and communist forces. These conflicts became hardwired into the cold war, which will be discussed next.

> **KEY POINTS**
>
> - Transitions from colonial rule in many cases gave way to conflicts related to political exclusion within the newly independent states.
> - Some transitions came with a war for independence. In parts of South East Asia and Southern Africa, wars for independence were transformed into protracted domestic conflicts.
> - Post-colonial secessionist struggles occurred, but colonial borders mostly held.

Social Order Conflicts and the Cold War

By definition, conflicts over the social order in a society—previously often called 'class conflict', now mostly understood in relation to political and socio-economic divisions—have local roots. Beyond the local dimensions of the social order conflicts of the 1970s and 1980s, however, was a common element that added coherence and destructive intensity: the conflicts interacted with a renewed intensification of the cold war. Conflicts over social change became expressed in the dominant discourse of the time—revolutionary socialism versus liberal democracy—which linked them to the ideologized power struggle between the Soviet Union and the United States. Recognizing that direct conflict between themselves would be mutually and unacceptably destructive given their nuclear parity, the superpowers instead intervened competitively in the global periphery. Local conflicts in what was then the 'Third World' became wars by proxies in which local protagonists received extensive military, economic, and political support.

In this logic, the United States supported military regimes in South America to crush actual or suspected leftist movements; in Chile, it helped to overthrow the democratically elected government of Salvador Allende in 1973. Washington supported anti-communist rebels in Nicaragua (the *contras*), and assisted the governments of Guatemala (see Chapter 26) and El Salvador in the long-running civil wars in these countries. The Soviet Union provided material support to the other side, mainly through Cuba. The communist regime in place there from 1959 onwards served as a funnel for assistance to rebel movements on the left, while leaders such as Fidel Castro and Che Guevara were sources of inspiration.

In Southern Africa, a similar pattern developed. The South African **apartheid** regime and the still white-ruled Rhodesia (today's Zimbabwe) both sided with the United States in the cold war while supporting armed opposition groups in the region that were seen as anti-communist. Thus the UNITA rebels in newly independent Angola were backed by South Africa, while RENAMO in Mozambique's civil war were backed by both South Africa and Rhodesia. On the other side of these conflicts, Cuba sent doctors, and the Soviet Union provided economic and military aid. Most independent African governments extended sanctuary for fighters and refugees. The result was an intricate web of interaction between local, regional, and international actors, often producing a self-reinforcing dynamic that sustained violence on the local level and increased hostility between the superpowers.

Even a more indirect backdrop of large power rivalry could fuel massive local violence, as in Indonesia in 1965 (see Box 13.1).

The most destructive of these local-cum-cold-war dynamics occurred when the superpowers moved from supporting **proxy wars** in the **developing world** to engage with their own troops on the ground. In Indochina, the United States became heir to the failed French attempt to prevent the Vietnamese from gaining independence after the Second World War. The French withdrew in 1954, leaving a country divided between a northern part ruled by the Vietnamese Communist Party and a southern part ruled by a

BOX 13.1 THE 1965 VIOLENCE IN INDONESIA

President Sukarno, who had led the independence struggle against the Dutch after the Second World War, had ruled with few serious challenges to his power until two other main forces emerged: the Communist Party of Indonesia (PKI) and the army. The delicate political balance collapsed in 1965, in a context of rising international tension between the United States and the main communist powers. China was accused of using the PKI as an instrument of global communist expansion, while the United States was increasing its military engagement in Vietnam to prevent the 'dominoes' from falling to communism throughout South East Asia. Against this background, the Indonesian armed forces set in motion a massive operation to physically eliminate the PKI. At least half a million people were killed—many in private vendettas that, in a familiar pattern, unfolded in the shadow of the overarching political conflict. The next president, General Suharto, abrogated the previous foreign policy of non-alignment and Indonesia became a main recipient of US military aid, as well as economic assistance from the International Monetary Fund (IMF) and the World Bank (see also Chapter 20).

staunchly anti-communist Catholic elite. To shore up the south, the United States gradually increased its troop commitments and air power to fight what it saw as global communism, thus giving the war a world-historical significance, as well as testing the **status** of the United States as a superpower.

The Vietnam War also spilled over into Laos and Cambodia, in the latter country setting in motion a chain of events that produced the Khmer Rouge and its social revolution. Seeking to turn Cambodia back to 'year zero', the Khmer Rouge rule in Cambodia (1975–79) cost between 1 million and 2 million lives (in a population of around 7 million) as people deemed useless to the revolution were killed or succumbed to its rigours. The excesses were stopped by another military intervention (led by a rival Khmer faction supported by neighbouring Vietnam), but ignited a new civil war as the Khmer Rouge and other Khmer factions fought on from sanctuaries in neighbouring Thailand.

A mirror image of the conflict dynamic in Vietnam appeared in Afghanistan, where a local communist party, the People's Democratic Party of Afghanistan (PDPA), seized power in April 1978 and proclaimed a revolution. The Afghan revolution violently eliminated its enemies, brooked no compromise with established landed elites and religious leaders, and sparked a counter-revolutionary movement of *muja-hidin* ('holy warriors') who assembled across the border in Pakistan. By late 1979, the Soviet Communist Party, which had close 'fraternal relations' (the term in the Communist Party lexicon for relations between communist governments, whether cordial or not) with the PDPA and a long-time interest in securing a strategic and economic foothold in Afghanistan, decided to send its own troops and airpower to impose some order. The result was a massive escalation of the war as the resistance movement gathered force, now significantly helped by the United States, its allies, and China (which by this time was in a deep conflict with the Soviet Union). After a decade of fighting, the Soviet Union withdrew its forces in 1989, but peace did not come to Afghanistan. The resistance movement now split into warring factions, starting a civil war of its own in the early 1990s, the excesses of which enabled the Taliban to gain power as a force of order and justice.

KEY POINTS

- The cold war intensified conflicts over the social order across the developing world, leading to 'proxy wars'.
- Conflicts involving the military forces of one or the other superpower directly were particularly destructive, as in South East Asia and Afghanistan.

The Nature of Conflicts in the post-Cold-War World

The end of the cold war gave decisive momentum to peace negotiations dealing with some of the most stubborn wars of proxy. Between 1991 and 1994, peace talks commenced or were concluded in Angola, Cambodia, El Salvador, Guatemala, and Mozambique; of these, only the Angola accords collapsed. The peace settlements—based on compromises between the contending parties—signalled the end of an era of revolutionary struggles. With the collapse of the Soviet bloc and the consequent blow to the status of state socialism, liberal democracy and the market economy became dominant paradigms for social change and foreign assistance.

Yet hopes that the 1990s would inaugurate a new world order without wars were not vindicated. The number and overall severity of conflicts, as measured by battle-related deaths, decreased overall, but varied by region (Human Security Report Project 2005; Lacina 2006). Civil war erupted in Liberia (1989) and Sierra Leone (1991), in both cases lasting for a decade or more. Wars in the Great Lakes region of Africa and the Balkans in the early 1990s were followed by **genocide** in Rwanda in 1994 and in Bosnia in 1995. Failure to prevent these disasters dashed the optimism of the early 1990s and heralded a rethink of policies of intervention (to which we return later in the chapter). Meanwhile Rwanda's major neighbour to the west, the Democratic Republic of the Congo (DRC), became the scene of two wars from 1996 to 2003, both involving a range of regional actors as well. In Angola, the peace of the early 1990s collapsed and war resumed in two phases (1992–94 and 1998–2002). In the Horn of Africa, the Ethiopian civil war came to an end in 1991, but unrest continued in Somalia.

What forces were driving these conflicts? The surface manifestations seemed chaotic. Military factions mobilized clan, tribe, or other ethnic supporters, fighting for no clear political agenda apart from capturing power. With the end of the globalized struggle between communism and capitalism, analysts struggled to understand the nature of the conflicts in the developing world. The explanations focused variously on ethnicity and tribalism, natural resources, **state failure**, poor **governance**, and rapid democratization. New analytical approaches to the study of conflict were generated (see Box 13.2). Some analysts argued that the wars of the 1990s were qualitatively different from previous wars, marked by extraordinary violence and barbaric attacks on civilians, the force of ethnicity, and the internationalized structure of funding (Kaldor 1999). The claim of newness in relation to violence against civilians was easily refuted (Kalyvas 2001), but other features were more novel.

The 'new wars' and their causes

The conflicts in Somalia, Rwanda, and the Balkans were at the forefront of international attention in the first half of the 1990s. The significance of ethnicity in these cases revived the notion that it was a principal driver of conflict. Yet, as noted earlier, ethnic identity alone does not cause conflict; it typically interacts with political and socio-economic factors. In Somalia, for instance,

BOX 13.2 STUDYING THE PROCESSES OF WAR

The study of the social and economic processes involved in war became more important from the 1990s onwards, partly as an entry point to understanding the post-cold war order. Some scholars focused on how wars were organized and financed, while others questioned the conventional distinctions between war and peace as discrete phenomena. Anthropologists and other social scientists studied war (and other forms of violence) as a social process, and the historical conditions that enabled and shaped conflicts in particular ways (for example Richards 2004; Wood 2008).

In this perspective, if there was something fundamentally new about the wars after the cold war, it was linked to changes in their historical settings. In particular, because financing from

superpowers largely ceased in the early 1990s, the need for new sources of funding for warfare gave rise to 'war economies' as armed groups engaged in resource accumulation. Some governments raised militias to fight wars on the cheap; others outsourced fighting to private contractors. As the discipline and cohesion of some national armies weakened, warfare became more decentralized, often intersecting with local and regional conflict dynamics. Militias were mobilized with appeal to tribal and **ethnic identities**. Demobilized military personnel also found jobs as mercenaries in conflict elsewhere. Many former soldiers of the army of the South African apartheid era, for instance, went to work for private military companies in Sierra Leone, Angola, and similar conflict scenes.

Siad Barre, president during the cold war era, was no longer able to sustain his rule with funding from superpowers that once had been eager to have a foothold in his strategically located state. His **patronage**-based regime collapsed and the state imploded. A protracted struggle for power ensued among major clans, with varying degrees of violence. Similarly, the end of Soviet funding to Afghanistan led to the fall of the communist government, opening the way for renewed civil war that now was fought largely along ethnic lines, between Pashtun, Tajik, Uzbek, and Hazara.

In Africa, natural resources were identified as a significant driver of violent conflict given the ready availability of diamonds, other minerals, and timber that helped to finance warring factions. Taking the point much further, some analysts claimed that contemporary wars were largely explained by the search for profit: the real purpose of war was not to win, but to engage in business ventures under cover of warfare (see Box 13.3).

The most elaborate and influential formulation of this claim was made by economist Paul Collier. Drawing on statistical analysis, Collier and colleagues (2003) argued that civil wars were driven by individual 'greed', rather than by collective grievances related to political exclusion and socio-economic conditions. Collier's economic model is derived from rational choice theory, in which the self-interested individual calculating cost–benefit is the starting point for explaining social behaviour. In this model of war, the existence of natural resources suggests ready availability of lootable goods, which makes rebellion a profitable undertaking, and a large number of unemployed and uneducated young men provide a pool of likely soldier-entrepreneurs.

Poverty and **underdevelopment** thus provide incentives for individuals to go to war, which in turn impoverishes the country. To exit from the perpetual conflict that traps countries, therefore, rapid economic growth, economic diversification, and foreign assistance were necessary (Collier et al. 2003).

The 'conflict trap' model was a more specific version of the long-standing theme in Western liberal discourse to the effect that poverty—or, more broadly, economic underdevelopment—causes conflict. The perspective had its critics. There were concerns about assumptions and methods (Humphreys 2005; Cramer 2006). A low level of education, for instance, did not necessarily mean that young males were joining a rebel group to make a living ('greed'); they might as well be joining to challenge exclusion or discrimination ('grievance'). The policy implications of the model were decidedly conservative: if rebels are driven only by personal greed, by implication, they have no claim to political legitimacy. By contrast, if rebellions in Africa and elsewhere were a response to lack of employment and educational opportunities, and anger over widespread **corruption** and bad governance—in effect, a crisis of the state—rebellion was a distinctly political and arguably legitimate action even if it lacked recognizable ideological claims or organizational cohesion (Keen 2012).

The economic interpretation of the 1990s conflicts in Africa and elsewhere largely overlooked the ways in which the international context shaped conflicts in the developing world. As in the case of Sierra Leone's 'blood diamonds', the looting and trading of valuables were made possible by international demand. The

BOX 13.3 SIERRA LEONE'S 'BLOOD DIAMONDS'

The civil war in Sierra Leone (1991–2002) was partly financed by the sale of diamonds, which the Revolutionary United Front (RUF) rebels in particular exploited. But the war was not simply driven by greed for profit. Political exclusion and deteriorating living conditions had led many to join the rebellion. The wartime diamond economy, moreover, did not represent a radical departure from peacetime practices in trade and production: a regional and international network of illicit trade and production in diamonds had existed for decades before the war. The RUF and other factions tapped into these structures, often entering into alliances with established traders, miners, and exporters. Many of the actors in Sierra Leone's diamond industry thus remained the same throughout war and peace.

same applied to the small arms trade that sustained the wars. Cheap and light weapons, partly pilfered from ex-Communist-Army stockpiles, were readily transported to conflict spots in the Global South by a network of arms traders. More generally, the increasingly deregulated global economy in the post-cold-war world, which accelerated global trade, communications, and financial transfers, also strengthened networks for arms trade, money laundering, and drug trafficking that were integral to the wars in the South. The industrialized world has been slow to recognize this; the more common reaction in the North has been to interpret instability as a symptom of underdevelopment. Nevertheless, there has been a growing willingness to regulate the global commons, as seen in the Kimberley Process for 'conflict diamonds', the United Nations' efforts to regulate the conventional arms trade by treaty, and, more recently, controls to prevent international financial flows from going to non-state armed groups defined as **terrorists**.

KEY POINTS

- The end of the cold war made space for the settlement of many protracted conflicts—notably, in Cambodia, Guatemala, El Salvador, and Mozambique.

- New wars erupted, however, and explanations were sought in the role of natural resources ('wars for profit') and underdevelopment.

- Claims that these 'new wars' were qualitatively different from 'old wars' were disputed.

New Forces

The attacks on Washington, DC, and New York on 11 September 2001 ('9/11') triggered a globalized, US-led military offensive against militant Islamic movements and their supporters. For students of contemporary history, it was a case of *déjà vu*, suggesting a conflict dynamic familiar from the cold war. Conducted initially in the Middle East, South West Asia, and the Horn of Africa, the **war on terror** became a globalized, deeply ideologized construct that penetrated and altered local conflicts, shored up local clients, demonized the adversary, and intensified the violence. The main difference was that the adversaries this time were, on the one hand, a *de facto* coalition of powerful states, with the United States, Russia, and China repeatedly finding themselves in agreement on the need to fight 'terrorists' and, on the other hand, a decentralized network of militant Islamists. Not openly backed by states, the militants sought to compensate for their material weakness by engaging in terrorist action, including in the homelands of their state adversaries. Asymmetric warfare—often sophisticated drones versus home-made bombs—was increasingly replacing the more conventional warfare of an earlier era. At the end of the decade, hugely destructive wars by proxy were fought as well, although this time primarily by the regional powers, as Iran and Saudi Arabia, in particular, intervened in the civil wars in Syria and Yemen, as well as in the renewed armed conflict in Iraq.

Militant Islam and the 'war on terror'

The first and principal front in the 'war on terror' was Afghanistan, which the United States invaded in 2001 to destroy Al Qaeda and its local Taliban allies. At the time, the Taliban regime controlled some 90 per cent of the countryside, while the main Afghan opposition had regrouped in the north. While the Taliban were easily driven from power in Kabul, building a new and legitimate administration was far more difficult. Efforts by the US-led coalition forces to hunt down suspected Taliban and Al Qaeda members in the countryside had limited success. Many had simply regrouped in neighbouring Pakistan or temporarily 'hung up' their arms, watching as US raids created local resentment. By mid-decade, the insurgency had re-established itself in the south-east; by the end of the decade, it affected most of the country.

The international forces led by the United States and the North Atlantic Treaty Organization (NATO) were gradually increased, reaching almost 150,000 by the end of the decade. The force level was comparable to the Soviet military presence at its peak during the 1980s. The Taliban and associated militant groups fought back, using asymmetric warfare, including attacks on civilians, to achieve their declared aim of driving out the 'infidel' invaders, defeating the 'puppet' government, and restoring Afghanistan as an Islamic emirate. By 2010, the international coalition recognized that this was not a winnable war, and that ambitions to transform Afghan state and society in a Western image were quite unrealistic despite the massive investment. By the end of 2015, most international combat forces had been withdrawn, leaving around 10,000 US troops and a smaller number of allied units to undertake special operations and train the Afghan armed forces. Violence continued, however. Barring a breakthrough in efforts to negotiate a peace, the future looked dim, with prospects at best for what had been aptly called a 'durable disorder' (Goodhand 2012).

The 9/11 attack on the United States had given the administration of George W. Bush a pretext to invade Iraq, where President Saddam Hussein had kept a fractured polity together primarily by repression and oil-fuelled patronage. The 2003 invasion brought down Hussein and dismantled the central coercive instruments of his state (the Ba'th Party and the army). A violent struggle for power defined by ethnic and sectarian lines ensued, alongside military resistance to the American occupation regime (see Chapter 22). Iraq soon became a magnet for militants, just as Afghanistan had been in the 1980s. Although the US occupation regime was dismantled and, by 2011, all US troops had withdrawn, violence continued. In a related development, Sunni insurgents coalesced with like-minded fighters across the border in Syria, where a civil war had erupted in 2011, leading to the emergence of the group today known as the so-called Islamic State. By 2015, the group controlled large swaths of territory straddling the Syria–Iraq border. Alongside the attempts to end the war in Syria, this triggered new military intervention by the United States and its allies in Iraq and Syria, and by Russia in Syria (see Chapter 21).

Local conflicts elsewhere had early on been brought into the orbit of the 'war on terror'. The Philippine government received US assistance to fight Muslim rebel movements that for years had been fighting for autonomy in the southern islands. In Somalia, the emergence of local Islamist bodies (the Islamic Courts Union) provoked an invasion by Ethiopian forces in 2006, assisted by the United States. A 'moderate' Somali government was installed in an attempt to deny Islamic militants the use of Somalia as a sanctuary. The government controlled little territory beyond the capital, however, while remaining factions of the Islamic Courts formed a separate, hard-line movement (*al-Shabaab*) to fight the government and its international supporters, including a peacekeeping force deployed by the African Union.

To ensure full coverage of the African continent in the new security paradigm, in 2007 the US government established a separate military command for the area (AFRICOM). Yet this did not prevent—and indeed may have helped to provoke—the continued growth of militant Islam in sub-Saharan Africa. Militant and Islamist groups launched violent attacks in Mali, Nigeria, and Kenya, networking with kindred militants in North Africa, the Horn, and the Middle East, and drawing on the ready supply of weapons that became available with the advancing state of conflict and disorder in much of that area. But they were also adept at exploiting local grievances and political agendas, as exemplified by the alliance between Al Qaeda affiliates and Tuareg separatists in Mali.

Fear of terrorism after 9/11 had set in motion a series of interventions across continents that left a trail of polarized and violent political landscapes. These interventions also posed challenges to the idea of impartiality of multilateral peace operations, which, after the cold war, had become the policy tool of choice for the **international community** to deal with 'failed states' and build peace (see Box 13.4).

The international peace-building regime

The end of the cold war had opened up space for new forms of international activism. The Western world had taken a renewed interest in ending conflicts in the developing world, but also found greater opportunities for military intervention. A reinvigorated United Nations had engaged itself early to make, secure, and build peace. The organization was involved in most of the major peace negotiations that took place in the aftermath of the cold war and took the lead in developing an international peace-building regime.

BOX 13.4 FAILED STATES—AND FAILED STATE-BUILDERS

From the early 1990s and onwards, the concept of 'state failure' had figured as a particular understanding of 'underdevelopment'. Early formulations were built around the divergence between *de jure* and *de facto* status. Robert Jackson (1990), for example, argued that while most countries in the developing world are formally recognized in the international system as states, they lack *de facto* statehood—that is, the capacity to perform basic functions associated with the modern state, above all providing security and basic services. As a result, they are only 'quasi-states'.

The 9/11 attacks and the US-led response caused a spike in the concept's popularity in Western policy discourse as a diagnosis of severe underdevelopment in the South that threatened international order. Western think tanks constructed indexes of 'failed', 'fragile', or 'collapsed' states. A large 'how to' literature laid out basic concepts, sequences, strategies, and tools with which to reconstruct states after misrule or upheavals. The high level of ambition was captured in the title of one widely cited book, *Fixing Failed States* (Ghani and Lockhart 2008).

A critical literature developed as well. So-called failed states, it was noted, were a very diverse group. Some, such as Haiti, hardly represented a threat to international peace and security. Some presumptively 'failed states' seemed to manage for a while through grass-roots governance and local authority structures, as seemed the case at one point in Somalia (Menkhaus 2006–07). The model also suggested that the causes of failure were all internal.

On a more theoretical note, critics of the 'failed state' concept argued that it led 'state-builders' mistakenly to see the state as a system—an empirically observable, functional organization—autonomous and separate from society (Heathershaw 2011). Attempting to transplant a model Western state into a wide range of different contexts was fundamentally misguided; it failed to recognize that 'the state' was, in fact, a name for a set of political relations that had emerged historically and were unique in each context. Imposing a formal **institutional** design in the hope that such relations would materialize was likely to fail and could well be counter-productive. Instead, external 'state-builders' needed to understand the 'elite bargains' (North et al. 2009) that underpinned a given political order, and recognize that foreign economic and military assistance influenced such settlements in important, but often unintended, ways.

Then UN Secretary-General Boutros Boutros-Ghali defined the agenda in a 1992 document entitled *An Agenda for Peace* (United Nations 1992). During the next two decades, the international peace-building regime expanded massively. By mid-2016, the United Nations had sixteen active peacekeeping operations around the world, involving just over 100,000 personnel and an annual budget of nearly US$8 billion (UN DPI 2016). While peacekeeping also had taken place during the cold war, it expanded massively in the 1990s and took on a number of new functions, including **human rights** monitoring, facilitation of elections, and reform of the armed forces and police. Initially called 'multidimensional peacekeeping', these operations were designed to support a country's own capacity to provide security, support development, and facilitate democratic participation—aims that also became central in the broader peace-building agenda. The UN Peacebuilding Commission was established in 2005 to direct and closely monitor peace-building in select countries emerging from armed conflict. Traditional development agencies reshaped some of their activities as peace-building as well. The World Bank and the UN Development Programme (UNDP), for example, established special organizational units to deal with so-called post-conflict situations. For donor agencies, international **non-governmental organizations (NGOs)**, and humanitarian and development organizations, peace-building represented a massive growth industry.

'Peace-building' soon came to mean a standardized package of post-war aid. It was designed to fulfil multiple aims in countries that had experienced armed conflict: to provide security in the initial phase after the war ended; to promote and monitor demilitarization of the ex-belligerent groups; to assist the return of refugees; to promote economic recovery; to help restore or reform state institutions; to hold elections; and to promote the establishment of **rule of law** and respect for human rights. In many cases, accountability mechanisms were established to address human rights violations perpetrated during the conflict. The package was developed by the major state aid agencies, the international financial institutions (the World Bank, the IMF, the regional development banks), and the specialized UN agencies (especially UNDP, the World Food Programme, and the United Nations High Commissioner for Refugees), as well as the UN Secretariat. It was further streamlined by international organizations such as the Organisation for Economic

Co-operation and Development (OECD), which, in the 2000s, started harmonizing guidelines for aid to peace-building activities.

In the 1990s, economic and political liberalization were strongly advocated by Western governments and international organizations as a foundation for a more peaceful world. Drawing on the democratic peace theory, which holds that war between states is less likely if the states have a democratic political system, the idea of democracy as a cornerstone of peace was celebrated in triumphalist terms by some scholars. In the words of Larry Diamond, a co-founder of the US *Journal of Democracy*:

> Countries that govern themselves in a truly democratic fashion do not go to war with one another . . . [They] do not 'ethnically' cleanse their own populations . . . [They] do not sponsor terrorism . . . [They] form more reliable, open and enduring trading partnerships . . . [They] are more environmentally responsible because they must answer to their own citizens.

(Diamond, cited in Paris 2004: 35)

Arguments along these lines underpinned Western support for democratization, which was a pillar in the international peace-building regime. The social science literature was more sceptical, noting that while established democracies tend to be internally peaceful and not to wage war on each other, they do go to war against non-democratic states (for example the NATO bombing of Serbia in 1999 and Libya in 2011, and the US-led invasions of Afghanistan and Iraq), albeit typically in the name of a higher value. Moreover, the road to a fully democratic stage is, statistically speaking, paved with violence and unrest (Hegre et al. 2001). In recent years, it has also been acknowledged that **democracy promotion** over the last two decades has had limited effect, as discussed in the twenty-fifth anniversary issue of the *Journal of Democracy* (Carothers 2015).

How, then, do we assess the impact on peace itself of this full inventory of activities covered by 'peace-building'? Quantitative studies suggest that the post-conflict package tends to prevent a relapse into full-scale war, at least early on (Doyle and Sambanis 2006). Historical analysis of the capacity of the UN system to meet the enormous challenges of peace-building confirms that peace operations usually have stabilizing functions, but note problems of legitimacy and effectiveness (Berdal 2009; Sisk 2013). Case studies

can be marshalled on either side of the balance sheet, but critics stress that intrusive missions typically have counter-productive effects. The emblematic case in this respect is Afghanistan, where massive international assistance generated dependence and resentment, overwhelmed local capacity, and undermined the legitimacy of Afghan authorities, thus failing to establish sustainable institutions. Most problematic were the inherent contradictions between the demands of building peace while waging war against a growing insurgency. The war necessitated alliances with abusive and corrupt local strongmen, justified military tactics that led to civilian casualties, and encouraged an intrusive international role to ensure 'control'. All were anathema to peace-building (Suhrke 2011).

The 'liberal peace' paradigm that framed peace-building centred on democratization and a market economy. Both systems are structured around competition and, critics maintained, are unsuitable for countries with wounds still raw from the violence of past conflicts. Instead of stabilizing conditions, more conflict was likely to occur (Newman et al. 2009). Liberalization before institutionalization was a particular recipe for conflict, concluded Paris (2004) in an oft-cited study of post-war situations, but with wider application.

A more radical critique claimed that the basic function of peace-building was to manage the effects of economic exclusion of the developing world that threaten Western interests in the form of refugee flows, transnational crime, epidemic diseases, and terrorism. As formulated by Mark Duffield (2001), peace-building in this perspective was a security intervention by the developed world to control and contain the global poor, thereby preserving the present international power structure.

'People power' and its aftermath

The 'Arab uprisings', or 'Arab Spring', that started in late 2010 in the Middle East and North Africa took most analysts by surprise, although in retrospect the historical logic appears reasonably clear (Joffe 2011). Autocratic regimes in Arab states had long been maintained by a coercive state apparatus, buttressed by Western support in the name of international stability—first against communism, and then, after 9/11, against militant Islam. For European states, it was also useful to have stable and capable state governments with which to partner in their attempts to control migration flows into Europe.

Yet corrosive forces had been at work since the early 1990s. In part as a response to demands for market reforms by the World Bank and the IMF, the Egyptian and Tunisian governments had started to privatize and deregulate the economy. The immediate benefits of reforms were captured by a small elite; the other side of this kind of 'crony capitalism' was deepening inequality and poverty. In Egypt, for instance, the **privatization** of the textile mill industry caused tens of thousands of workers to lose their jobs. In Tunisia in 1994, Abdelbaki Hermassi (1994: 241) had noted already a 'great bifurcation between those groups and classes that are incorporated in the world economy and those groups that are excluded from it'. The contradictions between economic **liberalism** and political authoritarianism—or what the anthropologist Clifford Geertz called 'authoritarian liberalism'—had indeed been building throughout the region. Aspiring middle classes and impoverished workers found a common ground for protest. The demographics of a rapidly expanding population of youth exerted additional pressure, as did unemployment and a sharp rise in the absolute number of poor. At the same time, **globalization** of communications helped to empower and connect the discontented with an emerging social infrastructure of protest, online and in the streets. The coercive state could no longer depend on controlling the flow of information.

The Arab uprisings affected almost all of the countries of the Middle East and North Africa, although to varying degrees. The aftermath was even more starkly varied: devastating civil war in Syria and Yemen; NATO military intervention and violent conflict in Libya; an interlude of Islamist rule followed by return of military rule in Egypt; and cautious political pluralism in Tunisia, where a street vendor's self-immolation had been the first sign of spring. Yet we can discern two main trajectories of change. In Tunisia and Egypt, the old regimes were overthrown rapidly and with little bloodshed, although the aftermath in Egypt turned violent as the Islamists and the army struggled for power and the latter reasserted its rule. Protracted conflict in Libya and Syria, by contrast, showed more clearly the limits of 'people power' (see Chapter 11). In Syria, the civil war that followed a brief popular uprising was, by 2014, by far the most lethal armed conflict worldwide (Pettersson and Wallensteen 2015; see also Chapter 21). In Libya, the opposition to Qaddafi's regime was bold, but divided; NATO's military intervention that brought down that regime in late 2011 was followed by years of extensive violence (see Box 13.5).

BOX 13.5 LIBYA AND THE RESPONSIBILITY TO PROTECT

In September 2005, the UN General Assembly endorsed the principle of an international **Responsibility to Protect (R2P)** populations exposed to particularly grave human rights violations. Libya became an important test case for how R2P could work in practice.

With uprisings ongoing in neighbouring Tunisia and Egypt, by early 2011 Libyans too dared to stand up against the regime of Muammar Qaddafi, which in response deployed its security forces. Because Libya is in the intersection between Africa and the Arab world, a transit state for migrants and a key oil exporter, the government's violent repression attracted much attention. Despite attempts by the African Union to mediate in Libya, in March 2011 the UN Security Council authorized the use of force in the name of protecting civilians. An Anglo-French initiative, the move was controversial. US President Obama did not push for intervention and powerful Council members—Brazil, Russia, India, China, and Germany—abstained from voting. The intervention itself went far beyond its mandate. NATO airpower was used to bomb government targets, leading

Qaddafi's regime to fall. And while some civilians were protected, others were killed or injured as 'collateral damage'. NATO's expansive interpretation of the mandate attracted fierce criticism and helped to trigger the deadlock in the Council over the emerging war in Syria.

Yet, on the streets of Tripoli, the fall of the dictatorship was greeted with relief. Turnout was high in the 2012 election. But the legacy of personalized rule proved hard to overcome, as NATO arguably should have considered before intervening. Qaddafi had instilled scepticism against the state, while skilfully playing groups against each other to retain power. Such regional and ethnic allegiances now took hold, complicating attempts to build institutions that could provide essential services. The small UN mission was unable to prevent tensions from escalating and, by 2014, Libya found itself in a conflict that attracted so-called Islamic State loyalists, as well as military intervention by the Arab League. Talks led to several peace agreements in 2015, but they remained fragile. As R2P reached its tenth anniversary, the initial enthusiasm about this idea seemed to have got lost somewhere between Tripoli and Damascus.

How are we to understand these transformations? The early literature focusing on the Arab Spring mostly saw events through the lens of societies transitioning to political democracy. The participation of Islamists in the elections in Tunisia (2011) and Egypt (2012) were viewed as particularly significant, heralding the change from banned opposition movements whose leaders were in jail or in exile to regular political parties. The massive Islamist victories in these early elections reflected the credibility they had gained whilst still in opposition to the dictatorships backed by the West, when they also had provided services to the poor and appeared as a fount of religious affirmation. Running a government was a different matter, however. In Egypt, the army capitalized on public protests against the Islamists for being authoritarian, yet unable to revive the economy, and seized power in 2013. In Tunisia, the Islamist party had steered a political middle ground while in power and, as a result, lost heavily in the 2014 elections.

As the obstacles on the road to political democracy became clearer, analysts adopted a lens for understanding events that showed the resilience of authoritarianism. When the Egyptian army fiercely repressed the Islamists and firmly reasserted its power, two close observers wrote that nothing seemed to have changed.

❝ Egypt of December 2015 is looking a lot like Egypt of late 2010 and the final months of Hosni Mubarak's three-decade rule. The country's long-time military president had little political sophistication; then as now, there were struggles between the military and businessmen for economic and political power, human rights abuses, economic woes, and jihadi groups in the Sinai. But today, these things appear more pronounced. **❞**

(Dunne and Nevin 2015)

In Tunisia, the army had never been a political force—a legacy of the Ottoman rule and French colonialism—but analysts questioned to what extent the previous one-party state had changed more than its face (Boubekeur 2016). That a group of **civil society** organizations received the Nobel Peace Prize in 2015 for their efforts to mediate a peaceful transition at a critical breaking point underlined the vulnerability of the new order.

As the aftermath of the Arab Spring became longer and the consequences clearer, analysts started to look for patterns of continuities *and* change relative to the past (Rivetti 2015), dropped the cognitive lenses of either authoritarian resilience or democratic change, and held up a lens through which political events appeared as 'contested, open-ended transformations' (Asseburg and Wimmen 2016). In this perspective, what would come after renewed top-down control in Egypt, cautious democratization in Tunisia, state failure and civil war in Libya and Yemen, and protracted war in Syria seemed uncertain.

Peace-building and military intervention in a multipolar world

By the opening of the twenty-first century, the distinction between peace-building and military intervention had become blurred—in policy discourse, as well as practice. The term 'peace-building' was appended to the aftermath of invasions to change the regimes in Afghanistan and Iraq, and UN-supported programmes to restore peace proceeded alongside military operations by the US-led coalition to neutralize remaining enemies or renewed opposition. In Mali in 2013, UN 'blue helmets' had a mandate to go after militant Islamist groups that had infiltrated from North Africa and the Middle East, and deployed nearby French forces to hunt down the militants. The long-time UN peacekeeping operation in the Democratic Republic of Congo (DRC) was given a similar mandate in 2013, euphemistically called 'peace enforcement', as was the UN peacekeeping force in Central African Republic. It was a marked departure from the traditional impartiality associated with peacekeepers that had been considered a principal condition for their effectiveness.

The reasons behind the change in UN practice were complex, but must be understood in the light of the international tensions and militancy of the post-9/11 world. As the United States and its allies went aggressively after terrorists, and new conflicts seemed to de-stabilize the Middle East, there was a sense in the United Nations that the organization also needed to demonstrate its assertiveness, whether in conflicts tied to the 'war on terror' (Mali) or strife of much older vintage. In the latter case, the failure to produce much result in the DRC during a decade of peacekeeping-cum-peace-building contributed to the change in 2013. The DRC mission had by then become the largest UN peacekeeping operation, with about 17,000 troops and an annual budget of more than US$1 billion, but without decisive results. It was time, it seemed, to change the approach. In the new modus, peace-building and peacekeeping became entwined with partisan pursuit

of conflicts and, in some cases, partisan military intervention. The United Nations is at war, one analyst
concluded (Karlsrud 2015).

At the same time, there was sharply declining enthusiasm among the United States and its allies for
massive military interventions that entailed both **regime change** and social transformation. The experiences in Iraq and Afghanistan indicated that the costs
and difficulties were prohibitive. The global financial
crisis of 2007–08 and its aftermath of economic austerity, combined with competing policy agendas such
as climate change and migration, reinforced a new
sense of prudence. The reorientation affected also the
ability of the United Nations to mount massive state-
and peace-building operations. New rising powers—
particularly, India and China—were not about to step
in and pick up the mantle. The scaling back of commitment was seen in Libya, where the 2011 Western
intervention consisted chiefly of a bombing campaign
to change the regime, followed by only limited UN
support for state- and peacebuilding (see Box 13.5).

Challenges to the peacebuilding regime that had
developed since the 1990s also came from other quarters. In 2009, the UN Secretary-General had called
for adjustment of peace-building strategies, emphasizing the importance of local context and ownership (United Nations 2009). Analysts and donors in
the wider peace-building community developed the
theme further. The focus was now on local values, actors, and interests, and ways of creating 'hybrid' structures (MacGinty and Richmond 2016).

Another correction to the idea of a standardized
Western-inspired template for creating peace was
seen in the growing involvement of regional actors
such as the African Union and the League of Arab
States in attempts to address conflicts in their areas.
In Latin America, regional legal instruments and organizational infrastructure to mediate conflicts on
the continent were both older and stronger. The rise
of the BRICS countries (Brazil, Russia, India, China,
and South Africa) represented another challenge.
The New Development Bank for BRICS, launched in
mid-2015, for example, presented itself as an alternative to the existing US-dominated World Bank and the
IMF, indicating that its founding members had alternative ideas for development and peace-building as well.

Yet it seems premature to announce the end of
peace-building as a Western-led project to remake
unstable or war-torn countries in the South in the
mould of liberal democracy and market economies.

Concerns expressed in the World Bank's 2011 World
Development Report are symptomatic. The report
presented the South as a deeply violent place, torn by
conventional civil wars, as well as violence from other
sources, such as drug trafficking and urban gangs. Its
message was clear: the rich and powerful states, and
the international financial institutions, must maintain a long-term commitment to deal with the twin
problem of security and development in the turbulent
parts of the world.

KEY POINTS

- Patterns of conflict changed. From 2001 onwards, the
  US-led global 'war on terror' interacted with local tensions
  in much of the Muslim-majority world.

- Uprisings in the Middle East and North Africa
  demonstrated the strength, but also the limits, of 'people
  power'. Global and regional forces shaped the causes and
  trajectories of the uprisings.

- International peace-building became an increasingly
  standardized package, which included economic and
  political liberalization, administrative reform, and
  institution-building.

- Shortcomings of peace-building interventions generated
  search for corrections, with more attention to local
  context and ownership, and to regional solutions.

- By the early 2010s, it appeared that a period of grand
  designs for transforming societies through external
  intervention had come to an end. At the same time,
  boundaries between peace-building and other agendas
  justifying intervention were becoming increasingly blurred.

Conclusion

This chapter has surveyed different phases of conflict
in the developing world, starting with the independence struggle. Decolonization itself was a driver of
violence, but most transfers were not violent. During
the cold war, local conflict dynamics were shaped in
decisive ways by the rivalry between the communist
and the capitalist worlds, with devastating effects
on local societies. Continued violence in developing
countries in the post-cold-war period raised new questions about the causes of these wars, including their
relationship to natural resource **exploitation**, state capacity, and poor governance. Yet these wars were also
profoundly shaped by global political and economic
developments, only more subtly. After 11 September

2001, conflict in the developing world yet again took a sharp geopolitical turn, with the 'war on terror' and a series of military operations designed to eliminate the threat posed by militant Islamists.

During the 1990s, novel international interventions in the form of 'peace-building' emerged as a concerted strategy to rebuild societies after war and to prevent renewed violence. By and large, the international peace-building regime was premised on the assumption that the main causes of conflict in the developing countries were a function of their underdevelopment and that this reflects conditions internal to the country. As this chapter has shown, however, the international setting of internal conflict is critically important: an internal focus alone is a poor basis for analysis and response.

A series of recent developments signalled the possible end to the 1990s type of peace operations that sought to transform societies, signifying a dilution of the international peace-building regime. The 'war on terror' and the increase in international military operations, the relative decline of Western economic and ideological dominance, and the corresponding emergence of a more multipolar world all posed challenges to the UN-led peace-building regime for addressing conflict.

? QUESTIONS

1. What were the most important factors determining whether colonized countries experienced a peaceful or violent transition to independence?

2. In what ways did the cold war impact on violent conflict in the developing world?

3. Was there a shift in the nature and patterns of conflict in the developing world after the end of the cold war, and if so, how can it be explained?

4. What are the potentials and limitations of 'people power' to change political systems?

5. What are the strengths and weaknesses of Western-led peace-building interventions?

6. How has the global 'war on terror' impacted on political change in affected regions of the South?

7. What are the advantages and potential pitfalls of more militarily robust UN peace operations?

8. How did the rise of countries such as China, India, and Brazil in the early twenty-first century shape decision-making processes about interventions in the name of peace and civilian protection?

9. What are the likely impact of the wars erupting in the aftermath of the 'Arab Spring'—as in Syria, Libya, and Yemen—on international, including UN, policies towards armed conflict?

FURTHER READING

Autesserre, S. (2014) *Peaceland: Conflict Resolution and the Everyday Politics of International Intervention* (Cambridge and New York: Cambridge University Press) Critically discusses the prevailing peace-building culture and practices.

Cederman, L.-E., Gleditsch, K. S., and Buhaug, H. (2013) *Inequalities, Grievances, and Civil War* (Cambridge: Cambridge University Press) Uses statistical analysis to show that certain patterns of inequalities and ethnic identity can lead to civil war.

Cramer, C. (2006) *Civil War is Not a Stupid Thing: Accounting for Violence in Developing Countries* (London: Hurst & Co.) Critically examines the assumptions that violent conflict is inimical to development.

Keen, D. (2012) *Useful Enemies when Waging Wars is More Important than Winning Them* (New Haven, CT: Yale University Press) Explores why civil wars—whether internationalized or not—are so numerous and protracted in the contemporary world.

North, D. C., Wallis, J. J., and Weingast, B. R. (2009) *Violence and Social Orders: A Conceptual Framework for Interpreting Recorded History* (New York: Cambridge University Press) Seeks to explain how societies can control violence through exclusive elite pacts, as well as open access and competition, and what conditions development of the latter kind of society.

Paris, R. (2004) *At War's End* (New York: Cambridge University Press) Critically assesses the impact of economic and political liberalization on post-war peace-building.

Zolberg, A., Suhrke, A., and Aguayo, S. (1989) *Escape from Violence: Conflict and the Refugee Crisis in the Developing World* (New York: Oxford University Press) Examines the nature of conflict in the developing world before and during the cold war.

WEB LINKS

http://www.hsrgroup.org/human-security-reports/human-security-report.aspx   Focusing on people rather than states, the Human Security Reports examine global and regional trends in wars and other forms of organized violence.

http://www.un.org/en/peace/peacebuilding   For UN Peacebuilding Commission efforts to garner international support for nationally owned and led peace-building efforts.

For additional material and resources, visit the Online Resource Centre at:
http://www.oxfordtextbooks.co.uk/orc/burnell5e/

14

Democratization and Regime Change

Lise Rakner

Chapter contents

Overview

The early 1990s saw a wave of former military and one-party regimes embracing political liberalization and democratization in Latin America, Africa, and Asia. Now into the third decade after the global 'democracy turn', many doubts and reservations have surfaced, and attention is turned to the quality of democracy, democratic erosion, and authoritarian persistence. We now understand that the fall of repressive authoritarian regimes does not necessarily procure lasting and consolidated democratic regimes. This chapter presents theories of democratization, summarizes recent trends, and compares understandings of democratic consolidation. It also discusses variations within democratic and autocratic regimes and various ways in which to measure democracy. Relations between democratization and development provide a central theme, not least because of worries that social and economic problems can undermine democratic progress. Finally, the chapter discusses how domestic and international factors interact to affect politics generally, and processes of democratization more specifically, inside developing countries.

Introduction

Democracy is an essentially contested concept. The long history of theorizing about its meaning provides few certainties about what 'democratization' means. Democratization refers to a process of change; most writers conceive of it as a journey without end. In a widely used metaphor, Huntington (1991) characterized the extension of democracy beginning around 1974 as the **third wave of democracy**, the two earlier waves (1828–1926 and 1943–62) each being followed by a reverse wave. For some countries, the experience has been attempted re-democratization following earlier democratic failure(s). Examples include Argentina's return to elected civilian rule in 1983 and Uruguay, which had military-controlled civilian government from 1973 to 1985. Ghana, now resembling a stable liberal democracy, made successive earlier attempts to re-establish elected civilian government following military rule in 1966–69, 1972–79, and 1981–92. Indonesia first enjoyed a period of 'Guided Democracy' in the 1950s; since the removal of President Suharto in 1998, it has maintained a democratic constitution and institutionalized, rule-based, multiparty elections.

Regime Change, Democracy, and Democratization

Democratization is not a unilinear movement from political authoritarianism to democracy. Simple dichotomizations of regime types are an oversimplification. Different kinds of authoritarian regime exist: monarchy, as in some Gulf states; personal dictatorships; military-bureaucratic rule; and *de jure* one-party states, as in Tanzania and Zambia before the 1990s (Geddes 1999). Authoritarian and semi-authoritarian regimes can enjoy **legitimacy** in the eyes of citizens. They draw on such sources as religious beliefs, as in theocratic Iran and Saudi Arabia, **nationalism**, and anti-imperialism, as in China and Cuba. Also a conviction may exist that the status quo serves personal security and material well-being better than the likely political alternatives, which could mean social conflict and political instability. While military rule has been replaced by democratically elected governments in Ghana, Argentina, and Nigeria, the military replaced an elected civilian government in Thailand in 2014. Whereas the military plays a significant role 'behind the scenes' in Pakistan, 2015 witnessed two

failed military coups in Burkina Faso and Lesotho. In Egypt, the 'Arab uprisings' proved short-lived as the military removed the first democratically elected president, Mohamed Morsi of the Muslim Brotherhood, in 2013.

In the aftermath of the cold war, euphoria about the power of democracy's global spread culminated, with some scholars predicting worldwide democratization as humanity's political endgame (Fukuyama 1992). However, expectations of democratization have undergone substantial shifts in the past decades and, by the early 2000s, many started to question the assumption that movements away from authoritarian rule would necessarily lead to democracy (Carothers 2002). That being said, the various forms of autocratic regimes have changed over time. In the 1970s, the authoritarian regimes of the world were predominantly of the military or one-party kind. This is no longer the case. After the end of the cold war and the demise of the communist one-party states, the most common forms of authoritarian regimes are of the hybrid variant and **electoral autocracies** have become the dominant form of autocratic rule. Today, almost 90 per cent of all countries in the world hold regular and competitive elections. Yet many elections are held under authoritarian conditions and incumbents manipulate the electoral process (see Box 14.1)—Robert Mugabe's Zimbabwe being an outstanding example. Military or one-party authoritarian rule has been replaced by a varied landscape of 'democracies with adjectives' in which multiparty elections and official recognition of

---

BOX 14.1 THE GROWTH AND SURVIVAL OF HYBRID REGIMES

Regimes cannot be neatly categorized into either being democratic or authoritarian (Teorell 2010). In the **developing world** today, the most common type of dictatorship is a regime 'dressed up' like a democracy. Often referred to as a 'hybrid' regime (Diamond 2002), an electoral autocracy (Schedler 2013), or a competitive authoritarian regime (Levitsky and Way 2010), we consider this to be a regime that holds elections and allows multiple parties to compete, but which, through processes of ballot rigging, repression, or other illicit tactics, chooses leaders in ways that do not resemble democracy. Despite an initial assumption that hybridity was a step on the path to democracy, many such regimes have shown a surprising longevity and ability to survive.

formal democratic institutions coexist with persistent autocratic practices and abuse of power by the incumbent (Schedler 2013).

Democracy (from the Greek *demokratia*, meaning 'rule by the people') has been called an inherently debatable and changeable idea. Yet ideas resembling the model of polyarchical democracy (**polyarchy**) advanced by American political scientist Robert Dahl in the 1970s (see Box 14.2) have dominated much of the democratization discourse at the expense of deliberative and emancipatory or more radical social ideas. Polyarchy centres on two main pillars: public contestation and the right to participate. Liberal democracy, which is akin to polyarchy, is the most commonly cited yardstick for judging the progress of democratization and is generally believed to avoid the **fallacy of electoralism**. Larry Diamond (1996), a prominent contributor to the democratization literature, usefully distinguished between 'liberal democracy', in which there is extensive provision for political and civic pluralism, as well as for individual and group freedoms, and mere **electoral democracy**, in which civil freedoms are less prized and minority rights are insecure, although elections could be largely free and fair.

Measuring democracy

How do we know which countries are democracies? Many scholars consult Freedom House ratings. Freedom House is a US non-profit organization that conducts annual evaluations of political rights and civil liberties throughout the world. It defines democracy, at minimum, as a political system in which people choose their leaders freely from among competitors who are not chosen by the government. Freedom is the chance to act spontaneously in a variety of fields outside the control of government and other centres of potential domination. Democracies are judged either free or partly free, as measured along a seven-point scale (1–2.5 = *free*; 3–5 = *partly free*; 5.5–7 = *not free*).

The Freedom House data indicates that, following a dramatic initial increase in democracies during the 'third wave', the number of liberal democracies levelled off by the early 1990s. While some countries, such as Vietnam, were never caught up in the tide, several emerging democracies soon began to show signs of democratic backsliding or 'hollowing out'. The latest *Freedom in the World*, Freedom House's annual report on the conditions of global political rights and civil liberties in the world, showed an overall decline for the ninth consecutive year (Puddington 2015).

Although the Freedom House methodology has attracted criticism, the ratings are widely used for depicting global trends in democratization, and for making national and intertemporal comparisons. But there are other alternative measurements to compare democratic development over time, and between countries and regions (see Box 14.3). When measuring democracy, an essential decision to make is whether

---

BOX 14.2 DEFINING DEMOCRACY: ROBERT A. DAHL

Citizens must have unimpaired opportunities to formulate their preferences, signify them and have them weighted equally. This requires certain institutional guarantees: freedom to form and join organizations; freedom of expression; right to vote; eligibility for public office; right of leaders to compete for support; alternative sources of information; free and fair elections; institutions for making government policies depend on votes and other expressions of preference.

(Dahl 1971: 2–3)

BOX 14.3 WAYS IN WHICH TO MEASURE DEMOCRACY

Some of the most applied democracy indices are:

- the Bertelsmann index—available since 2003, based on a 0–10 scale of subjective, expert perceptions, including five components;
- the Economist Intelligence Unit index—available since 1972, based on a 0–10 scale of expert and public perceptions, including five components;
- the Freedom House index—available since 1972, based on a 1–7 scale of subjective, expert perceptions, including two components and seven subcomponents (added in 2006);
- the Polity index—with data pointing back to 1800, with a scale from −10 to +10 of subjective expert opinion, including five components;
- the ACLP index, based on a dataset compiled by Alvarez and colleagues—includes data from 1946 to date, based on a scale of 0,1 and objective perceptions, including four components; and
- Vanhanen—includes data from 1810, based on a 1–100 scale of objective perceptions and including two components.

to measure only 'objective' indicators or whether also to include subjective measures, such as individual perceptions. Vanhanen (2000) provides a simple index of democracy that relies on two indicators: the number of votes cast for parties other than the biggest party in the most recent election; and the percentage of voting age population that cast a vote. The first indicator measures degree of competitiveness; the second, degree of inclusion. There are obvious advantages to an index that is minimal and can be measured in percentages. However, major aspects of democracy are not captured by this information, such as the degree of electoral fraud. To capture other central aspects of democracy, scholars rely on the opinion of experts. This has obvious problems, because two people may value the same aspect differently. Opinion surveys with a representative sample of the population are another way in which to measure subjective perceptions of democracy, but these are of little value in non-democratic regimes because we cannot know that respondents will feel sufficiently free or safe to respond honestly.

A criticism raised against all of the most established democracy indices is that they present a relatively narrow and Western liberal view of democracy, focused on whether a society conforms to a minimum level of competitiveness, as well as some level of control over the executive. In addition, since most measures are aggregated, it is not possible to ascertain what exact reform or incident in a country caused a change in the democracy measure. The Varieties of Democracy (V-DEM) project represents a novel approach to the regime classification debate by measuring 'seven principles of democracy'—electoral, liberal, majoritarian, consensual, participatory, deliberative, and egalitarian—made possible by increasingly sophisticated information technology and measurement tools. The V-DEM database first released in January 2016 comprises indices of all seven varieties and their components, as well as measures of 329 disaggregated indicators on a worldwide basis from 1900 until the present.

Why are measurements and democracy indices important? For one thing, it makes it possible to evaluate the effects of various forms of **democracy assistance**. If we were to want to know how to assist the development of democracy in Egypt most efficiently, where would we start? Would media freedom be the most important factor, or the development of political parties, or **civil society** organizations? Should we instead focus only on making elections as free and fair as

possible? These are questions to which we do not have good answers, but which better empirical data and democracy indices may help us to answer.

KEY POINTS

- Democracy defines political regimes in which citizens have unimpaired opportunities to formulate their preferences, signify them, and have them weighted equally. This requires **institutional** guarantees of freedoms to organize and hold fair electoral competitions.

- Democratization's progress in the developing world has been uneven and, since 2005, has seen a slight decline on average. There are, however, differences both within and between regions.

- In the developing world today, the most common type of authoritarian regimes are hybrid regimes that hold elections, but in which various forms of fraud and repression mean that leaders are chosen in ways that that do not resemble democracy.

- Most democracy indices are based on a Western liberal view of democracy, assessing how a society conforms to a minimum level of competitiveness, as well as some level of control over the executive.

Democratization as Process

Conceptual distinctions between political liberalization, democratic transition, and democratic consolidation are commonplace, but there is no necessary or inevitable sequence of events. As a prelude to 'political opening', authoritarian breakdown can happen in different ways—gradual or sudden, violent or peaceful—and may range from moderate to absolute. It can be brought about by pressure from below or by concessions from the incumbent autocrat. Most often, it is a combination of the two, as highlighted by the events in the Arab uprisings (see Box 14.4). 'Political liberalization' usually refers to a top-down process: political leaders aim to maintain power for themselves, reluctant to accept that institutionalized uncertainty over electoral outcomes should be the determining principle of who governs (and the possibility of alternation in office that implies). Liberalization advances political freedoms less than some civil liberties. In contrast, democratization introduces arrangements for genuinely competitive elections. Liberalization can become stalled, rather than lead on to democratization; it can also go into reverse. Conversely, largely free elections might be introduced without first establishing the **rule**

BOX 14.4 THE ARAB UPRISINGS: ILLUSIONS OF DEMOCRACY?

In the early parts of 2011, men and women took to the public squares throughout the Arab world. Their demands for dignity and voice transferred into calls for **regime change**. The popular uprisings forced regimes that had ruled for decades without showing any inclination towards democracy to make concessions or to resign. However, what came to be known as the 'Arab Spring' was largely confined to six countries: Bahrain, Egypt, Libya, Syria, Tunisia, and Yemen. Elsewhere, in Morocco, Jordan, and partly in Algeria, political concessions were made by the (semi-)authoritarian regimes, but the demands for regime change were soon suppressed. Rich Gulf states such as Saudi Arabia were not affected. Only Libya, Tunisia, Egypt, and Yemen actually experienced dictators leaving office, and of this small subset of Arab countries, only Tunisia has achieved and maintained a semblance of democracy.

The Arab uprisings highlight both the uncertainties and diversity with regards to the democratization effect of political openings. In Yemen, insurgencies in the north and south have produced a fragile power-sharing agreement and a **weak state**. Libya proved unable to erect a functioning state amid the ruins of the Qaddafi regime. In Syria (see Chapter 21), what started as protests for democracy in 2011 evolved into an ongoing civil war that has claimed 200,000 lives and seen 2 million people fleeing their homes. In Egypt, scarcely two years after the crowds gathered in Tahrir Square to compel Mubarak's resignation, they gathered again to demand the resignation of the country's first democratically elected president, Mohamed Morsi of the Muslim Brotherhood. Egypt's military had taken it upon itself to usher Morsi off the scene. Only Tunisia has been able to maintain the democratic reforms that people took to the market squares to demand (Brownlee et al. 2015).

---

of law, full executive accountability, and the flourishing civil society that are so important to democracy (see Chapter 10)—or what has been called **democratization backwards**. This occasions what Zakaria (1997) called 'illiberal democracy', citing Iran and President Fujimori's Peru as examples. Liberalization and democratic openings can also happen simultaneously, when authoritarian collapse is sudden and complete, as in **apartheid** South Africa. Rulers who at first allow some liberalization without intending to embrace democracy may lose control of the momentum, overtaken by demands for full democratic opening.

A related distinction made by some analysts is that democratization 'emerges from below', and involves political, although not necessarily violent, struggle, in contrast to some of the earliest 'third wave' cases of re-democratization in Latin America, in which **pacted transitions** were negotiated by the political elites. So there is not one, but several different routes to democratic reform; evidence about which ones provide the most durable change is mixed. Pro-democratic alliances that bridge different elements within the ruling elite and include civil society activists offer an optimum combination.

Democratic consolidation

Just as there can be political transition without transition to democracy, we know that there can be democratic transition without democratic consolidation.

Conversely, democratic decline need not lead to full-blown autocracy. But how do we recognize democratic consolidation? As Diamond (2015: 142) laments, a great irony in the growing scholarship on democratization is the accompanying disagreement on how to define and measure democracy. Answers range from equating consolidation with longevity to democratic 'deepening' or qualitative improvements in such indicators as the rule of law, minority rights, and **gender** issues (see Chapter 9). Schedler (1998) recommends restricting consolidation to 'negative' notions: avoiding democratic breakdown or democratic erosion. Put differently, democratic consolidation means an expectation of regime continuity—and nothing else. A minimal definition like this maximizes the number of developing countries qualifying for democratic consolidation. More demanding accounts that rest on democratic 'widening'—the incorporation of democratic principles in public *and* private spaces in economic and social arenas such as the family—impose criteria that few countries satisfy. Somewhere in between we find accounts that draw heavily on the people's political attitudes and perceptions. The Afrobarometer study of popular views about the supply of democracy in African countries consistently shows support for democracy and a citizen demand for more accountability, rule of law, and restraint of power of the executive. Three-quarters of adults sampled in the fifth round of the survey from across the continent expressed a preference for democracy (Gyimah-Boadi 2015: 111).

More significant for democratic consolidation than simple longevity may be the ability to withstand shocks—whether generated at home or abroad, either directly as in an attempted military coup or indirectly through dramatic deterioration in the economic climate. India's democracy, for example, shows great resilience in the face of **terrorist** provocations. One hypothesis is that democratic deepening strengthens resilience. However, if a new democracy has yet to be put to the test, can we know whether it is consolidated and whether expectations of continuity are justified? And what counts as a sufficient test? For some countries in southern Africa and the Sahel, the growing food insecurity that could come from climate change may well threaten political stability and democracy's survival in the coming years.

A more easily applied notion of consolidation is the double turnover test suggested by Huntington (1991: 266–7). This requires that a party that took office after a democratic election should relinquish office after losing a comparable election without seeking to resist or overturn the result. This definition of democratic consolidation would exclude Botswana, rated by Freedom House as a fully fledged democracy, but where the Democratic Party has yet to lose an election since gaining independence (in 1966). A more persuasive view sees consolidation as being achieved once democracy has become 'the only game in town'. This requires a permanent attitudinal shift rather than a temporary behavioural accommodation.

Some scholars regard legitimacy as one of democracy's most distinguishing properties (Diamond 2002) Legitimacy is like reinforcing glue: it helps democracy to survive shocks. Indeed, we could say that a democracy truly consolidates when it ceases to rely on 'performance legitimacy' (acceptance grounded on meeting society's material wants or needs), and achieves principled or 'intrinsic legitimacy' (grounded in respect for democracy's fundamental values, as well as adherence to the procedures that these inform—such as free and fair elections). Intrinsic legitimacy shelters democracy against such failings as weak developmental performance, India's experience for many years following independence. In a settled democracy, discontent with the performance of government is exacted on the government by peacefully removing it from office at the polls. So far, public support for many of Africa's new democracies appears to have weathered economic hardship (Gyimah-Boadi 2015). Yet, in Latin America, one view is that neither **populist** demagoguery nor the military pose the main threat to democracy now, but rather a 'continuing mediocre performance—the inability of democratic governments to meet the most important needs and demands of their citizens' (Hakim 2003: 122). This becomes more potent when combined with popular perceptions of bad **governance** and high-level **corruption** (see Chapter 15).

In conclusion, the conceptual baggage of democratic transition and consolidation may be too rigid a framework for analysing what, in reality, are multifaceted, multidimensional, and multidirectional processes of political change. In practice, these may resemble variable geometry: some of democracy's ingredients could be moving in one direction (possibly at different speeds); others may move in the opposite direction (again at different speeds); yet others may be standing still. For example, a stable competitive party system may emerge even as civic activism decreases from the heights that successfully brought down an autocracy.

KEY POINTS

- A minority of developing countries are liberal democracies, although many more approximate to electoral democracies.

- Conceptually, processes of democratization may be divided into distinctions between political liberalization, democratic transition, and democratic consolidation, but there is no necessary or inevitable sequence of events.

- Democratic consolidation has been defined in different ways, with implications for which developing countries qualify. The quality of democracy is as important as its longevity.

- We must not exaggerate democratization's usefulness as a lens through which to examine **politics** in the developing world; other political variables, such as the strength of the state and quality of government, are equally important.

Explaining Democratization and Regime Change

The ways in which democratization and regime change occur and why it takes particular forms generate considerable debate. Explanations of consolidation can be expected to diverge from democratic transition. Similarly, the reasons that illuminate stalled transition could differ from those that explain a democracy's collapse, which may connect to **state failure**, or authoritarian persistence through military or one-party regimes that do not shy away from oppression, as did Myanmar's until very recently.

One approach to explaining different experiences with democratization emphasizes the impact of historical, political, and other legacies, and **path dependence** (see Chapter 3). At its most elaborate, path dependence claims that the nature of the pre-existing regime and the mode used to change it influence the sequel, and ultimately can determine a new democracy's chances of survival. This confirms why it is important to distinguish between types of authoritarian and semi-authoritarian regime, and hybrid regimes too, to establish whether there were any previous, failed, attempts to democratize. Like much theorizing about democratization, path dependence provides more valuable insights for some countries than for others (see Box 14.5). To illustrate, failure to incorporate women on anything like equal terms in

the power structures that emerge following civil conflict, even when they contributed significantly to the freedom struggles, is not unusual, but can often be explained by in-depth historical and sociological analysis (see Chapter 9).

One of the most durable ideas is that national unity 'must precede all the other phases of democratization' (Rustow 1970: 351). By 'national unity', Rustow (1970: 351) meant that 'the vast majority of citizens . . . must have no doubt or mental reservation as to which political community they belong to'. Some developing countries, Afghanistan, Iraq, and Sri Lanka for example, appear to lack this simple condition. Indeed, transition to democracy may be cherished as a means of managing or resolving violent and endemic conflict between groups, but the route taken to introduce democracy can itself occasion increased (violent) domestic conflict. Minorities harbouring fears of a majority tyranny may be stirred to demand national self-determination for themselves. Sri Lanka's history has been one of both democracy and long-running civil war between the Sinhalese and Tamil separatists in the north. The Tamils were defeated militarily in May 2009, but, under the rule of President Mahinda Rajapaksa, Sri Lanka slid into an authoritarian path, characterized by political **patronage**, repression of media and civil society, and intimidation of the courts (DeVotta 2016). In the January 2015 presidential elections, a multi-ethnic and ideologically diverse coalition led by Maithripala Sirisena defeated Rajapaksa. The national unity government's attempt to revive independent institutions and effectuate justice signals that Asia's oldest democracy may be on a path towards restoring its historic democratic credentials.

More broadly, the literature explaining democratization can be divided into accounts emphasizing structure and accounts that dwell on agency. The first investigate the 'conditions', and even preconditions, whereby democratic trends are facilitated or actively promoted, or frustrated; the second focus on process, highlighting the role of actors. The impact of actors may be greater at key turning points, such as democratic transitions or their timing, than over the long haul. The important role played by institutions broadly defined (see Chapter 3) must be recognized too. All things considered, democratization is perhaps best understood as a complex interaction that links structural constraints and opportunities to institutions and the shaping of contingent choice (Karl 1990).

BOX 14.5 RUSTOW'S METHODOLOGICAL PROPOSITIONS

- The factors that keep a democracy stable may not be the ones that brought it into existence; explanations of democracy must distinguish between function and genesis.
- Not all causal links run from beliefs and attitudes to action; the flow can be in both directions.
- The genesis of democracy need not be geographically uniform; there may be many roads to democracy.
- The genesis of democracy need not be temporally uniform; different factors may become crucial during successive phases.
- Correlation is not the same as causation; a genetic theory must concentrate on the latter.
- Not all causal links run from social and economic to political factors; the flow can be in both directions.
- The genesis of democracy need not be socially uniform; even in the same place and time the attitudes that promote it may not be the same for all politicians and citizens.

(Rustow 1970: 346)

Socio-economic conditions

Lipset's seminal article on the social requisites of democracy first published in 1959 (revisited in 1994) presents a powerful theory of the positive relationship between socio-economic **modernization** and the persistence of stable democracy. 'Requisites' are not *pre*requisites or *pre*conditions: shared prosperity does not have to be established in advance. Democratic transition can occur amid poverty and economic backwardness. But the idea that material progress enhances the chances of extending democratic longevity continues to be strongly supported by evidence from the developing world. It is very relevant to democracy's future prospects in parts of the Middle East. In contrast, where economic misfortune persists—and especially where the burdens that women endure are compounded by the existence of many female-headed households—the drawbacks for democracy and its quality in poor societies are particularly evident.

More social scientists began to investigate seriously the possibility that development could be the dependent variable; they started treating democracy as the independent or 'causal' factor (see Box 14.6). The idea that certain sorts of freedoms—notably, economic freedoms—are beneficial to wealth creation goes

---

BOX 14.6 THREE VIEWS ON DEMOCRACY AND DEVELOPMENT

- Democracy is too conservative a system of power. It has a bias towards consensus and accommodation that cannot promote radical change in the system of wealth that is essential to establishing developmental momentum, especially in late developing societies. A truly **developmental state** needs more insulation from society (and world market forces) than democracy allows (Leftwich 2002).

- Developing countries differ from the West in that democratic contestants do not have to compromise with capitalists; instead, they capture power for their own enrichment. This **rent-seeking** behaviour by politicians destroys the chances of development (Khan 2002).

- Powerlessness and poverty go together. Democratic models might empower the poor and serve development, such as by attacking the corruption that benefits only a few (Grugel 2002).

Source: Adapted from Leftwich (2002)

---

back a long way, to Adam Smith (1723–90). But for many years the view that developing countries face a **cruel choice** proved very persuasive: either countries could do what was necessary to develop their economies, mainly by concentrating on saving and investing to expand the productive capital stock, or they could emulate the political systems of the West. The former requires government to take unpopular decisions—most notably, restraining current consumption. Authoritarian regimes that are well insulated from social pressures have an advantage. In contrast, the structure of political incentives posed by competitive party politics appears biased towards raising popular expectations about immediate consumption and public welfare spending. Politicians running for office will promise 'jam today' at the expense of doing what is needful for 'jam tomorrow'. In the long run, economic decline beckons—the experience of Argentina for much of the 1980s and 1990s, culminating in a spectacular financial crisis in December 2001.

The moral seemed to be that democracy is a luxury that poor countries can ill afford. Only after development has progressed beyond a certain threshold does sustainable democracy appear more viable. The term **wealth theory of democracy** captures the idea. The dramatic economic performance of East Asian 'tiger' economies, such as Taiwan and South Korea (see Chapter 24), in the cold-war era, followed by successful democratic transition, conforms to this general theory. Critics, however, point to examples of developing world democracies such as Mauritius (since independence in 1968) and Costa Rica (a democracy since 1899, with only brief interruptions in 1917 and 1948), which have a generally good record of economic and social development. East Asia's examples of an undeniably successful deployment of the authoritarian model, which are continued today by Vietnam and China (see Chapter 29), are perhaps the real exceptions. But some regimes in sub-Saharan Africa, such as Ethiopia and Rwanda, are now following this authoritarian state-led growth model. Rising prosperity does not guarantee transition to democracy. In oil-rich **rentier states** (see Chapter 12), such as those in the Gulf, and Equatorial Guinea and Angola in sub-Saharan Africa, the manipulation of rent-funded public spending by authoritarian regimes looks quite durable. But this **resource curse** seems not to apply where democracy is already established, as Botswana, blessed with diamond revenues, as well as income from cattle-raising, illustrates.

The significance of development for democratization

There is much statistical evidence that democracies can survive even in the poorest nations especially *if* they can generate development with widely distributed benefits, while meeting certain other conditions (Przeworski et al. 1996). But what is it about modernization and development that is so significant for democratization? Is it primarily a matter of resources, or a case of transforming attitudes, values, and patterns of behaviour, or the changes in class structure that come with capitalist development in particular? Or does the connection have more to do with development's integration of society into global structures and norms? Different theories emerge from concentrating on different aspects.

- Democratic institutions are expensive, and demand high organizational commitment and public involvement that affluent, well-educated societies can more easily provide. Technological and economic progress improves the physical infrastructure of political communication.

- Social modernization erodes old values that inculcate deference to traditional authority and generate self-confidence; people come to see themselves more as citizens than subjects. This increases the constituencies for rational-legal authority. Pragmatic values sympathetic to the politics of compromise and consensus lying at the heart of the 'democratic way' supplant non-negotiable values such as exclusive ethnic loyalties that divide society. Integration into the global economy also brings exposure to the liberal and democratic values already enjoyed elsewhere (the 'demonstration effect').

- There is a well-known aphorism: 'No bourgeoisie, no democracy.' Development breaks the exclusive power of feudal landlords. Capitalist development creates a plurality of potential centres of power and influence independent of the state. A property-owning middle class has a vested interest in checking the arbitrary use of executive power; it has the economic means and know-how to organize pressure for the redistribution of power. There is a caveat, however: economic growth can widen the economic inequalities that sustain inequalities of power. Middle-class

elements will defend an illiberal or undemocratic regime if they believe it serves their interests, for instance by providing stability. Prosperous Singapore, judged only partly free by Freedom House, is an example.

- Industrialization and urbanization help an organized working class to mobilize mass support to demand rights for ordinary people. Thus Rueschemeyer and colleagues (1992) disavow that democracy is created solely by the bourgeoisie, emphasizing instead the progressive role of the working class, acting together with middle-class elements. The relevance of this insight grows as more developing countries in Asia and Latin America become prominent industrial manufacturers.

The ambivalent relationship of market economy and democracy

A frequent assumption is that the market constitutes a necessary, but not sufficient, condition of democracy: there have been authoritarian regimes with market economies (President Pinochet's Chile, China, and Vietnam since the 1990s, for example), but no examples of non-market democracies. In reality, the relationship is ambivalent. As Beetham (1997) explained, there are some negative effects associated with the virtues of the market—and even its positive points must be qualified (see Box 14.7). This issue can be reformulated in terms of the effects on democracy's quality. Thus, for example, for Rueschemeyer (2004: 89): 'To deepen democracy in the direction of greater political equality requires systematic and strong policies promoting social and economic equality. The quality of democracy, then, depends on social democracy, on long-sustained policies of social protection and solidarity.' This is especially pertinent to countries such as Brazil and South Africa, which historically are among the most unequal of all societies, and even to India, where a substantial middle class develops alongside a large number of extremely poor people.

Political culture

The perceived significance of **political culture** dates from Almond and Verba's (1965) *The Civic Culture: Political Attitudes and Democracy in Five Nations.*

BOX 14.7 POSITIVE AND NEGATIVE CONNECTIONS BETWEEN DEMOCRACY AND THE MARKET

Positive connections

- The more extensive the state, the more difficult it is to subject to public accountability or societal control.

- The more that is at stake in elections, the greater is the incentive for participants to compromise the process or reject the outcome.

- Market freedoms and political freedoms are mutually supportive: both require the rule of law and ensuring it for one ensures it for both.

- Sovereignty of consumer and voter both rest on the same anti-paternalist principle.

- Market economy is necessary for long-term economic growth, which assists durable democracy.

Negative connections

- Independence of the market from the state distances the economy from democratic control.

- Free market competition intensifies socio-economic inequalities, which produce political inequalities and compromise democratic institutions.

- Market dispositions undermine the integrity of the democratic public sphere: market choices prevail over political choices; the logic of private self-interest colonizes the public sphere.

Source: Beetham (1997)

'Political culture' embodies the attitudes, beliefs, and values that underlie a political system. For Almond and Verba (1965), 'civic culture' supports democracy. After years during which the concept came under fire, democratization scholars now agree that sustainable democracy requires a special set of values, such as tolerance, mutual respect, and a willingness to trust in fellow citizens (**social capital**), not only acquaintance with democracy's procedures. Observers pay close attention to the public attitude surveys, such as Latinobarometer and Afrobarometer, and dissect discrepancies between support for democracy generally, and dissatisfaction with the particular institutions and political leadership specifically (Doorenspleet 2009).

The principal constituents of a democratic political culture and relations among them and their requisites are all contested. For instance, it was once thought that the Protestant ethic made famous by German sociologist Max Weber is more favourable to democracy than are Roman Catholicism and Confucianism, yet evidence from Latin America and Asia now refutes this. An especially topical debate is over whether it is the Muslim world, not the Arab world, which offers relatively inhospitable terrain for democracy. Attitudes towards women's rights and female equality are quite critical here: the political advancement of women generally in Muslim countries appears challenging (see Chapter 9). Progress depends as much on overcoming culturally and historically embedded

forms of disadvantage as on reforming the institutions of government, such as introducing female quotas in legislative representation.

If something like civic culture is essential to democracy, is it a prerequisite or can it be allowed to develop later, and if so, what can bring it about? This not only raises the idea of civic education, but also sparks other questions about whose culture is most important, particularly in democratization's early stages: that of the elite or that of the mass? One argument is that the primary threat to new democracies comes from the people in power—especially 'old generation' politicians, who assume democratic pretensions reluctantly and without conviction, of whom Kenya's President Arap Moi is an example. Bermeo's (2003) argument, drawing on Europe and the Americas in the 1960s and 1970s, is that small elite coalitions, not the ordinary people, bear major responsibility for democratic failure. This seems to be borne out by broader experience in the developing world, especially where high-level corruption and the jealous possession of power by a few (as in Zimbabwe), and great institutional or class-based privilege (as with Guatemala's military and wealthy elite), persist unchanged.

Institutional crafting

Chapter 3 introduced institutional perspectives on politics in developing countries. Clearly, institutional design can have significant consequences for the distribution of power generally, and democracy's quality and sustainability specifically. Formal organizational changes may barely affect the way in which things actually work, if inherited **informal institutions** or patterns of behaviour such as patronage and **clientelism** are impervious to change and prevent the economic advance that might otherwise flow from formal democratic transition. Moreover, as Chapter 13 suggests, tensions between crafting democracy's institutional architecture, on the one hand, and the larger imperatives of peace-building and state-(re) building or their requisites, on the other, can quickly surface in societies needing to escape internal violence. The recent troubled history of Iraq and Afghanistan are illustrative.

Two institutional concerns that have attracted special attention in new democracies are, first, the balance of power and mutual oversight among the executive, legislature, judiciary, and other constituents of a 'self-restraining state', and second, elections and party systems. A self-restraining state embraces multiple institutional mechanisms for making government accountable (Schedler et al. 1999). Latin American experience implies that presidentialism is more likely to be unstable than parliamentary democracy when combined with vigorous multipartyism, but others (such as Kapstein and Converse 2009) warn against simple correlations and re-emphasize that what matters most is the effectiveness of strong institutional constraints on executive power.

O'Donnell (1994) proposed the category **delegative democracy**, much cited in a Latin American context. It rests on the premise that whoever wins election to the presidency behaves as if he or she were entitled to govern as he or she thinks fit—constrained only by the hard facts of existing power relations and constitutional limits, which he or she may try to remove or relax. O'Donnell (1994) distinguished between vertical accountability and horizontal accountability. *Vertical accountability* makes government accountable to the ballot box and might even be extended to more direct forms of societal accountability, through the activities of civil society (see Chapters 10 and 11) and judicial power to enforce the rule of law—even, indeed especially, against democratically elected governments. *Horizontal accountability*, more generally, tends to be weak in delegative democracies and virtually non-existent in illiberal non-democracies.

KEY POINTS

- Different dimensions and phases of democratic change require their own explanations.
- Economic development may be one of the best guarantors of durable democracy, especially if the benefits are widely distributed, although the reasons are contested.
- The relationship of market-based or capitalist development to democratization is ambivalent.
- Institutional and cultural perspectives on democratization are complementary to more economistic explanations.

International Dimensions of Democratization

The end of the cold war and collapse of Soviet power help to explain the increase in agitation for political reform in the developing world from the late 1980s, although democracy's return to Latin America was already well advanced. Now, however, we see the growing economic and financial engagement of China (and India) with developing countries (see Chapters 29 and 30), and in international forums both China and Russia defend the principles of state sovereignty and non-interference in the internal politics of countries. These developments mean that growing attention should be paid to examining how domestic and international factors interact to affect politics inside developing countries.

External influences can work in many ways, such as by example, persuasion, and more direct involvement. The active engagement of prominent Western democracies in international democracy support is now well established, but the United Nations too has become a major actor as in arranging practical support to the staging, monitoring, and observing of elections, especially valuable in new states and post-conflict situations. The UN Development Programme (UNDP) is a substantial funder of projects in democratic governance.

The influence exerted by developments within a region should not be ignored either. Several regional organizations have undertaken to encourage—and defend from domestic attack—democratic institutions, values, and practices in their member states. In Latin America, the Organization of American States (OAS) sets out to uphold the Inter-American Democratic

Charter. The African Union's New Partnership for Africa's Development (NEPAD) established the African Peer Review Mechanism (APRM), with a view to advancing both economic and democratic governance of member states. This has yet to prove that it can make much impact, in the context of insurgencies, a diverse set of international states and actors competing for influence, and especially in large and influential countries such as Nigeria.

The role of the West has been discussed widely with regard to international **democracy promotion** in the developing world. Arguably, the global spread of **good governance** and democracy assistance counts as some of the most remarkable transformations in world politics in the twentieth century (Bush 2015). The end of the cold war opened space for new forms of international activism: led by a reinvigorated United Nations, Western governments and international organizations advocated economic and political liberalization as a foundation for a more peaceful world (Diamond 2015). From the early 1990s onwards, democracy aid evolved from a specialized niche into a substantial, well-institutionalized domain, and most Western governments provided some aid for democracy-building, whether through a foreign ministry, a bilateral aid agency, or other institutions. Levitsky and Way (2010) claim that the degree of linkage that a country has to the Western world, as well as the degree of leverage that Western countries hold over the country, is important for understanding democratization processes. They claim that leverage without linkage through interest and knowledge is not enough. In terms of how the West utilizes its leverage, two approaches stand out: one attaches democratic, **human rights**, and governance **conditionalities** to offers of development aid and other concessions, such as trade concessions; the other provides technical, financial, material, and symbolic support to democracy projects and programmes involving political parties, civil society, legislatures, and other institutions—namely, democracy assistance. By and large, governance conditionalities have been found to be ineffective when faced by determined opposition. Democracy assistance, now worth over US$5 billion worldwide, has a mixed record. Although support to elections has long been considered insufficient, building durable capacity in civil society too encounters difficulties (see Chapter 10): external involvement can easily compromise the independence of **non-governmental organizations** (**NGOs**), as has long been found in the world of international development cooperation. A growing number of authoritarian and semi-authoritarian governments obstruct external assistance to pro-democracy groups and human rights campaigners. According to data from the International Center for Non-Profit Law (ICNL), between 2004 and 2010, more than fifty countries considered or enacted measures restricting civil society (see Chapter 10).

A third alternative, the coercive imposition of democracy, is largely discredited. In fact, the conflating of democracy promotion with regime change, understood as ousting governments by force as in Afghanistan (2001) and Iraq (2003), is believed to have harmed the cause of international democracy promotion. It gave authoritarian rulers a reason to stir nationalist sentiment and to utilize anti-imperialist rhetoric against even non-coercive democracy promotion from outside. The current mood is that the legitimacy and credibility of international involvement have lost ground: a conscious relabelling of democracy 'promotion' as 'support' is one response. But this state of affairs is probably linked to the loss of momentum that worldwide democratization per se experienced before the 'Arab uprisings', even if the connections between the state of democratization and the state of democracy promotion, and the direction of causality, are exceptionally difficult to establish (Burnell and Youngs 2009).

It is important not to overstate the emphasis on democracy in the international good governance agenda (see Chapter 15). Nevertheless, the end of the cold war signalled a lower opportunity cost for aid donors to assert the importance of democratization and improved governance. This agenda is now contested. Shifting from its early start in the 1990s, the global good governance regime is adapting to a world that is no longer bipolar and in which US (Western) hegemonic power is reduced. Faced with the prospects of losing influence, Western governments are readjusting governance benchmarks and demonstrating an increasing reluctance to press for democratic governance reforms. In Africa, Western donors demonstrate increasing reluctance to press democratic governance reforms in misgoverned oil-rich states such as Chad, Angola, Nigeria, Sudan, and south Sudan (Gyimah-Boadi 2015).

Democratization's significance for international development

The idea of a 'cruel choice' between democracy and development no longer carries much weight. Many authoritarian regimes—especially weak and fearful autocracies, and some rentier states—badly mismanaged their economic and financial affairs, not least because of inadequate accountability. In contrast, party-based democracy can provide a more responsible approach whereby the parties judge that their electoral fortunes over the long run will be influenced by how they perform in office. Democratically elected governments can possess the legitimacy to take tough, but necessary, economic decisions. Accountability makes the gross abuse of public resources less likely: corruption surveys, such as those conducted by Transparency International, find that democracies generally are less corrupt, although significant variations exist across democracies. (See Chapter 15 for further discussions of the links between regime type and corruption.) To the extent that the sustained poverty reduction required for **human development** will happen only if poor people are empowered, the equal political rights and civil liberties that liberal democracy should bestow look more conducive compared to concentrating power in very few hands. A virtuous circle is possible: society exerts political pressure for an expansion of social and economic opportunities, which then improve the prospects for stable democracy. That said, our understanding of democratization's benefits for economic growth and development urges caution, and remains imperfect. In particular, democratization appears to offer no surety for a progressive redistribution of wealth and incomes. A shrewd insight claims that attempts to reduce economic inequality especially by populist leaders utilizing populist measures may come to threaten democracy's durability more than does inequality itself, especially if the measures actually damage the economic prospects of the poor in the long run (Bermeo 2009: 33). Furthermore, because the processes of democratization are not unilinear, it is important to remember that just because an authoritarian regime has broken down, there is no guarantee that a democratic regime will follow; as discussed earlier in this chapter, a 'hybrid' regime might be the outcome. Hybrid regimes often perform less well than more stable authoritarian regimes in terms of both development and economic growth (see Chapter 15). However, this does not mean that democratization and democracy are hostile towards growth and development; rather, it highlights the importance of knowing what we are comparing.

KEY POINTS

- The jury is still out on the potency of democratization to bring about socio-economic conditions that could underpin new democracies.

- There are many different routes by which the international environment can influence democratization in developing countries. Only some are supportive; others are unintentional—and their effects vary among countries.

- External influences can work in many ways, such as by example, persuasion, and more direct involvement.

- The global spread of good governance and democracy assistance counts as one of the most remarkable transformations in world politics in the twentieth century.

- Now shifting, the global good governance regime is adopting to a world that is no longer bipolar and in which US (Western) hegemonic power is reduced. Faced with the prospects of losing influence, Western governments are demonstrating an increasing reluctance to press for democratic reforms.

Conclusion

Key issues at the heart of contemporary debates about democratization in developing countries include: what is democratization? How much progress has there been? Is a reverse wave under way? What explains democratic developments, and the influences that determine forwards and backwards movements? What are democratization's relationships to development? And how important is the international environment? This chapter has argued that the meaning of democratization, like democracy itself, is contested. And while most developing countries have undergone political change over the last two decades or so, the number of new consolidated or stable liberal democracies is modest. In many countries, competing analytical frameworks such as **nation-building** and state-building may offer greater insights into their current-day politics.

Attention has turned away from explaining democratic transition and describing democratic consolidation towards specifying a democracy's quality, identifying democracies' hazard rates (the probability that they will decay), and explaining authoritarian persistence. Regime typologies have been enriched by the proliferation of hybrid regimes. There is a chicken-and-egg conundrum of how to sort out democratization's apparent requisites from its possible consequences. This underlines the need to establish how economic circumstances and external forces influence democratization's fortunes, and how much is determined by political choices (decisions and non-decisions) and institutional initiatives. In the long run, development appears to favour democracy, but there are reservations about the full effects of the market and global capitalism in particular, especially where popular aspirations for **human security** and human development are thwarted. Although substantial economic inequality appears not to be a barrier to democratic durability, it can reduce democracy's quality.

Arguably, at the core of many democratic setbacks over the past decades is the failure of institutionalization—put differently, the capacity of many new democracies in the developing world has not kept pace with popular demands for democratic accountability. Once a democratic government is in power, it has to actually *govern*. As we now turn to discuss in Chapter 15, 'governance', which is closely connected with matters intrinsic to the classification of types of political regime, legitimacy, and accountability, embraces a larger set of political issues that have now come to the fore.

? QUESTIONS

1. How do concepts of democratic consolidation and democracy's quality help us to understand politics in developing countries?

2. Does the existence of poverty explain the persistence of hybrid regimes?

3. Are there democratic alternatives to Western-style liberal democracy in the developing world?

4. How do democratic developing countries achieve legitimacy?

5. Is democracy in decline in the developing world? Why, if so?

6. Why did the Arab uprisings fail to bring about democracy in all countries, apart from Tunisia?

7. To what extent has democracy promotion assisted processes of democratization in the developing world?

FURTHER READING

Beetham, D., Bracking, S., Kearton, I., and Weir, S. (2002) *International IDEA Handbook on Democracy Assessment* (The Hague, London, and New York: Kluwer Law International) A foundation guide to how to assess democratic achievement, which can be supplemented with more recent guidance from the International IDEA website.

Bermeo, N. (2009) 'Does Electoral Democracy Boost Economic Equality?', *Journal of Democracy*, 20(4): 21–35 A compact survey of arguments and evidence pertaining to a relatively neglected, but important, issue.

Burnell, P., and Youngs, R. (eds) (2009) *New Challenges to Democratization* (New York and London: Routledge) Assesses linkages between challenges to democratization and challenges to international democracy support.

Diamond, L. (2015) 'Facing up to the Democratic Recession', *Journal of Democracy*, 26(1): 141–55 An important voice on the challenges facing democratic consolidation in the developing world today.

Rustow, D. A. (1970) 'Transitions to Democracy', Comparative Politics, 2(3): 337–63 A seminal article on how democratic transitions come about.

Schedler, A. (2013) *The Politics of Uncertainty: Sustaining and Subverting Electoral Authoritarianism* (Oxford: Oxford University Press) An excellent account of the foundation and spread of electoral authoritarian regimes.

WEB LINKS

http://www.afrobarometer.org   The site for national public attitude surveys on democracy, markets, and civil society in Africa.

http://www.freedomhouse.org   The site of the US-based Freedom House, which includes access to its annual comparative measures of freedom.

http://www.icnl.org/   The International Center for Non-Profit Law (ICNL) provides up-to date data and information on issues affecting civil society around the world.

http://www.idea.int   The site of the multi-member International Institute for Democracy and Electoral Assistance (Stockholm), and its democracy research and promotion activities.

http://www.latinobarometro.org   The site for national public attitude surveys in Latin America.

http://www.ned.org   The site of the Washington-based, non-governmental National Endowment for Democracy, which houses the International Forum for Democratic Studies.

http://www.oas.org   The site of the Organization of American States (OAS), containing statements on themes such as strengthening the democratic commitment and protecting human rights.

http://www.un.org/democracyfund/   Includes the UN Secretary-General's 'Guidance Note' applying to all UN democracy promotion activities.

http://www.undp.org/governance   Presents the work of the UN Development Programme (UNDP) on democratic governance.

https://v-dem.net/en/   Varieties of Democracy (V-DEM) offer a new approach to conceptualizing and measuring democracy; co-hosted by the Department of Political Science at the University of Gothenburg, Sweden, and the Kellogg Institute at the University of Notre Dame, IN.

http://www.journalofdemocracy.org and http://www.tandfonline.com/loi/fdem20   The *Journal of Democracy* (edited in the United States) and *Democratization* (edited in the UK) are two well-known journals, the second publishing an annual digest of the latest Freedom House survey.

For additional material and resources, please visit the Online Resource Centre at:
http://www.oxfordtextbooks.co.uk/orc/burnell5e/

15

Governance

Lise Rakner

Overview

Governance and debates about what constitutes good governance became central to development discourse in the early 1990s. Following from this, measurements of governance became key features of international foreign aid, and a condition for receiving aid from bilateral governments and multi-national institutions. The chapter discusses the concepts of governance and good governance. The good governance agenda and the indices developed to assess governance have been criticized for being too encompassing, and for not adequately separating between how power is obtained (the input side of politics) and how power is exercised once in office (the output side of politics). Increasingly, scholars are calling for a separation between governance and democracy. In part, the need to separate the input from the output side of politics is linked to the recognition that some authoritarian regimes may score highly on central indicators of governance, while some regimes that elect their leaders through free and fair elections may be unable to deliver effective services to their citizens and to curb corruption.

Introduction

The last chapter discussed how power is obtained (democratization and **regime change**); in this chapter, the focus shifts to discuss the concept of **governance**—or, put differently, how power is exercised and checked once a government is in office. The chapter begins with a discussion of the concepts of governance and **good governance**. In the context of developing nations, the governance debate dates back to the 1990s and the realization that the failure of the economic reform programmes was primarily a failure of the developing states to effectively implement reforms. However, while a consensus emerged arguing that governance is important in its own right, and as a means for achieving equitable and sustainable growth, what governance is, and how it relates to development processes, have remained issues of debate. According to Payne (2005: 55), the word governance 'is probably second only to **globalization** in use and abuse'. Governance, as it has evolved, may be understood as a fairly elaborate theory about how power is exercised and checked, through mechanisms of accountability, whereas democracy is about how power is attained through electoral processes and participatory **institutions**. However, in much of the literature on good governance reforms, this distinction is blurred, and many definitions blend *access* to power and *exercise* of power—or the input and output sides of **politics**. Acknowledging the wide variety of definitions and contents, for analytical purposes, this chapter distinguishes between democracy and governance, and defines governance as a government's ability to enforce rules and to deliver services, regardless of whether that government is democratically elected or not.

According to Francis Fukuyama (2013: 1), the comparative literature related to political development has paid too little attention to the institutions that accumulate and use power in developing nations. Building on a key concept of statehood discussed in Chapter 12, that of impartial bureaucracies, the chapter moves on to discuss how the concepts of governance and development are related. Two central features of governance considered crucial for development are emphasized: the capacity of a government to extract revenue from its citizens; and the ability to control **corruption**. The chapter shows that states that 'earn' income by taxing their citizens will need to be accountable to their citizens and to develop capable state bureaucracies, whereas a state that derives its revenue from rents such as natural resources and aid may not be required to answer to its citizens to the same extent or to build the same administrative capabilities. Similarly, the ability of the government to curb corruption is considered a key feature of quality of governance. In the final section, and building on the previous chapter on democracy, the chapter returns to the debate about governance and the input or output side of politics, discussing recent debates about the **developmental state**.

Conceptualizing Governance and Good Governance

Since the 1980s, the concept of *governance* has increasingly been employed to describe policymaking in the national, regional, and global arenas (Krahmann 2003: 232). The application of the term 'governance' at the global level emerged in the 1990s. Redefined as *good governance*, these principles were adopted by the World Bank and International Monetary Fund (IMF) as conditions for development aid. Disappointing results of the economic reforms advocated by the international finance institutions in the 1980s prompted the World Bank to identify poor governance in developing countries, rather than simply too much government, as a major problem. This shift was made possible by the end of the cold war, which opened up space for new forms of international activism. A series of new policy recommendations linked to civil services, parliamentary accountability, anti-corruption, **civil society**, **human rights**, and democracy were later added by Western governments in their roles as bilateral donors (Kjær 2004). Led by a reinvigorated United Nations, Western governments and international organizations advocated economic and political liberalization as a foundation for a more peaceful world.

Yet while good governance has become almost a mantra among developing organizations, there is no clear agreement on what exactly it entails (Fukuyama 2013). Governance has an economic dimension that usually refers to property rights, transparency of economic transactions, freedom of information, and public sector management. The political dimension of governance is usually taken to mean government **legitimacy**, human rights, **rule of law**, and government accountability (Grindle 2004). A common denominator in most understandings of governance is a focus on institutions (formal and informal) and 'rules of the game' (Hyden et al. 2004). *Good* governance, then, involves positive features within these institutions, often drawn from Western institutions. At the outset, the World Bank, in its idea of good govern-ance, focused on such qualities as transparency, fiscal accountability, and sound management of the public sector—in short, economic governance. Other actors, including foreign ministries in the West and bilateral aid agencies, quickly expanded the agenda towards political governance, bringing in issues of democracy and human rights in general, and political pluralism and free and fair elections specifically. However, even in the narrower definitions employed by the World Bank, the concept of governance came to include is-sues to do with the distribution of power in society, and between state and society—or what we refer to here as the 'input' side of politics. Table 15.1 shows how various development agencies have defined 'gov-ernance' in their development aid policies.

The study *Governance Matters* of Kaufmann and col-leagues (2010) (see Box 15.1) proceeds from a definition

of governance as the traditions and institutions that de-termine how authority is exercised in a country. This includes the process by which governments are se-lected, held accountable, monitored, and replaced, as well as the capacity to formulate and implement sound policies effectively, and the respect of citizens and the state for the institutions that govern economic and so-cial interactions among them. Now covering 212 coun-tries and territories, and compiled from thirty-five data sources and thirty-three different organizations, the most recent findings are displayed in *Governance Matters VIII: Governance Indicators for 1996–2008* (Kaufmann et al. 2010). The data falls into six dimensions: voice and accountability; political stability and absence of violence/terrorism; government effectiveness; regu-latory quality; rule of law; and control of corruption. The research overall confirms that good governance is correlated with better development and claims to

Table 15.1 Good governance defined by development agencies

Agency	Definition
World Bank (2000)	Inclusiveness and accountability established in three key areas: selection, accountability and replacement of authorities (voice an accountability, stability and lack of violence); efficiency of institutions, regulations, resource management (regulatory framework; government effectiveness); respect for institutions, laws and interactions among players in civil society, business and politics (control of corruption; rule of law).
SIDA (2002: 2)	A good system of government encompassing the state's way of exercising its political, economic and administrative powers. It maintains that both institutions and processes ought to be based on the principles of the rule of law and should be characterized by responsibility, openness, integrity and efficiency . . . it emphasizes that democratic state and its public sector ought to be characterized by a democratic culture and the rule of law.
IMF (2005)	Ensuring the rule of law, improving the efficiency and accountability of the public sector, and tackling corruption.
USAID (2005)	Democratic governance: transparency, pluralism, citizen involvement in decision-making, representation and accountability; focusing particularly on five areas: legislative strengthening, decentralization and democratic local governance, anti-corruption, civil–military relations, and improving policy implementation.
DfID (2007: 6)	Seven key governance capabilities to operate political systems which provide opportunities for all people . . . to influence government policy and practice; to provide macroeconomic stability . . . to promote the growth necessary to reduce poverty; to implement pro-poor policy, to guarantee the equitable and universal provision of effective basic services; ensure personal safety and security; to manage national security arrangements accountability; . . . to develop honest and accountable government.
Kaufman et al. (2010: 2–3)	Index measured along six dimensions (voice and external accountability, political stability and lack of violence, crime and **terrorism**; government effectiveness, lack of regulatory burden, rule of law, control of corruption).

Note: DfID = Department for International Development (United Kingdom); IMF = International Monetary Fund; SIDA = Swedish International Development Cooperation Agency; USAID = US Agency for International Development

Source: Rothstein and Tannenberg (2015), https://creativecommons.org/licenses/by/4.0/

BOX 15.1 *GOVERNANCE MATTERS VIII*: SOME LEADING FINDINGS

- Good governance can be found at all income levels. Developing countries such as Chile, Botswana, Uruguay, Mauritius, and Costa Rica score higher on certain dimensions such as government effectiveness, rule of law, and control of corruption than do countries such as Greece or Italy.

- Since 1998, countries showing substantial improvements have included: Ghana, Indonesia, Liberia, and Peru for voice and accountability; Rwanda, Algeria, Angola, and Sierra Leone for political stability and absence of violence/terrorism; and South Korea, Rwanda, and Ethiopia for government effectiveness. Regulatory quality in Iraq has improved, as has control of corruption in Tanzania.

- Since 1998, Zimbabwe and Thailand deteriorated in terms of voice and accountability, and Zimbabwe declined in respect of most other governance dimensions as well. Government effectiveness and regulatory quality both deteriorated in Bolivia, as has rule of law in Venezuela, and voice and accountability in Iran.

- Change does not always proceed in parallel across dimensions. Nigeria has, for example, recorded improvement in voice and accountability, but worsening of political stability and violence.

- The quality of governance globally has not improved much over the past decade.

Source: Kaufmann et al. (2010)

find a large causal effect running from improved governance to better development outcomes, rather than the other way around. The findings also support the belief that good governance significantly enhances the effectiveness of development assistance. While useful for cross-country and intertemporal comparisons, the methodology cannot say much about the specific **institutional** failures responsible for poor governance in particular settings, or whether 'good governance' leads to growth. As a result, increasingly scholars are turning to in-depth studies of individual countries to understand the causal relationship between governance and economic development.

The Governance Matters project is not the *only* source of information and analysis. The UN Development Programme (UNDP) Governance Centre in Oslo has, since 2008, carried out a Global Programme on Capacity Development for Democratic Governance Assessments and Measurements. This seeks to build on its existing Governance Indicators project—a project that set out to be more sensitive to **human development**, and to raise the profile of poverty and **gender**-sensitive indicators in particular, in a more country-contextualized way than other leading studies of governance. From a UNDP perspective, governance is the exercise of economic, political, and administrative authority to manage a country's affairs at all levels. Programmes funded by the UNDP for strengthening institutions of democratic accountability such as parliaments and judiciaries, along with support for decentralization and e-governance, are present in around 130 countries. The aim is to assist national processes of assessing and monitoring democratic governance.

This last ambition travels in the direction of recent research on a World Governance Assessment first trialled by Hyden and colleagues (2004), for whom political notions of governance must be ascribed at least as much importance as economic notions. The Quality of Government Institute in Sweden has developed a set of measures of quality of governance for 193 countries worldwide, based on expert surveys focusing on the level of a state's impartiality. Other research projects that collect data on bureaucratic quality include the Bertelsmann Transformation Index and the Varieties of Democracy project (see Chapter 14).

Table 15.1 shows that, for the World Bank and IMF, as well as for foreign ministries providing development assistance, good governance has become a concept that encompasses a large number of qualitative assessments, relating both to how power is obtained and what leaders do when in power. Owing to the vastness of the concept of governance and all of the dimensions to which it refers, it is arguably difficult—if not impossible—for developing countries to implement all of the changes that the good governance agenda prescribes. Grindle (2004: 525) argues that the 'laundry list' of the good governance agenda is simply unrealistically long and that it is particularly problematic when guidelines for what should come first, and what is feasible, are lacking. It is also a question of whether we know what we measure. Instead, Grindle calls for degrees of good governance, or 'good-enough governance', finding that the list of required institutions for development is simply too costly to sustain for the poorest developing nations. She presents a hierarchy of governance priorities, which gives an indication as to what should be a priority given the particular context of a country. For example, in a **collapsed state**, the best form of governance may be to ensure personal safety and conflict resolution first, ignoring accountability and responsiveness for the time being. Similarly, Rothstein and Teorell (2008) criticize many definitions of good governance for being too encompassing. In particular, they find that the wide definitions blend *access* to power and *exercise* of power—or the input and output sides of politics. As an alternative, they define governance as the government's ability to enforce rules and to deliver services, regardless of whether that government is democratic or not. For Rothstein and Teorell (2008: 170), good quality of government is when government acts impartially, which is defined as arising when 'implementing laws and policies, government officials [do] not take into consideration anything about the citizen/case that is not beforehand stipulated in the policy or the law'. This firmly puts the output side of politics at the forefront. But their 'quality of government' concept still relates to how state (institutions) and society interact.

KEY POINTS

- While there is general agreement that governance is important for achieving equitable and sustainable growth, what governance is and which elements of the governance agenda are most conducive to development remain debated.

- Many definitions of good governance merge governance and democracy; for analytical purposes, the two concepts should be kept separate.

- Some authoritarian **regimes** may score highly on central indicators of governance, while regimes that elect their leaders through free and fair elections may be unable to deliver effective services to their citizens.

- Global trends in governance overall show no improvement, but evidence from individual countries shows that it is possible to make significant improvements over fairly short periods.

- Some authors contend that good governance is best understood as the degree to which government exercises power in an impartial manner.

Governance and Development

The expectation that good governance is associated with development success has been given as a rationale for promoting a wide range of reforms from public financial management, property rights, and political regimes, to public administration. There are, however, still many unanswered questions about which types of institution positively influence development and which should be supported. Arguing that a correlation between governance and growth does not equate causality, Mushtaq Khan (2012) argues that many countries have followed a trajectory directly the opposite of that outlined in the governance agenda. In a recent, much-acclaimed book, Francis Fukuyama (2014: 25) writes that the international development aid community would like to turn Afghanistan, Somalia, Libya, and Haiti into idealized places like Denmark, but it does not have the slightest idea of how to bring this about.

Both China and Vietnam have a number of 'poor' governance features linked to authoritarian governments, high levels of corruption, and insecure property rights, yet both states have achieved economic growth, reduced levels of poverty, and improved public services in areas of education and health. An example of an established democracy with persistent problems of governance and inequality is India. India has one of the fastest growing economies on earth. Over the past three decades, socialism has been replaced by pro-business policies as the way forward. And yet, in this 'new' India, grinding poverty is still a feature of everyday life: some 450 million people subsist on less than US$1.25 per day and nearly half of India's children are malnourished. Atul Kohli (2012) blames poor governance on the narrow nature of the ruling alliance in India that, in its newfound relationship with business, has prioritized economic growth over all other social and political considerations.

The new **Sustainable Development Goals (SDGs)** emphasize the significance of governance for development by the **international community**. In 2015, the UN member states agreed to a new, universal set of goals, targets, and indicators to frame their development agendas over the next fifteen years. The UN Sustainable Development Goals (SDGs), replacing the 2015 Millennium Development Goals (MDGs), include, for the first time, specific goals on governance, aiming at building 'effective, accountable and inclusive institutions at all levels' (SDG 16). What this really entails and what the underlying challenges for development-friendly governance are is, however, a matter of dispute. When now turning to discuss two key determinants of good governance, the ability to extract revenue and to control corruption, we see that, in practice, it is difficult to separate the input and output sides of politics.

The role of taxation

What causes good governance and good quality of government? In the governance literature, a key feature of quality of government is the ability to generate revenue—or how a state is able to tax its citizens. Margaret Levi (1988: 1), emphasizing the centrality of taxation to state-building and state capacity, notes that 'the history of state revenue production is the history of the evolution of the state'. The history of modern state formation is closely tied to revenue creation and tax (see Chapter 12). American revolutionaries in the eighteenth century rallied around the slogan 'No taxation without representation' and history repeatedly shows how, when rulers have been in need of increasing taxes, they have agreed to constraints making them more accountable to their citizens (Tilly 1990). The need for the elite to raise revenues through taxes has often been proposed as a historically important reason for the development from authoritarianism to democracy, because states that do not need to generate taxes from its citizens are considered to be more autonomous from the people and thus less likely to democratize (see Box 15.2). Moore (2007) argues that

if governments do not depend on taxes to finance public services and state operations, they have few incentives to build political and organizational capacity to negotiate and collect revenue, and spend it, effectively. The likely outcome of such a situation is arbitrary and poor governance.

Taxation influences government capacity in two ways. First, collecting taxes demands governance capacity regardless of how taxes are collected and what forms of revenue are extracted. This gives governments incentives to develop such administrative capabilities. Second, taxation is considered central to the quality of governance as a key instrument for influencing economic and social redistribution through progressive taxation. Simply put, if they lack the ability to raise revenues effectively, states are not able to provide security and basic services or foster economic development (Bräutigam et al. 2008; Fukuyama 2013).

Taxation in the developing world

Tax extraction can be measured both by the percentage of taxes to gross national product (GNP), as well

BOX 15.2 COMPARING TAXATION AND ACCOUNTABILITY IN ETHIOPIA, GHANA, AND KENYA

Challenging a strict separation between the input and output sides of politics in relation to good governance, there are strong mechanisms that link taxation and pressures for increased responsiveness and accountability. This can happen through direct tax bargaining with citizens, leading to particular instances of political reform. Additionally, tax resistance by citizens may create indirect pressures for change and reform. Finally, taxation may become a catalyst for strengthening civil society organizations. The political context influences which of these mechanisms that become most prevalent.

In Ghana, an open political system, numerous instances of direct tax bargaining have taken place and the willingness to pay taxes seems related to the popularity of governments. When unpopular governments have attempted to increase revenue, citizens have undermined these measures by tax evasion or labour unrest, forcing changes, such as in 1999–2000, when increasing financial problems led to defeat in the presidential elections. Tax bargaining also directly increases government responsiveness, which can be seen when, during 1999 and 2003, increases in rates of value added tax (VAT) caused public protests, to which governments responded with promises to commit these tax revenues to specific popular social reforms.

Kenya, a less institutionalized political system, has experienced few such direct instances of tax bargaining. More indirect resistance to taxation by unpopular governments has, however, occurred. Unpopular governments were increasingly made fiscally weak by the explicit tax evasion of businesses linked to the opposition. This was seen in 2002 when the Moi government was ousted, and a more liberal and responsive government was put in place. Further, businesses whose profits were hurt by post-election violence in 2007–08 threatened to withhold tax revenues if the government did not find a solution to the problem.

The autocratic shape of modern Ethiopia has given citizens little bearing on revenue-raising. One example of tax bargaining nevertheless exists: in 2005, the government tried to introduce a tax on businesses, which provoked wide public outcry. In response, the government set up a commission to evaluate the fairness of the tax and, after the election, the government reduced taxes, increased participation in the assessment, and created new public forums for consultation about tax collection and expenditure.

Source: IDS (2010)

as by the nature of taxation—in other words, whether it is based on income or wealth, or more indirect taxation. Most developing countries struggle to collect taxes effectively and few developing countries have succeeded in creating a tax system with high levels of capacity. The tax systems of most developing countries are characterized by regressive and distortive taxation (Bräutigam et al. 2008). Moreover, tax administration is weak, often characterized by extensive evasion and corruption, and it often disregards the informal sector. This is considered detrimental for governance, because states lose out on substantial revenue, tax compliance within the formal sector may decrease, and people in the informal sector remain disengaged from an unresponsive state (Joshi and Ayee 2008: 187–8).

Considering the importance of taxation for development, taxation has played a rather limited role in terms of foreign development aid and aid **conditionality**. According to Bräutigam and colleagues (2008: 2), the World Bank and IMF have tended to focus more on cutting expenditure than on raising revenue. Since the 1990s, however, especially the IMF, but also regional organizations and various governments, have started to emphasize tax reform in its aid programmes—in particular the need to reform tax administration as a means for developing countries to increase revenue. In part, the involvement of global actors has meant that the ideas that shape tax reforms in developing countries today are heavily influenced by the norms of the international finance institutions. This suggests a significant *contrast* regarding revenue collection and state-building between developed and developing nations: the role of external actors such as the IMF has no counterpart in the historical models of how taxation has shaped governance capacity (Mahon 2004: 25). Fjeldstad and Moore (2008) find that the donor-initiated tax reforms intended to enhance governance capacity have done little for the developing nations. They argue that revenues lost to the global drive for trade liberalization for most developing countries have not been restored through other areas of tax reform such as VAT.

A taxation challenge that has received little attention from political actors, donors, and civil society in developing countries is that of widening the tax base (Fjeldstad and Moore 2008). This is particularly relevant in terms of incorporating the informal sector into the tax net. Developing nations often display low tax levels under which large sectors of the **informal economy** escape the tax net. Illustrating this, in 2006,

just over 80 per cent of the Zambian workforce was engaged in some form of economic activity in the informal sector. The tax base in Zambia is thus currently focused on a relatively few wealthy businesses, as well as public employees, who contribute the lion's share of all direct taxes. This is negative, because the state is not able to generate enough revenues to provide public services such as schools, roads, and health facilities. Further, the fact that only a fraction of the population is included in the tax net may suggest that Zambians hold the government accountable for the spending of revenue to only a limited extent.

But a given level of taxation does not necessarily translate into the efficient use of tax revenues. In developing countries depending on aid transfers, revenues can be wasted on poor administration or corruption. As a result, tax reform has been considered to be a governance reform, in particular by the World Bank. Tax reforms have often focused on simplifying taxes and removing those taxes that are hard to collect and easy to hide. Perhaps the most prominent reform of tax administration has been the creation of semi-autonomous revenue authorities, independent from finance ministries, and manned by well-paid professionals. According to Fjeldstad and Moore (2008: 239), the autonomous revenue authorities (more than thirty) that have emerged in the last two decades in the **developing world** have helped to privatize tax collection. The problem with the autonomous revenue authorities in some developing countries is that autonomy in practice has hidden the fact that the revenue authorities in fact are answerable only to one person: the president. The Uganda Revenue Authority (URA), for example, was initially very successful in terms of collecting more revenue more efficiently. After a period, however, the performance stalled, and observers link this to the fact that the URA in practice was directly accountable to President Museveni (Therkildsen 2004). In contrast, the South African Revenue Services (SARS), which has succeeded in increasing the level of taxation, has tended to work very closely with all relevant state agencies, including the treasury (Fjeldstad and Moore 2008: 253).

The difference between earned and unearned revenue

In Chapter 12, we saw that some developing states are described as **rentier states** because major parts of state revenues are derived from taxes on companies involved in the extraction of some valuable natural resource, such as oil, diamonds, or copper. However, contrary to taxes extracted from individuals and businesses (indirect and direct), rents on natural resources are considered to undermine governance and state capacity, and even to fuel intense conflict between groups determined to control the trade or the state to capture the rents. This further weakens, and sometimes simply destroys, the central power and authority of an already weak **post-colonial state**. Moore (2011: 1759) argues that 'political authorities which enjoy revenue that does not have to be "earned" politically are more likely to abuse their power and govern badly'. Referring to the **resource curse**, it is hypothesized that governments that do not depend on levying taxes on the population, but which get the bulk of their revenue from oil or other natural resources, are often unresponsive and unaccountable to their people (Ross 1999). The argument is that, because oil revenue accrues to a small number of big companies and central states, states become independent of citizen-taxpayers and thus, in effect, become unresponsive to them. There are therefore few incentives to promote broad economic responsiveness outside of the oil sector; instead, the revenues can be used to buy off opposition and to fund repressive internal security. Oil may also attract foreign military and political support that can disrupt internal dynamics. Further, revenues from natural resources are often opaque, with low oversight, increasing incentives for corruption. Because states do not depend on the effective extraction of revenue from their citizens through an effective bureaucracy, they have fewer incentives to build such institutions.

The differences between 'earned' and 'unearned' revenue can be illustrated by regional comparisons of Argentina and Tanzania (Moore 2007). Studies conducted in Argentina show that regions that depend on citizens for income are more democratic than regions depending on natural resources. Similarly, in Tanzania, in areas in which people pay taxes directly to authorities not indirectly to local tax collectors, more money is being spent directly on taxpayers.

A number of studies point to the fact that large levels of foreign aid have the same negative effects on developing countries' capacity to extract taxation as natural resources. Bräutigam and Knack (2004) argue that development aid decreases the incentive of governments to engage in the difficult negotiations with various social groups that would broaden the tax base. Research carried out by the World Bank similarly found that aid to African countries reduced government revenue by an average of 10 per cent (Devarajan et al. 1999). However, the effect of aid on governance is not clear. According to Moore (2011: 1771), we do not have conclusive evidence that aid makes countries less interested in increasing tax revenues, but aid does seem to weaken and fragment local administrative and political institutions—a tendency fuelled by the large increase in the number of aid channels, leading to a 'dispersal of the attentions, energies and resources of recipient governments'.

When states do not collect taxes from their citizens, these citizens may have few incentives to control the government and their spending. Kjær (2004) notes considerable controversy over the extent to which the payment of taxes in developing countries can be seen as a 'return' for better services. Public services that are deemed faulty, as in the case of corruption, can serve as an excuse for underpayment, which again leads to worse services. To break such vicious governance cycles, proper incentives must be put into place, including incentives for public servants to work more effectively and for punishing underpayment. Corruption may create a vicious cycle that hampers the extractive capacities of the state. The malign effects of corruption on governance are the topic to which we turn next.

KEY POINTS

- Improved governance is assumed to have a positive impact on development, but there are many unanswered questions about which types of institution positively influence development

- The UN Sustainable Development Goals (SDGs), replacing the 2015 Millennium Development Goals (MDGs), for the first time include specific goals on governance, aiming at building 'effective, accountable and inclusive institutions at all levels' (SDG 16).

- Taxation is central to the quality of governance as a key instrument for influencing economic and social redistribution through progressive taxation.

- The main challenge in many developing nations is to find cost-efficient ways in which to tax the informal sector.

- We should distinguish between revenue as 'earned' and 'unearned'. States that receive the bulk of their revenue from natural resources or aid do not depend on the effective extraction of revenue from their citizens through an effective bureaucracy and have fewer incentives to build efficient bureaucracies.

Corruption: A Key Governance Challenge

Perhaps the most important aspect of the quality of government is absence of corruption and, because of this, a low level of corruption is often used as a proxy for good governance (Rothstein 2011). Rose-Ackerman (2004: 1) defines corruption as the 'misuse of public power for private or political gain'. Corruption can be explicitly illegal, as in the case of bribing officials, or it can be on the border between legal and illegal. Rose-Ackerman (2004) distinguishes between two different kinds of corruption: one relates to administrative corruption and concerns, for example, using bribery and favouritism to lower taxes, to escape some form of regulation, or to win low-level procurement contracts; the other refers to a situation in which the state itself can be characterized as serving the interests of small segments of business or politicians—a situation in which the state is captured. Moreover, one can distinguish between 'grand corruption', relating to large-scale projects that generate massive rents, and 'petty corruption', such as bribing a police officer to escape a fine or a health worker to get faster treatment (see Box 15.3).

BOX 15.3 POLITICAL CORRUPTION IN CENTRAL AMERICA

Both high-level (grand) corruption and lower level (petty) corruption are widespread in Central America. But the use of different measures of corruption shows very different results. In 2008, the Corruption Perception Index (CPI) and the World Bank Control of Corruption (WBCC) rated Costa Rica as the least corrupt country in Central America. The Latinbarometer poll of the same year, however, found that a greater percentage of Costa Ricans than the people of any other Central American nations reported knowledge of corrupt acts in their country. This shows that competing measures of corruption based on expert perceptions and citizen's bribery experiences produce very different rankings of the Central American countries. According to these measurement tools, Costa Rica has the least grand corruption in the region, but the second most petty corruption. Panama and El Salvador experience serious high-level corruption, while petty corruption levels appear to be relatively low. The contrasting levels of grand and petty corruption exist because some of the factors that cause petty corruption (administrative and procedural burdens) may have little influence on grand corruption levels (Ruhl 2011).

High levels of corruption are associated with more unequal distribution of income—and while there is a general consensus among economists and policy analysts that corruption is a universal problem, the worst effects are felt in developing nations. Just as high levels of taxation are positively associated with development, corruption appears negatively associated with development, when measured by the Human Development Index (see Figure 15.1 and Table 15.2). The costs of corruption for developing countries were highlighted by the UN Secretary-General in his 2009 statement marking International Anti-Corruption Day:

" When public money is stolen for private gain, it means fewer resources to build schools, hospitals, roads and water treatment facilities. When foreign aid is diverted into private bank accounts, major infrastructure projects come to a halt. Corruption enables fake or substandard medicines to be dumped on the market, and hazardous waste to be dumped in landfill sites and in oceans. The vulnerable suffer first and worst. "

(Ki-moon 2009)

Corruption is considered to affect welfare and growth in developing countries through a range of mechanisms. Perceptions of, as well as experience with, corruption discourage business, investments, and growth. Foreign investment seems to be lower in corrupt societies and corruption distorts firms' production decisions, such as where to produce and where to purchase supplies. Corruption also increases budgetary costs of **public goods** and services, because informal payments—that is, 'kickbacks'—bring up costs. Owing to corruption, public development projects become more costly and affect development in a negative way. As discussed earlier, weak and corrupt tax collection agencies and tax evasion also affect revenue generation. Moreover, as a result of leaks out of the system, service delivery and **human capital** are negatively affected by corruption. In Indonesia, for example, at least 18 per cent of rice distributed to the poor through a social safety net programme was lost as a result of corruption (Olken 2006: 856). However, as Khan (2012) and others have pointed out, some developing states have achieved high growth rates despite high levels of corruption. South Korea (see Chapter 24) is a case in point.

But the costs of corruption are not only related to money, but also can prove detrimental for public trust. Corruption threatens democracy by corroding rule of

Figure 15.1 Relationship between corruption and development in the ten least and ten most corrupt countries

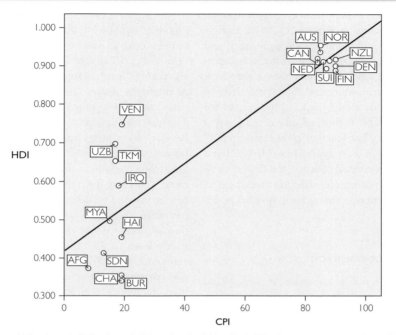

Note: AFG = Afghanistan; AUS = Australia; BUR = Burundi; CAN = Canada; CHA = Chad; CPI = Corruption Perceptions Index; DEN = Denmark; FIN = Finland; HAI = Haiti; HDI = Human Development Index; IRQ = Iraq; MYA = Myanmar; NED = Netherlands; NOR = Norway; NZL = New Zealand; SDN = Sudan; SUI = Switzerland; TKM = Turkmenistan; UZB = Uzbekistan; VEN = Venezuela
Sources: Human Development Report (UNDP 2013); Transparency International (2012)

Table 15.2 The ten most corrupt and least corrupt countries with corresponding HDI figures

Ten most corrupt countries	TI (2012)	HDI (2013)	Ten least corrupt countries	TI (2012)	HDI (2013)
Afghanistan	8	0.374	New Zealand	90	0.919
Sudan	13	0.414	Finland	90	0.892
Myanmar	15	0.498	Denmark	90	0.901
Turkmenistan	17	0.698	Sweden	88	0.916
Uzbekistan	17	0.654	Singapore	87	0.895
Iraq	18	0.590	Switzerland	86	0.913
Burundi	19	0.355	Norway	85	0.955
Chad	19	0.340	Australia	85	0.938
Haiti	19	0.456	Netherlands	84	0.921
Venezuela	19	0.748	Canada	84	0.911

Note: HDI = Human Development Index; TI = Transparency International

Sources: Human Development Report (UNDP 2013); Transparency International (2012)

law, democratic institutions, and public trust in leaders. For the poor, women, and minorities, corruption means even less access to jobs, justice, or fair and equal opportunity. According to Rothstein (2011), corruption may adversely affect democratic legitimacy, and install lower levels of interpersonal trust and belief in the political system among citizens, which may have wider governance consequences. Again, referring to the South Korean case study (see Chapter 24), we see that persistent corruption through all elected governments has led to very low levels of public trust in politicians. High levels of corruption may also increase the likelihood of protracted conflict (see Chapter 13). When public trust plummets, affecting the scope of government interventions, this again may affect political stability.

The causes of corruption

Corruption in developing countries is widespread not because people are different, but because conditions are ripe (Gray and Kaufman 1998). In the least-developed countries (LDCs), corruption tends to be endemic, because low income in itself is a cause. The basic causes of corruption are scarce public benefits, low wages, job insecurity, high levels of inflation, the presence of natural resources and foreign-owned companies, and difficulties of monitoring. Such a public benefit may be access to a particular service or having a law not apply to one's case (a traffic fine, for example). When rents are high and it is relatively easy to keep payoffs secret, opportunity for corruption is ripe. Corruption will also thrive where there are inadequate and ineffective controls. But, within a country, the level of corruption may vary greatly between sectors. In Ghana, for example, almost 50 per cent of citizens claim to have paid bribes when interacting with police, whereas only 5 per cent have done so when dealing with the health sector (Rose-Ackerman and Truex 2012: 53). Corruption will occur when the illicit benefits outweigh expected costs (Rothstein 2011). A problem with corruption, for developing countries in particular, is that it has a tendency of feeding on itself: the more corruption there is in society, the less formal and informal punishment of corrupt behaviour, and thus the easier it is for someone to commit corrupt acts. High levels of corruption affect development in a negative manner, just as low development may increase corruption, creating a vicious cycle in which

weak underlying economic conditions facilitate corruption (Rose-Ackerman 2004: 10).

The negative effects of corruption are illustrated in Figure 15.1, showing that the most corrupt countries in the world, as measured by the Corruption Perceptions Index (CPI), are also among the least developed and that the least corrupt are also the most developed. As the figure shows, corrupt countries record consistently lower development scores than the least corrupt. The least corrupt countries are found among the most developed countries and vice versa. As can be seen, however, among the most corrupt countries, there are strong variations regarding the level of development. This suggests that although corruption may be detrimental to development, even highly corrupt countries may score positively on various aspects of human development. Although this does not tell us if one leads to the other, it shows that the two concepts correlate substantially. Underlying the argument that corruption pervades a vicious development cycle, high inequality also spurs corruption. A range of other historical and social factors influences governance and corruption. For example, corruption is considered to be more prevalent in countries with higher ethnic fragmentation, in nations with few Protestants, and in societies characterized by socialist or French legal origin.

Reforms to reduce corruption

Considering the negative effects of corruption for the development of state capacity and services in the developing world, it is not surprising that curbing corruption has, since the 1990s, been a central concern for the World Bank and IMF, as well as bilateral governments and international **non-governmental organizations** (**NGOs**). Reflecting the broad definition of governance applied by the various international organizations, as discussed earlier, efforts to enhance oversight and transparency are considered key factors for reducing corruption. International aid agencies have put large sums of money into anti-corruption. Anti-corruption work involves preventing corruption by building transparent, accountable systems of government, and strengthening the capacity of civil society and the media (Cremer 2008). Corruption indices have become useful tools for drawing media attention to the problem of corruption (see Box 15.4). A common starting point has been the establishment

BOX 15.4 MEASURING CORRUPTION

Until the early 1990s, few empirical studies of corruption existed owing to lack of data. Since then, a number of corruption indices have emerged based primarily on assessments by experts and businessmen collected by a variety of organizations. Two often-used measures of corruption, Transparency International (TI) and World Government Indicators (WGI), are based on the perceptions of experts and surveys of the perceived level of corruption. They are based on a so-called poll of polls, meaning that they take the average of numerous polls and combine them. Since the data will always contain some degree of uncertainty, one should be careful to conclude that there are significant differences between countries that have similar scores (Kaufmann et al. 2010). However, as the distance increases, it will become more meaningful to speak of a real difference. For example, the difference between Somalia and Myanmar is negligible; the difference between Somalia and Denmark, however, is not. The perception-based indicators can nevertheless be problematic, because they may be measuring mere inferences by experts rather than actual levels of corruption—that is, if an expert believes a country to be democratic, then he or she may infer from this that corruption should be low, which will in turn validate the theory that democracy leads to less corruption (Treisman 2007).

KEY POINTS

- The absence of corruption is often used as a proxy for good governance and is understood as the misuse of public power for private or political gain.

- Research on corruption has improved and expanded rapidly in the last two decades because of better data. Recent research largely agrees that corruption is negatively associated with development, as measured by the Human Development Index (HDI).

- Corruption adversely affects democratic legitimacy, and leads to lower levels of interpersonal trust and belief in the political system among citizens, which may have wider governance consequences.

- International aid agencies have invested significant resources in anti-corruption strategies through building transparent, accountable systems of government, and strengthening the capacity of civil society and the media. To date, however, there have been few successes from the investments in countries most severely plagued by corruption.

The Relationship between Democracy and Governance

Do democracies in the developing world do a better governing job than autocracies? In other words, is there reason to expect that democratic states provide better services because they are more legitimate and depend on the consent of citizens? World economic leaders now argue that the biggest challenge facing the world is the increasing income gap between rich and poor. Not only is there an income gap between countries, but also many developing countries are currently experiencing dramatic income disparities between various groups. Against this background, some scholars have questioned whether democracy is a luxury that poor and developing countries can ill afford, arguing that policymakers should be more concerned with the quality of government and the public services that governments provide its citizens (see Box 15.5).

Civil liberties and democracy are often seen as the antidote for developmental deficiencies owing to the possibility of voicing one's opinion and holding officials accountable. The foregoing discussion about reforms to curb corruption and to enhance revenue collection indicates that many of the successful reforms to improve governance involved enhancing the voice of citizens and accountability of the political

of anti-corruption commissions, which sometimes have investigative functions; in other instances, anti-corruption agencies have awareness-raising and public education functions as their main purpose. The value of such commissions is debatable and many have suggested that they have had a limited effect in battling corruption (Persson et al. 2013), often serving primarily as an instrument of political score-settling. Countries that have successfully moved from corrupt to less corrupt systems of rule, such as Singapore and Hong Kong in recent times, share the characteristic that high-level public officials have served as role models. But we still have scant knowledge about what it takes for a country to move from a system of corrupt institutions to honest and impartial institutions. Because corruption and bad governance in many cases benefit a select few high up in the hierarchy, there is reason to believe that they will oppose such efforts. This leads to the question of whether it is really possible to separate good governance and the capacity to provide services in a just and equitable manner from the question of accountability and democracy. We will turn to this debate in the next section.

elites toward the citizens. This suggests that, in reality, it is difficult to separate the output side from the input side of politics when discussing governance reform in the developing world. The distinction is necessary, however, if we want to understand whether democracies perform better than autocracies. Scholars working within the concept of quality of government emphasize this distinction. The empirical evidence regarding the relationship between democracy and governance performance is not entirely conclusive. As an example, Rothstein (2011) contrasts the development paths of Jamaica and Singapore. Both countries gained independence from British colonial rule in the early 1960s and the two countries have approximately the same population size. But whereas Jamaica has abundant arable land, a homogenous population, and only one language spoken, Singapore has few natural resources, plus challenging ethnic and religious cleavages. Nevertheless, today Singapore's gross domestic product (GDP) is nine times higher than that of Jamaica, and Singapore outperforms Jamaica on most indicators of human well-being. Jamaica, however, has been a democracy since independence, while Singapore has never been democratic. Many quantitative studies, based on large data sets covering many nations, also seem to indicate that democracy has a negative impact on governance at least in the early phases of democratization processes (Charron and Lapuente 2010: 244). Quality of government appears to be highest in highly democratic countries, medium–high in strongly authoritarian regimes, and lowest in semi-democracies, or what Chapter 14 referred to as **electoral democracies** (Bäck and Hadenius 2008). This suggests a curvilinear relationship between democracy and quality of governance, meaning that, at low levels of democracy, a democratization process may in fact decrease the quality of governance, such as in Peru under Fujimori (McMillan and Zoido 2004). Because politicians aim to get re-elected, they will be responsive to citizen demands. At lower levels of economic development, citizens' demands will be centred more on short-term consumption than on long-term investments, which is not conducive to good governance. As economic development increases, citizens will be increasingly patient and concerned about future gains, and therefore favour more long-term investments. Theoretically, a democratic country should be more open and transparent, and it should be easier to hold politicians accountable. However, autocratic countries may, to a much larger degree, crack down

BOX 15.5 DEVELOPMENTAL PATRIMONIALISM

Critiques of the 'good governance' agenda have led to new research centring on two broad questions: first, what kinds of governance may enhance growth; and second, what kind of incentives may induce politicians in developing countries to implement growth-enhancing policies? An example is found in research on 'developmental **patrimonialism**', a term that describes centralized rent management in which economic transformation is favoured over political participation (Kelsall 2011: 80). Drawing on experiences of some East Asian countries such as South Korea and Indonesia, this perspective has recently been applied to the African context. Two countries, Rwanda and Ethiopia, have exhibited such traits. Both countries are characterized by centralized, top-down patron–client networks controlled by authoritarian governments, and this—it is assumed—has permitted far-sighted industrial policies for rent maximization, leading to high economic growth (Kelsall 2012: 679).

on corruption, thereby increasing the costs of corruption. Accordingly, in a democracy, the risks of getting caught are possibly higher and the possibility of bottom-up control is higher. In an autocracy, the risks of getting caught are lower, but the top-down punishment (that is, the cost) is potentially much larger. If corruption is more prevalent in economically underdeveloped countries, can one expect corruption to decline automatically as a country develops economically? Or is corruption actually such an impediment to growth that one first has to solve the corruption issue before economic development can start? These fundamental questions about the value of democracy, and its links to governance and development, continue to engage students of politics and development.

KEY POINTS

- The debate on whether autocracies or democracies perform better in terms of delivering services to its populations is not conclusive. Some studies indicate that democracy has a negative impact on governance in the early phases of democratization processes.

- Some scholars argue that since competitive elections can be detrimental to development measured as governance capacity, they should not be considered to be an important part of a developmental process.

Conclusion

In this chapter, we have seen that governance emerged as a key concept during the early 1990s. For international development organizations, the governance concept provided an opportunity to address social issues and government reform without 'meddling' with internal affairs or politics, and the concept of 'good governance' became a key indicator in aid allocations from multinational and bilateral donor agencies. A common denominator in most understandings of good governance is a focus on institutions (formal and informal) and 'rules of the game'. However, the concept has also come to embrace democratization, with a strong emphasis on state–society relations. Owing to the vastness of the concept of governance and good governance, it is very hard for developing countries to implement all of the changes that are prescribed. Some scholars have proposed an emphasis on 'good-enough governance', focusing on the minimal conditions of governance necessary to ensure political and economic development. Building from here, other scholars argue that definitions of good governance are too encompassing, making it impossible to establish what it exactly is. Emphasizing quality of government and the need for a government to act impartially, scholars recently have argued for a concept of governance that puts the output side of politics at the forefront. We have discussed two central aspects of governance: the ability to generate revenues through taxation and that to curb corruption. The discussions show that the abilities to generate revenue and to minimize corruption are closely linked to how state institutions and societies interact. Do democracies perform better than autocracies in terms of providing quality of public services? The evidence is inconclusive. The lesson learned about governance is that an essential condition for successful outcomes is that there is a domestic drive for development and that aid supports such a domestic drive. But if the political environment is unfavourable to providing effective leadership, governance reforms will have limited effect.

 QUESTIONS

1. Discuss the merits of the 'good-enough government' argument. Can it be argued that some aspects of governance are more important than others?

2. Why is there such great variation in respect of 'good governance' experienced by different countries in the developing world?

3. Why, and in what way, is a state's ability to extract taxes from its population an indication of the quality of governance?

4. In what way does corruption present an obstacle to development?

5. Study the Sustainable Development Goal (SDG) 16 on governance, aiming at building 'effective, accountable and inclusive institutions at all levels'. Discuss the definition of governance in SDG 16 in comparison with other definitions of governance found in this chapter.

6. Is climate change a governance challenge? Are democracies or autocracies better able to respond to climate change challenges? Why?

7. Is it possible for a country that is not democratizing to improve its governance and governance indicators?

 FURTHER READING

Fukuyama, F. (2014) *Political Order and Political Decay: From the Industrial Revolution to the Globalization of Democracy* (New York: Macmillan) A thought-provoking account of how and when societies develop strong, impersonal, and accountable political institutions.

Grindle, M. S. (2004) 'Good Enough Governance: Poverty Reduction and Reform in Developing Countries', *Governance*, 17(4): 525–48 Grindle shows how 'good enough governance' may be more appropriate for many developing countries.

Hyden, G., Court, J., and Mease, K. (2004) *Making Sense of Governance: Empirical Evidence from Sixteen Developing Countries* (Boulder, CO: Lynne Rienner) A comprehensive assessment informed by extensive evidence covering half the world's population.

Institute of Development Studies (2010) *An Upside down View of Governance* (Brighton: University of Sussex) Thoughtful collection of essays from the Centre for the Future State at Institute for Development Studies, suggesting that we need to stop viewing the world through the lens of the experiences of the Western world and instead look in a much more open-minded way at what is actually happening in particular 'fragile' contexts.

Kaufmann, D., Kraay, A., and Mastruzzi, M. (2010) 'The Worldwide Governance Indicators: Methodology and Analytical Issues', World Bank Policy Research Working Paper No. 5430, available online at http://papers.ssrn.com/sol3/papers.cfm?abstract_id=1682130 Gives an introduction into the methodology behind the widely used World Governance Indicators.

Khan, M. (2012) 'Governance and Growth Challenges for Africa', in A. Noman, K. Botchwey, H. Stein, and J. Stiglitz (eds) *Good Growth and Governance in Africa: Rethinking Development Strategies* (Oxford: Oxford University Press), 51–79 Khan offers a fundamental critique of the 'governance first' argument, or the idea that better governance will necessarily lead to economic growth.

Moore, M. (2004) 'Revenues, State Formation, and the Quality of Governance in Developing Countries', *International Political Science Review*, 25(3): 297–319 Explores the implications of fiscal sociology for governance in the developing world's rentier states.

Rothstein, B. (2011) *The Quality of Government: Corruption, Social Trust, and Inequality in International Perspective* (Chicago, IL: University of Chicago Press) Good introduction to the concept of quality of governance and an overview of governance debates.

Wrong, M. (2009) *It's Our Turn to Eat: The Story of a Kenyan Whistleblower* (London: Fourth Estate) An excellent account of corrupt practices and the problems combatting corruption in settings of poor governance.

 WEB LINKS

http://www.bti-project.org/home/index.nc   Site for the Bertelsmann Transformative Index.

http://www.transparency.org/cpi2015   The Transparency International Corruption Perceptions Index (2015).

http://www.institutions-africa.org/   Site for the African Power and Politics project.

http://www.odi.org.uk/wga_governance/About_WGA.html   Site for World Governance Assessment.

http://www.oecd.org/   Site includes the 2005 Paris Declaration on Aid Effectiveness: a shared vision of aid relations by international donors and developing world partners, including the idea of ownership by partners.

http://www.qog.pol.gu.se/   Site for the Quality of Government Institute.

http://www.u4.no   Provides anti-corruption material, including applied research, through an extensive web-based resource centre, based in Bergen, Norway.

http://www.undp.org/oslocentre/   Provides information on the Global Programme on Democratic Governance Assessments of the United Nations Development Programme (UNDP).

http://www.unodc.org/unodc/en/treaties/CAC/   Site for the United Nation Convention against Corruption (UNCAC).

http://www.worldbank.org/en/topic/governance   The World Bank Institute's site on governance and its activities in support of governance capacity-building.

http://info.worldbank.org/governance/wgi/index.asp   The World Bank World Governance Indicators Project.

https://www.youtube.com/watch?v=EdZOltzT8OE   Mushtaq Khan's lecture on governance in Africa, SOAS, London, December 2008.

For additional material and resources, please visit the Online Resource Centre at:
http://www.oxfordtextbooks.co.uk/orc/burnell5e/

PART 4
Policy Issues

In this part, several major policy domains in development are examined concerning development, environmental policies, and **human rights**. The themes do not concern developing countries only; across the world, they also represent key challenges to both state and non-state actors. Our concern is not with 'development' as a universal concept, although the increasingly holistic way in which development tends to be understood inevitably has implications for our presentation here; rather, this part has two main aims.

First, it aims to show how states, like other major actors in the economy and society, are confronted by certain key issues in development and face seemingly inescapable challenges. States in particular have to make significant decisions that involve political risks and impose considerable administrative burdens, concerning such matters as economic development, welfare, the environment, and human rights.

A *second* aim is to show the different ways in which governments and non-governmental actors and international bodies determine their responses, by comparing different strategies and their likely consequences. Here, the relevance of international influences to the way in which policy agendas are formed, and often to policy implementation, is undeniable, but nevertheless should be examined critically. The object of Part 4 is to illuminate the policy process, while necessarily being limited in how much detail it can convey about the policy substance. What choices really are open to developing countries and just how much scope for exercising choice independently have they experienced to date? Does state action necessarily offer the most appropriate way forward? Does 'one size fit all', or does the evidence suggest that the political response can embody distinct national and subnational frameworks for defining problems, devising solutions, and implementing a course of action?

16

Development

Tony Addison

Overview

This chapter discusses development policy objectives, noting how these have changed over the years, with a more explicit focus on poverty reduction coming to the fore recently. It also examines the relationship between economic growth and poverty reduction. The chapter then discusses ways in which to achieve economic growth, before considering what roles the market mechanism and the state should play in allocating society's productive resources. The chapter goes on to assess how economic reform has been implemented and the political difficulties that arise. It also considers the importance of transforming the structure of economies and the new global development landscape, including changes in development finance. The chapter concludes that getting development policy right has the potential to lift millions out of poverty.

Introduction

There are some 900 million people living in extreme poverty today, defined as having less than US$1.90 per day on which to survive, according to estimates and projections by the World Bank (Cruz et al. 2015: 1). There are large numbers of people living just above this (very low) poverty line, so at least a quarter of the population of the **developing world** is in, or close to, poverty. Hunger and malnutrition accompany poverty, as do ill-health and low life expectancy. Yet set against this grim picture there has also been considerable progress—notably, in East Asia, where extreme poverty is a fraction of its level thirty years ago, with China and Vietnam being outstanding successes. Even in South Asia, which has the largest numbers of poor people of all of the main regions, both the percentage and the number of people in poverty have fallen substantially over the last decade.

Much of the reduction in poverty has come through economic growth, especially when growth increases the demand for the labour and skills of poor people. East Asia has grown at rates that are historically unprecedented. Whereas it took the United Kingdom—the world's first industrial nation—fifty-four years to develop from a low per capita income economy to a middle-income economy, it is estimated that Hong Kong, Singapore, and Taiwan (the Asian 'tigers') achieved middle-income **status** in only ten years (Parente and Prescott 2000). China has grown at annual rates of around 6–9 per cent over the last two decades and India's growth has accelerated as well. Their growth pushed up the demand for oil and other commodities to the benefit of sub-Saharan Africa (which remains overwhelmingly dependent on commodity exports), as well as Latin America (where commodities still have a large export share). As a result, growth was strong in sub-Saharan Africa and Latin America over the last two decades after periods of severe economic crisis in these regions in the 1980s and 1990s. Oil wealth also raised living standards in the Middle East and North Africa, although this was unevenly distributed. However, Africa, the Middle East, and Latin America have, with few exceptions, largely failed to diversify their economies away from commodity-dependence and to provide employment for growing and young populations. The slump in commodity prices over 2014–16 has hit commodity exporters hard (especially the oil producers).

In sum, the developing world today presents a mixed picture: very fast growth and poverty reduction in much of Asia for many years; growth after long-term decline in sub-Saharan Africa, but high poverty and largely undiversified economies; growth, but considerable economic volatility, in Latin America; and the Middle East and North Africa living on abundant natural resources, but with often little economic progress (and now conflict affecting many countries as well). More fundamentally, economic and social progress cannot continue if climate change is allowed to accelerate, and a move towards 'green' growth, in which rising living standards are secured on the basis of environmentally sustainable economies, is imperative. Otherwise, climate change will intensify floods and droughts, thereby increasing poverty, especially in regions that are already environmentally stressed.

What role has development policy played in the variety of outcomes across the developing world? What policies are most important for accelerating development? Is the development past a guide to the development future? What lessons can we transfer across countries? As Nobel Laureate Robert Lucas (1988: 5) says: '[T]he consequences for human welfare involved in questions like these are simply staggering. Once one starts to think about them, it is hard to think about anything else.' And thinking about development policy has changed over time. On some issues, there is now considerable agreement about what needs to be done; many other issues remain deeply controversial, with starkly contrasting viewpoints.

KEY POINTS

- Some 900 million people live in extreme poverty, with many more just above the poverty line, so that about a quarter of the developing world's population is in, or close to, poverty.

- Poverty is falling in Asia, but remains high in sub-Saharan Africa and significant in Latin America.

- Growth has been achieved, but with insufficient diversification of economies, and climate change threatens economic and social progress.

Defining Development Policy Objectives

Much of today's debate is centred on poverty reduction as the primary objective for development policy. People differ as to how to define 'poverty': economists typically favour monetary measures, using data collected from household surveys of incomes and expenditures. If the household falls below a defined poverty line, then it is classified as poor. However, not all countries have the data to define poverty in this way, so measures of the 'dollar a day' variety (now US$1.90 to reflect the rise in the cost of living) are often used to calculate the global and regional aggregates. The World Bank has adjusted the poverty line over time to reflect the rising cost of living (of basic food, clothing, and shelter), so that the real value of US$1.90 in today's prices is the same as US$1.25, the poverty line used between 2008 and 2015, when the US$1.90 line was adopted. This poverty line is low and many millions of people live just above it, so that the calculation of global poverty numbers is quite sensitive to where the line is drawn. Shocks, such as a rise in food prices, can quickly drive many people into poverty, as can disaster within the household (the illness of a family worker, for example).

Non-monetary measures of poverty are increasingly used—measures such as infant mortality, life expectancy, and literacy—and people vary in terms of how well they are doing across these different dimensions. Some may have a rising income, but remain illiterate, for example, and women often do worse than men, reflecting **gender** discrimination (in access to education and jobs, for example). People in chronic poverty suffer from multiple deprivations, making it very difficult for them ever to escape, and poverty is passed down the generations: the children of the chronically poor generally remain poor when they become adults (Chronic Poverty Research Centre 2008). The Millennium Development Goals (MDGs), which were adopted by the world's leaders in the United Nations' Millennium Declaration of September 2000 as guiding principles for the international development community, reflect the multidimensional view of poverty. This approach has carried on with the adoption (in 2015) of the even more comprehensive UN **Sustainable Development Goals (SDGs)**. The SDGs also marked an attempt to promote the closer integration of environmental sustainability with conventional development goals such as poverty reduction (see Chapter 17). Whether the SDGs can be achieved is largely down to country efforts, together with help from the **international community**. States that are 'fragile' stand the least chance of success; this is especially so when conflict is prevalent (in Afghanistan, for instance). But this is not to say that significant progress cannot still be made in areas such as malaria—responsible for the deaths of more than 1 million people a year, most of them young children—in relation to which there are major initiatives and funding.

In the early days of development policy, during the era of decolonization from the late 1940s through to the 1960s, poverty reduction was often more implicit than explicit in development strategies. These tended to focus on raising gross domestic product (GDP)

per capita by means of economic growth—it being assumed that poverty reduction would then follow, more or less, from growth. Early development thinkers emphasized raising output—in particular, increasing overall labour productivity (output per person) by shifting labour from sectors in which productivity is low to sectors in which it is high. This led to a concentration on industry, which was seen as the dynamic sector, while many policymakers saw smallholder agriculture as hopelessly backward. Crudely put, industrialization and urbanization became synonymous with development in the minds of policymakers between the 1940s and the 1960s. This was reinforced by the Soviet Union's emphasis on industrialization. Aid donors enthusiastically supported big infrastructure projects, especially those benefiting the commercial interests of their own countries. As we shall see in this chapter, these ideas were increasingly challenged by other conceptions of what development should be and therefore what policy ought to achieve.

Income per capita is an *average* measure of a country's living standard, but income is unequally distributed, reflecting differences in the distribution of wealth (land, other property, and financial wealth) and **human capital** (peoples' skills and capabilities, which are partly a product of their education and which make them more productive). Accordingly, income inequality can show a wide variation across countries depending on their histories of colonization, war, and development policy.

There is an ethical dimension (how much inequality is 'just'—see Chapter 6), and high inequality can endanger social stability and democratization (see Chapter 14). Economists worry about high inequality because it can make economic growth less effective in reducing poverty. A Latin American landowner with millions of hectares will benefit much more from agricultural export growth than a smallholder eking out a living on just a few hectares, for example. Put differently, high-inequality societies need to grow a lot more quickly to achieve the same amount of poverty reduction per year as low-inequality societies.

So countries need to protect and build the assets of the poor—particularly their human capital, as well as the **natural capital**, such as the soils, forests, and fisheries, on which their livelihoods depend. Providing primary education, basic health care, water, and sanitation will not only raise the **human development** of poor people, but also raise their productivity. This will help them to diversify their livelihoods in both self-employment (for example from dependence on subsistence agriculture, and into cash crops and micro-enterprises) and wage employment (the poor will earn more as skilled workers than as unskilled workers). Asset *redistribution* may also be necessary to build the assets of the poor; land reform is most often cited as an example. Asset redistribution is much more challenging politically and large-scale redistributions tend to be associated with political revolutions.

In these ways, economic growth will start to become more pro-poor and each percentage point of growth will deliver more poverty reduction. This is not to say that all of the poor are in a position to benefit from growth; the chronically poor, who suffer from multiple deprivations, may be elderly or so sick that they are unemployable, and the illiterate are the least attractive to employers even in a growing economy. Many of the chronically poor live in remote regions far from the main economic centres and even strong economic growth can bypass them. For the chronically poor, it is important to use the additional public revenues generated from growth, collected through the tax system, to finance more social protection. State-building is therefore vital to achieving poverty reduction through public programmes.

Awareness of what holds poor people back came to the fore in the 1970s, in part because of disillusion with the outcomes of the first development decades. The high hopes of decolonization proved to be largely illusory in Africa, and poverty persisted in Latin America notwithstanding growth. This led to a radicalization of the development debate, with **dependency theory** much in vogue. In addition, by the 1970s, there was much more evidence from academic research on how poverty responds to economic and social change. This led to a new emphasis on the talents of poor people as farmers and micro-entrepreneurs and, for the first time, the knowledge of the poor themselves came to be valued. The World Bank focused more on poverty and moved away from its traditional emphasis on physical infrastructure.

Note that, in development strategy, direct attention to poverty reduction has a sharper political dimension than a focus on growth alone. For a start, the poor may be poor because they have very little, if any, political voice. This is true of many of Africa's rural poor, with development strategies often ignoring them or, perversely, taxing them (see Bates 1981). Politicians need to expend very little political capital when they talk about economic growth being 'like a tide that raises all

boats'. But when it comes to spending public money, basic pro-poor services are often left behind, after services that prioritize the needs of more vocal, and more effectively organized, middle- and higher-income people. A general **urban bias** against the rural areas was evident in much of post-independence Africa. Vocal and wealthy interests can effectively control the legislatures that determine the pattern of public spending and taxation (as in Central America), and the political power that accompanies wealth is another reason why many people worry about high inequality. When economic crisis strikes, governments often let the burden of adjustment fall on the services that benefit the poor. However, some governments do more for poor people than others, and there are substantial differences in outcomes for poverty and human development across countries at the same income per capita. Vietnam is one such success story (see Box 16.1). Moreover, within countries, there are strong regional differences in pro-poor spending, reflecting local **politics**: in India, the state of Kerala is an outstanding success, for example.

KEY POINTS

- Poverty reduction has become an explicit objective of development policy and economic growth is now seen as more of a means to an end, rather than a final objective in itself.
- Growth is important to reducing poverty, but not all poor people benefit and the chronically poor often miss out.
- Effective states are necessary to provide pro-poor services and infrastructure for development.

Markets and States

Achieving growth is far from easy, especially in countries that are landlocked and distant from markets (Bolivia and Niger, for example), subject to tropical diseases (West Africa in particular), and with climates and terrain that make them vulnerable to floods (Bangladesh, for example) or droughts (Africa's Sahel zone). Some countries therefore have more growth potential than others—but their prospects also depend upon the design of development strategy and whether the state is effective.

Most people agree that states have an important role to play in protecting property rights, enforcing

BOX 16.1 THE VIETNAM SUCCESS STORY

Vietnam, a country with a population of 84 million and one that suffered a devastating war, is Asia's best-performing economy after China. Vietnam is also one of the world's success stories in poverty reduction. Poverty has fallen from 58 per cent of the population in 1993 to under 20 per cent today.

Constructing a vigorous export economy, creating more opportunities for small enterprises, and investing in agriculture are the drivers of this success. Export growth has enabled the economy to diversify further, with considerable foreign investment in factories employing Vietnam's cheap and abundant labour, leading to a rise in wages over time. This trend accelerated after Vietnam's accession to the World Trade Organization (WTO) in 2007.

Following the end of the war in 1975 and the country's unification, the Hanoi government extended Marxist central planning, with its heavy restrictions on private enterprise, to the country's capitalist south (which had lost the war). The economy performed badly under this system, with hyperinflation and a sharp fall in living standards being the main results. Tentative reform began in the 1980s, with a move from collectivized agriculture to a market-orientated smallholder system, and gathered pace with the adoption of the *Doi Moi* ('new changes') strategy in 1986. Reform intensified in the early 1990s as aid from the Soviet Union, Vietnam's old cold war ally, dried up. The

government restored macro-economic stability, removed restrictions on small enterprises, and sought out foreign investment. However, the government is far from relinquishing all control over the economy and there are still many state-owned enterprises; these account for 40 per cent of GDP in what is officially called a 'socialist-orientated market economy'.

Export manufacturing has led to more urban jobs and less urban poverty. Vietnam has gone from a country of food shortages to become a leading exporter of rice and coffee, resulting in increased incomes and better rural livelihoods. But poverty remains higher in remoter regions such as Vietnam's Central Highlands. Policy is now giving more priority to these people via better education and health care, and more investment in transport and communications infrastructure, to improve market access.

Vietnam is a success, but its economic growth has come from a very low level of per capita income, reflecting the impact of the long war and the economic crisis of the immediate post-war years. Its government administration is too bureaucratic, **corruption** is a problem, and the Communist government's grip on power is threatened by the economy's opening-up and the accompanying increased flow of ideas and information from abroad. Vietnam therefore faces some tough challenges ahead in maintaining the momentum of its success.

contracts, and defending their citizens against external aggression. Economists have emphasized the importance of the first two of these in encouraging investment and in reducing the **transaction costs** of market exchange, both of which facilitate growth.

However, beyond a core set of **public goods**, such as law and order, and defence, people start to disagree about how much economic and social infrastructure the state should provide (public versus private education and health care, for example). And people often have radically different views about how far (if at all) the state should intervene in market mechanisms to set prices, control quantities, set standards, and regulate producers or act as a producer itself. Much of the debate about development strategy can be reduced to differences in views about what is the appropriate level of state provision and whether the state should mostly leave the market alone or intervene extensively.

These different viewpoints partly arise from different perspectives on how markets work. Much disagreement centres on how well market mechanisms yield poverty reduction—or, indeed, whether markets

sometimes work against poor people, making them poorer. Market optimists favour light regulation to let the market deliver the economic growth that best reduces poverty. Market pessimists favour state intervention, arguing that market outcomes reflect power and that this is often unfavourable to the poor (monopolies prevailing in unregulated markets, for example).

But people differ over the appropriate role for the state because they also hold different views over what constitutes the 'ideal society'. Nearly everyone agrees that an ideal society must achieve absolute poverty reduction, but some people favour state action to reduce overall income inequality as well. Others are vehemently opposed to such egalitarian ideas, citing individual freedom, including the right to accumulate wealth. Also controversial are the ability of market mechanisms to yield economic growth and whether a higher (or lower) growth rate will result from state intervention in the market mechanism.

Market optimists will favour a minimal state: one that provides protection for property rights, together with public goods that the market either does not supply or undersupplies, such as defence or transport infrastructure. In contrast, people who are pessimistic about the market's ability to deliver their ideal society will favour a more active state, but they vary widely in their conceptualization of what the state should do. At one extreme is central planning (practised by the former Soviet Union), under which society's productive factors are allocated according to a plan without reference to market prices, and under which state ownership of enterprises and property prevails (of which North Korea is one of the few examples left and even it has partially liberalized the economy). The 'European model' is at the other end of the scale of active states: continental European states provide very high levels of public goods and regulate the market 'in the public interest', but otherwise encourage a very vigorous private sector. The present difficulties in Europe illustrate the point that even the most successful models need renewal to cope with global economic change.

Most people now see a role for the state in meeting the challenge of environmental sustainability, because unregulated private markets can chronically undervalue (and therefore overuse) soils, water, fisheries, and other natural assets. Preventing climate change also implies much more state intervention, because the market is unlikely to create a green economy if left to itself. But there are still proponents of market **liberalism**—some politically powerful—who vehemently deny the need for extensive state involvement to meet these challenges.

Views on state effectiveness have swung like a pendulum over the last fifty years. As countries came to independence, they built national planning apparatuses and wrote national plans. The Soviet Union's example was very influential in China, Cuba, and Vietnam, and so was the state planning that even the capitalist economies introduced during the 1940s and many retained afterwards.

However, by the late 1970s, this confidence in the state's abilities was starting to erode as growth slowed down as a result of policy failure in many (but certainly not all) countries that pursued state-led development, together with the first (1974) and second (1979) oil price hikes by the Organization of Petroleum Exporting Countries (OPEC), and the associated world recessions, which tested state capacities to breaking point. During this time, the International Monetary Fund (IMF) became very important in providing balance-of-payments support. Several of the oil exporters also borrowed heavily using their oil revenues as collateral (for example Nigeria, Mexico, and Venezuela)

and they suffered macro-economic crises when the world oil price fell during the 1980s. The result was the debt crisis that stalled growth, especially in Latin America, for much of the 1980s (see Chapter 4).

The intellectual pendulum swung back (albeit with considerable resistance) towards the market mechanism in the 1980s and accelerated with the collapse of communism, and the start of the transition to market economies, in Eastern Europe and the Soviet Union. This was reinforced by the IMF and the World Bank, and their loan **conditionality** (often dubbed the **Washington consensus** on what constitutes good policy).

With so many of its client countries in deep distress, the World Bank was compelled to move beyond its traditional project lending and, in the 1980s, it started to provide balance-of-payments support through structural adjustment loans (SALs). These sought to change the fundamental structure of economies by introducing more market discipline into resource allocation. A SAL carried such policy conditionalities as: currency devaluation (to stimulate the supply of exports); the conversion of import quotas into import tariffs to reduce **rent-seeking** (and then tariff reduction in order to place more competitive pressure on inefficient infant industries); the removal (liberalization) of market controls in agriculture (to provide more incentives for farmers); and the reform of public expenditures and taxation (to shift more spending towards development priorities and to mobilize more public revenues to finance spending). The IMF's policy conditionality also included reduction of the fiscal deficit to curb inflation, because the latter impeded export competitiveness and economic growth.

Although World Bank and IMF adjustment lending was intended to deal with the immediate macroeconomic crises, it was also seen as a way of making poor economies more efficient and therefore better able to grow. Growth required a reduced role for the state in the productive sectors, as well as reduced controls on the private sector. Irrespective of the merits or otherwise of reform, countries in economic crisis had little alternative but to sign up to the conditionality, since private capital flows slowed dramatically with the onset of the debt crisis in the 1980s and official development flows became one of the few sources of external finance. This was especially true for the low-income countries.

The effects of reforms are never clear-cut. Many people oppose reform (*ex ante*) fearing a loss, even if this is not the case (*ex post*). Conversely, some people may gain a lot (for example those producing exports), but the gains are not immediate. Sometimes, a particular reform will benefit the majority of people, but if each person's gain is small, then they do not have much incentive to mobilize in support of reform, whereas the minority may stand to lose a lot and therefore has a much greater incentive to mobilize against change. Reform can therefore stall even if it benefits the majority. This is a 'collective action problem', which refers to the difficulties of organizing a group of people to achieve a common objective (Olson 2001).

Yet while the self-interests of elites or other small groups do often impede change, there are cases in which major reforms have been initiated despite elites having much invested in the status quo. Elite state actors may organize themselves into positions in which they profit from reform by investing in private enterprises that will benefit from liberalization, or by buying state assets on the cheap when they are privatized. Rulers may also initiate reform for reasons other than private financial gain. A concern for their reputation and legacy, patriotism, changing ideology, or a fear of more powerful neighbours are all drivers of elite behaviour. Ruling elites in China, Vietnam, and now Myanmar all initiated reforms despite having strong interests in the unreformed system. India undertook significant economic liberalization in the early 1990s, reflecting domestic criticism of the long-standing strategy of planning and state ownership. China and Vietnam's liberalizations have also been largely motivated by shifts in view within their ruling elites, rather than external pressures from the IMF, World Bank, and other donors.

The backlash against liberalization

Although it is highly controversial, liberalization is straightforward in its implementation: the state simply withdraws, partially or wholly, from the market. But some reforms require a strengthening of state capacity and better **governance** for their success. This is especially true of revenue and public expenditure reforms (see Chapter 15). The state's capacity to mobilize tax and customs revenues, and then to spend these resources effectively on pro-poor services and development infrastructure, requires a capable, well-motivated, and corruption-free government administration, at both central and local levels. However, the quality of civil services, together with their motivation, was in steep decline before reform began in many countries—especially in Africa, where inflation eroded real wages in the public sector. Governments were therefore attempting to implement demanding changes with very limited

institutional and human resources, and in some cases IMF fiscal conditionality weakened state capacities further. Reform breakdown and policy reversals are common. Zambia, for example, went through many donor-supported adjustment programmes that largely failed to achieve progress, notwithstanding there being greater political commitment by the government to this in the 1990s than previously. There is also a fierce debate on whether economic reform contributed to national breakdown in Sierra Leone and Somalia. (On conflict-prone societies, see Chapter 13.)

So-called second-generation economic reforms (**privatization** and financial reform, in particular) took place from the 1990s onwards in countries such as Ghana, Uganda, and Tanzania. Implementation of second-generation reforms was often problematic. For instance, privatization was often non-transparent, thereby transferring valuable assets to the politically connected. Financial reform was especially tricky. Asia's financial crisis in the 1990s and Africa's bank failures both highlight the need to build capacity for prudential supervision and regulation in central banks before major liberalization of financial controls. Tax reform and better public expenditure management were tough to implement.

Every shift in the intellectual debate sets up a counter-reaction, in part because proponents of the shift often overemphasize the likely benefits (or are simply wrong). Thus, from the mid-1990s onwards, a reaction against market liberalization and privatization set in, owing to sharp increases in inequality during reform, rising concern over liberalization's social effects, and the mismanagement of privatization. The intellectual pendulum then began to swing back towards the state and its role.

Liberalization was heavily criticized in Latin America, reflecting the very mixed outcome from reform programmes in the 1990s. Governments in Argentina, Bolivia, Peru, and Venezuela rejected the Washington consensus, and extended state control over their mining and energy sectors to boost government revenues. The commodity price boom after 2000—the result of China's demand for commodities to feed its rapid economic growth—enabled many governments to pay off their debts, and the improved credit rating of Latin America's sovereign borrowers reduced the influence of the IMF and the World Bank upon which Latin America relied for financing in times of economic crisis. However, the commodity price downturn of 2015–16 has once again demonstrated the vulnerability of commodity-dependent economies.

In the 1990s, economists increasingly came to recognize the importance of institutions to making the market mechanism work well for development and poverty reduction (see Chapter 3). This included the World Bank and the IMF. The experience of the transition economies of the former Soviet Union was central to this heightened awareness of the importance of institutions, as were the difficulties with second-generation reform in Africa. High-quality institutions are needed, such as an effective legal system that protects property rights and reduces the costs of market transactions, making markets more efficient and investment easier. All of this illustrates the importance of building effective state capacities and improving governance (see Chapter 15), to regulate markets in the public interest and to achieve improvements in the public goods that are essential to a well-functioning market economy, as well as for poverty reduction.

KEY POINTS

- The economic role of the state is one of the central issues dividing opinion on development strategy.
- An early emphasis on state-led development was eventually challenged by a market-liberal view, leading to widespread economic liberalization.
- Rising inequality led to a backlash against economic liberalization, especially when the fruits of the eventual growth were unequally distributed.
- Despite the rollback of the state, it still has many roles to play in providing public goods, as well as in regulating markets in the public interest.

Achieving Structural Transformation

The structure of an economy—the division of economic activity and employment across agriculture, natural resource extraction, manufacturing, and services—is central to whether it can achieve fast and sustained economic growth, as well as more jobs and less poverty. The role of SALs in the 1980s and 1990s in trying to change the structure of the developing economy has been noted already. In this section, we discuss structural transformation in more detail, for it remains a central issue of development policy to this day. Not surprisingly, there remain different views on the roles of the state and the market in achieving it. This is so even in low-income countries that have achieved better growth rates in recent years, for they mostly remain

very undiversified economies and therefore vulnerable to shocks that hit their narrow range of economic activities. Diversification in economic activity is a key metric of success in structural transformation.

For market liberals, developing countries that follow their **comparative advantage** will reap higher living standards by trading as much as possible with the developed countries and with each other (see Chapter 4). Their export earnings can then finance imports of products in which they have a comparative *disadvantage*. The market-liberal story of trade is one of mutual gains from trade for both the developing and the developed worlds. Comparative advantage is therefore the best guide to development policy, in this view.

For market liberals, comparative advantage also underpins their view of how trade contributes to economic growth, through **outward-oriented development**. Growth in developing countries' labour-intensive exports (their comparative advantage) will eventually bid up the price of labour (thereby contributing to poverty reduction) and encourage capital-for-labour substitution. The skill content of exports will also rise as educational investment builds human capital, allowing developing countries to start competitively producing what is presently made in the developed world. The state must assist this process through judicious public investment, in infrastructure for example, but it is the market that drives the process of structural transformation.

In the early years, many policymakers felt that such outward-orientated development would not yield much growth; instead, many saw the domestic market as the main growth driver, and they favoured inward-orientated development and import-substituting industrialization (see Chapter 4). Producers benefiting from protected markets also lobbied for the policy, and their influence increased over time as they used the **economic rents** associated with protection to fund sympathetic politicians and political parties, sometimes engaging in outright corruption. Critics of protection argue that rent-seeking comes to dominate the strategy, no matter how well intentioned initially, and this view underpinned the World Bank's efforts to open up economies in the 1980s.

In practice, the effects of lobbying and rent-seeking vary widely. They were at their worst in Africa, where **weak states** were easily captured by powerful rent-seekers, and where the smallness of domestic markets made import substitution unviable without high tariffs and very tight import quotas, which encouraged evasion and smuggling. Criticism of India's 'licence Raj' led to economic liberalization in the early 1990s, even if India's growth was respectable, if undramatic, prior to liberalization. And import substitution achieved some 'learning by doing', facilitated by India's enormous domestic market, which gives domestic manufacturers larger economies of scale. South Korea's planning mechanism effectively contained rent-seeking, and export subsidies offset the disincentive to export production inherent in import protection. Since South Korea is an outstanding development success, it is difficult to believe that it could have achieved even higher growth without import protection (see Chapter 24).

Today's low-income countries enjoy advantages that South Korea and other past success stories did not—namely, a larger global market of middle-income and rich countries in which to sell their products and services, a greater range of foreign investment partners (which now include the large middle-income countries themselves, which have become investors in poorer economies), and a much larger menu of technologies to help them to do so. At the same time, the success of China in the low-cost end of the global manufacturing supply chain can make it harder for smaller developing countries to break into labour-intensive manufacturing, the traditional first step in structural transformation. It can be done, as Vietnam shows, but it requires a good strategy to guide policy and investments, especially in the infrastructure required to connect national economies into global value chains.

Countries therefore need the right strategy for today's global economy. Yet there is a continuing weakness in development strategy, especially when it comes to economic diversification and employment creation. In the early days after independence, most developing countries created national plans. Sometimes, those plans were unrealistic, but they did at least focus the technocratic minds of governments, and in East Asia they generally worked well. Africa's development plans were the least well articulated, but there were exceptions; in Botswana, successive national plans have guided the allocation of the country's substantial revenues from diamonds, enabling it to achieve more economic diversification. The move away from such planning during the era of structural adjustment led to a dearth of hard thinking within countries about how to develop new economic sectors. Aid donors and many economists placed too much faith in the market's ability to diversify economies away from traditional sectors.

A national plan that sets out how to use aid, other capital inflows, and domestic tax revenues for development will ideally set out objectives for both human development and economic growth, linked to investments that promise high returns: investment in the health sector for human development (and by improving human capital, this should help growth as well) and infrastructure investment for economic growth, to take two examples.

However, the MDGs' agenda was almost entirely centred on the human development side of development strategy. The 'post-2015 agenda', contained in the SDGs, is now focusing more on economic development, especially job creation, but how is this best achieved? Market liberals would say 'leave it to the market', which will create the sectors that maximize growth and employment. Social entrepreneurs, such as Muhammad Yunus, founder of Bangladesh's innovative Grameen Bank, would say 'invest in micro-enterprises', especially through **micro-credit**. One group of increasingly influential economists would say 'conduct randomized control trials' (RCTs), in a similar way to the randomized control approach to testing new medicines, to better understand what works—for example different approaches to education provision and microfinance—and then use evidence from successes to scale up to larger programmes (these proponents of RCTs being known as the 'randomistas') (Ravallion 2009). Each of these approaches shares a limited view of what the state should do: that it should largely confine itself to basic service delivery to achieve human development and that entrepreneurs, whether motivated by profit or wider social goals, should drive development. Economic growth is then the resulting accumulation of many small-scale investments and successes.

However, East Asia still offers a bold vision that goes beyond this limited conceptualization of the state's role. The region's economic transformation is remarkable, defying the liberal view that states cannot be trusted to succeed when they move beyond providing public goods and protecting property rights. East Asia also challenges the randomistas, who argue that economists do not really know what produces economic growth. East Asia's transformation does not fit the social entrepreneur model either: states in partnership with the private sector created companies that eventually became very large-scale indeed—generating enormous numbers of jobs and in some cases becoming global brands (South Korea's Samsung and China's Lenovo are two examples).

East Asia has influenced the creation of a 'new structuralist economics'. This approach is also referred to as the 'new industrial policy', although the aim is to diversify the economy into sectors with higher value-added, which may be manufacturing, but also services (information technology for example), and agricultural crops with higher value-added than traditional subsistence farming. One influential Chinese proponent of new structuralist economics, Justin Lin (2011), argues that the state should help private enterprise to create 'leading sectors'—sectors in which a more advanced economy already holds the lead, but where the gap is not too large for the poor country to leap. Footwear and other light manufacture such as toys are examples. Lin argues that older state-led strategies failed when countries tried to move into sectors in which there was too big a gap between the latecomer and the more advanced economies, resulting in the latecomer never becoming competitive enough to gain global market share, leaving enterprises requiring continued state help. The new structuralist approach shares with older strategies a view that markets are imperfect; they will not deliver rapid economic development without vigorous state action to overcome market failures holding back private investment.

In contrast to the old paradigm of state-led development, the new structuralists see much less need for the state itself to own enterprises. It is also more positive about the prospects for exporting than older state-led development, which emphasized import substitution. It therefore incorporates elements of the market-liberal approach of SALs, including an outward-orientated focus, but blends them with a strong, but careful, role for the state in helping private enterprise to find new leading sectors.

KEY POINTS

- Import substitution works much better in countries with large domestic markets and in which policy encourages export production as well.

- While the failure of many countries to achieve growth through import protection increased support for outward-orientated development, this too requires a well-designed strategy, particularly in creating new skills to sell in the global marketplace.

- The new structuralist economics that emerged out of East Asian success argues for the state to help private enterprises in creating leading sectors—that is, those sectors in which the gap between poor countries and more advanced economies is not too large to leap.

The Global Development Landscape

Low-income countries have to make development policy in the world as it is, not as they wish it to be. Until they can diversify their economies, they remain subject to high levels of risk: even the best development plans can be knocked off course by commodity price shocks and climatic shocks. Middle-income countries with diversified economies are more robust and have more possibilities to shape the world economy, especially when their economies are large, such as China, and India. They can influence the global 'rules of the game' in finance, trade, and investment, and the international institutions that formulate and implement those rules.

Protectionism is still widespread in world trade despite the liberalization conducted under the auspices of the General Agreement on Tariffs and Trade (GATT) and WTO. The WTO's Doha Development Agenda negotiations, launched in 2001, are now dead, after years of fruitless talk. Trade protectionism reflects the balance of power between economies and economic blocs. Nowhere is this more apparent than in world agriculture. Rich countries pay large subsidies to their farmers and restrict imports from developing countries. This depresses the world prices of some major export earners for developing countries—notably, cotton and sugar, thereby reducing the incomes of their farmers. Brazil has used the WTO to successfully challenge US protectionism, but the smaller and poorer countries lack the resources to defend their interests. They also find it difficult to access the markets of the larger developing countries such as India, which also protects its farmers from foreign competition (although this protection has recently been reduced). The developing countries do not always have common interests in world trade negotiations and they face powerful political bodies, such as the European Union, which are adept at protecting their own interests.

Whereas the rules of the game governing global trade are slow to change, the last decade has seen rapid change in global development finance. The result has been increased power for the middle-income countries, a wider menu of external finance options for low-income countries and therefore greater scope for policy manoeuvre—thereby reducing the power of the rich world and the ability of aid donors to impose policy conditionality on low-income countries.

Development finance covers a wide spectrum from **official development assistance (ODA)**, usually to governments, of varying levels of concessionality, ranging from grants to loans at rates lower than market rates, portfolio flows (commercial bank lending, flows into government and corporate debt, and company equities via stock markets), foreign direct investment (FDI), which is longer term than portfolio flows, and remittances by households to each other. With their success in export markets, middle-income countries have built up substantial foreign exchange reserves. They were also motivated by the 1997 Asian financial crisis when it paid to have large reserves to ward off speculative currency attacks (and those that did not, such as Indonesia, fell into the care of the IMF). The reserves of the oil producers rose along with global oil prices and have provided them with some cushion as oil prices fell sharply over 2015–16. All of this has given the middle-income countries substantial financial power in bond and equity markets worldwide, and is evident in their 'sovereign wealth funds' that invest globally, including FDI in low-income countries. They have put some of this new financial muscle into aid programmes, so that the emerging donors have become significant players in foreign aid over the last decade (see Chapters 28 and 29).

Low-income countries are benefiting from these new sources of commercial finance and foreign aid. Their volume of remittances is at least triple the amount of ODA finance. South Asian countries benefit from the export of large amounts of labour to the wealthy Middle East and the resulting remittances home. The sovereign debt of developing countries has been in high demand, the result of hard-won economic reforms and, until recently, high commodity prices. Expansionary monetary policy in the rich countries in the aftermath of the 2007–08 global financial crisis has also driven down yields on rich country bonds to very low levels, making the much higher yields on developing country bonds even more attractive to investors. At the same time, countries must be careful that they do not overborrow to the point at which they cannot service the debt: in 2015, Ghana found itself back in the hands of the IMF, having done just that.

With a wider range of development finance now available, official aid is becoming less important to low-income countries as a group (with the exception of the small 'fragile' states). Many of the recipients are also tired of the complexity of aid, and the associated transactions costs that arise from the multiplicity of aid programmes and aid donors, each with its own procedures, and the lack of progress in rationalizing aid to make it more efficient despite successive attempts down the years.

Recipient countries have a great deal more room for manoeuvre with donors than in the era of structural adjustment, because many of their economies are much improved and the number of donors has risen. They can play the traditional Western donors off against China and other emerging donors. The ability of traditional donors to attach strict conditions to their aid has withered. In any case, traditional donors will provide aid to countries that are of strategic importance irrespective of whether these countries comply with any donor pressure on development policy. Ethiopia, Pakistan, and Afghanistan are such examples.

The recent graduation of countries from low-income to middle-income status, as a result of sustained economic growth and the likely graduation of more in the near future, also raises questions about the relevance of the international aid architecture, which was built around the transfer of resources from rich to poor countries. Whereas, at the turn of the millennium, some sixty-three countries were classified as low income, this number has now fallen to thirty-six (Sumner 2010). Yet many of the new middle-income countries still have large incidences of poverty and, since some of the new graduates to middle-income status have large populations (India, Nigeria, and Pakistan), this means that for the first time there are more poor people in middle-income countries than in low-income countries (Sumner 2010).

Graduation presents a difficulty in keeping foreign aid focused on poverty, since one of the largest sources of grant aid, the International Development Association (IDA), is reserved for low-income countries. More broadly, it can be asked: what is the added value of aid to middle-income countries that have rising revenues resulting from economic growth, which increases the size of their tax bases and therefore their ability to fund more pro-poor public spending? India illustrates how the world is changing. In the early 1990s, when India went through the balance-of-payments crisis that spurred eventual reform, it needed the World Bank and other official finance to ease its adjustment; today, India has ample access to international capital flows—and it even has a growing aid programme of its own (see Chapter 30). Yet it is still home to one third of the world's poorest people. It would seem unfair for international aid not to help these people even if they live in a country now defined as middle income rather than low income. At the same time, while India now has more tax revenue to fund anti-poverty projects, its tax revenues in relation to the large numbers of people still in poverty mean that it is not yet in a position to fund all of its poverty reduction effort from domestic revenues or from borrowing. Accordingly, there is a case for traditional aid donors to remain engaged with countries even as they graduate to middle-income status—but the nature of that relationship will have to change.

KEY POINTS

- Low-income countries now have a wider menu of development finance options and greater scope for policy.
- The ability of aid donors to impose conditionality on low-income recipients has declined.
- With more countries moving from the low-income to the middle-income groups, aid needs to be rethought.

Conclusion

There are issues over which there is considerable consensus and issues over which deep controversy remains. That development policy must have an explicit focus on poverty reduction is one of the main areas of consensus in today's development policy community. In contrast to the period up to the 1970s, when it was thought that economic growth would automatically deliver poverty reduction, it is now recognized that pro-poor policies are necessary to maximize growth's benefits for the poor. Moreover, it is widely agreed that poverty reduction entails not only higher incomes, but also improving human development indicators: poverty is a multidimensional concept. This implies improving the delivery of pro-poor services, particularly in basic health care, safe water and sanitation, and primary education, with a particular emphasis on delivery to rural areas (which contain high levels of poverty) and to women (see Chapter 9). Relatedly, it is widely agreed that the formation of human capital through better health and education is not only good for poverty reduction, but also contributes to growth by enabling diversification into skill-intensive manufactures and services. In this way, poor economies can seek to benefit from **globalization**.

Compared with the early years of development, there is now a greater recognition of the market's importance to growth. There is much less support for the state having a direct role in owning productive enterprises itself and more focus on the private sector. Market liberals would still confine the state's primary role to protecting the property rights of private investors, large and small, and the provision of public goods that are underprovided by markets alone. They fear the rent-seeking associated with market regulation. Social entrepreneurs favour micro-enterprise, with support through micro-credit and with states building basic service provision rather than attempting extensive direct involvement in the productive side of the economy. Economists of a randomista persuasion are in favour of states scaling up support to basic services and livelihood projects, once they have learned more about the best means to do so from RCTs. They do not generally favour a larger role for the state and are critical of economists with more ambitious aims for the state as a growth driver.

Yet the success of East Asia has demonstrated a more active role for the state in the productive economy and the potential for state success in supporting the private sector to build leading economic sectors, especially for export products and services. In contrast to proponents of early state-led development strategy, the new structuralist economists see less of a role for the state in owning and operating enterprises itself, and less of a focus on import substitution (unless the domestic market is large enough to deliver economies of scale). They are aware of the problems of rent-seeking that state intervention can create, but argue that institutions and mechanisms can be created to minimize the downside and maximize the upside of closer partnership between the state and the private sector. Certainly, the agendas of 'green growth' and adaption to climate change require the closer cooperation of state and private actors, together with communities.

Countries are now keener to attract private capital flows especially when they bring new technologies, as can be the case with FDI. Countries that were formerly considered to be poor debtors are now attracting international investor attention when they market their sovereign bonds. With more plentiful private capital available to them, they are much less dependent on foreign aid. Aid donors are less important in driving development strategy than in previous years in most, but not all, countries. This adds to the need for increased state effectiveness.

Getting development policy right has the potential to lift millions of people out of the misery of poverty. But making the right policy choices is not only a technical matter; it also requires careful political judgement about how to promote economic and social change in ways that stand the most chance of success, in a global economy that is becoming ever more complex and in the face of the mounting risks of climate change.

QUESTIONS

1. What are the main causes of East Asia's success in economic development? Can other countries adopt the East Asian model successfully?

2. Do the poor participate fully in economic growth? How can their participation be improved?

3. If economic reform does yield significant benefits for growth and living standards, as its proponents argue, then why is it often so difficult politically?

4. Why is the role of the state in economic development controversial, and what does development experience tell us about the respective roles of the state and the market?

5. Why has Africa found it so difficult to achieve economic development and what can be done to improve Africa's performance in future?

6. What lessons does China's development success offer to other countries?

7. Does the new structuralist economics offer a better perspective on development strategy than the older state-led development paradigm?

8. Is it better to be a low-income country in today's global economy than it was in the global economy of fifty years ago?

FURTHER READING

Addison, T. (2003) 'Economics', in P. Burnell (ed.) *Democratization through the Looking Glass* (Manchester: Manchester University Press), 41–55 Examines how democracy affects economic performance and contrasts democracy with autocracy in its development effects.

Addison, T. (2015) 'Thirty Years in Africa's Development: From Structural Adjustment to Structural Transformation?', UNU-WIDER Working Paper 2015/119, available online at https://www.wider.unu.edu/sites/default/files/wp2015-119.pdf Further discussion of Africa's experience with economic reform, reconstruction from conflict, and challenges ahead.

Banerjee, A. V., and Duflo, E. (2011) *Poor Economics: A Radical Rethinking of the Way to Fight Global Poverty* (New York: Public Affairs) A strong statement on the potential for randomized control trials to help to create better anti-poverty programmes.

Chronic Poverty Research Centre (CPRC) (2008) *The Chronic Poverty Report 2008-09* (London: CPRC) Discusses people who remain poor for much or all of their lives and who benefit least from economic growth.

Collier, P. (2007) *The Bottom Billion: Why the Poorest Countries Are Failing and What Can be Done about It* (Oxford: Oxford University Press) An influential analysis of success and failure in development, including Africa.

Kanbur, R. (2001) 'Economic Policy, Distribution and Poverty: The Nature of Disagreements', *World Development*, 29(6): 1083–94 A clear and balanced view of the contemporary poverty debate and why people differ over growth's effects on poverty. Includes very useful comparisons between the differing viewpoints of the World Bank and non-governmental organizations (NGOs) on poverty.

Lin, J. Y. (2012) *The Quest for Prosperity: How Developing Economies Can Take off* (Princeton, NJ: Princeton University Press) A discussion of the new structuralist economics by an influential Chinese economist.

Pritchett, L. (2013) 'The Folk and the Formula: Fact and Fiction in Development', UNU-WIDER Annual Lecture No. 16, available online at http://www.wider.unu.edu/publications/annual-lectures/en_GB/AL16/ On the importance of state capability for development and poverty reduction, and the struggle to improve it.

Rodrik, D. (2003) *The Globalization Paradox: Democracy and the World Economy* (New York: W.W. Norton) A good place to start on different development strategies in relation to globalization and some of the political tensions involved.

Wade, R. (1990; repr. 2003, with a new introduction by the author) *Governing the Market: Economic Theory and the Role of Government in East Asian Industrialization* (Princeton, NJ: Princeton University Press) An authoritative assessment of how East Asia achieved its economic success, which challenges the market-liberal view and emphasizes the role of the state.

 WEB LINKS

http://www.cgdev.org/   The Center for Global Development in Washington, DC, covers all aspects of development, including foreign aid and its effectiveness.

http://www.eldis.org   Very easy-to-use site, with downloadable research papers, reports, and many links to other sites.

http://www.ids.ac.uk/   The Institute of Development Studies (IDS) has large research programmes on many aspects of development.

http://www.imf.org   The International Monetary Fund (IMF) posts reports on its member countries and agreements with governments (such as 'letters of intent'), which spell out economic reforms in detail. The IMF's annual reports on the state of the world economy are also widely read.

http://www.odi.org.uk   The website of the Overseas Development Institute (UK), an independent think tank on development issues, which publishes briefing papers providing authoritative insight into the latest development issues.

https://sustainabledevelopment.un.org/sdgs   For progress towards the Sustainable Development Goals (SDGs).

http://www.wider.unu.edu   The website of the United Nations University's World Institute for Development Economics Research (UNU-WIDER), the working paper series of which offers a wide range of viewpoints on economic development issues, particularly in the areas of poverty measurement and inequality.

http://www.worldbank.org/en/topic/poverty   The poverty reduction website of the World Bank discusses poverty measures and presents cases of success in reducing poverty.

http://www.worldbank.org/en/topic/poverty/brief/global-poverty-line-faq   World Bank, 'FAQs: Global Poverty Line Update'.

 For additional material and resources, please visit the Online Resource Centre at:
http://www.oxfordtextbooks.co.uk/orc/burnell5e/

17

Environment

Peter Newell

Overview

This chapter explores how developing countries are managing the relationship between the environment and development. Often considered a threat to their economic development and prospects for growth, environmental issues have nevertheless come to feature centrally on policy agendas throughout the developing world. Driven by donors, public concern, and vocal environmental movements, responses to these issues have taken a number of different forms as they compete for 'policy space' with other pressing development concerns and are subject to changing thinking about the effectiveness of different policy tools to tackle environmental problems. This chapter explores these issues, connecting global agendas to national policy processes, explaining differences and similarities between how countries respond to these issues, and identifying patterns of continuity and change in the politics of environment in the developing world.

Introduction

From an issue on the periphery of the policy agendas of most governments in the **developing world**, the environment has assumed an important and rising **status** on the national political agendas of states in Africa, Latin America, and Asia. This shift results from a combination of pressures from global **institutions**, donors, and active citizen movements, and has evolved alongside a growth in both scientific understanding of environmental problems and rising levels of public concern, often generated by environmental disasters or conflicts. Regarding the issue of global warming in particular, there is a growing recognition that development gains may be systematically reversed by extreme and unpredictable climate change, which impacts most directly on the world's poor, whose livelihoods depend on agriculture, fishing, and other productive sectors especially vulnerable to changes in rainfall and temperature.

Yet the status of the environment as an issue on developing country agendas often remains precarious. Environmental issues in many areas of the world are only loosely embedded within national policy processes, incoherently related to wider economic and social agendas, and subject to displacement by issues that assume a greater priority for most countries. The theme of this chapter, then, is continuity and change. Most countries are operating in a context in which an increasingly globalized economy impacts more directly than ever before on the relationship between environment and development. Moreover, the institutions and structures of global environmental **governance** shape more strongly than ever before the nature of environmental policy within the developing world. At the same time, this is not a passive process: global environmental agendas have to be grafted onto existing policy agendas, national priorities, and decision-making processes that, in many cases, are characterized by bureaucratic inertia, organized opposition to reform, and reluctance to realign priorities. Yet some 'rising powers' such as India and China have also become highly proactive in global policy deliberations on the environment, as well as seeking to capitalize economically on the growing demand for environmental goods and services in the global economy. At the same time, they have become increasingly important players in global geopolitical competitions over natural resources in Africa and elsewhere.

The chapter is organized into five main sections. The first two sections sketch the increasingly important global context for debates about environment and development, and the links between them. Such links have been institutionalized through the growth of global bodies and areas of international environmental law produced through a series of United Nations negotiations. The third looks at policy processes at the national level: how these global agendas have been responded to and 'domesticated' by individual governments. It tackles questions about what is unique about policy processes in developing countries and what extra challenges are associated with tackling environmental problems in these settings. The fourth section looks at the range of tools and strategies that developing countries have adopted to combat environmental degradation. This includes discussion about the shifting roles of governments, market actors such as businesses, and **civil society** in natural resource use management and protection. The fifth section explores probable future directions of environmental **politics** in the developing world, pulling together these patterns of continuity and change.

KEY POINTS

- The environment has assumed an important and rising status on the national political agendas of states in Africa, Latin America, and Asia.

- Yet the status of the environment as an issue on developing country agendas is precarious. It is often displaced by issues that assume a greater priority for most countries.

- We can observe a process of continuity and change. Environmental challenges are handled within existing national policy frameworks, but **globalization** has changed the relationship between environment and development, and the balance of power among the actors charged with delivering **sustainable development**.

Global Context

In an unequal and fragmented international society, it is perhaps not surprising that it has been very difficult to construct a global consensus about which environmental issues are most urgent. It is often assumed that differences of opinion on this issue fall along North–South lines, whereby developed countries are more concerned with global problems, such as climate change and ozone depletion, and conservation issues, such as whaling and forest protection, while developing countries attach greater priority to rural issues, such as desertification and soil erosion, and localized environmental threats, such as water pollution and air quality in cities. Even a cursory look at the politics of global negotiations on these issues suggests that these categorizations are, at best, only partially accurate.

First, we need to consider issues of causation and impact. Many of those people who contribute most to global environmental degradation are not those who will suffer its worst effects. While climate change will have global impacts, wealthier countries are better placed to adapt to its adverse consequences. Whereas the Netherlands can build sea defences against sea-level rise, Bangladesh does not have the same resources to protect itself against widespread flooding of low-lying agriculturally important areas. Yet it is the developed world that contributes to global environmental problems to a proportionally much greater extent. For example, 80 per cent of the world's climate-changing carbon dioxide is produced by less than 25 per cent of the world's population. One country alone, the United States, which makes up just 4 per cent of the world's population, is responsible for 20 per cent of global emissions, while 136 developing countries together account for 24 per cent. We should also recall, however, that exposure to environmental harm and culpability for causing it is highly uneven and differentiated within countries in which inequalities along class, **gender**, and racial lines are often magnified and exacerbated by global environmental change.

Second, the economic importance of natural resources to a country's economic development is a significant determinant of its position on a particular environmental policy problem, making it difficult for developing countries to form common policy positions. Brazil has traditionally resisted calls to view the Amazonian rainforests as part of the common heritage of humankind because of their strategic importance to the country's economic development. Many other developing countries, however, have called for this principle of **global stewardship** to apply to a range of common pool resources, such as Antarctica and the deep seabed, on the basis that if those resources are to be exploited, they should be for the benefit of all and not only those richer countries that are in a position to exploit them. Similarly, while the Alliance of Small Island States (AOSIS), threatened by sea-level rise associated with global climate change, has strongly advocated controls on greenhouse gas

emissions, the Organization of Petroleum Exporting Countries (OPEC) bloc, the economies of which are heavily dependent on the export of oil, has resisted such controls.

While some developing countries view environmental policy as an opportunity to secure additional aid and new forms of technology transfer, others feel threatened by agendas that appear to constrain their prospects for growth. The Group of 77 (G77) bloc of least-developed countries (LDCs)—formed at the United Nations after a meeting of the UN Conference on Trade and Development (UNCTAD) in 1964, for the purpose of promoting the collective economic interest of 'Third World' countries—has traditionally placed the responsibility for short-term action on climate change upon the global North in the negotiations on the subject. But the rapid growth of industrial powerhouses such as India, China, and Brazil has further fractured the unity of the G77 bloc. It has become increasingly difficult, in light of their rising contribution to the problem of global warming, (for example China is now the single largest emitter of greenhouse gases, although not on a per capita basis), for these countries to refute the need to adopt their own emissions reduction obligations. Indeed, the Paris Agreement on climate change concluded in 2015 is the first 'universal' climate agreement that requires action from all countries to keep warming well below 2°C compared with pre-industrial levels, which they articulated in their own intended nationally determined contributions (INDCs).

Third, aside from areas in which core national economic interests may be at stake, global environmental institutions have played a key role in shaping the national environmental policy agendas of many developing countries. Box 17.1 summarizes the mandates and key activities of some of the more prominent global environmental institutions. It is their access to financial resources and the mandate that they have to oversee the implementation of key global environmental accords that allows these bodies to play this role. As Box 17.1 shows, the Global Environment Facility (GEF) has responsibility for overseeing the transfer of aid and technology to developing countries to help them to meet their obligations under the Rio Agreements, for example on climate change and biodiversity conservation. The provision of aid and technology to developing countries to meet these commitments recognizes that these countries require assistance in making a contribution to global efforts to tackle forms of

BOX 17.1 KEY GLOBAL ENVIRONMENTAL INSTITUTIONS

United Nations Environment Programme (UNEP)

- Created following the Stockholm Conference on the Human Environment in 1972

- Initially conceived as a clearing house of environmental data and research, and to set up demonstration projects

- Has no statute or charter to describe its function and role

- Has a Governing Council of fifty-eight members elected by the UN General Assembly based on a regional formula for four-year terms

- Council is mandated to promote cooperation on environmental issues and to recommend appropriate policies

- Has a budget of only US$10.5 million a year drawn from the regular United Nations budget

- Depends on voluntary contributions from member countries for financing specific projects

- Has no structured system of dispute settlement

- Enforcement is reliant on peer review and moral pressure

Global Environment Facility (GEF)

- Is a key financing body for actions on climate change, biodiversity loss, ozone depletion, international waters, land degradation and persistent organic pollutants (POPs)

- Set up with a budget of US$1.3 billion prior to the Earth Summit as a global fund to oversee the financing of the Rio Agreements

- Has allocated US$9.2 billion, supplemented by more than US$40 billion in co-financing, for more than 2,700 projects in more than 165 developing countries and countries with economies in transition

- Implemented by three agencies: UNEP, United Nations Development Programme (UNDP), and the World Bank

- Administered by the World Bank on a day-to-day basis, which is a trustee of the GEF Trust Fund

- Makes decisions by consensus; in case of dispute, makes decisions on double-majority basis

Green Climate Fund (GCF)

- Established by 194 governments, following the Copenhagen Climate Summit in 2009, to limit or reduce greenhouse gas emissions in developing countries and to help vulnerable societies to adapt to the unavoidable impacts of climate change

- Accountable to the United Nations and governed by a board of twenty-four members, comprising an equal number of members from developing and developed countries

- Is promised US$100 billion per year from 2020, US$10.2 million of which has been pledged to date

- Of the money channelled through the GCF, half will go to funding adaptation measures in developing countries, such as better flood defences, drought monitoring schemes, and water management systems, and at least half of that to countries most at risk from the impacts of climate change. The other half of the GCF's money will go towards helping developing countries to curb their emissions, by decarbonizing their energy and transport infrastructure

---

environmental degradation to which most currently contribute very little. Concern was expressed at the time of the UN Conference on Environment and Development in Rio in 1992 that aid for the implementation of these international environmental agreements should be 'additional' to that which developing countries receive for other development purposes. This concern continues today in relation to calls for 'new and additional' finance for climate change mitigation and adaptation. Developing countries are concerned that, in a context of financial austerity in donor countries, and in the absence of clear benchmarks and effective tracking, it will be tempting for richer countries to divert or relabel **official development assistance** (**ODA**) intended for other development purposes as aid for climate mitigation and adaptation.

Increasingly, however, these institutions and the conventions that they seek to enforce have sought to facilitate the integration of environmental and developmental concerns rather than see them as competing issues. There has been a clear shift towards addressing development concerns that can be traced from the Stockholm Conference on the Human Environment in 1972 onwards (see Box 17.2). This prepared the ground for the famous Brundtland Report (1987) *Our Common Future*, which first coined the phrase 'sustainable development', defined as '[d]evelopment which meets the needs of the current generation without compromising the ability of future generations to meet their own needs'. The title of the Rio Conference that followed five years later encapsulated the rhetorical integration of environmental

BOX 17.2 CHRONOLOGY OF ENVIRONMENT AND DEVELOPMENT ON THE INTERNATIONAL AGENDA

1972: Stockholm Conference on the Human Environment

- Created UNEP
- Established key principles of responsible global environmental stewardship
- Set in train global scientific cooperation

1980: Brandt Commission

- Resulted in report entitled *North–South: A Programme for Survival* (Brandt 1980)
- Addressed North–South elements more clearly, including trade, debt, energy, and food

1987: World Commission on Environment and Development

- Resulted in report entitled *Our Common Future* (Brundtland 1987)
- Gave birth to a concept: 'sustainable development'

1992: United Nations Conference on Environment and Development (UNCED)

- Resulted in:
  - UN Framework Convention on Climate Change (UNFCCC)
  - Convention on Biological Diversity
  - Rio Declaration

- Statement of Forest Principles
- Agenda 21

2002: World Summit on Sustainable Development (WSSD)

- Resulted in:
  - Agreement on water and sanitation (to halve the number of people without access to basic sanitation by 2015)
  - Agreement on fisheries (plan to restore world's depleted stocks by 2015; to create marine areas around the world by 2012)

2012: Rio+20

- Produced a non-binding document entitled *The Future We Want*
- Emphasized 'green growth' and need to strengthen **institutional** frameworks for sustainable development as major themes, but failed to agree on new targets or concrete actions

2015: Sustainable Development Goals (SDGs)

- Agreed the *Transforming Our World: The 2030 Agenda for Sustainable Development*, which includes seventeen goals
- Produced goals relating explicitly to environmental issues, such as climate change and the protection of forests and oceans, as well as calling for access to water, energy, and food be secured in a sustainable manner

---

and developmental objectives: the 'United Nations Conference on Environment and Development'. Ten years on, the language of sustainable development was placed centrally in the naming of the follow-up to Rio, the World Summit on Sustainable Development (WSSD) in Johannesburg in 2002. At the Rio+20 Summit in 2012, great emphasis was placed on the idea of a 'green economy' to promote the idea, once again, that growth could be green. Likewise, the shift towards integration is notable when comparing the **Sustainable Development Goals (SDGs)** agreed in 2015 and the more narrowly defined Millennium Development Goals (MDGs) of 2000.

Despite this rhetorical shift, many developing countries and activists have been critical of the way in which certain issues have been actively kept off the agenda of these summits. The Rio Conference of 1992 attracted criticism for not addressing issues such as debt, terms of trade, or the regulation of multinational corporations (MNCs)—issues that some developing countries have sought to advance since the early 1970s, initially through the platform of the 'new international economic order'. The US delegation to the Conference fought hard to remove references to unsustainable levels of consumption in the Rio documents in 1992 and again in 2012, during the WSSD, there were attempts to thwart the negotiation of a new convention on corporate accountability.

Rather than viewing environmental issues as stand-alone concerns, it is becoming increasingly clear that it is necessary to mainstream environmental concerns into the activities of leading development actors. As far back as 1987, the World Bank had set up an environmental department; it now insists on detailed environmental impact assessments (EIAs) of all of its lending programmes. Yet it continues to draw fire for a perceived failure to mainstream environmental issues throughout its operations. For example, a 2015 report from the Institute for Policy Studies found that despite it serving as the interim trustee of the Green Climate Fund, the largest share of the World Bank's funding still supports fossil fuels, and that the overall volume of financing for oil, coal, and gas has increased almost four-fold over the last four years (IPS 2015).

The World Trade Organization (WTO), for its part, has created a Committee on Trade and Environment. This first met in 1995 to look at the relationship between environmental standards and trade liberalization—although, notably and controversially, not the environmental impacts of trade. The emphasis has therefore been on defining the legitimate circumstances in which environmental and human health concerns can be invoked as exceptions to the normal obligations that countries assume through membership of the WTO, rather than the ecological cost of transporting greater volumes of goods across ever larger distances, for example. The question is whether environmental considerations should be allowed to drive decisions about which types of trade are desirable and necessary from the point of view of sustainable development, or whether all environmental measures that impact upon trade have to be compatible with WTO rules. For developing countries, one of the key concerns has been the growth in environmental standards that many fear will be used as barriers to trade and disguised forms of protectionism to protect Northern producers from competitive exports from the South. High-profile cases that have come before the WTO's Dispute Settlement Body (DSB), such as the Tuna–Dolphin dispute, have reflected this fear. In this case, the United States sought to ban yellowfin tuna imports from Mexico on the grounds that the nets being used by the Mexican fishing industry to catch tuna fish were also killing dolphins.

KEY POINTS

- There is now a wide range of global environmental agreements that developing countries have signed and are in the process of implementing.

- Although development issues have gained a higher profile in global environmental summits and agreements, there is still some concern that Northern countries continue to control the agenda.

- Countries' positions on these issues do not fall neatly along North–South lines, however, and key differences exist between developing countries on many high-profile global environmental issues.

- There have been moves towards **mainstreaming** environmental concerns into the lending practices of multilateral development agencies, but critics suggest that these have not gone nearly far enough.

Environment and Development: An Uneasy Relationship

The relationship between environment and development is not an easy one, and many conflicts are subsumed under the convenient banner of 'sustainable development', the aims of which are difficult for anyone to refute. Many have therefore questioned the value of 'sustainable development' as an analytical concept, when it can be invoked so easily to justify 'business as usual' polluting activities. The term disguises conflicts over priorities between environment and development, gives few, if any, indications about which forms of development are sustainable, and is inevitably interpreted by different actors to mean different things. Fundamental conflicts over the causes and appropriate solutions to environmental degradation persist. These include the debate about the extent to which population growth is a cause of environmental degradation. Malthusian analysis (so named after eighteenth-century thinker the Reverend Thomas Malthus) of resource degradation, popular in certain strands of 1970s environmental thinking (Ehrlich 1972), suggested that rapid increases in population were driving the planet towards ecological collapse because of the strain on natural resource systems. The influential report of the Club of Rome (a global think tank) entitled *The Limits to Growth* (Meadows et al.

1972) suggested instead that unsustainable patterns of resource use would ultimately bring about ecological collapse because of the finite nature of the natural resource base upon which we all depend. Many developing countries and more radical environmental groups target overconsumption and affluence in Western societies, rather than population, as the key cause of the global environmental crisis.

Given this lack of consensus on the causes of environmental degradation, it is unsurprising that consensus eludes attempts to find appropriate solutions. Old conflicts in development over aid, trade, debt, and the role of technology get replayed through discussions about how to combat environmental degradation. Those believing that poverty leads people to use resources unsustainably have looked to ideas such as debt-for-nature swaps, whereby debt relief is provided in exchange for commitments to preserve areas of forest, as a way out of this cycle. This model informs current initiatives on reducing emissions from deforestation and forest degradation (REDD), and payments for ecosystem services (PES), which compensate local host communities for the environmental service that they provide in preserving forests that serve as important global carbon sinks.

Critiques of the effects of aid and technology transfer on developing countries also get rehearsed in environmental debates. For example, it is alleged that technologies that are transferred as part of global environmental agreements are often out of date, inappropriate to local needs, and serve only as a subsidy to Northern producers of technologies for which markets no longer exist. In environmental terms, it is also argued that technologies are no substitute for tough action aimed at reducing unsustainable patterns of production and consumption, and that developed countries often prefer to transfer technologies to developing countries rather than take measures to address the source of environmental degradation in their own countries.

This, then, is the global historical and contemporary context that shapes the ways in which developing countries have been tackling environmental issues at the national level. The next section looks in more detail at the commonalities and differences in the ways in which developing countries have responded to these global environmental agendas, while grappling with their own unique environmental problems and development needs.

> **KEY POINTS**
>
> - The term 'sustainable development' disguises key conflicts over priorities between environment and development.
>
> - There are ongoing disagreements about the importance that should be attached to population growth in the South, as opposed to unsustainable consumption in the North.
>
> - Fundamental disagreements arise concerning the role of aid, trade, and technology as appropriate solutions to environmental problems.

Policy Processes

Political diversity

It is impossible to make generalizations about environmental policy that would apply across the entire developing world. Although nearly all developing countries are involved in global negotiations on the aforementioned issues, the processes by which they translate those commitments into workable policies at the national level are very different. First, there is the issue of power. There is clearly a difference between countries such as China or India, with significant scope for independent action and power to assert their interests in global forums, and smaller and less powerful countries such as Uruguay or Zambia. This difference relates in part to the resources that can be committed to participating in global processes, which can be highly time-consuming and resource-intensive. Environmental negotiations take place all around the world and are therefore costly to attend, and to participate effectively in them requires a large delegation with access to high levels of scientific and legal expertise. Many developing countries are often only able to send smaller delegations to these negotiations, which are often run with parallel meetings that it becomes difficult to attend. But it is also about the leverage that countries wield. At critical moments, such as in the final hours of the Copenhagen Climate Change Summit in December 2009, it was larger developing countries such as Brazil, South Africa, India, and China that were invited to participate in a closed meeting to advance progress in the talks. They were the actors whose cooperation and support was most required. Likewise, in the run-up to the Paris climate summit in 2015, the United

States and China issued a joint presidential statement on climate change intended to clear the path to securing a global agreement.

But the degree of power that a country has in global economic terms and the extent to which it is aid-dependent also affects its vulnerability to pressure to take environmental action. Countries such as Mozambique or Ethiopia find that their policy priorities regarding energy and agriculture are strongly affected by such bilateral financial ties. Countries such as Brazil, on the other hand, have a larger degree of discretion in determining policy positions, and they can draw on greater economic weight in trade and industrial terms to resist calls from the **international community** to do more to combat deforestation in the country.

Second, but related, are issues of capacity for the enforcement of policy. Many developing countries, such as India, have some of the most impressive legislative Acts on environmental issues in the world. But lack of resources and training, and the **corruption** of local pollution control officials, often conspire to delay implementation. Sometimes, the nature of the problem and the size of the country are the key constraints. For example, regulating the cultivation and trade in genetically modified (GM) seeds is almost impossible in a country the size of China and many instances of illegal growing of non-authorized seeds have been reported. Managing the transborder movement of GM seeds, as is required by the 2000 Cartagena Protocol on Biosafety (under the Convention on Biological Diversity), presents many problems for developing countries, where seed markets are often poorly regulated and even basic equipment with which to test movements of seeds across borders is unavailable. Where countries have a strong economic and developmental incentive to ensure active compliance, extra steps may be taken. Kenya is keen to be seen as an attractive tourist location for wildlife safaris. Because tourism provides a large source of revenue, officials have gone to controversial lengths to tackle the problem of illegal poaching of elephants and rhinos for their ivory and horns. These include shooting poachers and banning tribal groups from culling animals for food, even on their own ancestral lands.

Third, the degree of importance that will be attached to environmental concerns, at the expense of broader development goals, will reflect the nature of democratic politics in the country. The strength of environmental groups in a country, pushing for new policy and acting as informal 'watchdogs' of compliance with environmental regulations, will be determined by the degree of democratic space that exists within the country. Countries such as India and Mexico have strong traditions of active civil society engagement in environmental policy. India, for instance, hosts the globally recognized **non-governmental organization (NGO)**, the Centre for Science and Environment, which is active in global policy debates, as well as domestic agenda-setting. In Singapore and China, by contrast, the avenues for policy engagement are few and tightly restricted. The scope and effectiveness of environmental policy will also be shaped by the extent to which the interests of leading industries are affected by proposed interventions. Where policy directly impinges on the interests of a particularly powerful industry, policy reform is often stalled or environmental concerns are kept off the agenda altogether. The close ties between logging companies and state officials that often have personal commercial stakes in the companies is an oft-cited reason for the lack of progress to reverse unsustainable logging in South East Asia (Dauvergne 1997).

The way in which governments formulate and implement policy also reflects a broad diversity of styles of environmental policymaking. Each country has a unique history when it comes to its approach to regulation, the organization of its bureaucracy, and the extent to which public participation in policy is encouraged and enabled. The Chinese government is able to act decisively and in a 'command and control' fashion to sanction industries failing to comply with pollution control regulations. In India, the Supreme Court has played a decisive role in moving environmental policy forward, often in controversial circumstances, setting strict and sometimes unrealistic targets, for example for the phasing out of non-compressed-natural-gas (non-CNG) vehicles in Delhi. Approaches to environmental policy also reflect the different ways in which knowledge—especially scientific knowledge—informs policy. Scientific knowledge does not provide a neutral and value-free guide to which environmental problems are the most serious or how they should be addressed. It is employed strategically by government officials to support their position within the bureaucracy, but can also change political practice and priorities by highlighting some areas of concern, while ignoring others. The power of expert communities in this regard explains why developing countries have sought greater representation of Southern-based scientists in international environmental bodies providing advice to policymakers such as the Intergovernmental Panel on Climate Change (IPCC).

Given these factors, there is sometimes also a mismatch between the expectations contained in multilateral environmental agreements about the way in which commitments should be implemented and the realities of what is possible in many developing country settings. There is the problem of capacity, whereby the resources and skills to oversee micro-level implementation of environmental regulations emanating from central government to meet global commitments are often lacking. In addition, many agreements, including the Cartagena Protocol on Biosafety, specify the process by which national environmental frameworks should be designed with respect to public consultation and participation; yet many are poorly placed to meaningfully set up participatory processes for deliberative and inclusive decision-making across a wide range of issues, involving a cross-section of their societies. Democratic values are weakly embedded in many societies and publics in many places remain sceptical of interaction with official bodies, such that good global intentions may not translate well into local practice.

Common challenges

Despite these differences in the policy positions and policy styles that developing countries have adopted, it is worth highlighting some common challenges that nearly all developing—and, of course, many developed—countries face in the design and execution of environmental policy. First, there is the scale of resources required to tackle environmental problems. Undertaking scientific research and monitoring the enforcement of pollution control places large resource demands on developing countries in particular. International environmental agreements create new demands of governments for more regulation, more monitoring, and an efficient and effective bureaucracy to oversee these, often across multiple levels of governance right down to the local level. Despite the availability of global funds to support some of these activities (see Box 17.1), it remains difficult even for larger developing countries to meet these expectations.

Second, in spite of the efforts of active environmental movements within developing countries, as well as globally, it remains the case that political constituencies with a strong preference for more effective environmental policy are often very weak. The issue is not only that the beneficiaries of environmental policies are not present in policy debates (future generations) or not adequately represented (indigenous peoples for example), but also that political parties with strong commitments to environmental issues are not well developed in most parts of Asia, Africa, and Latin America. Conversely, the presence of green parties in some parts of Europe has served to keep environmental issues on the agendas of the main parties.

Where **social movements** have taken up environmental issues, they often touch on deeply sensitive issues—for example access to resources such as forests and water or land reform—bringing them into conflict with state elites. *Campesino* (peasant-based) movements in Latin America often incorporate environmental issues into broader campaigning platforms for land redistribution and greater levels of compensation for the appropriation of natural resources (see Chapter 11). Movements for environmental justice that oppose the location of often hazardous and highly polluting industries in poorer communities often frustrate the development ambitions of policy elites. The ability of movements to use environmental issues to advance broader political agendas serves to entrench the suspicion that many governments have of environmental agendas. Occasionally, however, governments see in environmental issues an opportunity to gain political capital on an issue of national concern. The Argentine government became locked in conflict with neighbouring Uruguay over pulp mills set up there, which, Argentina alleged, are contaminating the Uruguay River that the two countries share. Argentina even initiated proceedings at the International Court of Justice (ICJ) in The Hague over the issue following large popular protests, despite claims that it hosts many equally polluting pulp mills within its own territory.

Third, it is important to recognize the global economic pressures that all countries face, but which developing countries face more acutely. Crushing debt burdens and the conditions attached to **structural adjustment programmes (SAPs)** (see Chapter 16) often create incentives for economic activities that are highly destructive of the environment. Export-led growth patterns, which often require intensive use of land with heavy applications of chemical fertilizers, and the creation of **export-processing zones (EPZs)**, in which environmental standards are often lower, are indicative of this. Deteriorating terms of trade for timber, minerals, and agricultural produce can also drive developing country economies, dependent on single commodities and monoculture production, to exploit that resource unsustainably.

The broader issue is what has been termed the 'race to the bottom' in environmental standards as developing countries compete to lower environmental regulations to attract increasingly mobile investors. The evidence for this is mixed. Some argue that increased patterns of trade interdependence have the effect of raising standards as developing country exporters seek access to lucrative Western markets that require higher environmental standards (Vogel 1997). However, there are many examples of regulatory reforms not being introduced or not implemented for fear of deterring investors (Newell 2012). In other cases, lack of environmental regulation has been used as a **comparative advantage** to attract environmentally hazardous production of substances, such as toxic wastes and asbestos, which are banned in richer countries. The desperation of many developing countries to attract investment on any terms, therefore, clearly both affects their ability to prioritize action on the environment and, in certain situations, will lead them to lower standards to attract mobile capital.

It is also the case that many developing countries have abundant natural resources that make them key locations for extractive industries. For years, activists have berated the mining industry for its environmental pollution, **human rights** violations, and displacement of indigenous peoples. The oil industry too has been accused of double standards when it operates in developing countries. The activities of firms such as Shell in Nigeria's Niger Delta and Texaco in Ecuador have attracted global attention as a result of activist exposure and high-profile legal actions against the companies (Newell 2001).

By way of response, many firms have developed corporate social responsibility (CSR) programmes to defend and promote their reputations, and to present themselves as a force for good. It is now commonplace for larger companies to claim that they incorporate sustainable development in their investment decision-making. This discourse is being picked up by export-oriented Southern-based MNCs and state-owned firms as they come under pressure from Northern corporate buyers and consumers to improve their own social and environmental performance. However, it remains the case that many of the drivers of corporate environmental responsibility, including government incentives, civil society watchdogs, and consumer and investor pressure, are currently underdeveloped in many parts of the

developing world. Firms within countries with strong trading ties to overseas markets in which compliance with tougher environmental regulations is expected will often have higher standards than many firms in parts of sub-Saharan Africa, for example, which are more isolated from such global pressures.

Fourth, the **underdevelopment** of the scientific expertise that underpins environmental policy is a characteristic common to many developing countries. While there are many international scientific research programmes on environmental issues and many international environmental agreements have panels or rosters of experts, the representation of scientists from developing countries is often low. There have been initiatives from UNEP to try to address this problem by ensuring, for example, that a percentage of scientists on such bodies are from developing countries. But the problem endures, and the implication is that the agendas of Northern researchers and their policy networks attract greater attention and resources than issues and concerns that are more pertinent to the developing world.

KEY POINTS

- Despite facing similar international pressures to integrate environmental issues into development policy, the willingness and ability of developing countries to address environmental challenges is highly uneven.

- There are important differences in priorities, power and policy autonomy, resources and capacity, and policy styles between governments in the developing world, and in relation to the role of environmental and business groups in policy formulation and implementation.

- There are, however, many common challenges that developing countries face when it comes to environmental policy: weaknesses in enforcement capacity; economic vulnerability, which means that trade and aid leverage can be used to influence policy; and an underdeveloped knowledge base from which to develop environmental policy.

New Policy Instruments for Environmental Protection

We have already noted the different policy styles that developing countries around the world have employed in the design and implementation of environmental policy. It is also the case, however, that they have been affected by shifts in prevailing thinking about the most efficient and effective way in which to provide environmental goods—particularly an increased emphasis on the use of market-based mechanisms. This is not to suggest that strong **developmental states** are not, on occasion, able to intervene forcibly to close down polluting industry, or to overlook the important role of legal systems in driving environmental policy reform and in protecting the rights of citizens against their own government. Courts have been a key site for poorer groups to seek compensation for socially and environmentally destructive investments that have undermined their livelihoods (see Chapter 11). They have provided a venue in which to draw attention to grievances that have not been recognized elsewhere. Where successful, legal cases can uphold key rights to environmental information, ensure that EIAs are undertaken in advance of large industrial projects, or contest the forced displacement that is associated with infrastructural projects such as dams. In Nigeria, numerous cases have been brought against oil companies by communities seeking compensation for damage to land caused by oil spillages from company pipelines in the Niger Delta. Companies exploiting lower health and environmental standards in developing countries, providing their workers with less protection than their counterparts in the North, have also ended up paying large out-of-court settlements to victims of industrial hazards. More positively and proactively, poorer groups have also been able to use legal remedies to realize their rights to key resources such as water (see Box 17.3), or to access forests (Newell and Wheeler 2006).

Relying on legal remedies to tackle environmental problems is often inadequate, however. People frequently resort to the law only after the pollution has occurred. There are also limits to how poorer groups can use the law to their benefit. Poorer communities frequently lack the financial resources to bring a case. They lack the 'legal literacy' necessary to appreciate their rights under the law and how they can be realized. These problems of access are often compounded by long backlogs of cases and distrust in the independence of the legal system. There are many legal barriers to successfully demonstrating cause and effect between a polluting activity and evidence of damage to human health or the environment, particularly when poorer groups are exposed to such a range of hazards in their day-to-day lives.

In general, however, state-based environmental regulation has been subject to sustained criticism from key development actors such as the World Bank on the grounds that it is inflexible, inefficient, and often ineffective at delivering the change in behaviour that it intends. Increasingly, the preference is for the use of the market as a tool for incentivizing positive action and deterring polluting activities. Carbon emissions trading schemes are now being rolled out in a number of developing countries, from China to Mexico to Kazakhstan. Market tools such as labelling have also been accepted in many developing countries as a means by which to assure global buyers of the environmentally responsible way in which the product has been produced, as well as to facilitate consumer choice. For example, certification has been used in the forestry sector in the form of the popular Forestry Stewardship Council (FSC) scheme and the World Bank has led a 'Lighting Africa' programme to certify solar lighting products.

Another general trend in environmental policy that is catching on in the developing world is the adoption of voluntary measures by industry. Codes of conduct among leading companies are now commonplace in

BOX 17.3 THE RIGHT TO WATER IN SOUTH AFRICA

- South Africa recognizes the human right to water at the constitutional and policy level through its Free Basic Water policy.

- The Water Services Act of 1997 provides for a basic level of water for those that cannot pay. People are entitled to 25 litres of water free per day for personal and domestic use.

- There is, nevertheless, uneven access to water. Problems of capacity of local authorities to deliver on the commitment and financial constraints have led to undersupply and to people being cut off. This has led some people to get water from unprotected sources—leading to health problems.

- The government is also under immense pressure to introduce user fees and cost recovery in line with market-based approaches to water provision.

- Many people are also unaware of their constitutional right to water and therefore when their rights are violated.

- Although some legal cases have secured interim relief from disconnections by invoking the right to water, the onus on proving inability to pay rests with the water user and depends on his or her access to legal representation.

Source: Mehta (2006)

the North, and many of those firms investing overseas are insisting that their suppliers and partners adopt them. The trend forms part of the rejection of the alleged inefficiencies and ineffectiveness of central government 'command and control' policy measures; it also reflects the preference of firms to set their own standards appropriate to their own circumstances in a way that avoids or pre-empts state intervention. In the environmental context, environmental management systems such as ISO 14001 created by the International Organization for Standardization (ISO) are increasingly popular and have been revised many times. While, traditionally, such standards have tended to apply only to larger firms that can afford the compliance costs and those seeking access to developed country markets, small and medium-sized enterprises (SMEs) are increasingly seeking ISO certification to serve as subcontractors for ISO-certified enterprises. There are also sector-specific programmes, such as 'Responsible Care' in the case of the chemical industry, which have been adopted in countries such as Mexico and Brazil, as well as roundtables on responsible soy, palm oil, biofuels, and beef production. It is clear, then, that global market pressures from buyers and consumers increasingly exercise as significant an influence on environmental policy practice in many parts of the developing world as the international agreements to which governments sign up.

As a reaction to the limitations of market-based and voluntary mechanisms, there has also been a growth in what has been termed **civil regulation**—that is, civil-society-based forms of business regulation. The increasing use of such tools as shareholder activism and boycotts, and the growth of watchdog groups such as OilWatch based in Nigeria, are illustrative of the trend. New forms of engagement in constructing codes of conduct and building partnerships between business and civil society also fall under the umbrella of civil regulation. Concern has been expressed that many of these tools are available only to well-resourced groups with good access to the media and in societies with strong traditions of free speech. But there does seem to be evidence of these strategies being employed on an increasing scale in most parts of the global South. Strategies of resistance and exposure of corporate wrongdoing date from colonial times, but there has also been a notable proliferation in groups across the entire spectrum adopting them, ranging from confrontation to collaboration. Many of these groups are also increasingly globally well connected. This means that companies engaging in environmentally controversial activities in the developing world can also expect to face shareholder resolutions and embarrassing media publicity in their home countries.

It is unclear at this stage what the net effect of these forms of civil regulation will be on the environmental performance of investors in developing countries. The hope is that groups with the expertise and capabilities to plug gaps and weaknesses in systems of government pollution control and monitoring will play an important complementary role as informal regulators. One study of community-based regulation in Vietnam shows how this has been possible when 'the energies and actions of average community members and the responses of front-line environmental agencies' have been brought together (O'Rourke 2004: xvii). This may encourage firms to respect the environmental standards of the countries in which they operate to a greater degree than if they were not there and so help to dissuade companies from adopting double standards when they operate in developing countries. The extent to which groups will be allowed to perform this role will depend on the strength of civil society in a given setting and the extent to which its activities are tolerated by the state. Issues of whom the groups represent and to whom they are accountable will also have to be faced if they are to be seen as legitimate actors in environmental policy.

KEY POINTS

- Many countries continue to use central government 'command and control' environmental policy measures.

- Despite their limitations, poorer groups have sought to use legal remedies to claim rights to resources, to contest planning processes, and to seek compensation for loss of livelihood.

- There has been a shift, however, in thinking about how best to tackle environmental pollution away from state-based approaches, towards the use of market instruments and voluntary approaches.

- Many companies in developing countries are seeking certification for their products to get access to Northern markets.

- In recent years, there has been a trend towards civil regulation by civil society groups. The long-term impact of this will vary by country, and the extent to which such groups are able to address issues of their own accountability and representation.

Futures

Attempting to predict the likely future of environmental policy in the developing or developed world with any degree of accuracy and precision is a fruitless endeavour. It is, however, possible to identify certain patterns of continuity and change. We have seen how many developing countries face common challenges in terms of how to reconcile pressing development needs with environmental goals. Countries have inevitably responded in different ways that reflect, among other things, their political systems, the nature of their economies, and the level of civil society engagement. But we have seen similar problems of enforcement at the national level—constraints that arise from economic relationships of trade, aid, and debt, and conflicts over which environmental issues should assume the highest priority.

Through global processes of negotiation, increasingly integrated supply chains, and globally interdependent trading patterns, we have seen how pressures come to be exerted on developing countries to design and implement environmental policies in ways that reflect the priorities of Northern governments, businesses, and international organizations. Shifts in thinking about environmental policy, and what makes it more effective and efficient, are transmitted through donor lending and the global reach of transnational companies. These are the sorts of pressures that bring about conformity and harmonization in environmental politics in the developing world.

But there is much that is subject to change, such is the fragile and often ephemeral status of environmental issues on the policy agendas of countries the world over. The profile of such issues is as vulnerable to the state of the world economy as it is to the health of the planet. Despite calls in the North for a 'green new deal' (increased public investment in new jobs and green technology in the wake of the 2007–08 global financial crisis), government spending on environmental programmes notoriously decreases in times of recession as other issues assume a higher profile. The links between security and the environment continue to attract increasing attention. Resources such as oil and water are often cited as a cause of geopolitical conflicts in the Middle East, for example, while the way in which drought exacerbated the conflict in Darfur has led some to call it, controversially, the world's first 'climate war'. Priorities shift according to global events as much as they reflect

changes in domestic politics following changes of government. A realignment of donor priorities in the wake of these shifts may have a significant impact on resource allocations for environmental projects, or the extent to which some regions of the developing world come to be favoured over others on the basis of their strategic value to Western interests. Nevertheless, with or without donor support, developing countries face many environmental challenges of their own, including water pollution, land degradation, and urban air quality. It is often the human impact of these problems that attracts attention and acts as the driver for change. The increasingly high human cost of environmental degradation exacts an economic price: costs to health systems increase and an unhealthy workforce is an unproductive workforce. Despite increasing acknowledgement of the human and developmental case for tackling environmental degradation, stark trade-offs between environmentally damaging investment and no investment at all continue to force governments to put profit before the needs of their own people or the planet. Global economic pressures from highly mobile companies and global economic institutions further load the dice towards investment and exports over the imperatives of sustainable development.

Sometimes, of course, environmental problems draw attention to themselves and demand action from governments. Floods in Mozambique, droughts in Ethiopia, and forest fires in Indonesia, the intensity of which will increase as our climate changes, prompt short-term emergency measures. Rarely, however, do they initiate deeper reflection about the deeper causes of the crisis. Nevertheless, the increased incidence of such human-induced, yet seemingly 'natural', events may, more than any other single factor, serve to focus the world's attention on the environmental consequences of current patterns of development.

Conclusion

Developing countries face a range of often contradictory pressures from international institutions, market actors, and civil society regarding how to reconcile environmental protection with broader development goals. How they handle these challenges will be a function of both domestic political factors and global political influences. Access to diminishing supplies of resources such as oil and conflicts over water, exacerbated by climate change, will link environmental issues ever more closely to questions of national and international security. A key driver of policy responses will continue to be environmental disasters, which focus public attention on the impacts of particular types of development. The challenge is to harness this concern towards longer-term change aimed at tackling the causes of environmental degradation, rather than merely to address some of its immediate symptoms.

? QUESTIONS

1. Why has the relationship between environment and development been so uneasy?

2. Is it still meaningful to refer to the global South in international environmental negotiations?

3. Discuss the relationship between environment and national and international security.

4. How far does climate change force us to rethink conventional models of development?

5. Under what circumstances might environment and development challenges be reconciled more effectively in the future?

6. Which institutional reforms could improve the international community's ability to promote sustainable development effectively?

7. What reasons are there to believe that the Sustainable Development Goals (SDGs) will be more successful than previous attempts to promote sustainable development?

8. What are the prospects of the green economy?

FURTHER READING

Adams, W. M. (2008) *Green Development: Environment and Sustainability in the Third World,* 2nd edn (London: Routledge) Provides a detailed history of the concept of sustainable development, and the different ways in which it has been interpreted and applied in the mainstream and by its critics.

Bryant, R. L., and Bailey, S. (1997) *Third World Political Ecology* (London: Routledge) Provides a useful actor-based introduction to the key forces shaping environmental politics in the developing world, from business and multilateral institutions, to non-governmental organizations and the role of the state.

Elliott, L. (2004) *The Global Politics of the Environment* (London: Macmillan) Wide-ranging textbook that covers not only the global environmental agenda, but also issues of trade, debt, and aid, which bring together environmental and development agendas.

Keeley, J., and Scoones, I. (2003) *Understanding Environmental Policy Processes: Cases from Africa* (London: Earthscan) Drawing on research in Ethiopia, Mali, and Zimbabwe, this book examines the links between knowledge, power, and politics in understanding how environmental issues come to be framed and the consequences of this for how they are acted upon.

Newell, P. (2012) *Globalization and the Environment: Capitalism, Ecology and Power* (Cambridge: Polity Press) Emphasizes the centrality of politics and social relations to understanding the nature of the relationship between globalization and the environment, focused particularly on trade, production, and finance, and their environmental impacts, governance, and contestation.

Peets, R., Robbins, P., and Watts, M. (eds) (2010) *Global Political Ecology* (London: Routledge) Collection of essays that provides theoretical perspectives from political ecology and political economy, and empirical case studies of a range of urban and rural environmental issues from the developed and developing world.

Scoones, I., Leach, M., and Newell, P. (eds) (2015) *The Politics of Green Transformations* (London: Routledge) Collection of essays, including many cases from the developing world and covering a range of issues, exploring the politics of different pathways to sustainability in relation to the state, business and finance, innovation, and civil society.

 WEB LINKS

http://www.act.or.ke   The African Centre for Technology Studies, Nairobi, Kenya, provides useful studies, resources, and news items on issues such as agriculture and food security, climate change, and biotechnology.

http://www.cseindia.org   The site of the Centre for Science and Environment, Delhi, India, contains reports and details of campaigns on key environmental challenges facing India, but also maintains a global focus.

http://www.iied.org   The site of the London-based International Institute for Environment and Development (IIED) offers research and publications on a range of environment and development issues.

http://www.iisd.org   Among other useful databanks, the site of the International Institute for Sustainable Development (IISD), based on Winnipeg, Canada, gives access to the *Earth Negotiations Bulletin*, which provides updates on all of the leading international environmental negotiations.

http://practicalaction.org/home   The site of Practical Action, UK, contains details on the organization, its project and research work, and reports and publications on a range of environment and development issues.

http://www.steps-centre.org   This University of Sussex research centre on social, technological, and environmental pathways to sustainability produces research on a range of environmental and development issues. The site also provides access to the Eldis gateway from where searches for information and studies on particular environmental issues in specific developing countries can be undertaken.

http://www.unep.org   The United Nations Environment Programme (UNEP) site is a mine of information about global environmental issues and the negotiations aimed at tackling them.

http://www.worldbank.org   Contains information about the World Bank's work on a range of environmental issues in the developing world.

 For additional material and resources, please visit the Online Resource Centre at:
http://www.oxfordtextbooks.co.uk/orc/burnell5e/

18

Human Rights

Michael Freeman

Chapter contents

Overview

The language of human rights is a pervasive feature of contemporary international politics. This chapter offers an analysis of the concept, a brief account of its history, and a description of the international human rights regime. It proceeds to examine two persistent problems that arise in applying the concept to developing countries: the relations between the claim that the concept is universally valid and the realities of cultural difference around the world; and the relations between human rights and development.

Introduction

The concept of **human rights** derives primarily from the Charter of the United Nations, which was adopted in 1945 immediately after the Second World War. The Preamble to the Charter declares that the United Nations was determined to 'reaffirm faith in fundamental human rights, in the dignity and worth of the human person, in the equal rights of men and women, and of nations large and small'. In 1948, the

UN General Assembly adopted the Universal Declaration of Human Rights, which sets out a list of human rights 'as a common standard of achievement for all peoples'. The list includes such civil and political rights as: those to freedom from slavery, torture, arbitrary arrest, and detention; freedom of religion, expression, and association; and a number of economic and social rights, such as the rights to education and an adequate standard of living. These rights were intended to protect everyone from tyrannical governments like that of Nazi Germany and from the economic misery that was thought to have facilitated the rise of fascism.

Although the countries of Latin America, Asia, and Africa formed the majority of those that produced the Declaration, many of the world's people lived at that time under colonial rule and were thus excluded from this process. The concept of human rights was derived from a Western philosophical tradition and was shaped mainly by European historical experience. Colonialism was itself condemned for its human rights violations and, when worldwide decolonization brought many new states to the United Nations, the **post-colonial states** accepted human rights in principle, although their priorities differed from those of the West, emphasizing self-determination, development, economic and social rather than civil and political rights, and anti-racism.

Disagreements about which human rights should be legally binding led to the adoption of two UN human rights covenants in 1966: the International Covenant on Civil and Political Rights (ICCPR); and the International Covenant on Economic, Social and Cultural Rights (ICESCR). Each covenant has now been ratified by more than 80 per cent of UN member states. The United Nations has also adopted several more specialized conventions. There are additionally regional human rights conventions, although these do not cover the whole world, especially the Middle East and Asia (see Box 18.1).

Many developing countries have poor human rights records. There are internal and external explanations of this. The internal explanations include poverty, ethnic tensions, and authoritarian government. Some of the internal problems of developing countries are legacies of colonialism. The external explanations include support for dictatorships by the great powers, and the global economic system, which many believe is biased against developing countries and thereby hinders their capacity to develop the **institutions** necessary to protect human rights. Since the end of the cold war and

BOX 18.1 UNIVERSAL AND REGIONAL HUMAN RIGHTS TREATIES

- European Convention on Human Rights and Fundamental Freedoms 1950
- UN Refugee Convention 1951
- UN International Convention on the Elimination of Racial Discrimination 1965
- UN International Covenant on Civil and Political Rights 1966
- UN International Covenant on Economic, Social and Cultural Rights 1966
- American Convention on Human Rights 1969
- UN Convention on the Elimination of Discrimination against Women 1979
- African Charter on Human and Peoples' Rights 1981
- UN Convention against Torture 1984
- UN Convention on the Rights of the Child 1989
- UN International Convention on the Protection of the Rights of Migrant Workers 1990
- UN Convention on the Rights of Persons with Disabilities 2006
- UN International Convention for the Protection from Enforced Disappearances 2006

the discrediting of the Soviet state socialist model of development, **neoliberalism**—the ideology of free markets—has dominated global economics. Whether neoliberalism promotes respect for, or violation of, human rights is highly controversial. The Universal Declaration's conception of human rights, however, presupposed effective states; neoliberalism tends to weaken states, and especially their capacity to protect social and economic rights. The harmful effects of such policies disproportionately affect women and children. Since the United Nations adopted its Millennium Development Goals (MDGs) in 2000, replaced in 2015 by the **Sustainable Development Goals (SDGs)**, the **international community** has committed itself to reducing world poverty, but the results of this commitment have been mixed.

Developing countries have been vulnerable to military coups and to ethnic conflict, both of which lead to serious human rights violations. While the dominant human rights discourse is highly *legalistic* and emphasizes legal solutions to human rights problems, social scientists have recently revived the concept of **civil society** (see Chapter 10) as a barrier to tyranny. Developing countries vary considerably in the strength of their civil societies, but some observers see civil society as the best hope both for development and the improvement of human rights protection. Human rights seem to require a balance between effective states and strong civil societies, which is difficult to achieve when resources are scarce.

The experience of Western imperialism has led developing countries to accord greater priority to economic development and state sovereignty than to human rights. This tendency has been strengthened by internal struggles for power that have often led to highly authoritarian governments. Resistance to implementing the **international human rights regime** is often justified by the claim that the concept of human rights is itself part of Western imperialism, although this argument is strongly resisted by many human rights activists in developing countries.

KEY POINTS

- The concept of human rights, promoted by the United Nations after the Second World War to combat dictatorship, was embodied in the UN Charter (1945) and the Universal Declaration of Human Rights (1948).

- At that time, people living under colonial rule were excluded from participating in the concept's elaboration; thereafter, new, post-colonial states accepted human rights in principle, but prioritized development and state sovereignty.

- In the decades after 1948, the United Nations developed a large body of international human rights law.

- Many developing countries have poor human rights records, often caused by the economic and political challenges of development, and sometimes aggravated by the policies of developed countries.

The Concept of Human Rights

There are two main conceptions of human rights favoured by philosophers. The more traditional conception holds that every human being has certain moral rights, such as the rights to life, freedom, and the material basis for 'a life of dignity'. This conception has been criticized because the philosophical basis of such rights is uncertain and controversial. The alternative is the so-called political conception, which finds the basis of human rights in international agreement. This has the advantage of providing a basis for the claim that

human rights are 'universal' and perhaps its justification is clearer. Its disadvantage is that what is politically agreed may be morally wrong and the 'agreement' may not be sincere. No philosophical agreement exists, therefore, on the 'foundations' of human rights or on whether there are any. The concept of human rights has a powerful intuitive moral appeal to millions around the world, and is supported by an uneasy political and legal agreement that the Universal Declaration provides us with an authoritative list of human rights as a reference for international policy.

The two 1966 Covenants distinguish between civil and political rights, on the one hand, and economic, social, and cultural rights, on the other. Western governments tend to prioritize the first type; developing countries, the second. The distinction is, however, controversial: the right to property, for example, is often regarded as a civil, rather than an economic, right, which seems absurd. The United Nations' Vienna Declaration (1993) sought to overcome the distinction by proclaiming that all human rights are 'indivisible'. This idea has become increasingly influential as the United Nations, its member governments, and international institutions, such as the World Bank, have come to recognize that neglect of human rights is at least sometimes a barrier to development.

A brief history

Some say that the concept of human rights is ancient and found in all, or most, of the world's cultures. This claim usually confuses the concept of human rights with related concepts, such as those of justice and human dignity. These concepts are found in many cultures. The idea of human rights is more unusual and consequently more controversial.

The concept of 'citizens' rights', but not that of 'human rights', is found in ancient Greek and Roman thought. The modern concept of human rights derives from that of natural rights, which appeared in Europe in the late Middle Ages and featured prominently in the political struggles of seventeenth-century England. Natural rights were derived from natural law and were known by reason. This idea burst onto the stage of world **politics** with the American and French revolutions in the late eighteenth century. In the nineteenth century, it fell out of favour, because it was thought to be unscientific and subversive of social order. The concept of human rights evokes that of natural rights, but differs in at least two important

ways: first, it is not necessarily derived from the controversial philosophy of natural law; and second, it presupposes the existence of certain political, legal, economic, and social institutions, and in this sense the rights are not 'natural'.

Contemporary conceptions

The contemporary conception of human rights derives from Western liberalism, which gives priority to individual freedom. Human rights are the rights of every individual. It is often said that Western cultures are individualistic, whereas non-Western cultures are collectivistic, but while there may be some truth in this claim, both Western and non-Western cultures balance individual and collective values.

KEY POINTS

- Human rights may be considered to be the fundamental moral rights held by all human beings or a specific set of rights established by international agreement.

- International law has distinguished between civil and political rights, on the one hand, and economic, social, and cultural rights, on the other. This distinction is both influential and controversial.

- Human, as distinct from citizens', rights are modern, deriving from the late medieval idea of natural rights, which fell out of favour after the French Revolution, but was revived by the United Nations in the form of human rights.

- The dominant conception of human rights is controversial in developing countries, because it is thought to express the Western philosophy of liberal individualism.

Human Rights Regimes

Human rights regimes exist at international, regional, and national levels.

The UN system

The international human rights regime consists of a large body of international law and a complex set of institutions to implement it. Chief among these institutions was the UN Commission on Human Rights, established in 1946. Its members represented governments and it was criticized for political bias. In 2006,

the United Nations replaced the Commission with the Human Rights Council. The Council has improved on the work of the Commission in some respects and has remained controversial in other respects. The United Nations employs independent experts as members of working groups, or as rapporteurs on specific themes and countries. The members of the committees that monitor the various treaties are also independent experts. **Non-governmental organizations** (**NGOs**) play an important role in providing information, and campaigning for the development and implementation of human rights standards. It is difficult to evaluate the effectiveness of the international regime, but the consensus of scholars is that it is rather weak.

Regional and national regimes

There are regional human rights regimes in Europe, the Americas, and Africa. The European is the most developed, although it has recently been subject to various criticisms, and the African is the least developed, although it has begun to progress.

Many scholars believe that the most effective level of protection for human rights is that of national constitutions, legislation, and independent courts. International human rights authorities strongly encourage national legal enforcement of human rights. There is strong evidence in social science that civil and political rights are best protected where there is a high level of economic development, governments are democratic, the **rule of law** is reliably enforced by an independent judiciary, and there is a strong civil society.

There has been much debate about whether economic and social rights are 'justiciable'—that is, suited to judicial decision-making. Until recently, judicial decisions on these rights were rare. Recent scholarship has, however, discovered up to 2,000 such decisions in the last two decades, many of them in developing countries, covering a wide range of rights (Langford 2008). These rights, therefore, definitely *are* justiciable. Many scholars, however, doubt whether they *ought to be*.

Three main objections are made to the judicialization of economic and social rights:

- decisions about these rights involve the allocation of scarce resources and these allocations should be made by democratically accountable politicians;
- such decisions involve technical knowledge not always available to courts; and

- court decisions tend to benefit the rich at the expense of the poor.

The following responses have been made to these objections:

- courts properly protect the fundamental rights of citizens in democracies, and these include at least minimal economic and social rights;
- courts have access to as much expert advice as the other branches of government do; and
- the rich may benefit from court decisions, as they do from many other social institutions, but at least some judicial decisions on economic and social rights have benefited the poor.

We lack sufficient evidence to evaluate the constitutionalization and judicialization of economic and social rights adequately. One study of 188 states from 1960 to 2010 concluded that neither the incorporation of such rights into constitutions nor making them justiciable led to significant improvements in the enjoyment of these rights (Bjørnskov and Mchangama 2013). This challenges the simple view that judicialization of these rights improves their enjoyment significantly, but leaves open the question as to which combinations of political mobilization and judicial enforcement are optimal for these rights. There are many forms of human rights politics and many ways in which courts can respond to human rights complaints. Lawyers may overemphasize legal approaches to human rights implementation, whereas social scientists tend to emphasize the political and legal obstacles, while exploring political and legal paths to progress.

KEY POINTS

- Human rights are regulated legally at international, regional, and national levels.
- The international human rights regime is fairly weak and, where human rights receive strong legal protection, it is usually at the national level.
- The effectiveness of the legal approach to human rights implementation is uncertain. Strong political and economic forces are barriers to implementation, but progress probably requires the well-judged combination of political mobilization and litigation.

Development and Human Rights

There is a widely held view that 'development' should have priority over human rights. Various reasons are given for this view. It is said that, in the absence of certain material goods such as food and health, non-material goods such as freedom of speech have no value. It is also claimed that human rights are too expensive for poor countries. It is argued, further, that human rights subvert social order and thus hinder development, especially in developing countries with problematic ethnic divisions. The so-called Asian tigers—South Korea, Taiwan, Malaysia, and Singapore, plus, more recently, China—are cited as examples of successful economic development under authoritarian rule.

Conceptions of development

'Development' is often assumed to mean economic development and economic development has often been measured by per capita income. Recently, however, development has been reconceptualized as **human development**, with emphasis on quality of life. The economic development of states is compatible with the misery of many people. The new conception of development sees human rights and development as *conceptually* overlapping. Development is seen as improvement in the quality of life for everyone and thus development includes respect for human rights. This new conceptualization of development has been influential at the United Nations. The UN Development Programme (UNDP), for example, has recently included the protection of human rights in its policies. This new conception of development has been closely associated with an increased emphasis on **gender** equality.

Arguments that restrictions of human rights are necessary for development are not well supported by the evidence. They often rely on selective use of case studies, especially from East Asia. South Korea and Taiwan achieved rapid economic development under authoritarian governments, but both developed into liberal democracies. Singapore has also been economically successful, with a so-called soft authoritarian **regime**. Other cases are ambiguous. Some Latin American countries—such as Pinochet's Chile—had some economic growth, but also some economic setbacks, under authoritarian rule, while

China has achieved rapid economic growth in recent years, but in combination with serious human rights violations. Authoritarian regimes can sometimes achieve rapid economic development. Most repressive regimes, however, have failed to deliver development. The causal connection between human rights violations and development has never been established. Some countries that have combined economic development with restrictions of civil and political rights—such as South Korea, Singapore, and China—have relatively good records with respect to economic and social rights, such as education and health. Some development economists believe that democratic political rights and social rights, such as those to health and education, are conducive to success in development.

The relations between development and human rights may well be mediated by other factors, including the economic strategies adopted by governmental elites and the country's security situation. Taiwan, South Korea, and Singapore all faced external and/or internal security threats that made authoritarian government more likely, and all were able to locate themselves favourably within the global economic system.

Respect for human rights is therefore not generally necessary for economic development and violation of human rights is certainly not sufficient for economic development. Most countries that have persistently and seriously violated human rights have been unsuccessful in developing their economies. The increasing political repression in Zimbabwe, for example, has been accompanied by economic collapse and the former is certainly a cause of the latter. It is very difficult to generalize about the relations between development and human rights, and we should be very cautious about inferring policies for particular countries from generalizations and, *a fortiori*, from the experience of selected countries.

Attempts to establish statistical relations between human rights and development in large numbers of countries have also produced inconclusive, and sometimes apparently contradictory, results. Famous Indian economist Amartya Sen (1999a, 1999b) has argued that the evidence suggests little correlation, positive or negative, between respect for civil and political rights and economic growth, and that the violation of such rights is not *necessary* to economic development. He reminds us that human rights have a value that is independent of development and argues

consequently that the available evidence is no barrier to the policy of pursuing development-with-human-rights. It is nonetheless true that the gravest human rights disasters of recent years have taken place in developing countries, such as Cambodia, Rwanda, and Syria—so why is this?

Developing countries are poor and vulnerable to the power of rich states and non-state actors, such as transnational corporations (TNCs). This makes economic development difficult. Without economic development, the resources for implementing human rights are scarce. Where resources are not scarce (as in countries with valuable natural resources), the temptations of **corruption** and authoritarianism will be great.

The achievement of independence from colonial rule, the ethos of the United Nations and world culture, and the spread of information through modern media of communication have raised expectations of economic progress among the peoples of the developing countries. The persistent inability of governments to meet them has created widespread social frustration, active opposition to governments, and consequent repression. These problems are aggravated in many developing countries by ethnic divisions. Although ethnic diversity does not necessarily lead to conflict and human rights violations, such divisions are difficult to manage where ethnicity is a potent source of conflict.

Developing countries should not be seen simply as dependent victims of domination by rich states, international institutions, TNCs, or global capitalism. They have some autonomy, however limited, as the success of the Asian tigers demonstrates. Corrupt and incompetent government has contributed to the economic failures of many developing countries, and human rights violations are partly explained by the desire of powerful and corrupt rulers to remain in power, as in China, Indonesia, Iraq, Saudi Arabia, Nigeria, and Zimbabwe, for example.

Most developing countries lack traditions of human rights (see Box 18.2). They may have traditional cultures with morally admirable features, such as mutual solidarity, and they may also have active human rights organizations—which are found throughout much of Asia, Africa, and Latin America—and even individual 'human rights heroes' (such as Aung San Suu Kyi in Myanmar). But, in contrast with Europe, the value of human rights may not be deeply embedded in the

BOX 18.2 BARRIERS TO HUMAN RIGHTS IMPLEMENTATION BY DEVELOPING COUNTRIES

- Most developing countries are poor and cannot afford the full implementation of human rights.
- Most developing countries have little power in the global economic system, and are consequently vulnerable to the policies of powerful states and non-state actors that are often hostile to human rights.
- In the conditions of contemporary global culture and media of mass communication, under which the expectations of many people in developing countries for economic progress are high, the inability of governments to meet those expectations stimulates protest and repression.

- Most developing countries have ethnic divisions that predispose them to conflict in conditions of scarcity and consequently to repression.
- Corrupt and incompetent government has been common in developing countries, and human rights violations are explained in part by the desire of corrupt rulers to remain in power.
- Many developing countries have had traditional cultures under which human rights enjoyed little place and have developed a modern human rights culture only in a weak form.

public culture of the society. Even where the government has ratified international human rights treaties and human rights are written into national constitutions, human rights may not be a strong feature of the **political culture**.

The Vienna Declaration maintained that democracy, development, and human rights were interdependent. This claim, however, oversimplifies a complex set of relations: democracy is probably not necessary to development, but may improve its chances (see Chapter 14). The problem is that it is very difficult to establish democracy at very low levels of development. Empirically, democracies respect human rights better than do other forms of government, but all democracies violate human rights sometimes, and so-called facade democracies, which hold formally fair and free elections, but exclude sections of the population from effective political participation, are likely to have fairly poor human rights records. The protection of human rights by legal institutions may run counter to the democratic will of the people. The human rights of suspected criminals, refugees, and ethnic and political minorities are particularly vulnerable to democratic violations, in both developed and developing countries. In developing countries with ethnic divisions and weak human rights traditions, the process of democratization itself may lead to serious human rights violations. Democratization played a role in ethnic conflict and **genocide** in Rwanda, for example. Finally, the responses of Western democratic governments to **terrorist** attacks has led to restrictions of human rights at home and support for serious human rights violations abroad under cover of the **war on terror(ism)**.

KEY POINTS

- It is commonly argued that development should have priority over human rights, although when development is defined by reference to the quality of life, it overlaps with the concept of human rights.
- Although the empirical relationship between human rights and development is not well understood, the available evidence suggests that it is weak. There are independent reasons for valuing human rights.
- Democracies generally respect human rights better than do authoritarian regimes, but sometimes violate them. The war on terrorism led to human rights violations by both democratic and authoritarian governments.

Universalism and Cultural Diversity

The Preamble to the Universal Declaration of Human Rights refers to 'the equal and inalienable rights of all members of the human family', and the Declaration proclaims itself to be 'a common standard of achievement for all peoples'. It goes on to state, in Article 1, that all human beings 'are born free and equal in dignity and rights'. The Vienna Declaration reaffirmed the universality of human rights.

Cultural imperialism and cultural relativism

The belief that human rights are universal appears to conflict with the obvious cultural diversity of the world. Moral and political ideas, many people say, derive from culture, and different societies have different cultures; to impose human rights on everyone in the world is therefore intolerant, imperialistic, and unjustified. This moral logic may be supported by the *historical* claims that: first, the concept of human rights is a Western concept; and second, the West has a history of political, economic, and **cultural imperialism** that is not yet over. Some non-Western critics of human rights argue that not only is the concept of human rights alien to non-Western cultures, but also its use by the West is part of a project of global political and economic domination.

In the 1990s, a number of governments and intellectuals from East and South East Asian countries that had achieved considerable economic success called into question the dominant interpretation of human rights by appealing to what they claimed were distinctively Asian values. This claim was somewhat puzzling, because the cultures of East Asia are extremely diverse, ranging from officially atheist China to predominantly Muslim Indonesia and Malaysia. One of the leading proponents of 'Asian values', Dr Mahathir Mohamad, then prime minister of Malaysia, acknowledged that Asian values were similar to conservative Western values—that is, order, harmony, and respect for authority. The Asian values argument was partially acknowledged by the Vienna Declaration, which reaffirmed the universality of human rights, but conceded that 'the significance of national and regional particularities and various historical, cultural and religious backgrounds should be borne in mind' (Article I.5). Read literally, this statement is uncontroversial, for it would be foolish to interpret and implement human rights without bearing in mind the significance of these cultural differences. However, many Asian NGOs continued to affirm the universalist orthodoxy. Thus two different Asian approaches to human rights were produced during this controversy. Some human rights scholars and activists saw the appeal to Asian values as an ideological attempt to justify authoritarian government, but it did provoke a debate about how the universal values of human rights should be reconciled with the world's cultural traditions.

The argument that the concept of human rights is an example of cultural imperialism is very problematic, for it assumes that at least one principle is universally valid: that imperialism is wrong. If we ask why imperialism is wrong, a plausible answer is that it violates certain human rights—particularly the **right to self-determination** and the prohibition of racial discrimination, but very likely also a further set of rights, such as those to freedom of expression, association, and protection from arbitrary arrest and imprisonment. The critique of imperialism does not justify the full dominant interpretation of human rights, but it does refute one common line of argument against universalism.

Another approach would be to reject all forms of universalism and to claim that all moral principles derive from *particular* cultures, that particular cultures are *diverse*, that some cultures reject at least some human rights principles, and that the dominant conception of human rights is valid only within the culture of the modern West. On this view, there is a human rights culture. But it is only one culture among many and, because it derives from Western secular liberalism, it is not particularly appealing, still less *obligatory*, for those who, perhaps on the basis of their religious beliefs, subscribe to non-liberal moral and political codes.

This argument avoids the self-contradiction of the anti-imperialist approach, but at considerable cost. The first difficulty is that the argument that all actual moral principles are justified by the cultures of which they form a part is another universal principle that cannot be used against universalism as such without self-contradiction. The next difficulty is that if all principles are justified by their cultures, then imperialism would be justified by imperialistic cultures—a view that is anathema to critics of human rights universalism. They could argue that, according to the criteria of their culture, imperialism is wrong, but they could not show would-be imperialists why they should act according to these criteria. In practice, most critics of human rights universalism accept that racism is universally wrong and cannot be justified by racist cultures like that of **apartheid** South Africa. A further difficulty with the 'culturalist' conception of morality is that actual cultures are complex, contested, and overlapping. There are, for examples, many schools of Islamic thought; there are disputes about the requirements of the religion and Islamic ideas have mixed with other ideas in different ways in different societies. The idea of a homogeneous culture that justifies particular moral ideas is a myth. The world is full of a great diversity of complex moral ideas, some of which cohere in different ways into patterns that are themselves subject to change, in part as the result of interaction with other cultures.

These arguments do not themselves provide a justification of human rights. Only a justificatory theory of human rights could do that, and any such theory is likely to be controversial not only between the West and the rest, but also within Western thought, and even among human rights supporters. They also imply no disrespect for culture as such. Culture provides meaning, value, and guidance to human life, and there is a human right to participate in the cultural life of one's community. They do show that cultures are not self-justifying and that we commit no logical or moral error in subjecting actual cultures to critical scrutiny. **Feminist** human rights scholars have argued that the appeal to culture has often been made in an attempt to justify the oppression of women.

Islam, human rights, and the war on terror(ism)

There have been tensions between the Islamic Middle East and the Christian West since at least the times of the medieval crusades. Modern problems arose in the First World War, when the conflicting parties sought to mobilize Muslim peoples to their cause. The victorious West, especially Britain and France, divided the Middle East into spheres of influence under the mandate system of the League of Nations. These territories became the familiar modern states of the Middle East, with considerable ethnic, religious, and political diversity, consequent instability, and difficulties in implementing policies of development.

The rise in oil prices in the early 1970s, the Islamic Revolution in Iran in 1979, the continuing Israel–Palestine conflict, and the relative failure of secular, **nationalist** governments in the Middle East to achieve development contributed to the rise of politico-religious Islamist parties and movements. In Afghanistan, Osama bin Laden, son of a rich Saudi businessman, had recruited non-Afghans to support the Afghan resistance to the Soviet occupiers. When Soviet troops withdrew from the country in 1988, bin Laden formed Al Qaeda to continue a *jihad* (holy war) against the perceived enemies of Islam. In 1990, the forces of the secular Iraqi regime of Saddam Hussein invaded Kuwait, the population of which is almost wholly Muslim. A US-led force, acting with UN authority and based in Saudi Arabia, expelled the Iraqi invaders from Kuwait. Following this war, several attacks on US and other targets were attributed to Al Qaeda, culminating in the attacks of 11 September 2001 ('9/11'). The United States responded by invading Afghanistan, the extremely conservative and authoritarian Islamic government of which, the Taliban, was believed to have

protected Al Qaeda. President Bush declared a 'war on terror'. The United States set up a detention camp in Guantanamo Bay, Cuba, where it held several hundred suspected terrorists without due process of law. Many countries introduced new anti-terrorists laws, which were criticized by NGOs for their neglect of human rights protections. After the United States and some of its allies invaded Iraq in 2003, serious human rights violations were committed by US troops and their allies. Allegations of torture by US forces in Afghanistan, Iraq, and at Guantanamo Bay, and charges of the 'rendition' (transportation) of suspects to other countries in which torture was common, were made by well-informed observers. Pictures of the mistreatment of Iraqi prisoners in the Abu Ghraib prison in Baghdad created an international scandal.

These events changed the context of the global human rights struggle, because the United States had become the only superpower; administration officials had, in both internal memoranda and public pronouncements, shown contempt for the United Nations, international law, and human rights. Many governments have used the war on terrorism as an excuse for increasing human rights violations. Although most Muslims oppose terrorism, the use of Islam by Al Qaeda to justify its actions, the widespread targeting of Muslims as suspected terrorists, and increasing tensions between Western secular liberals and many Muslims over the proper limits of freedom of expression all contributed to a crisis in the relations between Islam and the West. Human rights activists had to come to terms both with the war on terrorism and their own relations with Islam. This challenge was made more difficult both by the complexity of Islamic beliefs and the unwillingness of human rights activists to work out fully the philosophical basis of their commitments. The election of Barack Obama as US president in November 2008 was based in part on promises to end the human rights violations associated with the 'war on terror'. Expert observers generally believe that he has kept these promises only in part, although the limits of his achievements are partly the result of opposition both within and outside his own country. Thus, although there may be differences in values between some versions of Islam and human rights, especially relating to the **status** of women, the problems of human rights and Islam are probably more political and economic than philosophical.

Beginning in December 2010, protests broke out throughout the Middle East, popularly known as the

'Arab uprisings' or 'Arab Spring'. At the time of writing (mid-2016), the hopes of the protesters for democracy, an end to corruption, the protection of human rights, and more effective and just development policies had been largely frustrated throughout the region, with the possible exception of Tunisia. Egypt has reverted to a form of military dictatorship even more authoritarian than that against which the Arab uprisings demonstrators protested. Initially peaceful protests against the authoritarian rule of President Bashar al-Assad in Syria broke out early in 2011, but, following violent repression by government forces, these fractured into a multisided civil war, in which an extremely violent and conservative Islamist group, the so-called Islamic State, seized control of territory in Syria and Iraq, and perpetrated the most atrocious forms of human rights violations in the name of its version of Islam (see Chapter 21). The so-called Islamic State attracted recruits from many countries, including those of the West, and several terrorist attacks took place claiming support for that group or for Al Qaeda. At the time of writing, no solution to the civil war in Syria and Iraq was in sight, while governments and Muslim groups sought mutually acceptable forms of reconciliation.

> ## KEY POINTS
>
> - The argument that attempts to universalize human rights are imperialistic fails because it presupposes certain universal human rights.
>
> - The argument that all values are relative to culture is unconvincing, because cultures are not self-justifying and hardly anyone believes that anything done in the name of culture is justified.
>
> - The concept of human rights includes the right to practise one's culture, and thus human rights and culture may be compatible. Some cultural practices may, however, violate human rights standards.
>
> - The rise of **political Islam** and the so-called war on terror(ism) have raised new challenges for the human rights movement.

The New Political Economy of Human Rights

Marxists have traditionally argued that human rights conceal real inequalities of wealth and power. The inclusion of economic and social rights in the list of human rights has been intended to meet this criticism,

but its success has been very problematic: first, economic and social rights have been relatively neglected in international politics, compared with civil and political rights; and second, great inequalities of wealth and power persist worldwide. Nevertheless, some attempts have been made recently to integrate human rights with development and to improve poverty-reduction strategies.

Globalization

The concept of **globalization** is complex and controversial in the social sciences. It is nevertheless essential to understand the contemporary state of human rights. The idea of 'human rights' is a global idea and is supported by a global movement. Globalization has been opposed by a worldwide protest movement expressing various concerns, including world poverty, environmental degradation, and human rights. The targets of this movement have been primarily rich states, intergovernmental organizations dominated by rich states such as the World Trade Organization (WTO), and TNCs. The human rights movement has recently increased its concern about the role of TNCs in human rights violations, either directly (for example in relation to the employment of child labour) or in collaboration with repressive government. In 2005, the UN Commission on Human Rights asked the UN Secretary-General to appoint a Special Representative on human rights and TNCs and other business enterprises. In 2011, the Human Rights Council unanimously endorsed the Guiding Principles on Business and Human Rights based on the standards proposed by the Special Representative. An excellent NGO, the Business and Human Rights Resource Centre, tracks more than 6,000 companies and reports on human rights violations. The United Nations also has a Global Compact that invites companies to commit themselves to ten human rights, labour, environmental, and anti-corruption principles.

Empirical research on the impact of TNCs on human rights in developing countries has produced mixed results according to the different research methods used. There is no doubt that some TNCs are involved in human rights violations in developing countries, but the only generalizations about the effect of TNCs on human rights in developing countries that are justified by the evidence are that the impact of TNCs can be positive and can also be negative, and that no simple generalizations are valid.

There is also a global economic regime, consisting of organizations such as the Group of Seven (G7), the Group of Twenty (G20), the World Bank, the International Monetary Fund (IMF), and the WTO, which attempts to regulate global capitalism and the economies of the developing countries. The World Bank and the IMF are powerful actors in the international economy, and have traditionally been unconcerned with human rights. Critics have alleged that their policies have often been very harmful to human rights, especially economic and social rights. The World Bank has opened up a dialogue with NGOs and independent experts on human rights, but the outcomes of this process remain uncertain. The WTO is also accused of working to the disadvantage of the developing countries. The UN conception of human rights is a statist, social democratic idea, whereas the global economy, and the international financial institutions that are supposed to regulate it, are based on a neoliberal ideology that prefers vibrant markets and **weak states**. Recently, extreme neoliberalism has been somewhat modified by the belief that **good governance** and poverty reduction are necessary to development (see Chapter 15). The United Nations and the World Bank have claimed some success in poverty reduction, but the causes of this reduction are unclear, and almost certainly complex, and development successes are unevenly distributed both among and within countries.

A new approach to globalization and human rights is based on the concept of **human security** (see Chapter 13). This idea first appeared in the 1994 Human Development Report (UNDP 1993), which defined 'human security' as safety from a wide range of threats to human well-being, such as hunger, disease, and repression, as well as new threats, such as terrorism and climate change. The discourse of human security was intended to transform the familiar concept of state security, which was often used to violate human rights, to suggest that state security was best promoted by protecting the security of everyone. It was also intended to integrate humanitarian relief, development assistance, human rights promotion, and conflict resolution. The special vulnerability of women and children to the effects of conflict and poverty is often emphasized (see Box 18.3). The concept has, however, been criticized on several grounds: it is too broad and vague to generate clear obligations; it repeats, while ignoring, the established concept of human rights; it threatens to replace the legal obligations of states to protect human rights with policy options to protect human security; it undermines the discourse of the international human rights movement; and, by switching the

---

BOX 18.3 HUMAN SECURITY: THE CASE OF DARFUR

It took three months for Fatouma Moussa to collect enough firewood to justify a trip to sell it in the market town of Shangil Tobayi, half a day's drive by truck from here. It took just a few moments on Thursday for janjaweed militiamen, making a mockery of the new cease-fire, to steal the [US]$40 she had earned on the trip and rape her.

Speaking barely in a whisper, Ms Moussa, who is 18, gave a spare account of her ordeal.

'We found janjaweed at Amer Jadid,' she said, naming a village just a few miles north of her own. 'One woman was killed. I was raped.'

Officially, the cease-fire in Darfur went into effect last Monday.

[. . .]

But the reality was on grim display in this crossroads town, where Ms Moussa and other villagers were attacked Thursday as they rode home in a bus from Shangil Tobayi.

The Arab militiamen who attacked them killed 1 woman, wounded 6 villagers and raped 15 women, witnesses and victims said.

(Polgreen 2006)

Darfur is a region of western Sudan, about the size of France, with a population of approximately 6 million. It is composed of many ethnic groups, all Muslim, and has suffered from economic and social neglect since colonial times. The relative stability of Darfur was undermined by increased competition for diminishing land resources as a result of desertification, the emergence of a racist Arab ideology in Sudan, expansionist policies by Libya's Colonel Qaddafi in neighbouring Chad, and the intrusion of southern Sudanese rebels into Darfur. Darfurian self-defence organizations developed into a number of rebel forces. The Sudanese government sought to repress these rebellions by a savage counter-insurgency, employing Arab militias known as the *Janjaweed* ('evil horsemen'). A peace agreement was signed in Abuja, Nigeria, on 5 May 2006 by the Sudanese government and the largest rebel group, but not by other rebels. Estimates of those killed in the period 2003–06 range from 200,000 to 500,000; those displaced, more than 2 million; and those suffering deprivation, nearly 4 million. In July 2015, the United Nations reported that 2.7 million Darfuris remained in internally displaced persons camps and more than 4.7 million relied on humanitarian aid (UNHCR 2015).

emphasis from rights to security, it may legitimate the violation of rights in the name of security. Nevertheless, the concept may include threats to human well-being not adequately addressed by human rights, such as climate change, and to persons not well protected by human rights law, such as transnational migrants, refugees, and stateless persons. The concept of human security, carefully defined, could improve the concept of human rights and its implementation by connecting it systematically to problems, such as international crime, global finance, and climate change, which have not traditionally been addressed by the human rights movement. (See Chapter 19 for further discussion of this in relation to Pakistan.)

Globalization has also greatly increased migration. There are human rights to travel, and to seek and enjoy asylum from persecution in other countries. The UN Refugee Convention 1951 offers protection to refugees who can show a well-founded fear of persecution; it does not, however, recognize as refugees those fleeing war, starvation, or persecution who remain in their own country. The UN High Commissioner for Refugees (UNHCR) and many NGOs provide assistance to refugees, but their work is hampered by inadequate resources and the strict immigration policies of most developed countries. Development failures, increasing global inequality, improved communications and transportation technologies, persisting human rights violations, and conflict have increased global migration and asylum-seeking. The number of people displaced by war, conflict, or persecution reached a record of nearly 60 million in 2014; the proportion of women and children among the world's refugees has increased rapidly (UNHCR 2015). Some migrants benefit from migration, but many others are exploited and suffer from various human rights violations both during their migration and on arrival at their destination. Far more migrants die *every year* crossing from Mexico to the United States and from North Africa to southern Europe than died trying to cross the Berlin Wall *throughout its whole history* (Brian and Laczko 2014). Women and children migrants are particularly vulnerable to violations of their human rights.

Migrants often benefit 'host' countries economically by filling skill gaps and introducing entrepreneurship, although these effects are small. Immigration can lead to competition for jobs and services with less skilled and lower income citizens. Immigration can enrich the host culture, but also lead to cultural tensions. The benefits and costs of large-scale migration make it a controversial political issue, and give rise to anti-immigrant politics.

Migration also creates a 'brain drain' of skilled workers from developing countries, but remittances sent back to home countries, which amount to many times all aid sent by developed to developing countries, contributes to economic development. Most migrants move from developing to developed counties, but there are large-scale migrations within the **developing world**, for example from south Asia to the Persian Gulf. In 2014, developing countries hosted 86 per cent of the world's refugees; the least-developed countries (LDCs) provided asylum to 25 per cent of the global total (UNHCR 2015). Mass migration is a major political issue of the contemporary world, but, because it is driven by deep political and economic problems of globalization, it cannot be solved by anti-immigrant politics or restrictive immigration law. Solutions should recognize the human rights of all migrants, and address the political and economic causes of mass migration.

KEY POINTS

- Marxists have criticized human rights for obscuring inequalities of wealth and power inherent in capitalism, while, more recently, the anti-globalization movement has criticized globalization's implications for human rights.

- Global capitalist institutions are quite frequently involved in human rights violations, but the general relations between global capitalism and human rights are complex.

- The global economic regime that seeks to regulate global capitalism almost certainly has a major impact on human rights, but the nature of this impact is controversial.

- UN institutions and NGOs have recently placed more emphasis on transnational business organizations and human rights.

Conclusion

The concept of human rights became important in world politics only with the adoption of the Charter of the United Nations in 1945. Although it was derived from Western moral, legal, and political philosophy, it was declared to be universal. On the foundation of the UN Universal Declaration of Human Rights (1948), a large body of international human rights law has been elaborated. Most of this is legally binding on most states and the principles of the Declaration have been reaffirmed by all UN member states. Nevertheless, international procedures for implementing human rights are weak, human rights violations are common, and the concept of human rights is not universally accepted as culturally legitimate.

The main question raised by human rights in the developing countries is the relationship between development and human rights. This is a complex issue. There is more than one definition of 'development' and some definitions include human rights. There is, however, a widespread view that some restriction of human rights is a precondition of development and that development should take priority over human rights. There is no doubt that some countries have achieved rapid rates of economic development while violating civil and political rights. However, most rights-violating countries have poor records of development. The relations between human rights and development are still not well understood, but the evidence suggests that, generally, factors other than human rights are more important in promoting or obstructing development. The case for violating human rights for the sake of development is therefore much weaker than it has often been thought to be. The view that human rights are necessary for economic development is, however, not well supported by the evidence. There are also strong reasons for respecting human rights independently of their relation to development. Recently, international efforts have been made to integrate human rights and development.

Developing countries are often poor, which makes it difficult to fund the implementation of human rights. They may not want to do so because their governments are corrupt and unconcerned with human rights. They may not be able to because external agents, such as donor governments and/or international financial institutions, limit their capacity to do so by insisting on the reduction of state budgets.

The United Nations is right in seeing development and human rights as interdependent, in the sense that improvements in each makes the achievement of the other easier. Crises of development are often accompanied by crises of human rights, as countries such as Somalia, the Democratic Republic of Congo, and the countries of the 'Arab uprisings' show. Development success is good news for human rights—as South Korea and Taiwan illustrate—although the interests of elites and local cultures may limit human rights achievements, as in Singapore. Rwanda and Zimbabwe show that apparent initial success in development accompanied by human rights violations may lead to disaster for both human rights and development.

The process of globalization has been associated with the assertion of cultural difference. This has meant that the claim that human rights are universal, although often reaffirmed by UN member states, is constantly challenged. Some of these challenges express the interests of the powerful, who are reluctant to allow a voice to dissenters; others raise difficult questions about legitimating universal principles in a culturally diverse world. Debates about Asian values in the 1990s have been succeeded by debates about Islam and terrorism, but the underlying problems may be political and economic, rather than cultural or religious.

Arguments that the concept of human rights expresses the interests of the West or the rich are generally not convincing. Taking human rights seriously would most benefit the poorest and most oppressed. There is a danger, however, that Western states may discredit the concept by associating it with their own foreign policies motivated by their own interests. The cause of human rights will be damaged if it is—or if it is perceived to be—a new form of imperialism. Although human rights are now well established in great power politics, it may be that the best hope for their future lies with the increasing number of grass-roots movements in the developing countries.

?   QUESTIONS

1.   In what sense, if any, are human rights 'universal'?

2.   Is international human rights law adequate to address contemporary human rights problems?

3.   Are popular movements the best hope for the future of human rights?

4.   Is concern for human rights a help or a hindrance for development policies?

5.   Are the problems of Islam and human rights religious or political?

6.   Are Western governments blameworthy for human rights violations in developing countries?

7.   Should the human rights obligations of international institutions be strengthened?

8.   Is development a precondition of respect for human rights?

 FURTHER READING

Alston, P., and Robinson, M. (eds) (2005) *Human Rights and Development: Towards Mutual Reinforcement* (Oxford: Oxford University Press) Essays on the integration of human rights and development.

Bjørnskov, C., and Mchangama, J. (2013) 'Do Social Rights Affect Social Outcomes?', Aarhus Economics Working Papers No. 2013-18, available online at ftp://ftp.econ.au.dk/afn/wp/13/wp13_18.pdf Raises an empirical challenge to the value of legalizing economic and social rights.

Brian, T., and Laczko, F. (eds) (2014) *Fatal Journeys: Tracking Lives Lost during Migration* (Geneva: International Organization for Migration) Comprehensive study of migration deaths.

Brownlie, I., and Goodwin-Gill, G. S. (eds) (2010) *Basic Documents on Human Rights*, 6th edn (Oxford: Oxford University Press) Authoritative collection of international legal texts.

Collier, P. (2013) *Exodus: Immigration and Multiculturalism in the 21st Century* (London: Penguin Books) A learned and thought-provoking survey of contemporary migration issues.

Donnelly, J. (2013) *Universal Human Rights in Theory and Practice*, 3rd edn (Ithaca, NY: Cornell University Press) An introduction to the international conception of human rights and the principal issues of human rights implementation.

Forsythe, D. P. (2012) *Human Rights in International Relations*, 3rd edn (Cambridge: Cambridge University Press) An authoritative introduction to the topic.

Freeman, M. A. (2011) *Human Rights: An Interdisciplinary Perspective*, 2nd edn (Cambridge: Polity Press) A comprehensive introduction for social science students and law students who want a non-legal approach.

Howard-Hassmann, R. E. (2012) 'Human Security: Undermining Human Rights?', *Human Rights Quarterly*, 34(1): 88–112 Critical assessment of human security from a human rights perspective.

Langford, M. (ed.) (2008) *Social Rights Jurisprudence: Emerging Trends in International and Comparative Law* (Cambridge: Cambridge University Press) A wide-ranging survey of legal decisions on social rights.

Office of the United Nations High Commissioner for Human Rights (OHCHR) (2004) *Human Rights and Poverty Reduction* (New York and Geneva: United Nations) An influential analysis of the relations between human rights and development.

Pogge, T. (ed.) (2005) 'Symposium: World Poverty and Human Rights', *Ethics & International Affairs* 19(1): 1–83 Various approaches to the ethics of world poverty.

Sen, A. (1999a) *Development as Freedom* (Oxford: Oxford University Press) A thought-provoking argument for the mutual relations between development and freedom.

Sen, A. (1999b) 'Human Rights and Economic Achievements', in J. R. Bauer and D. A. Bell (eds) *The East Asian Challenge for Human Rights* (Cambridge: Cambridge University Press), 88–99 Reflections on 'Asian values'.

United Nations High Commissioner for Refugees (UNHCR) (2015) *World at War: UNHCR Global Trends—Forced Displacements in 2014* (Geneva: UNHCR) Valuable source of refugee trends.

Uvin, P. (2004) *Human Rights and Development* (Bloomfield, CT: Kumarian Press) A provocative critique of various attempts to integrate human rights and development.

 **WEB LINKS**

http://www.amnesty.org Amnesty International.

http://business-humanrights.org/ Business and Human Rights Resource Centre.

http://www.hrw.org Human Rights Watch (HRW).

http://www.ohchr.org Site of the Office of the UN High Commissioner for Human Rights (OHCHR), which is the best way into the UN human rights system.

 For additional material and resources, please visit the Online Resource Centre at:
http://www.oxfordtextbooks.co.uk/orc/burnell5e/

PART 5
Regime Change

This section includes three chapters providing case studies of regime change. As Chapter 14 has described, during the 1980s and 1990s there was huge academic interest in, and hopes for, a seemingly global 'third wave' of democratization. The term 'democratization' itself was central to analysis of political change in developing countries, with the understanding that democratic regimes were emerging out of preceding authoritarian regimes, whether based on personal dictatorships, or single-party or military rule.

As time passed, it became clear that there was no irresistible tide of democratization—except perhaps in the very, very long run. There were still significant countries, even regions, largely untouched by this trend and, at the same time, in many other countries, democratic beginnings were soon mired or corrupted, leading, as we have seen, to the coining of a range of neologisms indicating the different ways in which democracy had been compromised (for example **electoral authoritarianism**).

Accordingly, the focus in Part 5 is on **regime change**—or indeed the limits to regime change—without any necessary prior assumption of an underlying democratization process. Here, we understand a regime as a form or system of government (as distinct from the individual governments that take or yield power within its terms). Regimes can be defined in formal terms, but for a fuller characterization we may need to consider less formal, underlying characteristics and continuities. Our case study chapters—on Pakistan, Indonesia, and Syria, respectively—enable us to explore and illustrate these different aspects of the theme of regime change, in contrasting circumstances.

In the case of Pakistan, as David Taylor relates, there has been an almost bewildering succession of regimes, in formal terms at least. Post-independence, early, broadly democratic forms soon gave way to military, or military-bureaucratic, types of rule. There followed a brief and troubled quasi-democratic interlude in the 1970s, a decade of military rule under Zia, unstable democratic government through much of the 1990s, a further military coup led by Musharraf, and only from 2008 more freely contested government elections. Whilst on one level, then, Pakistan is characterized by regime instability, on another more profound level, according to Taylor, the military has remained a dominant force—possibly *the* dominant force—either directly or indirectly, in Pakistan's **politics**.

Indonesia appears to provide a contrasting case study. After more than thirty years of military-based rule under Suharto, democratic elections in 1998 ushered in a sustained era of competitive party politics. Gyda Marås Sindre argues that, from that time, Indonesian democracy remains a relative success story within the region. Even so, significant authoritarian elements persist.

Syria provides a contrast to both the other two countries: formally under extreme authoritarian rule, it allows of no democratic developments, but has effectively descended into a chaotic civil war, in which external powers play a key role. Authoritarian rule under the Ba'ath Party originated in the coup of 1963. Decades later, the popular 2011 uprising was inspired by democratic movements in other parts of the region—but, in the face of brutal suppression, it rapidly took on a militarized and sectarian form.

19

Pakistan
Regime Change and Military Power

David Taylor

Chapter contents

Overview

Since its creation in 1947, Pakistan has struggled to develop a system of sustainable democratic government. She has experienced a succession of regime changes, alternating between qualified or electoral democracy and either military or quasi-military rule. But underlying apparent instability and regime change, a continuing feature has been the central role of the military in the political process. This pattern is in stark contrast to India, despite their sharing the same colonial background. Ironically, the reintroduction of military rule has often been welcomed in Pakistan as a relief from the factional disputes among the civilian political leaders and accompanying high levels of corruption. This chapter describes Pakistan's history of regime change and explains the military's persistent influence, culminating in the period of rule by General Pervez Musharraf, from 1999 to 2008.

Figure 19.1 is a map of Pakistan and Box 19.1 provides an overview of key dates in Pakistan's history.

Introduction: From Independence to State Breakup in 1971

Pakistan's military forces—principally the army, which, numerically and politically, has always been the key player—have dominated the country for most of its history since independence. This has meant not only political power for extended periods, both direct and indirect, thus dominating the process of **regime change**, but also the pre-emption of a substantial share of economic resources. Defence expenditure was estimated by the Stockholm International Peace

Figure 19.1 Pakistan

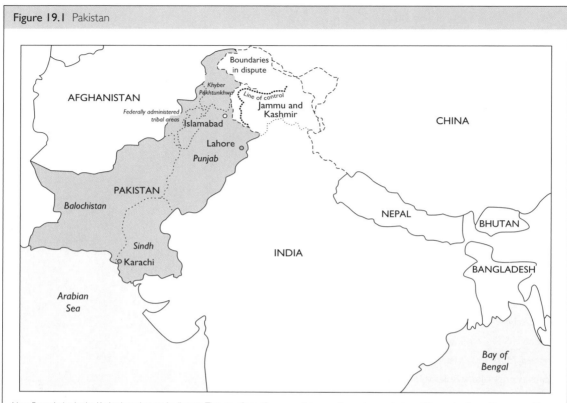

Note: Boundaries in the Kashmir region are in dispute. The use of specific nomenclature and boundary symbols on this map implies neither recognition nor non-recognition of the legality of the political regions or boundaries to which they refer.

BOX 19.1 KEY DATES IN PAKISTAN'S HISTORY

15 Aug 1947	Pakistan independence	Dec 1970	Elections give absolute majority to Awami League based in East Pakistan
11 Sept 1948	Independence leader Muhammad Ali Jinnah dies	Dec 1971	Indian intervention brings about defeat of Pakistan army and separation of Bangladesh
Feb 1954	Pakistan joins a US-led cold war military alliance	Jan 1972	Zulfikar Ali Bhutto, leader of the Pakistan People's Party (PPP), becomes president (later prime minister)
Mar 1956	First constitution passed (but never fully implemented)	Apr 1977	General election returns Bhutto to power, but opposition launches agitation, claiming results were rigged
Oct 1958	General Ayub Khan carries out first military coup		
Feb 1960	Ayub Khan becomes president through indirect election	July 1977	Military coup led by General Zia-ul-Haq
Mar 1962	New constitution passed	Apr 1979	Bhutto executed
Sept 1965	Indecisive war with India	Dec 1984	Referendum gives Zia basis to become president
Mar 1969	Ayub Khan forced to hand over power to General Yahya Khan	Aug 1988	Zia killed when his plane is blown up

Nov 1988	Elections bring Benazir Bhutto (daughter of Zulfikar Ali Bhutto) to power	Oct 2007	Musharraf stands down as army chief
May 1998	Pakistan tests nuclear devices	Dec 2007	Benazir Bhutto assassinated
Oct 1999	Military coup led by General Pervez Musharraf	Feb 2008	Elections bring PPP back to power
Apr 2002	Referendum makes Musharraf president	Aug 2008	Musharraf resigns as president, succeeded by PPP leader, Asif Ali Zardari, widower of Benazir Bhutto
Oct 2002	Elections bring to power the Pakistan Muslim League (Quaid) (PML(Q)), a party sympathetic to Musharraf	Mar 2013	Elections won by Pakistan Muslim League; its leader, Nawaz Sharif, forms coalition government and becomes prime minister
Mar 2007	Chief justice of Pakistan suspended by president		

Research Institute at 3.1 per cent of gross domestic product (GDP) in 2015, a figure that remains the highest in the region (SIPRI 2015). Defence consumes almost as much as the total federal expenditure on social and economic development. The army (excluding paramilitary forces) is 550,000-strong and many more depend on the army directly or indirectly for employment. Internationally, the image of Pakistan as a **garrison state**, although acceptable at times to the United States and other Western powers, has often created difficulties, for example the country's suspension from the Commonwealth after the 1999 military coup until 2004. A garrison state is a state maintained by military power and, in some definitions, is a state organized primarily around the need for military security.

The dominance of the military in Pakistan has been explained in different ways. Some analysts note the way in which Pakistan inherited a strong army from the colonial state (which based its policy on a racially based classification of Indians into martial and non-martial groups); others see it as an aspect of a social order still dominated by landowning groups. The two arguments come together in the fact that the army has traditionally been recruited very heavily from rural areas of the Punjab—the most populous of the country's four provinces—and from adjacent areas of the North-West Frontier Province (renamed Khyber Pakhtunkhwa in April 2010), although the officer corps is increasingly coming from more urban and middle-class families, and efforts have been made to broaden the base of the rank-and-file. The army thus tends to share a strong sense of Pakistan as a unitary state. Regional and international factors are also important, with Pakistan's long-running conflict with India over Kashmir and the cold war both influential in enhancing the role of the army.

When British India became independent in 1947, and was simultaneously divided into the two successor states of India and Pakistan, the armed forces were similarly divided. As a result of previous recruitment policies, Pakistan got more than its proportionate share of soldiers. It also inherited a social structure in which control of land and of the people who worked the land was the single most important basis of political power. Political parties were weak.

At first, the unchallenged authority wielded by Muhammad Ali Jinnah, who had led the Pakistan movement from its inception, kept tensions between provinces, and between locals and newcomers, in check. However, after his death in 1948, the country lacked political leadership of national standing. While popular leaders emerged in the eastern wing of the country (now Bangladesh), in the west (from where the army was recruited) provincial politicians battled for local control with little regard to national issues.

At the same time as Pakistan was facing difficulties in establishing stable structures of government, there was a belief that India's leaders did not truly accept the existence of Pakistan and would miss no opportunity to sabotage it. The distrust soon found a focus in the conflict over the princely state of Jammu and Kashmir, which erupted into war in October 1947 until a truce under United Nations auspices was negotiated in August 1948.

The weakness of Pakistan's political **institutions** and perceived need for security against a more powerful India meant that the army as an institution became increasingly important in Pakistan's public life. General Ayub Khan, the first Pakistani commander-in-chief of the army, became minister of defence for a period in 1954 and played a key role in bringing Pakistan into the US-led military alliance system that was constructed in Asia in the early 1950s. A complementary development was the assertion of the role of the bureaucracy and judiciary as guardians of the state in the absence of strong national leadership and in the face of challenges to the dominance of the established social order, in particular of the Punjab. While not identical, the social base of the army and the bureaucracy overlapped, and their perceptions of Pakistan were similar.

Under the constitution that had been adopted in 1956, Pakistan's first parliamentary elections were due in 1958. To avoid the accession to power of H. S. Suhrawardy, a politician based in East Bengal, President Iskander Mirza declared martial law. Shortly afterwards, Ayub Khan assumed political control, sending Mirza into exile. Ayub Khan was able to obtain a judgment from the Supreme Court authorizing his rule. He also conducted a campaign against the political leaders whom he had displaced. Hundreds of politicians were disqualified from further political activity, on the grounds of **corruption**. This was complemented by an analysis of the situation that seemed to draw both on colonial assumptions and on some of the contemporary thinking in the United States, for example by political scientist Samuel P. Huntington, about economic and political development. Pakistan was seen as a society that needed firm leadership if it was to enjoy healthy national development.

Building on this analysis, Ayub Khan initiated what was called the 'basic democracies' system, which brought around 80,000 local leaders and notables as so-called basic democrats into **politics** on a non-party basis. As well as electing a national assembly, they formed an electoral college for the presidency and, in 1960, Ayub Khan was duly elected to this office. This enabled him to dispense with martial law and to formulate a new constitution for the country—brought into effect in 1962. This defined Pakistan as a progressive Muslim state, pursuing policies that reflected a dynamic interpretation of religious values. In line with this, in 1961 Ayub Khan's government issued the Family Laws Ordinance, which introduced reforms in the area of marriage and divorce, significantly improving the rights of women. Ayub Khan was nevertheless unable to cope with the increasing alienation of East Bengal, and in elections for the basic democrats and subsequently for the presidency in 1964–65, he was unable to gain a majority there.

Growing discontent in both parts of the country, especially after an abortive attempt to seize Kashmir led to war with India in September 1965, appeared to indicate that a democratic upsurge was about to dislodge Ayub Khan, but this was pre-empted in March 1969 by a fresh military intervention, again led by the army chief—on this occasion, General Yahya Khan.

In a break with his predecessor's policy, General Khan promised direct parliamentary elections, which were held in December 1970—the first to be held since independence and the first on the basis of 'one person. one vote'. East Pakistan, which held a demographic majority, voted overwhelmingly for Sheikh Mujibur Rahman's Awami League; Zulfikar Ali Bhutto, a former protégé of Ayub Khan who had established his own Pakistan People's Party (PPP) in 1967, won convincingly in the west, but on a smaller scale. Sheikh Mujibur Rahman's insistence on his right to unfettered power was rejected both by the army and by West Pakistan's politicians, and in March 1971 the army deployed force to assert the authority of the (west) Pakistan state and to terrorize the population. By most estimates, there were hundreds of thousands, or even millions, of civilian deaths (in some cases, the victims of retaliatory attacks) and many more crossed the border to India as refugees. Indian intervention led to a decisive military defeat for Pakistan, providing the opportunity for Bhutto to take over in the west and ushering in the creation of Bangladesh in the east.

KEY POINTS

- Pakistan has been dominated by the army since its creation in 1947. Social and political factors, as well as the cold war context, have contributed to this situation.

- Pakistan's state structures derive from the colonial period; the colonial army was recruited heavily from the areas of British India that became Pakistan in 1947—especially the Punjab.

- Because conflict with India, especially over Kashmir, has fostered insecurity, the army has been able to place its needs and requirements at the centre of political life.

- Ayub Khan, Pakistan's first military ruler following the 1958 coup, attempted to develop an alternative political structure based on mobilization of rural leadership.

- The unsuccessful 1965 war with India ultimately led to Ayub Khan's downfall. The failure of his successor, General Yahya Khan, over Bangladesh led to the latter's displacement by a civilian politician, Zulfikar Ali Bhutto.

Unstable Government from 1971 to 1999

The Bhutto era represented an attempt at a politics of **populism**, but by using the apparatus of the state to achieve his ends, Bhutto remained caught within its folds. The army, as an institution, remained a central actor, being used in 1974 to put down an internal rising in the province of Balochistan. The personalization of power by Bhutto alienated many army officers. In 1977, he faced a political crisis largely of his own making when he was accused by the opposition parties of rigging elections. Following three months of continuous agitation in the main cities, the army, headed by General Zia-ul-Haq (whom Bhutto had promoted ahead of more senior generals in the belief that Zia had no political ambitions), intervened and called for fresh elections.

Bhutto's evident popularity among his supporters led Zia to have him rearrested and the elections postponed. Bhutto was controversially arraigned on murder charges and executed in April 1979, after a split judicial decision. A feature of the Zia period was the expansion of the armed forces' intelligence service, the Directorate of Inter-Services Intelligence (ISI). As well as managing Pakistan's involvement in the Afghan conflict, as a result of which it developed close links with selected Islamist leaders, the ISI began systematically to monitor the activities of political parties. More generally, Zia gave strong encouragement to the growth of Islamist sentiment in the army, a shift most noticeable among the more junior ranks.

During the early 1980s, Zia pressed ahead with the Islamization of the country's institutions, for example introducing changes to the banking system to eliminate the payment of interest. One major series of initiatives that attracted worldwide attention was a redefinition of the legal position of women. Their standing as witnesses in legal cases was reduced to half that of men, and rules on pre- and extramarital sexual relations were made more punitive in ways that especially disadvantaged women. This was in direct contrast to the progressive stance on **gender** issues taken by Ayub Khan and other senior army figures. (For an account of the women's movement in Pakistan, see Chapter 9.)

In 1985, Zia felt strong enough to end the period of direct martial rule, reintroducing a heavily modified constitution that gave the president sweeping discretionary powers. This had been preceded by a referendum that was widely regarded as bogus, but which enabled him to claim a five-year term as president. In August 1988, he was killed by a bomb planted on his plane. Many theories have been advanced, but it is still not certain who the perpetrators were.

After Zia's death, elections brought the PPP back to power, under the leadership of Bhutto's daughter Benazir, and she alternated in office with Nawaz Sharif, the other major civilian political leader, whose power base lay in the Punjab and who had originally been inducted into politics by Zia. A major role was also played by the Muttahida Qaumi movement, a party representing the Urdu-speaking population of Karachi and in whose creation Zia had again played a part. In eleven years, there were four elections. This might appear an interlude of democratic politics, with political parties competing for control of government, but throughout effective power was, in fact, shared between the political leadership, the army, and sections of the civilian bureaucracy. This uneasy arrangement produced constant difficulty. In 1993, a deadlock between President Ghulam Ishaq Khan, a former senior civil servant who had been close to Zia, and Prime Minister Nawaz Sharif was eventually resolved through the intervention of the army chief, who insisted that both resign prior to new elections under a neutral caretaker prime minister. Nawaz Sharif returned to power in 1997 and succeeded in amending the constitution to restrict the powers of the president. He also forced General Jehangir Karamat, the army chief, to resign in 1998 and appointed as his successor General Pervez Musharraf. Musharraf nevertheless reasserted the right of the army to take part in policymaking by unilaterally embarking on a military adventure in the Kargil district of Kashmir in 1999. The fighting—the most intense since 1971—was brought to an end through US diplomatic pressure and without any gains by Pakistan. This left the army and the government deeply suspicious of each other. In October, General Musharraf launched a military coup to prevent his own dismissal.

KEY POINTS

- Bhutto's failed attempt at populist politics, bypassing the military, triggered a coup by General Zia-ul-Haq in 1977 and Bhutto's execution in 1979.

- Zia's political strategy relied heavily on presenting himself and the army as the guardians of Pakistan's Islamic goals.

- Following Zia's assassination, the period 1988–99 saw unstable civilian governments, with the army and the bureaucracy continuing to exercise power behind the scenes.

- A failed military adventure over Kashmir in 1999 ultimately generated a further military coup led by General Pervez Musharraf.

General Musharraf's Rule from 1999 to 2008

Coming after a period of instability, Musharraf's rule began with substantial popular support. He promised action against the more notoriously corrupt politicians and bureaucrats, and seemed in tune with the aspirations of many of Pakistan's urban population for a more liberal lifestyle. He gained credit for a bold move to open up the electronic media to private ownership, although his willingness to support US intervention in Afghanistan after the **terrorist** attacks of 11 September 2001 ('9/11') was unpopular in many quarters. The question that he had to resolve, however, was how quickly to return to civilian rule while maintaining his own and the army's decisive power to intervene in areas that were deemed critical to national interests.

Musharraf's initial political moves echoed previous military rulers' strategies, for example by holding a referendum in 2002 to make himself president and increasing devolution of administration to the local level. Elections in 2002 were fought on a party basis, but the leaders of the two main parties, who were both based abroad, were unable to participate directly, and a government-backed breakaway faction of the Pakistan Muslim League (PML(Q)), known popularly as the 'King's Party', was able to win a plurality of seats and form a government. Musharraf also came to a tactical agreement with the main Islamist parties. These moves only heightened the contradictions in his efforts to remain above civilian politics. They also acted as a brake on his efforts to reform the law on sexual offences, in which regard only a very modest measure could be passed in 2006. Both of the main political parties continued to demand that he leave office.

In March 2007, Musharraf took the dramatic step of suspending the chief justice of Pakistan, allegedly because of abuse of power, but in reality for fear that the Supreme Court would rule against him on key political and constitutional issues. The decision provoked nationwide protests led by the lawyers and, in November, Musharraf imposed a state of emergency. The assassination of Benazir Bhutto at the end of the year, apparently by Islamist militants, changed the political landscape yet again and the PPP won the elections that were eventually held in February 2008. In August, Musharraf was forced to resign and Benazir Bhutto's widower, Asif Ali Zardari, succeeded him.

One major reason for Musharraf's long survival was that he enjoyed the political and financial support of the United States, anxious to retain Pakistani support in its battle with militant groups in Afghanistan and in Pakistan itself; towards the end of his period in office, however, the United States, concerned about the need for civilian cover, put increasing pressure on Musharraf for a negotiated handover of power to elected politicians. Another reason for his survival was the relatively strong performance of the economy, buoyed by increased inflows of funds both from official donors following Pakistan's strategic importance in the wake of 9/11 and from diaspora Pakistanis. Inflation was brought under control and industrial production picked up, although poverty levels remained stubbornly high.

KEY POINTS

- Musharraf responded to 9/11 by giving full support to the United States, although this was unpopular with some sections of the population.
- Like his predecessors, Musharraf sought to discredit existing political leaders and to build a party loyal to himself; he amended the constitution to increase his discretionary powers as president.
- Musharraf's popular support declined steadily; he tried to divide the political parties, but in the end was unable to maintain his juggling act.

Conclusion: Military Rule or Military Influence

Since the 2008 elections, Pakistan has seen continuous civilian rule based on regular elections and universal suffrage. In elections held in 2013, Zardari's PPP was defeated by Nawaz Sharif's Muslim League—the first time in the country's history that such a transition had taken place. A major factor in the re-establishment of civilian rule has been the evident desire by the army, headed from 2008 to 2013 by General Ashfaq Kayani and since 2013 by General Raheel Sharif, to withdraw from direct political involvement. It has also been reinforced by the growth of a middle class, based in Pakistan's rapidly expanding cities. Yet there is no clear consensus on what sort of state Pakistan should be and the existence, for example, of a strong lobby for the strict implementation of the blasphemy laws demonstrates some of the tensions that cannot easily be resolved. Civilian governments, despite their democratic mandate, are seen by many as corrupt and self-serving.

Despite the appearance of a return to civilian dominance, the army has remained deeply involved in the political process, both through insisting on a major say in policymaking in areas such as defence, foreign policy, and anti-corruption, and by manipulating political forces to ensure favourable conditions for the armed forces. Examples of this involvement include the reconstitution of the national security council in August 2013 with a strong armed forces representation, the army's role in mediating a political crisis in August 2014, and the decisions in 2014 and 2015 to launch major attacks ('Operation Zarb-e-Azb') on militant groups along the frontier with Afghanistan. The armed forces have also resisted attempts to raise questions of abuse of **human rights** in the course of military action. This has been a special issue in the course of their extended campaigns against separatist groups in Balochistan, where it is claimed that the armed forces have been responsible for hundreds of extrajudicial killings.

This continuing involvement of the armed forces can be seen in the context of a discourse on politics that has developed since 1947 and is shared not only by the military, but also by some other sections of society who distrust democracy as it currently functions in Pakistan. Politics, as it has commonly been practised, is conceived as an aspect of the 'feudal' phase of Pakistani history. To break its hold, the argument is made that the army may need to intervene to help the process along. The 'ordinary' Pakistani is a key figure in this discourse and is brought into politics through carefully tailored institutions from which party politics are excluded, at least on the surface. The acquisition by Pakistan of nuclear weapons in the late 1990s, carefully guarded by the army, has heightened the sense that the armed forces have a unique role to play in the survival of the state.

In the words of one recent analyst, Aqil Shah, the armed forces of Pakistan have arrogated to themselves a tutelary role in the country's affairs. This gives the senior ranks—especially the powerful leadership of the ISI—some of the characteristics of what has been described in countries such as Egypt and Turkey as the 'deep state'—that is, a set of structures that have the capacity to override the agenda of elected regimes and to impose their own priorities on them. This raises a major issue for the analysis of electoral politics and the transition from one set of political leaders to another: if the armed forces play such a major role in key areas of political life, do elections and changes of government really matter that much?

While the army leadership projects itself as the guardian of the national interest, it is often seen by others as primarily concerned with its own interests. Retired officers are frequently appointed to senior administrative positions and given preferential treatment—most significantly, the allocation of prime rural and urban land. The armed forces—the army, in particular—have major business interests, such as the Fauji (Military) Foundation, the profits of which go to support welfare programmes, primarily, but not exclusively, aimed at army veterans and their families. Nothing has changed in this respect in recent years.

A key challenge to the army since the beginning of the 2000s is the initiation of internal security operations against Islamic militant groups, some of whom have, since the end of 2007, fought under the banner of the Tehrik-i-Taliban Pakistan (TTP). In 2008–09, the army fought major battles in the Swat valley in Khyber Pakhtunkhwa before it could be recaptured from the militants. There has also been fierce fighting along the Afghan border. Army losses in these campaigns and the evident difficulty of bringing the insurgency under control are themselves worrisome, but more serious is the risk that they pose to the internal coherence of the army itself. Some members of the armed forces are sympathetic to Islamist ideas, and also resent the actions of the Americans in Iraq and Afghanistan, especially the targeting of militants on Pakistani territory and the deaths of innocent bystanders in US drone attacks. The death of Osama bin Laden at US hands in an army-dominated town near Islamabad was both an embarrassment and also, to many, a provocation. The possibility of a coup within the army (as against the pattern to date, whereby all four coups have been carried out by the army as an institution) cannot be ruled out. The massacre of 141 people, most of them pupils, at an army school in Peshawar in December 2014 by militants associated with the TTP brought the army and public opinion together in outrage, but nevertheless illustrates the depth of the challenges posed by militants.

Some army leaders believe that Pakistan cannot sustain a political system that does not give a major role to the armed forces. Turkey is often cited as a parallel example. Some civilians share this view, but many more reject it, especially in the smaller provinces.

However, until there has been a lengthy spell of civilian rule under a prime minister or president who has the skills to wean the army away from its current set of assumptions without provoking a backlash, while promoting the further development of **civil society** organizations and **social movements**, further direct or indirect military intervention in politics remains a constant possibility.

QUESTIONS

1.   What policies did the colonial state pursue that prepared the way for recurrent military intervention in politics after independence?

2.   'More apparent than real.' Comment on this assessment of frequent regime change in Pakistan.

3.   Compare and contrast the political strategies of Generals Ayub Khan, Zia-ul-Haq, and Pervez Musharraf.

4.   Discuss the implications of military rule and influence for gender relations in Pakistan.

5.   Assess the prospects for democratic consolidation in Pakistan over the next five years.

6.   What factors constrain the Pakistan army's ability to repress Islamist militancy?

FURTHER READING

Ali, T. (1983) *Can Pakistan Survive? The Death of a State* (Harmondsworth: Penguin) Highly critical analysis by a leading journalist and political activist.

Cohen, S. P. (2002) *The Pakistan Army* (Karachi: Oxford University Press) Based on extensive interactions with the Pakistan army's leadership, this carefully documented analysis of the history and development of the army is coupled with a discussion of its political attitudes.

Dewey, C. (1999) 'The Rural Roots of Pakistani Militarism', in D. A. Low (ed.) *The Political Inheritance of Pakistan* (Basingstoke: Macmillan), 255–83 The author is a historian of the Punjab and relates the persistence of military influence to the army's embeddedness in the structures of power in rural society.

Fair, C. (2014) *Fighting to the End: The Pakistan Army's Way of War* (New York: Oxford University Press) The author is a prominent American specialist on Pakistan who, in this work, explores in detail the Pakistan army's self-image as the defender of the nation.

Jaffrelot, C. (2015) *The Pakistan Paradox: Instability and Resilience* (London: Hurst & Co.) A reflective and insightful history of contemporary Pakistan that includes substantial discussion of the relationship between the army and the state.

Jalal, A. (1990) *State of Martial Rule: The Origins of Pakistan's Political Economy of Defence* (Cambridge: Cambridge University Press) A detailed study of the process by which the Pakistan army became central to the Pakistan state. The author locates internal processes within the general cold war context.

Lieven, A. (2012) *Pakistan: A Hard Country* (London: Allen Lane) Written by a journalist-turned-academic, the book provides an up-to-date survey of the issues facing Pakistan.

Musharraf, P. (2006) *In the Line of Fire* (London: Simon & Schuster) General Musharraf's own (ghostwritten) account of his life and times.

Shah, A. (2014) *The Army and Democracy: Military Politics in Pakistan* (Cambridge, MA: Harvard University Press) A comprehensive, fine-grained study of the subject.

Siddiqa, A. (2007) *Military Inc.: Inside Pakistan's Military Economy* (London: Pluto Press) This work documents and analyses the extent of the Pakistan army's involvement in the civilian economy.

Talbot, I. (1998) *Pakistan: A Modern History* (London: Hurst & Co.) The most reliable of recent histories of the country. Talbot has a strong sense of the provincial roots of contemporary Pakistan.

WEB LINKS

http://countrystudies.us/pakistan/   A detailed US-based compilation of information on the history, economy, society, and politics of Pakistan.

http://www.sacw.net/   The South Asia Citizens Web is an independent space that provides exchanges of information between and about citizen initiatives in South Asia.

For additional material and resources, please visit the Online Resource Centre at:
http://www.oxfordtextbooks.co.uk/orc/burnell5e/

20

Indonesia
Dynamics of Regime Change

Gyda Marås Sindre

Overview

Since the start of the new millennium, Indonesia has been rated one of the few success stories in the post-1970s wave of democratization in the Global South. This chapter traces the dynamics of regime change in Indonesia since 1998, focusing on the dynamics of political mobilization against the backdrop of institutional reform.

Figure 20.1 is a map of Indonesia, Box 20.1 provides an overview of key dates in Indonesia's history, and Box 20.2 is a glossary of Indonesian terms used throughout this chapter.

Introduction

In the decade since the collapse of the 'New Order'— that is, the authoritarian military-based regime that governed Indonesia in the period 1966–98—Indonesia has become one of the few success stories in the post-1970s wave of democratization in the Global South. It is not only deemed the most stable and the freest democracy in South East Asia, but also remains the region's largest and fastest growing economy (Reid 2012). The 2014 presidential elections saw Joko Widodo ('Jokowi'), a former businessman, win over his

Figure 20.1 Indonesia

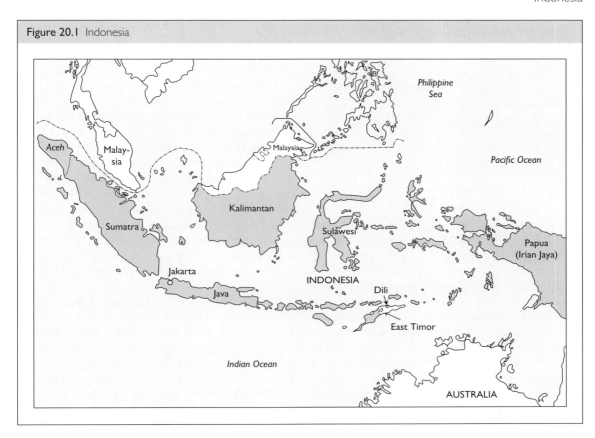

BOX 20.1 KEY DATES IN INDONESIA'S HISTORY

1942	Japanese military forces occupy Netherlands East Indies—territory that will become Indonesia
1945	Nationalist leaders proclaim Indonesia's independence
1945–49	Nationalists mobilize against Dutch colonial powers and ruling elite in bloody war of independence known as 'National Revolution'
1949	Dutch colonial forces withdraw; nationalist leader Sukarno becomes first president of Republic of Indonesia
1955	Indonesia's first parliamentary elections and only democratic elections until 1998
1965	Following a failed coup attempt in Jakarta, army begins massacres of communists and leftists
1966	President Suharto takes power; New Order begins
1997	Asian financial crisis, in which Indonesia is one of countries hardest hit
1998	Nationwide protests force resignation of President Suharto, marking beginning of reform period and transition to democracy
1999	First post-New-Order democratic elections; East Timor votes to become independent
2002	Indonesia recognizes East Timor's independence
2004	Susilo Bambang Yodhoyono (SBY) from Partai Demokrat is elected president in first direct elections for president
2005	Separatist conflict in Aceh ends with signing of peace agreement between Free Aceh Movement (GAM) and Indonesian government
2009	Third democratic elections held; SBY elected for second term
2014	Joko Widodo, former mayor of Jakarta (PDI-P), is elected president, defeating former New Order General Prabowo Subianto from Gerindra

BOX 20.2 INDONESIAN GLOSSARY

aliran Political cleavages reflecting social streams.
pancasila The New Order's state ideology based on five principles: belief in one god; humanitarianism; national unity; consultative democracy; and social justice.
pilkada Direct elections for governors, mayors, and regents.
Sharia Islamic law.
transmigrasi A New Order policy aimed at moving people from overpopulated areas to less densely populated areas.

contender Prabowo Subianto, a former special forces general and son-in-law of New Order leader General Suharto. Jokowi has no links to the past regime; rather, Jokowi is a product of the 'new' democratic Indonesia. His political career started when he became mayor of a small town. He rose to political prominence as governor of Indonesia's capital, Jakarta, and was subsequently endorsed as presidential candidate by the Indonesian Democratic Party of Struggle (PDI-P), one of the largest parties in Indonesia. Although, in many ways, Jokowi's victory is a sign that Indonesian democracy remains stable and is progressing in some arenas, the small margin by which he won the electoral race (a mere 53 per cent of the vote), is a sign that authoritarian tendencies still prevail. More important than his past as a former military general with a shady **human rights** record was the fact that Prabowo mobilized on a political platform that would set Indonesia back several steps in terms of democratic freedoms. Thus the 2014 presidential race encapsulated a general trend of post-authoritarian political dynamics in Indonesia—namely, the contestation between new and old political forces, between those moving the democratization process forward and those holding on to authoritarian tendencies. That the country fell from being ranked 'Free' for eight consecutive years since 2006 to become 'Partly Free' in 2014 is a sign that Indonesian democracy is facing severe challenges (Freedom House 2014).

Authoritarian Legacies

The archipelago that makes up Indonesia today was a former Dutch colony, the Dutch East Indies, which was, for a brief period, under Japanese control (1942–1945).

The war of independence, or the National Revolution as it is also known, lasted from 1945, when Indonesian **nationalists** declared independence, until 1949, when the Netherlands withdrew. In the period 1945–57, Indonesia's first president, Sukarno, experimented with liberal democracy, but increased political instability and intra-elite rivalry saw Sukarno assume authoritarian powers in 1957. In 1965, the army, led by General Suharto, crushed an apparent coup by the Indonesian Communist Party (PKI). During the next two years, acts of mass violence were perpetrated against suspected PKI members, resulting in an estimate of between 500,000 and 1 million deaths (Cribb and Kahin 2004: 264), and the eradication of one of the world's largest communist movements. With military backing, Suharto formally became president in 1968, marking the onset of a regime that came to be known as the 'New Order'.

To grasp the dynamics of **regime change** and democratization in Indonesia, it is imperative to understand some of the key features of the New Order regime. The legacies of the New Order include the predominance of oligarchic business elites that control the country's natural resources, endemic **corruption** at all levels of government, a weak and fractured political opposition, the politicization of Islam, and a strong military that continues to interfere in civilian **politics**. The New Order was a military dictatorship, but not in the strictest sense; rather, Suharto ruled through civilian structures with support of the military. The regime is classically characterized as a neo-patrimonial system, depicting a patron–client system in which a ruling coalition occupied the state apparatus and controlled the national economy. The neo-patrimonial arrangements of the New Order reflected the interplay of **clientelistic** and capitalist mechanisms. Naming himself 'the Father of Development', Suharto ensured that his circle of family and friends from the business community and the military were granted control over state corporations, monopolies, and government agencies (Bünte and Ufen 2009). He ruled by the guiding principle *pancasila*, a concept that emphasized national unity and cohesion. The image was of a 'family state' (*Negara Keluargaan*), underlining cooperation and the absence of conflict. In the long run, this strategy was a way of depoliticizing society by limiting opportunities and room for political mobilization. The depoliticizing of society entailed the formalization and incorporation of political parties and associations into the state. For instance, all political parties were forced to undergo a fusion into three political parties that were meant to represent three main segments in society: the state party—that is, President Suharto's own party—*Golongan Karya* (Functional Group), known as 'Golkar'; the United Development Party (PPP), which endorsed all Muslims; and the Indonesian Democratic Party (PDI), which was meant to represent secular nationalists (Ufen 2009). The Party Law of 1975 allowed for only Golkar to establish party branches across the county, while the other two parties fulfilled the function of highly restricted opposition parties in parliament. The regime also controlled and incorporated into the state other associations such as trade unions, women's groups, youth groups, and religious groups. This strictly controlled system of regime-sanctioned associations and the creation of a well-organized and well-funded catch-all party, Golkar, which remains one of the dominant parties in post-Suharto Indonesia, were key legacies of the New Order regime (Tomsa 2008). The regime's political **legitimacy** came from its ability to maintain rapid economic growth. The regime's hold on power resulted from social control enabled by the military's dominance within all streams of political, social, and economic life.

In the 1990s, this system became increasingly unstable. The politics of liberalization and protectionism encouraged by organizations such as the World Bank and the International Monetary Fund (IMF) created an unstable economic climate, which contributed to Indonesia being particularly hard-hit by the 1997 Asian economic crisis. At the same time, Suharto faced increased opposition both from moderates within his own regime and from an increasingly active **civil society**. What followed was an economic collapse that triggered student-led uprisings and the forced resignation of Suharto in May 1998. Hence the transition itself was based on a pact between moderates within the regime and the opposition, to the exclusion of the regime-friendly hardliners who supported continued authoritarianism. The year 1998 therefore marks the end of authoritarianism and the beginning of *reformasi*—that is, the period characterized by the rapid and relatively smooth implementation of widespread democratic reforms. In just a few years, political parties multiplied, the military formally withdrew from national politics, the press became one of the freest in Asia, and power was decentralized to the regions.

KEY POINTS

- The New Order regime was a neo-patrimonial system with power distributed between Suharto's extended family members and friends from business and the military.

- Suharto's legitimacy was tied to his ability to ensure economic growth, while enforcing social cohesion and suppressing dissent secured his hold on power.

- Economic collapse, internal dissent by moderates, and popular dissent contributed to the end of the New Order regime.

Democratization and Decentralization

Immediately after 1998, the new government undertook a radical reform agenda of decentralization with the aims of making governments more responsive to local needs and of appeasing regional dissent. Prior to 1998, all political power had been centred almost exclusively in Jakarta, where more than 70 per cent of the money of the national economy circulated; with decentralization, the relationship between the centre and the regions changed dramatically. The process was supported by the international agencies such as the World Bank, under the pretext that less state involvement would result in more and better markets, and by **non-governmental organization (NGO)** activists who argued that the suppressive state could be counterbalanced by moving power closer to the people (see Aspinall and Fealy 2003; Aspinall 2013). Thus democracy and decentralization became two mutually reinforcing processes that were expected to enhance **good governance**, strengthen the role of civil society, forward economic development, and ensure more accountable government (Aspinall 2013).

Decentralization was a complex and multifaceted process. Administratively, decentralization involved the transfer of political authority and administrative powers to provinces, districts, and municipalities. Regional autonomy laws gave increased powers to elected parliaments at the local level over their own budgets in areas such as infrastructure, health care, and the administration of land and environmental issues. Many argued that key stakeholders such as the World Bank ignored the entrenched nature of regional interests and intra-elite competition, and that there is by no means an automatic correlation between decentralization and the provision of good governance (for example Schulte Nordholt and van Klinken 2007). Scholars of local politics in Indonesia identified two interlinked problems: the immediate rise of regional identity politics, and the entrenchment of economic interests at the local level.

The rise and resolution of communal and separatist conflicts

The immediate onset of democratization was accompanied by a rise in internal communal conflicts in the areas of West and Central Kalimantan, Central Sulawesi, and the Moluccas during 1999–2001 (van Klinken 2007: 4) and escalation of separatist conflicts in Aceh, East Timor, and Papua (Aspinall and Berger 2001). Many observers in the media and elsewhere pointed to the so-called primordial nature of the conflicts, arguing that ethnic violence was a sign that Indonesia's survival depended on the upholding of a strong centralized state. While it is clear that communal and separatist violence occurred (or reoccurred) during a period when the power of the central state was temporarily weakened, most scholars agree that the causes of intra-group violence were more complex. One prevalent argument emphasizes the political economy of conflict rather than primordial differences. Van Klinken (2007) argues that communal violence erupted in provincial towns, which, over recent decades, had experienced rapid, but state-dependent, economic growth, in combination with a high level of immigration as part of the government-sponsored programme of *transmigrasi*. The result was a local economy that depended on state investment and government employment and a highly diverse urban environment (van Klinken 2007). Beginning with the 1997 Asian economic crisis and culminating with the collapse of the New Order regime, local elites no longer had a stable source of power. One avenue for local urban elites, often described as influential politicians-cum-bureaucrats with good connections to local business people, was to seize power by mobilizing their ethnic or religious constituencies. This pattern of mobilization contributed to escalation in intra-group violence (van Klinken 2010).

However, most of what had been deemed ethnic violence ended in 2001–02 when the state was regaining sufficient strength to intervene. Subsequent governments invested a lot of resources in conflict resolution. For instance, decentralization reforms involved the implementation of new **institutional** mechanisms intended to address some of the discrepancies in power relations. In West Kalimantan and Central Sulawesi, separate districts were created for each ethnic group; elsewhere, with the introduction of direct elections of district heads and mayors, people were able to defeat unpopular candidates at the ballot box (Tomsa 2009a). To some extent, therefore, it can be argued that what was initially interpreted as a sign of failed decentralization reforms proved quite successful in terms of creating a relatively stable platform for political competition at the lower levels of government.

The collapse of the New Order regime also saw the resurgence of separatist groups in the regions of East Timor, Aceh, and West Papua. The temporary opening of political space and weakening of the military meant that armed separatist groups were able to mobilize more widely and openly in support of independence. How the state approached these three conflicts differed to a remarkable extent.

East Timor was a Portuguese colony, meaning that it was subject to a historical trajectory of decolonization that was different from that of the rest of Indonesia. Indonesia invaded East Timor in 1975 after the Portuguese pulled out. When the New Order ended, the United Nations backed East Timor's right to carry out a referendum on the **status** of the province, which it did in 1999. Following the referendum, in which a large majority of East Timorese voted in favour of independence, Indonesia withdrew from the territory. East Timor was placed under UN-administration until 2002 when powers were handed over to East Timorese-elected authorities.

In Aceh, the end of the New Order meant the opening up of political space and the resurgence of the province's demand for independence. In 1998–99, the Free Aceh Movement (GAM) was able to mobilize more broadly, but in contrast to such efforts in East Timor, the group lacked international support. Armed conflict between GAM and the Indonesian military escalated during 1999–2004. In the aftermath of the Indian Ocean tsunami of 2004, which caused massive devastation to the province of Aceh, GAM engaged in peace talks with the Indonesian government and eventually the former protagonists agreed on a framework for special autonomy. The 2005 Memorandum of Understanding (MoU) between the government and GAM (that is, the peace agreement) and the subsequent Law on the Governing of Aceh stipulated increased control over natural resources and the opportunity for local political parties to stand for election. To some extent, this resolution of the separatist conflict in Aceh is a sign of the newfound flexibility in Indonesia's decentralization policies.

Yet this flexibility has not yet been seen in Papua. Here, the government has failed to address the many grievances raised by human rights activists and the military remains heavily vested in local politics. One reason could be that while East Timor and Aceh both received massive international attention, the unresolved political crisis in Papua has not attracted international concern to a similar degree.

Decentralized corruption and local elites

Despite the fact that decentralization has had a positive effect on the level of stability across Indonesia, it has not automatically resulted in good governance. An important body of research on local politics in post-authoritarian Indonesia shows that even though the state has undergone a massive restructuring, authoritarian practices and corruption continue to linger at the lower levels of government (for example Schulte Nordholt and van Klinken 2007; van Klinken and Barter 2009).

During the New Order, the role of local administrators was to hand out permits and licences to trade and exploit natural resources. Within the neo-patrimonial logic of the New Order state, this opened up a variety of lucrative 'private–public' arrangements between the bureaucracy, members of the security forces, and private business. The introduction of local elections did not untangle these connections; instead, wealthy individuals paid off parties and parliamentarians so as to win seats and positions in local governments (Mietzner 2009: 233). To address this issue, both reformers and activists pushed for electoral reforms to move power away from local parliaments and into the hands of the people. Replacing the system of indirect voting via parliaments, a major electoral reform introducing direct elections for district heads, mayors, and governors was introduced in 2004. Although much work still needed to be done to improve the quality of local governance, *pilkada* has been a popular reform that has served to diminish vote-buying, and has given voters the chance to oust unpopular governors and mayors from office

(Buehler and Tan 2007; Tomsa 2009a). The law passed in 2014 to end *pilkada* and to return to indirect elections via parliaments has consequently been wildly unpopular amongst ordinary Indonesians, and critics view it as an attempt by established elites to retake control over regional-level political processes and resources.

KEY POINTS

- Decentralization was accompanied by regional conflicts. Violence erupted not because the state disintegrated, but because elites sought to reposition themselves within the new political order.

- Decentralization created new frameworks for conflicts to be resolved; hence most conflicts that erupted after 1998 have ended.

- While decentralization did not automatically lead to good governance, reforms such as the introduction of direct elections provided newfound flexibility for ordinary people to influence politics.

Political Mobilization and Participation

In Indonesia, regime change was accompanied by the manifestation of a highly fragmented multiparty system. The system is a combination of many newly established parties, although many of their leaders rose to prominence during the New Order period. The decision to implement proportional representation (PR) resulted from the high number of relevant political actors representing different cleavages and interests, often referred to as *aliran* ('streams'), in Indonesian society (Geertz 1976). *Aliran* first manifested themselves during the 1950s as cleavages between secular and Islamist forces, as well as between the centre (the main island of Java) and the periphery (the 'outer' islands) (Ufen 2009). The political left has never re-established itself after the eradication of the Indonesian Communist Party (PKI) in 1965–66.

Political parties: Drivers of change?

The fear of national disintegration that had dominated during the New Order period was also reflected in the ways in which reformers sought to regulate parties through party-system engineering that promoted national parties over local and regional parties

(Hicken 2008). Since 2004, political parties have been required to establish branches in at least two-thirds of the provinces and in two-thirds of the municipalities within the provinces, and each party branch must have a minimum of 1,000 members. The only exception is in Aceh, where the 2004 peace settlement between GAM and the Indonesian government allowed local political parties to operate. This exception from the otherwise strict regulations has enabled the former separatist group (GAM) to transform into a political party (Partai Aceh).

Despite the strict attempts at party regulations, the post-New-Order period has seen the growth of several new political parties. Box 20.3 provides an overview of the relevant parties and their share of the vote in the four elections held since 1998, as well as where they are located on the ideological spectrum (secular, pluralist Islamic, or Islamist). Instead of reflecting cleavages, or *aliran*, many of the parties are established as political vehicles for key figures with money and influence, and with connections to the past regime. One example is the Democratic Party (PD), the party established by former President Susilo Bambang Yodhoyono (SBY), who ruled for two terms between 2004 and 2014. Despite his past as a senior military general of the New Order, SBY had emerged from the Suharto era with a reputation relatively untainted by allegations of human rights abuses and corruption. Another newcomer is Gerindra, the party established by Prabowo Subianto, the losing candidate in the 2014 presidential elections. Gerindra was backed by former military elites and big business, including Prabowo's own business empire (Aspinall 2015).

A key feature is that few parties are associated with a clear ideology or political manifesto. The only exception are the Islamist parties—especially the Prosperous Justice Party (PKS), which has been able to combine a clear ideological stance with a rather efficiently organized party apparatus (Tomsa 2009b: 180). While the secular–Islamist division is clearly represented within the party system, the significance of Islamist ideology should not be overestimated. For instance, although the PKS remains staunchly Islamic in its ideology and draws its supporters from mostly pious segments of the population, it has been moderate on several core religious issues. One example is the retreat from promoting **Sharia** law, substituting instead good governance (Buehler 2013).

Amongst the secular parties, the PDI-P, the largest party in the legislature, draws legitimacy from its historical ties to the independence era, while Golkar is a catch-all party with a strong party organization that attract voters from outside of Java. Parties such as PD, Gerindra, and Hanura are all led by former military generals who control large business empires (see Box 20.3).

What is clear is that the dynamics of political mobilization in Indonesia is regulated from the top down. Only those parties with an already national organizational structure and elite connections in place, or the new parties whose leaders have mustered enough financial backing across the archipelago to fulfil the requirements of the party laws, have evolved into relevant political parties. In 1999, forty-eight parties passed the verification process to compete in the elections; in 2013, only thirteen parties passed. Party regulations have achieved precisely what they set out to—namely, to reduce the number of political parties, while securing nationwide parties. Meanwhile, the regulations have also produced a party system in which the linkages between voters and parties are weakening. This process is often described as *dealiranisasi*, meaning the eradication of *aliran* (Ufen 2009). This is further reflected in how parties behave and operate in parliament. The lack of clear manifestos has led to a tendency among parties to form so-called grand coalitions, or rainbow coalitions, in which parties water down their manifesto commitments to secure and share at least some of the spoils of office.

KEY POINTS

- The decision to use proportional representation (PR) was a result of the high number of relevant political *aliran*, meaning 'cleavages' or 'streams'.

- The party laws are designed so as to favour large national party organizations over smaller regional political parties.

- Influential new parties are established by former military generals backed by big business (for example PD, Gerindra).

Civil Society: The Narrowing of Space for Political Mobilization

The second pillar for political mobilization that influences Indonesia's democratization is civil society. Indonesia has generally been credited with a vibrant

BOX 20.3 POST-NEW ORDER PARTY SYSTEM

Election results for the Peoples Representative Council (*Dewan Perwakilan Rakyat*, or DPD)	1999 (%)	2004 (%)	2009 (%)	2014 (%)
Secular parties				
Gerindra (Greater Indonesia Movement Party), founded in 2008 as personal vehicle for Prabowo Subianto, former general and Suharto's son-in-law, contender for president in 2014			4	12
Golkar (Party of the Functional Group), the New Order ruling party	22	22	14	15
Hanura (People's Conscience Party), established in 2006 as personal vehicle for former General Wiranto	–	–	4	5
Partai Nasdem (Nasdem Party), founded in 2011 as personal vehicle for Surya Paloh, media mogul and owner of MetroTV,	–	–	–	7
PDI-P (Indonesian Democratic Party of Struggle), President Jokowi's party, led by Megawati Soekarnoputri, former president (2001–04) and daughter of Sukarno, first president of the Republic	34	19	14	19
PD (Democratic Party), founded in 2001 as personal vehicle of former President Susilo Bambang Yudhoyono (2004–14)	–	7	21	10
Pluralist Islamic parties				
PKB (National Awakening Party), aligned with main traditionalist Islamic organization, Nadhatul Ulama	13	11	5	9
PAN (National Mandate Party), aligned with main modernist Islamic organization, Muhammadiyah	7	6	6	8
Islamist parties				
PPP (United Development Party), Islamic party first formed under the New Order	11	8	5	7
PKS (Justice and Welfare Party), puritan party with voter base amongst religious urban intellectuals	1	7	8	7

Source: Komisi Pemilihan Umum (General Elections Commission), online at http://www.kpu.go.id

civil society that played a critical role during and after the transition period. In the period 1998–2005, the pro-democracy student movement was spearheading the expansion of democracy, forcing elites to adopt democratic reforms, as well as ensuring the establishment of important institutions such as the Corruption Eradication Commission (KPK) and the Independent Election Commission (KPU) (Mietzner 2012). Since 1998, pro-democracy activists have also operated crucial advocacy groups that investigate past human rights abuses as well as oversee basic freedoms such as freedom of association, of the press, and of minorities.

In recent years, however, many observers have noted that the pro-democracy movement has become increasingly fragmented and less able to fend off democratic setbacks. Pro-democracy activists and former key figures within the student movement generally refrain from joining formal politics, in part because they continue to see politics as 'dirty business', but also because they lack the required ties to big business to do so (Törnquist 2013). Mietzner (2012) further notes that where civil society had previously been able to shape the political agenda directly, after 2008 activists were increasingly sidelined as the alliance between reform-minded politicians and pro-democracy activists unravelled. Even so, civil society is still able to fend off attempts by conservative factions of the political elite to roll back already implemented reforms. For example, mobilization by civil society activists was important in curbing attempts by conservative parliamentarians to weaken the Corruption Eradication Commission (KPK), which in 2008 had begun to target and arrest members of parliament in high-profile anti-corruption operations. Civil society activists were also able to halt the reduction of resources to the independent election commission proposed in 2009 (Mietzner 2012; Freedom House 2014, 2015).

Within other arenas, civil society is targeted directly. One example is the Law on Mass Organizations of 2013, which states that the government can dissolve any civic association, religious or non-religious, which does not espouse the ideology of *pancasila*, an ideological principle that is associated with anti-democratic period of the New Order. The Law further requires associations to register with the government, and to register and report their activities to prove their adherence to the state ideology, which includes the rejection of Marxism-Leninism, giving the government increased control of civic space (Freedom House 2015).

KEY POINTS

- While civil society was integral to the democratic transition and maintaining oversight of the implementation of democratic reform, few pro-democracy activists have entered formal politics.
- In recent years, civil society has been unable to curb the developments that threaten minority rights and the freedoms of association and of religion.

Conclusion

With almost twenty years having passed since Indonesia transitioned to democracy, the process of regime change has faced many contradictions. The first decade after the collapse of the New Order was marked by optimism among reformers, a vibrant civil society, and a relatively well-functioning electoral system—all accompanied by relatively stable economic growth. One of the most far-reaching of the democratic reforms was that of decentralization, aimed at moving power away from the centre towards the regions, enhancing good governance and more inclusive development across the archipelago by seeking to break down the centralized state structure that had dominated the New Order period. Despite dangers of vote-buying and intra-elite competition, observers generally agree that direct elections for governors, mayors, and regents have enhanced the opportunities for ordinary voters to impact on local politics; hence the return to indirect elections is likely to increase the powers of established political parties and make it more difficult for figures outside of the traditional elites, such as President Jokowi, to gain office. Likewise, while political parties remain a key avenue for access to formal power, the party laws favour large parties. At the same time, political parties are weakly institutionalized and party platforms unclear.

The experiences of Indonesia demonstrate not only the relative success of reformers, but also the ease with which authoritarian tendencies can persist within a democratic framework. It also shows that, without real representation via political parties, civil society activists remain on the outside of formal politics, lacking the organizational infrastructure and economic resources with which to truly shape post-authoritarian reform.

? QUESTIONS

1. What instigated regime change in Indonesia in 1998?
2. How do the legacies of the New Order regime continue to shape post-New-Order politics?
3. In what areas can Indonesia's decentralization reform be deemed successful? Where has it been less successful?
4. What are the main characteristics of Indonesia's parties and party system?
5. What are the main obstacles facing Indonesia's pro-democracy movement?

FURTHER READING

Aspinall, E., and Mietzner, M. (eds) (2012) *Problems of Democratisation in Indonesia: Elections, Institutions and Society* (Singapore: Institute of Southeast Asian Studies) A collection of chapters providing an overview of the workings of Indonesia's democracy.

Horowitz, D. (2013) *Constitutional Change and Democracy in Indonesia* (New York: Cambridge University) A detailed analysis of political developments before and after the collapse of the New Order.

Törnquist, O. (2013) *Assessing Dynamics of Democratisation: Transformative Politics: New Institutions, and the Case of Indonesia* (New York: Palgrave MacMillan) Analysis of the failures and successes of the Indonesian pro-democracy movement based on nationwide expert surveys.

van Klinken, G. (2007) *Communal Violence and Democratization in Indonesia: small Town Wars* (Leiden: KITLV) A case study of six episodes of communal violence in the post-New Order era.

WEB LINKS

http://cip.cornell.edu/Indonesia   *Indonesia* is an academic journal devoted to the study of Indonesian affairs.

https://freedomhouse.org/country/indonesia   Freedom House offers annual country reports assessing progress and setbacks related to human rights and democracy.

http://www.insideindonesia.org   *Inside Indonesia* is an online magazine that focuses on Indonesian politics, human rights, and environmental issues.

For additional material and resources, please visit the Online Resource Centre at:
http://www.oxfordtextbooks.co.uk/orc/burnell5e/

21

The Onset of the Syrian Uprising and the Origins of Violence

Reinoud Leenders

Chapter contents

Overview

Starting from December 2010 in Tunisia, Arabs from various walks of life took to the streets in protest against decades-long authoritarian rule, repression, and corruption in what came to be known as the 'Arab uprisings'. These waves of protest reached Syria in March 2011. The current chapter presents an analysis of the early stages of mass mobilization in Syria, and attempts to explain the onset of popular mobilization in what is perhaps the region's most authoritarian and repressive state. While Syria's protests initially were largely peaceful, they soon gave way to violence, which culminated in an armed insurgency by the end of 2011 and, combined with regime brutality, a civil war that is ongoing at time of writing. How, when, and why that happened is the second main theme of this chapter.

Figure 21.1 is a map of Syria and Box 21.1 provides an overview of key dates in Syria's history.

Figure 21.1 Syria

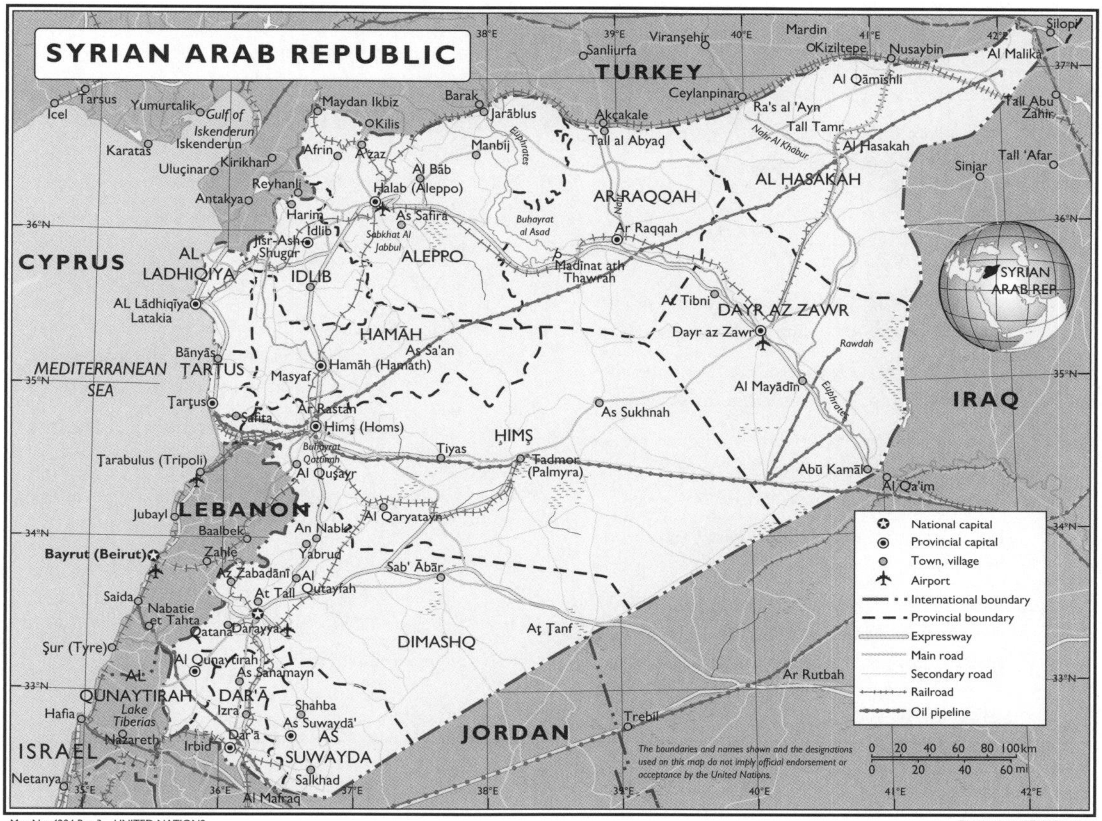

Map No. 4204 Rev.3   UNITED NATIONS
April 2012

Department of Field Support
Cartographic Section

Source: Syria, Map No. 4204 Rev. 3, United Nations (April 2012)

BOX 21.1 KEY DATES IN SYRIA'S HISTORY

1920–46	Syria under French mandate
1958–61	Syria and Egypt join United Arab Republic
1961	Syrian army officers seize power and dissolve union with Egypt
1963	Ba'thist army officers seize power
1967	Israeli forces seize Syrian Golan heights in Six Day War
1970	Hafez al-Assad seizes power
1973	Syria and Egypt go to war with Israel
1980	Muslim Brotherhood leads violent uprising
1982	Regime forces violently repress insurrection in Hama
1991	Following Ta'if Peace Accord in Lebanon (1989), Syria gains supremacy in Lebanon
2000	Hafez al-Assad dies and is succeeded by his son Bashar
2001	Crackdown on opposition activists of the 'Damascus Spring'
2003–04	Syrian regime opposes US-led occupation of Iraq
2005	Syrian forces leave Lebanon under pressure of UN Security Council
Mar 2011	Mass protests commence in southern city of Dar'a and quickly spread throughout the country
July 2011	Defected officers announce formation of Free Syrian Army (FSA)

Jan 2012	Jabhat al-Nusra announces its formation as Syria's Al Qaeda affiliate	June 2013	Syrian regime joins forces with Lebanon's Hezbollah and retakes strategically important town al-Qusayr
Feb 2012	Regime forces shell FSA-held Bab al-Amr neighbourhood in Homs	Aug 2013	Damascus suburb of Ghouta attacked with chemical weapons; regime troops held responsible; United States threatens air strikes
Mar 2012	FSA pulls out of Bab al-Amr	Sept 2013	Syrian government allows its chemical weapons to be dismantled by Organization for the Prohibition of Chemical Weapons (OPCW)
Apr 2012	Former UN Secretary-General Kofi Annan brokers ceasefire; UN observers deployed, but truce breaks down	Jan 2014	Geneva peace talks attended by Syrian government and SNC fail to provide breakthrough
May 2012	Sectarian-motivated massacres, including in the village of Houla; UN investigators accuse regime forces	May 2014	Regime troops retake Homs under terms of a ceasefire
June 2012	United Nations suspends observer patrols in Syria owing to deteriorating security conditions	June 2014	So-called Islamic State announces 'caliphate' in territory it controls in Iraq and Syria
July 2012	Massive bomb attack in Damascus kills key regime incumbents, leading to regime crackdown efforts	Oct 2014	US-led airstrikes counter IS advances in Kurdish town of Kobani and IS strongholds elsewhere in Syria
Nov 2012	Syrian opposition broadens into 'National Coalition for Syrian Revolutionary and Opposition Forces' (Syrian National Coalition, or SNC)	Mar 2015	Rebel forces deal significant blows to regime forces throughout country
Feb 2013	Rebel groups continue to make territorial gains largely thanks to new supplies of foreign weaponry	Feb 2016	Renewed international efforts to initiate talks between regime and opposition forces in Geneva suspended; US-Russian-brokered partial ceasefire
Apr 2013	Iraqi jihadist Abu Bakr al-Baghdadi announces formation of so-called Islamic State (IS), merging Iraqi jihadists with Jabhat al-Nusra; Jabhat al-Nusra leader Abu Muhammad al-Julani denies merger and insists on allegiance to Al Qaeda.	Mar 2016	Regime forces retake Palmyra from IS

Introduction

Mass mobilization and protests aimed at **regime change** in Syria, one of the most authoritarian and repressive states in the Middle East, followed in the wake of unprecedented popular uprisings in a number of Arab countries. Pent-up grievances among large sections of the Syrian population are associated with the ways in which Syria's ruling Ba'th Party and, increasingly, a small circle of relatives and associates around the presidency had monopolized political decision-making and scarce resources since they seized power in a coup in 1963. Yet such popular grievances alone cannot fully explain how, when, and why Syrians managed to mobilize en masse, starting from the end of March 2011; neither was the uprising's mutation into a sustained armed insurgency inevitable. It can be argued that the wider context of the 'Arab uprisings' generated some important opportunities for Syrian mobilizers, causing the 'wall of

fear' to crumble. The protests elsewhere in the Arab world became a source of inspiration for Syrian mobilizers in the ways in which demonstrators framed their challenge to the **regime** and roused many others to join in. The Syrian regime's security forces responded with ruthless repression. Commencing in relatively remote areas, the protests quickly swelled and spread throughout the country. Loose social networks were key to such rapid diffusion, because they escaped full regime control, became a source of protest recruitment, and generated values and forms of solidarity that proved indispensable in defying and challenging regime power. Some of the same social networks— particularly those embedded in sectarian identities encouraged by regime repression and the release of Salafist-jihadist detainees—also served as the background against which the uprising in Syria became increasingly violent and, by the end of 2011, had started to mutate into a vicious armed insurgency.

Syria: A Short History of Growing Popular Discontent

Cobbled together by British and French colonial designs, the dotted patches of territory that today comprise Syria gained formal state independence in 1946. Until the late 1960s, the country had witnessed recurring coups and profound political instability as successive rulers, mostly resorting to ruthless, authoritarian measures, struggled to keep the country together and to impose central authority. In 1963, a small group of military officers aligned to the Pan-Arabist and staunchly secular Ba'th Party seized power and imposed one-party rule. A decade of fierce elite infighting until 1970 prompted the 'corrective movement' initiated by air force commander Hafez al-Assad and a small faction of like-minded officers.

Assad and most of his supporters were born into poor families in the countryside near Latakia, in the northwest of the country. Predominantly belonging to the Alawite sect, an offshoot of Shi'a Islam, they used their military backgrounds to help to further the political and economic emancipation of their minority group, which today comprises some 11 per cent of Syria's population. Some regime figureheads and senior officers, however, were drawn from the Arab Sunni community, today comprising some 60 per cent of the population (Minority Rights Organisation 2011). The regime's reliance on stiff repression of any form of dissent, in combination with its refusal to allow political power beyond the Ba'th Party and a small cohort of regime supporters, formed the background in the mid-1970s to an armed uprising led by Syria's branch of the Islamist Muslim Brotherhood. The regime subsequently tried to restore some of its **legitimacy** or support base by allowing a select group of urban entrepreneurs to benefit from limited economic liberalization in collusion with regime strongmen and their relatives. The regime took care, however, to ensure that the country's sizeable public sector employment, its state-owned enterprises, and a relatively generous welfare system remained intact, because these helped to undermine efforts by an Islamist and left-wing opposition to gain a real foothold among the population at large. The regime also managed to draw support from within some of the country's other minorities, including the Druze (approximately 3 per cent) and Christians (12 per cent), because the latter preferred the regime's authoritarian secularism to the Islamist ideology of the Muslim Brotherhood. In contrast, the country's Kurds (10 per cent), most of them residing in the northeast, were met with repression and discriminatory treatment.

When Hafez al-Assad died in 2000, he was succeeded by his son Bashar. Bashar inherited a fortress that had finessed authoritarian rule to the degree that virtually no organized opposition was able to pose a real threat to the regime. Yet the fortress was built on a series of contradictions that Bashar ultimately failed to address or overcome. For one thing, the oil revenues that had enabled the state's relative generosity toward the poorer classes were declining. Bashar responded, especially after 2003, with unprecedented economic reforms in the hope of reinvigorating private sector-led economic growth. Yet, fearful that this would empower a predominantly Sunni Arab business class that could rise up against his rule, economic privileges were doled out to regime strongmen and their relatives, soon earning the regime a reputation for unbridled cronyism and **corruption**. Meanwhile, fewer jobs and state subsidies reached the regime's more popular constituencies. Furthermore, not all of his father's aides, from within the Ba'th Party and among the country's security agencies, had been pleased with Bashar's hereditary succession. Bashar responded by marginalizing—even, in some instances, assassinating—such inner regime critics and by appointing members of his own entourage, mostly from Alawite backgrounds, to key regime positions. As a result, sectarian resentment strengthened when most ordinary Alawites were as deprived from power and wealth as the other communities.

KEY POINTS

- The 2011 uprising and insurgency emerged against a backdrop of long-standing popular grievances with the Ba'th regime's repressive policies since the early 1960s.

The Onset of the Syrian Uprising

Despite assurances by observers and regime incumbents alike that Syria would be immune to the revolutionary mobilization unfolding elsewhere in the region, and following several false starts, Syria's popular uprising commenced on 18 March 2011 in a place no one had foreseen (and indeed some had never heard of): the sleepy, provincial town of Dar'a, situated on the plateau of Hawran spanning southwestern Syria and northwestern Jordan. Protests swelled and spread quickly throughout the Dar'a governorate, extending first to Latakia and then, in more sustained fashion, to the Homs, Idlib, and Deir az-Zur governorates.

Until the summer of 2011, Syria's early uprisers succeeded in bringing about unprecedented levels of mass mobilization, thereby collectively posing the most serious challenge against authoritarian rule by the Ba'th Party and its strongmen since they seized power in 1963. Equally remarkable, the early mobilization was predominantly peaceful, as protestors underscored in their slogans—*silmiya, silmiya!* ('peaceful, peaceful')—in the face of power. The regime immediately sent its security forces and troops to clamp down on the protests. Its response failed to deter further mobilization and triggered new waves of heightened repression, which in turn fuelled more protests. Statistics on fatalities during the Syrian crisis are disputed and problematic in many ways; Syrian **human rights** and opposition activists variously claim, however, that, in the course of only a few months, the regime forces killed thousands of protestors and bystanders (see Figure 21.2).

Explaining the onset of popular mobilization in a context of severe and sustained authoritarianism and repression like that in Syria is no easy task. But the loose or informal, multiple, and overlapping social networks in which mobilization and mobilizers were embedded provide key insights to the mobilization witnessed. (For a full account of **social movement** theory, or SMT, on which this explanation builds, see Chapter 11.) These social networks were built around, respectively, family clan and quasi-tribal structures of solidarity, (circular) labour migration, cross-border traffic and linkages, and (petty) crime. Such social networks had important implications for the ways in which the uprising commenced and evolved.

Via processes of **framing**, transnational networks associated with (circular) labour migration were key in making revolutionary mobilization in Egypt and elsewhere in the region highly relevant to Syria's early uprisers. The social networks associated with the early uprisers' clan structure help to explain why the regime's threats and violence were seen as a cause for mobilization, rather than submission. Especially in Dar'a, but elsewhere too, protestors framed the regime's repression as an affront and insult to the values embedded in their clan networks. Notably, the scale of threat mattered as much as the ways in which repression was experienced, especially because it comprised the arrest, abuse, torture, and killing of women and children. Further, informal social networks generally—being relatively insulated from regime surveillance—can also be viewed as having laid a foundation for protestors' open and defiant articulation of their grievances and demands in the relative absence of a solid repertoire of open contention.

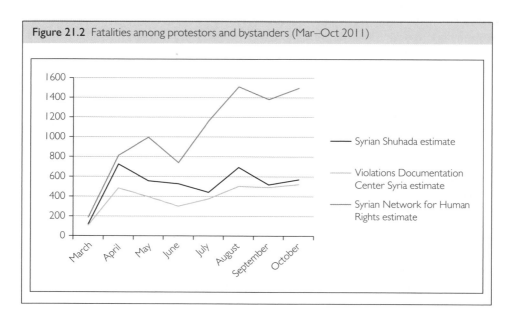

Figure 21.2 Fatalities among protestors and bystanders (Mar–Oct 2011)

As significantly, an appreciation of the qualities of the social networks of Syria's early uprisers goes a long way towards explaining protestors' effective use of perceived opportunities and their success in gaining critical mass while withstanding intense regime violence. The early uprisers' social networks provided an important sense of solidarity and presented the background against which recruitment for mobilization took place. Meanwhile, social networks supplied key skills and resources for mobilization to be effective and to be sustained under prohibitive conditions. Petty criminals began to provide protection and intelligence as quickly as the regime augmented its violence. The elusive nature of the dispersed and leaderless networks added to the regime's failing response as it struggled to find 'instigators' to arrest or kill. In summary, all of this helps to explain why Syria's uprising commenced in what appears a periphery, or borderland, exactly because the latter was so richly endowed with the social networks and associated resources that proved essential to mobilization.

Beyond their social networks, protestors' ingenuity and framing efforts were indispensable. In essence, they addressed the dearth of a solid repertoire of contentious **politics** by patching together elements from various scripts and registers, and putting them to the use of their cause. Protestors' efforts included copying, amending, tinkering with, responding to, and appropriating slogans and protest acts from Egypt and Tunisia: the Assad regime's utterances in response to the unrest; the regime's own worn-out, but therefore widely familiar, slogans and chants; common Arab and Muslim narratives and symbols of resistance and commemoration (martyrdom); and cultural expressions and folklore, such as traditional poetry recitals and songs. Finally, Syria's early uprisers quickly developed a simple, but powerful, framing tactic to address the challenge of national fragmentation, in turn helping to spread and sustain mobilization throughout the country. Routinely invoking protests, mobilization, and regime violence in other parts of the region, strong solidarity in this context became key to framing the *national* relevance of early and arguably 'localized' mobilization, and helped to create a national playing field in the process.

During the first months of the uprising, mobilization spread and a complex set of mutually reinforcing mechanisms were set in motion. Protest framing was one factor and a repeat of the 'repression–mobilization' nexus in numerous locations, whereby regime repression invited more mobilization, was another. Interestingly, the regime's harsh response to the uprising contributed to diffusion in more indirect ways too. Soldiers were sent all over the country and could establish with their own eyes that the regime's narrative of it confronting an armed rebellion dominated by **terrorists** held no ground. People displaced by regime violence went to quieter areas, such as the suburbs of Damascus, where they gave a first-hand account of the regime's atrocities. This gave rise to solidarity networks in their place of refuge that quickly got involved in mobilization locally. In vain, the regime responded by literally trying to compartmentalize the country, establishing countless checkpoints in the hope of containing mobilization. None of these policies could prevent the fact that the prominence gained by Syria's early mobilizers allowed them to offer a tested and legitimate toolkit to be drawn upon and extended for the purposes of intense mobilization throughout the country. The use of social media facilitated the quick development of this toolkit and amplified its reach to an ever-widening audience.

KEY POINTS

- Loose or informal, multiple, and overlapping social networks in which mobilization and mobilizers were embedded provide key insights into how and why popular mobilization commenced and spread throughout Syria.

The Roots of the Uprising's Militarization

Syria's initial and predominantly peaceful mobilization has, however, now mutated into an organized and sustained insurgency involving hundreds of armed groups, many of them pursuing extremist Salafist-jihadist agendas, such as Ahrar al-Sham, Jabhat al-Nusra, and the so-called Islamic State. In the course of more than four years, the Syrian regime applied ever-increasing doses of indiscriminate military force. While the onus for the vast scale of human suffering since March 2011 lies predominantly with the regime, the origins of the uprising's militarization should be part and parcel of an analysis of early mobilization.

To properly analyse the origins of the Syrian uprising's militarization, we would need to engage in a

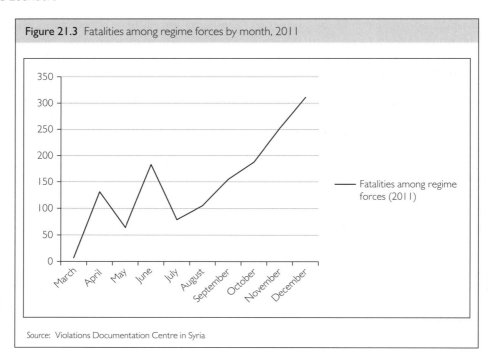

Figure 21.3 Fatalities among regime forces by month, 2011

Fatalities among regime forces (2011)

Source: Violations Documentation Centre in Syria

detailed exercise of 'process tracing'—that is, to conduct a detailed analysis of events, contexts, and actors relevant to, in this case, the militarization of the Syrian uprising. This would give us a kind of roadmap with which to investigate and elucidate the answer to the question, as Tilly (2003: 12) put it: 'When, how, and why do shifts between nonviolent and violent interaction occur?' What we can do here is begin to assess some common and competing accounts of early political violence in the Syrian uprising. Table 21.1 lists some of the most commonly expressed views on early violence in Syria.

Although each of the arguments presented in Table 21.1 may, at first sight, contain a grain of truth and some may be compatible, assessing their plausibility and weighing their significance relative to one another remains an arduous task.

Perhaps unsurprisingly, the first argument on the 'Salafist-jihadist conspiracy', primarily put forward by the Syrian regime itself, is the most problematic. On the one hand and judging from eye-witness accounts, social media footage and data on fatalities among regime forces violent contention is indeed likely to have accompanied more peaceful mobilization from as early as April 2011.

Between March and October 2011, the Violations Documentation Centre in Syria recorded more than

900 regime casualties. Social media footage of the same period recorded early ambushes, improvised attacks, and other forms of violence directed against the regime and its supporters. Regime claims on total or accumulated fatalities among its forces are somewhat lower, but consistent with the observation that anti-regime violence occurred at modest, but still significant, levels from the onset of the uprising (Reuters 2011; Permanent Mission of the SAR 2011; UN Independent International Commission of Inquiry 2011). Again, caution is warranted here, because estimated or claimed regime fatalities are likely to include an unknown number of armed personnel killed by their own superiors for refusing to obey orders.

However, even if one were to take the lower-end estimates of fatalities among protestors and bystanders shown in Figure 21.2 to denote armed rebels killed in combat, regime fatalities dwarf in comparison. In short, it appears that there was no violent plot, let alone a Salafist-jihadist conspiracy, of a magnitude such that the regime was forced to respond with brutal repression. Even if there were small ambushes, improvised raids on checkpoints, and some small-arms fire from the onset, their scale was grossly exaggerated by a regime that responded with extreme, disproportionate violence. This, of course, is

Table 21.1 Common arguments on early political violence in Syria

View	Argument
The Salafist-jihadist conspiracy	The Syrian uprising, although involving peaceful protests, was militarized from the start as armed Salafist-jihadist groups took on security forces with weapons and other forms of assistance they received from abroad.
The legacy of Iraq	Early violence against regime forces mainly occurred in areas inhabited by conservative Muslims who had already become radicalized when they took part as jihadist fighters in the civil war in neighbouring Iraq (2006–08).
Defecting soldiers came as saviours	The Syrian uprising inevitably militarized as large numbers of defecting soldiers, disgusted by and refusing to take part in the use of indiscriminate force against peaceful protestors, joined unarmed protestors and began to protect them in self-defence.
Sectarian conflict	Early violence was primarily a function of local sectarian tensions heightened by regime–protestor clashes and exacerbated by the regime's resort to crude sectarianism.

not to deny the much more plausible argument that at a *much later stage*—that is, at the end of 2011 and early 2012, when the uprising had fully militarized—Salafist-jihadists began to drive violent contention. It is indeed around this time that such groups began to present themselves by declaring their existence or by carrying out attacks.

The related argument of the 'legacy of Iraq' (see Table 21.1) is harder to assess. Again, it is conceivable that past skills and experiences gained by those Syrians involved in the war in Iraq became relevant, especially at a later stage of militarization. Yet, based on what we know about the geographical concentration of Syrian jihadists who fought in and returned from the civil war in Iraq—based largely on a survey of 500 such imprisoned Salafists and/or alleged jihadists in the period 2003–08 (Zaytuneh 2009)—their key areas of residence, including, foremost, Damascus suburbs (30 per cent) followed by Raqqa, Deir az-Zur, Homs, Aleppo, and Idlib, show only a weak match with the scale or intensity of early armed contention. Some early violence indeed involved 'Iraqi' jihadists, including by those whom the regime released from prison in March and May 2011, ostensibly deliberately to drive the uprising towards extremism and, accordingly, to become a legitimate target of regime clampdown (Lister 2015: 53–4). Yet much violent contention, at least up until October 2011, does not seem to have implicated these Iraq veterans on any significant scale.

Syrian opposition activists within Syria and abroad have repeatedly suggested the third argument, highlighting 'defecting soldiers as saviours' (see Table 21.1). It also has been largely accepted in mainstream Western media, at least to account for armed conflict in Syria from the start of the uprising until the end of 2011. There certainly is some truth to the argument: defections did indeed cause soldiers to join protestors and to become engaged in their armed protection. Yet if militarization of the uprising is to be viewed as resulting from defecting soldiers joining opposition ranks, defections should have reached significant levels before regime opponents used considerable violence. Judging from available reports and witness accounts of defections, that does not seem to have been the case (Abouzeid 2011; Human Rights Watch 2011: 20; Albrecht and Koehler 2016). For months, the number of defections remained extremely modest; it seems to have gathered pace only in October–November 2011. Moreover, many defectors fled or went into hiding, while only few brought their weapons with them, because they deserted when on leave. Thus, from October to November 2011, army defectors are likely to have intensified anti-regime violence, facilitating the uprising's militarization, but they cannot explain lower, but significant, levels of violent contention prior to these developments.

That leaves us with the remaining argument on the role of sectarianism. To avoid essentialist assumptions—that is, ascribing certain 'inherent' qualities to

supposedly fixed or ancient identities—we need to
tread carefully. Even when protestors were at pains
to emphasize their non-sectarian intentions, one cannot deny that an overwhelming majority of them
were Sunni Arabs. Neither can it be disputed that
the regime's security and intelligence forces are predominantly led by Alawite officers, a phenomenon
aggravated by a series of high-level appointments
after Bashar al-Assad came to power. As pointed out
earlier, before the uprising, the regime and its core
Alawite incumbents had made efforts to incorporate
Sunni Arabs. Yet when the uprising broke out, the regime's stated policy of keeping inter-sectarian peace
and stability was quickly abandoned. Newly created
pro-regime militias, the *Shabiha*, comprised mostly
of Alawite supporters (al-Hajj Saleh 2014). Swept up
and mobilized by an increasingly sectarian narrative
by the regime, they unleashed unprecedented levels
of aggressive violence against protestors. As a result
of these and other developments, sectarian 'boundary activation'—that is, the heightening of awareness
of perceived differences between members of the in-
group and the out-group (Tilly 2003: 21)—quickly became an overpowering response to increased levels of
insecurity (real or perceived) on all sides. Protestors increasingly adopted anti-Alawite slogans, or recited in
praise the name of exiled and staunchly anti-Alawite
cleric Adnan al-'Arur. Nir Rosen (2011), a correspond-
ent for Al Jazeera who visited Syria during the early
months of the uprising, documented in detail how, in
this context of increased polarization, sectarian ste-
reotyping and prejudice found their way to the local
level as neighbouring villages and communities within
villages engaged in mutual sectarian violence. Nayruz
Satik (2013), a Syrian author, similarly chronicled the
rise of sectarian sentiments and associated incidents
of early opposition violence—including abductions
and assassinations—in Homs, Latakia, Hama countryside, and Baniyas in the Tartus governorate. All of
these places are inhabited by a mix of sectarian communities living side by side—foremost, Alawites and
Sunni Arabs. In short, one does not have to subscribe
to crude primordialist or essentialist assumptions to
see the significance of sectarianism in early political violence during the Syrian uprising. In this respect, there
are ample reasons to take collective identities and related processes of 'boundary activation' seriously.
Further analysis anchored in SMT and incorporating
detailed process tracing will be essential to further un-
packing these linkages and relevant mechanisms.

KEY POINTS

- The Syrian uprising militarized largely because of pro-regime militias triggering sectarian 'boundary activation', which in turn increased levels of insecurity on all sides, especially in mixed sectarian areas.

Conclusion: A Vicious and Protracted Civil War

When tasked with the daunting challenge of eluci-
dating a civil war as brutal, complex, and protracted
as the one in Syria, social scientists often turn to its
origins and onset, as has been the case in this chapter. The Syrian people—protagonists and bystanders
alike—have done no differently as they have developed
their own narratives of what brought them to a state
of destruction and despair that has affected their lives
so dramatically. Accordingly, the insights gained from
an analysis of the onset of mobilization and the origins of its militarization form an essential component
of a broader understanding of what caused the Syrian civil war, how it developed, and how or why it endured. Yet these insights should not be equalled with a
broader explanation of the Syrian conflict as the latter
evolved, mutated, and became protracted. Thus the
Syrian insurgency as we know it today has become a
predominantly Salafist-jihadist affair—a fact made all
the more arresting by the rise of Al Qaeda affiliate Jabhat al-Nusra, and the brutality of its offshoot and rival,
the so-called Islamic State (Lister 2015). Responding to
the sectarian turn of the conflict, and exacerbating it
in the process, were external powers including Saudi
Arabia, Qatar, and Turkey, which began to support fellow Sunni Muslim rebel groups, while Iran, Hezbollah
from Lebanon, and Shi'ite fighters from Iraq came to
the rescue of the regime. While drawing on the region's fault-lines, the Syrian conflict further gained
transnational dimensions as tens of thousands of
Muslim volunteers from the region and beyond came
to fight with Jabhat al-Nusra and the so-called Islamic
State. As the Syrian conflict kept mutating and became
increasingly complex, the regime skilfully played
its cards on all fronts. Although losing territory and
bringing the country to ruin, the regime has managed
to survive and withstand formidable challenges—foremost, the call for regime change so powerfully expressed during the first months of the uprising.

In time, a focus on popular mobilization in all of its multifarious manifestations and mutations may tell us something about how, when, and why people in specific settings, such as Syria, resist authoritarian rule, revolt, and sustain their challenge against injustice and oppression. The Syrian uprising must be understood against the background of the country's five decades of authoritarian rule. For the Syrians themselves, the implications of heightened sectarianism and related violence, combined with the regime's readiness to use all of its force no matter the civilian costs, are dire as the country enters its sixth year of civil war.

? QUESTIONS

1. Why did Syria's uprising commence in a peripheral area of the country and not the capital, Damascus?

2. How, and to what extent, were features of the clan system in Syria instrumental in the early mobilization against the authoritarian regime?

3. Why did the initial Syrian uprising escalate into a civil war and military insurgency?

4. What counter-measures did the Syrian regime take to fight off the popular uprising and how can these be argued to have contributed to the country's civil war?

FURTHER READING

Beinin, J., and Vairel, F. (eds) (2013) *Social Movements, Mobilization, and Contestation in the Middle East and North Africa*, 2nd edn (Stanford, CA: Stanford University Press) The leading volume on social movements in the Middle East, with contributions on the Arab uprisings, including in Syria.

Burgat, F., and Paoli, B. (eds) (2013) *Pas de printemps pour la Syrie: Les clés pour comprendre les acteurs et les défis de la crise (2011–2013)* (Paris: La Découverte) Anthology of analysis on the Syrian uprising and its mutation into a civil war, the regime's and protestors' strategies, and the conflict's regional and international dimensions.

Heydemann, S., and Leenders, R. (eds) (2013) *Middle East Authoritarianism: Governance, Contestation and Regime Resilience in Syria and Iran* (Stanford, CA: Stanford University Press) Includes contributions written largely before the uprising on the interplay between Syria's resilient authoritarianism and its economy, state-religion relations, judicial politics, and foreign relations.

Hokayem, E. (2013) *Syria's Uprising and the Fracturing of the Levant* (London: International Institute for Strategic Studies) A general, but accurate, account of the background to the Syrian uprising and its mutation into a full-fledged civil war, with regional involvement.

Kerr, M., and Larkin, C. (eds) (2015) *The 'Alawis of Syria: War, Faith and Politics in the Levant* (London: Hurst & Co.) Multi-authored volume exploring the sectarian and religious dimensions of the Syrian conflict.

Lister, C. (2015) *The Syrian Jihad: Al-Qaeda, the Islamic State and the Evolution of an Insurgency* (London: Hurst & Co.) A detailed account and analysis of the rise of Salafi jihadist groups and how they came to dominate the Syrian insurgency.

Wedeen, L. (1999) *Ambiguities of Domination: Politics, Rhetoric, and Symbols in Contemporary Syria* (Chicago, IL: University of Chicago Press) A penetrating analysis of Syrian regime propaganda, the 'wall of fear', and how ordinary Syrians became complicit in confirming the regime's increasingly improbable claims on legitimacy.

 **WEB LINKS**

http://www.creativememory.org/?lang=en   Site of the Creative Memory of the Syrian Revolution, archiving protest art and related footage from Syria since March 2011.

http://www.crisisgroup.org/en/regions/middle-east-north-africa.aspx   The International Crisis Group (ICG) reports on the Arab uprisings, including in Syria.

http://syria.jadaliyya.com   Jadaliyya offers commentary and op-eds on the Syrian uprising and its civil war, including by Syrian writers and activists.

http://video.pbs.org/video/2364993210/   The PBS documentary *Syria: Behind the Lines*.

http://www.youtube.com/watch?v=s5BhaF6MjRo   The BBC documentary *The Syrian Revolution*.

 For additional material and resources, please visit the Online Resource Centre at:
http://www.oxfordtextbooks.co.uk/orc/burnell5e/

PART 6
Fragile versus Strong States

Whereas the focus of Part 5 was on a country's **regime** or system of government, in Part 6 emphasis is placed on the state. Whilst regime and state are closely linked concepts, 'regime' refers to the type of rule—for instance democratic or authoritarian—and the 'state' is understood as a summary term for the assemblage of ruling **institutions** and organizations. Referring back to Chapter 12, Anna Persson argues that whereas an increasing number of states subscribe to the legitimating doctrine of national sovereignty, states across the **developing world** vary significantly in terms of state strength. We find, on the one hand, states that have the capacity to extract huge amounts of taxes, to adopt highly functional policies to avoid human tragedies such as mass starvation and civil war. On the other hand, many sovereign states are faced with prolonged and bloody civil strife, a **weak state** bureaucracy, dysfunctional policies, and low levels of **public goods** provision. Owing to the international norm of sovereignty—and the resulting maintenance of territorial borders of even the weakest states—states today are more varied in their capacities and capabilities than ever before. The country case studies presented in Part 6 illustrate both the complexity of notions and assessments of state strength and weakness, and also the precariousness of state strength in practice. Nadje Al-Ali and Nicola Pratt focus on Iraq in the wake of the 2003 invasion. They argue that, under Saddam Hussein, the Iraqi state had been not so much strong as 'hard', or even 'fierce', with the emphasis on its capacity for repression. Despite constitutional reforms and democratic elections, violence and **corruption** have been hallmarks of post-Saddam Iraq; some have wanted to call it a 'failed state'. The authors argue, however, that the concentration of oil revenues and security forces in the hands of the executive under the prime minister are more reminiscent of Saddam's 'fierce state'.

Andreas Schedler describes how, in Mexico, something like a modern state was already emerging under Porfirio Diaz. Following a period of turbulence and revolution, the PRN/ PRI (Institutional Revolutionary Party) emerged as the dominant force in government, at the head of a centralized patrimonial bureaucracy and enjoying a degree of **legitimacy**. A process of democratization culminated in defeat of the PRI in the presidential elections of 2000, but the Mexican state has subsequently faced a massive challenge to its internal sovereignty and security from organized crime, associated notably with the drugs trade, again leading Schedler to argue that it is 'failing'.

Of the three countries presented in this section, South Korea comes closest to the notion of a 'strong state'. Peter Ferdinand describes the emergence of an almost 'textbook' **developmental state**, under General Park Chung Hee, featuring a close relationship between the state and industry in the interests of national development and defence. Even in this case, the state has faced a mounting challenge from social forces with democratization from the 1990s; it has failed to confront the entrenched power and associated corruption of the ***chaebols*** in the wake of the Asian financial crisis, whilst its international position is overshadowed by China and the continuing threat posed by North Korea.

22

Iraq
A Failing State?

Nadje Al-Ali and Nicola Pratt

Overview

This chapter explores whether Iraq is a failed state and how it arrived at that possible characterization. It examines the period since the US-led invasion of Iraq in 2003, which resulted in the fall of the dictatorship of Saddam Hussein. It focuses on three areas: the reconstruction of Iraq's political institutions; post-invasion violence and security; and human and economic development. The chapter demonstrates how the failure to reconstruct political institutions capable of reconciling Iraq's different political groupings has weakened central government, increased corruption within state institutions, and fed into ethnic/sectarian violence, thereby creating a favourable environment for the emergence of the so-called Islamic State (IS). The Iraqi state is failing to provide necessary services and infrastructure for economic and human development and even basic security for much of the population.

Figure 22.1 is a map of Iraq and Box 22.1 provides an overview of key dates in Iraq's history.

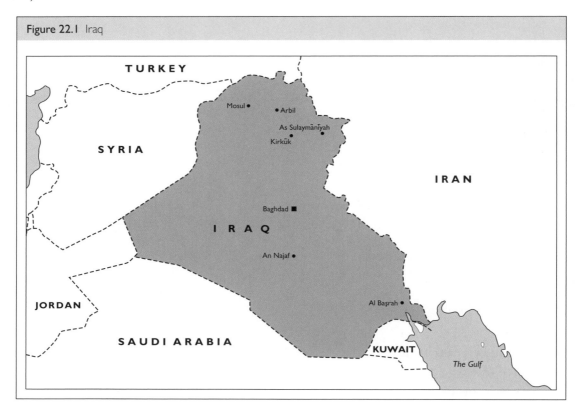

Figure 22.1 Iraq

BOX 22.1 KEY DATES IN IRAQ'S HISTORY

1920	British mandate of Iraq created from former provinces of Ottoman Empire	Jan–Feb 1991	'Operation Desert Storm'—US-led international military coalition forces Iraqi troops out of Kuwait by means of air bombardment of Iraq
July 1958	Military coup against monarchy and British presence; establishment of republic		
July 1979	Saddam Hussein becomes president	May 1991	Iraqi government crushes popular uprisings in north and south of country; United Nations creates 'safe haven' in Kurdish north; UN weapons inspections begin
1980	Following 1979 Iranian revolution, Iraqi government cracks down on Shi'a Islamist groups, including the Da'wa Party; expels 40,000 Shi'a to Iran		
1980–88	Iran–Iraq War	Mar–Apr 2003	United States and United Kingdom invade Iraq; topple Ba'th regime
1987–88	Iraqi government wages Al-Anfal campaign, which includes chemical warfare, in Kurdish areas in northern Iraq, resulting in up to 60,000 deaths	June 2004	Handover of US power to Iraqi interim government
		Oct 2005	New constitution passed in national referendum—although with significant numbers of 'no' votes in majority Sunni provinces
Aug 1990	Iraq invades and annexes Kuwait; United Nations imposes strict sanctions regime against Iraq (in place until April 2003)		
		Dec 2005	Elections to new parliament, the Council of Representatives

Feb 2006	Attack on Al-Askari Mosque in Samarra triggers widespread sectarian violence	Jan–June 2014	So-called Islamic State (IS) captures large swathes of Iraqi territory, including Fallujah and Mosul, leading to forced resignation of Prime Minister Nuri al-Maliki
Jan 2007	US President Bush announces deployment of 30,000 US troops to Iraq (generally known as 'the surge') to defeat the insurgency	Aug 2014	So-called Islamic State abducts thousands of Yezidi men, women, and children; Sinjar massacre of thousands of Yezidi men
Dec 2011	Withdrawal of US forces	2015	Government troops regain control of Tikrit (April) and most of Ramadi (December) from IS
Dec 2012	Large-scale Sunni demonstrations to protest marginalization by Shi'a-led government of Nuri Al-Maliki		
Apr 2013	Insurgency resumes with levels of violence matching those of 2008	May 2016	Iraqi army and Shi'ite militias launch 'Third Battle of Fallujah'

Introduction

From its independence in 1958 until the imposition of international sanctions in 1990, Iraq benefited from a large and highly educated population (see Box 22.2 for demographic information), excellent infrastructure and welfare services, and a large and well-equipped army, paid for by significant revenues from the sale of oil. Yet this success came at a political price. The **regime** of former President Saddam Hussein (1979–2003) was one of the most authoritarian in the region and political dissent was brutally suppressed. According to the typology of late political economist, Nazih Ayubi (1995: 449), Iraq could be

BOX 22.2 THE IRAQI POPULATION

Iraq's population, like those of other countries in the Middle East, is very young, with nearly 50 per cent of the population under the age of 19. Relatively high birth rates (about four per woman), as well as high death rates of adult males as a result of wars, violence, and political oppression over the past decades, have created not only a young population, but also a demographic imbalance between men and women. While no official statistics are available, estimates of the proportion of the population that is female range between 55 per cent and 65 per cent. The more recent violence linked to the invasion and occupation of Iraq, as well as sectarian and criminal violence, has increased this demographic imbalance in terms of both age and **gender**. According to Iraq Body Count (2016), which provides conservative estimates of non-combatant deaths, 16,115 civilians were recorded killed in Iraq during 2015, 20,030 in 2014, 9,851 in 2013, and 4,622 in 2012. In 2014 and 2015, the so-called Islamic State was a major cause of death of civilians, along with the Iraqi military and US and coalition air forces involved in the conflict.

In terms of ethnic and religious make-up, Iraq has historically been diverse and mixed. Shi'a Arabs make up the majority of the Iraqi population, followed by Sunni Arabs, Kurds (predominantly Sunni), Iraqi Turkmen, and Assyrian and Chaldean Christians, as well as Yazidis. Historically, Iraq also had a large indigenous Jewish population, the majority of whom emigrated from Iraq in the 1950s and 1960s. Arabic (Iraqi dialect) is the most widely spoken language, followed by Kurdish, Turkish, Aramaic, Syriac, and Armenian. The south is predominantly inhabited by Arab Shi'i, whilst the north is mainly inhabited by Sunni Kurds. Nevertheless, in the north, there also live Shi'a Kurds called Faili Kurds, as well as Iraqi Turkmen and Assyrian and Chaldean Christians. Meanwhile, central Iraq has always been very mixed.

Sectarianism, especially in its overt violent form, is predominantly a post-invasion phenomenon; Iraqis had been living as neighbours and even intermarrying for decades. However, since Saddam Hussein's assumption of the presidency in 1979, divide-and-rule tactics increased sectarian divisions inside Iraq (Farouk-Sluglett and Sluglett 2003). There is no doubt that Kurds and Shi'a bore the brunt of the atrocities committed by the regime (see Box 22.1). Yet Sunni Arabs in political opposition parties and, increasingly, even within the Ba'th Party were also subjected to arrests, torture, and executions, as were members of other minorities such as Chaldeans, Assyrians, Turkmen, and Mandeans if they were part of opposition groups, or suspected to be so. Based on accounts of Iraqis of different ethnic and religious backgrounds, social class played a more important role in terms of defining social difference (Al-Ali 2007). Post-2003, religious and ethnic minorities, such as Christians, Yazidis, and Mandeans, have been targeted by Islamist groups, including Al Qaeda and, more recently, the so-called Islamic State, and have fled the country in large numbers.

categorized as a 'hard state' and a 'fierce state', but not a 'strong state'.

Saddam Hussein came to power as the head of the Ba'th Party in 1979. He employed techniques of power utilized by previous Iraqi regimes: the exclusion of rivals; the promotion of communal mistrust; the development of **patronage** networks; and violence (Tripp 2002: 194). He privileged his extended clan, whilst also developing communal and tribal relations as mechanisms of patronage and coercion (Tripp 2002: 194). Opposition to the Ba'th Party came from various political tendencies, including communists, secular liberals, Arab **nationalists**, democrats, and Islamists, and cut across ethnic and sectarian lines, including many Sunni political dissidents. However, Kurdish nationalists and Shi'a **political Islamists** were particular targets of regime repression and crimes against humanity.

The US-led invasion of 2003 triggered a number of processes, some of which were intentional, but others of which were unintended, which have led some to label Iraq a 'failed state'. At the time of writing, the Iraqi state is certainly a paralysed state when it comes to providing essential services and security to its citizens. As a result of **corruption**, the Iraqi military was easily defeated by so-called Islamic State (IS) in 2014 and is dependent on US support. Moreover, the conflict with IS since 2014 has further exacerbated trends towards state fragmentation, even within the Iraqi Kurdistan region, which previously enjoyed relative stability.

Reconstructing Iraq's Political Institutions

On 20 March 2003, in the face of significant opposition, the United States, supported by the United Kingdom, launched a 'pre-emptive' military attack on Iraq ostensibly to disarm the country of its weapons of mass destruction (WMDs) and end its support for international **terrorism**. Since then, the evidence for these claims has been largely discredited. The regime of Saddam Hussein was toppled on 20 April 2003; by 1 May 2003, US President George Bush had declared the end of hostilities, designating Iraq a 'post-conflict' zone. Yet, in reality, Iraq was entering a new phase of conflict—one that has combined elements of anticolonial insurgency with the 'new wars' of the postcold-war period.

Before the invasion, the US administration of President George Bush had assumed that it would hand over power to an Iraqi government within a short time frame. However, shortly after the invasion, it became clear to the United States that this would not be straightforward. After decades of dictatorship, there were no local Iraqi leaders, except for the Kurdish parties in northern Iraq, and there was limited local acceptance of the former opposition in exile that were brought into Iraq with the coalition forces (Melia and Katulis 2003). With the aim of creating a government that would be legitimate in the eyes of the Iraqi population, the United States entered into discussions with Iraqi political and religious leaders. With involvement from the United Nations, a plan for the introduction of democracy to Iraq was agreed, which would begin with the drafting of a transitional constitution, followed by multiparty elections to a transitional assembly and the drafting of a new constitution, and ending with elections to a new legislature—the Council of Representatives. Indeed, a political process took place, more or less following the timetable agreed at the end of 2003. However, this process, despite its apparently liberal underpinnings and UN technical support, failed to engender a transition to democracy; instead, it contributed to fostering perhaps even wider corruption and sectarianism within the political system than had previously existed.

Explanations of the failure of the post-invasion political transition may be divided between flawed implementation and flawed design. The timing of the elections and the constitution-drafting process were too early and/or too hurried, thereby undermining possibilities for reconciliation and confidence-building amongst Iraq's different communities. There was little consultation with Iraqi **civil society** over the contents of the constitution, as had been practised in other post-conflict countries. In addition, the United States attempted to shape the transition process according to its strategic interests: initially marginalizing the Sunni population, which it regarded as the source of the anti-US insurgency (International Crisis Group 2004) and later bringing unelected Sunni representatives into the process in an attempt to dampen the insurgency (International Crisis Group 2005).

Arguments criticizing the design of the political transition cite the nature of the electoral system adopted for the transitional assembly, which resulted in underrepresentation for the Sunni population (many of whom had boycotted the elections) (Diamond 2004; Rubin 2004). There are also concerns that the United Nations, United States, and other major donors attempted to implement what has become a standard post-cold-war liberal peace-building package with little recognition of the specific complexities of Iraq (Richmond 2009)—a country emerging from over a decade of sanctions, decades of dictatorship, and a recent war.

Post-invasion political **institutions** have proved ineffective in rebuilding the Iraqi state; instead, the political system has helped to engender corruption and paralysis of decision-making. Most political parties do not represent different political ideologies or ideas, but rather ethnic/sectarian-defined communities. Attempts at power-sharing within the cabinet, through the allocation of ministerial posts to different parties/ethno-sectarian groups in proportion to seats in parliament (called the *muhasasa* system), has become an opportunity for asset-grabbing and zero-sum **politics**, rather than cooperation (Dodge 2014). This has greatly delayed the formation of governments following different rounds of elections, presenting obstacles to effective decision-making. Perhaps even more worryingly, there were clear trends towards increasing dictatorship under former Prime Minister Nuri al-Malaki (2006–14) (Dodge 2012).

The failure of the post-2003 political system is illustrated by ongoing political crises in Iraq. There are unsolved tensions between the Kurdistan regional government and the Iraqi central government over the distribution of oil revenues and disputed territories (International Crisis Group 2012). The most serious problem has been the political marginalization of Iraq's Sunni community after 2003. In 2013, peaceful protests against Prime Minister Nuri al-Malaki were violently repressed by security forces, opening the way for the resurgence of the 'Islamic State in Iraq' (International Crisis Group 2013), which would later become the 'Islamic State of Iraq and the Levant' or the 'so-called Islamic State' (IS). By the summer of 2014, IS had captured substantial swathes of territory in northwest Iraq, including the major city of Mosul. The United States and members of al-Malaki's own coalition pressured him to step down in August of that year, and he was replaced by Haider al-Abadi. The ongoing war between the Baghdad government and IS has further exacerbated the sectarian tensions dividing Iraq's political elites, even threatening the future unity of the country.

In addition, since 2011, there have been growing popular demonstrations against the central government and the Kurdistan regional government, protesting against corruption and poor services. Civil society associations, journalists, and women's rights activists who express dissent and opposition to corruption, lack of transparency, and lack of proper infrastructure have come under attack by the regime. Arrests, harassment, imprisonment, torture, and even executions have become almost everyday occurrences in this new 'fierce' state, just as they were during the time of Saddam Hussein (Jamail 2012). At the beginning of 2016, it was reported that 'two-thirds of Iraqis think that their country is headed in the wrong direction, and party and leader favorability ratings are at all-time lows' (Al-Damaluji et al. 2016).

KEY POINTS

- Following the overthrow of the Ba'th regime, the United States helped to establish a multiparty democracy by organizing elections and drafting a constitution, which favoured the Shi'a religious and Kurdish parties, whilst alienating the Sunni community.

- The design and implementation of the political transition process resulted in institutionalizing political competition along ethnic/sectarian lines, encouraging corruption and undermining state effectiveness.

- Ineffective political institutions have paved the way for the re-emergence of dictatorship, **human rights** abuses, and increasing dissatisfaction amongst Iraqis. Sunni jihadist group the so-called Islamic State has benefited from this environment, further fuelling ethno-sectarian tensions.

Post-Invasion Violence and Security

Violence and insecurity has been endemic within Iraq since 2003, and has included the anti-US insurgency, sectarian conflict, and criminality. Much of the violence in Iraq after 2003 was initially directed against the US-led occupation, including the multinational forces and Iraqi police force, as well as Iraqi and foreign civilians working for Iraqi state institutions and foreign agencies. This insurgency was made up of different groups (mainly Iraqi, with some foreign fighters) that combined, to different degrees, patriotic and political Islamist motivations (International Crisis Group 2006). The surge in US troop numbers in 2008, combined with divisions between insurgent groups over tactics and the arming of Sunni militia (called the 'National Council for the Awakening of Iraq') in the fight against 'Al Qaeda in Iraq', dampened anti-US insurgency-related violence in early 2009. Almost all US troops were withdrawn at the end of 2011. In the summer of 2014, following the spectacular success of the so-called Islamic State in capturing large parts of Iraqi territory, the United States restarted its military intervention in Iraq, including a bombing campaign against IS, and military support and training for the Iraqi army and the Kurdish *peshmerga* fighters.

In 2006–08, sectarian violence by different militia groups—either those linked to political parties in government, such as the Badr Brigade, Mahdi Army, and *peshmerga*, or other neighbourhood militia—resulted in daily deaths on the streets of Baghdad and other cities in central Iraq, with individuals being summarily executed and their bodies dumped in sewage plants, irrigation canals, or the middle of the street (Abdul-Ahad 2006). The majority of killings occurred on a 'tit-for-tat' basis between Shi'i and Sunni groups. During this period, more than 40,000 families were displaced as minorities were 'cleansed' from neighbourhoods, particularly in Baghdad, to make them religiously homogeneous. After 2008, sectarian violence significantly decreased.

Since 2014, with the rise of the so-called Islamic State, ethnic and sectarian violence has once again flourished in Iraq, with 15,000 civilians killed between 2014 and 2015 (OHCHR and UNAMI 2015). The group has targeted religious minorities and non-Sunni Muslims with brutal punishments and killings, including the use of systematic sexual violence against women from religious minorities. Meanwhile, Shi'a militias, encouraged by the government to fight against IS to compensate for the weakness of the Iraqi army, have been accused of conducting extrajudicial killings and targeting Sunnis (BBC News 2014a).

The success of the so-called Islamic State is not only a result of the grievances of the Sunni community, but also of the corruption and politicization of the army, which quickly collapsed in the face of the IS offensive (Dodge 2014). This is despite the fact that the United States spent more than US$19 billion to train and equip the Iraqi armed forces after 2003, topped up by more than US$16.6 billion from the Iraqi government (International Institute for Strategic Studies 2008: 226). The Iraqi Ministry of Defence's budget rose yearly after 2003 and, by 2013, Iraq emerged sixth in terms of world rankings for military spending (CIA 2013).

Whilst the violence of the so-called Islamic State and ongoing sectarian conflict attracts the lion's share of media attention, Iraqis suffer from ongoing insecurity as a result of crime. Criminal gangs kidnap Iraqis for financial gain, and women and young girls have been particularly vulnerable to trafficking for prostitution and forced marriage. If they manage to survive the ordeal, the stigma attached to rape deters women from reporting cases of sexual violence, since they could be killed by their families to protect their 'honour'. As a result of the security situation, many women have stopped going to work or university and young girls have been pulled out of school.

KEY POINTS

- The sources of violence in Iraq are multiple and have included the insurgency against the US-led occupation, jihadists (Al Qaeda and, since 2014, the so-called Islamic State), sectarian violence, and general lawlessness and organized crime.

- In 2007, the United States managed to decrease the violence through a surge of troops and arming Sunni tribes to fight Al Qaeda. However, the so-called Islamic State emerged after 2012 and, by 2014, controlled large parts of Iraq.

- The remilitarization of the Iraqi state and huge numbers of Iraqi security personnel has not managed to eliminate the relatively high incidence of violent deaths in Iraq.

- Women are affected in particularly negative ways by continuing violence and insecurity.

Human and Economic Development

Following the invasion and thirteen years of economic sanctions, which both had a devastating impact on human and economic development, Iraq was in dire need of rebuilding and humanitarian assistance. However, reconstruction was undermined by a range of factors. The first few years after the downfall of Saddam Hussein were punctuated by changes in state personnel. Many experienced Iraqi civil servants were either dismissed from their jobs as part of the de-Ba'thification orders or fled the country as a result of the widespread violence. Meanwhile, staff were hired and fired with the changes in interim governments in the first few years following the invasion. In many cases, the political parties dominating national politics used state institutions to build up networks of patronage and nepotism, rather than hiring the most competent people to implement much-needed reconstruction (Al-Ali and Pratt 2009: 66). Slow disbursement of funding owing to the dire security situation, as well as lack of expertise, also contributed to undermine reconstruction. These factors were exacerbated by the widespread use of US contractors, rather than local companies, to undertake the rehabilitation of essential services and infrastructure. They became a target for insurgent attacks, as well as often inflating costs, whilst failing to achieve their objectives (Herring and Rangwala 2006; Al-Ali and Pratt 2009).

In line with notions of liberal peace-building, the Coalition Provisional Authority (CPA) attempted to dismantle Iraq's state-dominated economy and to establish a free market. It promoted **neoliberal economic reforms**, such as liberalizing prices and removing subsidies. However, some critics have argued that such reforms undermined, rather than supported, economic reconstruction and **human development** (Herring and Rangwala 2006). As a result of price liberalization, food prices increased considerably after 2004, leading to malnutrition amongst the poorest households. According to one report, over 10 per cent of children below the age of 5 in nine Iraqi districts suffer from acute malnutrition (Agency for Technical Cooperation and Development et al. 2010: 7).

There has emerged a significant problem of corruption within Iraq's state institutions. A report by international watchdog Transparency International (2005: 87) claimed as early as 2005 that Iraq could 'become the biggest corruption scandal in history'. The corruption ranges from petty bribery of civil servants, which was already increasingly common under the sanctions regime, to the misuse of millions of dollars of reconstruction funds owing to a lack of oversight by donors or by Iraqi institutions. Under former Prime Minister al-Malaki, corruption became entrenched and endemic throughout the Iraqi state. In 2009, it was estimated that 10 per cent of the central government's revenues were lost through corruption (Dodge 2012: 162). Meanwhile, al-Malaki hindered anti-corruption cases (International Crisis Group 2011).

As foreign troops have been withdrawn, international aid and the commitment to sustainable recovery for the country has almost stopped. Officially, Iraq has become a 'middle-income country' (World Bank 2012), yet the Iraqi government has so far been unable to develop the economy beyond the oil sector or to secure the basic needs of its population. Iraq's economy remains heavily dependent on its oil industry (90 per cent) and has so far failed to diversify. By 2015, the price of oil had fallen by more than half and the volume of Iraq's oil exports had fallen by a fifth, while the government had to embark on a costly military campaign against the so-called Islamic State in the north and the west of Iraq. These factors, together with the rising cost of imports, have already seen the Central Bank of Iraq's foreign-currency reserves shrink from US$78 billion at the end of 2013 to around US$50 billion in late 2016. The Iraqi dinar also fell sharply during this period (Al-Khatteeb 2015).

By 2010, only 45 per cent of the population had access to clean drinking water; food prices and food insecurity had risen; the health system was overburdened, and in need of both equipment and professional staff; education was deemed inadequate at all levels, from primary school to universities, and illiteracy and school dropout rates had risen significantly (Agency for Technical Cooperation and Development et al. 2010). By 2015, the situation became even worse owing to 3.2 million internally displaced people, in addition to Iraq hosting about a quarter of a million Syrian refugees (Mackenzie 2016). The humanitarian situation in Iraq continues to deteriorate: 10 million people—nearly a third of the total country's population—were in need of lifesaving assistance by the end of 2015; as a result of the conflict with the so-called Islamic State, the protection of civilians became a major challenge (European Commission 2015). Health capacities are severely overburdened and disrupted, while severely limited water and sanitation services have triggered a high risk of disease (UNOCHA 2015: 3).

Poverty and unemployment are serious problems throughout the country. The conflict with the so-called Islamic State has led to an increase in poverty levels: the number of people living below the poverty line increased by an estimated 2.8 million by end of 2014, to become 22.5 per cent of the population, while an additional 800,000 became unemployed—and increased levels of violence after 2013, combined with years of severe economic and social fragmentation, led a World Bank report to suggest that ending extreme poverty would be challenging (Krishnan et al. 2014: 2).

Years of insecurity, violence, and lack of protection have seriously affected the health and well-being of Iraqis—particularly children, women, and internally displaced populations, as well as disabled people. The ongoing political violence, lawlessness, militarization of society, and increased authoritarianism continue to generate insecurity, and to seriously hamper human and economic development.

KEY POINTS

- Iraq had already experienced a humanitarian crisis and deterioration of infrastructure as a result of thirteen years of economic sanctions.

- While national security has been high on the agenda, **human security** has been neglected.

- Lack of expertise, neoliberal economic reforms, widespread corruption, and poor security have been obstacles to economic reconstruction and human development.

- The crisis and violence linked to the so-called Islamic State has increased the humanitarian crisis in Iraqi society.

- Iraq's dependence on oil makes it particularly vulnerable in the current economic climate.

Conclusion

Since the toppling of the Ba'th regime in April 2003, Iraq has faced multiple challenges that are interconnected and unresolved. The experience of Iraq illustrates the complex relationship between the political process, law and order, and socio-economic development (Burnell 2009). The political process, rather than encouraging cooperation, has contributed to conflict and failed to resolve key issues about the future of the country. The ongoing violence, as well as the weakness and corruption of Iraq's government, has presented huge obstacles to the economic reconstruction process, thereby impacting upon human and economic development. Simultaneously, the failure of human and economic development feeds grievances against the government and the political process more generally. Whilst Iraqi political leaders shoulder much blame for contributing to the failures of the political process and stoking ethno-sectarian tensions, the case of Iraq also underlines the significant role played by external actors, particularly the United States, in shaping the post-conflict reconstruction process, including the design of political institutions that have structured the behaviour of Iraq's elites.

 QUESTIONS

1. Do you think that Iraq is a 'failed state'? If so, in what ways?

2. What are the reasons for the high levels of violence in Iraq?

3. Despite significant oil reserves, why are Iraq's human development levels so poor?

4. Evaluate the success of multiparty elections after 2003 in bringing democracy to Iraq.

5. To what degree have the international community's post-conflict reconstruction measures contributed to Iraq's problems since 2003?

 FURTHER READING

Abdullah, T. A. J. (2003) *Short History of Iraq* (London: Pearson-Longman) A concise, insightful, and rigorous history of Iraq since the Iran–Iraq war by a well-respected Iraqi intellectual.

Al-Ali, N. (2007) *Iraqi Women: Untold Stories from 1948 to the Present* (London and New York: Zed Books) An accessible modern history of Iraq told in the voices of different Iraqi women.

Al-Ali, N., and Pratt, N. (2009) *What Kind of Liberation? Women and the Occupation of Iraq* (Berkeley, CA: University of California Press) Exploration of US reconstruction efforts in Iraq after 2003, focusing on their impact on women and women's activism.

Dodge, T. (2013) *Iraq from War to New Authoritarianism* (London: International Institute for Strategic Studies) An incisive and astute analysis of the major challenges facing post-invasion Iraq, with a focus on Iraq's remilitarization and the re-emergence of authoritarianism.

European Commission (2015) Humanitarian Implementation Plan (HIP) Iraq Crisis, http://ec.europa.eu/echo/files/funding/decisions/2015/HIPs/iraq_en.pdf

Farouk-Sluglett, M., and Sluglett, P. (2003) *Iraq since 1958: From Revolution to Dictatorship* (London and New York: I. B. Tauris) Provides the historical background to political, social, and economic developments in the post-invasion period.

Fawn, R., and Hinnebusch, R. (eds) (2006) *The Iraq War* (Boulder, CO: Lynne Rienner) A collection that explores the international dimensions of the invasion of Iraq, including the reasons why the United States went to war, and the impact of the war on international and Middle East regional relations.

Haddad, F. (2011) *Sectarianism in Iraq: Antagonistic View of Unity* (London: Hurst & Co.) A nuanced discussion of sectarianism based on empirical research in Iraq.

Herring, E., and Rangwala, G. (2006) *Iraq in Fragments: The Occupation and its Legacy* (London: Hurst & Co.) A detailed account of political developments in Iraq during the first few years following the invasion, focusing on the ways in which the US occupation shaped political outcomes.

OHCHR and UNAMI (2015) Report on the Protection of Civilians in the Armed Conflict in Iraq, 11 December 2014-30 April, http://www.ohchr.org/Documents/Countries/IQ/UNAMI_OHCHR_4th_POCReport-11Dec2014-30April2015.pdf

Tripp, C. (2002) *A History of Iraq* (Cambridge: Cambridge University Press) A history of modern Iraq that focuses on the development of Iraqi state structures and their implications for how politics has played out. A very important background to understanding post-invasion developments.

World Bank (2015) 'A Risk Worth Taking: Supporting Iraq's Stability and Economy to Avoid Greater Risks', 17 December, http://www.worldbank.org/en/news/feature/2015/12/17/supporting-iraq-s-stability-and-economy-to-avoid-greater-risks

WEB LINKS

http://www.forcedmigration.org/research-resources/regions/iraq   Forced Migration online offers resources on the humanitarian situation and forced migration.

http://iwpr.net/programme/iraq   The site of the Institute for War and Peace Reporting's Iraq programme.

http://www.uniraq.org/index.php?lang=en   United Nations Iraq offers access to UN reports on Iraq.

For additional material and resources, please visit the Online Resource Centre at:
http://www.oxfordtextbooks.co.uk/orc/burnell5e/

23

Mexico
Transition to Civil War Democracy

Andreas Schedler

Overview

With a population of more than 120 million, a vast and heterogeneous territory, and an extended common border with the United States, Mexico commands the attention of international policymakers. In the closing decades of the twentieth century, the big challenge of the country was political democratization. Today, less than two decades afterwards, it is organized criminal violence. In the presidential elections of 2000, the victory of conservative opposition candidate Vicente Fox sealed the end of more than seven decades of hegemonic party rule. It culminated a protracted process of democratization by elections. Yet, as its fledgling democracy was struggling to find its way, Mexico slid first imperceptibly, then dramatically, into a situation of civil war. It suffered a pandemic escalation of violence related to organized crime. The democratization of the Mexican state was followed by serious challenges to its internal sovereignty (see Chapter 12). This chapter analyses this double transition: the country's incremental and largely peaceful transition to democracy, followed by its sudden descent into civil war.

Figure 23.1 shows a map of Mexico and Box 23.1 provides an overview of key dates in Mexico's history.

Figure 23.1 Mexico

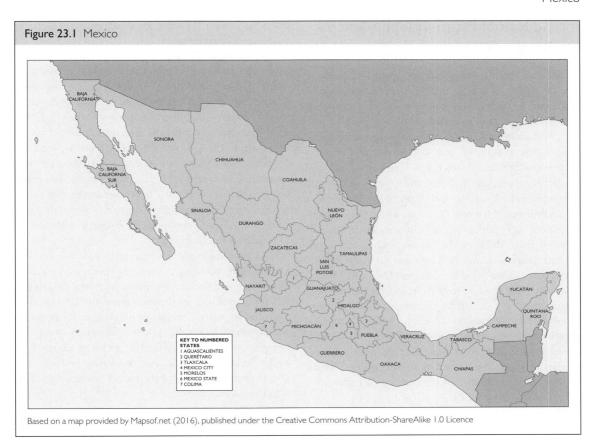

KEY TO NUMBERED
STATES
1 AGUASCALIENTES
2 QUERÉTARO
3 TLAXCALA
4 MEXICO CITY
5 MORELOS
6 MEXICO STATE
7 COLIMA

Based on a map provided by Mapsof.net (2016), published under the Creative Commons Attribution-ShareAlike 1.0 Licence

BOX 23.1 KEY DATES IN MEXICO'S HISTORY

1810–21	War of Independence against Spain
1846–48	War between Mexico and United States
1857	New republican constitution
1876–1910	Presidency of Porfirio Díaz
1910–20	Mexican Revolution
1917	New constitution (still in force)
1929	Foundation of National Revolutionary Party, succeeded by Institutional Revolutionary Party (PRI)
1934–40	Land redistribution, social reforms, and oil nationalization under President Lázaro Cárdenas
1982	Debt crisis
1988	PRI presidential candidate obtains a bare majority in 'earthquake election' among allegations of fraud
1990	Foundation of Federal Electoral Institute (IFE)
1994	North American Free Trade Agreement (NAFTA); Zapatista rebellion
1996	Crossing democratic threshold: 'decisive' electoral reform
2000	Opposition candidate Vicente Fox, from conservative National Action Party (PAN), wins presidency
2006	Felipe Calderón preserves presidency for PAN; deepens and extends 'war on drugs'; descent into economic civil war
2012	Enrique Peña Nieto from PRI wins presidential election

Introduction: From Independence to Revolution

As Mexico reached independence from Spain after a decade of war in 1821, it faced the triple challenge of redefining its political regime, constructing a modern state, and laying the foundations of a capitalist economy. Failure in establishing a regime—in institutionalizing accepted rules of access to power and exercise of power—precluded success in building a state and developing a market. In its first thirty years of political independence, the country fell prey to the vicissitudes of *caudillismo*. Between 1821 and 1850, the country was (nominally) ruled by fifty different governments, most of them delivered by military rebellions. Internal instability was matched by external vulnerability. In the war against the United States (1846–48), Mexico lost around half its territory. At home, civilian **politics** was increasingly driven by the major cleavage common to most of nineteenth-century Latin America: conflict between conservatives and liberals. Conservatives sought to protect the inherited political, economic, and cultural power of the Catholic Church; liberals strove to limit it and to create an autonomous sphere of secular politics.

The developmental dictatorship under Porfirio Díaz (1876–1910), while harshly repressive, brought an unprecedented measure of stability and **institutional modernization**. Having taken power by a coup, General Díaz proceeded to set up an early variant of **electoral authoritarianism** (see Box 23.2). Regular (indirect) presidential elections confirmed his continuity in power. At the same time, something like a modern state started to take shape, with a central government, a national military, and a permanent bureaucracy extending its reach to the country's periphery. Foreign investment aided by public infrastructure (railways) enabled some incipient dependent industrialization through the development of an extractive enclave economy.

The Mexican Revolution (1910–20) is customarily explained as a response to the growing impoverishment of the rural masses. Its first impulse, however, was entirely political. After three decades of developmental dictatorship, liberal reformer Francisco I. Madero demanded democratic elections and alternation in power. In the 1911 (indirect) elections, he won the presidency with 99.3 per cent of total votes. He was murdered two years later in a military coup. The ensuing civil war is commonly described as the first social revolution of the twentieth century; during the war, some 1.4 million people out of a total population of 15.2 million lost their lives.

The revolutionary constitution, enacted in 1917 and still in force today, enshrined a mixture of political **liberalism** and social reformism. It copied almost the full set of political institutions from the US constitution, and stipulated extensive social rights for peasants and workers. Ironically, under subsequent one-party hegemony, it proved ineffective in its procedural, as well as its substantive, aspects: it worked neither as an effective institutional constraint on politics nor as an effective policy programme.

> ### KEY POINTS
>
> • During much of the nineteenth century, Mexico's difficulties in institutionalizing a political regime frustrated its efforts at state-building and economic development.
>
> • Revolutionary civil war in the second decade of the twentieth century led to a new constitution, the liberal restraints and social aspirations of which were rendered ineffective by subsequent hegemonic party rule.

The Foundations of Electoral Authoritarianism

Post-revolutionary politics continued to be disorderly and violent. The bullet, alongside the ballot, enjoyed acceptance as a valid currency for gaining and losing public office. Violent protest, military rebellion, and the physical elimination of adversaries remained common. But regular elections took place at all levels, although nothing resembling a structured party system existed. Politics remained a game of elite competition mediated by force, not by formal institutions.

> ### BOX 23.2 ELECTORAL AUTHORITARIANISM
>
> **Electoral autocracies** display a nominal adherence to the principle of democratic rule, while denying democracy in practice. They hold regular multiparty elections, yet constrain and subvert them so deeply as to render them instruments not of democracy, but of authoritarian rule. Modern examples are Indonesia under Suharto and Russia under Putin (see Chapter 14).

The crisis of presidential succession in 1928 marked a turning point. After the assassination of President Elect Alvaro Obregón, outgoing President Plutarco Elías Calles announced his intention to institutionalize the revolutionary government. In 1929, he founded the National Revolutionary Party (PRN) as an umbrella organization of all revolutionary leaders, factions, and parties.

Twin institutionalization

The PRN was to pacify electoral disputes by providing a transparent mechanism of electoral coordination: it would select winning candidates from among the 'revolutionary family', reward their followers, and crush their opponents. By the mid-1930s, the PRN had centralized candidate selection by dissolving local parties and prohibiting the immediate re-election of deputies. Within a few years, what was initially a loose alliance of local factions established itself as a centralized hegemonic party that was to rule Mexico for the rest of the century.

Before quitting power peacefully in the 2000 presidential elections, the successor party of the PRN, the Institutional Revolutionary Party (PRI), was the longest-ruling political party in the world. It had clearly excelled in fulfilling its original mission of pacifying and stabilizing the country—but how did the PRI achieve this extraordinary success in party and regime institutionalization? Like all institutions, it had to achieve two basic objectives: 'stability' and 'value' (Huntington 1968). The former is a matter of expectations; the latter, one of evaluations. People had to know that the PRI was there to stay, but they had to value it, too.

The institutional infrastructure

Over seven decades, the PRI sustained a regime that looked as exceptional as its longevity. In essence, it rested upon three institutional pillars: a hierarchical state party; state corporatism; and electoral gatekeeping.

In the first regard, the hegemonic party operated as a big 'linkage mechanism' that turned the Mexican state into a unitary hierarchical organization. By controlling all branches and levels of government, the hegemonic party effectively cancelled the constitutional separation of state power. It annulled the horizontal division of power between the executive, legislative, and judicial branches, as well as the vertical division of power between central government, federal states,

and municipalities. The fusion between state and party granted almost unlimited powers to the president, who acted as the supreme patron at the peak of a **clientelist** pyramid—the Mexican state.

The state in turn controlled **civil society** by co-opting and corrupting potential dissidents and opponents. The party patronized and domesticated labour unions, peasant organizations, and popular movements by incorporating them into tightly controlled corporatist arrangements. It kept businesspeople content by means of subsidies, market protection, and informal access to power.

Electoral autocracies like the PRI regime reproduce and legitimate themselves on the basis of periodic elections that show some measure of pluralism, but fall short of minimum democratic standards. Their violations of liberal-democratic norms may be manifold (see Schedler 2013), and post-revolutionary Mexico had nearly all of them in place: limitations of civil and political liberties; restrictions on party and candidate registration; discriminatory rules of representation; electoral fraud; **corruption**; and coercion—as well as an incumbent enjoying close to monopolistic access to media and campaign resources.

The ideological infrastructure

Following Sartori (1976), scholars commonly portray Mexico's post-revolutionary regime as 'pragmatic' authoritarianism. It is true that the PRI did not institute a mobilizational dictatorship that tried to coerce its subjects into ideological uniformity; its relative tolerance of pluralism should not, however, be mistaken for the absence of ideology. Its revolutionary **nationalism** was not a mere echo chamber. Actually, the PRI was able to create what Antonio Gramsci (1992 [1929–35]) called 'cultural hegemony'. The state party defined lasting coordinates of **national identity**. Its ideology—a combination of liberalism, nationalism, and the corporative defence of the welfare state—continues to define the terms of national political correctness.

> **KEY POINTS**
>
> - Post-revolutionary Mexico developed an electoral authoritarian regime held together by a hegemonic party, the PRI.

- The party oversaw the state, as well as civil society. Through its centralized control of elections, it acted as the sole gatekeeper to public office.
- The PRI did not exercise its power 'naked', but draped in national-revolutionary ideology.

The Structural Bases of Regime Change

The relationship between economic development and political democracy has been subject to intense debate (see Chapter 14). Although it was a democratic under-achiever for a long time, Mexico seems to confirm the structural congruence between socio-economic and political modernization. Modern societies are complex and diverse. Autocracies strive to suppress their social and political heterogeneity, while democracies offer a peaceful way of processing it.

Societal transformation

Not unlike Porfirio Díaz—even if less personalistic, repressive, and exclusionary—the PRI established its own version of developmental dictatorship. Especially during the 'Mexican miracle' between 1940 and 1970, it achieved steady rates of economic growth and expanding public services. Seven decades of modernizing authoritarian rule by the PRI produced profound societal transformations. At the end of the revolution, Mexico was a poor, rural country with no more than 16.5 million inhabitants; at the turn of the century, it had grown to become an urban middle-income country with almost 100 million inhabitants. Although about half of the population still counts as poor and the country displays one of the most unequal income distributions in the world, societal modernization was bound to create strong pressures for democratization. Societal pluralism could hardly be contained within the confinements of a single party. The structural dissociation between a hegemonic party and a complex society was further deepened by economic mismanagement and crisis.

Economic crises

After 1970, a mixture of structural disequilibria and performance failure pushed Mexico into periodic economic recessions. Each presidential succession from

1976 to 1994 was marked by economic crisis. The oil boom and external debt first postponed, and then aggravated, the big crash that hit the country in 1983, which in retrospect appears as the starting point of democratization. There was nothing inevitable about it, however: neither structural pressures nor recurrent economic failures translate automatically into democratizing progress. During the 1970s and 1980s, the talk of the day was about *crisis*. Anything seemed possible, including a return to the violence of the past. It was only in the late 1980s that this diffuse sense of alarm receded. Actors and analysts started talking about democratic *transition*, and started playing the game of peaceful, incremental political democratization.

KEY POINTS

- Socio-economic modernization created multiple pressures for democratization.
- Cycles of economic crisis eroded the regime's **legitimacy**.

Democratization by Elections

Under electoral autocracies like the PRI regime, elections are not 'instruments of democracy' (Powell 2000), but battlefields of democratization. Unlike democratic elections, manipulated elections unfold as two-level games in which parties compete for votes at the same time as they struggle over basic rules. Democratization 'by elections' ensues when opposition parties succeed at both levels, when they manage to undermine both pillars of authoritarian rule: its popular support, as well as its anti-democratic institutions (Schedler 2013). Mexico's emergent opposition parties—the right-wing National Action Party (PAN) and the left-wing Party of the Democratic Revolution (PRD)—were able to start such a self-reinforcing spiral of rising competitiveness and democratic reform. As they turned into serious contenders, they were able to remove successive layers of authoritarian control through negotiated electoral reforms.

Electoral competition

Until 1982, all Mexican revolutionary and post-revolutionary presidents were elected by acclamation (other than in 1946 and 1952, when they faced popular splinter candidates). Plurality elections prevented opposition parties from winning legislative seats until the early 1960s, when the PRI introduced some element of proportional representation to keep the PAN in the electoral game.

In the wake of the 1982 debt crisis, however, the governing party's hegemony began to crumble. First, the PAN started to win and to defend its victories, in a series of post-electoral confrontations, at the municipal and state levels in northern Mexico. Then, in the 1988 presidential election, the performance of PRI dissident Cuauhtémoc Cárdenas shattered the image of PRI invincibility at the national level. His followers continue to think that he actually won the contest, being denied victory only by blatant electoral fraud. Afterwards, opposition parties conquered more and more sites of subnational power, at the same time as they strengthened their presence in the bicameral national legislature. In 1997, the official party lost its absolute majority in the chamber of deputies, inaugurating a period of divided government. Finally, in 2000, PAN candidate Vicente Fox won the really big prize in Mexican politics—the presidency.

Electoral reform

The rising competitiveness of the party system made possible (and was made possible by) profound changes in the institutions of electoral **governance**. Today, vote-rigging and the state control of elections belong to the past. Within less than a decade, Mexico effectively remodelled its electoral institutions. The electoral reforms added up to a veritable institutional revolution within the (self-denominated) regime of the institutional revolution.

The new electoral system rested upon three institutional columns: a new independent election body; the judicialization of conflict resolution; and comprehensive oversight by parties. Mexican parties decided to delegate the organization of elections to a permanent and independent election management body, the Federal Electoral Institute (IFE), founded in 1990 (and since 2014 renamed the National Electoral Institute, or INE). Electoral reformers also set up a new system for the judicial resolution of election disputes: the Electoral Tribunal of the Judicial Power of the Federation (TEPJF) now has the last say in all electoral disputes, national as well as subnational. Finally, parties institutionalized a 'panoptic regime' of surveillance that allows them to monitor the entire electoral process closely, step by step.

KEY POINT

- Mexico's democratic advance resulted from the interplay between democratizing reform and increasing interparty competition.

Transition to Civil War

With the 2000 alternation in power, Mexico turned into a 'normal' Latin American democracy operating in the context of a **weak state** and an unequal society. Like most democracies in the region, it has faced serious challenges of consolidation, deepening, and performance. Yet one dramatic development has blown up all expectations of democratic normality: the country's vertiginous descent into economic civil war (see Box 23.3).

BOX 23.3 ECONOMIC CIVIL WARS

Civil wars are large-scale lethal conflicts between collective actors within a country. In conventional civil wars, insurgents fight against central governments to achieve political goals, such as secession or the capture of state power. In economic civil wars, armed groups employ lethal violence for private gain, to exploit markets, populations, and states (see De la Calle and Schedler 2016). Although it had not been an issue during the election campaign, President Calderón decided to make the combat against drug cartels the defining policy of his presidency. It was to turn into its defining failure. Heavily relying on military support, Calderón essentially escalated the one-sided strategies pursued by his predecessors: bolstering the security apparatus, without strengthening the justice system; drawing the military into police functions, without subjecting it to oversight; chasing down cartel leaders, without dismantling cartel networks; pursuing drug trafficking, while giving traffickers a licence to kill each other; conducting massive arrests of suspected criminals, while lacking the capacity to subject them to fair and effective trials; and seeking mass confiscations of drug money and arms, while lacking serious strategies against money laundering and the importation of arms.

The escalation of violence

In 2006, after a close and contentious election, conservative Felipe Calderón assumed the Mexican presidency amidst a lingering security crisis. During the Fox government, violent competition between drug-trafficking organizations (so-called cartels) had been provoking more than 1,000 homicides per year, with a rising tendency (see Figure 23.2). In the academic literature, we speak of 'civil war' when confrontations between armed groups within a state cost a minimum of 1,000 'battle-related deaths' per year.

Policy incoherence permitted the creeping civil war to escalate—qualitatively, as well as quantitatively. In qualitative terms, modes of assassination moved towards demonstrative cruelty, routinized and ritualized. In certain parts of the country, the public display of tortured, dismembered, and decapitated bodies became part of ordinary life. In quantitative terms, the number of annual homicides attributed to criminal

organizations shot up from more than 2,000 in 2006 to more than 15,000 in 2010. In 2011, these figures reached a peak. They have been steadily declining since then (see Figure 23.2). We do not know how reliable they are, however, for data problems are massive. Many newspapers have stopped reporting on organized violence and, according to official figures, more than 20,000 persons have 'disappeared' after forced abductions.

The morphology of war

It is true that the new Mexican civil war is not a classical civil war in which ideological insurgencies strive to topple state power; rather, it is a prototypical 'new' civil war, fought for material gain, not social justice. Its motives are economic, not political. Its societal protagonists strive to evade or capture the state as much as to confront it. Moreover, the war is not one, but many. Its major lines of conflict run between criminal enterprises.

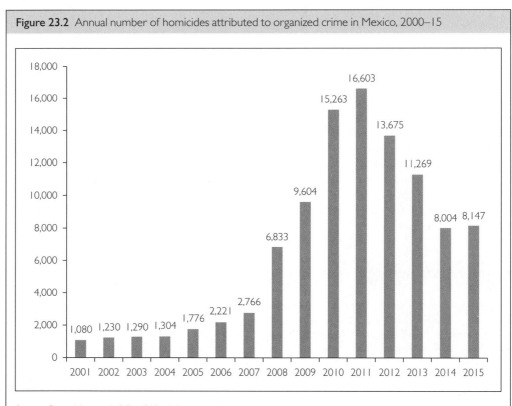

Figure 23.2 Annual number of homicides attributed to organized crime in Mexico, 2000–15

Sources: General Attorney's Office (2001–06), cited in Moloeznik (2009); Presidency of the Republic, 'Dataset of Deaths by Presumptive Criminal Rivalry' (2007–10); General Attorney's Office, 'Dataset of Deaths by Presumptive Criminal Rivalry' (Jan–Sep 2011), http://www. pgr.gob.mx; Lantia Consultores, 'Dataset of Violence of Organized Crime' (Oct 2011–Dec 2015), http://www.lantiaconsultores.com

The Calderón administration routinely attributed 90 per cent of drug-related assassinations to informal justice (the 'settling of scores') between criminal organizations. This figure was merely impressionistic, not to say propagandistic. Only 10 per cent of victims are innocent, it said; the rest are guilty. In what amounted to a tacit **privatization** of the death penalty, their cases were generally not prosecuted (Schedler 2015).

While the war involves various interacting 'non-state' conflicts, it also contains elements of 'one-sided' violence that predatory criminals unleash against civilian actors. Organized homicides have been only the tip of the violent iceberg. As criminal organizations have diversified their activities, the country has seen the dramatic expansion of violent crimes such as kidnapping, human trafficking, and extortion (mafia-like protection rackets).

The Mexican state, of course, is a warring party, too. In theory, it is the monopoly holder of legitimate violence; in practice, it commits criminal violence on a large scale. International **human rights** associations coincide in diagnosing 'widespread grave human rights violations committed by the military and police' (Amnesty International 2012: 234). In part, these violations are expression of state *abuse*. They are the non-intended, but inevitable, consequence of acting with brute force, little intelligence, and no oversight in an 'irregular war' characterized by endemic problems of information (Kalyvas 2006). In part, illegal state violence is a symptom of state *collusion*. Public officials are known to collaborate with criminal organizations (see, for example, Human Rights Watch 2013: 29–33). The 'criminalization of the state' (Bayart et al. 1999) feeds on the interplay of coercion and corruption. At some places, it results from the direct capture of local governments by armed groups. By colonizing local politics, criminal organizations expand their power, as well as their resource bases, as they obtain direct access to federal tax transfers. Not the entire state apparatus is at the service of criminal organizations, of course. During the Calderón administration, more than 2,500 security officials and more than 200 military personnel were murdered by criminal organizations. The 'collateral damages' to democracy have been massive, too (Schedler 2014). Dozens of mayors, former mayors, and candidates have been assassinated. Civil society activists have been intimidated and murdered. And 127 journalists and media-support workers were killed between 2000 and 2014, making Mexico one of the most dangerous places for journalism and political activism (Heinle et al. 2015: 25).

Explaining organized violence

Why has Mexico turned, within a few short years, into a 'violent democracy' (Arias and Goldstein 2010)—that is, a democracy besieged by civil war? Some might say that there is no puzzle to be explained: Mexico's plunge into societal violence has been a process of Latin American 'normalization'. Today, the country's homicide rate of 18.6 per 100,000 inhabitants lies close to the regional average of 15.6 (data for 2010 by OAS Hemispheric Security Observatory 2012: 18). Yet even if we were prepared to habituate ourselves to a new level of 'structural' violence, we would still want to explain its recent surge.

One set of arguments points to rising access to the *material resources* necessary to wage a civil war.

- *Money* The trade with illegal drugs is a lucrative business. It creates the wealth that permits criminal 'oligarchs' (Winters 2011) to organize their violent self-defence. While the tradition of drug production and trade in Mexico reaches back to the late nineteenth century, the market received a massive expansionary shock in the closing decades of the twentieth century, when cocaine-trafficking routes shifted from the Caribbean to Mexico. Illicit wealth sustains the organization of violence; yet the private organization of violence also produces wealth. According to estimates, less than half of the income of so-called drug cartels derives from actual drug sales. The rest comes from other violence-based illicit activities, some market-oriented, others predatory.

- *Arms* Since the late 1990s, Mexican drug cartels have been engaged in a kind of subnational armament race, expanding and professionalizing their structures of defence and repression. Given the porousness of the border and the free availability of small weapons on the US market (even more so since the ban on assault weapons was lifted in 2004), they have enjoyed unlimited access to means of destruction.

- *Personnel* The Mexican drug industry is estimated to employ about half a million people. An unknown number of professionals of violence work in the paramilitary branches of criminal organizations—as bodyguards, kidnappers, torturers, killers. Common clichés of poor young men who have nothing to lose suggest that the cartels' proletarian reserve army is unlimited—which may or may not be true. We know little about the identity and recruitment of killers. Up to now, though, labour supply for the Mexican killing field has been abundant.

A second set of explanations points to the *field of actors*. Both the state and organized crime have gone through processes of *fragmentation*. In the 'good old times' of hegemonic peace, state officials and criminal organizations institutionalized corrupt exchanges: the former agreed to tolerate illicit enterprises; the latter, to pay for official protection and follow certain rules of conduct. These 'state-sponsored protection rackets' (Snyder and Durán-Martínez 2009) have broken down. Both sides have been destabilized by the multiplication of actors. On the one side, the spread of electoral competition replaced hegemonic party discipline by party pluralism at all levels of the political system; on the other side, the governmental strategy of leadership decapitation destabilized the entire system of criminal actors. It fractured all relationships: within cartels, among cartels, and between cartels and the state. It provoked the 'disorganization' of organized crime. In 2006, six major transnational drug cartels were operating in Mexico; four years later, it was twice as many. In addition, more than sixty local criminal organizations had sprung up, developing any kind of activity that organized violence can render profitable, from mass kidnapping to private protection. The destabilization and multiplication of violent actors intensified violence within cartels (succession crises), among cartels (market competition), against the state (self-defence), and against society (predation).

The demand shock of the cocaine boom explains what made the war ignite; the structural availability of money, arms, and personnel, what has made it feasible; and the fragmentation of actors, what made it escalate. Together, these bundles of factors explain why the war is likely to go on for the long haul.

KEY POINTS

• Already, at the official inauguration of its democracy in 2000, Mexico faced a creeping low-intensity civil war between drug cartels. Fuelled by the cocaine boom of the 1990s, it also rested upon structural factors: easy access to arms and recruits.

• During the presidency of Felipe Calderón (2006–12), societal violence escalated. Almost 70,000 assassinations attributed to criminal organizations were registered during his term. Tens of thousands of individuals were reported missing. Dozens of mayors, journalists, and civil society activists were murdered.

• While strengthening the security apparatus, the government did little to strengthen the justice system. Its strategy of leadership decapitation destabilized the field of criminal actors. It intensified violence among cartels, between cartels, and against the state.

• The state has been a victim, as well as an agent, of criminal violence. Abuse of power, as well as collusive behaviour, have been widespread. At the local level, the boundaries between state and crime have often blurred.

Conclusion

At the turn of the twenty-first century, after traumatic experiences of instability and violence, followed by seven decades of authoritarian stability, Mexico finally seemed to have found a way of reconciling political stability and democracy. After the tranquil alternation in power of 2000, democracy seemed to be blessed by instantaneous consolidation. The democratic consensus within the political elite seemed firm. No anti-system actors were threatening the fledgling democracy.

Today, the picture looks much less encouraging. Rather than direct challenges to democracy, direct challenges to the state have arisen. Once again, the country has descended into fratricidal violence. The Mexican state is not a failed state. There are many things that it manages to accomplish rather well and there are vast regions, including the capital city, that have been spared the fall into the abyss of public insecurity. Yet both the state and democracy have come under siege. They are damaged and debilitated.

Within the current security crises, the PRI, the former authoritarian hegemon and grand champion of peace and order, has returned to national power. While former President Calderón chose to dramatize criminal violence, President Peña Nieto (2012) has been trying to downplay it. However, the dynamics of violence have been clamouring for periodic attention. In early 2014, the spread of armed self-defence groups in Michoacán led the president to turn the state into a federal protectorate. Later that year, the forced disappearance of forty-three students from Ayotzinapa by a local syndicate of criminals, politicians, and police in the city of Iguala, Guerrero, provoked a nationwide wave of protests. Citizen mobilization was fleeting, though, and has achieved little despite its intensity. Very quickly, the federal government, the Mexican state, political parties, and ordinary citizens have gone back to 'business as usual'. Apparently, Mexican elites, as well as a majority of citizens, still feel safe enough from organized criminal violence to accept it as a normal fact of life.

? QUESTIONS

1. What were the central political and economic challenges of post-independence Mexico?

2. How do you account for the institutional and ideological foundations of Mexico's post-revolutionary authoritarianism?

3. How did Mexico's socio-economic modernization in the twentieth century create pressures for political democratization?

4. Which were the core features of 'democratization by elections'?

5. Which are the main features of the internal war that drug cartels wage among themselves and against the Mexican state?

6. Why did this new civil war emerge? Why did it escalate? Why is it likely to persist in the near future?

7. Which are the implications of organized criminal violence for democratic rights and liberties? How does it affect the quality of Mexican democracy?

FURTHER READING

De la Calle, L., and Arjona, A. (ed) (2016) 'Conflict, Violence, and Democracy in Latin America', *Política y Gobierno*, thematic issue Empirical studies on political and criminal violence in the region.

Escalante, F. (2012) *El crimen como realidad y representación* (Mexico City: Colegio de México) An insightful analysis of the treatment of violence in the Mexican public sphere.

Greene, K. F. (2007) *Why Dominant Parties Lose: Mexico's Democratization in Comparative Perspective* (Cambridge: Cambridge University Press) A theoretical and empirical analysis of hegemonic party demise in Mexico.

Grillo, I. (2011) *El Narco: Inside Mexico's Criminal Insurgency* (New York: Bloomsbury) A succinct recount of historical drug trafficking and contemporary drug violence in Mexico.

Heinle, K., Molzahn, C., and Shirk, D. (2015) *Drug Violence in Mexico: Data and Analysis through 2014* (University of San Diego, CA: Trans-Border Institute) A data-rich discussion of organized criminal violence in Mexico.

Human Rights Watch (HRW) (2011) *Neither Rights nor Security: Killings, Torture, and Disappearances in Mexico's 'War on Drugs'* (New York: HRW) One documentation among several of human rights abuses by Mexican security agencies.

International Crisis Group (ICG) (2015) 'Disappeared: Justice Denied in Mexico's Guerrero State', 23 October, available online at https://www.crisisgroup.org/latin-america-caribbean/mexico/disappeared-justice-denied-mexico-s-guerrero-state A report on forced disappearances in Guerrero before and after the disappearance of the forty-three students from Ayotzinapa.

Ley, S. (2014) 'Citizens in Fear: Political Participation and Voting Behavior in the Midst of Violence', PhD dissertation, Duke University, Durham, NC A study of electoral and protest behaviour under the shadow of violence in Mexico.

Shirk, D., and Wallman, J. (eds) (2016) 'Understanding Mexico's Drug Violence', *Journal of Conflict Resolution*, thematic issue Empirical studies on the Mexican drug war.

Turati, M., and Rea, D. (eds) (2012) *Entre las cenizas: Historias de vida en tiempos de muerte* (Mexico City: Sur + Ediciones) Narrative accounts of civic initiatives in a context of uncivil violence.

Valdez Cárdenas, J. (2012) *Levantones: Historias reales de desaparecidos y víctimas del narco* (Mexico City: Aguilar) Narrative accounts of organized violence from the perspective of victims.

 WEB LINKS

http://articulo19.org/   Offers news and annual reports on freedom of expression in Mexico.

http://www.gob.mx/presidencia/   Site of the Mexican presidency.

http://www.ine.mx/   The chaotic website of the Mexican National Electoral Institute.

http://justiceinmexico.org   News and data on violence and the rule of law in Mexico compiled by the Trans-Border Institute, University of San Diego.

https://losqueremosvivoss.wordpress.com/   Short case histories of murdered or disappeared journalists.

http://menosdiasaqui.blogspot.mx/   Daily reports on violent deaths in Mexico.

http://movimientoporlapaz.mx/   Movement for Peace, Justice and Dignity, founded by Javier Sicilia, with links to other societal initiatives against violence.

 For additional material and resources, please visit the Online Resource Centre at:
http://www.oxfordtextbooks.co.uk/orc/burnell5e/

24

South Korea
Strong State, Successful Development

Peter Ferdinand

Chapter contents

Overview

In 1945, the Korean peninsula was freed from Japanese colonial rule by the United States and the Soviet Union. It was divided into two states—one communist, in the north; one capitalist, in the south. In 1950, North Korea—the Democratic People's Republic of Korea (DPRK)—invaded South Korea—the Republic of Korea (ROK). In three years, more than 1 million people died as a result of the conflict and it devastated the Korean economy. In 1961, it left per capita income in South Korea, at approximately US$92 per year (in nominal terms), among the lowest in the world. By 2015, that figure had risen to US$27,222, according to the World Bank (2015). In 1995, South Korea became only the second Asian state after Japan—and the second former colony anywhere—to be admitted to the Organisation for Economic Co-operation and Development (OECD), just after Mexico. In 2009, it became the first former aid recipient to join the OECD's Development Assistance Committee (DAC). This makes it one of the success stories of economic development, in which the state itself played a central role. What explains South Korea's remarkable development trajectory? In this chapter, we will discuss South Korea's developmental state emerging from an authoritarian political base, toward its democratic openings in the 1990s.

Figure 24.1 is a map of South Korea and Box 24.1 provides an overview of key dates in South Korea's history.

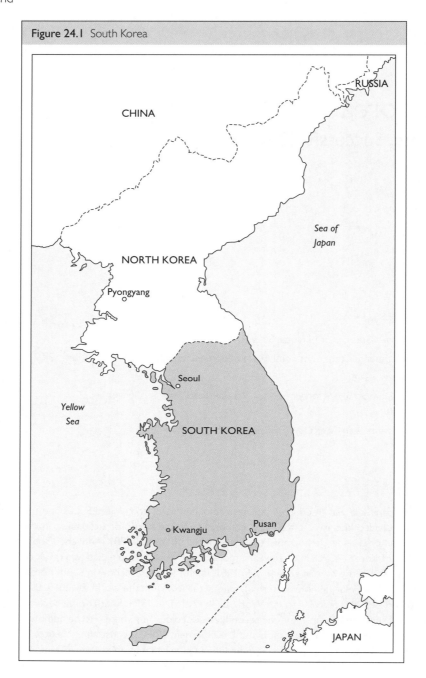

Figure 24.1 South Korea

Introduction: Historical Sources of National Strength

Four legacies from before 1953 contributed to the drive in South Korea for national economic development, especially after 1961: social traditions; centralization; the impact of Japanese colonialism, partition,

and civil war; and South Koreans' perception of their place in the East Asian region and the world.

In terms of social traditions, South Korea has the distinct advantage of being ethnically homogeneous. Out of a population of 50 million, only 20,000 Chinese living there with Korean nationality are not considered ethnic Koreans (Ferdinand 2013). Although the

BOX 24.1 KEY DATES IN MODERN KOREA'S HISTORY

1910	Colonized by Japan	2002	Roh Moo Hyun's election as president marks rise of new political generation
1945	Creation of two separate independent Korean states in north and south	2007	Lee Myung Bak elected president (Grand National Party)
1950–53	Korean War	Feb 2008	Lee Myung Bak's inauguration
1961	General Park Chung Hee seizes power in South Korea	2011	US Congress approves free trade agreement with United States
1987	Democracy re-emerges as General Roh Tae Woo allies with former oppositionist Kim Young Sam to form Democratic Liberal Party and rule through it	2012	Park Guen-hye (daughter of General Park Chung Hee) elected president (Saenuri Party, formerly Grand National Party) and becomes first female president in South Korea
1988	Olympic Games in Seoul; first free parliamentary elections	Nov–Dec 2015	Mass protests in Seoul against government's economic policy and insistence on state-approved history books in schools
1992	Kim Young Sam becomes first civilian president since 1961	2015	Prime minister resigns after involvement in corruption scandal
1997	Asian financial crisis; Kim Dae Jung elected president		

civil war generated millions of refugees and separated families across the new border, there has been no contestation of the right of a Korean state to exist. No significant group in society wanted to leave. The only unresolved business was: which Korean state should represent the whole of the Korean nation? This has meant that ethno-nationalism has been the dominant kind in Korea (see Chapter 7), although this has led to considerable ambivalence in South Korean society about their 'fellow' Koreans in the North, especially among those who still have relatives there. It is striking, for example, that, in the United Nations (UN) General Assembly, South Korea votes the same way as North Korea more often than it votes in line with the United States (Ferdinand 2013).

Also, over the centuries, Confucianism became the dominant ideology of social organization in Korea. Over half of the present-day population of the Republic of Korea (ROK) are either Christian or Buddhist, but principles of Confucian social organization are deeply embedded in Korean society. These respect a hierarchy of relationships within the family, in which everyone knows his or her obligations towards everyone else, as the basis for a well-ordered society. The **patriarchal** head of the family was entitled to absolute respect; so too was the emperor or ruler. Filial piety— the devotion of the son to the father—was the core relationship. The word for 'state' in Korean (*guk'ka*) is an amalgam of 'nation' and 'family', as it is in Chinese.

In terms of centralization, an early analysis of South Korean **politics** identified a 'vortex' of centralization as the dominant dynamic determining Korean political development into the modern era. This meant the dominance of the court (in imperial times) and the capital (Seoul) over the rest of a country of villages—that is, a lack of intermediate social organizations. Traditionally, Korea was polarized between rulers and the mass of society. There was weak horizontal organization (Henderson 1968). This enhanced the potential power of the new state.

The impact of colonialism launched Korean **modernization** and development. Until the twentieth century, the Korean peninsula—the 'hermit kingdom'—was a poor backwater, largely ignored by its neighbours; after 1910, Japanese colonialism introduced a wider set of regional relations and industrialization in the North, but in consequence the Japanese occupied all of the important managerial and administrative posts. The colonial experience generated a very powerful sense of patriotism among Koreans, in both the North and the South. The injustices that had been inflicted by the Japanese—their treatment as inferiors—created a strong unifying factor. Nevertheless, a small middle class of Korean entrepreneurs emerged. After 1945, they laid the foundation for Korea's indigenous industrialization drive in the South. Korean business corporations (the *chaebol*) came strongly to resemble the pre-war *zaibatsu* of Japan.

Finally, a desire to remake the country after the civil war underpinned the development drive in both North and South, where both felt overshadowed by near-neighbours China and Japan, and respective superpower protectors. The social whirlwind of the civil war, followed by land reform, had the effect of eroding social support for traditional elites, even if habits of deference persisted. Support could be transferred to the modernizing state.

Nevertheless, historical experience left challenges, as well as potential strengths. The civil war bequeathed a legacy of political turbulence and social mistrust, as well as the legacy of a northern border that was as arbitrary as those of former colonial states in Africa. Some in the South had collaborated with occupation by the North and resentments persisted. The victors exploited their victory to distribute spoils to their supporters, which encouraged **corruption**. The economy stagnated. Nationalist President Rhee Syngman (in Korean, the surname comes first) was widely regarded as corrupt and, in 1960, he attempted to rig elections again, only to be overthrown by popular demonstrations led by students. In turn, this led fairly swiftly to a military takeover led by General Park Chung Hee, who ruled the country until his assassination in 1979. It was President Park who laid the foundations for Korea's economic 'take-off'.

KEY POINTS

* Following independence, Korean society possessed many traditional elements that contributed to national unity.

* This unity provided a core strength for national development, yet the civil war also left a concomitant legacy of division and mistrust.

* It took the efforts of presidential strongman Park Chung Hee to impose the order that served as the basis of national economic development.

The Korean Developmental State: Dictatorship, Development, and National Restoration

Under the banners of national reconstruction and anti-communism, Park Chung Hee's **regime** set out to make the country 'rich and strong'. The main goals were economic development, but President Park

packaged this into a bigger project of 'national restoration' to match what had happened in Japan in the nineteenth century. He justified prioritization of national economic development, arguing that 'the Asian peoples want to obtain economic equality first and build a more equitable political machinery afterward' (Jones and Sakong 1980: 43).

Generals dominated government until 1992. This meant that development and industrialization were pursued as much for purposes of national defence against an ever-threatening North as for improving living standards. For example, in 1973, the regime set up a national shipbuilding industry; Korea is now the world's largest shipbuilder and Hyundai, the largest shipbuilding company. General Park imposed what has subsequently been termed a **developmental state** (see Chapter 12). Its main features have been described as: a **nationalist** agenda; state direction of finance for priority development projects; an effective and technocratic bureaucracy; a partnership between state and business; authoritarianism; and favourable international circumstances (Woo-Cummings 1999: 1–31). The major development decisions were formulated by the Economic Planning Board (EPB), founded in 1961. For the next fifteen years, the economy grew even more quickly than 'planned'.

A key factor was the state's **embedded autonomy** (Evans 1995): aimed at developing capitalist enterprises, the state was insulated from excessive pressure from those interests. The military's political domination helped. During the 1960s and 1970s, a solid, more merit-based, bureaucracy was created, replacing the political appointees of the 1950s. This was accompanied by what has been called a 'hardening' of the state's structures and operating practices (Myrdal 1968). Myrdal (1968: 66) has said that, in 'soft' states, 'policies are often not enforced, if they are enacted at all'. In 'hard' states, by contrast:

> [T]he success of planning for development requires a readiness to place obligations on people in all social strata to a much greater extent . . . [and] requires . . . rigorous enforcement of obligations, in which compulsion plays a strategic role.

(Myrdal 1968: 66–7)

The Korean military strengthened the state apparatus: between 1960 and 1970, the number of state officials nearly doubled—rising from 240,000 to 450,000

(Kohli 2007: 89)—and relied on trusted businessmen for economic success. To use the title of the book by Kim (1997), it was a case of 'big business, strong state'. Some companies had been established under the Japanese; others took advantage of the new opportunities created by a shortage economy that ran on permits and licences. They were able to accumulate business empires, the most successful building *chaebol*—that is, business groups or conglomerates.

The *chaebol* were family-based companies with cross-holdings of shares in subsidiaries. They benefited from government favouritism; financing remained the preserve of state banks. General Park was able to direct the nation's economy and to initiate industrial projects by summoning the thirty top business leaders for meetings within one room; cartels were encouraged to form and compete among themselves. Individual *chaebol* were compensated for government-induced financial losses (Lee 1997). However, as Kim (1997: 123) emphasizes:

❝ The story of South Korea's remarkable economic achievement is not simply that the state summarily reformed itself and gave marching orders to the private sector and that the private sector complied. The success was in part due to the private sector, which went over and beyond the state's mandate and actively took advantage of the favorable economic environment created by the state . . . Those *chaebol* that grew most rapidly did more than simply invest in sectors that the state had recommended; they employed their shrewd entrepreneurial skills. ❞

Most crucially, where businesses before 1961 grew primarily through **rent-seeking**, afterwards they were forced to focus on production.

A few families grew exceedingly rich and were also widely resented (Eckert 1990). In 1989, the Ministry of Finance estimated that, in each of the ten largest *chaebol*, the main family held roughly 50 per cent of all of the shares, whether directly or through cross-holdings (Janelli 1993: 84). The relationship between the regime and leading *chaebol* was one of both mutual support and vulnerability, with the balance of power gradually tipping towards the *chaebol*, although government kept control of financial resources, thereby stunting the development of an independent financial sector. Debt-to-asset ratios of *chaebol* soared, but few, if any, thought about the likely consequences until the Asian financial crisis of 1997. The government also tightly controlled the labour unions; memories of the civil war and military service, and fear of communist infiltration, were all invoked to strengthen **legitimacy** (Janelli 1993).

Korea followed Japan in concentrating upon full employment policies to raise welfare, rather than introducing a welfare state for which there was no popular demand, in part because of the Confucian tradition of family obligations. Large construction and infrastructure policies, rather than welfare programmes, were used to stimulate economic activity when the business cycle turned downwards.

To sum up:

❝ Park re-created the cohesive-capitalist state inherited from a colonial past and used it with a vengeance to push industrialization. Renewed contacts with Japan and the availability of Japanese capital and technology proved indispensable for these efforts. Within this framework, Park engineered a growth-oriented alliance of state and capital, recorporatized labor, and used economic nationalism to exhort the entire society into the service of economic advancement. ❞

(Kohli 2007: 123).

According to the World Bank, average annual per capita growth in gross national income (GNI) between 1960 and 1995 was around 7.5 per cent (see Table 24.1).

Table 24.1 South Korea's average annual growth rate of gross domestic product (GDP)

1950–59	1960–69	1970–79	1980–89	1990–99	2000–08
5%	8.5%	9.5%	9.4%	5.4%	4.8%

Source: World Bank, *World Development Report* (various years); EconStats

3848 Peter Ferdinand

KEY POINTS

- An intensive period of economic development and industrialization between 1961 and 1979 created a powerful business sector, but also solidified business dependence upon the state.

- From the early 1980s onwards, successive administrations tried to shift support towards small and medium-sized businesses, but were stymied by the entrenched power of the *chaebol*, upon which the government became increasingly dependent to deliver national prosperity.

Development Policies

In 1953, the economy was still overwhelmingly agricultural. The first task, land reform, was accomplished relatively easily because larger landowners were tarred with the brush of having collaborated with the Japanese. The second priority was rebuilding the country—a nationalist project, the execution of which created rents for businessmen who supported the government.

The government also strongly encouraged large-scale savings by imposing punitive taxes on expensive consumer imports and periodically mobilized the media to urge people to be 'patriotic' in their spending. The results were impressive (see Table 24.2) and the savings were channelled towards government-determined investment priorities.

Initially, the government pursued **import-substitution industrialization (ISI)** (see Chapter 4), as much for reasons of national security as because of the prevailing orthodoxy of development economics. In 1965, however, the government was forced to change strategy, as the United States reduced its aid to Korea to pay for the Vietnam War. Korea reacted by concentrating more upon exports, with the blessing of the United States, and increasing access to world markets. The selective targeting of industries for

national development succeeded handsomely: by the early 1970s, the government was sufficiently confident to introduce a policy to develop heavy and chemical industries (HCI). Following a temporary setback from oil price shocks, exports to the United States doubled between 1985 and 1988. Also, Korean corporations were now able to tap international financial markets for investments.

As Korean industry began to catch up with technologically more sophisticated international competitors, it also began to distance itself from government direction. The *chaebol*, now frequently obtaining cheaper funds abroad than from the government, increasingly began to talk of 'economic democracy'—that is, autonomy from state interference.

KEY POINTS

- South Korea's adoption of a state-led strategy for development has been outstandingly successful.

- As the economic strategy changed from import-substitution industrialization (ISI) to exports, business gradually distanced itself from government, calling for 'economic democracy'.

The Emergence of Democracy: Stronger Society, Weaker State, and Challenges of Corruption

During the 1990s, Korea turned into a functioning multiparty democracy, which withstood the 1997 Asian financial crisis without any attempt by the military to regain control. In elections in 1997, power changed hands from one party to another for the first time, and peacefully, allowing Kim Dae Jung, a veteran oppositionist to the military's rule, to become president.

Table 24.2 Gross domestic savings as a percentage of South Korea's growing GDP

1960	1970	1980	1990	2000	2008	2014
2%	16.2%	20.8%	36.1%	33%	30.1%	34.50%

Sources: World Bank, *World Development Report* (various years); EconStats

Political reform can be attributed in part to pressure from the labour movement and students, followed by white-collar workers, in part to increased pressure from the US administration, and in part to a greater willingness of later military leaders to make compromises. Until the late 1980s, it was commonly said of Korea (and other countries in the region) that democracy was an alien, Western concept. Yet the military leaders never abolished the national legislature, and they tried to enhance their legitimacy by organizing their own parties and winning elections—although President Park did declare himself 'president for life' in 1972.

Such was the country's economic development in the 1980s that, in 1988, gross domestic product (GDP) exceeded US$3,000 per capita—the threshold beyond which, for Huntington (1996b: 7–8), military coups scarcely succeed (see Chapter 14). Even in 1980 the overwhelming majority of the population said that they felt 'middle class' (Choi 1997: 106), although still heavily dependent on state largesse. There was no permanently active **civil society** counterposed to the state—something that began to appear only in the 1990s, as much a consequence of democratization as a cause.

However, the owners of *chaebol* were becoming restive about state control, feeling better equipped than government bureaucrats to determine development strategy. As Moon (1994) puts it, the relationship was becoming increasingly 'unruly'. Yet the main catalysts for change were workers and students. The labour unions saw democracy as essential to asserting their members' interests after decades of repression. And although students benefited from the massive expansion of the education system in response to Confucian values and the needs of a more technologically advanced economy, they were less deferential to their elders than previous generations. There were also far more of them. By the late 1980s, there were 1.4 million university students; in 1960, when students brought down Rhee Syngman, there were only 101,000. Repression by the riot police and the army alienated parents, especially middle-class ones. And organized religion became a more potent factor in democratization. Christianity attracted many more believers among the newly urbanized. By the mid-1980s, roughly a quarter of the population had converted to Christianity. Both Protestant and Catholic churches openly challenged the military leaders, and the church became the chief forum for political protest in the early 1980s.

In 1980, students in Kwangju City took to the streets to show solidarity with striking industrial workers. The riot police reacted with force, leading to at least 240 deaths. The regime survived the crisis, but as the eyes of the world fixed on Korea and its preparations to host the 1988 Olympic Games, a new crisis emerged: in 1987, General Park Chung Hee provoked widespread public anger and street protests by nominating General Roh Tae Woo as the next president. White-collar workers also joined in the demonstrations. US President Reagan specifically telephoned President Park to warn against bloodletting. The authorities embarked upon protracted secret negotiations, at the end of which Roh Tae Woo agreed with Kim Young Sam, the leader of the largest opposition party, to form a new party, with the understanding that Kim would become president after Roh. They called the new merged party the 'Democratic Liberal Party', deliberately echoing the name of the Liberal Democratic Party that had ruled Japan for more than thirty years. They hoped to inaugurate a similar period of conservative ruling-party dominance.

The 1990s saw democratic consolidation. The military withdrew from politics. Kim Young Sam replaced Roh Tae Woo as president and launched an anti-corruption campaign. Military officers were accused of misappropriating public funds, which harmed the image of the armed forces. The two preceding presidents, Chun Doo Hwan and Roh Tae Woo, were sentenced to long prison terms for massive corruption and responsibility for the Kwangju massacre. To break the tradition of over-centralization, Kim introduced elected **institutions** for local government, which in turn provided opportunities for the parties to extend their activities and to create additional posts to reward party members. But because political habits change slowly, this increase in elected officials also increased the amount of 'consideration' needed to achieve 'favourable' decisions. So while Korea remained a comparatively 'hard' state, democracy made it somewhat softer and more opaque.

In 1995, Kim led Korea into the OECD, which many pro-democracy activists had long advocated as a means by which to strengthen the democratic basis of politics, as well as to entrench a more market-oriented approach to economic management. Nevertheless, Kim's term of office ended in ignominy; the hopes of creating a hegemonic ruling party were dashed and Kim Dae Jung replaced Kim Young Sam. He, in turn, promised to deepen democracy and root out corruption. He guided Korea's responses to the Asian financial crisis that engulfed the country in 1997—but then his term of office ended ignominiously too, with two sons arrested on charges of corruption.

Korean politics was beginning to undergo a generational transformation, as leaders who had dominated the opposition movement for thirty years left the scene. The new president, Roh Moo Hyun, also from Kim Dae Jung's party, was in his 50s and offered electors a fresh start. He appointed other newcomers to national office. But his presidency ended in yet further ignominy amid allegations of corruption, which drove him to commit suicide in 2009. The corruption challenges have also marked the presidency of Park Geun-hye. In 2015, the prime minister (Lee Wan-koo) was forced to resign because of his part in a large corruption scandal involving the top echelons of the South Korea's private business. New legal codes have been implemented to combat corruption and to stem the growing discontent with government, but the close ties between government and the business conglomerates poses significant challenges to anti-corruption policies.

KEY POINTS

- Economic development reconfigured social forces and gradually constrained military rule; then, a changing external environment acted as a key catalyst in South Korea's transition to democracy.

- Democratic consolidation has yet to witness a marked decrease in high-level corruption.

Conclusion: Travails after Achieving Development

South Korea's development over the past sixty years has been impressive. In 1950, the country was poorer than Bolivia, but with a current per capital income above US$27,000, it is now richer than Spain and the fifteenth largest economy in the world (World Bank 2015). Along with Mexico, South Korea was touted by Goldman Sachs as one of the four largest and most promising states among the 'next eleven' for further economic success and for foreign investors—that is, as having the potential to join the largest economies in the world (Wilson and Stupnytska 2007). Nevertheless, an underlying sense of political malaise is noticeable.

In the World Values Survey carried out at the end of the 1990s, admittedly in the aftermath of the Asian financial crisis, only 17 per cent of ROK respondents said that they were 'very proud' to be Korean, while 27 per cent believed that 'most people can be trusted' (although the world average was only 28 per cent) (Inglehart et al. 2004: tables G006, A165). According to Lee (2011: 402), despite the ethnic homogeneity, 'Korea suffers from endless conflict and chaos, and Korean society is fractured by small, competing, and unyielding special interest groups'. Despite the **Gini coefficient** of household incomes of 0.302 in 2014, which made the ROK twenty-ninth in the world and more equal than most European states, Koreans still widely complained about inequality (Ferdinand 2012). Despite all of the development that has taken place, the average Korean worker still works the most hours per year of any country in the OECD (Ferdinand 2012: 152). Its politics are still dominated by men. Standards of living have still not caught up with those of the developed West. And, in years to come, these problems are likely to be exacerbated by generational conflicts of interest, as Korean society ages rapidly.

To a significant extent, this fretfulness reflects the ambivalence that many Koreans still feel about the place of the *chaebol* and their family owners in Korean society—especially their cosy relationship with the state—and it is a lingering legacy of the Park Chung Hee era. It was a source of pride that China took the *chaebol* as a template for reform of its state-owned enterprises at the end of the 1990s. However, the widespread Korean perceptions of interlocking corruption in these companies and the state has fuelled popular cynicism (Kang 2002), even though the 2012 Corruption Perception Index (CPI) ranked the ROK only forty-fifth out of ninety (Transparency International 2012). Most of all, it suggests that the state is either not strong enough or not willing enough, or neither strong nor willing enough, to deal with it. Kang (2002) graphically expresses the relationship between political and business elites as one of 'mutual hostages': each is dependent on the other. Ever since the 1980s, the Korean government has declared an intention to bring about a rebalancing of the economy by reducing the weight of the *chaebol* and increasing that of small and medium-sized enterprises (SMEs), yet it never happens. After the 1997 Asian financial crisis, Koreans accepted the severe austerity imposed by the liberal Kim Dae Jung administration in part because it promised to do something about the *chaebol*.

The electoral victory in 2007 of Lee Myung Bak from the conservative Grand National Party was in part based on the hope that he would run the country and the economy more successfully, because he would be able to get government and business to cooperate. Yet, at the end of his term, he had an even lower approval rating than his predecessors. And then, in 2012, as much out of nostalgia for the dynamism of the Park Chung Hee era as out of belief in her platform of policies, Koreans elected as president Park's daughter, Park Geun-hye, from the same party (now called the Saenuri Party), with the highest proportion of votes of any candidate since democracy was introduced in 1987. Yet the continuing corruption scandals through liberal and conservative administrations have persuaded the electorate that little has changed and, according to the OECD (2015), 70 per cent of the population now reports that they distrust the government. In the 2016 legislative elections, the Saenuri Party lost its majority.

Lastly, for all of its successes, the ROK has not grown into a self-confident, rising power in the world as have the BRICS countries—that is, Brazil, Russia, India, China, and South Africa. Partly, this reflects its regional perspective, in that it has traditionally seen itself as a 'prawn among whales' (that is, China, Russia, and Japan) in North East Asia; partly, it reflects anxiety over China's recent rapid rise and its touchy relations with Japan. Above all, it reflects fear of the unpredictable, and now nuclear-capable, North Korea just across the border. South Korea is still fundamentally dependent on the United States to defend it in case of invasion, yet its leaders have always harboured doubts about the unconditional willingness of the United States to come to its aid. So although the ROK is now a member of the OECD and has even signed a landmark free-trade agreement with the United States, it is still not considered a global 'player'.

QUESTIONS

1. What were the main features of Korea's developmental state?

2. In what ways was the state strong and society weak?

3. How far has this changed?

4. How far has Korea abandoned the developmental state and why?

5. Which was more important in the transition to democracy in Korea, long-term socio-economic change or short-term political crisis?

6. Why is it so difficult to stamp out corruption in politics in Korea?

FURTHER READING

Amsden, A. H. (1989) *Asia's Next Giant: South Korea and Late Industrialization* (Oxford: Oxford University Press) Examines how and why Korea got prices 'wrong', and yet achieved dramatic economic growth.

Eckert, C. J. (1990) 'The South Korean Bourgeoisie: A Class in Search of Hegemony', *Journal of Korean Studies*, 7: 115–48 Outlines the rise of the families owning *chaebol*.

Evans, P. (1995) *Embedded Autonomy: States and Industrial Transformation* (Princeton, NJ: Princeton University Press) Focuses on a key element of the developmental state.

Henderson, G. (1968) *Korea: The Politics of the Vortex* (Cambridge, MA: Harvard University Press) A very influential early attempt to theorize politics in Korea.

Janelli, R. L. (1993) *Making Capitalism* (Stanford, CA: Stanford University Press) The internal life of a Korean *chaebol* based on extended fieldwork.

Jones, L. P., and Sakong, I. (1980) *Government, Business and Entrepreneurship in Economic Development: The Korean Case* (Cambridge, MA: Harvard University Press) A revealing early account of the key role of government in Korean development.

Kim, E. M. (1997) *Big Business, Strong State: Collusion and Conflict in South Korean Development, 1960-1990* (Albany, NY: State University of New York Press) An excellent analysis of this key relationship during Korea's high-growth period.

Pirie, I. (2005) 'Better by Design: Korea's Neoliberal Economy', *Pacific Review*, 18(3): 355–74 A good and provocative summary of the changes in Korean political economy after the 1997 Asian financial crisis.

Shin, D. C. (1999) *Mass Politics and Culture in Democratizing Korea* (Cambridge: Cambridge University Press) The best single account of the emergence of Korea's democracy.

Shin, D. C., and Park, C.-M. (2008) 'The Mass Public and Democratic Politics in South Korea', in Y. Chu, L. Diamond, and A. J. Nathan (eds) *How East Asians View Democracy* (New York: Columbia University Press), 39–60 Updates the previous work.

Woo-Cummings, M. (ed) (1999) *The Developmental State* (Ithaca, NY: Cornell University Press) Outlines the basic principles and their realization in various countries around the world.

WEB LINKS

http://www.acrc.go.kr/eng_index.html   The Anti-Corruption and Civil Rights Commission.

http://english.yonhapnews.co.kr/   The main news service in Korea.

http://www.kdi.re.kr   The Korean Development Institute.

http://www.korea.net   The South Korean government's official home page.

http://www.koreaherald.com/   The *Korea Herald* (Seoul).

http://www.nec.go.kr/engvote/main/main.jsp   The National Electoral Commission.

http://www.saenuriparty.kr/web/eng/index.do   The main conservative party, Saenuri.

For additional material and resources, please visit the Online Resource Centre at:
http://www.oxfordtextbooks.co.uk/orc/burnell5e/

PART 7

Development and Human Rights

This part highlights the relationship between development and **human rights** in three different empirical contexts-namely, Nigeria, Guatemala, and Sudan. As earlier chapters have shown (Chapters 16 and 18 on development and human rights, respectively), there is a somewhat ambiguous relationship between these two concepts. A strong argument has been made that development is more feasible in strong states, where human rights are limited. Some have made the claim that economic development is more likely in states that limit human rights, especially related to civil and political rights. Human rights should become an integral part of **governance** later on in the development process, because it is simply too expensive for poor countries to implement the necessary reforms. However, as Chapter 18 further illustrates, the main empirical basis for such claims has come from a few well-discussed cases in South East Asia, such as South Korea and China. There is no conclusive evidence that violations of human rights in any case will *lead* to development, but, as the previous examples show, there is no clear-cut positive relationship between human rights and development either. However, in many cases, the two concepts are also overlapping. Development is increasingly defined more broadly than solely economic development. When **human development** is discussed, it is clear that human rights play an integral part. Additionally, human rights are not exclusively related to civil and political rights. By including aspects related to economic and social rights, it becomes apparent that the two concepts are closely linked. With regard to the relationship between development and human rights, Nigeria presents an interesting puzzle. Nigeria is a very oil-rich country, but has not been able to translate its immense natural resources into sustainable economic development and respect for human rights. As a result, Nigeria is an example of **resource curse** in that tremendous riches have resulted in an undiversified economy served by a corrupt elite (as discussed in Chapter 15 on governance). Ethnic and religious tensions, a result of colonialism, have been exacerbated by disastrous economic development, which has in turn led to a deteriorating human rights situation and intense violence. Although **civil society** remains strong, the country is mired by bad governance, low development, and a worsening security context.In Guatemala, human rights abuse and **underdevelopment** seem to go hand in hand. The civil war that tormented the country for several decades left several hundred thousand dead. The peace treaty achieved in 1996 was by many seen as a welcome respite and hopes were high. However, as the chapter shows, the security situation leaves much to be desired, and the country exhibits one of the world's highest murder rates and a high degree of underdevelopment. Because the state has failed to prevent, and has often even encouraged, human rights abuses, the system of formal democracy is not well regarded by Guatemala's citizens. Civil society has remained weak and unable to check the gross human rights violations. Development, both economic and otherwise, has been hampered by the security situation.The case of Sudan has similarities with both Nigeria and Guatemala, but also involves distinctive features. Like Nigeria, Sudan has oil, offering the potential for development. However, since independence in 1956, Sudan has been dominated by a northern Muslim 'ethnocracy'-a factor helping to precipitate secession of the Christian south in 2011. This northern elite siphoned off oil revenue, failing to reinvest it in either economic diversification or the public sector and leaving the marginal regions of Sudan still desperately poor. Long periods of military rule and civil war have further contributed a culture of authoritarianism and violence, in which democratic political rights and human rights have struggled to take root.

25

Nigeria
Consolidating Democracy and Human Rights

Stephen Wright

Overview

The relatively peaceful transfer of power to President Muhammadu Buhari in March 2015 provides hope of the consolidation of democracy in Nigeria. This is the first time in Nigeria's history that an incumbent leader and political party were voted out of office. Successive governments have struggled to promote democracy and human rights in the face of significant societal divisions, and have not produced the level of economic and human development commensurate with the country's vast earnings from natural resources. Military governments ruled the country for a total of almost thirty years, curtailing many political and civil rights, but civilian governments since 1999, alongside a vibrant civil society, have provided some cause for optimism. This chapter analyses these strands of Nigeria's political and economic development, focusing upon critical aspects of human security and civil society. It concludes on a cautiously optimistic note, recognizing the progress that has been made, but pointing to ongoing challenges.

Figure 25.1 is a map of Nigeria and Box 25.1 provides an overview of key dates in Nigeria's history.

Introduction

Prior to colonial rule, the territory that was to become Nigeria consisted of numerous empires and political entities, but British colonists gradually absorbed these into three administrative regions. In turn, these regions were amalgamated into the colony of Nigeria in 1914, although each maintained a strong degree of identity and separation. Tensions between the three regions deepened in the 1950s, as ethnicity became a political vehicle in the jostling for power in a post-independent Nigeria. This struggle to manage ethnic

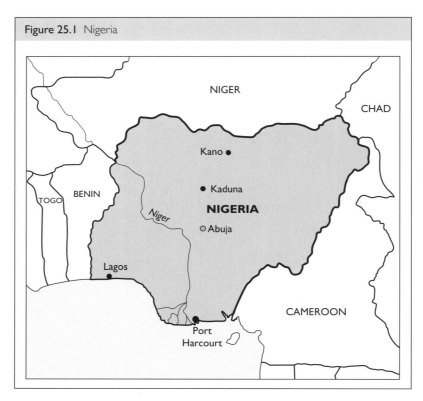

Figure 25.1 Nigeria

BOX 25.1 KEY DATES IN NIGERIA'S HISTORY

1960	Independence from Britain
1966	Two military coups end first civilian republic
1967	Start of three-year civil war over Biafran secession
1976	Head of state Murtala Muhammed assassinated; Olusegun Obasanjo takes over
1979	Second civilian republic inaugurated, under President Shehu Shagari
1983	Military coup on New Year's Eve ushers in sixteen years of military rule, first led by Muhammadu Buhari
1985	Ibrahim Babangida takes over in palace coup
1993	Moshood Abiola wins presidency, but elections annulled by Babangida; later that year, Sani Abacha seizes power in coup
1999	Following death of Abacha in 1998, new transition undertaken that elects Obasanjo to presidency and new civilian era begins
2007	Umaru Yar'Adua elected president in disputed election; first successful civilian transfer of power
2010	Following Yar'Adua's death, Vice-President Goodluck Jonathan appointed president
2011	President Goodluck Jonathan wins elections
2015	Muhammadu Buhari elected president, with first ever electoral defeat of an incumbent

and religious tensions has been a constant feature, and has significantly contributed to the country's political and **human rights** difficulties.

Political development

The British installed a parliamentary democracy in Nigeria prior to their departure in 1960, but this imported system could not function effectively in the highly combative political environment. The first of many military *coups d'état* took place in January 1966, sweeping the civilians from office. A second coup later in the year slid the country towards a brutal civil war between 1967 and 1970, during which as many as 3 million civilians died. Despite efforts to ease ethnic and religious tensions—notably by breaking up the three powerful administrative regions into smaller units, eventually ending up with thirty-six internal states—instability remained. The civilian government installed in 1979 barely lasted four years before the military swept back and a despotic era of military rule emerged with severe abuses of human rights. This period ended in 1999, when the civilian government of President Olusegun Obasanjo (himself a former military head of state) was elected to office. His re-election in 2003 was considered a hopeful sign of a maturing democratic system, although the election of President Umaru Yar'Adua in 2007, which was widely perceived to have been manipulated, cast a shadow over such progress. Obasanjo had attempted to change the constitution to allow him to contest a third term in office, but was defeated by the Senate in May 2006 in a victory for political rights. He then went on to muscle Yar'Adua into office in arguably the most corrupt election in Nigeria's history. Yar'Adua's three years in office were undermined by ill health and, in the last three months, he was absent from the country, hospitalized in Saudi Arabia, but refused to cede power to his vice president, Goodluck Jonathan. Such chicanery, shaped largely by elite and ethnic concerns, undermined the constitution, but a semblance of stability resumed after Yar'Adua's death and Jonathan's installation. Jonathan's term in office was mired by allegations of **corruption** and by the poor handling of domestic insurgencies, but his quick and somewhat graceful acceptance of electoral defeat by Buhari in March 2015 helped to stave off major disturbances. All of this is indicative of the challenge of entrenching democracy and human rights in a severely fractured state.

Regional influence

Nigeria's prominence in the West African region stems largely from two key factors: population and petroleum. Ethnicity politicizes the census process and makes an accurate headcount problematic, but the population is estimated to be around 180 million, a little under a sixth of the continent's total population, and places the country as the world's eighth largest. Geological good fortune enabled Nigeria to be a prominent producer and exporter of oil and gas, making Nigeria's the largest economy in the region (roughly equal to the other West African states combined) and one of the largest in Africa. Currently, Nigeria stands as the world's eleventh largest producer of oil and the sixth largest in the Organization of Petroleum Exporting Countries (OPEC), with 4 per cent of the world's proven reserves.

Nigeria has been the leading member of the Economic Community of West African States (ECOWAS) since its founding in 1975. All of Nigeria's immediate neighbours are former French colonies, and ECOWAS is perceived in Nigeria as an attempt to check French influence in the region and to promote its own. During its forty years, ECOWAS has attempted to improve trade and movement of people within the region. Official trade figures remain low, around 10 per cent of total trade, whereas unofficial (illegal) trade has flourished, with the porosity of the Nigerian borders being an important contributory factor. The control of trade policy and routes provides a major avenue for corruption by elites.

Nigeria has taken up leadership causes on behalf of the continent as a whole. During the 1960s and 1970s, these focused upon non-alignment, African independence, liberation in southern Africa, and economic rights. After 1980, as economic problems weakened Nigerian leverage, the country's global impact was less certain. During the 1990s, Nigeria's position as Africa's proclaimed 'champion' was further undermined by the rise of South Africa, which was a stronger economic power and which, in Nelson Mandela, had a leader who far surpassed in stature Nigeria's despotic military leaders. Nigeria's isolation peaked during the mid-1990s, when minor sanctions were imposed by the West and Nigeria was suspended from the Commonwealth. Nigeria's failure to democratize until 1999 also served to undermine its **legitimacy** to lead.

The new civilian era opened up by the election of Obasanjo helped to restore some credibility, and also to repair frayed relations with the United States, the European Union, and the international financial **institutions**. Investment in the oil and gas sectors increased considerably, although they had not been affected much during the 1990s. Nigeria also benefited from the United States' strategy to lessen its dependence upon Middle Eastern oil and, today, some 40 per cent of Nigeria's oil exports go to the United States.

KEY POINTS

- British colonization created a 'new' country of Nigeria, the people of which had lived separately prior to colonial rule.

- Nigeria's population is the largest in Africa.

- Nigeria has significant influence in West Africa via ECOWAS and tries to shape African political initiatives.

The Political Economy of Oil

Economic transformation

At independence, agriculture dominated the economy. The British had created export production of single crops for each region: groundnuts in the north; palm oil in the southeast; and cocoa in the southwest. Oil production, focused in southeastern Nigeria, began in earnest in the 1960s and was a factor in the country's civil war. Once peace was attained, oil production accelerated rapidly, contributing to an economic boom in the 1970s, helped significantly by soaring prices after 1973. Agriculture quickly lost its prominence as oil revenues contributed 90 per cent of export revenues, a figure that has remained fairly constant ever since. Massive development schemes were started, including dams, roads, airports, universities, and hospitals, but some of these projects were of more political significance than economic benefit to the country.

The combination of oil wealth and a large consumer population led to considerable foreign investment and tighter integration in the global political economy. By the end of the 1970s, Nigeria utilized its growing diplomatic and economic **status** to pursue important foreign policy initiatives, notably working for the 'liberation' of Zimbabwe and South Africa, and attempting to represent the views of developing countries in their call for a transformed and more egalitarian global political economy. Its true economic clout, however, was somewhat of an illusion, as subsequent events showed.

Elusive development

The hopes and ambitions of the 1970s were undermined after 1980 by a series of events. The most important of these was the glut of oil in world markets, which contributed to the collapse of Nigerian revenues. Development projects quickly became expensive white elephants and import dependence racked up large national debt. Oil revenues had not only been squandered, but were siphoned off to corrupt civilian and military elites, taking billions of dollars out of the development process. Oil sucked investment from other areas of the economy, as Nigeria became a textbook example of the **resource curse**. The governments of the 1980s, civilian and military, were forced to limit their outspoken role in world **politics**, and to take up structural adjustment funding and debt support from the World Bank and International Monetary Fund (IMF). These adjustments, particularly affecting health care and education, had a harsh impact on large swathes of the Nigerian population, undermining social and economic rights.

The 1990s was a difficult decade in Nigeria's political and economic development. Continuing low oil revenues served to debilitate social and **human development**. Infrastructure and transport crumbled, despite efforts at **privatization** and liberalization of critical sectors following World Bank and IMF orthodoxy. External debt rose to a level of US$34 billion, then the largest in Africa. Compounding the problem was the country's military leader between 1993 and 1998, General Sani Abacha, whose brutal rule and suppression led to Nigeria's ostracism from many international bodies for heinous human rights abuses.

The election of Obasanjo in 1999 helped to stabilize the economic environment. His initial attempt to crack down on corruption brought some limited success. Obasanjo was able to pay down the country's debt considerably, and facilitated large investment inflows into the oil and gas sectors. His attempts at partnership with the West brought a respite within the global arena, but did little to promote economic justice or redistribution to the majority inside Nigeria. The policies of his successors have also done little to transform the economy, with Jonathan's presidency marked by corruption and scandal. In December

2015, according to the United Nations, Nigeria ranked a lowly 152 out of 187 countries in terms of its human development, with average life expectancy just 52.8 years.

Current political economy challenges

Many challenges remain to promote a more balanced, stable, and equitable economy. These include massive economic inequalities, alongside huge unemployment, poor levels of human development, and a rampant abuse of economic rights. Although telecommunications have been a bright spot in Nigerian economic growth, crumbling and insufficient infrastructure and transportation, along with endemic power shortages, continue to undermine confidence. Diversification away from a dependence upon oil and multinational corporations has not occurred. The thorny problem of revenue allocation within Nigeria still pits local communities against the federal government—most notably, in the oil-producing areas of the Delta region, where an insurgency has been led by the Movement for the Emancipation of the Delta (MEND), the members of which feel cheated out of a greater share of resources. The government's response (allegedly in collusion with some of the oil corporations) has tended to be violent, undermining **human security** and disrespecting rights, even though a truce declared in October 2009 with MEND, followed by subsequent administrations, has helped to curb some of those excesses.

Corruption continues to undermine genuine economic development and a fairer economic system. The World Bank estimated in 2012 that Nigeria had lost some US$400 billion in oil revenues to corruption over the previous four decades. Lucrative contracts remain in the hands of patrimonial elites. Transparency International ranks Nigeria 136 out of 175 countries in its 2014 Corruption Perceptions Index (CPI). The gross domestic product (GDP) per capita stands at only US$3,203 in 2015, according to the World Bank (half that of South Africa). The more democracy is pursued, the more entrenched and resistant the forces of corruption appear to be, and it will be interesting to see if Buhari makes headway against this challenge. Furthermore, the collapse in global oil prices in 2015 is increasing economic and budgetary pressures within the country, and led to a two-thirds cut in capital spending.

KEY POINTS

- The mainstay of the Nigerian economy is oil, accounting for the vast majority of export revenue.

- Economic development is not spread evenly across the population and many indicators illuminate continuing development challenges.

- The 2000s witnessed a slight upturn in macro-economic conditions, partly helped by the presence of civilian government, although the downturn in oil prices in 2015 is causing problems at time of writing.

Human Security and Civil Society

Social and religious fabric

Nigeria is made up of a complex mosaic of ethnic, regional, and religious identities, all of which have served at some time or other to undermine the country's stability. British colonialism forged together a country of disparate people, and also helped to create a heightened sense of **ethnic identity** and competition. The three regions—north, west, and east—of colonial Nigeria contained a single dominant ethnic group in each—Hausa, Yoruba, and Igbo, respectively—who often viewed politics as a battle for resources between the ethnic groups. The fledgling federal state at independence could not contain this animosity and the early experiment in democracy was brought to an abrupt halt with the 1966 military coup. Tensions between these three powerful ethnic groups form only a part of the story. Minority ethnic groups, particularly from the centre of the country and the country's oil belt, have increasingly become a major factor in politics. Superimposed upon this ethnic tension is religion. A rough division sees the country split into a Muslim north and a Christian south, although the reality is much more complex. Religious differences have become increasingly politicized, and the establishment of **Sharia** (or Islamic) law in many northern states exacerbates an already tense situation and appears to threaten religious freedom and civil rights for Christians in those states. Such religious tensions are also exacerbated by severe economic deprivation, poverty, and disaffection. Religious riots, normally led by unemployed and alienated youth, killing hundreds at a time, are now commonplace. The Nigeria

Social Violence Project at Johns Hopkins University recorded 32,943 deaths from social violence in the country between January 1998 and December 2014. These high levels of human insecurity provide a problem that no Nigerian government has been able to solve and has often led to repressive retaliation by security forces.

Boko Haram

The most recent manifestation of these problems is the emergence of radical Islamic group Boko Haram (meaning 'Western education is bad/sacrilegious') in the north. Drawing strength from radicalized and unemployed youth, this organization has resorted to terror tactics, with bombings and assassinations in government offices, international agencies (such as the United Nations' compound in Abuja), Christian churches, and other random attacks. In February 2013, for example, the organization killed nine aid workers inoculating children against polio. In April 2014, the group abducted about 270 schoolgirls from Chibok. Over the next two years, some escaped, while others were feared killed—and frustration in the country grew at the inability of the government to make progress. The government was finally able to negotiate the release of twenty-one students in October 2016, with the hope of more to follow. The overall death toll since 2008 from Boko Haram's actions is estimated at 20,000. In 2014 alone, fatalities caused by its attacks stood at 6,664 and placed the group as the world's most deadly **terrorist** group (ahead of the so-called Islamic State).

Boko Haram's actions have undermined human security, destabilized border regions, and weakened political and civil rights. Retaliatory actions by security forces have often not respected human rights either, and continue to undermine broad civil and political rights. President Jonathan's inept handling of the crisis was a major contributing factor to his electoral defeat in 2015. Since his election, President Buhari has launched coordinated military action against Boko Haram, though with slow progress. Although this insurgency is often viewed as religious, a strong case can be made to explain this in terms of the failure to provide economic rights and development across broad areas of northern Nigeria, and also as an indictment of government corruption and incompetence. Defeating Boko Haram remains a stern test for the Buhari presidency.

Beyond fragility?

Since 1960, Nigeria has had four different constitutions and republics, both parliamentary and presidential forms of government, at least eight governments overthrown by the military, and numerous different sets of political parties. The internal federal structure has evolved from three regions to thirty-six states in an effort to undermine the strength of regional and ethnic politics (and to offer more politicians the opportunity to extract wealth). In this environment of experimentation and instability, it is little surprise that democratic institutions and structures of government have found it difficult to establish themselves to provide stable and predictable political and civil rights (see chapter 3).

At independence, Nigeria was bestowed the **Westminster model** of government. This failed to contain the conflicts between government and 'opposition', which were exacerbated by the struggle between the fledgling federal government and established ethnically driven regional governments. Military governments ruled for all but four years between 1966 and 1999, and ranged considerably in capability and probity. Political parties were proscribed during much of military rule, undermining political rights and freedoms, and little progress was made in solving the social, ethnic, and religious problems facing the country. The civilian Second Republic (1979–83) was, like the first, dominated by northern power groups, and exhibited extreme corruption, ethnic bias, and electoral fraud before being swept from office on New Year's Eve 1983. This republic was very much fashioned upon the American presidential model, with an executive president, a senate, and a house of representatives, and was adopted for the Fourth Republic in 1999.

The 1990s were arguably the pinnacle of state repression and human rights abuses. In elections for the Third Republic in 1993, results pointed to a win by Chief Moshood Abiola, a Yoruba Muslim businessman. Alarmed at the possible consequences to their interests, the military government under Ibrahim Babangida annulled the elections, and transferred power to a military and civilian coalition that lasted a few months before being overthrown by Sani Abacha. Plans for a return to civilian government were repeatedly postponed, as civilian political leaders were handpicked and dropped by Abacha. By 1998, Abacha had manipulated the political process to the extent that he was the sole presidential candidate of all five parties allowed by his **regime**. Upon Abacha's surprise death, yet another transition was started and a new slate of political parties created. The success of Obasanjo, a former military head of state who had been imprisoned for three years by Abacha, indicates the residual power of military leaders in the political process (as does the election of Buhari in 2015).

The April 2007 presidential election provided the first-ever transfer of power from one civilian government to another, although within the ruling People's Democratic Party (PDP). The PDP selected Umaru Yar'Adua, a relatively unknown governor from the northern state of Katsina, to be its presidential candidate, probably because Obasanjo hoped to maintain his influence over party and country. The 2007 elections were marred by widespread fraud and violence, as Yar'Adua was guided into office. He largely continued Obasanjo's policies, although in a more subdued, low-profile manner, primarily because of his poor health. The uncertainty regarding the constitutional transition of power from Yar'Adua to Jonathan underlines the fragility of the system. The 2011 elections, although more peaceful than those of 2007, again polarized the country. Jonathan's government achieved relatively little over the next four years, with few successes against militant insurgencies and little headway in promoting economic development. Widespread frustration with the government's inadequacies led to its defeat in 2015, the first ever of a ruling party in office. Buhari's promises to eliminate Boko Haram and end corruption provided hope to a disillusioned electorate, and he won by more than 2.5 million votes, sweeping most of the states across the north and southwest of the country. Buhari's All Progressive Congress also won majorities in the house of representatives and senate.

Civil society

Despite long periods of oppressive rule and human rights violations, **civil society** groups have remained active and strong promoting civil rights. The media have been outspoken during even the darkest times, and help to maintain a healthy dialogue about national and local policies. The universities have also played a strong role in voicing opinions about governments and policies, and student and faculty protests and strikes are common. Similarly, trade unions are relatively well organized and not afraid to take action when their interests are threatened, and judges strive to maintain their independence. During the Abacha administration, repression of these groups was at its height, with many jailed without trial, but large numbers fought back against the regime, often from exile. Human rights and democracy organizations flourished, and worked with external groups to maintain pressure upon the regime. Unfortunately, these groups were sometimes divided upon ethnic lines, rather than united on social class, but nevertheless indicated the strength and vitality of civilian society, resisting blatant oppression. Prominent Nigerian writers such as Chinua Achebe, Ken Saro-Wiwa, and Wole Soyinka were also important in maintaining pressure upon the corrupt regimes. With such a vibrant civil society, aided by the use of social media, one perhaps might expect significant advances in the political arena in terms of **good governance** and accountability. Unfortunately, to date, this has not fully transpired.

Women's groups are also well represented in civil society, although their focus is often shaped along regional and ethnic lines. For example, the Federation of Muslim Women's Associations in Nigeria (FOMWAN) focuses upon education and health within an Islamic framework. Nationally, women's groups argue that they are worse off than in pre-colonial times, because their economic and political rights have been usurped by men. Few women reach the highest rungs of politics, especially in the north of the country. In 2015, women held only 6 per cent of the seats in Nigeria's house of representatives, an actual decrease on the previous year. Much work still needs to be done to improve the status of women, even though they do play significant roles within the formal and **informal economies**.

KEY POINTS

- Significant political experimentation with institutions and structures of government has occurred.
- Civil society groups have maintained a consistently strong role in promoting human rights in Nigerian political life.
- The election of civilian governments since 1999 gives hope that the cycle of military rule has been broken.

Conclusion: Development Challenges

Nigeria struggles to fulfil its promise. Despite its demographic size and economic potential, the country has been dogged by political, social, economic, and human rights problems. Development is linked to the need to improve political and human rights. Successive democratic elections since 1999 provide optimism that the country has broken the cycle of military government and may pursue better governance emanating from a democratic dividend. Inflows of foreign investment into the oil and gas sectors, as well as into telecommunications, indicate economic strength, even though significant economic inequalities remain, as does potential vulnerability within the global economy.

Corruption has to be tackled more vigorously. Ethnic and religious intolerance and violence also remain problematic and undermine human security, with successive governments showing only small gains and often resorting to violence against these groups. Human development indicators remain relatively poor. Democracy needs continual nurturing, with civil society's role vital. Efforts need to be made to consolidate civil, political, economic, and religious rights, and human security needs improvement. Nigeria is often seen as a bellwether for other African countries and so how it develops is of vital importance to the West African region, if not to the continent as a whole.

? QUESTIONS

1. What structures of government have been used in Nigeria since independence?

2. How have issues of national cohesion affected development in Nigeria?

3. To what extent has oil benefited or detracted from development in Nigeria? Is there a 'resource curse'?

4. How effective are civil society groups in promoting democracy and human rights in Nigeria?

5. Does the 2015 election confirm that democracy is entrenched in Nigeria today?

FURTHER READING

Adejumobi, S. (2010) *Governance and Politics in post-Military Nigeria* (New York: Palgrave Macmillan) An assessment of the problems facing democratization in Nigeria.

Balogun, M. (2009) *The Route to Power in Nigeria* (New York: Palgrave Macmillan) An empirical analysis of failed leadership in Nigeria.

Campbell, J. (2011) *Nigeria: Dancing on the Brink* (Lanham, MD: Rowman & Littlefield/Council on Foreign Relations) An assessment of contemporary Nigeria through the eyes of a US ambassador to the country.

Cunliffe-Jones, P. (2010) *My Nigeria: Five Decades of Independence* (New York: Palgrave Macmillan) A journalist's account of Nigeria.

Falola, T., and Heaton, M. (2008) *A History of Nigeria* (Cambridge: Cambridge University Press) An overview of the historical development of Nigeria and the legacies of history faced today.

Iliffe, J. (2011) *Obasanjo, Nigeria and the World* (Woodbridge: James Currey) A focus on Olusegun Obasanjo's role in Nigeria's political life since the 1960s.

LeVan, C. (2015) *Dictators and Democracy in African Development: The Political Economy of Good Governance in Nigeria* (New York: Cambridge University Press) A discussion of political groups within domestic Nigerian politics and their ability to influence policy.

Okome, O. (2013) *State Fragility, State Formation, and Human Security in Nigeria* (New York: Palgrave Macmillan) An analysis of Nigeria as an (un)civil society and a failed state.

Okonta, I., and Oronto, D. (2003) *Where Vultures Feast: Shell, Human Rights, and Oil* (London: Verso) An account of oil issues in the Nigerian Delta.

Smith, D. J. (2007) *A Culture of Corruption: Everyday Deception and Popular Discontent in Nigeria* (Princeton, NJ: Princeton University Press) An examination of the methods and impact of corruption in Nigeria.

WEB LINKS

http://www.theguardian.com/world/2014/may/07/twitter-hashtag-bringbackourgirls-nigeria-mass-kidnapping-
On the global social media campaign focusing on Boko Haram's mass kidnappings.

http://nass.gov.ng   Official website of the federal National Assembly.

http://www.ngrguardiannews.com   *The Guardian* (Lagos) newspaper.

http://www.onlinenewspapers.com/nigeria.htm   Offering access to numerous Nigerian news sources.

http://www.vanguardngr.com   *Vanguard* news media.

For additional material and resources, see the Online Resource Centre at:
http://www.oxfordtextbooks.co.uk/orc/burnell5e/

26

Guatemala
Enduring Underdevelopment and Insecurity

Rachel Sieder

Overview

This chapter examines Guatemala as a persistent case of underdevelopment, defining development in terms of social, economic, cultural, and political rights. It argues that the roots of Guatemala's underdevelopment lie in its domination by external powers, and historical patterns of state formation and economic accumulation premised on acute social and cultural inequality, violence, and impunity. The 1996 peace agreement represented an attempt to reverse historical trends, to 'engineer development', and to secure the human rights of all Guatemalans. Some key development indicators have improved since the 1990s, but basic needs, human rights, and security continue to be denied to most Guatemalans. The final section signals the main contemporary causes of the country's persistent underdevelopment: a patrimonialist and predatory state underpinned by a strong, conservative private sector, an extremely weak party system, the continued influence of active and retired members of the armed forces in politics, entrenched counterinsurgency logics, and the increasing presence of transnational organized crime. Today, the widespread insecurity and systemic corruption generated by long-run historical patterns of state formation and contemporary patterns of globalization constitute serious obstacles to development.

Figure 26.1 is a map of Guatemala and Box 26.1 provides an overview of key dates in Guatemala's history.

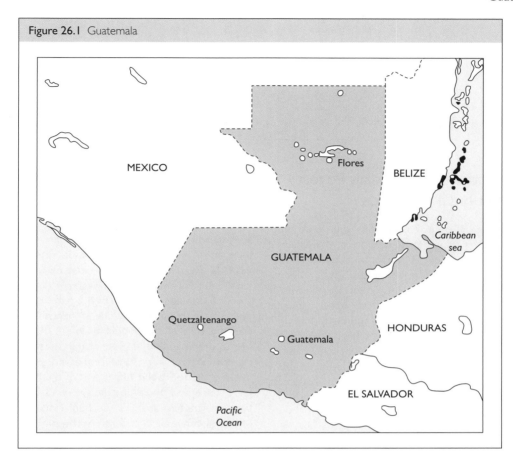

Figure 26.1 Guatemala

BOX 26.1 KEY DATES IN GUATEMALA'S HISTORY

1944	Forced labour abolished; universal male suffrage introduced
1952	Agrarian reform law approved
1954	Democratically elected government of Jacobo Arbenz overthrown in coup backed by US Central Intelligence Agency (CIA)
1960	First guerrilla insurgency
1978–83	Height of counter-insurgency war; 100,000 civilians killed or disappeared 1981–83
1984–85	Military oversees guided transition to elected, civilian government
1990	Oslo Accord between government and Unidad Revolucionaria Nacional Guatemalteca (URNG) establishes framework for national peace negotiations
1994–96	United Nations mediates peace process; agreements reached on human rights, indigenous rights and identity, resettlement of displaced populations, clarification of human rights violations, agricultural modernization, and reform of military and state
1996	Final peace settlement signed
1999	UN truth commission finds Guatemalan state guilty of acts of genocide during armed conflict; recommends prosecutions
1999	Frente Repúblicano Guatemalteco (FRG), led by former dictator Ríos Montt, wins presidential elections
2006	United Nations and Guatemalan government sign agreement to create International Commission against Impunity in Guatemala

2007	Social democrat candidate Álvaro Colóm wins presidential elections	2014	Attorney General Claudia Paz y Paz, who had spearheaded efforts to fight impunity, forced out of office
2011	Former military intelligence chief Otto Pérez Molina wins presidential elections	2015	Pérez Molina resigns; arrested on corruption charges after Congress removes his immunity
2013	Constitutional Court overturns verdict of genocide against former dictator Ríos Montt		

Introduction: Guatemala's Poverty and Multiple Inequalities

The influence of rights-based approaches to development (see also Chapter 18) in recent years has ensured that our understanding of development and **underdevelopment** has become more holistic. Where, previously, development was measured simply in terms of economic variables, assessments today tend to include composite measures of the socio-economic, cultural, and political rights enjoyed by its inhabitants, and the extent to which their inclusion, well-being, and security are guaranteed. Thinking on development policy has evolved accordingly (see Chapter 16). Guatemala can be characterized as a country with persistent underdevelopment (see Box 26.2).

Ethnic, regional, and gender inequality

Economic differences between different regions of the country, sectors of the population and ethnic groups—in a country in which indigenous people constitute nearly half the population—are huge. The predominantly rural indigenous areas of the country have the worst conditions of poverty, health, education, and land shortages. Government spending on welfare provision is lower in rural areas, although it has increased in recent years. Between 1980 and 2014, Guatemala's life expectancy at birth increased by 14.6 years (to 71 years), mean years of schooling increased by 3.2 years, and expected years of schooling increased by 4.7 years. Nonetheless, three-quarters of the population of 16 million people live in poverty and some 58 per cent of the population in extreme poverty. Some 90 per cent of indigenous people live in poverty. Around 70 per cent of the population is under the age of 30 and, by the age of 15, a third of all Guatemalans have abandoned school. Half (50 per cent) of all children under 5 suffer from chronic malnutrition (UNDP 2015).

Guatemala is classified as a middle-income country, but has a long history of low social spending. This is partly accounted for by historically low rates of tax

---

BOX 26.2 KEY DEVELOPMENT INDICATORS FOR GUATEMALA

UN Human Development Index	0.627 (128 out of 188 countries)
UN Human Poverty Index (HPI-1)	19.7% (76 out of 135 countries)
Gini index	55.1
Share of national income of top quintile of population	60.3%
Share of income of bottom quintile of population	2.9%
Percentage of population in poverty	75%
Percentage of population in extreme poverty	58%
Numbers of people living in poverty	12 million (of total population of 16 million)

Sources: http://hdr.undp.org/sites/all/themes/hdr_theme/country-notes/GTM.pdf; UNDP Human Development Reports and country reports (UNDP 2008, 2010, 2015); World Bank (2009); http://hdr.undp.org/sites/all/themes/hdr_theme/country-notes/GTM.pdf

collection: Guatemala's tax coefficient has remained at around 10 per cent of gross domestic product (GDP) in the post-war period, despite commitments in the peace accords of 1996 to increase it to 12 per cent by 2002. (For the significance of taxation for good government, see Chapter 15.) Public spending on education, health, and infrastructure improved somewhat after the mid-1990s, but remains very low by regional standards (CESR-ICEFI 2009). The legacy of **gender** and ethnic discrimination is evident in literacy statistics: although literacy rates for women improved between 1989 (when 67.5 per cent of women were literate) and 2006 (when 84.8 per cent of women were in this category), women still lag behind men (91.4 per cent of whom are literate), and indigenous women in the rural areas have even lower literacy rates (at 68.9 per cent). Women also occupy more precarious and less well-paid jobs: in 2006, 75.7 per cent of women worked in the informal sector and 53.4 per cent of these earned less than the basic minimum wage (UNDP 2008).

Growth and employment

For much of its recent history, Guatemala has enjoyed relative macro-economic stability and reasonable growth: an annual average of around 3 per cent growth in the post-war period. Nonetheless, with one of the highest population growth rates in the region (around 2.6 per cent per annum), income per capita growth rates were significantly lower (and even negative during the 1980s), averaging around 1 per cent annually over the past fifty years. Economic development has not generated sufficient low-skilled jobs to absorb the poor. Consequently, between 700,000 and 1 million Guatemalans are forced to migrate for seasonal harvest work. Working conditions for migrant workers are extremely tough: they are often paid less than the minimum wage, and have little or no access to health and educational facilities. In recent years, the structural crisis of coffee and sugar markets (two of Guatemala's main agro-exports) drastically reduced national and regional employment opportunities. Correspondingly, the numbers of those attempting to reach the United States as undocumented migrants has increased, despite the dangers and predations they face at the hands of organized crime and corrupt state officials as they cross Mexico. Rape, kidnapping, and extortion of migrants is commonplace (it is estimated that some 20,000 migrants are kidnapped in Mexico each year). But the flow continues and poor families in Guatemala increasingly rely on dollar remittances from family members working in the United States, which represent around 10 per cent of the country's overall GDP. In 2012, Guatemalans sent home the highest per capita remittances in the region.

Democratic disenchantment

Like most of Latin America, Guatemala is now formally a democracy. However, while respect for political and **human rights** has improved compared to the 1980s, these rights are still far from secure. Since restoration of electoral rule in 1986, elections have become freer and fairer, and an increasingly broad spectrum of political opinion has been represented at the polls, particularly following the successful conclusion of a negotiated settlement to the armed conflict in December 1996. During the 1990s and 2000s, decentralization and electoral reforms increased opportunities for citizen participation in municipal government. Yet Guatemalans' levels of political participation and faith in the **institutions** of government are extremely low compared to other countries in the region. Voter turnout is comparatively poor and regional public opinion surveys, such as the Latinobarometer, regularly find that Guatemalans have some of the lowest regard for democratic norms in the region. Explanatory factors include chronic impunity, citizen insecurity, and systematic **corruption**: Guatemala has one of the highest homicide rates in the region (40 per 100,000 in 2014—more than double the annual average during the thirty-six years of the armed conflict) and extremely high levels of so-called common, especially violent, crime. Many citizens, particularly the poor, are the victims of crime and gender-based violence on a daily basis. The judicial system is weak, impunity is routine, and those responsible for criminal acts are rarely prosecuted. In recent years, some advances have been made in securing high-profile prosecutions for gross violations of human rights and organized crime, but these have met with powerful opposition. For most Guatemalans, democracy clearly has yet to deliver.

KEY POINTS

- Guatemala has among the highest rates of poverty and inequality in Latin American and Caribbean.

- Indigenous people, rural inhabitants, women, and children are amongst the poorest and most disadvantaged sectors of the population.

- Despite relative macro-economic stability, tax collection and social spending rates over the last three decades have been dismally low.
- A return to **electoral democracy** occurred in 1986, but citizen disenchantment with government remains high.

Patterns of State Formation

Guatemala's economic fortunes were built on agro-exports and based on a highly exploitative form of rural capitalism, which in turn was reflected in authoritarian and exclusive forms of **politics** and development. The dispossession of indigenous people from their historic lands began with Spanish colonization in the sixteenth century and accelerated during the late nineteenth-century coffee boom. The capitalist planter class in Guatemala relied on forced wage labour, becoming increasingly dependent on the coercive power of the central state, dominated by the armed forces, to ensure its supply of workers. Economic downturns necessitated repression by the military to quell wage demands and to ensure profitability margins. Ruling elites did not view the poor and particularly the indigenous as citizens, but rather as subjects to be disciplined, controlled, and 'civilized'. Race and class discrimination were mutually reinforcing and underpinned the economic system.

The cold war: Reform reversed

Between 1944 and 1954, reformist governments were elected, following a coup by junior military officers. The administration of Juan José Arévalo (1944–51) introduced universal male suffrage, abolished forced labour and indentured servitude, and sponsored progressive labour and social security legislation. The more radical government of Jacobo Arbenz (1952–54) introduced an agrarian reform law in an effort to stimulate agricultural production and to address rural poverty. However, the expropriation of large, underutilized estates and their distribution to landless peasants angered both rich landowners and the US-based United Fruit Company, one of the largest landowners in Guatemala. United Fruit conspired with US President Eisenhower's administration and elements of Guatemala's armed forces to overthrow the reformers, accusing the Arbenz government of communist sympathies. In 1954, Guatemala gained the dubious distinction of being the second country subject to a CIA-sponsored 'cold war coup' (Iran being the first in 1953).

Following the overthrow of Arbenz, the Guatemalan armed forces were supported by the United States within the regional framework of counter-insurgency training. The state became increasingly dominated by the military, which, by the 1970s, had become a powerful economic actor in its own right. Espousing a virulent anti-communism, the private sector relied on the army to repress workers' demands for improved wages or better working conditions. Delegating the business of government to the military, it nonetheless exercised a permanent veto on social reform.

Insurgency, counter-insurgency, and genocide

Such acute socio-economic and political exclusion contributed to the emergence of a guerrilla insurgency in the 1960s. This was brutally repressed by the army. State violence increased throughout the 1970s, targeting trade unionists, social activists, and reformist politicians, reaching a peak in the early 1980s when *de facto* military **regimes** fought an all-out war against the civilian population to stamp out a second guerrilla insurgency. This involved hundreds of army-led massacres, 'scorched earth' measures, the forced displacement of thousands of Guatemalans, mandatory paramilitary 'civil patrols' for all indigenous men in the countryside, and the militarization of the entire state apparatus; it constituted one of the most extreme cases of state repression in twentieth-century Latin America. In total, during thirty-six years of armed conflict, some 200,000 people were killed (2 per cent of the 1980 population), nearly a quarter of whom were forcibly 'disappeared'. Another million were displaced, either internally or into Mexico. In 1999, the United Nations found that the Guatemalan state was responsible for over 90 per cent of gross human rights violations documented throughout the armed conflict, and was guilty of acts of **genocide** against the indigenous population between 1981 and 1983. This massive destruction of human and **social capital** had significant negative consequences for Guatemala's development prospects.

Electoral democracy and peace negotiations

In the mid-1980s, the military returned the country to civilian rule in a 'guided transition' to democracy designed to improve the country's standing before the **international community**, while perpetuating effective control by the armed forces over national affairs. Presidential elections held in 1985 were won by the centre-right Christian Democrat Party; a new constitution was adopted in 1986. Yet political parties remained weak and fragmented, the influence of the military was undiminished, and state-perpetrated political repression of political opponents and trade union and human rights activists continued.

The armed conflict was not resolved until December 1996, when the pro-business sector government of President Alvaro Arzú signed a definitive peace settlement with the insurgent Unidad Revolucionaria Nacional Guatemalteca (URNG), bringing nine years of stop–start peace talks to a successful conclusion. The final phase of the negotiations was overseen by the United Nations and, after 1994, an on-site UN mission was charged with verification of the accords. Through its sponsorship of the peace settlement, the international community became highly involved in attempts to kick-start development in Guatemala.

> ### KEY POINTS
>
> - Guatemala's republican history is characterized by authoritarian rule, coercive rural capitalism, and racist discrimination.
> - The counterinsurgency led to militarization of the state and extreme violence against the civilian population.
> - The return to elected civilian government and close of the civil war did not end the political influence of the military.

The Peace Accords: A Turning Point?

The peace accords aimed not only to end the armed conflict formally, but also to reverse the country's historically exclusionary pattern of development. They comprised thirteen separate accords, involving four main areas:

- the resettlement of displaced populations, the reincorporation of former guerrillas, and reconciliation regarding past violations of human rights;
- an integrated programme for **human development**, which mandated a 50 per cent increase over five years in health and education spending;

- goals for productive and **sustainable development**, including market-led reform of the agricultural sector; and
- **modernization** of the democratic state, including reduction in the role of the armed forces, strengthening the **rule of law**, and increasing **civil society** participation, particularly in implementing the accords themselves.

Three cross-cutting elements were emphasized: the rights of indigenous communities; commitments regarding the rights and position of women; and greater social participation. The international community pledged more than US$3.2 billion in aid—over 60 per cent as grants to implement the accords.

Lack of domestic commitment

The peace accords constituted important achievements in their own right, but implementation was slow and uneven. Given the country's violent past, and history of socio-economic and ethnic and gender exclusion, meeting the comprehensive goals of the peace settlement was bound to be challenging. However, lack of commitment by key domestic actors further constrained prospects for success. While the international community and civil society organizations backed the agreements, the commitment of the main political parties, the military, and the private sector to the settlement was weak. The powerful and conservative private sector staunchly defended its privileges blocking land and tax reforms, despite the more progressive stance of certain reformist elements within the business community.

Implementation: A mixed record

Other aspects of the peace settlement were more successful. The guerrillas were reincorporated into civilian life—the ceasefire was not breached and the URNG became a political party. Displaced and returned refugee populations were resettled, although many complained of being allocated poor land and of insufficient access to credit. A UN-led truth commission was completed in 1999—a major achievement that signalled army responsibility for gross violations of human rights and recommended legal prosecutions. Yet despite the sustained efforts of human rights organizations to secure justice, impunity remains the norm. In May 2013, former dictator Ríos Montt was convicted of genocide in a historic ruling, yet the country's constitutional court subsequently accepted an appeal by the former dictator's lawyers, overturning the conviction. Attacks have occurred against human rights organizations and indigenous communities struggling to secure prosecutions for human rights violations carried out during the armed conflict. And, in recent years, social protest against the negative effects of large-scale development projects such as mining or hydroelectric dams has been increasingly met with repression; community leaders have been murdered, intimidated, and imprisoned. Spending on health and education did increase in the 2000s, and a number of important structural reforms were implemented, particularly in education. However, this has not yet had an appreciable impact on social indicators. The global economic downturn in 2000–01, combined with the fall in agro-export prices, severely hampered even the limited development plans for the rural sector set out in the peace accords. The rural poor continue to lack access to land. In some cases, large landowners made a healthy profit from the peace funds provided by the international community by selling unproductive lands at inflated prices to the national peace fund. Landless peasants settled on these lands found that they were unable to feed themselves and were saddled with debt repayment obligations that they could not meet.

> ### KEY POINTS
> * Implementation of the peace agreements was beleaguered by private sector opposition.
> * Social indicators have failed to improve significantly and social conflict has increased in recent years.

Human Security and Development

Since the end of the armed conflict, insecurity has worsened; homicide rates have climbed, as have other indicators of crime, such as violence against women. In contrast to the period of the armed conflict, human rights violations are increasingly perpetrated by private agents rather than by state forces. In general, judicial and police authorities fail to investigate, try, and punish crimes, and ordinary Guatemalans lack faith in the ability of the state to guarantee the rule of law and human rights. Organized crime is an increasingly important source of capital accumulation, and transnational criminal networks have penetrated politics, the private sector, and government in the post-war period (Panner

and Beltrán 2010; Grupos de Poder en Petén 2011). In recent years, the UN International Commission against Impunity in Guatemala (CICIG) has worked together with the Attorney General's office to investigate corruption and organized crime. In 2015, their investigations and urban mobilizations led to the indictment and imprisonment of former President Otto Pérez Molina and Vice-President Roxana Baldetti on charges of involvement in *La Línea*, a far-reaching criminal network that involved political and economic elites in misappropriation of public funds, bribery, tax evasion, and trafficking. These developments are important, but it is unlikely they alone will reverse existing trends.

A patrimonialist state and weak party system

In addition to private sector intransigence, the failure to modernize the state and the weakness of democratic institutions provide clues to Guatemala's continuing underdevelopment. The internationally prescribed formula of **institutional** strengthening and 'civil society participation' contained in the peace accords failed to transform an exclusive, **patrimonialist** state into a **developmental state** (see Chapters 3 and 12). This reflects the balance of political forces, the inherent difficulty of changing historically entrenched patterns, and the spread of new forms of economic accumulation linked to corruption and transnational organized crime. The nature of Guatemala's party system is both cause and effect of the patrimonialist state.

During the 1990s, a core nucleus of political parties on the right and centre-right of the political spectrum contested elections, signalling a degree of stability of the party system, but these parties continued to be dominated by personalist politics within the private sector. Some centre-left parties gained ground after 1995, including the former guerrilla URNG, but command a negligible share of the vote.

In general, political parties tend to be dominated by powerful individuals who campaign on the strength of their personal **clientelist** networks, rather than by programmatic coherence or the representation of different groups in society. Subject to continuous division and fragmentation, many are little more than electoral alliances of convenience to support the interests of one or another economic sector. In the absence of congressional majorities, governments are forced to rely on opportunistic coalitions between the different parties. Party discipline is extremely lax, elected deputies often switching their allegiance during their term of office, and clientelism is rife. Many elected representatives use their congressional immunity to avoid investigation on criminal charges ranging from embezzlement to drug-trafficking. In broad terms, two blocs currently dominate Guatemalan politics. The first is a **populist** coalition of forces that relies on clientelist networks, particularly in the rural areas. This loose alliance represents a new economic elite linked to sectors of the military and organized crime. In the early 2000s, the political vehicle for this bloc was the right-wing populist Frente Republicano Guatemalteco (FRG), led by former military dictator Ríos Montt. In the latter part of the decade, that bloc dominated the government of Social Democrat Alvaro Colóm, which held power between 2007 and 2012 (and which was represented in the 2015 elections by Sandra Colóm, Colóm's ex-wife). The opposing bloc, dominated by traditional private sector interests and multinational companies, was represented by the governments of Oscar Berger (2003–07) and former General Otto Pérez Molina (2013–15). Following the scandal of *La Línea* and the imprisonment of Otto Pérez Molina, political newcomer Jimmy Morales, a comedian and television personality, was elected on a wave of anti-politician sentiment. Yet Morales is backed by the National Convergence Front (FCN), a right-wing party set up by retired military officers implicated in corruption, criminal activity, and involvement in gross violations of human rights during the armed conflict. In January 2016, former military officer Edgar Ovalle, a key member of Morales' team and head of the FCN, was indicted on charges related to mass forced disappearances of civilians during the armed conflict.

Military power, weak civil society, and continued human rights abuses

The armed forces largely retained their power following the peace settlement. Troop numbers were reduced during the late 1990s, but the military budget increased and the army has again been employed in public security functions, directly contravening the peace accords. The police remain weak, corrupt, and underfunded. Police and army units have also been implicated in extrajudicial executions and so-called social cleansing operations, including one notorious massacre of prison inmates in 2006.

Serving and former military officers form part of a network of associations of so-called parallel powers, which have influence within the highest spheres of government. These mafia-style networks are implicated in wide-scale corruption scandals, organized crime, and maintaining impunity for those guilty of gross violations of human rights. The UN Commission to Combat Abuses by Clandestine Groups (CICIG) began work in 2007 and its mandate was repeatedly extended by the UN Secretary-General, with the support of the US Embassy in Guatemala. While CICIG, together with key individuals in the Attorney General's office, has played a central role in combating these 'parallel powers', it is unclear whether its mandate will be extended beyond 2017. While civil society organizations have become more vocal advocates of government transparency and accountability in recent years, violence and intimidation against rights activists continue, and popular awareness of the historically high costs of dissent means that Guatemalan civil society remains comparatively weak. Indigenous Mayan organizations gained a national presence after the early 1990s, and promoted important national and local development initiatives, but their influence has declined as formal politics has been colonized by clientelist interests and organized crime. According to the framework for peace negotiations, all reforms to the constitution had to be approved by congress and then passed by a majority in a national referendum. A poll held in May 1999 (with a turnout of less than 20 per cent) rejected a package of constitutional reforms that included the official recognition of Guatemala as a multicultural and multi-ethnic nation-state. Elements of the private sector campaigned vociferously against recognition of indigenous peoples' rights, arguing that it would lead to 'reverse discrimination' and **balkanization** of the country. Guatemala has ratified the International Labour Organization (ILO) Convention No. 169 on the rights of indigenous and tribal peoples, but has failed to honour its international commitments to respect indigenous rights. Conflicts over large-scale infrastructural developments in indigenous regions—such as gold mining and hydroelectric dams—have led to increasingly violent clashes in recent years.

In spite of the end of the armed conflict, the human rights situation in Guatemala remains bleak. High levels of violent crime, continued impunity, and the ineffectiveness of the police and the judiciary mean weak civil rights protection for the majority of Guatemalans. The growth of rival armed gangs linked to drug trafficking during the 1990s worsened the security situation for ordinary citizens. Tough-on-crime policies against gang members have failed to generate significant improvements. Male homicide rates are amongst the highest in

Latin America and the Caribbean; violent murders of women also increased in the 2000s, leading campaigners to talk about 'femicide'. More than 5,000 murders a year are committed in Guatemala—more than during the final years of the armed conflict; most are never investigated. United Nations officials have accused the Guatemalan government of fostering a culture of impunity and have pointed to the costs of violence for development: the UN Development Programme for Guatemala estimated in 2006 that violence cost 7.3 per cent of GDP—costs that were associated with health care, lost production, and public and private security.

KEY POINTS

- The 1996 peace accords set out a programme aiming to reverse exclusionary development and to improve social participation, especially of women and indigenous peoples.

- The accords were backed by the international community and civil society groups, but the commitment of the Guatemalan armed forces, private sector, and political parties to the settlement was low.

- Some progress on implementation has been made, but targets have not been met. Private sector resistance to raising fiscal revenues remains high.

- Key factors impeding emergence of a developmental state include opportunist, clientelist, and fragmented political parties, a powerful and autonomous military, and relatively weak civil society.

- Confrontational party politics, and the rise of organized crime and 'parallel powers', continue to pose serious obstacles to development and undermine a more democratic politics.

Conclusion

Guatemala is a **predatory state**, rather than a developmental state. The US-supported derailing of the reformist administration of Jacobo Arbenz produced one of the most violent and authoritarian regimes in the region. The state lacked autonomy and was effectively colonized by powerful private interests. During the cold war, it was supported by the regional superpower under the aegis of anti-communism. Despite transition to electoral rule two decades ago, such predatory tendencies have not disappeared; indeed, many now point to the increasingly mafia-style operation of the Guatemalan state.

The peace process of the 1990s provided an important opportunity for reorienting historically exclusionary patterns of development. However, such a shift lacked the political commitment of the most powerful domestic actors, sufficient or effective international pressure, and the support of civil society. Guatemala today is a weak and illiberal democracy: the population may enjoy suffrage or political rights, but civil rights are not enforced, and the rule of law is routinely flouted by powerful actors within and outside government. Historical patterns of ethnic and economic exclusion, combined with the legacy of extreme levels of state violence against the civilian population, mean that citizen participation is low. The strength and conservatism of the private sector, its historic reliance on the armed forces, and the systematic persecution of the left and centre-left has engendered a particularly weak and venal political class and party system, constituting another impediment to development. More progressive elements face powerful opposition and seem unable to consolidate effective parties capable of winning elections.

Finally, long-term structural factors have not favoured the Guatemalan economy. Historically reliant on a particularly exploitative form of rural capitalism, the private sector has largely failed to adapt to new global conditions despite the relative decline of traditional agro-exports. Commodity prices rises have helped to secure macro-economic stability, but the historic lack of investment in **human capital** remains a serious impediment to future economic development. Prevailing economic policies have proved singularly incapable of generating greater development and equality.

QUESTIONS

1. What are the impacts of violence and insecurity on politics?
2. What is the relationship between politics and development?
3. How does impunity affect development prospects?

4.   Was the peace agreement successful in fulfilling its goals? Why, or why not?

5.   Are the main causes of underdevelopment in Guatemala largely economic or mainly political?

 FURTHER READING

Center for Economic and Social Rights (CESR) and Instituto Centroamericano de Estudios Fiscales (ICEFI) (2009) *Rights or Privileges? Fiscal Commitment to the Rights to Health, Education and Food in Guatemala*, available online at http://www.cesr. org/downloads/Rights%20or%20Privileges%20Executive%20Summary%20final.pdf An insightful source on social and economic rights in Guatemala.

 WEB LINKS

http://hdr.undp.org/en/countries/profiles/GTM   UNDP Human Development Reports, Guatemala.

 For additional material and resources, please visit the Online Resource Centre at:
http://www.oxfordtextbooks.co.uk/orc/burnell5e/

27

Sudan
Human Rights, Development, and Democracy

Liv Tønnessen

Overview

Sudan is 'Africa in microcosm', with multiple languages, religions, and ethnicities. The largest geographic nation-state in Africa, spanning nearly 1 million square miles, has had a complex and conflictual political history since its independence from British colonial rule in 1956. Formerly a single country, political conflict between the north and south spawned Africa's longest civil war, which culminated in a peace agreement in 2005 and the secession of South Sudan in 2011. A year after South Sudan's secession, new conflicts over oil erupted along disputed borders between the two states. A civil war erupted in Africa's newest nation South Sudan in 2013. Sudan has remained embroiled in conflict in the western province of Darfur since 2003.

The political and economic marginalization of the regions in the south, east, and west has been a constant feature in Sudan's political history, and has significantly contributed to the country's instability, underdevelopment, and human rights difficulties. Competition for economic resources (both oil and land), as well as ethnic, cultural, and religious divisions, are basic ingredients of Sudan's conflictual history. The Islamist-military regime of Omar al-Bashir has ruled Sudan the last twenty-seven years.

Figure 27.1 is a map of Sudan and Box 27.1 provides an overview of key dates in Sudan's history.

Figure 27.1 Sudan

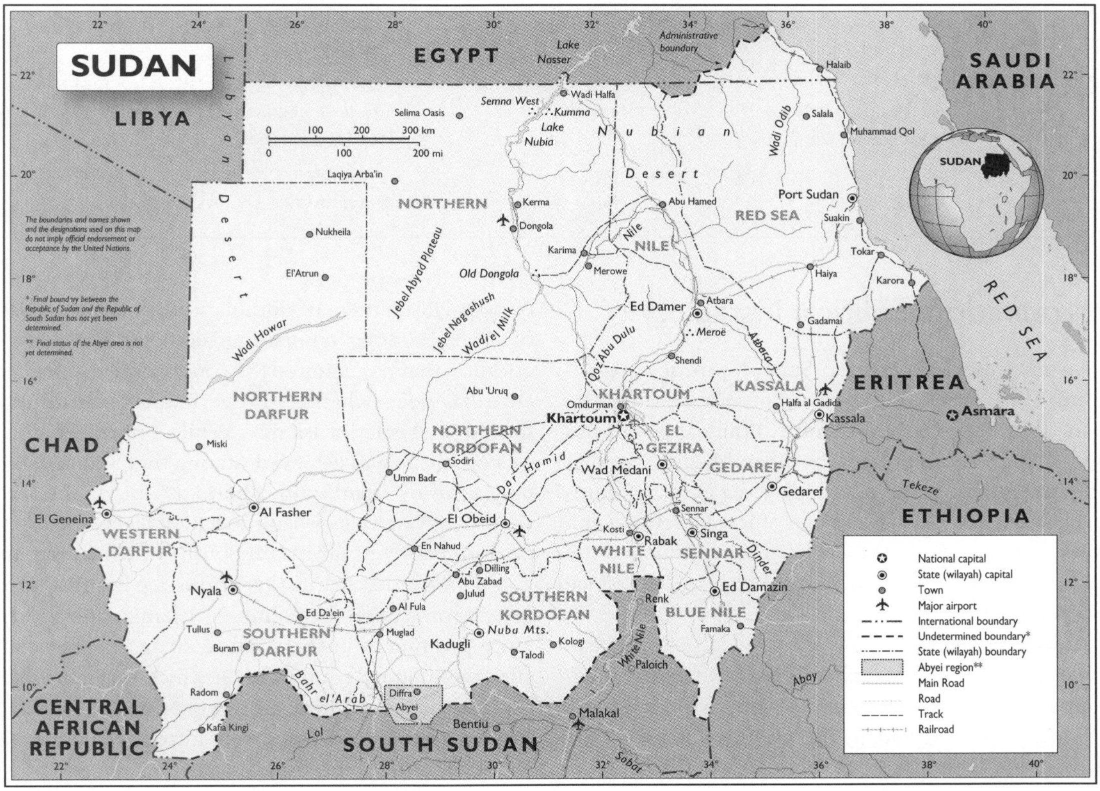

Source: Sudan, Map No. 4458 Rev.2 UNITED NATIONS, March 2012

BOX 27.1 KEY DATES IN SUDAN'S HISTORY

1899–1955	Anglo-Egyptian colonial rule
1955	First civil war between north and south Sudan begins
1956	Sudan's independence and establishment of democratic processes
1958	General Ibrahim Abboud leads military coup against civilian government elected earlier in year
1964	October Revolution results in new attempt at democracy
1969	Jaafar Nimeiri leads 'May Revolution' military coup
1973	Addis Ababa peace agreement between north and south ends first civil war
1983	September laws (Islamic penal code, or *hudud*) introduced, leading to commencement of second civil war in same year
1985	April uprisings result in end of Nimeiri's regime and attempt at democracy
1989	Military *coup d'état* installs Islamist regime of Omar al-Bashir in power
2003	Outbreak of armed conflict in Darfur between government-backed militia *janjaweed* and Sudan Liberation Army/Movement and Justice and Equality Movement
2005	Comprehensive peace agreement between north and south ends second civil war

2009	International Criminal Court issues arrest warrant for President Omar al-Bashir, citing war crimes, crimes against humanity, and genocide in connection with atrocities in Darfur conflict	2013	Civil war erupts in South Sudan between supporters of President Salva Kiir and supporters of former Vice-President Riek Machar
2011	South Sudan's secession; Salva Kiir becomes president of Africa's youngest nation	2015	President Bashir re-elected in poll marked by low turnout and boycotted by most opposition parties
2012	Outbreak of armed conflict between Sudan and South Sudan	2016	Sudan opens border with South Sudan for first time since 2011 secession

Introduction: Political Instability

It is sometimes said that, in Sudan, 'politics are different every week, but if you come back after ten years, they are exactly the same'. Political power has indeed been monopolized by Arab-Muslim riverine elites in Khartoum, who have played a game of musical chairs in competing for state office. Described as a Muslim 'ethnocracy', these elites have dominated the country socially, politically, and economically since independence.

At independence, the British handed over political power, control of the army and civil service, and management of economic resources to two traditional political parties in Sudan: the Umma Party and the Democratic Unionist Party, both supported by Muslim sectarian groups. These two political parties came to dominate the political scene (Warburg 2003). They were eventually challenged by Jafaar Nimeiri and Omar al-Bashir, who both assumed power by means of military coup in 1969 and 1989 respectively. The failure of the several contending elites to take effective control of the state has rendered Sudan chronically unstable. Sudan has been governed by a number of regimes that have fluctuated between short periods of multiparty rule and longer periods of military dictatorship. The last period of military dictatorship by Omar al-Bashir (1989–present) encompassed the period in which the comprehensive peace agreement (CPA) was implemented and South Sudan became sovereign (Sørbø and Ahmed 2013).

Another main feature of Sudanese politics has been the powerful influence of religion. Successive regimes since independence in 1956 have attempted to unite disparate peoples and regions of Sudan around Islam and Arabism as ideological identities. Islam has been not only the principal base of legitimacy for the major political parties (which have used religion as their principal instrument of domination), but also the basis of rivalry among competing ideological groups. A question that has haunted the country since independence has been whether the permanent constitution should be secular or Islamic. While a northern political consensus was achieved, stating that Sudan was to be guided by Islam, with Sharia as one of the main sources of law, this was immediately dismissed by the predominantly non-Muslim South, which feared limited rights under Sharia. Over time, the Islamist forces grew stronger and the politics of Islamization became more prominent in the political struggle—especially after the military coup in 1989, which brought Islamists into the driver's seat. Comprehensive Islamization and Arabization processes were introduced under the banner of a monolithic and exclusionary vision of the Sudanese nation-state (Ahmed 2007).

Civil War and Sudan's Perpetual Conflicts

On the eve of its independence from Britain, Sudan was plunged into prolonged violent conflict that is still raging. The British deprived south Sudan of a share of power, which led to the first civil war, named *Anyanya*. This first civil war ended when the Addis Ababa peace agreement was signed in 1973, granting south Sudan regional autonomy.

Sudan's second civil war erupted in 1983 when Jafaar Nimeiri abrogated the Addis Ababa agreement by declaring that revenues from oil recently discovered in the south were to accrue to the central government, rather than to the south. Nimeiri had come to power in 1969 as a socialist, but later recast himself as an Islamist. In 1983, Nimeiri repealed the secular 1973 constitution and imposed Sharia law. In response, southerners launched their own state-building project in opposition to the Islamization and Arabization policies of the centralized government. Southern grievances eventually crystallized around the Sudan People's Liberation Army and the related Sudan People's Liberation Movement (SPLM/A), a rebel group led by Dr John Garang. For SPLM/A, the goal was not the south's secession, but to establish a secular, non-racial, federal Sudan.

Repeated peace initiatives during the 1990s were gridlocked over the relationship between religion and the state. The SPLM/A insisted that a unitary Sudanese nation-state should be secular; the Islamist-military regime insisted that Sharia remain the supreme law in a unified Sudan. During these years, Islamic terminology such as *jihad* and martyrdom became essential features of the government's official discourse on the war against the south, particularly in mass media.

In January 2005, the northern National Congress Party (NCP) and the southern SPLM/A signed the CPA. Peace talks had started already in the early 2000s under the auspices of the Intergovernmental Authority on Development (IGAD) under Kenyan leadership, supported by a 'troika' of the United States, United Kingdom, and Norway (Johnson 2011). Throughout the IGAD-led negotiations, the United States played a particularly key role: not only did it provide funding and technical assistance, but it also intervened at critical stalemates during the peace negotiations.

The CPA established a one-state, two-system rule, in which the north imposed Sharia law, while the south remained secular. It granted the south the right to a referendum on self-determination following a six-year interim period. A new federal government was sworn in, and the south's autonomous legislature and government became operational. A new interim constitution was ratified the same year, which, for the first time in Sudan's history, included a bill of rights establishing principles of non-discrimination and **gender** equality.

In January 2011, the overwhelming majority of southern Sudanese opted for secession in a popular vote and a new nation was born in Africa. The referendum left unresolved a number of delicate and potentially combustible issues, including how the two sides would share the revenue from sizeable reserves of crude oil. The secession has sparked new debates about Sudan's constitution and the role of Sharia. There is vast mobilization by conservative religious forces for a reinstatement of an Islamic constitution now that Sudan (that is, North Sudan) has the potential to become an 'unsullied' Islamic state.

While the CPA may have resolved the war between the north and the south in the short term, it was not a comprehensive solution. The piecemeal approach to making peace failed to address the fundamental issue of the centre's marginalization of the periphery (De Waal 2007). **Framing** the peace negotiations as between a unified north and a unified south alienated other marginalized peripheries, emboldening some to take up arms. These sentiments made a significant contribution to the outbreak of war in Darfur in 2003. Darfur emerged as Sudan's next crisis when two rebel groups, the Sudan Liberation Army/Movement and the Justice and Equality Movement, took up arms against the government amidst ongoing peace negotiations with the south.

Peace remains elusive in Sudan. Violence continues in Darfur. The International Criminal Court (ICC) has charges pending against five individuals, including Sudan's president, for war crimes, crimes against humanity, and **genocide** in Darfur. (For more information on genocide in Darfur, see Chapter 18.) In 2012, renewed war erupted between Sudan and South Sudan over disputed oil fields along the border, resulting in countless civilian casualties, sexual violence as a weapon of war, and displacement of masses of people. Sudan has currently one of the highest populations of internally displaced persons in the world. In an attempt to normalize relations, Omar al-Bashir opened Sudan's border with South Sudan in 2016 for the first time since the 2011 secession. Sudan's new neighbour, South Sudan, is struggling: only five years old, Africa's youngest nation tops the rank of failed states worldwide. In 2013, a civil war erupted between former allies President Salva Kiir and Vice President Riek Machar, splitting South Sudan along ethnic lines. Despite its vast oil reserves, the country is best described as a protracted humanitarian crisis that has left 3.8 million people without enough food—raising the spectre of famine.

KEY POINTS

- Sudan was Africa's largest country until the secession of South Sudan in 2011.
- Sudan has experienced Africa's longest civil war (1983–2005).
- State power has been dominated by Arab-Muslim elites in Khartoum since independence in 1956.

Human Development and Political Economy

Underdevelopment and the politics of oil

With rising oil revenues, the Sudanese economy was booming in the years before South Sudan's secession. Nonetheless, while the country's oil resources are located elsewhere, oil revenues have flowed to the political and economic elites of Khartoum, while outlying states remain neglected and impoverished. Khartoum and some northern states along the Nile show performance above the sub-Saharan average on key measures of **human development**, but Sudan's disadvantaged regions rank among the lowest in the world. During its oil boom, Sudan failed to diversify economically, and oil reserves were not converted into robust public investment in education, health, and infrastructure. Sudan is considered one of the world's most corrupt countries, ranking third from the bottom of Transparency International's Corruption Perceptions Index (CPI).

Uneven development among regions and groups is not new. In fact, it was a major feature of Sudan's colonial economy. British colonists initiated projects in and around Khartoum, including setting up the world's largest irrigation scheme in the Gezira area for the cultivation of export crops (mainly cotton). Little was done elsewhere and the resulting unevenness translated into gross economic disparities between Sudan's regions. Not much changed during the post-colonial period; economic policy followed the colonial blueprint and inequality was, in many cases, exacerbated. The Unregistered Land Act of 1970 abolished customary rights of land use and land allocation, thereby allowing the state to lease large tracts of land to private interests. Successive governments used this practice in their drive to modernize agriculture. The resulting land dispossession led to impoverishment and displacement of large populations, which in turn gave rise to conflict in several parts of the country (Sørbø and Ahmed 2013).

While, historically, agriculture remains the main source of income and employment, oil has been Sudan's main export since the late 1990s and early 2000s. The oil industry went through two phases prior to the South's separation from the North in 2011: first, the period from the 1950s until the exit of the US firm Chevron from Sudan in 1992; and second, the decade of substantial oil production from 1999 to 2011. Production increased dramatically during the 2000s when peace talks between the north and the south were initiated. During the civil war, armed groups saw the oil pipelines as legitimate military targets, since they helped to keep the regime in power. Because the oil fields were primarily in South Sudan, the economic opportunity provided by oil also encouraged the regime to seek political stability through genuine peace negotiations with SPLM/A. The CPA included an agreement on wealth-sharing that bore directly on the question of oil revenues. In the second oil production phase, a partnership with China was established after an aborted attempt at an agreement with Iran. Oil production has brought Sudan into closer integration with the world economy and politics, and has included a significant alliance with China. It has also provided essential revenues that have enabled Omar al-Bashir's Islamist regime to withstand economic sanctions imposed by Western countries.

The South's separation from the North in 2011 marks the beginning of a new phase. The secession meant that Sudan immediately lost 75 per cent of its oil revenues. This had direct economic repercussions for Sudan, including depreciation of the national currency and the need to resort to economic austerity measures that, in 2012 and 2013, sparked anti-regime demonstrations by those voicing opposition against the escalation of prices and economic hardship in Sudan (Sidahmed 2013). With the majority of oil production in the South, but essential export routes and processing facilities in the North, the two countries have strong incentives for collaboration; instead, contention over the division of oil revenues led to renewed conflict in 2012. However, an agreement was negotiated between the two countries at a time when oil prices were high, granting Sudan a set price for exporting oil through its pipelines at US$25 per oil barrel. Combined with recent falls in oil prices internationally, this means that South Sudan is currently receiving the lowest price internationally for its oil. This has had catastrophic consequences for South Sudan, which is one of the most oil-dependent countries in the world. Because of the outbreak of a civil war in South Sudan in 2013, oil production has fallen dramatically, which has further negative impacts on both Sudan's and South Sudan's economies.

Democracy and Human Rights

Sudan has fluctuated since independence between military dictatorships and 'democratic', or civil multiparty, rule. Democracy was attempted at independence in 1956 (lasting until 1958), again after the October Revolution in 1964 (lasting until 1969), and again after the April uprisings in 1985 (lasting until 1989). Because of the north–south civil war, most of the southerners were unable to participate in the elections, so the periods of multiparty rule can hardly qualify as democratic. In an environment of perpetual armed conflict since independence, it is little surprise that democratic **institutions** have found it difficult to establish themselves. Moreover, the central state's limited capacity to dominate its territory has forced a reliance on **patron–client relationships**. This has encouraged competition over resources, and thereby a lack of unity among Sudan's heterogeneous ethnic and cultural groups (Woodward 1990).

Political institutions and parties

The present authoritarian regime led by Omar al-Bashir has endured for the last twenty-seven years. This Islamist-military regime has proven to be a most challenging period of political development in Sudan. The 1990s, in particular, were the pinnacle of state repression and **human rights** abuses. The military officers and Islamists who seized power in 1989 were determined to complete the Islamization process that had begun when Nimeiri promulgated an Islamic penal code (*hudud*) in September 1983. This Islamization process had later faltered under the civil government led by Sadiq al-Mahdi and the Umma Party, which stopped enforcing the *hudud* between 1985 and 1989. Before the CPA in 2005, non-Muslims residing in northern Sudan were subjected to punishments under the Islamic penal code. Islamization also had a detrimental effect on women's rights under Bashir's early leadership. Among other things, headscarves became mandatory for women in 1991, women's movement in public spaces was restricted in 1994 and 1996, and child marriages were legalized in the name of Islamic law in 1991. In many areas, this was a backlash against rights that Sudanese women had previously attained (Fluehr-Lobban 2012).

Bashir's regime used religious justifications to institute control measures typical of authoritarian governments and 'political resistance' become synonymous with 'religious apostasy'. During the 1990s, the government suppressed trade unions and **civil society**, banned political parties and newspapers, and sought to restructure social and cultural life to conform to its monolithic vision of an Islamic society and state. The political and economic power base of the traditional parties was erased. The Sudanese Communist Party, historically the main political contender to the Islamists, was severely oppressed and many of its members were forced into exile (Gallab 2008).

Sudan held presidential and multiparty elections in 2010 as part of the CPA, and again in 2015 after the South's secession. While the CPA opened up political space for political opponents to criticize and challenge Bashir's regime, the elections can hardly be described as free and fair. While the SPLM/A was rather disinterested in the 2010 elections in advance of secession, the northern political opposition boycotted both elections, resulting in the dominance of the NCP and the re-election of Omar al-Bashir as Sudan's president.

Popular uprisings

Sudan has experienced two popular uprisings in attempts to take down military dictatorships. The so-called October Revolution in 1964 brought an end to Ibrahim Abbud's military regime. It began with a symposium on the civil war at the University of Khartoum. When the police cracked down on the gathering, killing student activist Ahmad al-Qurashi, a mass non-violent movement was sparked. Al-Qurashi's funeral procession led to a rally and protests throughout Khartoum. Three days into the growing uprising, trade unions announced a general strike that spread throughout the country. One of the great achievements of the revolution noted in Sudanese history books was the extensive participation of women in the protests, among other things demanding universal suffrage and the right to be elected to office; both granted by the new civilian government.

Growing economic problems, combined with Nimeiri's Islamist turn and the reigniting of civil war, led to his downfall during the April uprisings in 1985. Fuelled by the introduction of Sharia law in 1983 and the execution of one of Sudan's most liberal Islamic thinkers, Mahmoud Muhammed Taha, in 1985, anti-regime protests spread and paralysed the country.

The next attempts at popular uprisings came in the aftermath of the 'Arab Spring', first in 2011, and later in 2012 and 2013, but demonstrators were unsuccessful in bringing down Omar al-Bashir's dictatorship. Protests erupted in 2011 in the wake of the Arab uprisings in Egypt and Tunisia. On 30 June, to commemorate the day on which Bashir came to power, approximately 2,000 protesters, both men and women, gathered in the capital and shouted 'Down with the regime!' Protests followed in 2012 and 2013 throughout the country, and the declining economy was the main concern of protestors. While demonstrations took place since 2013, none were on the same scale as the uprisings of the preceding two years. The regime suppressed protesters with gunfire, and thousands of protesters were arrested and tortured. As a response to national pressure and anti-regime demonstrations, Omar al-Bashir strengthened his authoritarian grip. The NCP's dominance of the political system was reinforced by South Sudan's secession, which signalled the end of a power-sharing government with the SPLM/A. This was followed by a general crackdown on political parties and civil society. Sudan is ranked by Freedom House as 'not free'.

Civil society

Trade unions have historically been influential in Sudan, beginning during the country's anti-colonial struggle. After independence, trade unions led to the toppling of the military dictatorships of Ibrahim Aboud in 1964 and Nimeiri in 1985. A new generation of civil society organizations started to emerge in response to drought, famine, and displacement caused by the renewal of the war in the South. In addition, large numbers of international **non-governmental organizations** (**NGOs**) and relief agencies arrived, directing their efforts to serving the victims of famine and war. These NGOs' efforts were directed towards addressing the symptoms, rather than causes, of war. Following the 1989 coup, however, the new regime dissolved all trade unions and NGOs. This disrupted and destroyed the vibrant civil society that had been emerging in Sudan between 1985 and 1989, and effectively silenced opposition to Bashir's rule.

For the most part, northern civil society and NGOs have operated separately from their southern counterparts. During the civil war, the southern NGOs remained mostly Nairobi-based and affiliated with SPLM/A. Most of the northern NGOs were Khartoum-based, largely non-political, service-oriented, and dependent on external funding from international donors. The same pattern is repeated in the Sudanese women's movement, which has been mainly Khartoum-based and situated among the Arab-Muslim elites, and thereby has excluded, in particular, southern women. One recent and notable exception has been Sudanese Women Empowerment for Peace, established in 1997, which includes both southern and northern women.

The 2005 CPA allocated some political space to civil society and this resulted in a significant growth of NGOs, including both human rights-based groups, as well as new and conservative religious ones. Women's groups were particularly vocal in demanding legal reform of a series of discriminatory laws codified in the name of Sharia by Bashir's regime. However, with the exception of a 25 per cent quota on seats reserved for women in parliament, introduced in 2008, few demands have resulted in legislative reforms. There have also been few policy changes aimed at rectifying women's developmental challenges, such as Sudan's high maternal mortality rates, the high prevalence of female genital mutilation, and child marriage.

While the CPA allocated some space for political opposition, including for women's groups, a series of laws have recently been enacted and/or strategically used by the regime to restrict civil society's room for manoeuvre. The Voluntary and Humanitarian Work Act of 2006 imposes severe restrictions on NGOs, both international and national, and gives the government excessive discretionary and regulatory powers over the work of NGOs. The National Security Act of 2010 gives security forces broad powers of arrest and detention, and many other laws contravene basic human rights norms. The Anti-terrorism Law of 2001 has in recent years been used strategically to clamp down on civil society, especially Darfur-based groups. In particular, after the ICC issued a warrant for the arrest of President Bashir, not only has independent civil society been viewed as a threat to the regime, but also activists have been viewed as collaborators with the ICC. In 2015, a new amendment to the Criminal Law redefined an 'apostate', a crime punishable with the death penalty, as anyone questioning the credibility or otherwise misrepresenting the Quran. This makes it difficult for civil society to criticize the current Islamist regime, even if they are careful to frame demands within Islam.

In spite of this, there is an emerging landscape of human rights and youth movements. A new generation of activists is emerging with an appetite for change, and few believe in the old political parties based on a narrow vision of the Sudanese nation-state as Arab and Muslim. While some organizations are shut down and members are forced into exile or put under arrest, many continue to operate in informal networks that push for **regime change**.

KEY POINTS

- Despite popular uprisings and periods of multiparty rule, democracy has failed to consolidate.

- The current authoritarian regime led by Omar al-Bashir has been the pinnacle of state repression and human rights abuses.

- Civil society has played a key role in Sudan's popular uprisings.

Conclusion: Human Rights and Development

The best way in which to describe Sudan is as a country of perpetual conflict and violence. Instability and rivalry among Khartoum's Muslim Arab elites—combined with political, cultural, and economic marginalization of the peripheries—have been constant features of Sudanese politics, and perhaps the most important cause of political instability and armed rebellion. Despite the 2005 peace agreement, peace remains elusive and **human security** has remained threatened even after the South's secession in 2011.

Even with Sudan's oil boom and economic potential, human development indicators remain poor. In particular, Sudan's disadvantaged regions rank among the lowest in the world. **Corruption** remains endemic.

Despite periods of multiparty rule and several popular uprisings, democracy remains a distant vision. During most of Sudan's independence, military dictatorships have been the rule. In terms of violating human rights, the current regime of Omar al-Bashir has been exceedingly challenging. Development in the Sudanese context is clearly linked to the need for improving human rights.

? QUESTIONS

1. Why has Sudan been in a state of perpetual conflict since independence in 1956?

2. What role does Islam play in Sudanese politics?

3. To what extent has oil benefited or detracted from development in Sudan?

4. Why has democracy failed to consolidate in Sudan?

5. What is the role of civil society in popular uprisings in Sudan? What restrictions do they face under the current authoritarian regime?

 FURTHER READING

Ahmed, E. (2007) 'Political Islam in Sudan: Islamists and the Challenge of State Power (1989–2004)', in B. F. Soares and R. Otayek (eds) *Islam and Muslim Politics in Africa* (New York: Palgrave Macmillan), 189–208 A detailed case study on the changing role of Islamism in Sudanese politics.

De Waal, A. (2007) *War in Darfur and the Search for Peace* (Cambridge, MA: Harvard University Press) A thought-provoking account of the failed negotiations between the Sudanese government and opposition movements, and the resulting genocide.

Fluehr-Lobban, C. (2012) *Sharia and Islamism in Sudan: Conflict, Law and Social Transformation* (London: I. B. Tauris) Addresses the complex questions of the development of Sharia and Islamism, and their relations with social transformation in Sudan.

Gallab, A. A. (2008) *The First Islamist Republic: Development and Disintegration of Islamism in the Sudan* (Aldershot: Ashgate) Comprehensive treatment of the Sudanese Islamists' experience.

Johnson, H. F. (2011) *Waging Peace in Sudan: The Inside Story of the Negotiations that Ended Africa's Longest Civil War* (Eastbourne: Sussex Academic Press) Provides a unique insider perspective from one of the chief negotiators between the opposing parties on the negotiations that brought an end to the civil war in Sudan.

Sørbø, G., and Ahmed, G. A. (eds) (2013) *Sudan Divided: Continuing Conflict in a Contested State* (New York: Palgrave Macmillan) Examines the 2011 secession of South Sudan and how the Islamist project has shaped developments in Sudan.

Tønnessen, L., and al-Nagar, S. (2013) 'The Women's Quota in Conflict-Ridden Sudan: Ideological Battles for and against Gender Equality', *Women's Studies International Forum*, 41(2): 122–31 Detailed analysis of women's substantive representation in Sudan's National Assembly.

Warburg, G. (2003) *Islam, Sectarianism, and Politics in Sudan since the Mahdiyya* (London: Hurst & Co.) Thought-provoking analysis of the history of Sudan's Islamic politics to illuminate current conflicts in the region.

Woodward, P. (1990) *Sudan 1898–1989: The Unstable Border* (Boulder, CO: Lynne Rienner) Careful analysis of the principal factors that have shaped the Sudanese state since the establishment of the condominium.

 WEB LINKS

http://africanarguments.org/category/making-sense-of-sudan/   An excellent website/blog including critical debate on Sudanese politics.

https://www.crisisgroup.org/africa/horn-africa/sudan   The International Crisis Group (ICG) on Sudan.

https://www.theguardian.com/world/sudan   For updated news on Sudan (and South Sudan).

https://www.hrw.org/africa/sudan   Human Rights Watch (HRW) on Sudan.

https://www.icc-cpi.int/darfur   The International Criminal Court (ICC) on Darfur, Sudan.

https://www.irinnews.org/afrique/afrique-de-lest/sudan   Irin on Sudan.

http://riftvalley.net/   Site of the Rift Valley Institute.

http://www.securitycouncilreport.org/sudansouth-sudan/   Security Council Report offering monthly coverage of issues in Sudan/South Sudan.

http://sihanet.org/   Site of the Strategic Initiative for Women in the Horn of Africa (SIHA).

http://www.sudantribune.com   Aims to promote plural information, and democratic and free debate on the two Sudans.

http://www.transparency.org/cpi2015   The Transparency International 2015 Corruption Perceptions Index, based in expert opinion, measures the perceived level of public sector corruption.

 For additional material and resources, please visit the Online Resource Centre at:
http://www.oxfordtextbooks.co.uk/orc/burnell5e/

PART 8

South–South Relations

Over the past few years, increasing attention has been given to the development of stronger South–South relations. The international scene is changing. Through country case studies of Brazil, China, and India, this part shows how new powers claim their place in international **politics**, and present challenges and opportunities for other developing countries and developed countries alike. These three countries form part of the BRICS (along with Russia and South Africa), which are all emerging economies challenging the economic and political hegemony of traditional Western powers. They are becoming increasingly significant global partners and, in 2009, the BRICS called for a greater voice for developing countries in international financial **institutions**. This is not to say that these countries are homogenous in any way; their economies, incentives, and political systems all differ. They do, however, present a challenge to the old North–South divide.

Brazil has emerged as a regional, as well as a global, power. Through her chapter, Leslie Armijo shows how Brazil has striven to play a bigger role on the international scene. This is seen through the active campaigning for continental integration in which Brazil has played an important role by means of several initiatives. Brazil has also conducted an active foreign policy on a global scale, linked to trade, climate, finance, and nuclear proliferation. The increased prominence of Brazil on the international scene can also be explained by increasing relative capabilities compared with Western countries.

China's relations with other developing countries have been given significant attention. Deborah Bräutigam displays how, by means of foreign aid, economic cooperation, **soft power** (such as the Confucius Institutes), and (more importantly) trade, China aims to be seen as a responsible global power. More precisely, China wants to secure territorial integrity and sovereignty, and to prevent Taiwan from gaining international standing. It also wants to be seen as a leader of developing countries, although not a threatening one. Lastly, it wants to secure a stable political environment within which to provide economic development. Many people voice fears that this international engagement resembles a form of new colonialism, because it revolves around importing cheap raw materials and exporting cheap manufactured goods.

The final chapter shows how India and other developing countries are becoming bigger players in the international foreign aid **regime**. Emma Mawdsley contends that, until recently, foreign aid was mainly seen as stemming from Western, developed countries. Recently, however, many non-traditional donors have either appeared or come to attention. A central feature of aid from southern partners is that it comes with few **conditionalities**. India started its foreign aid activities in the 1950s. The main reason for such an early commitment was a willingness to create regional goodwill among hostile neighbours, to provide energy security, and to create relations of solidarity with developing countries and a resulting increasing international stature. The paradox here remains that even though India increases its international efforts and decreases its own dependence on aid, a large part of its population still remains very poor. As with traditional development partners, there are also mixed motivations behind the involvement of India in foreign aid.

28

Brazil as a Global Player?

Leslie Elliott Armijo

Chapter contents

Overview

Brazil is a big country. With a land mass similar in size to that of continental United States, a population of 200.4 million in 2013, and gross domestic product (GDP) of US$2.4 trillion in 2014, Brazilians make up half the population and generate over half the economy of South America. In the eyes of much of the world, as recently as the early 1990s, Brazil remained a 'banana republic', with annual price inflation over 1,000 per cent and chaotic politics. Yet Brazil today has a large and growing presence on the international scene, as a key player in international climate forums, an active participant in the major economies' Group of 20 (G20) (see Chapter 5), a member of the BRICS group of countries (Brazil, Russia, India, China, and South Africa), and, since 2010, a creditor of the International Monetary Fund (IMF). It has been governed in recent years by a moderately left-leaning coalition under Presidents Luíz Inácio ('Lula') da Silva (2003–10) and Dilma Rousseff (2011–16). Despite significant governance challenges, linked to high-level political corruption, Brazil is a stable democracy, with a growing middle class, and a policy and business elite eager to expand their country's influence in the world. Brazilian leaders cherish their foreign policy autonomy, and have enthusiastically embraced 'South–South' diplomacy especially under Presidents Lula and Dilma—both universally referred to by their given names in Brazil. Nonetheless, Brazil remains a fundamentally Western and liberal power, whose policies bear a family resemblance to those of today's major advanced industrial countries. Following a brief historical introduction, this chapter focuses on contemporary Brazilian foreign policy—especially its leaders' vision of the country as a consequential global player in an increasingly multipolar world.

Figure 28.1 is a map of Brazil and Box 28.1 provides an overview of key dates in Brazil's history.

Figure 28.1 Brazil

BOX 28.1 KEY DATES IN BRAZIL'S HISTORY

1500	Portuguese explorer Pedro Alves Cabral, seeking a passage to India, instead encounters Brazil	1808	Fleeing Napoleon, Portuguese court relocates to Brazil
Mid-17th century	Sugar exports, worked with slave labour, dominate Brazil's economy; largely failed attempt to enslave indigenous population, who are instead pushed into interior	1821–89	Independent Brazilian kingdom, evolving toward constitutional monarchy; slavery ended in 1888
		1889–1930	Brazil becomes oligarchic republic, economy of which depends on coffee exports
1550–1866	Nearly 5 million enslaved Africans disembark in Brazil—almost half of all slaves brought to Americas	1930–64	Urban populist government, dominated by President Getúlio Vargas until his suicide in 1954

1964–84	Modernizing military rule, including high growth period 1967–73, known as 'Brazilian miracle'	2008–09	First leaders' summits of major economies' G20 (October 2008) and BRICs (April 2009)
1985–89	Peaceful transition to civilian, democratic rule with universal suffrage	2010	Brazil elects its first female president, Dilma Rousseff (Workers Party)
1994–95	*Real* Plan economic policies end decades of recurrent high inflation	May 2016	Rousseff impeached by parliamentary vote

Introduction: A Brief History

The Portuguese colonized lightly populated Brazil, first arriving at the turn of the sixteenth century. Three centuries later, Brazilian elites took advantage of the Napoleonic Wars to declare independence in 1822. The new country constituted itself as a monarchy, ruled by a prince of the Portuguese royal family, thus avoiding the bloody wars among rival *caudillos* that spawned seemingly endless conflicts in much of newly independent Spanish-speaking Latin America throughout the nineteenth century. African slaves provided much of the labour in its primary-product export economy. Brazil's Princess Isabel announced the abolition of slavery in 1889, the final straw that led local elites to overthrow the monarchy. Thereafter, regionally based landowner coalitions ruled Brazil, under rules of political competition that were sometimes democratic, although often not, through the mid-twentieth century. By the time of the Second World War, Brazil had significant industrial centres and an activist international diplomacy. Brazilians remain proud of having been the only Latin American country to participate as a combatant in the war, which it entered on the side of the Allies, and to have been a founding member of the United Nations.

In the latter half of the twentieth century, Brazil struggled with the challenges of the military in **politics** and democratization (see Chapter 14). After twenty years in power, the army peacefully relinquished political power in 1985. Brazil today is a democracy with a federal, bicameral, and presidential system. Under the military, Brazil pursued import-substituting industrialization (ISI) (see Chapter 4). The big economic policy successes since democratization have been ending multi-digit annual inflation (in 1995), reigniting growth (beginning in 2000), and reducing Brazil's horrendous income inequality (see Chapter 6). In 1991, 40 per cent of Brazilian households were poor and 20 per cent indigent (extremely poor), but by 2009 the respective figures had fallen to 16 and 6 per cent (IPEA 2013). With Brazil's relatively 'easy' passage through the global financial crisis of 2007–08, the country seemed possessed of the prerequisites of a serious global player. Nonetheless, in the short run, economic stagnation, beginning in 2012 and continuing through to time of writing (2016), has combined with the simultaneous explosion of political **corruption** scandals and uncertain leadership at the top to muddy Brazil's lustre.

Brazil in the World: Pursuit of Continental Integration and Global Voice

Since the country's return to democratic government in 1985, Brazilian political and opinion leaders have gradually elaborated their vision of promoting multipolarity and democratization in the international system—an outcome they believe to be both morally superior to, and more stable than, the current concentration of global influence in the major advanced industrial countries of the West (or the North). Centre-right President Fernando Henrique Cardoso (1995–2002) sought greater South American cooperation and hoped to counter the region's historic vulnerability to the United States with enhanced links to the European Union. His centre-left successors, Presidents Lula da Silva (2003–10) and Dilma Rousseff (2011–16) of the *Partido dos Trabalhadores* (PT, or Workers' Party), de-emphasized Europe and expanded South–South cooperation beyond the region.

South American integration

The early twenty-first century saw three differing hemispheric integration projects being pursued simultaneously. Brazil is a pivotal country in influencing which of these will prevail. Both its economic and political policies are centrist in terms of their placement on a Latin American and Caribbean spectrum, which lends its leaders credibility.

The hemisphere-wide project led by the United States reflects the most politically and economically conservative vision of regional cooperation. The United States prefers political cooperation through the long-established Organization of American States (OAS), which, under US pressure, excluded Cuba between 1962 and 2009. Through annual Summits of the Americas, begun in the mid-1990s, the United States hoped to promote a Free Trade Area of the Americas (FTAA), featuring 'deep' economic integration, similar to that of the North American Free Trade Area (NAFTA), linking the United States, Canada, and Mexico. The proposed FTAA would include very liberal rules governing international trade and capital flows, bringing the legal frameworks of all countries into economic regulatory convergence with the generally pro-free enterprise and business-friendly rules prevailing in the United States, yet would *not* seek political integration, collective decision-making, or region-wide citizenship or immigration rights. Major Latin American countries, including Brazil, Argentina, and Venezuela, have resisted this neoliberal vision. Consequently, the United States instead has pursued bilateral and mini-regional trade and investment treaties with countries accepting more free market economic integration. In 2011, Peru, Colombia, Chile, and Mexico—the four largest Latin American countries with relatively open ('neoliberal') trade and economic policy **regimes**—formed the Pacific Alliance, which subsequently provided the Latin American core of the US-organized Trans-Pacific Partnership (TPP) trade deal with the Association of Southeast Asian Nations (ASEAN), Japan, and South Korea, but without China. (At time of writing—mid-2016—the US Congress had not, however, ratified the TPP.)

On the left was a Venezuela-led project, the Bolivarian Alliance of Latin America (ALBA), growing out of Venezuelan–Cuban contacts in 2004, and envisioning a mutual aid union of socialist and popular-progressive Latin American and Caribbean states. ALBA was sustained by the willingness of Venezuelan President Hugo Chávez (1999–2013) to employ Venezuelan petroleum wealth to subsidize smaller states of the circum-Caribbean and the Andes. The end of the commodity super-cycle and subsequent death of the iconic Chávez effectively ended Venezuela's bid

to refashion hemispheric identity. Yet some of ALBA's symbols have been appropriated by a new political grouping, which held its leaders' summit in 2013. The Community of Latin American and Caribbean States (CELAC), like ALBA before it, pointedly excludes the United States and Canada, and roundly criticizes US political policies in the region. Because CELAC members include countries that lean both right and left, its performance in practice is likely to be pragmatic—an outcome that will suit Brazil.

The third integration project aims at continental cooperation within South America. The Common Market of the South (MERCOSUR), founded in 1991 with Argentina, Brazil, Paraguay, and Uruguay, grew out of the late 1980s' cooperation between Brazilian President José Sarney and Argentine President Raúl Alfonsín, each of whom hoped to subdue his country's military and institutionalize its democratic transition by deepening cross-border trade ties. Initially only a forum for negotiating tariff reductions, MERCOSUR has expanded cautiously into political cooperation and, since 2009, boasts a nascent, although relatively powerless, parliament. Venezuela joined MERCOSUR in 2012, while Chile, Bolivia, and Peru are associates. Brazilian Presidents Cardoso and subsequently Lula da Silva also envisioned greater continental cooperation. In 2004, all twelve leaders, including those of Dutch-speaking Suriname and Anglophone Guyana, created the Union of South American Nations (UNASUR), the principal, if somewhat vaguely articulated, aim of which is political cooperation. Officially, UNASUR builds on two existing multilateral economic groupings in South America—MERCOSUR and the Andean Community (CAN), a cold-war-era and largely moribund trade agreement linking the (currently centre-right) governments of Colombia and Peru and the (left-leaning) leaders in Bolivia and Ecuador. In 2007, Brazil and Venezuela further announced the formation of the South American Defence Council (CDSA) under UNASUR auspices. Colombia, the most consistently politically conservative large Latin American country, almost did not join, as a result of ongoing tensions with its neighbour Venezuela. However, personal diplomacy by senior Brazilian and other officials kept the negotiations and institutions alive, and in March 2009 the CDSA held its first meeting, with representatives of all twelve member states in attendance. The CDSA is not a mutual aid treaty or plan to mount joint operations; thus far it is merely a joint political process, ostensibly to discuss common and relatively apolitical defence concerns such as coordinated responses to natural disasters and pandemics, and airline safety, as well as to facilitate intraregional defence procurement—the latter a significant potential benefit for Brazil's large defence industry.

Each of these three overlapping integration projects—the more conservative, hemisphere-wide project preferred by the United States, the left-leaning Latin American and Caribbean project today loosely centred in CELAC, and the continental South American integration process championed by Brazil—will continue on paper, yet some will shape outcomes more than others. Among these alternatives, Brazilian leaders have played an assertive, but centrist, diplomatic game. For example, Brazil has resolutely and publicly opposed overt coups or questionably legal impeachments against an elected head of state—even a clearly flawed one, as in Honduras in 2009 or Paraguay in 2012—yet has been loath to criticize lesser anti-democratic moves by incumbent leaders, such as actions by Venezuelan President Chávez or his successor President Madero to reduce press freedoms and harass the political opposition. In terms of the hemispheric distribution of material capabilities among states, there are reasons to anticipate a growth of the South American (possibly Latin American) identity. In late 2015, reflecting the worries in most South American countries over their economic vulnerability to fluctuating Chinese demand for their commodity exports, leaders of the free trade Pacific Alliance and the hitherto more protectionist MERCOSUR countries began talks over cooperation and gradual policy alignment.

Brazil's pursuit of global voice

Brazil's post-1990 rise in relative material capabilities has also fuelled the ambitions of its leaders to engage more actively in global diplomacy. A joint bid with Germany, Japan, and India in 2012 to include these three countries plus Brazil as permanent members of the UN Security Council (UNSC) came to naught, but Brazil continues to dream of this goal. A significant barrier is that Brazil's own Latin American neighbours—however much they may, on some occasions, appreciate Brazilian leadership in continental and hemispheric issues—have no wish to see Brazil's power advantages over them further institutionalized.

Consequently, Argentina, Colombia, Mexico, and others have formally opposed permanent Brazilian UNSC membership.

Particularly under President Lula da Silva, Brazil created or joined several cross-regional groupings of 'Southern' states, including the India, Brazil, and South Africa (IBSA) grouping, which held its initial leaders' summit in 2006. Although IBSA's statements of purpose emphasize the members' commitments to democracy, **human rights**, and peaceful diplomacy, in practice its members have mainly cooperated around economic issues, such as taking joint positions within the World Trade Organization (WTO), despite the substantial structural differences in their economies. In 2006, Brazil joined the BRICs countries, later BRICS (when South Africa was added), the first leaders' summit of which took place in early 2009. Brazil also has collaborated with the BASIC countries (Brazil, South Africa, India, and China) in multilateral climate negotiations. President Rousseff's Foreign Minister Antônio Patriota (2011–13) articulated and sought to promote among other 'Southern' states a **human security** doctrine ('Responsibility *while* Protecting') that would balance Western concerns for human rights with the stricter respect for national sovereignty preferred by many developing countries. Other forays into South–South diplomacy have generated ad hoc cooperation around specific issues (Abdenur 2014).

KEY POINTS

- Brazil has articulated a foreign policy strategy for the Western hemisphere focusing on South American regional cooperation.

- Brazil's vision of multilateral cooperation in the Americas constitutes an ideological middle ground between the neoliberal preferences of the United States and the popular socialist hopes of Venezuela and other left-leaning countries.

- Brazil believes rising global multipolarity to be normatively desirable and engages in South–South cooperation outside its geographic region to promote this goal.

Key International Issues for Brazil

This section summarizes Brazilian foreign policy initiatives in four global issue arenas: trade; climate; financial **governance**; and nuclear proliferation.

Trade

As noted earlier in the chapter, Brazil participated in the FTAA negotiations, but also acted to try to construct its own groupings, such as MERCOSUR. A very long-running, off-and-on series of trade negotiations between MERCOSUR and the European Union, informally commenced in 1995, but long stalled because of Western European unwillingness to liberalize agricultural trade and South American fears of lowering industrial tariffs, could bear fruit eventually. Brazilian and other MERCOSUR leaders conceptualize their ties with the three major global economic poles (the United States, the European Union, and China) as maximizing their autonomy and minimizing their vulnerability both politically and in response to future fluctuations in global demand.

Brazilian leaders also have clear preferences for their own national trade strategy. While they accept that trade promotes growth, they also prefer to have an export surplus and a rising share of exports that is manufactured goods rather than primary products such as food and natural resources. In 2009, China overtook the United States to become Brazil's single most important trading partner, generating angst in Brazil. In the view of Brazilian policymakers, the main problem with trade with China specifically, and Asia more generally, is that these countries purchase mainly raw materials such as soybeans, iron ore, and coal, while selling Brazil mainly manufactured goods. The share of manufactured and semi-processed goods in total Brazilian merchandise exports fell from 69 per cent in 2003 to only 50 per cent in 2012. Trade concerns provide an additional reason for Brazil's efforts to strengthen regional ties: over 80 per cent of Brazilian exports to Latin America and the Caribbean in 2012 were industrial products—as compared to only about 20 per cent to Asia.

Climate and environment

A second arena for Brazil's multilateral involvement has been that of negotiations over cutting greenhouse gas emissions. The Amazon River Basin, the vast majority of which is in Brazil, contains the world's largest rainforest, a hugely important global carbon sink. Beginning in the late 1980s, Brazil became a principal target of global ecological campaigners, mostly from the industrialized world, who condemned its high and rising rates of deforestation, associated with gold prospecting by poor migrants and especially with the illegal, but mostly unpoliced, burning of huge swathes of virgin forest for cattle ranches.

Yet, in the twenty-first century, Brazil began to claim the mantle of being a 'green' energy power (Harvey 2010). Its domestic energy matrix minimizes greenhouse gas emissions. Currently, more than half of Brazil's total energy used comes from renewable sources and over 70 per cent of electricity from hydropower. Brazil is a world leader in the production and use of biofuels. Its sugar-cane ethanol is the world's most efficiently produced and all new cars since the late 1990s have been engineered to run on a gasoline–ethanol mix.

Moreover, via a two-track process of beginning to enforce its own environmental laws and the development of concrete proposals for multilateral solutions in global negotiations—formally known as the United Nations Framework Convention on Climate Change (UNFCCC)—Brazil has become an active and respected participant in the global climate regime. In 2004, for example, Brazil attempted to mediate between the advanced industrial countries (whose view has been that countries whose pollution is absolutely largest and/or growing fastest, such as China and India, must make the largest cuts), and developing countries, who understandably demand that per capita energy consumption should first become more equal worldwide (Friman 2006). At the December 2010 UNFCCC negotiating round in Copenhagen, an informal meeting of leaders of the United States and the BASIC countries generated a non-binding accord, including the first concrete promises of cuts by both developed and developing countries (see Chapter 17).

In the most recent period, Brazil's policies again have become more problematic in the eyes of environmentalists, who claim that the federal government's plan to expand hydropower—such as through the huge new Belo Monte Dam on the Xingu River, a major tributary of the Amazon—will have very negative implications for both local habitat and the livelihood of nearby indigenous groups (see Chapter 11). While hydroelectric power is renewable, it nonetheless incites controversy. The other significant shift is that Brazil has suddenly become wealthy in fossil fuels. In 2006, prospectors found the first of several enormous underwater oil fields off the Rio de Janeiro coast. If these 'pre-salt' finds are fully confirmed, Brazil will become one of the top ten countries worldwide in terms of petroleum reserves. Because the current administration—and almost any plausible alternate—is more committed to rapid economic growth, which it views as essential for poverty reduction, than to maximizing its green credentials, we may expect increasing conflicts, involving both Brazilians and external actors, over new dams and deep-sea drilling.

At time of writing, conflicts over deep-sea drilling have been inadvertently postponed, because Brazil's majority-state-owned national petroleum company, Petrobras (the country's largest firm and long considered one of its best managed), has been at the centre of the political corruption scandal that has brought down many senior figures in the Workers' Party (the party of Presidents da Silva and Rousseff). Unrelated allegations of fiscal manipulations by President Rousseff worsened the economic crisis in 2015 and led to her impeachment in May 2016. Petrobras' stock remains deeply depressed, and its ability to borrow in global markets and pursue long term investment, already hit by low world oil prices, are stalled in the medium term. In early 2016, Petrobras accepted a US$10 billion loan from the China Development Bank, pledging future oil exports in exchange. This was Brazil's first such Chinese loan since 2009, which some observers have viewed as implicitly placing Brazil in the company of countries, such as Venezuela, long shunned by market lenders, while others instead view it as an indicator of faith in Petrobras'—and Brazil's—coming economic recovery. Brazil's long-term role in the global climate adjustment regime thus remains ambivalent.

Finance

A third international realm in which Brazilian governments are desirous of leaving their mark is that of global financial and economic regulation. Prior to the recent slowdown in Brazil's economy, the country's strong private banks competed actively with Spanish banks to become the leading financial institutions in Latin American markets. Yet a place in the significant global governance clubs is not something that the global economy's major powers hand out easily; instead, Brazil and other emerging powers have been invited into the tent only as the Group of Seven (G7) countries have come to recognize that they need these countries' cooperation.

The 1997 Asian financial crisis led to the founding of two new multilateral organizations—the Financial Stability Board (FSB) and the financial Group of Twenty (G20), also known as the 'large economies' G20'—to consider reforms of the global financial architecture. The FSB was sited at the Bank for International Settlements (BIS) in Basel, and for the first decade it had only two developing country members: the financial *entrepôts* Singapore and Hong Kong. The FSB quickly developed into a multilateral body for detailed technical consultations among regulators. The financial G20, which included both advanced industrial and major emerging economies, was more representative than the FSB, but initially influenced public policy less. After issuing a cautious report on needed reforms of the global financial architecture, the financial G20 seemed destined for obscurity.

The global financial crisis of 2007–08 provided the shock that elevated the financial G20 to global significance (see Chapter 5). Following the September 2008 crash of Lehman Brothers investment bank, economic policymakers in Washington, DC, abruptly recognized that the balance of global financial and economic capabilities had shifted toward developing countries, particularly in East Asia. The only appropriate multilateral group available was the financial G20, which assumed many of the *de facto* global economic governance functions hitherto exercised by wealthy democracies club the G7. The international financial crisis also provided the impetus for the BRICs (later BRICS) to begin regular leaders' summits. Acting as a coherent lobby within the financial G20, the BRICs pressed for larger quotas and voting shares in the International Monetary Fund (IMF) and World Bank, and criticized the national monetary policies of the United States and other advanced industrial countries for their often destabilizing side-effects on the currency and financial stability of emerging economies.

The BRICs, along with the remaining emerging economies in the G20, were invited into the FSB. At their 2014 summit in Brazil, the BRICS also announced their intention to create two new multilateral financial institutions owned and managed by themselves: the New Development Bank (NDB), which will focus on infrastructure and large project lending to developing economies, an area that the World Bank has de-emphasized in recent decades in favour of anti-poverty and governance reform projects; and the Contingent Reserve Arrangement (CRA), an agreement of the five to loan one another foreign exchange reserves in times of crisis, perhaps without the onerous conditions imposed by the IMF (see Chapter 4). Partially in response to BRICS financial statecraft, in late 2015 the IMF agreed in principle to include China's currency in the basket of monies comprising its own quasi-currency, known as 'special drawing rights' (SDRs). Almost immediately, the US Congress finally agreed to ratify the 2010 IMF quota readjustment, which had been painstakingly negotiated by all IMF member governments, but subsequently languished awaiting US approval. The BRICS, including Brazil, could plausibly count this a collective victory (Roberts et al. forthcoming). Nonetheless, Brazil's celebration of this milestone was tainted by the loss, also in late 2015, of its investment-grade credit rating for sovereign debt as a result of the combination of recession and the spreading corruption scandals.

Nuclear proliferation

In the early 1990s, Brazilian President Fernando Collor da Mello ceremoniously buried a casket symbolizing the secret nuclear weapons development programme of Brazil's military government in the 1970s. Although Brazil now has credibly renounced all intentions to produce nuclear weapons and is a party to the Non-Proliferation Treaty (NPT), successive governments have refused to participate in the full range of its additional inspection protocols, to the intense annoyance of the United States, for which the NPT has been the litmus test of 'responsible' international behaviour by emerging powers. Brazil, although lacking regional military worries, and firmly democratic, capitalist, and culturally 'Western', nonetheless views its symbolic nuclear independence as a key indicator of foreign policy autonomy. In 2010, during the ongoing war of words and economic sanctions between Iran and the West, Brazil and Turkey attempted to broker a face-saving compromise: allowing Iran to store spent nuclear fuel in Turkey, as a guarantee that it would not be secretly enriched to make weapons. When the United States and European Union angrily rejected the proposed deal, President Lula da Silva backed down, noting that Brazil did not approve of economic sanctions on Iran, but would 'abide by international law' (Fleischer 2010). While this episode was hardly a success for Brazilian diplomacy, it clearly illustrates the country's efforts to be seen as a global player.

KEY POINTS

- Since the country's democratic transition in 1985, Brazilian leaders have taken a much more active role in global diplomacy, cooperating with other emerging powers including India, South Africa, China, Russia, and Turkey.
- Brazil's negotiating positions have already altered outcomes in the global regimes for trade, climate change, and financial governance.
- Although Brazil wishes to maintain an independent stance vis-à-vis the United States, Brazil is nonetheless a Western, liberal, and capitalist power.

Toward Global Multipolarity?

This chapter's preceding sections have emphasized assertive Brazilian diplomacy and the presence of plausible foreign partners among other emerging powers in both the region and the world. A third reason that Brazil has become more globally visible than before is its relatively greater command of material capabilities than in the past. The majority of Brazilian opinion leaders are convinced that the world is becoming more multipolar and that Brazil is thus objectively entitled to a greater voice in global affairs.

There are many possible ways in which it might be suggested that relative capabilities among sovereign states may be shifting. Table 28.1 shows a shifting distribution of 'hard power' capabilities among the major traditional powers of the Group of Five (G5)—that is, France, Germany, Japan, the United Kingdom, and the United States—and large emerging powers, including Brazil. The Contemporary Capabilities Index, v2 (CCI2), is computed as the mean of each country's annual share in world totals of five equally weighted types of material resources that, arguably, are useful for exerting international influence: production of goods and services (measured as gross domestic product, or GDP); population; technology (an indicator combining industrial value-added, telephone subscriptions, and patents); and world military spending (Armijo et al. 2014). The CCI2 undoubtedly understates the true international influence of the wealthy democracies such as the G5, because it excludes crucial **soft power** resources such as institutionally determined influence in global governance organizations and possession of an internationally attractive language, culture, educational system, or political system (Nye 2004).

Table 28.1 Contemporary Capabilities Index, v2 (% of world total)

	1995	2002	2009	2013
Traditional powers				
United States	24.7	27.7	24.8	21.3
Japan	12.7	9.3	6.5	5.1
Germany	7.3	5.7	5.2	4.4
France	5.2	4.1	3.7	3.2
United Kingdom	4.4	4.6	3.4	3.1
Emerging powers				
China	7.6	10.4	14.0	17.5
India	5.2	5.7	7.2	7.4
Russia	2.5	2.0	3.0	3.5
Brazil	2.4	2.0	2.6	2.8
Mexico	1.2	1.8	1.5	1.6

Nonetheless, it is noteworthy that the BRICS countries—especially, but not exclusively, China—have increased their relative command of material resources very dramatically, while the G5's share has been drifting downwards.

KEY POINTS

- In terms of material power resources and influence, Brazil was not a global power in the twentieth century.
- In the early twenty-first century, Brazil aspires to become a major international player.

Conclusion

Brazil has become more internationally consequential over the past twenty years, as judged by the frequency with which it is routinely included in regional and global governance summitry. While the most significant reason is the relative increase in its material capabilities vis-à-vis other states, Brazil's greater confidence and diplomatic creativity since its democratic transition also have been important. While economic decline and wide-ranging political corruption may have dire short-term consequences, over the medium term Brazilian leaders increasingly, and plausibly, see themselves as players on a global stage.

? QUESTIONS

1. Many Brazilian policymakers aspire to have their country considered a major global power. Is this a reasonable goal?

2. What might be the costs and benefits of South American regional integration for Brazil?

3. Compared to China, India, and Russia, Brazil is geographically situated in a peaceful, unthreatening neighbourhood. What difference might this make to its foreign policy positions?

4. In which international policy arenas—from climate policy, to trade, to democratic development—might Brazil provide leadership? Why?

FURTHER READING

Burges, S. W. (forthcoming) *Brazil in the World: The International Relations of a South American Giant* (Manchester: Manchester University Press) A full-length treatment of contemporary Brazilian foreign policy through the first Dilma Rousseff administration.

Fausto, B. (1999) *A Concise History of Brazil* (Cambridge: Cambridge University Press) A scholarly, yet highly readable, summary of Brazilian history since colonial times.

Kingstone, P., and Power, T. J. (forthcoming) *Democratic Brazil Divided* (Pittsburgh, PA: University of Pittsburgh Press) Assesses the impact of contemporary competitive politics on Brazilian government, institutions, economics, and society.

Nadkarni, V., and Noonan, N. C. (eds) (2013) *Emerging Powers in a Comparative Perspective: The Political and Economic Rise of BRIC Countries* (New York: Bloomsbury) A careful introduction to each of the BRICs and their relations with the G5 powers.

Stuenkel, O., and Taylor, M. M. (eds) (2015) *Brazil on the Global Stage: Power, Ideas, and the Liberal International Order* (New York: Palgrave Macmillan) Brazilian and North American specialists analyse Brazil's evolving foreign policy vision of multilateralism and multipolarity.

Taylor, M. M. (2016) 'Brazil in the Crucible of Crisis', *Current History*, Feb: 68–74 A perceptive analysis of the deep political and economic crisis of President Rousseff's second administration.

 WEB LINKS

http://www.cfr.org/region/index.html   The portal of the United States' Council on Foreign Relations, an independent think tank, closely representative of the 'foreign policy establishment' in Washington, DC.

http://www.cipamericas.org   News and views from the left-leaning investigative journalists of the Americas Program at the Center for International Policy.

http://www.coha.org/   News and views from the investigative journalists at the Council on Hemispheric Affairs (COHA).

http://www.theguardian.com/world/americas   News and views from British newspaper *The Guardian*.

http://wilsoncenter.org   Home page of the Woodrow Wilson International Center for Scholars, which offers access to the Brazil Center for centrist news and opinion.

 For additional material and resources, please visit the Online Resource Centre at:
http://www.oxfordtextbooks.co.uk/orc/burnell5e/

29
China and the Developing World

Deborah Bräutigam and Yunnan Chen

Chapter contents

Overview

China's rise as a world power marks the coming of age of a country that has, in recent years, been considered part of—and yet different from—the rest of the developing world. This chapter examines China's South–South relations and how it has been shaped by the nature of the Chinese state: a highly capable, developmental state that uses an array of instruments to promote its interests. We examine the history behind China's engagement with countries of the Global South and the instruments that it has employed in this regard. In addition to foreign investment and commercial loans, the Chinese have developed soft power tools to engage other developing countries. Chinese ties are shaped by long-standing foreign policy principles, including non-interference in the internal affairs of others, equality, and mutual benefit. China's need for raw materials and resources, the political imperative of reassuring other developing countries that China's rise will not pre-empt their opportunities, and China's embrace of globalization and the growth of its own multinational corporations (MNCs) also condition its ties with other developing countries. Some applaud the rise of China as an investor and financier, noting that China provides an alternative to the Washington consensus; others worry that Chinese competition, and lower concern for environmental, social, and governance standards, may set back progress in other developing countries.

Figure 29.1 is a map of China and Box 29.1 provides an overview of key dates in China's history.

Figure 29.1 China

BOX 29.1 KEY DATES IN CHINA'S HISTORY

1949	Founding of People's Republic of China (PRC)
1950	China intervenes on North Korea's side in Korean War
1955	Bandung Afro-Asian Conference in Indonesia
1958–59	Great Leap Forward
1959	China sends troops to suppress revolt in Tibet
1960	Soviet Union withdraws aid and advisers from China
1962	Border war with India over Tibet
1963	Chinese premier Zhou Enlai visits ten African countries
1966–76	Cultural Revolution led by Mao Zedong and 'Gang of Four'
1972	War with Vietnam (February–March)
1976	Chinese-funded Tanzania–Zambia Railway opens in East Africa
1978	Chinese pragmatists win over radicals; market-oriented reforms begin
1982–83	Chinese premier Zhao Ziyang visits eleven countries in Africa
1989	Tiananmen Square demonstrations violently suppressed
1996	President Jiang Zemin state visit to six African countries
1997	Britain returns Hong Kong to China
2000	Forum on China–Africa Cooperation (FOCAC) established; first overseas mission of Chinese UN peacekeepers
2004	President Hu Jintao state visit to Brazil, Argentina, Chile, and Cuba
2005	President Hu Jintao pledges US$10 billion finance for Millennium Development Goals (MDGs)

2006	Beijing Summit of FOCAC; forty-four African heads of state participate
2008	Beijing hosts summer Olympics; unrest in Tibet
2011	Exxon discovers oil in South China Sea; regional disputes escalate
2012	China Central Television (CCTV) Africa launches in Nairobi, Kenya

2013	President Xi Jinping visits Russia and Africa on first foreign trip; announcement of 'one belt, one road' initiatives.
2014–15	Launch of BRICS New Development Bank and Asian Infrastructure Investment Bank (AIIB); President Xi pledges US$2 billion for Sustainable Development Goals (SDGs) in new South–South Cooperation Fund; second FOCAC Summit held in Johannesburg, South Africa

Introduction

At least since the founding of the People's Republic of China (PRC) in 1949, the Chinese have considered themselves to be part of the **developing world**. China lost portions of its territory to the colonial ambitions of others, suffered armed invasion and revolution, and endured more than a decade as a failed state in the '**warlord** period' between 1916 and 1928. Yet China's history as a developing country is also quite distinct from that of other parts of the global South.

China has, historically, been an effective regional power. The roots of its capable state bureaucracy can be traced back to the third century bc. Agriculture was relatively productive and well beyond the level of subsistence, while manufacturing was highly developed in some urban areas even before the Second World War. Although, after 1949, China was subjected to political sanctions and trade embargos, it has never been dominated by foreign multinational corporations (MNCs), grown dependent on foreign aid, or succumbed to external pressures to liberalize its economy or to democratize.

In recent decades, as China has moved to regain its historic prominence as a centre of world trade, culture, and political influence, these differences have helped to shape the framework for its contemporary South–South engagement. In addition, China is both a centralized **developmental state**, in the mode of Japan or South Korea, and a socialist country still undergoing economic liberalization. This tension means that while Beijing continues to plan its overseas engagements and has many tools with which to promote its interests, it no longer exercises complete control over state-owned companies and provincial governments. It has even less influence with the growing number of private Chinese and Hong Kong firms operating overseas (Gill and Reilly 2007).

Chinese foreign policy is influenced by the 'five principles of peaceful coexistence' (Box 29.2). These principles emphasize sovereignty, non-interference in each other's internal affairs, non-aggression, equality, and mutual benefit. With some notable exceptions, such as Chinese support for left-wing rebellions abroad during the Cultural Revolution (1966–76) or sporadic clashes along the borders with the former Soviet Union, Vietnam, and India, Chinese leaders have generally shied away from overseas political or military intervention, prizing norms of non-interference and state sovereignty over those of universal **human rights** or **Responsibility to Protect (R2P)**. Even so, since the 2000s, China has taken a growing role in the United Nations' peacekeeping operations overseas.

As a weaker counterpart to both the hegemony of the Soviet Union and the Western powers during the cold war, China emphasized the equality of nations as promised by the United Nations and advocated multilateral forums for international negotiations concerning the rules of world order. Concerned about overdependence on the Soviet Union during the 1950s, China emphasized economic cooperation and mutual assistance, rather than the one-way transfer of resources through foreign aid. However, as China grows in power and influence, its development cooperation has also shifted from knowledge transfer to capital-based instruments. As Chinese loans and

BOX 29.2 FIVE PRINCIPLES OF PEACEFUL COEXISTENCE (1954)

1. Mutual respect for each other's territorial integrity and sovereignty
2. Mutual non-aggression
3. Mutual non-interference in each other's internal affairs
4. Equality and mutual benefit
5. Peaceful coexistence

investments are put at risk in politically tense environments, assumptions of equality, and the principles of mutual benefit and non-interference, are increasingly difficult to maintain.

China's South–South partnerships today build on a substantial history of foreign aid and economic cooperation, new instruments of **soft power**, and skyrocketing increases in trade, loans, and investment over the past decade. This involvement with other developing countries has at least four overarching goals. First, China aims to preserve its own sovereignty and territorial integrity. This security concern also helps to explain why Chinese assistance has always been concentrated in Asia—particularly in the countries on its border: North Korea, Cambodia, Burma, and Pakistan, for example.

Second, China has long used economic diplomacy to counter efforts by its breakaway province of Taiwan to gain international standing. This explains Beijing's emphasis on the 'One China' policy: a consistent practice of cutting off formal ties with all countries that give official diplomatic recognition to the government in Taiwan as 'China'.

Third, China wants to enhance its long-standing role as a leader among developing countries, assuaging fears that its rise will threaten other countries, whilst also creating its own sphere of influence against the hegemony of Western powers. Knitting together regional groupings and building up tools of public diplomacy are part of this effort.

Finally, Beijing is keen to create a stable global environment that will allow China to focus on its own economic development and thus promote internal stability. This includes secure access to raw materials, new markets, and opportunities for Chinese companies overseas.

KEY POINTS

- China considers itself to be a developing country, yet there are many differences between China's history and that of others in the global South.

- China is a developmental state and has many instruments with which to reach its national goals. But, as China liberalizes its economy, it has less control over its companies and their behaviour overseas.

- The five policies of peaceful coexistence influence Chinese foreign policy and economic cooperation. These stress non-interference in the internal affairs of other countries and mutual benefit.

A Brief History

Ethnic Chinese traders and labourers have ventured abroad for many centuries, settling in dense communities in South East Asia and establishing 'Chinatowns' in many other parts of the developing world. During most of its imperial history, however, the Chinese state was uninterested in venturing abroad—with the exception of the voyages of the Muslim admiral Zheng He, who travelled to Africa between 1418 and 1433.

In the mid-nineteenth and early twentieth centuries, the Chinese lost portions of their territory in what has been called the 'century of humiliation': the island of Taiwan was lost to Japan; Macao to Portugal; and Hong Kong to Great Britain. The last imperial dynasty ended in 1911 with the founding of the Republic of China (ROC). Battles with warlords between 1916 and 1928 gave way to a civil war between the ROC and the Chinese communists. In 1949, with the communists close to victory, the government of the ROC fled to the island of Taiwan, where it remains today. The United States intervened in the conflict by sending the Seventh Fleet to patrol the waters between Taiwan and the mainland. The United States was also able to muster enough international support to keep the ROC (that is, Taiwan) in China's Security Council seat at the United Nations until 1971.

The Chinese Communist Party (CCP) initially had close ties with the Soviet Union, which sent advisers and helped to build China's economy. Deteriorating ties led Moscow to cut its assistance in 1960, just as the Chinese had begun to back away from the Great Leap Forward (1958–59), a disastrous effort to mobilize the population to create collective farms, rural mines, and rudimentary small-scale industries. More than 20 million Chinese are believed to have died in the famine resulting from the Great Leap.

At the same time, the break with the Soviet Union helped China to solidify a role as part of the 'Third World'—neither part of the capitalist camp nor in the Soviet camp. The origins of this idea of non-alignment can be traced to the 1955 Afro-Asian Solidarity Conference in Bandung, Indonesia, where Chinese leaders met with those from India, Egypt, and other newly independent countries emerging from colonialism. Bandung helped to mark out a space for countries that wished to avoid the two cold war camps. The five principles of peaceful coexistence proposed by China's premier Zhou Enlai were later espoused by the Non-Aligned Movement (NAM).

During the 1950s and even in the 1960s, Chinese engagement with other developing countries emphasized the advancement of socialism. When Zhou Enlai visited Africa in 1964, he declared the continent 'ripe for revolution'. Chinese assistance to communist North Vietnam, locked in combat with the United States, took up 40 per cent of China's aid budget during this period. However, the goal of regaining China's seat in the United Nations became an equally important objective, which gained the support of non-socialist countries in places like Africa. Aid became an important tool in China's economic diplomacy. In 1975, four years after winning its seat back in the United Nations, China had aid programmes in more African countries than did the United States (Bräutigam 2011). In contrast, Chinese ties are newer in Latin America, a legacy of the cold war and of American hegemony. In 1972, Chile, under socialist President Salvador Allende, became the first Latin American country to switch diplomatic ties from Taipei to Beijing. As of 2015, most Central American countries continued to maintain diplomatic ties only with Taiwan, although in 2007 Costa Rica recognized Beijing.

In the late 1970s, under reformist leader Deng Xiaoping, the Chinese began a long road of gradual economic reforms. In 1982, Chinese premier Zhao Ziyang embarked on a trip to eleven African countries to discuss what China's economic reforms would mean for its relationships on the continent. Instead of aid, he said, China would now emphasize 'South–South cooperation'. It would experiment, beginning with joint ventures, construction projects, and other forms of engagement aimed at mutual benefit and practical results.

Thirty years on, Chinese companies were making headlines with multibillion-dollar business deals in developing countries. China's relationship with other developing countries had evolved a great deal. The world had begun to see a small group of emerging powers, Brazil, Russia, India, and China, as the BRICs (see Chapter 5): not as developed as the West and Japan, but not 'Third World' either (Glosny 2010: 129). Being part of this group allowed China to follow Deng Xiaoping's advice: 'Hide your light and grow quietly in the shadows.'

KEY POINTS

- Like many other developing countries, China suffered colonial incursions, periods as a failed state, and civil war during the twentieth century.

- After the founding of the People's Republic of China (PRC) in 1949, the Chinese communists broke away from the Soviet Union and tried to build a non-aligned movement.

- In the 1970s, aid shifted from being primarily a tool to support other socialist countries to become primarily a tool to win diplomatic recognition.

- As China shifted toward the market, its overseas engagement began to stress business opportunities and economic cooperation.

Instruments of Engagement

Although it attracted little notice until after the millennium, Chinese business engagement in Asia, Africa, and elsewhere in the developing world had been steadily growing since the 1990s. As early as 1979, Chinese construction companies had already started to win contracts in other countries. Meanwhile, in 1993, China's oil imports exceeded its oil exports for the first time (Downs 2007). By the end of the 1990s, it was clear that South–South cooperation would need to be vastly increased if China were to find the new markets and access to resources required to sustain its rapid **modernization**.

Following in the footsteps of Japan and other developmental states, the Chinese established new instruments to meet these goals. China Export Import Bank (China Eximbank), set up in 1994, offered preferential government loans to facilitate trade and investment, particularly in poorer countries. It would also manage a new foreign aid instrument: low-interest (concessional) loans. China Development Bank (CDB), set up in 1994 primarily to serve development needs within China, gradually began to support China's efforts to go global. In 2006, CDB set up the US$5 billion China–Africa Development Fund, an equity fund to promote Chinese investment. It has also extended very large lines of credit to Chinese companies active overseas, such as telecoms company Huawei. In 2014, President Xi announced the New Silk Road Fund, a private equity fund, to complement the Silk Road Economic Belt and the twenty-first-century Maritime Silk Road ('one belt, one road') initiatives launched in 2013. In 2015, Beijing pledged to establish a new US$10 billion China Africa Production Cooperation equity fund to boost manufacturing investment in Africa:

Beijing also began to set up new regional organizations to boost political, cultural, and economic ties. The Forum on China–Africa Cooperation (FOCAC) was established in 2000 and the Shanghai Cooperation Organization (SCO)—a group concerned with mutual security, comprising China, Russia, Uzbekistan, Kazakhstan, Kyrgyzstan, and Tajikistan—was established in 2001. Forums were founded for the Caribbean, Portuguese-speaking countries, Arab states, and the Pacific Islands. These have many similar features, often including promises of aid, trade benefits, and debt relief. China's commitment to the BRICS countries (so named after the addition of South Africa) has also been solidified through the joint establishment of the BRICS New Development Bank. China also spearheaded the 2015 creation of the Asian Infrastructure Investment Bank (AIIB), making these the first two multilateral development banks (MDBs) to be led by countries of the global South.

Free trade agreements (FTAs) are another instrument of engagement. As of 2015, China has finalized eleven bilateral FTAs, including with other developing countries such as Chile, Pakistan, and Peru, and the members of the Association of Southeast Asian Nations (ASEAN). China is also driving the development of a Free Trade Area of the Asia-Pacific (FTAAP), a China-centred counterpart to the Trans-Pacific Partnership (TPP), which many saw as a US-led instrument for containing China.

The selection of regions for engagement reflect three goals:

• the drive to secure access to resources—in particular, oil;

• strategic interests, through the diplomatic isolation of Taiwan and the counterbalancing of US dominance in the Asia-Pacific region; and

• promoting Chinese business—for example business networks in the Portuguese-speaking Chinese enclave of Macao were enlisted to give Chinese companies an important **comparative advantage** in concluding deals with countries such as Brazil.

Soft power

In addition, China's soft power has expanded. Confucius institutes, like the Alliance Française or Goethe institutes, have been set up overseas with the aim of promoting Chinese language and culture. More than 500 Confucius institutes were established between 2004 and 2015, in more than 108 countries. Between 2006 and 2012, university scholarships for African students increased from 2,000 to 5,500 per year. Since 1963, Chinese medical teams have also been dispatched on a rotating basis to more than seventy-three countries, where each team spends two years offering traditional Chinese and Western medical treatments in local hospitals. Chinese state media branches are also 'going out': in 2012, China Central Television (CCTV) launched its first African news bureau in Nairobi, since when it has expanded to bureaus in Egypt and South Africa.

As their international influence has grown, Chinese leaders have become increasingly visible as benefactors in multilateral forums. In 2005, former Chinese President Hu Jintao made a pledge during a speech at the United Nations to provide US$10 billion in finance for the Millennium Development Goals (MDGs). China has also proactively engaged with the post-2015 **Sustainable Development Goals (SDGs)** process, voicing support for goals of poverty reduction and sustainable and inclusive growth, but remaining opposed to the inclusion of political reform and **governance** in the post-2015 agenda. In his first speech to the United Nations in 2015, President Xi Jinping pledged up to US$12 billion of investment in the least-developed countries (LDCs) by 2030 and an initial US$2 billion assistance fund supporting South–South cooperation. After many years as a recipient of World Bank assistance, China became a donor to the **institution** in 2007, and it has gained membership in a number of other MDBs, including the African Development Bank, the Inter-American Development Bank, and the European Bank for Reconstruction and Development. These moves can be seen as reflections of a Chinese commitment to multilateralism.

China's efforts to position itself as a 'responsible power' are also reflected in its contributions to humanitarian aid, reflected in its unprecedented response to the Indian Ocean tsunami disaster and the Pakistan earthquake in 2005. China's foreign aid, in the form of concessional and interest-free loans, as well as grants, has risen substantially over the decades. While China is not very transparent about its aid programme, according to its second White Paper on foreign aid, China provided over US$14 billion of foreign aid between 2010 and 2012 (State Council Information Office 2014).

Arms and peacekeeping: China's military presence

China's military presence in the developing world is characterized by contrasts: China is an emerging global force for peacekeeping—but it is also an arms exporter, and its military presence in the South and East China Sea has caused controversy with neighbours. China is a major arms supplier to other developing countries, especially Pakistan, Bangladesh, and Myanmar, which together receive nearly 70 per cent of Chinese arms exports (Wezeman and Wezeman 2015). Beijing has not published information on its export of arms, while arms traders have sometimes mislabelled shipments of Chinese arms as agricultural equipment to escape arms embargoes (Taylor 2009a: 126). Although Chinese spokespersons insist that they respect the UN arms embargo on South Sudan, Chinese-made military equipment has been recovered from sites in the troubled province of Darfur. The exposure of Chinese arms sales and attempted sales to the repressive governments of Robert Mugabe in Zimbabwe and Muammar Qaddafi in Libya also generated controversy.

This portrait of China as arms supplier to rogue **regimes** is offset by another: of China as a supplier of UN peacekeepers. More than 17,390 Chinese peacekeepers have served nineteen UN peacekeeping missions and China is the largest contributor to peacekeeping forces of the UN Security Council members. At the end of 2014, according to UN figures, some 2,181 Chinese were serving in the UN police or military missions, mainly in Lebanon, Sudan, Liberia, and the Democratic Republic of the Congo. Although Chinese personnel primarily serve in non-military roles, as medical staff and engineers, 2013 saw the first deployment of Chinese combat troops to Mali and, in 2015, a Chinese infantry battalion was dispatched to the UN mission in South Sudan, indicating a growing military capacity in its international peacekeeping engagements.

In 2009, responding to a sharp rise in attacks by Somali pirates on ships moving through the Arabian Gulf, the Chinese dispatched two naval ships to help to escort merchant vessels through the troubled waters. The Chinese navy coordinates with the United States and other countries whose ships also patrol the Arabian Gulf. In 2015, China announced plans to establish its first overseas naval base in Djibouti, citing the need for logistical support for its peacekeeping and anti-piracy operations. The base also signifies China's growing capacity for power projection overseas.

China's territorial assertions in the South China Sea have led to rising tensions with neighbours Vietnam, the Republic of China (Taiwan), the Philippines, Malaysia, and Brunei. China has overlapping historical and legal claims over a number of small islands, including the Spratly and Paracel archipelagoes. The relatively unexplored seabed is believed to have significant oil and gas resources, fuelling contention over legal boundaries. Escalating territorial disputes have spurred land reclamation efforts from China and Asian neighbours, where islands have been artificially created over neighbouring reefs to support military bases and bolster territorial claims.

KEY POINTS

- Chinese policy banks were established to provide finance to meet government objectives. This follows the 'developmental state' model pioneered by Japan.

- China set up a number of regional organizations as strategic forums for interaction. Soft power and China's military presence also increased.

China's Economy Goes Global

Since China's own economic reform and subsequent boom, it has assumed an increasingly central and interdependent position in the world economy. China's growing partnerships with other developing countries are based on its economic interests, both in securing access to raw materials and world markets. The 'Going Global' policies launched in 2001 aimed to encourage Chinese companies to diversify their markets by investing abroad and to become global leaders, helping Chinese domestic industries to move up the value chain away from labour and energy-intensive manufacturing, and to secure raw materials for domestic needs.

Trade is central in this effort. From 2000 to 2014, China's trade with Latin America grew from US$12 billion to US$264 billion, and trade with Africa, from US$10.5 billion to US$220 billion. This surge was partly a result of high prices for natural resources, stimulated by China's growing demand. However, in both regions, Chinese exports made up nearly half of this trade, demonstrating the success of Chinese companies overseas. This has been controversial in both regions, where local deindustrialization has been blamed on China's export push.

Chinese banks have ratcheted up their loans in developing countries. In Brazil and Venezuela, CDB has signed lines of credit worth, respectively, US$10 billion and US$20 billion, backed by regular exports of oil. Researchers have identified over US$75 billion in resource-linked lending commitments from Chinese banks in Africa and Latin America since 2005 (Bräutigam and Gallagher 2014). Many of these loans are linked to construction projects carried out by Chinese firms. In resource-backed loans such as these, and by winning contracts financed by the World Bank, other donors, and African governments, Chinese engineering companies have earned billions in revenues in recent years, including US$47.9 billion in Africa, US$64.4 billion in Asia and the Middle East, and US$137.1 worldwide in 2013 alone. Some of these construction contracts were secured by flagship telecoms companies such as ZTE and Huawei, because the Chinese state helped them to profit by assisting Africans and others to bypass fixed line telephones and jump directly into wireless technology.

Beyond its overseas enterprises, China's domestic economy has also become an important economic centre of gravity for developing economies. China's domestic growth and continued demand for raw materials served to insulate much of the developing world from the recession that afflicted Western economies in the 2007–08 global financial crisis. On the other hand, any slowdown in Chinese growth is likely to deeply affect the economies of natural resource-exporting countries, especially in Africa and Latin America.

Many developing countries have agreements to use China's currency, the renminbi (RMB), in at least some of their trade. The addition of the renminbi

to the International Monetary Fund's (IMF's) special drawing rights (SDR) basket of reserve currencies in 2015 was another forward step in Beijing's long-term goal towards the internationalization of the renminbi. The renminbi's new **status** is a political symbol of China's global rise and a shift towards China's vision of multipolar world. Having reserve currency status also carries tangible economic benefits, facilitating lower borrowing costs for domestic firms, as well as boosting renminbi-denominated trade.

KEY POINTS

- The 'Going Global' policies involve trade diversification, secure access to raw materials, overseas investment and contracting, and the building up of Chinese multinational corporations (MNCs).
- Chinese trade has risen enormously, reaching US$220 billion in Africa and US$264 billion in Latin America in 2014.
- Chinese banks have made very large, long-term loans, many linked to repayment in natural resources. In Africa, some of these loans pay for much-needed infrastructure.

Controversies

Chinese engagement with other developing countries is more controversial than that of any of the other BRICS. In Latin America and Africa especially, critics charge that Chinese economic engagement replicates 'colonial' patterns: exports of manufactured goods and imports of raw materials. Chinese textiles, plastic products, and other simple manufactured goods threaten the weak industrial sectors in some countries. Colombia imposed tariffs on Chinese textiles and South Africa asked China for temporary voluntary export restraints. While Chinese demand benefits commodity exporters through higher prices, Chinese goods have been damaging to many local manufacturers. In Africa, local traders and businesses complain about competition from Chinese traders and small enterprises in their own markets. To counter these political frictions, the Chinese have announced programmes such as the construction of at least fourteen overseas economic zones, in which Chinese companies will be encouraged to invest in manufacturing.

Social and environmental complaints about Chinese companies are common. Many enterprises, particularly in Africa, use Chinese nationals for management and technical positions: on average, about 20 per cent of employment in a project or investment will be Chinese. In 2013, at least 214,534 Chinese were officially working in Africa and these numbers have been rising steadily (National Bureau of Statistics 2014). Others have criticized Chinese companies' low environmental, safety, and labour standards. In one infamous case, an explosion in a Chinese-owned factory killed more than fifty Zambian workers. Poor work conditions have led to strikes and host government reprimands from Peru to Papua New Guinea. Chinese companies are blamed for overfishing in the coastal waters of other developing countries and for buying illegally harvested timber. Chinese demand for ivory and rhino horn has fuelled poaching of endangered species in Africa. The rise of Chinese private companies, provincial firms, and increased independence for non-state actors (including Hong Kong companies) means that Beijing now has fewer levers with which to control the actions of its companies overseas (Gill and Reilly 2007).

Finally, **civil society** groups in developing countries and in the global North (along with northern governments) have charged that Chinese policies of aid and commercial engagement with 'no strings attached' propped up rogue regimes in places such as Sudan, Iran, North Korea, and Zimbabwe. The Chinese response is that active engagement works better than embargoes, that they abide by sanctions when imposed by the United Nations, and that their diplomats have played constructive roles in getting warring parties to agree to peace talks in the conflict between Sudan and South Sudan. They also point out that, when it is convenient for them, Western companies and governments themselves engage with many reviled regimes.

KEY POINTS

- Chinese patterns of trade in many developing countries have led to accusations of 'neocolonialism', with China exporting manufactured goods and importing raw materials.
- Concerns raised about Chinese companies overseas include their tendency to employ Chinese in management and skilled labour roles, and their failure to adopt high social and environmental standards.
- China's policy of investment and aid without political conditions means that it actively engages with some pariah regimes such as North Korea and Sudan.

Conclusion

China's economic boom has made it an influential global actor and an important partner for developing countries whose economies have become interdependent with China. Despite its rise, Beijing has been reluctant over the decades to take on international responsibilities; however, it is mindful of being seen as a 'responsible power' as its overseas interests necessitate an increased international role. As it grows wealthier, Beijing does not want to replicate the familiar 'North–South' relations based on foreign aid. Yet it runs the risk of being seen as reproducing 'neo-colonialism' through patterns of trade and investment based on raw materials and low-level manufactured goods. Because China's engagement with other developing countries has grown so rapidly, it is difficult to find more than anecdotal evidence of the impact of China's ties on governance, debt, environment, employment, or social standards. This makes it challenging to find balanced and accurate analysis, but it also means that the field is open for evidence-based research on an important new phenomenon.

QUESTIONS

1. As China grows in power, is it likely to follow existing global rules or will it challenge existing institutions to create new rules?
2. How do China's patterns of engagement with developing countries differ from those of Western countries? How does China's distinct history shape its present behaviour?

3.   How durable is China's adherence to norms of sovereignty and non-intervention?

4.   Is China's rise a threat—or an opportunity—for other developing countries? In which areas?

5.   What implications does China's ongoing economic transformation have for other developing countries?

 FURTHER READING

Bräutigam, D. (2011) *The Dragon's Gift: The Real Story of China in Africa* (Oxford: Oxford University Press) A comparative introduction to Chinese aid and economic engagement in Africa. Tackles the myths and misunderstandings, as well as the dimensions of engagement and how it works.

Gallagher, K. (2016) *The China Triangle: Latin America's China Boom and the Fate of the Washington Consensus* (Oxford: Oxford University Press) Examines China–Latin America relations, with a focus on economic and political engagement. Pays special attention to challenges to the region's dominant Washington consensus development ideas.

Hayton, B. (2015) *The South China Sea: The Struggle for Power in Asia* (New Haven, CT: Yale University Press) Thorough and engaging study of how China's rise has affected an important neighbourhood issue.

Nathan, A. J., and Scobell, A. (2012) *China's Search for Security* (New York: Columbia University Press) Focus on China's relations with its immediate neighbours, as well as other states in Asia and beyond.

 WEB LINKS

http://www.chinaafricarealstory.com   Website and blog exploring Chinese aid, investment, and economic engagement in Africa.

http://www.chinadialogue.net/reports   Site focusing on China, environment, food security, and development issues.

http://www.thedialogue.org/chinaandlatinamerica   Website devoted to Chinese engagement in Latin America.

 For additional material and resources, please visit the Online Resource Centre at:
http://www.oxfordtextbooks.co.uk/orc/burnell5e/

30

India's Development Partnerships in the Twenty-First Century

Emma Mawdsley

Chapter contents

Overview

Many countries of the global South have established development cooperation policies and programmes with other low- and middle-income countries. A few started as long ago as the late 1940s (including India), while others are more recent entrants to the field. Often bundled closely with trade, investment, and diplomatic agendas, such South–South partnership includes debt relief, concessional loans, grants, humanitarian assistance, technical support, and educational and training provision. The '(re-)emerging' donors and development partners raise a series of opportunities and challenges for the so-called traditional aid community, while the direct and indirect impacts of their development cooperation programmes have profound implications for the world's poor and for the politics of development. This chapter outlines the main trends and issues of South–South development cooperation, using India as a case study.

Figure 30.1 is a map of India and Box 30.1 provides an overview of key dates in India's history.

Figure 30.1 India

Note: Boundaries in the Kashmir region are in dispute. The use of specific nomenclature and boundary symbols on this map implies neither recognition nor non-recognition of the legality of the political regions or boundaries to which they refer.

BOX 30.1 KEY DATES IN INDIA'S HISTORY

1857	'Revolt', 'Mutiny', or 'First War of Independence' suppressed	1920–22	Civil disobedience movement against British rule launched by Congress, led by Mahatma Gandhi
1858	India comes under direct rule of British Crown (assumed from East India Company)	1947	India achieves independence, but country is violently split in Partition; East Pakistan (later Bangladesh) and West Pakistan (later Pakistan) also created; Jawaharlal Nehru becomes independent India's first prime minister
1885	Indian National Congress formed by emerging nationalists		

1949–52	Constitution of India declares it to be secular, federal republic	2000	India's population reaches 1 billion
1962	India loses short border war with China, despite earlier declarations of friendship	2006	Hu Jintao visits India, first Chinese president to do so for a decade
1964	Jawaharlal Nehru dies	2007	Launch of India's first commercial space rocket
1966	Indira Gandhi, Nehru's daughter (no relation to Mahatma Gandhi), becomes prime minister, leading ruling Indian National Congress Party	2008	Closer United States–India ties signalled by nuclear deal; India–Africa Forum Summit launched
1971	Third war with Pakistan, this time over secession of East Pakistan to form Bangladesh	2009	Indian National Congress, with Manmohan Singh as prime minister, re-elected to central government
1984	Indira Gandhi assassinated; her son Rajiv Gandhi elected prime minister	2011	India joins United Nations Security Council as non-permanent member; second meeting of India–Africa Forum Summit held in Addis Ababa
1989	Congress loses national elections to coalition of other parties	2012	Manmohan Singh offers line of credit to Burma in first official visit by an Indian prime minister since 1987; Development Partnership Administration launched within Ministry of External Affairs
1991	Major economic reforms implemented by Prime Minister Narasimha Rao mark decisive shift towards neoliberalism	2013	BJP leader and Narendra Modi elected prime minister
1998	Bharatiya Janata Party (BJP), a Hindu nationalist party, wins national elections; controversial nuclear tests carried out shortly afterwards	2015	Third India–Africa Forum Summit held in Delhi

Introduction

Over the last few decades, India has been not only a recipient of foreign aid (at one time, the largest in the world), but also a provider of concessional loans, grants, technical assistance, peacekeeping forces, humanitarian assistance, debt relief, and so on. This chapter explores how and why a country that still has more absolutely poor people than the whole of sub-Saharan Africa gives development assistance to countries in Asia, Africa, and beyond. It will start with a brief introduction to the issue of the '(re-)emerging' development actors and then move on to a more detailed analysis of India's development cooperation.

The 'Rising Powers' as Development Actors

Commentators tend to disagree—often virulently—about every conceivable aspect of 'traditional' foreign aid, including stated and real motivations, effective and appropriate modalities, desirable recipients, direct and indirect impacts, and much more. The depth and range of disagreement is not surprising given the enormous complexity of the global foreign aid architecture, the vast range of actors—from the World Bank, to bilateral aid agencies, to global **non-governmental organizations (NGOs)**, right down to small grass-roots local organizations—and its multiple, contingent, and often conflicting stated rationales—humanitarian, developmental, commercial, and geopolitical. But what almost all of these contending evaluations share is a dominant geographical imaginary that views foreign aid as given by rich industrialized countries to poorer countries. Until recently, with few exceptions, Western analysts almost entirely overlooked the large number of other countries that offer development assistance to other poorer countries. However, this is a situation that has changed rapidly and large numbers of so-called non-traditional development partners (see Box 30.2 for a discussion of terminology) are now very much on the agenda.

The DAC donors

The Organisation for Economic Co-operation and Development (OECD) is made up of thirty-five countries, all of which are relatively industrialized and high income. Of these, twenty-eight are members of the Development Assistance Committee (DAC), while the twenty-ninth member is the European Union (see

BOX 30.2 TERMINOLOGICAL DILEMMAS

'Emerging' donors or 'new' donors? Some countries are only recently embarking upon development assistance programmes (for example Thailand), but many have a long history of development partnership (for example Saudi Arabia, Vietnam, and Poland).

'Post-colonial' donors In some ways, this is an attractive term, because it explicitly reverses **orientalist** binaries that set up the North as giver and the South as receiver. However, if the term is used in the sense of 'countries that were once formally colonized, but which are now independent', it is not universally accurate.

'Non-DAC' donors (NDDs) Although accurate, as a residual category (that is, something that is defined by what it is *not*), this

term appears to promote the centrality of the Development Assistance Committee (DAC) of the Organisation for Economic Co-operation and Development (OECD); what unites all of the other donors is their non-DAC **status**, suggesting a peripheral location, or even an unfulfilled aspiration. It does not signal the active critique of DAC ideologies and practices, and the wider discontent with the dominant structures of foreign aid, felt by many around the world and especially within the global South. Moreover, many NDDs are cautious about the label of 'donor', with some firmly rejecting it. 'Donor' is burdened with associations of paternalism, hierarchy, and neo-colonial interference. Similarly, many reject the term 'foreign aid', preferring 'development assistance'.

Box 30.3). All are Western, with the exception of Japan (which, at one point, was the largest aid donor in the world) and, since January 2010, South Korea. The DAC has traditionally acted as a powerful forum for formulating dominant bilateral aid policies and practices around the world.

Many Southern, Gulf, and Central and East European states have been development partners for decades and, in some cases, quite substantial donors. In 1978, for example, the Organization of Petroleum

Exporting Countries (OPEC) donors alone provided one third of all official foreign aid. Current calculations suggest that the NDDs contribute around 15 per cent of 'foreign aid', although extreme difficulties with both definitions, and with the availability and robustness of data, mean that this can be estimated only with considerable caution. Although dwarfed by the DAC total, this is still a significant absolute and relative amount. Moreover, for some recipient countries, assistance from the (re-)emerging development partners

BOX 30.3 DAC AND NON-DAC DONORS

DAC members

Australia	Austria	Belgium	Canada	Czech Republic
Denmark	European Union	Finland	France	Germany
Greece	Iceland	Ireland	Italy	Japan
Luxembourg	Netherlands	New Zealand	Norway	Poland
Portugal	Slovak Republic	Slovenia	South Korea	Spain
Sweden	Switzerland	United Kingdom	United States	

Main non-DAC donors/development partners

Brazil	Bulgaria	China	Cuba	Cyprus
Estonia	Hungary	India	Israel	Kuwait
Latvia	Lithuania	Malta	Mexico	Romania
Russia	Saudi Arabia	Slovenia	South Africa	Taiwan
Thailand	Turkey	United Arab Emirates	Venezuela	

constitutes a high proportion of the total—notably, the Occupied Palestinian Territories and North Korea. Another way of looking at it is to compare absolute amounts with those of DAC donors. Park (2011) points out that, in 2011, Saudi Arabia provided more **official development assistance (ODA)** than fifteen DAC donors, and China, more than eight DAC donors. The growing numbers of Southern donors was starkly demonstrated after the Indian Ocean tsunami of 2004, when more than seventy countries offered humanitarian assistance.

Today's (re-)emerging development partners have a variety of historical ties and contexts for their development assistance. In the post-war era, a large number of communist countries provided various forms of development assistance to other communist countries and to 'friendly' **regimes**, including Vietnam, Yemen, and Indonesia, amongst others. The Arab OPEC donors significantly expanded their development cooperation **institutions** following the oil price rises of the 1970s. Driven by regional geopolitical and economic considerations, and shaped by Islamic cultures of charitable giving, some have been substantial donors for more than forty years.

The historical lineages of other donors lie in more specific interests. For example, the origins of Taiwan's foreign aid activities are highly specific to its competition with the People's Republic of China (PRC) for diplomatic recognition, but they also reflect its achievement of rapid and very successful industrial development and economic growth, and the view that it has valuable experiences to share.

It is notable that it is only in the last decade or so that the broader development community has really woken up to these 'other' development actors. What has jolted Western academics and policymakers out of their amnesia in the last few years has much to do with the growing role and presence of China (Bräutigam 2009). China is a major, long-standing development assistance partner to many countries, and its growing development partnership activities actively complement its wider economic, diplomatic and geopolitical ambitions (see Chapter 29). The visibility of these other donors/partners was also been driven by Venezuela's substantial aid programme under Hugo Chávez, which was openly constructed as a challenge to US hegemony, as well as simply the growing numbers of development actors. Furthermore, in 2004, ten new states joined the European Union. Most had previous experience of foreign aid during the socialist period, but re-established their aid institutions and policies in compliance with the Union's norms and standards.

We can now observe within the heavily Western-dominated international foreign aid architecture, including the DAC, its member states, the World Bank Group, and various UN bodies, a huge new interest in this more diverse set of development actors. This chapter offers a case study of Indian development cooperation. India is obviously not representative of these 'new' partners—they are simply too diverse in their origins, histories, interests, capabilities, ideologies, and cultures—but what we sacrifice in breadth, we gain in some depth through this case study.

KEY POINTS

- There is no easy way in which to capture or categorize the diversity of the (re-)emerging development partners.

- Although these donors have historically contributed a significant share of official 'aid', Western academic and policy analysts have tended to overlook their roles and activities—something that is now changing rapidly.

- South–South development cooperation is not the same as 'foreign aid'. It usually includes 'aid' and 'aid-like' flows and activities, but is frequently explicitly bundled and blurred with investment, trade, and diplomatic agendas.

India and South–South Relations

Over the last sixty years, India has been at the centre of a series of attempts to contest the ordering of the world along the economic and political hierarchies established during the colonial period, which deepened in the period after the Second World War. India was a key architect of the Non-Aligned Movement (NAM), for example, which was founded in 1961 and which insisted on the sovereign right of the newly decolonizing nations to resist subordination to the cold war superpowers. At the Bandung Conference of 1955, the principles of South–South solidarity were set out as: mutual respect for territorial integrity and sovereignty; mutual non-aggression; mutual non-interference in domestic affairs; equality and mutual benefit; and peaceful coexistence. These discourses of non-interference and mutual benefit remain the stated values underlying South–South development cooperation approaches, and although practice certainly departs from principle at times, they continue to be deeply held cultural-historical referents for South–South development partnerships in the twenty-first century.

Over the last ten or fifteen years, sustained high economic growth (albeit socially and regionally uneven) has enabled India to put greater financial and diplomatic weight behind these assertions of global stature. Whereas, in the first few decades of independence, India had to mobilize other strengths—Prime Minister Nehru's charisma and the exercise of **soft power**, India's size, its ability to play the United States and Soviet Union off against each other, and its technological and scientific strengths—now, its growing wealth and the confidence of its increasingly assertive middle classes and elites are underpinning a new vigour in its foreign policy (Ogden 2014). During the 1990s and twenty-first century, for example, India has been a controversially disruptive voice in the World Trade Organization (WTO), demanding a better deal for developing countries. However, despite claims to 'Third World' leadership:

> **❝** India's foreign policy has always exhibited a dichotomy between principle and practice: an ideological opposition to formal institutionalized discrimination in the international system—such as UNSC [United Nations Security Council] permanent membership and nuclear weapon status in the Nuclear Non-Proliferation Treaty—has gone hand-in-hand with a pragmatic willingness to seek the best possible deal for India within a hierarchical international system that is not egalitarian. **❞**

(Sahni 2007: 23)

This would suggest that India's claim to leadership, and to South–South partnership and solidarity, must be critically and carefully appraised in all arenas, including its development cooperation efforts. Singh (2007: 10), for example, argues that 'ever since economic liberalization started in 1991 India's foreign policy has been increasingly driven towards finding export markets, and attracting foreign capital and technological know-how', and observes the growing place of development cooperation in facilitating these trends. While there are indeed many potential direct and indirect benefits from India's development cooperation efforts, it would be naive to see these as necessarily positive simply by virtue of India's post-colonial status and rhetoric of developing country solidarity, as some less critical commentators claim.

> **KEY POINTS**
>
> - India has long positioned itself as a leader of the **developing world** and has been an active, and sometimes effective, challenger of neo-imperialistic hierarchies that characterize the current world order.
> - India's strategic imperatives (as with any other state) mean that the pursuit of its interests may sometimes align and sometimes clash with the interests of other Southern states and groups within them.

India as a Development Assistance Partner

After independence in 1947, India was very quickly targeted by both the United States and the Soviet Union as a potential cold war ally, although, over the succeeding decades, the United States was to turn much more strongly to India's neighbour and rival, Pakistan. Even so, both offered substantial amounts of aid to India and it became one of the largest aid recipients in the world. Despite this status, India rapidly took on a development partner mantle, for example in the early 1950s with regard to its Himalayan neighbours, Nepal and Bhutan. As well as funding infrastructure development, India assistance included the provision of technical experts in a wide range of fields to partner countries, and the offer of scholarships and training. Despite budget constraints, Nehru was determined that India would invest in science and technology, and to that end he made sure that scarce funding was directed towards universities and research institutions—expertise that India has been able to deploy abroad. In 1964, India created the Indian Technical and Economic Cooperation (ITEC) scheme. The scheme supports projects, deputations of experts, and study tours, but its main focus is on providing training programmes in areas as diverse as small and medium-sized enterprises (SMEs), rural credit programmes, food processing, textiles, information technology, and women's entrepreneurship. The scheme now runs in 158 countries and, through it, the Indian government offers thousands of placements a year.

What explains India's early entry into international development activities? Clearly, it was in part motivated by the desire to create regional goodwill, especially given the hostile embrace of West Pakistan (now Pakistan) and East Pakistan (now Bangladesh) following Partition in 1947. Moreover, after Sino–Indian friendship crumbled in the early 1960s, India wished to promote strong and stable buffer states between itself and China. Thus India looked to secure regional allies, and its development cooperation played some part by funding goodwill and transport infrastructure. A second incentive was energy security, which helps to explain the early focus on hydropower projects in Bhutan and Nepal. A third motivation arose from India's desire to take its place in the world as not only a regional, but also an international, power. Being a development partner helped to build relations of solidarity with other newly independent countries and signalled India's aspirant status to international stature.

India's own technological achievements continue to be reflected in its development cooperation profile. One of its current flagship technology transfer programmes is the pan-Africa e-network. The scheme aims to provide facilities for tele-education, tele-medicine, and network video conferencing for heads of state in all fifty-three members of the African Union. The network will also connect fifty-three learning centres, ten super-speciality hospitals (three of which are in India), fifty-three other hospitals, and five universities (two in India). India has committed at least US$100 million to this scheme, although it is currently limited by a variety of implementation deficits. Other forms of development assistance include debt write-offs, and a substantial set of contributions to food aid and peacekeeping personnel. The pursuit of 'soft power' continues to be a major incentive for development cooperation, as a resurgent India acts as a key player in the growing challenge to current hegemonies.

The last few years have also witnessed some significant developments in India's cooperation modalities. In particular, lines of credit are becoming an increasingly favoured route of channelling development assistance. These are a form of state-sponsored subsidy for Indian or recipient country firms (or governments), and are intended to facilitate trade and investment. Lines of credit are often tied to the purchase of Indian goods and services. Since 2003, these have been managed by the Export–Import Bank of India, which is managed indirectly by the Ministry of Finance. The Ministry of Commerce is also playing a growing role—indicative of the increasingly economically strategic profile of Indian aid. India's development cooperation is evidently being increasingly leveraged to support commercial and trade objectives. Mutual benefits with 'partner' countries are entirely possible within this new dispensation—being strategic does not necessarily undermine effectiveness, just as being altruistic does not

necessarily achieve positive change—but the claims to a 'win–win' scenario are not always substantiated.

The changing geography of Indian development cooperation is also suggestive of its increasingly strategic intent. After Asia, Africa has long been a major destination for India's developmental assistance, with the anglophone Commonwealth countries historically the favoured partners. However, one of the interesting shifts in India's engagement with Africa has been its growing interest in West Africa (Singh 2007). While India has had long linkages with Nigeria and Ghana, historically there has been less diplomacy and trade with francophone countries. What has changed is the growing demand for resources—above all oil—and the search for investment opportunities. Reflecting these new imperatives, in 2004, the 'Techno-Economic Approach for Africa-India Movement' (TEAM-9) initiative was launched by the government of India, together with eight resource- and energy-rich West African countries. That said, India's African engagement is also about market-seeking, and takes in a wide range of economic sectors and activities.

India also contributes to regional and global development institutions, and is now a net creditor to the International Monetary Fund (IMF), and a major contributor to the World Food Programme and to UN peacekeeping forces. In the last few years, India has also engaged in development cooperation with other donors, although so far only in a limited number of arenas—notably, Afghanistan, in which it is a member of the Afghanistan Donors Group. India was also one of the Group of Four (G4), together with Australia, Japan, and the United States, which coordinated the post-tsunami emergency relief response in 2004–05. One area in which there has been little change to date has been that of NGOs and other **civil society** organizations. Aside from the Indian Red Cross, India has not yet sought to make use of NGOs as a channel for development funding and assistance. The government has an uneasy relationship with its own NGO community and in the past has appeared reluctant to devolve any overseas functions in this direction—although this may be something that changes in the next few years.

India has also been involved in emerging pressures on the global architecture of foreign aid. In 2007, for example, India helped to promote the creation of the Development Cooperation Forum in the United Nations Economic and Social Council (ECOSOC), which, unlike the DAC, represents a grouping of donors *and* recipients, and which seeks to identify *mutually* acceptable principles and priorities. India, like other (re-)emerging development partners, has signalled its independence from dominant aid ideologies and practices, deliberately articulating different principles of development engagement. Thus, in 2003, India announced that it no longer needed the assistance of the majority of its own donors, although they are still able to fund NGOs in India, under government supervision and through multilateral organizations. The remaining donors (Germany, Japan, Russia, the United Kingdom, the United States, and the European Union) are subject to considerable scrutiny and direction from the government, and in 2012 a timeline for the end of British aid to India was agreed. India has recently paid off its debts to fifteen bilateral funders, and large parts of its debt to the Asian Development Bank and the World Bank. However, the paradox of India's own vast levels of poverty remains unresolved. For some commentators, India's development cooperation is all about diplomatic and commercial support for the 'rising power' constituency of India—the politicians, policymakers, and increasingly affluent middle classes who benefit most from its booming neoliberal economy and increasingly assertive global presence. At present, these benefits appear not to be trickling down to the mass of India's poor. Questions are also being raised about who benefits from Indian development cooperation in recipient countries. In some cases, it certainly supports wider 'development' benefits; in other cases, Indian development assistance appears to be providing financial and technical support for land acquisition and resource extraction that benefit donor and recipient elites, while often displacing and exploiting poor and marginalized peoples (Rowden 2011).

KEY POINTS

- India has a long history of development assistance in Asia and Africa—in some cases, dating back to the 1950s.
- India argues that it differs from Western donors in that it promotes 'genuine' partnership and mutual benefit.
- Many commentators suggest that the motivations for Indian development assistance are increasingly tilting from promoting South–South solidarity and diplomatic alliances, towards more commercial and resource-oriented needs. However, these are not necessarily mutually exclusive.
- The benefits of India's development cooperation are shared unevenly, both domestically and abroad.

Conclusion

Political analysts of foreign aid are becoming increasingly aware of the opportunities and problems raised by the diverse set of 'non-traditional' development partners. For their supporters, these (re-)emerging development actors represent an alternative to the discredited intentions and outcomes of Western-dominated foreign aid. As Woods (2008: 1220) suggests:

> In Africa and elsewhere, governments needing development assistance are sceptical of promises of more aid, wary of conditionalities associated with aid, and fatigued by the heavy bureaucratic and burdensome delivery systems used for delivery of aid. Small wonder that the emerging donors are being welcomed with open arms.

However, despite claims by some to a selfless postcolonial solidarity, there is no doubt that Southern partners share the complex mix of motivations that characterize Western donors—humanitarian, geopolitical, and commercial. The differences between them reside more in modalities and discourses. The relative lack of **conditionalities** is key here: no **structural adjustment programmes (SAPs)** or insistence on **good governance** accompanies the bulk of South–South assistance. Supporters argue that this more honest relationship represents genuine partnership, as opposed to what many see as the hollow use of the term by the World Bank and others, allowing partner countries to benefit much more from investment in training opportunities, infrastructure development, trade growth, and local investment. Critics, on the other hand, fear that Southern development partners will contribute to an unravelling of the fragile process towards greater transparency, effectiveness, and well-targeted anti-poverty efforts.

Most analytical attention is understandably directed at China, but India, like other Southern providers, offers a fascinating example of a challenge to Western-dominated institutions, practices, and ideologies of foreign aid. The **politics** of the developing world is changing, and development cooperation is one constituent element and reflection of this, bringing new challenges and opportunities for poorer peoples and poorer countries around the world.

QUESTIONS

1. What will be the impacts of the (re-)emerging development actors on humanitarian intervention, longer-term development, poverty reduction, and economic growth in poorer countries?

2. What will be the impacts of these donors and development partners on the existing architecture of foreign aid—the ideologies, policies, and practices of the dominant institutions?

3. What part will 'non-traditional' development assistance play in the changing global geographies of economic and geopolitical power that are taking place and predicted to accelerate?

4. What challenges do these shifts imply for theorizing politics and development in a new global era?

FURTHER READING

Chaturvedi, S., and Mulakala, A. (eds) (2016) *India's Soft Power: The Emerging Dynamics of Indian Development Cooperation* (London: Routledge) The first comprehensive analysis of India's soft power from an international relations perspective.

Manning, R. (2006) 'Will "Emerging" Donors Challenge the Face of International Cooperation?', *Development Policy Review*, 24(4): 371–83 A view on the emerging donors from the former director of the Development Assistance Committee.

Mawdsley, E. (2012) *From Recipients to Donors: Emerging Powers and the Changing Development Landscape* (London: Zed Books) A comprehensive and accessible account of the 'rising powers' as development actors.

Ogden, C. (2014) *Indian Foreign Policy* (Cambridge: Polity Press) A critical and robust overview of Indian foreign policy in the round.

Woods, N. (2008) 'Whose Aid? Whose Influence? China, Emerging Donors and the Silent Revolution in Development Assistance', *International Affairs*, 84(6): 1205–21 Critically summarizes the 'emerging donors' and the response of the 'traditional' donor community.

WEB LINKS

http://www.oecd.org/dac/stats/aid-at-a-glance.htm   Based on the Development Assistance Committee (DAC) definitions of 'official development assistance' (ODA), this page provides calculations of all DAC and some key non-DAC donor contributions.

http://ssc.undp.org/content/ssc.html   Home page of the United Nation's special unit for South–South cooperation.

For additional material and resources, please visit the Online Resource Centre at:
http://www.oxfordtextbooks.co.uk/orc/burnell5e/

Appendix A

Case Study Countries: Basic Indicators

	Population 2014 (million)[1]	Average annual population growth 2010–15 (%)[1]	GNI 2015, (US$bn), Atlas Method[2]	GNI per capita 2014 (US$), PPP[1]	GDP per capita growth 2015 (%)[2]	% of population on less than US$1.90 a day, PPP (most recent)[2]	Gini index (most recent)[2]	HDI value 2014[1]	Political rights 2016[3]	Civil liberties 2016[3]
Brazil	202.0	0.8	2,047.1	15,175	−4.7	4.9	52.9 (2013)	0.755	2	2
China	1,393.8	0.6	10,724.0	12,547	6.4	11.2	42.1 (2010)	0.727	7	6
Guatemala	15.9	2.5	58.6	6,929	2.1	11.5	52.4 (2011)	0.627	4	4
India	1,267.4	1.2	2,084.4	5,497	6.3	21.3	33.9 (2009)	0.609	2	3
Indonesia	252.8	1.2	887.0	9,788	3.5	15.9	35.6 (2010)	0.684	2	4
Iraq	34.8	2.9	202.0	14,003	−1.1	N/A	29.5 (2012)	0.654	5	6
Mexico	123.8	1.2	1,233.7	16,056	1.2	2.7	48.1 (2012)	0.756	3	3
Nigeria	178.5	2.8	514.0	5,341	0.0	53.5	43.0 (2009)	0.514	4	5
Pakistan	185.1	1.7	272.6	4,866	3.4	8.3	29.6 (2010)	0.538	4	5
South Korea	49.5	0.5	1,389.0	33,890	2.2	N/A	31.6*	0.898	2	2
United Kingdom	63.5	0.6	2,823.3	39,267	1.5	N/A	32.6 (2012)	0.907	1	1
United States	322.6	0.8	17,663.6	52,947	1.6	N/A	41.1 (2013)	0.915	1	1

* Old data from 1998–2000

Note: GDP = gross domestic product; GNI = gross national income; HDI = Human Development Index; PPP = purchasing power parity

Sources: [1] UNDP (2015) Human Development Report; [2] World Bank (2016); [3] Freedom House (2016)

Appendix B

Case Study Countries: Gender-Related Indicators

	HDI rank 2014[1]	GDI 2014[1]	Maternal mortality 2013, deaths per 100,000 live births[1]	Female population with at least secondary education (2005–14), (% ages 25 and older)[1]	Male population with at least secondary education (2005–14), (% ages 25 and older)[1]	Labour force participation rate women 2013 (% ages 15 and older)[1]	Labour force participation rate men 2013 (% ages 15 and older)[1]	Women seats in parliament 2014 (%)[1]	Total fertility rate (births per woman 2014)[2]
Brazil	75	0.997	69	54.6	52.4	59.4	80.8	9.6	1.8
China	90	0.943	32	58.7	71.9	63.9	78.3	23.6	1.6
Guatemala	128	0.949	140	21.9	23.2	49.3	88.2	13.3	3.2
India	130	0.795	190	27.0	56.6	27.0	79.9	12.2	2.4
Indonesia	110	0.927	190	39.9	49.2	51.4	84.2	17.1	2.5
Iraq	121	0.787	67	27.8	50.2	14.9	69.8	26.5	4.6
Mexico	74	0.943	49	55.7	60.6	45.1	79.9	37.1	2.2
Nigeria	152	0.841	560	—	—	48.2	63.7	6.6	5.7
Pakistan	147	0.726	170	19.3	46.1	24.6	82.9	19.7	3.6
South Korea	17	0.930	27	77.0	89.1	50.1	72.1	16.3	1.2
United Kingdom	14	0.965	8	99.8	99.9	55.7	68.7	23.5	1.8
United States	8	0.995	28	95.1	94.8	56.3	68.9	19.4	1.9

Note: HDI = Human Development Index; GDI = Gender-related Development Index

Sources: [1] UNDP (2015) *Human Development Report*; [2] World Bank (2016)

Glossary

alternative politics Political activity that emerges 'from below', in the sense that it centrally involves ordinary people, as opposed to political elites, and takes place outside of formal **politics** and established political channels, such as parties, elections, and parliamentary politics.

apartheid An Afrikaans word meaning 'separateness', in South Africa expressed as the official government policy of racial segregation between 1948 and 1989.

ascriptive identities Groupings to which people belong by birth rather than by choice.

autonomy of politics/political autonomy The extent to which **politics**, as a level or sphere of social life, is determined by economic and/or social/cultural dimensions of society or is able independently to impact on those dimensions.

balkanization Referring to the breaking up of a region or country into small territorial units, often as a means to 'divide and rule'.

Beijing consensus Also called the 'Chinese model'; the economic policies of the People's Republic of China (PRC) since 1976; based on three overarching ideas of Chinese development—innovation, the pursuit of dynamic goals/rejection of per capita gross domestic product (GDP), and self-determination.

caste A system of social stratification characterized by hereditary **status**, endogamy, and social barriers sanctioned by custom or law.

caudillismo Historically referring to the organization of political life in parts of Latin America by local 'strongmen' (caudillos) competing for power and its spoils.

chaebols The family-based business groups or conglomerates, many of them with cross-ownership, that have been South Korea's primary source of capital accumulation.

Christian democracy The application of Christian precepts to electoral **politics**.

civic nationalism Involving unity among citizens of an autonomous state.

civil regulation In the environmental arena, referring to a range of activities undertaken by **civil society** actors aimed at creating new frameworks of expectation and obligation for companies.

civil society A highly contested term, concerning the realm of voluntary citizen associations that exists between the family and the state, enjoying independence of the latter and seeking to influence public policy without aspirations to public office; **modern civil society** comprises formal, professionalized **non-governmental organizations** (NGOs) typical of the late twentieth century; **traditional civil society** is organized more informally, and may follow patterns with deep and enduring roots in history and society.

clash of civilizations Referring to Samuel P. Huntington's (1993, 1996a) prediction that, after the end of the cold war, international conflicts would increasingly have cultural characteristics—most notably, setting the Christian 'West' against the mostly Muslim, mostly Arab, 'East'.

clientelism/clientelist Referring to the exchange of specific services or resources (usually publicly funded) between individuals in return for political support such as votes and essentially a relationship between unequals.

collapsed state See **state collapse**

comparative advantage The economic theory that countries should specialize in the production and export of those goods and services in which they have a *relative* production cost advantage compared with other countries.

competitive authoritarianism A kind of 'illiberal democracy' in which formal democratic **institutions** are widely viewed as the principal source of political authority, but rulers violate the rules so strikingly that the **regime** fails to meet conventional minimum standards of democracy.

conditionality/conditionalities Referring to the attachment of policy and/or other conditions to offers of financial and other assistance, with the possibility of aid sanctions for non-compliance.

corruption Involving the private use of public office and resources, and generally considered illegal.

cruel choice Jagdish Bhagwati's term for the dilemma that he believed faced developing countries: either concentrate on economic development, or emulate the political systems of the West.

cultural imperialism The domination of vulnerable peoples by the culture of economically and politically powerful societies.

decentralized despotism A pattern of colonial and post-colonial government identified by Mahmood Mamdani (1996) as arising from the colonial practice of **indirect rule**.

delegative democracy According to Guillermo O'Donnell (1994), resting on the premise that whoever wins election to the presidency is thereby entitled to govern as he or she thinks fit, constrained only by the hard facts of existing power relations and a constitutionally limited term of office.

democracy assistance Comprises largely consensual and concessionary international support to democratic reform chiefly by way of specific projects and programmes, such as **civil society** capacity-building endeavours.

democracy promotion Encompasses a wide range of approaches including not only **democracy assistance**, but also diplomatic pressure and, in some accounts, much more coercive forms of intervention of which democratization is the stated goal.

democratization backwards Describing situations in which largely free elections are introduced in advance of such basic **institutions** of the modern state as the **rule of law**, full executive accountability, and a flourishing **civil society**.

dependency theory An argument that the weak structural position of developing countries in the international capitalist system influences important variables in their political life, as well as explains their failure to achieve stronger development.

descriptive representation Representation that 'stands for' the represented (or constituency) by reflecting their shared identity, such as race, **gender**, level of education.

despotic power The power to control and suppress (as Michael Mann has called it); cf. **infrastructural power**.

developing world A term conventionally referring to the predominantly post-colonial regions of Africa, Asia, Latin America and the Caribbean, and the Middle East, perceived to be poorer, less economically advanced, and less 'modern' than the developed world.

developmental state According to Adrian Leftwich (1995), concentrating sufficient power, autonomy, and capacity at the centre to bring about explicit developmental objectives, whether by encouraging the conditions and direction of economic growth or by organizing it directly; hallmarks include a competent bureaucracy and the insulation of state **institutions** from special interests in society—in other words, the state enjoys **embedded autonomy**; while there are significant differences among the cases commonly cited as examples of the development state, the most successful examples in East Asia have tended to be authoritarian.

economic rents Incomes derived from the possession of a valuable licence or permit, particularly for the import of foreign goods.

electoral authoritarianism/autocracy In which elections are an instrument of authoritarian rule, an alternative to both democracy and naked repression.

electoral democracy A fairly minimalist conception of democracy that highlights electoral competition and a degree of popular participation, but understates the civil liberties and some other distinguishing features associated with liberal democracy.

embedded autonomy According to Peter Evans (1995), characterized by the relative facility of the **developmental state** to transcend sectional interests in society, providing a sound basis for pursuing national industrial transformation.

entitlements Justified rights or claims belonging to individuals or groups.

equality of outcome An approach that aims to make people equal whatever their original differences.

ethnic identities Socially constructed identities that follow when people self-consciously distinguish themselves from others on the basis of perceived common descent and/or shared culture; many, but not all, such identities are politicized.

ethnic morphology Refers to the form and structure of groups.

ethno-national identities Defining the nation in ethnic terms, attaining unity through the merger of **ethnic identities** and **national identities**, and demanding autonomy for ethnic nations.

ethnopolitical identities Those **ethnic identities** that have been politicized—that is, made politically relevant.

exploitation Defined by the *Oxford English Dictionary* as 'a situation in which somebody treats somebody else in an unfair way, especially in order to make money from their work'.

export processing zones (EPZs) Economic enclaves often set up in developing countries to attract investment; specialize in manufacturing for export, and offer incentives such as free trade conditions and liberal regulatory conditions.

extents of freedom In Amartya Sen's terminology, the capabilities or the *freedom* to achieve whatever functionings an individual happens to value.

extractive state The idea that the extraction of the nation's (natural resource) wealth for the benefit of its ruler(s) becomes the primary goal of the ruler(s).

extraversion A theory of African political behaviour developed by Jean-François Bayart (1993) that argues that, historically, the relatively weak development of the continent's productive forces and its internal social struggles made African political actors more disposed to mobilize resources from their relationship with the external environment.

failing state A state that is failing in respect of some or all of its functions without yet having reached the stage of 'collapse'.

fallacy of electoralism Privileging electoral contestation as though that were a sufficient condition for democracy to exist.

feminism/feminist Comprising recognition and action on women's common bonds and inequalities between men and women.

framing Processes giving meaning to the actions of a movement, drawing on shared cultural understandings.

garrison state A state maintained by military power and, in some definitions, a state organized to secure primarily its own need for military security.

gatekeeper state A term coined by African historian Frederick Cooper (2002) to denote a form of state focused on controlling the intersection of the territory with the outside world, collecting and distributing the resources that that control brought.

gender Referring to ideas about male and female, and the relations between them as social constructions rather than the product of biological determinants only.

gender quotas voluntary or legal mechanisms aimed at addressing the historical under-representation of women in public and political life.

genocide Referring to deliberate extermination of a social group selected on grounds of culture, ethnicity, or race.

Gini coefficient A commonly used measure of inequality (household income or consumption); the higher the figure, the more unequal the distribution.

global justice movement A loose, increasingly transnational network of non-governmental and **social movement** organizations opposed to neoliberal economic **globalization**, violence, and North–South inequalities; they support participatory democracy, equality, and **sustainable development**.

global stewardship Referring to resources that are said to be part of the common heritage of humankind and which should be managed for the benefit of all.

globalization Highly contested term, defined in different ways that range from increasing global economic integration—in particular, international trade—to processes whereby many social relations become relatively delinked from territorial geography and human lives are increasingly played out in the world as a single place.

globalization theory Focusing on a process of accelerated communication and economic integration that transcends national boundaries, and increasingly incorporates all parts of the world into a single social system.

good governance Originated in World Bank discourse to mean the sound management of public affairs with a bias towards neoliberal conceptions of the state's role in the economy, but went on to acquire broader connotations sharing many of the ideas and **institutions** associated with accountability, **human rights**, and democracy, and hence democratic **governance**.

governance A fairly elaborate theory about how power is exercised and checked, through mechanisms of accountability; a term with a variety of contested meanings that reflects its usage in diverse disciplines and practices ranging from new public management to international development cooperation, and spanning **institutions** at both the local and the global levels; best defined contextually, and best understood with reference to both the objective and normative purposes of the definer.

Hindu caste system A complex and ancient, although evolving, system of social stratification in which people's **caste** status is determined at birth.

HIV/AIDS Refers to human immunodeficiency virus, a retrovirus that infects cells of the human immune system; it is widely accepted that infection with HIV causes AIDS (acquired immunodeficiency syndrome), a disease characterized by the destruction of the immune system.

human capital Referring to the knowledge, skills, and capabilities of individuals.

human development According to the United Nations Development Programme (UNDP), about the freedom, well-being, and dignity of people everywhere; the UNDP's Human Development Index (HDI) measures longevity, educational attainment, and standard of living.

human rights Either the rights that everyone has because they are human or those generally recognized as such by governments or in international law.

human security An emerging paradigm that links development studies and national security, and which is defined as the protection of human lives from critical and pervasive threats; a wide-ranging version claims that human security is 'freedom from want'—extreme poverty precludes real security; more narrowly, human security is 'freedom from fear'—the emphasis is on safety from violence, including wars and violent crime.

Ikhwan Meaning 'the brethren', religious followers of *Wahhabism*.

import-substitution industrialization (ISI) Referring to the economic strategy of protecting the growth of manufacturing industry by reserving the home market for domestic producers ('infant industries'), through introducing barriers to imports.

indirect rule A mode of rule developed especially, although not only, by Britain, under which the colonial power allowed native rulers and chiefs to exercise limited authority.

informal economy Referring to employment and wealth creation that is not captured by the official data, offering opportunities for people who are unable to participate in the formal economy; governments find it difficult to regulate and tax the informal sector.

informal institutions Rules and procedures that are created, communicated, and enforced outside the officially sanctioned channels; they may undermine, reinforce, or even override the formal **institutions**.

infrastructural power The power to penetrate and transform society.

institutional See **institutions**

institutions Collections of (broadly) agreed norms, rules, procedures, practices, and routines, either formally established or written down and embodied in organizations, or as informal understandings embedded in culture.

intentional institutional design Refers to situations in which political **institutions** are deliberately, consciously, and explicitly designed or reformed, often with a particular object in view.

international community A loose term denoting the main Western powers and the international organizations in and over which they exert considerable influence, for example in the United Nations.

international human rights regime A large body of international law and a complex set of institutions to implement it.

legitimacy A psychological relationship between the governed and their governors, which engenders a belief that the state's leaders and **institutions** have a right to exercise political authority over the rest of society.

liberal imperialism The idea that powerful advanced Western states should intervene, if necessary by force, in other countries to spread good government and liberal democratic values.

liberal peacekeeping The belief that the route to peace-building is to promote liberal democratic governing systems and market-orientated economic growth.

liberalism A political philosophy that gives priority to individual freedom.

liberation theology A school of theological thought with widespread influence in Latin America beginning in the 1960s, which explores the relation between Christian theology and political activism in the areas of poverty, social justice, and **human rights**.

mainstreaming In the context of gender and environment, infusing public policies with a gender or environmental focus.

micro-credit The provision of small loans to poor people who cannot obtain normal commercial credit for entrepreneurial activities.

Millennium Development Goals (MDGs) Established by the UN Millennium Declaration (September 2000) in eight areas: to eradicate extreme poverty and hunger; to achieve universal primary education; to promote gender equality and to empower women; to reduce child mortality; to improve maternal health; to combat **HIV/AIDS**, malaria, and other diseases; to ensure environmental sustainability; and to develop a global partnership for development.

modern civil society See **civil society**

modernization Referring to a complex set of changes in culture, society, and economy characterized by urbanization, industrialization, and, in some cases, **secularization**, although one response to it may be religious revival.

modernization revisionism A critique of **modernization** theory, centred on its oversimplified notions of tradition, modernity, and their interrelationship.

multi-ethnic/multicultural national identities Defining the nation in terms of several ethnic or cultural

identities contained within citizenship, political interaction, and an overarching **national identity** in an autonomous state.

national identities Inherently political, emphasizing the autonomy and unity of the nation as an actual or potential political unit.

nation-building Referring to building a sense of national belonging and unity.

nationalists/nationalism Advocacy for the political independence of a country or belief in the superiority of one's country over others.

natural capital Comprising nature's free goods and services.

neoliberal economic reforms See **neoliberalism**

neoliberalism Stressing the role of the market in resource allocation and a correspondingly reduced role for the state, together with integration into the global economy; aspects of the neoliberal agenda are exhibited in the **Washington consensus** associated with the Bretton Woods **institutions**.

neo-patrimonialism Combining **patrimonialism** and legal-rational bureaucratic rule, which gives formal recognition to the distinction between the public and the private.

new protectionism Referring to the measures of developed countries to reserve their domestic markets for home producers by means of non-tariff barriers such as imposing environmental standards.

newly (or new) industrialized/industrializing countries (NICs) Referring to those developing countries primarily, but not exclusively, in East Asia (also sometimes called 'dragon', or 'tiger', economies) that experienced dramatic industrialization soonest after 1945.

non-governmental organizations (NGOs) Organizations that operate in **civil society** and are not part of government or the state (although they may sometimes be dependent, in part, on government for funding).

official development assistance (ODA) Comprising resources transferred on concessional terms with the promotion of the economic development and welfare of the developing countries as the main objective.

ontological equality The assumption that all people are born equal.

orientalism Referring to Edward Said's (1995 [1978]) influential account of Western dominance of the East and how images of the Orient (the 'Other') helped to define the West as its contrasting image.

outward-oriented development Looking to the global economy as a driving force for economic growth, through the creation of a favourable policy environment for exports.

pacted transition In which transition to democracy comes about by agreement among political elites integral to the precursor **regime**.

Pancasila The official ideology of Suharto's Indonesia, enjoining belief in a supreme being, humanitarianism, national unity, consensus democracy, and social justice.

path dependence Claiming that point of origin, the method of change, and choices made or not made along the way significantly influence the outcome and final destination.

patriarchy Referring to the ideology and **institutions** of male rule, male domination, and female subordination.

patrimonialism Treating the state as the personal patrimony or property of the ruler (hence 'patrimonialist state'), and all power relations between ruler and ruled as personal relations.

patronage The politically motivated distribution of favours, intended to create and maintain political support among groups.

patron–client relations Connecting **patronage** and **clientelism**

political culture Embracing the attitudes, beliefs, and values that are said to underlie a political system.

political Islam Refers to a political movement with often diverse characteristics that, at various times, has included elements of many other political movements, while simultaneously adapting the religious views of Islamic fundamentalism or Islamism.

political opportunity structure Term derived from sociology to determine exogenous factors that may limit or empower collective actors (**social movements**), such as degree of state repression, groups access to political **institutions**, etc.

politicide Referring to extermination of political enemies.

politics On a narrow understanding, a kind of activity associated with the process of government and, in modern settings, also linked with the 'public' sphere; on a broader understanding, it is about 'power' relations and struggles not necessarily confined to the process of government or restricted to the public domain.

politics of order A critique of political development theory that focused on the need for strong government and political order.

polyarchy Robert Dahl's (1971) influential idea of democracy that rests on the two pillars of public contestation and the right to participate.

populism A political ideology or approach that claims to be in the interests of 'the people'.

post-colonial state A state that came into being as a consequence of the dissolution of the European colonial empires.

post-structuralism/post-structuralist Sometimes also referred to as 'post-modernism', a broad philosophical approach that questions the epistemological foundations of 'rational' enlightenment thinking.

post-Washington consensus A movement away from the **neoliberalism** of the **Washington consensus** towards a development policy that emphasizes a more active role for the state and the crucial role that institution-building and democratic **governance** can play in successful development; accompanied by a shift to stressing the importance of policies to deal with social problems such as unemployment, poverty, and inequality, in addition to a focus on growth and efficiency.

predatory state Close to the idea of an **extractive state**, one that exploits the people for the benefit of the rulers and holds back development.

privatization The transformation of something that is communally or publicly owned to private property.

proxy wars Conflicts carried out on behalf of, and supported by, the great powers, as was often the case in developing areas during the cold war era.

public goods Goods, such as defence, which, if supplied to anybody, are necessarily supplied to everybody, as a consequence of which the market is unlikely to provide them in sufficient quantity.

public institutions The **institutions** of the modern state are all 'public' institutions and include 'the government' and legislature, the courts, the civil service, the army and the police, plus any state-owned agencies.

realists In international relations theory, include classical realists, who define security as national security; they emphasize military threats to the state and inter-state conflict.

regime A set of rules and practices that regulate the conduct of actors in a specified field (as distinct from political regime, understood as a system of government).

regime change Came to be applied to the practice of removing a government by external force, as in the military invasion of Afghanistan and Iraq to topple the Taliban and Saddam Hussein's government, respectively; some opponents of international intervention in developing countries choose to identify it with the aspirations behind **democracy promotion** and **democracy assistance** from the West.

religio-politics Political activity with religious dimensions.

rentier state A state the income of which takes the form primarily of rents from a resource such as oil, or from foreign aid, rather than from taxing the subjects, which gives it high autonomy from society and may restrain citizens from demanding democratically accountable government.

rent-seeking Referring to the pursuit of gains (**economic rents**) to be derived from control over scarce goods or services—a scarcity that might be artificially created for the purpose.

resource curse Refers to the paradox that countries with an abundance of natural resources (oil, minerals, etc.) tend to have less economic growth, less democracy, and poorer development outcomes than countries with fewer natural resources.

Responsibility to Protect (R2P) Refers both to states' responsibility to protect their own citizens and the **international community**'s responsibility to engage in humanitarian intervention when a state fails in its responsibilities.

right to self-determination The claimed right of a distinct group of people to determine their own political, economic, and cultural destinies.

robust peacekeeping Used by the North Atlantic Treaty Organization (NATO) to define the new type of peacekeeping in which its troops in Afghanistan are engaged, under which they have more leeway to make peace, as well as to undertake peacekeeping and monitoring functions.

rule of law The idea that all citizens, including the lawmakers and all other government officials, are bound by the law and no one is above the law.

scramble for Africa The late nineteenth-century territorial expansion of European powers in Africa, leading to the Congress of Berlin (1884–85), which formally adopted the division of the new colonies and protectorates.

secularization The gradual diminution of the influence of religion on public affairs; liberal secularism advocates separation of church and state, with the second power being dominant and no one religion having official priority.

Sharia Islamic religious law, incorporated to varying degrees in the legal systems of states with large Islamic populations.

social capital Referring to the social networks, norms, and trust that enable participants to function more effectively in pursuing a common goal; arguably, high levels are valuable both for political and economic cooperation.

social movements Loose networks of informal organizations that come about in response to an issue, crisis, or concern, and which seek to influence social and other public policy, such as environmental policy, often through using direct action, which may or may not employ violence.

soft power In its original formulation by Joseph Nye Jr (2004), the ability of a country's culture, ideals, and policies to influence others by attraction and without deliberate resort to bribery or coercion.

state collapse Occurring where a functioning state system ceases to exist.

state failure Indicating a less-than-complete collapse of the state system.

status A quality of social honour or a lack of it, which is mainly conditioned by, as well as expressed through, a specific style of life.

structural adjustment programmes (SAPs) Designed to shift economic policy and management in the direction of the **Washington consensus**, sometimes leading to more narrowly focused sectoral adjustment programmes, and often associated with structural adjustment loans (SALs) from the Bretton Woods **institutions** and other aid donors.

subsistence economy Referring to activity outside the cash economy for barter or home use.

substantive representation Representation 'acting for' the interests of a group/constituency regardless of shared characteristics.

sustainable development A disputed term, which was defined by the Brundtland Report (1987) as development that meets the needs of the present without compromising the ability of future generations to meet their own needs; environmental degradation is minimized while ecological sustainability is maximized.

Sustainable Development Goals (SDGs) Goals in the **UN 2030 Agenda for Sustainable Development**.

terrorism A tactic designed to achieve an objective (usually political) by using violence against innocent civilians to generate fear.

third wave of democracy Samuel P. Huntington's (1991) term for the third major surge of democracy in history starting with the transitions to democracy in Portugal, Spain, and Greece in the mid-1970s.

traditional civil society *See* **civil society**

transaction costs The costs of doing business in a market economy, including the cost of finding market information, as well as the costs incurred when parties to a contract do not keep to their agreement.

transfer pricing Refers to transactions within companies (not between) and is one of the most central concerns of international taxation.

UN 2030 Agenda for Sustainable Development Adopted in September 2015 to replace the **Millennium Development Goals (MDGs)**. The agenda set out a fifteen-year plan with seventeen goals and 169 targets to eradicate poverty, fight inequality, and tackle climate change.

underdevelopment Lack of development, according to **dependency theory**, which is a consequence of capitalist development elsewhere.

unequal exchange The idea that international trade between developed and developing countries is an instrument whereby the former exploit the latter and capture the greater part of the benefits.

unsecularization A global religious revitalization.

urban bias Bias in public policy and spending against the rural areas in favour of urban areas or urban-based interests, owing to their greater political influence.

war on terror(ism) The term given by the United States and its allies to an ongoing campaign with the stated goal of ending global **terrorism**; launched in response to the 11 September 2001 ('9/11') terrorist attacks on the United States.

warlord Powerful regional figure possessing coercive powers, inside a country.

Washington consensus The term applied to a package of liberalizing economic and financial policy reforms deemed essential if Latin America (and subsequently other parts of the **developing world**) are to escape debt and rejuvenate their economic performance; quickly became attached to the policy approach in the 1990s of the Bretton Woods **institutions** especially—namely, the International Monetary Fund (IMF) and World Bank; the central elements are fiscal discipline, reorientation of public expenditures, tax reform, financial liberalization, openness to foreign direct investment (FDI), **privatization**, deregulation, and secure property rights.

weak state According to Joel Migdal (1988), a state lacking the capability to penetrate society fully, to regulate social relations, to extract and distribute resources, or to implement policies and plans.

wealth theory of democracy Claiming that the prospects for stable democracy are significantly influenced by economic and socio-economic development.

Westminster model Referring to the **institutional** arrangement of parliamentary government bequeathed by Britain to many of its former colonies.

women's (or gender) policy interests Referring to official decisions or practices in which women have a special stake because of need, discrimination, or lack of equality.

women's policy machinery Units within government, such as women's bureaux, commissions of women, ministries of women, and women's desks.

References

Abdelal, R., Herrera, Y., Johnston, I., and McDermott, R. (2009) 'Identity as a Variable', in R. Abdelal, Y. Herrera, I. Johnston, and R. McDermott (eds) *Measuring Identity: A Guide for Social Scientists* (New York: Cambridge University Press), 203–36.

Abdenur, A. E. (2014) 'Emerging Powers as Normative Agents: Brazil and China within the UN Development System', *Third World Quarterly*, 35(10): 876–93.

Abdul-Ahad, G. (2006) 'Inside Iraq's Hidden War', *The Guardian*, 20 May.

Abouzeid, R. (2011) 'Syria's Most Wanted: A Glimpse of Life on the Run with Army Defectors', *Time*, 18 August, available online at http://www.raniaabouzeid.com/Rania_Abouzeid/Clips/Entries/2011/8/18_Syrias_Most_Wanted__A_Glimpse_of_Life_on_the_Run_with_Army_Defectors.html

Acemoglu, D., and J. Robinson (2012) *Why Nations Fail: The Origins of Power, Prosperity, and Poverty* (New York: Crown Business).

Acharya, A. (1999) 'Developing Countries and the Emerging World Order', in L. Fawcett and Y. Sayigh (eds) *The Third World beyond the Cold War* (Oxford: Oxford University Press), 78–98.

Adeney, K., and Wyatt, A. (2004) 'Democracy in South Asia: Getting beyond the Structure–Agency Dichotomy', *Political Studies*, 52(1): 1–18.

Agency for Technical Cooperation and Development, Antares Foundation, Danish Refugee Council, Handicap International, Internal Displacement Monitoring Centre, International Rescue Committee, Italian Consortium of Solidarity, Knowledge for Iraqi Woman Society, Kurdistan Civil Rights Organization, Medecins du Monde—France, Mercy Corps, Mercy Hands, Muslim Aid, Muslim Hands, NGO Coordination Committee for Iraq, Premiere Urgence, and War Child (2010) *Fallen off the Agenda? More and Better Aid Needed for Iraq Recovery*, Policy Brief, available online at http://www.internal-displacement.org/assets/library/Middle-East/Iraq/pdf/Iraq-more-and-better-aid-needed-jul-2010.pdf

Ahluwalia, P. (2001) *Politics and post-Colonial Theory: African Inflections* (London: Routledge).

Ahmed, E. (2007) 'Political Islam in Sudan: Islamists and the Challenge of State Power (1989–2004)', in B. F. Soares and R. Otayek (eds) *Islam and Muslim Politics in Africa* (New York: Palgrave Macmillan), 189–208.

Al-Ali, N. (2007) *Iraqi Women: Untold Stories from 1948 to the Present* (London: Zed Books).

Al-Ali, N., and Pratt, N. (2009) *What Kind of Liberation? Women and the Occupation of Iraq* (Berkeley, CA: University of California Press).

Al-Damaluji, M., Al-Kubaisi, Y., Mulla Chaid, S., Haddad, F., Jabar, F., and Mansour, R. (2016) 'The Crisis of Representation in Iraq', 8 January, available online at http://carnegie-mec.org/2016/01/08/crisis-of-representation-in-iraq/ioeb

Al-Haj Saleh, Y. (2014) 'The Syrian Shabiha and Their State: Statehood and Participation', 3 March, available online at https://lb.boell.org/en/2014/03/03/syrian-shabiha-and-their-state-statehood-participation

Al-Khatteeb, L. (2015) 'Iraq 2016 Outlook: Reality Bites', 25 November, available online at http://www.brookings.edu/research/articles/2015/11/25-iraq-in-2016-alkhatteeb

Alavi, H. (1979) 'The State in Post-Colonial Societies', in H. Goulbourne (ed.) *Politics and the State in the Third World* (London: Macmillan), 38–69.

Alavi, H. (1988) 'Pakistan and Islam: Ethnicity and Ideology', in F. Halliday and H. Alavi (eds) *State and Ideology in the Middle East and Pakistan* (New York: Monthly Review Press), 64–111.

Albrecht, H., and Koehler, K. (2016) 'Going on the Run: What Drives Military Insubordination in Violent Domestic Conflict?', Paper presented at Belfer Centre for Science and International Affairs, 2 March, available online at http://belfercenter.ksg.harvard.edu/

files/Albrecht_Koehler%20Desertion%20Syria%20MEI2016.pdf

Alden, C. (2007) *China in Africa* (London: Zed Books).

Allison, R., and Williams, P. (1990) *Superpower Competition and Crisis Prevention in the Third World* (Cambridge: Cambridge University Press).

Almond, G., and Bingham Powell, G. (1966) *Comparative Politics: A Developmental Approach* (London: Little, Brown).

Almond, G., and Verba S. (eds) (1965) *The Civic Culture: Political Attitudes and Democracy in Five Nations* (Newbury Park, CA: Sage).

Alvarado, F., and Piketty, T. (2010) 'The Dynamics of Income Concentration', in L. Lopez-Calva and N. Lustig (eds) *Declining Inequality in Latin America: A Decade of Progress?* (New York and Washington, DC: UNDP and Brookings Institute), 72–100.

Alvarez, S. E. (1990) *Engendering Democracy in Brazil: Women's Movements in Transition Politics* (Princeton, NJ: Princeton University Press).

Amenta, E., and Young, M. (1999) 'Making an Impact: Conceptual and Methodological Implications of the Collective Goods Criterion', in M. Giugni, D. McAdam, and C. Tilly (eds) *How Social Movements Matter* (Minneapolis, MN: University of Minnesota Press), 22–41.

Amenta, E., Caren, N., Chiarello, E., and Su, Y. (2010) 'The Political Consequences of Social Movements', *Annual Review of Sociology*, 36: 287–307.

Amnesty International (2012) *Amnesty International Report 2012: The State of the World's Human Rights* (London: Amnesty International).

Anderson, B. (1983) *Imagined Communities* (London: Verso).

Anderson, B. (1991) *Imagined Communities: Reflections on the Origin and Spread of Nationalism*, rev'd edn (London: Verso).

Andrews, M. (2008) 'The Good Governance Agenda: Beyond Indicators without Theory', *Oxford Development Studies*, 36(4): 379–407.

Andrews, M. (2013) *The Limits of Institutional Reforms in Developing Countries: Changing the Rules for Realistic Solutions* (Cambridge: Cambridge University Press).

Arias, E. D., and Goldstein, D. M. (eds) (2010) *Violent Democracies in Latin America* (Durham, NC: Duke University Press).

Armijo, L., Muehlich, L., and Tirone, D. (2014) 'The Systemic Financial Importance of Emerging Powers', *Journal of Policy Modeling*, 36(Supplement 1): S67–S88.

Aspinall, E. (2013) 'A Nation in Fragments: Patronage and Neoliberalism in Contemporary Indonesia', *Critical Asian Studies*, 54(1): 27–54.

Aspinall, E. (2015) 'Oligarchic Populism and Economic Nationalism: Prabowo Subianto's Challenge to Indonesian Democracy', *Indonesia*, 99: 1–28.

Aspinall, E., and Berger, M. (2001) 'The Break-up of Indonesia? Nationalisms after Decolonisation and the Limits of the Nation-State in post-Cold War Southeast Asia', *Third World Quarterly*, 22(6): 1003–24.

Aspinall, E., and Fealy G. (eds) (2003) *Local Power and Politics in Indonesia: Democratization and Decentralization* (Singapore: Institute of Southeast Asian Affairs).

Asseburg, M., and Wimmen, H. (2016) 'Transformation, Elite Change and New Social Mobilization in the Arab World', *Mediterranean Politics*, 21(1): 1–22.

Atkinson, A. (2015) *Inequality: What Can be Done?* (Cambridge, MA, and London: Harvard University Press).

Avaaz (2016) 'About Us: Our Community', available online at http://www.avaaz.org/en/community.php

Ayers, A. J. (2009) 'Imperial Liberties: Democratisation and Governance in the "New" Imperial Order', *Political Studies*, 57(1): 1–27.

Ayubi, N. (1995) *Overstating the Arab State: Politics and Society in the Middle East* (London: I. B. Tauris).

Bacevitch, A. (2011) 'The U.S. Withdrawal from Iraq Marks the End [of] America's Great Expectations', *Washington Post*, 16 December, available online at http://www.washingtonpost.com/opinions/the-us-withdrawal-from-iraq-marks-the-end-of-american-supremacy/2011/12/12/gIQAStpTyO_story.html

Bäck, H., and Hadenius, A. (2008) 'Democracy and State Capacity: Exploring a J-Shaped Relationship', *Governance*, 21(1): 1–24.

Badran, M. (2002) *Feminism in Islam. Secular and Religious Convergences* (Oxford: One World).

Balaam, D. N., and Dillman, B. (2014) *Introduction to International Political Economy*, 6th edn (London: Routledge).

Banarjee A., and Somanathan, R. (2007) 'The Political Economy of Public Goods: Some Evidence from India', *Journal of Development Economics*, 82(2): 287–314.

Barkan, J. D. (2009) *Legislative Power in Emerging African Democracies* (Boulder, CO: Lynne Rienner).

Basedau, M., and Stroh, A. (2008) *Measuring Party Institutionalization in Developing Countries: A New Research Instrument Applied to 28 African Parties* (Hamburg: German Institute of Global and Area Studies).

Bassil, N. (2013) *The post-Colonial State and Civil War in Sudan. The Origins of Conflict in Darfur* (London: I. B. Tauris).

Bastian, S., and Luckham, R. (eds) (2003) *Can Democracy Be Designed? The Politics of Institutional Choice in Conflict-Torn Societies* (London: Zed Books).

Bates, R. H. (1981) *Markets and States in Tropical Africa: The Political Basis of Agricultural Policy* (Berkeley, CA: University of California Press).

Bates, R. H. (1989) *Beyond the Miracle of the Market: The Political Economy of Agrarian Development in Kenya* (Cambridge: Cambridge University Press).

Bates, R.H. (2008) *When Things Fell Apart: State Failure in Late-Century Africa* (Cambridge: Cambridge University Press).

Bauer, P. T. (1981) *Equality, the Third World and Economic Delusion* (London: Methuen).

Bayart, J.-F. (1993) *The State in Africa: The Politics of the Belly* (London: Longman).

Bayart, J.-F., Ellis, S., and B. Hiou (1999) *The Criminalization of the State in Africa* (Bloomington, IN: Indiana University Press).

Bayat, A. (2015) 'Neo-orientalism', 19 September, available online at http://futureswewant.net/asef-bayat-neo-orientalism/

Baylis, J., and Smith, S. (eds) (2001) *The Globalization of World Politics*, 2nd edn (Oxford: Oxford University Press).

Bayly, S. (1999) *The New Cambridge History of India, IV.3: Caste, Society and Politics in India from the Eighteenth Century to the Modern Age* (Cambridge: Cambridge University Press).

BBC News (2012) 'Profile: Mercosur—Common Market of the South', 15 February, available online at http://news.bbc.co.uk/1/hi/world/americas/5195834.stm

BBC News (2014a) 'Iraq: Shia Militias "Killing Sunnis in Reprisal Attacks"', 14 October, http://www.bbc.co.uk/news/world-middle-east-29603272

BBC News (2014b) 'The MINT Countries: Next Economic Giants?', 6 January, available online at http://www.bbc.co.uk/news/magazine-25548060

BBC News (2015) 'Brics Countries Launch New Development Bank in Shanghai', 21 July, available online at http://www.bbc.co.uk/news/33605230

BBC News (2016) 'Hundreds Forcibly Disappeared in Egypt Crackdown, Says Amnesty', 13 July, available online at http://www.bbc.com/news/world-middle-east-36775035

Beckwith, K. (2005) 'A Common Language of Gender?', *Politics and Gender*, 1(1): 128–37.

Beddoes, Z. M. (2012) 'For Richer, for Poorer', *The Economist*, 13 October, available online at http://www.economist.com/node/21564414

Beetham, D. (1997) 'Market Economy and Democratic Polity', *Democratization*, 4(1): 76–93.

Beinin, J., and Vairel, F. (2011) *Social Movements, Mobilization, and Contestation in the Middle East and North Africa* (Stanford, CA: Stanford University Press).

Benford, R., and Snow, D. (1988) 'Ideology, Frame Resonance, and Participant Mobilization', in B. Klandermans (ed.) *International Social Movement Research* (Greenwich: Jai Press), 197–217.

Benford, R., and Snow, D. (2000) 'Framing Processes and Social Movements: An Overview and Assessment', *Annual Review of Sociology*, 26: 611–39.

Berdal, M. (2009) *Building Peace after War* (London: The International Institute for Strategic Studies).

Bereketeab, R. (ed.) (2015). *Self-Determination and Secession in Africa. The post-Colonial State* (London: Routledge).

Berger, M. (1994) 'The End of the "Third World?"', *Third World Quarterly*, 15(2): 257–75.

Bermeo, N. (2003) *Ordinary People in Extraordinary Times: The Citizenry and the Breakdown of Democracy* (Princeton, NJ: Princeton University Press).

Bermeo, N. (2009) 'Does Electoral Democracy Boost Economic Equality?', *Journal of Democracy*, 20(4): 21–35.

Bertrand, J. (2008) 'Ethnic Conflicts in Indonesia: National Models, Critical Junctures and the Timing of Violence', *Journal of East Asian Studies*, 8(3):425–49.

Béteille, A. (ed.) (1969) *Social Inequality* (Harmondsworth: Penguin).

Bhalla, S. S. (2002) *Imagine There's No Country: Poverty, Inequality and Growth in the Era of Globalization*

(Washington DC: Institute for International Economics).

Billig, M. (1995) *Banal Nationalism* (London: Sage).

Birmingham, D. (1995) *The Decolonization of Africa* (London: UCL Press).

Birnir, J. (2007) *Ethnicity and Electoral Politics* (Cambridge and New York: Cambridge University Press).

Birnir, J., Fearon, J., Laitin, D., Gurr, T., Saideman, S., Brancati, D., Pate, A., and Hultquist, A. (2015) 'Socially Relevant Ethnic Groups, Ethnic Structure and AMAR', *Journal of Peace Research*, 52(1): 105–9.

Birnir, J., Laitin, D., Wilkenfeld, J., Hultquist, A., Waguespack, D., and Gurr. T. (2016) 'Socially Relevant Identity: Addressing the Selection Bias Issues and Introducing the AMAR (All Minorities at Risk) Data', draft paper, available online at http://www.mar.umd.edu/data/amar/AMAR%208.21.%202016.for.websitedocx.pdf

Bjørnskov, C., and Mchangama, J. (2013) 'Do Social Rights Affect Social Outcomes?', Aarhus Economics Working Papers No. 2013–18, available online at ftp://ftp.econ.au.dk/afn/wp/13/wp13_18.pdf

Blofield, M. (2008) 'Women's Choices in Comparative Perspective: Abortion Policies in Late-Developing Catholic Countries', *Comparative Politics*, 40(4): 399–419.

Bob, C. (2012) *The Global Right Wing and the Clash of World Politics* (Cambridge: Cambridge University Press).

Boubekeur, A. (2016) 'Islamists, Secularists and Old Regime Elites in Tunisia: Bargained Competition', *Mediterranean Politics*, 21(1): 107–27.

Boyd, D. R. (2012) *The Environmental Rights Revolution: A Global Study of Constitutions, Human Rights, and the Environment* (Vancouver, BC: UBC Press).

Brahm, E. (2007) 'Uncovering the Truth: Examining Truth Commission Success and Impact', *International Studies Perspectives*, 8(1): 16–35.

Brandt, W. (ed.) (1980) *North–South: A Programme for Survival* (London: Macmillan).

Bratton, M., and van de Walle, N. (1994) 'Neopatrimonial Regimes and Political Transitions in Africa', *World Politics*, 46(4): 453–89.

Bratton, M., and van de Walle, N. (1997) *Democratic Experiments in Africa* (Cambridge: Cambridge University Press).

Braunstein, E. (2006) *Foreign Direct Investment, Development and Gender Equity: A Review of Research and Policy* (Geneva: United Nations Research Institute for Social Development).

Bräutigam, D. (2009) *The Dragon's Gift: The Real Story of China in Africa* (Oxford: Oxford University Press).

Bräutigam, D. (2011) *The Dragon's Gift: The Real Story of China in Africa* (rev'd edn, Oxford: Oxford University Press).

Bräutigam, D., and Gallagher, K. (2014) 'Bartering Globalization: China's Commodity-backed Finance in Africa and Latin America', *Global Policy*, 5(3): 346–52.

Bräutigam, D., and Knack, S. (2004) 'Foreign Aid, Institutions, and Governance in sub-Saharan Africa', *Economic Development and Cultural Change*, 52(2): 255–85.

Bräutigam, D., Fjeldstad, O.-H., and Moore, M. (2008) *Taxation and State-Building in Developing Countries: Capacity and Consent* (Cambridge: Cambridge University Press).

Brian, T., and Laczko, F. (eds) (2014) *Fatal Journeys: Tracking Lives Lost during Migration* (Geneva: International Organization for Migration).

Brown, J. (1985) *Modern India: The Origins of an Asian Democracy* (Oxford: Oxford University Press).

Brownlee, J., Masoud, T., and Reynolds, A. (2015) *The Arab Spring: Pathways of Repression and Reform* (Oxford: Oxford University Press).

Brundtland, G. (ed.) (1987) *Our Common Future: The World Commission on Environment and Development* (Oxford: Oxford University Press) (the 'Brundtland Report').

Buehler, M. (2013) 'Revisiting the Inclusion–Moderation Thesis in the Context of Decentralized Institutions: The Behavior of Indonesia's Prosperous Justice Party in National and Local Politics', *Party Politics*, 19(2): 210–29.

Buehler, M., and Tan, P. (2007) 'Party–Candidate Relationships in Indonesian Local Politics: A Case Study of the 2005 Regional Elections in Gowa, South Sulawesi', *Indonesia*, 84: 41–69.

Bünte, M., and Ufen, A. (2009) 'The New Order and Its Legacy', in M. Bünte and A. Ufen (eds) *Democratization in post-Suharto Indonesia* (London: Routledge), 3–29.

Bureau of Investigative Journalism (n.d.) 'Drone Strikes in Pakistan', available online at https://www.

thebureauinvestigates.com/category/projects/drones/drones-pakistan/

Burnell, P. (2009) 'The Coherence of Democratic Peace-building', in T. Addison and T. Bruck (eds) *Making Peace Work: The Challenges of Social and Economic Reconstruction* (Basingstoke: Palgrave Macmillan), 51–74.

Burnell, P., and Youngs, R. (eds) (2009) *New Challenges to Democratization* (New York and London: Routledge).

Burra, A. (2010) 'The Indian Civil Service and the Nationalist Movement: Neutrality, Politics and Continuity', *Journal of Commonwealth and Comparative Politics*, 48(4): 404–32.

Bush, S. (2015) *The Taming of Democracy Assistance: Why Democracy Promotion Does Not Confront Dictators* (Cambridge: Cambridge University Press).

Calhoun, C. (1993) 'What's New about New Social Movements? The Early 19th Century Reconsidered', *Social Science History*, 17(3): 385–427.

Calvert, P., and Calvert, S. (2001) *Politics and Society in the Third World*, 2nd edn (Harlow: Pearson Education).

Cammack, P. (1997) *Capitalism and Democracy in the Third World: The Doctrine for Political Development* (Leicester: Leicester University Press).

Cammack, P., Pool, D., and Tordoff, W. (1993) *Third World Politics: A Comparative Introduction* (Basingstoke: Macmillan).

Campbell, H. (2008) 'China in Africa: Challenging US Global Hegemony', *Third World Quarterly*, 29(1): 89–105.

Carothers, T. (2002) 'The End of the Transition Paradigm', *Journal of Democracy*, 13(1): 5–21.

Carothers, T. (2015) 'Democracy Aid at 25: Time to Choose', *Journal of Democracy*, 26(1): 59–73.

Carranza, M. (2004) 'Mercosur and the End Game of the FTAA Negotiations: Challenges and Prospects after the Argentine Crisis', *Third World Quarterly*, 25(2): 319–37.

Casanova, J. (1994) *Public Religions in the Modern World* (Chicago, IL, and London: University of Chicago Press).

Cassola, A., Raub, A., Foley, D., and Heymann, J. (2014) 'Where Do Women Stand? New Evidence on the Presence and Absence of Gender Equality in the World's Constitutions', *Politics and Gender*, 10(2): 200–35.

Castells, M. (2012) *Networks of Outrage and Hope: Social Movements in the Internet Age* (Cambridge: Polity Press).

Cederman, L.-E., Gleditsch, K. S., Buhaug, H. (2013) *Inequality, Grievances, and Civil War* (New York: Cambridge University Press).

Central Intelligence Agency (CIA) (2013) 'World Fact Book: Iraq—Military', available online at https://www.cia.gov/library/publications/the-world-factbook/geos/iz.html

Center for Economic and Social Rights (CESR) and Instituto Centroamericano de Estudios Fiscales (ICEFI) (2009) *Rights or Privileges? Fiscal Commitment to the Rights to Health, Education and Food in Guatemala*, available online at http://www.cesr.org/downloads/Rights%20or%20Privileges%20Executive%20Summary%20final.pdf

Chabal, P. (2009) *Africa: The Politics of Suffering and Smiling* (London: Zed Books).

Chakrabarty, D. (2003) 'Postcoloniality and the Artifice of History: Who Speaks for "Indian" Pasts?', in J. D. LeSueur (ed.) *The Decolonization Reader* (London: Routledge), 428–48.

Chandra, B., Mukherjee, M., and Mukherjee, A. (1999) *India after Independence* (New Delhi: Viking Penguin India).

Chandra, K. (ed.) (2012) *Constructivist Theories of Ethnic Politics* (Oxford: Oxford University Press).

Chandra, K., and S. Wilkinson (2008) 'Measuring the Effect of "Ethnicity"', *Comparative Political Studies*, 41(4/5): 515–63.

Chang, H. (2014) *Economics: The User's Guide* (London: Pelican).

Chapman, A. R., and Ball, P. (2001) 'The Truth of Truth Commissions: Comparative Lessons from Haiti, South Africa, and Guatemala', *Human Rights Quarterly*, 23(1): 1–43.

Charron, N., and Lapuente, V. (2010) 'Does Democracy Produce Quality of Government?', *European Journal of Political Research*, 49(4): 443–70.

Chatterjee, P. (1986) *Nationalist Thought and the Colonial World: A Derivative Discourse?* (London: Zed Books).

Chatterjee, P. (1989) 'Colonialsm, Nationalism, and Colonialized Women: The Contest in India', *American Ethnologist*, 16(4): 622–33.

Chatterjee, P. (1993) *The Nation and Its Fragments: Colonial and Postcolonial Histories* (Princeton, NJ: Princeton University Press).

Cheibub, J. A. (2007) *Presidentialism, Parliamentarism and Democracy* (Cambridge: Cambridge University Press).

Chibber, V. (2005) 'The Good Empire: Should We Pick up Where the British Left off?', *Boston Review*, 1 February, available online at http://www.bostonreview.net/chibber-good-empire

Childs, S., and Krook, M. (2009) 'Analysing Women's Substantive Representation: From Critical Mass to Critical Actors', *Government and Opposition*, 44(2): 125–45.

Chiriyankandath, J. (1992) '"Democracy" under the Raj: Elections and Separate Representation in British India', *Journal of Commonwealth and Comparative Politics*, 30(1): 39–63.

Choi, S. (ed.) (1997) *Democracy in Korea: Its Ideals and Realities* (Seoul: Korean Political Science Association).

Chronic Poverty Research Centre (CPRC) (2008) *The Chronic Poverty Report 2008–09* (London: CPRC).

Clapham, C. (2000) 'Failed States and non-States in the Modern International Order', Paper presented at Failed States III: Globalization and the Failed State–A Conference, Florence, Italy, 7–10 April, available online at http://www.comm.ucsb.edu/faculty/mstohl/failed_states/2000/papers/clapham.html

Clapham, C. (2002) 'The Challenge to the State in a Globalized World', *Development and Change*, 33(5): 775–95.

Cohen, J. L., and Arato, A. (1994) *Civil Society and Political Theory* (Cambridge, MA: MIT Press).

Cohn, B. S. (1996) *Colonialism and Its Forms of Knowledge: The British in India* (Princeton, NJ: Princeton University Press).

Collier, P. (2006) *The Bottom Billion: Why the Poorest Countries Are Failing and What Can be Done about it* (Oxford: Oxford University Press).

Collier, P., and Hoeffler, A. (2006) 'The Political Economy of Secession', in H. Hannum and E. F. Babbitt (eds) *Negotiating Self-Determination* (Lanham, MD: Lexington), 37–59.

Collier, P., Elliott, V. L., Hegre, H., Joeffler, A., Reynal-Querol, M., and Sambanis, N. (2003) *Breaking the Conflict Trap* (Washington, DC: World Bank).

Collier, R. B., and Collier, D. (1991) *Shaping the Political Arena: Critical Junctures—The Labour Movement and Regime Dynamics in Latin America* (Princeton, NJ: Princeton University Press).

Cooper, F. (2002) *Africa since 1940: The Past of the Present* (Cambridge: Cambridge University Press).

Cooper, F. (2003) 'Conflict and Connection: Rethinking Colonial African History', in J. D. Le Sueur (ed.) *The Decolonization Reader* (London: Routledge), 23–44.

Cooper, F. (2005) *Colonialism in Question: Theory, Knowledge, History* (Berkeley, CA: University of California Press).

Cooper, R. (2004) *The Breaking of Nations: Order and Chaos in the Twenty-First Century* (London: Atlantic).

Coulon, C. (1983) *Les musulmans et le pouvoir en Afrique noire* (Paris: Karthala).

Cox, G. W. (1997) *Making Votes Count: Strategic Coordination in the World's Electoral Systems* (New York: Cambridge University Press).

Craig, A. L., and Cornelius, W. A. (1995) 'Mexico', in A. Mainwaring and T. R. Scully (eds) *Building Democratic Institutions* (Stanford, CA: University of California Press), 249–97.

Cramer, C. (2006) *Civil War is Not a Stupid Thing: Accounting for Violence in Developing Countries* (London: Hurst & Co.).

Cremer, G. (2008) *Corruption and Development Aid: Confronting the Challenge* (Boulder, CO: Lynne Rienner).

Cribb, R., and Kahin, A. (2004) *Historical Dictionary of Indonesia* 2nd edn (Oxford and Toronto, ON: Scarecrow Press).

Crivelli, E., De Mooij, R., and Keen, M. (2015) 'Base Erosion, Profit Shifting and Developing Countries', International Monetary Fund Working Paper No. WP/15/118, available online at http://imf.org/external/pubs/ft/wp/2015/wp15118.pdf

Cromwell, M. A. (1986) *An African Victorian Feminist: The Life and Times of Adelaide Smith Casely Hayford, 1868–1960* (London: Frank Cass).

Crook, R. C. (2005) 'The Role of Traditional Institutions in Political Change and Underdevelopment', Center for Democratic Development/Overseas Development Institute Policy Brief No. 4, available online at https://www.odi.org/sites/odi.org.uk/files/odi-assets/publications-opinion-files/1967.pdf

Croucher, S. L. (2003) 'Perpetual Imagining: Nationhood in a Global Era', *International Studies Review*, 5: 1–24.

Cruz, M., Foster, J., Quillin, B., and Schellekens, P. (2015) *Ending Extreme Poverty and Sharing Prosperity: Progress and Policies* (Washington, DC: World Bank Group).

Dahl, R. (1971) *Polyarchy: Participation and Opposition* (New Haven, CT, and London: Yale University Press).

Dahlerup, D., and Friedenvall, L. (2005) 'Quotas as Fast Track to Equal Representation for Women', *International Feminist Journal of Politics*, 7(1): 26–48.

Dauvergne, P. (1997) *Shadows in the Forest: Japan and the Politics of Timber in South East Asia* (Cambridge, MA: MIT Press).

Davenport, C. (2007) 'State Repression and Political Order', *Annual Review of Political Science*, 10: 1–23.

Davidson, B. (1992) *The Black Man's Burden: Africa and the Curse of the Nation-State* (New York: Times).

Davis, M. (2001) *Late Victorian Holocausts: El Niño Famines and the Making of the Third World* (London: Verso).

De la Calle, L., and Schedler, A. (2016) 'Political and Economic Civil Wars', Unpublished typescript.

De Waal, A. (2007) *War in Darfur and the Search for Peace* (Cambridge, MA: Harvard University Press).

Della Faille, D. (2011) 'Discourse Analysis in International Development Studies: Mapping Some Contemporary Contributions', *Journal of Multicultural Discourses*, 6(3): 215–35.

Della Porta, D., and Diani, M. (2006) *Social Movements: An Introduction* (Malden: Blackwell).

Denny, E., and Walter, B. (2014) 'Ethnicity and Civil War', *Journal of Peace Research*, 51(2): 199–212.

Department for International Development (DfID) (2007) *Governance, Development and Democratic Politics: DFID's Work in Building More Effective States*, available online at http://webarchive.nationalarchives.gov.uk/+/http://www.dfid.gov.uk/pubs/files/governance.pdf

Deshpande, A., and Nurse, K. (2012) 'Introduction', in A. Deshpande and K. Nurse (eds) *The Global Economic Crisis and the Developing World* (London: Routledge), 1–18.

Devarajan, S., Azam, J. P., and O'Connell, S. A. (1999) 'Aid Dependence Reconsidered', World Bank Policy Research Working Paper Series 2144, available online at http://elibrary.worldbank.org/content/workingpaper/10.1596/1813-9450-2144

Devlin, C., and Elgie, R. (2008) 'The Effect of Women's Increased Representation in Parliament: The Case of Rwanda', *Parliamentary Affairs*, 61(2): 237–54.

DeVotta, N. (2016) 'The Win for Democracy in Sri Lanka', *Journal of Democracy*, 27(1): 152–66.

Diamond, L. (1996) 'Is the Third Wave over?', *Journal of Democracy*, 7(3): 20–37.

Diamond, L. (2002) 'Thinking about Hybrid Regimes', *Journal of Democracy*, 13(2): 21–35.

Diamond, L. (2004) 'What Went Wrong in Iraq', *Foreign Affairs*, 83(5): 34–56.

Diamond, L. (2012) 'The Coming Wave', *Journal of Democracy*, 23(1): 5–13.

Diamond, L. (2015) 'Facing up to the Democratic Recession', *Journal of Democracy*, 26(1): 141–55.

Dicken, P. (2003) *Global Shift: Reshaping the Global Economic Map in the 21st Century* (London: Sage).

Dicken, P. (2011) *Global Shift: Mapping the Changing Contours of the World Economy*, 6th edn (London: Sage).

Dickson, A. K. (1997) *Development and International Relations: A Critical Introduction* (Cambridge: Polity Press).

Dirks, N. (2001) *Castes of Mind: Colonialism and the Making of Modern India* (Princeton, NJ: Princeton University Press).

Dirks, N. (2004) 'Colonial and Postcolonial Histories: Comparative Reflections on the Legacies of Empire', UNDP Human Development Report Office Occasional Paper No. 2004/4, available online at http://hdr.undp.org/sites/default/files/hdr2004_nicholas_dirks.pdf

Dodge, T. (2003) *Inventing Iraq* (London: Hurst).

Dodge, T. (2012) 'Iraq's Road back to Dictatorship', *Survival: Global Politics and Strategy*, 54(3): 147–68.

Dodge, T. (2014) 'Can Iraq be Saved?', *Survival*, 56(5): 7–20.

Doorenspleet, R. (2009) 'Public Support versus Dissatisfaction in New Democracies?', in P. Burnell and R. Youngs (eds) *New Challenges to Democratization* (London and New York: Routledge), 95–117.

Downs, E. (2007) 'The Fact and Fiction of Sino-African Energy Relations', *China Security*, 3(3): 42–68.

Doyle, M. W., and Sambanis, N. (2006) *Making War and Building Peace: United Nations Peace Operations* (Princeton, NJ: Princeton University Press).

Duffield, M. (2001) *Global Governance and the New Wars: The Merging of Development and Security* (London: Zed Books).

Duffield, M. (2006) 'Racism, Migration and Development: The Foundations of Planetary Order', *Progress in Development Studies*, 6(1): 68–79.

Dunne, N., and Nevin, N. (2015) 'Egypt Now Looks a Lot Like it Did in 2010, Just before 2011 Unrest', *Wall Street Journal*, 16 December, available online at http://blogs.wsj.com/washwire/2015/12/16/egypt-now-looks-a-lot-like-it-did-in-2010-just-before-2011-unrest/

Dunning, T., and Nilekani, J. (2013) 'Ethnic Quotas and Political Mobilization: Caste, Parties and Distribution in Indian Village Councils', *American Political Science Review*, 107(1): 35–56.

Eckert, C. J. (1990) 'The South Korean Bourgeoisie: A Class in Search of Hegemony', *Journal of Korean Studies*, 7: 115–48.

Eckl, J., and Weber, R. (2007) 'North–South? Pitfalls of Dividing the World by Words', *Third World Quarterly*, 28(1): 3–23.

The Economist (2013) 'A Continental Divide', 18 May, available online at http://www.economist.com/news/americas/21578056-region-falling-behind-two-alternative-blocks-market-led-pacific-alliance-and

Ehrlich, P. (1972) *The Population Bomb* (London: Pan/Ballantine).

Elkins, Z., Ginsburg, T., and Melton, J. (2008) 'Baghdad, Tokyo, Kabul . . . Constitution-Making in Occupied States', *William & Mary Law Review*, 49(4): 1139–78.

Elson, D., and Pearson, R. (1981) 'Nimble Fingers Make Cheap Workers: An Analysis of Women's Employment in Third World Export Manufacturing', *Feminist Review*, 7(1): 87–107.

Elster, J. (1997) 'Ways of Constitution-Making', in A. Hadenius (ed.) *Democracy's Victory and Crisis* (Cambridge: Cambridge University Press), 123–42.

Englebert, P. (1997) 'The Contemporary African State: Neither African nor State', *Third World Quarterly*, 18(4): 765–97.

Englebert, P. (2000) 'Solving the Mystery of the AFRICA Dummy', *World Development*, 28(10): 1821–35.

Englebert, P. (2002) *State Legitimacy and Development in Africa* (Boulder, CO, and London: Lynne Rienner).

Englebert, P. (2009) *Africa: Unity, Sovereignty and Sorrow* (Boulder, CO, and London: Lynne Rienner).

Englebert, P., and Hummel, R. (2005) 'Let's Stick Together: Understanding Africa's Secessionist Deficit', *African Affairs* 104(416): 399–427.

Eriksen, T. H. (1993) *Ethnicity and Nationalism: Anthropological Perspectives* (London: Pluto Press).

Escobar, A. (1995) *Encountering Development: The Making and Unmaking of the Third World* (Princeton, NJ: Princeton University Press).

European Commission (2015) 'Humanitarian Implementation Plan (HIP): Iraq Crisis', 2 October, available online at http://ec.europa.eu/echo/files/funding/decisions/2015/HIPs/iraq_en.pdf

Evans, P. B. (1995) *Embedded Autonomy: States and Industrial Transformation* (Princeton, NJ: Princeton University Press).

Evans, P. B., Rueshmeyer, D., and Skocpol, T. (eds) (1985) *Bringing the State back in* (Cambridge: Cambridge University Press).

Fanon, F. (1967) *The Wretched of the Earth* (Harmondsworth: Penguin).

Farouk-Sluglett, M., and Sluglett, P. (2003) *Iraq since 1958: From Revolution to Dictatorship* (London and New York: I. B. Tauris).

Fawcett, L., and Sayigh, Y. (eds) (1999) *The Third World beyond the Cold War: Continuity and Change* (Oxford: Oxford University Press).

Fearon, J. D. (2003) 'Ethnic and Cultural Diversity by Country', *Journal of Economic Growth*, 8(2): 195–222.

Fearon, J. D. (2006) 'Ethnic Mobilization and Ethnic Violence', in B. R. Weingast and D. Wittman (eds) *Oxford Handbook of Political Economy* (Oxford: Oxford University Press), 852–68.

Fearon, J. D., and Laitin, D. D. (2003) 'Ethnicity, Insurgency, and Civil War', *American Political Science Review*, 97(1): 75–90.

Ferdinand, P. (2012) *Governance in Pacific Asia* (New York: Continuum).

Ferdinand, P. (2013) 'Foreign Policy Convergence in Pacific Asia: The Evidence from Voting in the UN General Assembly', *British Journal of Politics and International Relations*, 16(4): 662–79.

Ferguson, J. (1997) *The Anti-Politics Machine* (Minneapolis, MN: University of Minnesota Press).

Ferguson, J. (2002) *Global Shadows: Africa in the Neoliberal World Order* (Durham, NC, and London: Duke University Press).

Ferguson, N. (2004) *Colossus: The Rise and Fall of the American Empire* (London: Allen Lane).

Feuerwerker, A. (1983) 'The Foreign Presence in China', in J. K. Fairbank and D. C. Twitchett (eds) *The Cambridge History of China, Vol. 12: Republican China 1912–1949, Part 1* (Cambridge: Cambridge University Press), 128–207.

Fjeldstad, O.-H., and Moore, M. (2008) 'Tax Reform and State-Building in a Globalised World', in D. Bräutigam, O.-H. Fjeldstad, and M. Moore (eds) *Taxation and State-Building in Developing Countries: Capacity and Consent* (Cambridge: Cambridge University Press), 235–61.

Fleischer, D. (2010) 'Brazil to Comply with UN Sanctions against Iran', *Brazil Focus*, 7 August.

Fluehr-Lobban, C. (2012) *Sharia and Islamism in Sudan: Conflict, Law and Social Transformation* (London: I. B. Tauris).

Forsberg, E. (2008) 'Polarization and Ethnic Conflict in a Widened Strategic Setting', *Journal of Peace Research*, 45(2): 283–300.

Fowler, M. R., and Bunck, J. M. (1995) *Law, Power, and the Sovereign State* (University Park, PA: Penn State University Press).

Frank, A. G. (1969) *Capitalism and Underdevelopment in Latin America: Historical Studies of Chile and Brazil* (New York: Monthly Review Press).

Frank, A. G. (1971) *The Sociology of Development and the Underdevelopment of Sociology* (London: Pluto Press).

Frank, A. G. (1998) *Reorient: Global Economy in the Asian Age* (Berkeley, CA: University of California Press).

Fraser, N. (1997) *Justice Interruptus: Critical Reflections on the 'Postsocialist' Condition* (New York: Routledge).

Freedom House (2012) *Countries at the Crossroads 2011: An Analysis of Democratic Governance, Vol. 11* (Lanham, MD: Rowman & Littlefield).

Freedom House (2014) 'Indonesia, 2014', available online at https://freedomhouse.org/report/freedom-world/2014/indonesia

Freedom House (2015) 'Indonesia, 2015', available online at https://freedomhouse.org/report/freedom-world/2015/indonesia

Freedom House (2016) 'Freedom in the World 2016', available online at https://freedomhouse.org/report/freedom-world/freedom-world-2016

Friman, M. (2006) 'Historical Responsibility: The Concept's History in Climate Change Negotiations and Its Problem-Solving Potential', MA thesis, Linköping University, Faculty of Arts and Sciences, Sweden.

Fuest, V. (2009) 'Liberia's Women Acting for Peace: Collective Action in a War-Affected Country', in S. Ellis and I. van Kessel (eds) *Movers and Shakers: Social Movements in Africa* (Leiden: Brill), 114–38.

Fukuyama, F. (1989) 'The End of History', *The National Interest*, 16: 3–18.

Fukuyama, F. (1992) *The End of History and the Last Man* (Harmondsworth: Penguin).

Fukuyama, F. (2004) *State Building: Governance and World Order in the 21st Century* (New York: Cornell University Press).

Fukuyama, F. (2006) 'Nation-Building and the Failure of Institutional Memory', in F. Fukuyama (ed.) *Nation Building beyond Afghanistan and Iraq* (Baltimore, MD: John Hopkins University Press), 1–16.

Fukuyama, F. (2011) *The Origins of Political Order: From pre-Human Times to the French Revolution* (New York: Farrar, Straus & Giroux).

Fukuyama, F. (2013) 'What is Governance?', *Governance*, 26(3): 347–68.

Fukuyama, F. (2014) *Political Order and Political Decay: From the Industrial Revolution to the Globalization of Democracy* (New York: Farrar, Straus & Giroux).

Gallab, A. A. (2008) *The First Islamist Republic: Development and Disintegration of Islamism in the Sudan* (Aldershot: Ashgate).

Gamble, A., and Payne, A. (eds) (1996) *Regionalism and World Order* (London: Palgrave).

Ganguly, S. (2012) 'An Enduring Threat', *Journal of Democracy*, 23(1): 138–48.

Gbowee, L., and Mithers, C. (2011) *Mighty be Our Powers: How Sisterhood, Prayer, and Sex Changed a Nation at War* (New York: Beast Books).

Geddes, B. (1999) 'What Do We Know about Democracy after 20 Years?', *Annual Review of Political Science*, 2(June): 115–44.

Geertz, C. (1973) *The Interpretation of Culture* (New York: Basic Books).

Geertz, C. (1976) *The Religion of Java* (Chicago, IL: Chicago University Press).

Ghani, A., and Lockhart, C. (2008) *Fixing Failed States: A Framework for Rebuilding a Fractured World* (Oxford and New York: Oxford University Press).

Ghosh, A. (2002) *The Imam and the Indian* (New Delhi: Ravi Dayal & Permanent Black).

Gill, B., and Reilly, J. (2007) 'The Tenuous Hold of China, Inc. in Africa', *The Washington Quarterly*, 30(3): 37–52.

Gilmartin, D. (2003) 'Democracy, Nationalism and the Public: A Speculation on Colonial Muslim Politics', in J. D. Le Sueur (ed.) *The Decolonization Reader* (London: Routledge), 191–203.

Ginsburg, T., Elkins, Z., and Blount, J. (2009) 'Does the Process of Constitution-Making Matter?', *Annual Review of Law and Social Science*, 5(5): 201–23.

Giugni, M. (2004) *Social Protest and Policy Change: Ecology, Antinuclear, and Peace Movements in Comparative Perspective* (Lanham, MD: Rowman & Littlefield).

Glosny, M. (2010) 'China and the BRICs', *Polity*, 42(1): 100–29.

Go, J. (2003) 'Global Perspectives on the US Colonial State in the Philippines', in J. Go and A. L. Foster (eds) *The American Colonial State in the Philippines: Global Perspectives* (Durham, NC: Duke University Press), 1–42.

Goetz, A. M. (2007) 'Political Cleaners: Women as the New Anti-Corruption Force', *Development and Change*, 38(1): 87–105.

Goldstone, J. (2003) *States, Parties and Social Movements* (Cambridge: Cambridge University Press).

Goodhand, J. (2012) 'Contested Transitions: International Drawdown and the Future State in Afghanistan', 26 November, available online at http://www.peacebuilding.no/About-NOREF/Authors/Jonathan-Goodhand

Goodin, R. (1996) *The Theory of Institutional Design* (Cambridge: Cambridge University Press).

Goodwin, J., and Jasper, J. M. (2003) *The Social Movements Reader: Cases and Concepts* (Malden: Blackwell).

Gopin, M. (2000) *Between Eden and Armageddon: The Future of World Religions, Violence and Peacemaking* (New York and London: Oxford University Press).

Gopin, M. (2005) 'World Religions, Violence, and Myths of Peace in International Relations', in G. Ter Haar and J. Busutill (eds) *Bridge or Barrier? Religion, Violence and Visions for Peace* (Leiden: Brill), 35–56.

Gradín, C. (2009) 'Why is Poverty so High among Afro-Brazilians? A Decomposition Analysis of the Racial Poverty Gap', *Journal of Development Studies*, 45(19): 1426–52.

Gramsci, A. (1992 [1929–35]) *Prison Notebooks* (New York: Columbia University Press).

Gray, C. W., and Kaufmann, D. (1998) 'Corruption and Development', *Finance and Development*, 35(1): 7–10.

Gray, J. (2003) *Al Qaeda and What it Means to be Modern* (London: Faber & Faber).

Green, E. D. (2010) 'Ethnicity and Nationhood in pre-Colonial Africa: The Case of Buganda', *Nationalism and Ethnic Politics*, 16(1): 1–21.

Grewal, I. (1999) 'Women's Rights as Human Rights: Feminist Practices, Global Practices and Human Rights Regimes in Transnationality', *Citizenship Studies*, 3(3): 337–54.

Grindle, M. S. (2004) 'Good Enough Governance: Poverty Reduction and Reform in Developing Countries', *Governance*, 17(4): 525–48.

Grossman, G., and Paler, L. (2015) 'Using Field Experiments to Study Political Institutions', in J. Gandhi, and R. Ruiz-Rufino (eds) *Handbook of Comparative Political Institutions* (London: Routledge), 84–97.

Grugel, J. (2002) 'Conservative Elites and State Incapacities', *New Political Economy*, 7(2): 277–9.

Grugel, J., and Riggirozzi, P. (2012) 'Post-Neoliberalism in Latin America: Rebuilding and Reclaiming the State after Crisis', *Development and Change*, 43(1): 1–21.

Grupos de Poder en Petén (2011) *Territorio, política y negocios* (the 'Peten Report'), available online at https://www.plazapublica.com.gt/sites/default/files/the-peten-report.pdf

Guha, R. (1989) 'Dominance without Hegemony and Its Historiography', in R. Guha (ed.) *Subaltern Studies VI: Writings on South Asian History and Society* (New Delhi: Oxford University Press), 210–309.

Gulbrandsen, Ø. (2012) *The State and the Social: State Formation in Botswana and its Precolonial and Colonial Genealogies* (New York: Berghahn Books).

Gurr, T. R. (1993) *Minorities at Risk* (Washington, DC: US Institute of Peace).

Gurr, T. R. (2000) *Peoples versus States: Minorities at Risk in the New Century* (Washington, DC: US Institute of Peace Press).

Gyimah-Boadi, E. (2015) 'Africa's Waning Democratic Commitment', *Journal of Democracy*, 26(1): 101–13.

Hakim, P. (2003) 'Latin America's Lost Illusions: Dispirited Politics', *Journal of Democracy*, 14(2): 108–22.

Hall, P. A., and Taylor, R. C. R. (1996) 'Political Science and the Three New Institutionalisms', *Political Studies*, 44(5): 936–57.

Hall, S. (1996) 'When Was "the post-Colonial"? Thinking at the Limit', in I. Chambers and L. Carti (eds) *The post-Colonial Question: Common Skies, Divided Horizons* (London: Routledge), 242–60.

Halliday, F. (1989) *Cold War, Third World: An Essay on Soviet–US Relations* (London: Hutchinson).

Halliday, F. (2002) *Two Hours that Shook the World: September 11, 2001—Causes and Consequences* (London: Saqi).

Halliday, F. (2005) *The Middle East in International Relations: Power, Politics and Ideology* (Cambridge: Cambridge University Press).

Hanna, W. M. (2012) 'Clouded U.S. Policy on Egypt', in Project on Middle East Political Science (ed.) *Arab Uprisings: The Egypt Policy Challenge*, POMEPS Briefings No. 18, 17–19, available online at http://pomeps.org/wp-content/uploads/2013/03/POMEPS_Brief-Booklet18_Egypt_web-REV.pdf

Harff, B. (2003) 'No Lessons Learned from the Holocaust? Assessing Risks of Genocide and Political Mass Murder since 1955', *American Political Science Review*, 97(1): 57–73.

Harvey, F. (2010) 'The Long Road to Rainforest Conservation', *Financial Times*, 28 June.

Haynes, J. (1996) *Religion and Politics in Africa* (London: Zed Books).

Haynes, J. (2007) *Introduction to Religion and International Relations* (Harlow: Pearson Education).

Hearson, M. (2015) *Tax Treaties in sub-Saharan Africa: A Critical Review* (Nairobi: Tax Justice Network—Africa).

Heathershaw, J. (2011) *Post-Conflict Tajikistan: The Politics of Peacebuilding and the Emergence of Legitimate Order* (New York: Routledge).

Hegel, G. W. F. (1942 [1821]) *Philosophy of Right*, trans. (with notes) T. M. Knox (Oxford: Clarendon Press).

Hegre, H., Ellingsen, T., Gates, S., and Gleditsch, N. P. (2001) 'Democracy, Political Change and Civil War', *American Political Science Review*, 95(1): 16–33.

Heinle, K., Molzahn, C., and Shirk, D. (2015) *Drug Violence in Mexico: Data and Analysis through 2014* (University of San Diego, CA: Trans-Border Institute).

Helmke, G., and Levitsky, S. (eds) (2006) *Informal Institutions and Democracy: Lessons from Latin America* (Baltimore, MD: Johns Hopkins University Press).

Henderson, G. (1968) *Korea: The Politics of the Vortex* (Cambridge, MA: Harvard University Press).

Heo, M. (2010) 'Women's Movement and the Politics of Framing: The Construction of Anti-Domestic Violence Legislation in South Korea', *Women's Studies International Forum*, 33(3): 225–33.

Herbst, J. (2000) *States and Power in Africa* (Princeton, NJ: Princeton University Press).

Herbst, J. (2003) 'States and War in Africa', in P. Ikenberry and J. Hall (eds) *The Nation-State in Question* (Princeton: Princeton University Press), 166–82.

Hermassi, A. (1994) 'Socio-Economic Change And Political Implications', in G. Salamé (ed.) *Democracy without Democrats? The Renewal of Politics in the Muslim World* (London: I. B. Tauris), 225–42.

Herring, E., and Rangwala, G. (2006) *Iraq in Fragments: The Occupation and its Legacy* (London: Hurst & Co.).

Hicken, A. (2008) 'Political Engineering and Party Regulation in Southeast Asia', in B. Reilly and P. Nordlund (eds) *Political Parties in Conflict-Prone Societies: Regulation, Engineering and Democratic Development* (New York: United Nations University Press), 69–94.

Hirst, P., Thompson, G., and Brompley, S. (2009) *Globalization in Question*, 3rd edn (Cambridge: Polity Press).

Hobbes, T. (2008 [1651]) *Leviathan* (Oxford: Oxford University Press).

Hobson, J. A. (2004) *The Eastern Origins of Western Civilization* (Cambridge: Polity Press).

Holmarsdottir, H. B., Moller Eken, I. B., and Augestad, H. L. (2011) 'The Dialectic between Global Gender Goals and Local Empowerment: Girls' Education in Southern Sudan and South Africa', *Research in Comparative and International Education*, 6(1): 14–26.

Holsti, K. J. (1996) *The State, War, and the State of War* (Cambridge: Cambridge University Press).

Holton, R. J. (2014) *Global Inequalities* (London: Palgrave).

Hoogvelt, A. (1997) *Globalization and the Postcolonial World* (Baltimore, MD: Johns Hopkins University Press).

Horowitz, D. (1985) *Ethnic Groups in Conflict* (Berkeley, CA: University of California Press).

Horowitz, D. (2014) 'Ethnic Power Sharing: Three Big Problems.' *Journal of Democracy*, 25(2): 5–20.

Howard, P. N., and Hussain, M. M. (2013) *Democracy's Fourth Wave? Digital Media and the Arab Spring* (New York: Oxford University Press).

Htun, M. N. (2002) 'Puzzles of Women's Rights in Brazil', *Social Research*, 69(3): 733–51.

Htun, M. N. (2004) 'Women, Political Parties and Electoral Systems in Latin America', in J. Ballington and A. Karam (eds) *Women in Parliament: Beyond Numbers* (Stockholm: International IDEA), 111–21.

Human Rights Watch (HRW) (2011) *'By All Means Necessary!' Individual and Command Responsibility for Crimes against Humanity in Syria*, 15 December, available online at https://www.hrw.org/report/2011/12/15/all-means-necessary/individual-and-command-responsibility-crimes-against-humanity

Human Rights Watch (HRW) (2013) *Mexico's Disappeared: The Enduring Cost of a Crisis Ignored* (New York: HRW).

Human Security Report Project (2005) *Human Security Report 2005: War and Peace in the 21st Century* (New York and Oxford: Oxford University Press).

Humphreys, M. (2005) 'Natural Resources, Conflict, and Conflict Resolution: Uncovering the Mechanisms', *Journal of Conflict Resolution*, 49(4): 508–37.

Huneeus, C., Berrios, F., and Rodrigo C. (2006) 'Legislatures in Presidential Systems: The Latin American Experience', *The Journal of Legislative Studies*, 12(3/4): 404–25.

Hunter, E. (2015). *Political Thought and the Public Sphere in Tanzania: Freedom, Democracy and Citizenship in the Era of Decolonization* (New York: Cambridge University Press).

Huntington, S. P. (1968) *Political Order in Changing Societies* (New Haven, CT: Yale University Press).

Huntington, S. P. (1971) 'The Change to Change', *Comparative Politics*, 3(3): 283–332.

Huntington, S. P. (1991) *The Third Wave: Democratization in the Late Twentieth Century* (Norman, OK, and London: University of Oklahoma Press).

Huntington, S. P. (1993) 'The Clash of Civilizations?', *Foreign Affairs*, 72(3): 22–49.

Huntington, S. P. (1996a) *The Clash of Civilizations and the Remaking of World Order* (New York: Simon & Schuster).

Huntington, S. P. (1996b) 'Democracy for the Long Haul', *Journal of Democracy*, 7(2): 3–14.

Hurrell, A., and Narliker, A. (2006) 'A New Politics of Confrontation? Brazil and India in Multilateral Trade Negotiations', *Global Society*, 20(4): 415–33.

Hutchinson, J., and Smith, A. D. (eds) (1994) *Nationalism* (Oxford: Oxford University Press).

Hyden, G. (2006) *African Politics in Comparative Perspective* (Cambridge: Cambridge University Press).

Hyden, G., Court, J., and Mease, K. (2004) *Making Sense of Governance: Empirical Evidence from Sixteen Developing Countries* (Boulder, CO: Lynne Rienner).

Ikenberry G. J. (2011) 'The Future of the Liberal World Order', *Foreign Affairs*, 90(3): 56–68.

Inglehart, R., Basáñez, M., Díez-Medrano, J., Halman, L., and Luijkx, J. (2004) *Human Beliefs and Values: A Cross-Cultural Sourcebook Based on the 1999–2002 Values Surveys* (Mexico: Siglo XXI Editores).

Institute for Applied Economic Research (IPEA) (2013) 'IPEA Data: Brasília', available online at http://www.ipeadata.gov.br

Institute for Policy Studies (IPS) (2015) *Walking the Talk: World Bank Energy-Related Policies and Financing 2000–2004 to 2010–2014* (Washington: IPS).

Institute of Development Studies (IDS) (2010) *An Upside down View of Governance* (Brighton: University of Sussex).

International Crisis Group (ICG) (2004) *Iraq's Transition on a Knife Edge* (Baghdad and Brussels: ICG).

International Crisis Group (ICG) (2005) *Unmaking Iraq: A Constitutional Process Gone Awry* (Amman and Brussels: ICG).

International Crisis Group (ICG) (2006) *In Their Own Words: Reading the Iraqi Insurgency* (Amman and Brussels: ICG).

International Crisis Group (ICG) (2011) *Failing Oversight: Iraq's Unchecked Government* (Brussels: ICG).

International Crisis Group (ICG) (2012) *Déjà Vu All over Again: Iraq's Escalating Political Crisis* (Brussels: ICG).

International Crisis Group (ICG) (2013) 'Make or Break: Iraq's Sunnis and the State', 14 August, available online at https://www.crisisgroup.org/middle-east-north-africa/gulf-and-arabian-peninsula/iraq/make-or-break-iraq-s-sunnis-and-state

International IDEA (2014) *Atlas of Electoral Gender Quotas*, available online at http://www.idea.int/publications/atlas-of-electoral-gender-quotas/index.cfm

International Institute for Strategic Studies (2008) 'Middle East and North Africa', *The Military Balance*, 108(1): 225–72.

International Labour Organization (ILO) (2013) *Global Wage Report 2012/13* (Geneva: ILO).

International Monetary Fund (IMF) (2005) 'Good Governance: The IMF's Role', available online at http://www.imf.org/external/pubs/ft/exrp/gvern/govindex.htm

International Monetary Fund (IMF) (2016) 'Commodity Market Monthly', 15 January, available online at http://www.imf.org/external/np/res/commod/pdf/monthly/011516.pdf

Inter-Parliamentary Union (IPU) (2015) 'Sluggish Progress on Women in Politics Will Hamper Development', 10 March, available online at http://www.ipu.org/press-e/pressrelease201503101.htm

Iraq Body Count (2016) 'Iraq 2015: A Catastrophic Normal', 1 January, available online at https://www.iraqbodycount.org/analysis/numbers/2015/

Isaak, R. A. (2005) *The Globalization Gap: How the Rich Get Richer and the Poor Get Left Further behind* (London: FT Prentice Hall).

Jackson, R. H. (1990) *Quasi-States: Sovereignty, International Relations and the Third World* (Cambridge: Cambridge University Press).

Jackson, R. H., and Rosberg, C. (1982) 'Why Africa's Weak States Persist: The Empirical and the Juridical in Statehood', *World Politics*, 35(1): 1–24.

Jacques, M. (2012) *When China Rules the World*, 2nd edn (London: Penguin).

Jalal, A. (1995) *Democracy and Authoritarianism in South Asia: A Comparative and Historical Perspective* (Cambridge: Cambridge University Press).

Jamail, D. (2012) 'Iraq Execution Spree under the Spotlight', *AlJazeera English Online*, 11 September.

James, C. L. R. (1977) *Nkrumah and the Ghana Revolution* (London: Allison & Busby).

Janelli, R. L. (1993) *Making Capitalism* (Stanford, CA: Stanford University Press).

Jayawardena, K. (1986) *Feminism and Nationalism in the Third World* (London: Zed Books).

Jensenius, F. (2013) 'Power, Performance and Bias: Evaluating the Electoral Quotas of Scheduled Casts in India', PhD dissertation, University of California, Berkeley, CA.

Joffe, G. (2011) 'The Arab Spring in North Africa: Origins and Prospects', *The Journal of North African Studies*, 16(4): 507–32.

Johnson, H. F. (2011) *Waging Peace in Sudan: The Inside Story of the Negotiations that Ended Africa's Longest Civil War* (Eastbourne: Sussex Academic Press).

Johnson, M., and Blas, J. (2009) 'China Drives Commodity Price Rises', *Financial Times*, 19 June.

Jones, A. (2010) *Globalization: Key Thinkers* (Cambridge: Polity Press).

Jones, L. P., and Sakong, I. (1980) *Government, Business and Entrepreneurship in Economic Development: The Korean Case* (Cambridge, MA: Harvard University Press).

Joshi, A., and Ayee, J. (2008) 'Associational Taxation: A Pathway into the Informal Sector?' in D. Bräutigam, O.-H. Fjeldstad, and M. Moore (eds) *Taxation and State-Building in Developing Countries: Capacity and Consent* (Cambridge: Cambridge University Press), 183–212.

Juergensmeyer, M. (2003) *Terror in the Mind of God: The Global Rise of Religious Violence* (Berkeley, CA: University of California Press).

Kaag, J., and Kreps, S. (2014) *Drone Warfare* (Cambridge: Polity Press).

Kaldor, M. (1999) *New and Old Wars: Organized Violence in a Global Era* (Stanford, CA: Stanford University Press).

Kalyvas, S. (2001) '"New" and "Old" Civil Wars: A Valid Distinction?', *World Politics*, 54(1): 99–118.

Kalyvas, S. (2006) *The Logic of Violence in Civil War* (New York: Cambridge University Press).

Kandiyoti, D. (1991) 'End of Empire: Islam, Nationalism and Women in Turkey', in D. Kandiyoti (ed.) *Women, Islam and the State* (London: Macmillan), 22–47.

Kandiyoti, D. (2007) 'Between the Hammer and the Anvil: Post-Conflict Reconstruction, Islam and Women's Rights', *Third World Quarterly*, 28(3): 503–17.

Kang, D. C. (2002) *Crony Capitalism: Corruption and Development in South Korea and the Philippines* (Cambridge: Cambridge University Press).

Kaoma, K. (2009) *Globalizing the Culture Wars: US Conservatives, African Churches, and Homophobia* (Somerville, MA: Political Research Associates).

Kapstein, E., and Converse, N. (2009) 'Why Democracies Fail', *Journal of Democracy*, 19(4): 57–68.

Karl, T. L. (1990) 'Dilemmas of Democratization in Latin America', *Comparative Politics*, 23(1): 1–21.

Karlsrud, J. (2015) 'The UN at War: Examining the Consequences of Peace-Enforcement Mandates for the UN Peacekeeping Operations in the CAR, the DRC and Mali', *Third World Quarterly*, 36(1): 40–54.

Kashyap, S. C. (1989) *Our Parliament: An Introduction to the Parliament of India* (New Delhi: National Book Trust).

Kaufmann, D., Kraay, A., and Mastruzzi, M. (2010) 'The Worldwide Governance Indicators: Methodology and Analytical Issues', World Bank Policy Research Working Paper No. 5430, available online at http://papers.ssrn.com/sol3/papers.cfm?abstract_id=1682130

Kavada, A. (2012) 'Engagement, Bonding, and Identity across Multiple Platforms: Avaaz on Facebook, YouTube, and MySpace', *MedieKultur*, 28(52): 28–48.

Keck, M., and Sikkink, K. (1998) *Activists beyond Borders: Transnational Activist Networks In International Politics* (Ithaca, NY: Cornell University Press).

Keen, D. (2012) *Useful Enemies: When Waging Wars is More Important than Winning Them* (New Haven, CT: Yale University Press).

Kelsall, T. (2011) 'Rethinking the Relationship between Neo-Patrimonialism and Economic Development in Africa', *IDS Bulletin*, 42(2): 76–87.

Kelsall, T. (2012) 'Neo-Patriomonialism, Rent-Seeking and Development: Going with the Grain?', *New Political Economy*, 17(5): 677–82.

Khan, M. (2002) 'Fundamental Tensions in the Democratic Compromise', *New Political Economy*, 7(2): 275–7.

Khan, M. (2012) 'Governance and Growth Challenges for Africa', in A. Noman, K. Botchwey, H. Stein, and J. Stiglitz (eds) *Good Growth and Governance in Africa: Rethinking Development Strategies* (Oxford: Oxford University Press), 51–79.

Khan, N. S. (1999) 'Up against the State: The Women's Movement in Pakistan—Implications for the Global Women's Movement', Dame Nita Barrow Lecture, Toronto University, November, available online at https://www.oise.utoronto.ca/cwse/UserFiles/File/UpAgainstTheState.pdf

Khanna, P. (2009) *The Second World: How Emerging Powers are Redefining Global Competition in the Twenty-First Century* (London: Penguin).

Ki-moon, B. (2009) 'Secretary-General's Message on International Anti-Corruption Day', 9 December, available online at http://www.un.org/sg/statements/?nid=4293

Kim, E. M. (1997) *Big Business, Strong State: Collusion and Conflict in South Korean Development, 1960–1990* (Albany, NY: State University of New York Press).

Kim, S.-K., and Kim, K. (2011) 'Gender Mainstreaming and the Institutionalization of the Women's Movement in South Korea', *Women's Studies International Forum*, 24: 390–400.

Kipling, R. (1987 [1890]) 'Tods' Amendment', in *Plain Tales from the Hills* (London: Penguin), 179–84.

Kitschelt, H. P. (1986) 'Political Opportunity Structures and Political Protest: Anti-Nuclear Movements in Four Democracies', *British Journal of Political Science*, 16(1): 57–85.

Kjær, M. (2004) *Governance* (Cambridge: Polity Press).

Knight, J. (2014) 'Inequality in China', *The World Bank Research Observer*, 29(1): 1–19.

Kohli, A. (2004) *State-Directed Development: Political Power and Industrialization in the Global Periphery* (Cambridge: Cambridge University Press).

Kohli. A. (2007) *State-Directed Development: Political Power and Industrialization in the Global Periphery* 2nd edn (Cambridge: Cambridge University Press).

Kohli, A. (2012) *Poverty amid Plenty in the New India* (Cambridge: Cambridge University Press).

Kohli, A., and Singh, P. (eds) (2013) *Routledge Handbook of Indian Politics* (New York: Routledge).

Kothari, U. (2009) 'Spatial Practices and Imaginaries: Experiences of Colonial Officers and Development Professionals', in M. Duffield and V. Hewitt (eds)

Empire, Development and Colonialism: The Past in the Present (Woodbridge: James Currey), 160–75.

Kraft, H. J. S. (2006) 'China and Democracy in the Asia Pacific', UNISCI Discussion Paper No. 11, available online at http://revistas.ucm.es/index.php/unis/article/download/uniso606230071a/28109

Krahmann, E. (2003) 'National, Regional, and Global Governance: One Phenomenon or Many?', *Global Governance*, 9(3): 323–46.

Krauthammer, C. (1991) 'The Unipolar Moment', *Foreign Affairs*, 70(1): 23–33.

Kriesi, H., Koopmans, R., Duyvendak, J. W., and Giugni M. G. (1995) *New Social Movements in Western Europe: A Comparative Analysis* (Minneapolis, MN: University of Minnesota Press).

Krishnan, N., Olivieri, S., and Lima, L. (2014) *Iraq: The Unfulfilled Promise of Oil and Growth—Poverty, Inclusion and Welfare in Iraq, 2007–2012* (Washington, DC: World Bank).

Krook, M. L. (2010) 'Women's Representation in Parliament: A Qualitative Comparative Analysis', *Political Studies*, 58(5): 886–908.

Kurlantzik, J (2014) 'The Rise of Elected Autocrats Threatens Democracy', *Bloomberg Businessweek*, 23 January.

Lacina, B. (2006) 'Explaining the Severity of Civil Wars', *Journal of Conflict Resolution*, 50(2): 276–89.

Lake, D., and Rothchild, D. (1996) 'The Origins and Management of Ethnic Conflict', *International Security*, 21(2): 41–75.

Lal, D. (2004) *In Praise of Empires: Globalization and Order* (Basingstoke: Palgrave).

Landman, T. (2008) *Issues and Methods in Comparative Politics*, 3rd edn (London: Routledge).

Langford, M. (ed.) (2008) *Social Rights Jurisprudence: Emerging Trends in International and Comparative Law* (Cambridge: Cambridge University Press).

Lange, M. K. (2004) 'British Colonial Origins and Political Development', *World Development*, 32(6): 905–22.

Lange, M. K. (2009) *Lineages of Despotism and Development: British Colonialism and State Power* (Chicago, IL: Chicago University Press).

Large, D. (2008) 'All over in Africa', in C. Alden, D. Large, and R. Soares de Oliviera (eds) *China Returns to Africa: A Rising Power and a Continent Embrace* (London: Hurst & Co.), 371–6.

Lauth, H. J. (2000) 'Informal Institutions and Democracy', *Democratization*, 7(4): 21–50.

Lawson, L. (2009) 'The Politics of anti-Corruption Reform in Africa', *Journal of Modern African Studies*, 47(1): 73–100.

Lebon, N. (2013) 'Taming or Unleashing the Monster of Coalition Work: Professionalization and the Consolidation of Popular Feminism in Brazil', *Feminist Review*, 39(3): 759–89.

Lee, A.-R., and Chin, M. (2007) 'The Women's Movement in South Korea', *Social Sciences Quarterly*, 88(5): 1205–26.

Lee, K.-S. (2011) *The Korean Financial Crisis of 1997: Onset, Turnaround, and Thereafter* (Washington, DC: International Bank for Reconstruction and Development, World Bank, and Korea Development Institute).

Lee, Y. H. (1997) *The State, Society and Big Business in South Korea* (London and New York: Routledge).

Leftwich, A. (1993) 'Governance, Democracy and Development in the Third World', *Third World Quarterly*, 14(3): 603–24.

Leftwich, A. (1995) 'Bringing Politics Back in: Towards a Model of the Developmental State', *Journal of Development Studies*, 31(3): 400–27.

Leftwich, A. (2000) *States of Development: On the Primacy of Politics in Development* (Cambridge: Polity Press).

Leftwich, A. (2002) 'Democracy and Development', *New Political Economy*, 7(2): 269–81.

Leftwich, A. (2014) 'Theorizing the State', in P. Burnell, L. Rakner, and V. Randall (eds) *Politics in the Developing World* (Oxford: Oxford University Press), 181–95.

Levi, M. (1981) 'The Predatory Theory of Rule', *Politics & Society*, 10(4): 431–65.

Levi, M. (1988) *Of Rule and Revenue* (Berkeley, CA: University of California Press).

Levi, M. (2006) 'Why We Need a New Theory of Government', *Perspectives on Politics*, 4(1): 5–19.

Levitsky, S., and Way, L. A. (2010) *Competitive Authoritarianism: Hybrid Regimes after the Cold War* (New York: Cambridge University Press).

Lin, J. Y. (2011) 'From Flying Geese to Leading Dragons: New Opportunities and Strategies for Structural Transformation in Developing Countries', World

Bank Policy Research Working Paper No. 5702, available online at http://elibrary.worldbank.org/content/workingpaper/10.1596/1813-9450-5702

Lindberg, S. (2006) *Democracy and Elections in Africa* (Baltimore, MD: Johns Hopkins University Press).

Linz, J. J. (1990) 'The Perils of Presidentialism', *Journal of Democracy*, 1(1): 51–69.

Linz, J. J., and Stepan, A. (1996) *Problems of Democratic Transition and Consolidation: Southern Europe, South America, and post-Communist Europe* (Baltimore, MD: Johns Hopkins University Press).

Lipset, S. M. (1959) 'Some Social Requisites of Democracy: Economic Development and Political Legitimacy', *The American Political Science Review*, 55(1): 69–105.

Lipset, S. M. (1994) 'The Social Requisites of Democracy Revisited', *American Sociological Review*, 53(1): 1–22.

Lister, C. (2015) *The Syrian Jihad: Al-Qaeda, the Islamic State and the Evolution of an Insurgency* (London: Hurst & Co.).

Lopez-Calva, L. (2012) 'Declining Income Inequality in Brazil: The Proud Outlier', *Inequality in Focus*, 1(1): 5–8.

Lopez-Calva, L., and Lustig, N. (2010) 'Explaining the Decline in Inequality in Latin America', in L. Lopez-Calva and N. Lustig (eds) *Declining Inequality in Latin America* (New York and Washington, DC: UNDP and Brookings Institute Press), 1–24.

Lowndes, V. (2010) 'The Institutionalist Approach', in D. S. Marsh and G. S. Stoker (eds) *Theory and Methods in Political Science*, 3rd edn (Basingstoke: Palgrave), 60–79.

Lucas, R. E., Jr (1988) 'On the Mechanics of Economic Development', *Journal of Monetary Economics*, 22(1): 3–42.

Lugard, Lord (1965 [1922]) *The Dual Mandate in British Tropical Africa* (London: Frank Cass).

Lustig, N., Lopez-Calva, L., and Ortiz-Juarez, E. (2013) 'Deconstructing the Decline in Inequality in Latin America', World Bank Policy Research Working Paper No. 6552, available online at http://documents.worldbank.org/curated/en/79249146804 7055310/Deconstructing-the-decline-in-inequality-in-Latin-America

MacGinty, R., and Richmond, O. (2016) 'The Fallacy of Constructing Hybrid Political Orders: A Reappraisal of the Hybrid Turn in Peacebuilding', *International Peacekeeping*, 23(2): 219–39.

MacQueen, B. (2013) *An Introduction to Middle East Politics: Continuity, Change, Conflict and Co-operation* (London: Sage).

McAdam, D. (1982) *Political Process and the Development of Black Insurgency 1930–1970* (Chicago, IL: University of Chicago Press).

McAdam, D., McCarthy, J. D., and Zald, M. N. (1996) *Comparative Perspectives on Social Movements: Political Opportunities, Mobilizing Structures, and Cultural Framings* (Cambridge: Cambridge University Press).

McCarthy, J. D., and Zald, M. N. (1977) 'Resource Mobilization and Social Movements: A Partial Theory', *American Journal of Sociology*, 82(6): 1212–41.

McCauley, J. (2014) 'The Political Mobilization of Ethnic and Religious Identities in Africa', *American Political Science Review*, 108(4): 801–16.

McEwan, C. (2009) *Postcolonialism and Development* (London: Routledge).

McGrew, A. (1992) 'A Global Society?', in S. Hall, D. Held, and A. McGrew (eds) *Modernity and Its Future* (Cambridge: Polity Press), 62–102.

McMichael, P. (2008) *Development and Social Change: A Global Perspective*, 4th edn (Los Angeles, CA: Pine Forge).

McMillan, J., and Zoido, P. (2004) 'How to Subvert Democracy: Montesinos in Peru', *Journal of Economic Perspectives*, 18(4): 69–92.

Mackenzie, L. (2016) 'Iraq: Reaching Isolated Children on Sinjar Mountain', 6 January, https://blogs.unicef.org/blog/reaching-isolated-children-on-sinjar-mountain/

Maddison, A. (2007) *Contours of the World Economy, 1–2030 AD* (Oxford: Oxford University Press).

Madrid, R. (2012) *The Rise of Ethnic Politics in Latin America* (New York: Cambridge University Press).

Mahon, J. (2004) 'Causes of Tax Reform in Latin America, 1977–95', *Latin America Research Review*, 39(1): 3–30.

Mahoney, J. (2010) *Colonialism and Postcolonial Development: Spanish America in Comparative Perspective* (Cambridge: Cambridge University Press).

Mahoney, J., and Thelen, K. (2010) *Explaining Institutional Change: Ambiguity, Agency and Power* (Cambridge, Cambridge University Press).

Mahoney, J., and vom Hau, M. (2005) 'Colonial States and Economic Development in Spanish America', in M. Lange and D. Rueshmeyer (eds) *States and Development: Historical Antecedents of Stagnation and Advance* (New York: Palgrave Macmillan), 92–116.

Mair, P. (1996) 'Comparative Politics: An Overview', in R. E. Goodin and H. Klingemann (eds) *A New Handbook of Political Science* (Oxford: Oxford University Press), 309–35.

Malek, C. (2013) 'International Conflict', May, available online at http://www.crinfo.org/coreknowledge/international-conflict

Maluf, S. W. (2011) 'Brazilian Feminisms: Central and Peripheral Issues', *Feminist Review Conference Proceedings*, e36–e51.

Mamdani, M. (1996) *Citizen and Subject: Contemporary Africa and the Legacy of Late Colonialism* (London: James Currey).

Mani, L. (1987) 'The Debate on Sati in Colonial India', *Cultural Critique*, 7: 119–56.

Mann, M. (1984) 'The Autonomous Power of the State: Its Origins, Mechanisms and Results', *European Journal of Sociology*, 25(2): 185–213.

Mann, M. (1990) *States, War and Capitalism* (Oxford: Basil Blackwell).

Manor, J. (ed.) (1991) *Rethinking Third-World Politics* (London: Longman).

Mao, Z. (1977) *Selected Works of Mao Tse-tung* (Peking: Foreign Language Press).

March, J., and Olsen, J. (1984) 'The New Institutionalism: Organisational Factors in Political Life', *American Political Science Review*, 78(3): 734–49.

March, J., and Olsen, J. P. (1989) *Rediscovering Institutions: The Organizational Basis of Politics* (New York: Free Press).

March, J., and Olsen, J. (2006) 'Elaborating the "New Institutionalism"', in R. A. W. Rhodes, S. Binder, and B. A. Rockman (eds) *The Oxford Handbook of Political Institutions* (Oxford: Oxford University Press), 3–22.

Marshall, T. H. (1965) *Class, Citizenship, and Social Development* (New York: Doubleday).

Marx, K. (1970) *The German Ideology* (London: Lawrence & Wishart).

Marx, K., and Engels, F. (2002) *The Communist Manifesto* (London: Penguin).

Masoud, T. (2015) 'Has the Door Closed on Arab Democracy?', *Journal of Democracy*, 26(1): 74–87.

Mayall, J., and Payne, A. (eds) (1991) *The Fallacies of Hope: The post-Colonial Record of the Commonwealth Third World* (Manchester: Manchester University Press).

Mazrui, A. (1986) *The Africans: A Triple Heritage* (London: BBC).

Meadows, D. H., Meadows, D. L., Randers, J., and Behrens, W. W., III (1972) *The Limits to Growth* (New York: Universe).

Mearsheimer, J. (2010) 'The Gathering Storm: China's Challenge to US Power in Asia', *The Chinese Journal of International Politics*, 3(4): 381–96.

Mehta, L. (2006) 'Do Human Rights Make a Difference to Poor and Vulnerable People? Accountability for the Right to Water in South Africa', in P. Newell and J. Wheeler (eds) *Rights, Resources and the Politics of Accountability* (London: Zed Books), 63–79.

Melia, T. O., and Katulis, B. M. (2003) *Iraqis Discuss Their Country's Future: Post-War Perspectives from the Iraqi Street* (Washington, DC: National Democratic Institute).

Menkhaus, K. (2006–07) 'Governance without Government in Somalia: Spoilers, State Building, and the Politics of Coping', *International Security*, 31(3): 74–106.

Merrill, D. (1994) 'The United States and the Rise of the Third World', in G. Martel (ed.) *American Foreign Relations Reconsidered 1890–1993* (London: Routledge), 166–86.

Mesbahi, M. (ed.) (1994) *Russia and the Third World in the post-Soviet Era* (Gainesville, FL: University Press of Florida).

Michels, R. (1962) *Political Parties: A Sociological Study of the Oligarchical Tendencies of Modern Democracies* (New York: Collier).

Midgley, J., and Piachaud, D. (2011) *Colonialism and Welfare. Social Policy and the British Imperial Legacy* (Cheltenham: Edward Elgar).

Mietzner, M. (2009) 'Indonesia and the Pitfalls of Low-Quality Democracy: A Case Study of the Gubernatorial Elections in North Sulawesi', in A. Ufen and M. Bünte (eds) *Democratization in post-Suharto Indonesia* (London and New York: Routledge), 124–50.

Mietzner, M. (2012) 'Indonesia's Democratic Stagnation: Anti-Reformist Elites and Resilient Civil Society', *Democratization*, 19(2): 209–29.

Migdal, J. S. (1988) *Strong Societies and Weak States: State–Society Relations and State Capabilities in the Third World* (Princeton, NJ: Princeton University Press)

Migdal, J. S. (2001) *State in Society* (New York: Cambridge University Press).

Milanovic, B. (2011) *The Haves and the Have Nots* (New York: Basic Books).

Milanovic, B. (2012a) 'Global Income Inequality by the Numbers: In History and Now—An Overview', World Bank Policy Research Working Paper No. 6259, available online at http://elibrary.worldbank.org/content/workingpaper/10.1596/1813-9450-6259

Mill, J. S. (1888) *A System of Logic* (New York: Harper & Row).

Milliken, J., and Krause, K. (2002) 'State Failure, State Collapse, and State Reconstruction: Concepts, Lessons, and Strategies', *Development & Change*, 33(5): 753–74.

Minorities at Risk Project (MAR) (2009) 'Minorities at Risk Dataset', available online at http://www.mar.umd.edu/mar_data.asp

Minority Rights Organisation (2011) 'World Directory of Minorities and Indigenous People', available online at http://www.minorityrights.org/?lid=5266

Mitlin, D., and Mogaldi, J. (2013) 'Social Movements and the Struggle for Shelter: A Case Study of eThekwini (Durban)', *Progress in Planning*, 84: 1–39.

Moghadam, V. M. (2013) 'What is Democracy? Promises and Perils of the Arab Spring', *Current Sociology*, 61(4): 393–408.

Moloeznik, M. P. (2009) 'Militarizing Mexico's Public Security', William J. Perry Center for Hemispheric Defense Studies Regional Insights No. 11.

Molyneux, M. (1985) 'Mobilization without Emancipation? Women's Interests, the State and Revolution in Nicaragua', *Feminist Studies*, 11(2): 227–54.

Moon, C. (1994) 'Changing Patterns of Business–Government Relations in South Korea', in A. MacIntyre (ed.) *Business and Government in Industrializing Asia* (Sydney: Allen & Unwin), 142–66.

Moon, S. (2002) 'Carving out Space: Civil Society and the Women's Movement in South Korea', *The Journal of Asian Studies*, 61(2): 473–500.

Moore, M. (2007) 'How Does Taxation Affect the Quality of Government?', IDS Working Paper No. 280, available online at http://www2.ids.ac.uk/gdr/cfs/pdfs/Wp280.pdf

Moore, M. (2011) 'Globalisation and Power in Weak States', *Third World Quarterly*, 32(10): 1757–76.

Morris, A. (1993) 'Birmingham Confrontation Reconsidered: An Analysis of the Dynamics and Tactics of Mobilization', *American Sociological Review*, 58(5): 621–36.

Morris-Jones, W. H. (1987) *The Government and Politics of India* (Huntingdon: Eothen Press).

Mosley, L. (2005) 'Globalization and the State: Still Room to Move?', *New Political Economy*, 10(3): 355–62.

Mozaffar, S. (1995) 'The Institutional Logic of Ethnic Politics: A Prolegomenon', in H. Glickman (ed.) *Ethnic Conflict and Democratization in Africa* (Atlanta, GA: African Studies Association Press), 34–69.

Mozaffar, S., Scarritt, J. R., and Galaich, G. (2003) 'Electoral Institutions, Ethnopolitical Cleavages, and Party Systems in Africa's Emerging Democracies', *American Political Science Review*, 97(3): 379–90.

Muñoz, P. (2014) 'An Informational Theory of Campaign Clientelism: The Case of Peru', *Comparative Politics*, 47(1): 79–98.

Muriaas, R. L., and Wang, V. (2012) 'Executive Dominance and the Politics of Quota Representation in Uganda', *Journal of Modern African Studies*, 50(2): 309–38.

Myrdal, G. (1968) *Asian Drama: An Enquiry into the Poverty of Nations* (Harmondsworth: Penguin).

Nash, K. (2010) *Contemporary Political Sociology: Globalization, Politics, Power* (Chichester: Wiley-Blackwell).

National Bureau of Statistics (2014) *China Statistical Yearbook 2014* (Beijing: China Statistics Press).

Nehru, J. (1942) *An Autobiography* (London: The Bodley Head).

Nehru, J. (1961) *The Discovery of India* (Bombay: Asia).

Neuman S. G. (ed.) (1998) *International Relations Theory and the Third World* (Basingstoke: Macmillan).

New York Times (2014) 'Under Francis, a Bolder Vision of Vatican Diplomacy Emerges', 19 December, available online at http://www.nytimes.com/2014/12/19/world/europe/pope-francis-vatican-diplomatic-mediator-cuba.html

Newell, P. (2001) 'Environmental NGOs, TNCs and the Question of Governance', in D. Stevis and V. Assetto (eds) *The International Political Economy of the Environment: Critical Perspectives* (Boulder, CO: Lynne Rienner), 85–107.

Newell, P. (2012) *Globalization and the Environment: Capitalism, Ecology and Power* (Cambridge: Polity Press).

Newell, P., and Wheeler, J. (eds) (2006) *Rights, Resources and the Politics of Accountability* (London: Zed Books).

Newman, E., Paris, R., and Richmond, O. P. (2009) *New Perspectives on Liberal Peacebuilding* (Tokyo: United Nations University Press).

Nilsen, A. G., and Motta, S. C. (2011) *Social Movements in the Global South: Dispossession, Development, and Resistance* (London: Palgrave).

Niner, S. (2011) 'Hakat Klot, Narrow Steps', *International Feminist Journal of Politics*, 13(3): 413–35.

Nkrumah, K. (1965) *Neo-Colonialism: The Last Stage of Imperialism* (London: Panaf).

Nolutshungu, S. C. (1991) 'Fragments of a Democracy: Reflections on Class and Politics in Nigeria', in J. Mayall and A. Payne (eds) *The Fallacies of Hope* (Manchester: Manchester University Press), 72–105.

North, D.C. (1981) *Structure and Change in Economic History* (New York: Norton).

North, D. C. (1990) *Institutions, Institutional Change and Economic Performance* (Cambridge: Cambridge University Press).

North, D. C., Wallis, J. J., and Weingast, B. R. (2009) *Violence and Social Orders: A Conceptual Framework for Interpreting Recorded History* (New York: Cambridge University Press).

Nozick, R. (1974) *Anarchy, State and Utopia* (Oxford: Blackwell).

Nunn, N. (2008) 'The Long-Term Effects of Africa's Slave Trades', *The Quarterly Journal of Economics*, 123(1): 139–76.

Nye, J. S. (2004) *Soft Power: The Means to Success in World Politics* (New York: Public Affairs Press).

O'Brien, R., and Williams, M. (2013) *Global Political Economy: Evolution and Dynamics*, 4th edn (Basingstoke: Palgrave Macmillan).

O'Donnell, G. (1994) 'Delegative Democracy', *Journal of Democracy*, 5(1): 55–69.

O'Neill, J. (2001) *Building Better Global Economic BRICs*, Goldman Sachs Global Economic Paper No. 66, available online at http://www.goldmansachs.com/our-thinking/archive/archive-pdfs/build-better-brics.pdf

O'Rourke, D. (2004) *Community-Based Regulation: Balancing Environment and Development in Vietnam* (Cambridge, MA: MIT Press).

Office of the United Nations High Commissioner for Human Rights (OHCHR) and United Nations Assistance Mission for Iraq (UNAMI) (2015) *Report on the Protection of Civilians in the Armed Conflict in Iraq: 11 December 2014–30 April 2015*, available online at http://www.ohchr.org/Documents/Countries/IQ/UNAMI_OHCHR_4th_POCReport-11Dec2014-30April2015.pdf

Ogden, C. (2014) *Indian Foreign Policy* (Cambridge: Polity Press).

Olinto, P., and Saavedra, J. (2012) 'An Overview of Global Inequality Trends', *Inequality in Focus*, 1(1): 1–4.

Olken, B. A. (2006) 'Corruption and the Costs of Redistribution: Micro Evidence from Indonesia', *Journal of Public Economics*, 90(4–5): 853–70.

Olson, M. (1965) *The Logic of Collective Action: Public Goods and the Theory of Groups* (Cambridge, MA: Harvard University Press).

Olson, M. (1993) 'Dictatorship, Democracy, and Development', *The American Political Science Review*, 87(3): 567–76.

Olson, M. (2001) *Power and Prosperity: Outgrowing Communist and Capitalist Dictatorships* (New York: Basic Books).

Organisation for Economic Co-operation and Development (OECD) (2015) 'Government at Glance: Country Fact Sheet—Korea', available online at http://www.oecd.org/gov/Korea.pdf

Organization of American States (OAS) Hemispheric Security Observatory (2012) *Report on Citizen Security in the Americas 2012* (Washington, DC: OAS).

Ottaway, M. (2003) *Democracy Challenged: The Rise of Semi-Authoritarianism* (Washington DC: Carnegie Endowment for International Peace).

Ottaway, M., and Carothers, T. (eds) (2000) *Funding Virtue: Civil Society Aid and Democracy Promotion* (Washington, DC: Carnegie Endowment for International Peace).

Palma, J. G. (2011) 'Homogenous Middles vs Heterogenous Tails, and the End of the "Inverted-U": It's All about the Share of the Rich', *Development and Change Forum*, 42(1): 87–153.

Panner, M., and Beltrán, A. (2010) 'Battling Organized Crime in Guatemala', *The Americas Quarterly*, available online at http://www.americasquarterly.org/node/1899

Parente, S. L., and Prescott, E. C. (2000) *Barriers to Riches* (Cambridge, MA: MIT Press).

Paris, R. (2004) *At War's End* (New York: Cambridge University Press).

Park, K. (2011) 'New Development Partners and a Global Development Partnership', in H. Kharas, K. Makino, and W. Jung (eds) *Catalysing Development: A New Vision for Aid* (Washington, DC: Brookings Institute), 38–60.

Payne, A. (2004) 'Rethinking Development inside International Political Economy', in A. Payne (ed.) *The New Regional Politics of Development* (Basingstoke: Palgrave), 1–28.

Payne, A. (2005) 'The Study of Governance in a Global Political Economy', in N. Phillips (ed.) *Globalizing International Political Economy* (Houndmills: Palgrave Macmillan), 55–81.

Payne, A., and Phillips, N. (2010) *Development* (Cambridge: Polity Press).

Perham, M. (1963) *The Colonial Reckoning: The Reith Lectures 1961* (London: Fontana).

Permanent Mission of the SAR (2011) 'Note Verbale Dated 27 June 2011 and 16 August 2011 from the Permanent Mission Addressed to the UN High Commissioner for Human Rights', available online at http://www.ohchr.org/Documents/countries/SY/Syria_Report_2011-08-17.pdf

Persson, A., and Sjöstedt, M. (2012) 'Responsive and Responsible Leaders: A Matter of Political Will', *Perspectives on Politics*, 10(3): 617–32.

Persson, A., Rothstein, B., and Teorell, J. (2013) 'Why Anticorruption Reforms Fail: Systemic Corruption as a Collective Action Problem', *Governance*, 26(3): 447–71.

Peters, G. D. (2005) *Institutional Theory in Political Science: The New Institutionalism*, 2nd edn (London: Continuum).

Pettersson, T., and Wallensteen, P. (2015) 'Armed Conflicts, 1946–2014', *Journal of Peace Research*, 52(4): 536–50.

Phillips, A. (1995) *The Politics of Presence* (Oxford: Oxford University Press).

Phillips, A. (1999) *Which Equalities Matter?* (Cambridge: Polity Press).

Phillips, N. (ed.) (2005) *Globalizing International Political Economy* (Houndmills: Palgrave Macmillan).

Pichardo, N. A. (1997) 'New Social Movements: A Critical Review', *Annual Review of Sociology*, 23: 411–30.

Pierson, P. (2000) 'The Limits of Design: Explaining Institutional Origins and Change', *Governance*, 13(4): 475–99.

Pieterse, J. N. (2015) *Globalization and Culture: Global Melange*, 3rd edn (Lanham, MD: Rowman & Littlefield).

Piketty, T. (2014) *Capital in the Twenty-First Century* (Cambridge, MA, and London: Harvard University Press).

Pitcher, M. A., and Askew, K. M. (2006) 'African Socialisms and Postsocialisms', *Africa*, 76(1): 1–14.

Piven, F. F., and Cloward, R. A. (1977) *Poor People's Movements: Why They Succeed, How They Fail* (New York: Pantheon Books).

Polgreen, L. (2006) 'Truce is Talk, Agony is Real in Darfur War', *New York Times*, 14 May.

Pope Francis (2014) 'Letter . . . to the Christians in the Middle East', available online at https://w2.vatican.va/content/francesco/en/letters/2014/documents/papa-francesco_20141221_lettera-cristiani-medio-oriente.html

Porter, B. (1996) *The Lion's Share: A Short History of British Imperialism 1850–1995*, 3rd edn (London: Longman).

Posner, D. (2005) *Institutions and Ethnic Politics in Africa* (Cambridge: Cambridge University Press).

Posner, D., and Young, D. J. (2007) 'The Institutionalization of Political Power in Africa', *Journal of Democracy*, 18(3): 126–40.

Pourmokhtari, N. (2013) 'A post-Colonial Critique of State Sovereignty in IR [International Relations]: The Contradictory Legacy of a "West-Centric" Discipline', *Third World Quarterly*, 34(10): 1767–93.

Powell, G. B. (2000) *Elections as Instruments of Democracy: Majoritarian and Proportional Visions* (New Haven, CT: Yale University Press).

Prakash, G. (1999) *Another Reason: Science and the Imagination of Modern India* (Princeton, NJ: Princeton University Press).

Prichett, L., and Woolcock, M. (2004) 'Solutions when the Solution is the Problem: Arraying the Disarray in Development', *World Development*, 32(2): 191–212.

Przeworski, A., Alvarez, M., Cheibub, J., and Limongi, F. (1996) 'What Makes Democracies Endure?', *Journal of Democracy*, 7(1): 39–55.

Puddington, A. (2015) 'The Return to the Iron Fist: The Freedom House Survey 2014', *Journal of Democracy*, 26(1): 122–38.

Putnam, R. (1993) *Making Democracy Work: Civic Traditions in Modern Italy* (Princeton, NJ: Princeton University Press).

Pye, L. W. (1966) *Aspects of Political Development* (Boston, MA: Little, Brown).

Rai, S. M. (2002) *Gender and the Political Economy of Development: From Nationalism to Globalization* (Cambridge: Polity).

Rakner, L., and van de Walle, N. (2009) 'Opposition Weakness in Africa', *Journal of Democracy*, 20(3): 108–21.

Ramo, J. C. (2004) *The Beijing Consensus* (London: The Foreign Policy Centre).

Randall, V. (2004) 'Using and Abusing the Concept of the Third World: Geopolitics and the Comparative Study of Development and Underdevelopment', *Third World Quarterly*, 25(1): 41–53.

Randall, V., and Svåsand, L. (2002) 'Party Institutionalization in New Democracies', *Party Politics*, 8(1): 6–29.

Ravallion, M. (2001) 'Growth, Inequality and Poverty: Looking beyond Averages', *World Development*, 29(11): 1803–15.

Ravallion, M. (2005) 'Inequality is Bad for the Poor', World Bank Policy Research Working Paper No. 3677, available online at https://openknowledge.worldbank.org/handle/10986/8625

Ravallion, M. (2009) 'Should the Randomistas Rule?', *Economists' Voice*, 6(2), available online at http://www.degruyter.com/view/j/ev.2009.6.2/ev.2009.6.2.1368/ev.2009.6.2.1368.xml

Rawls, J. (1971) *A Theory of Justice* (Oxford: Oxford University Press).

Reid, A. (ed.) (2012) *Indonesia Rising: The Repositioning of Asia's Third Giant* (Singapore: ISEAS).

Reilly, B. (2006) 'Political Engineering and Party Politics in Conflict-Prone Societies', *Democratization*, 13(5): 811–27.

Remmer, K. (1997) 'Theoretical Decay and Theoretical Development: The Resurgence of Institutional Analysis', *World Politics*, 50(1): 34–61.

Reuters (2011) 'Syria's Assad Issues Amnesty: State TV', 31 May, available online at http://af.reuters.com/article/worldNews/idAFTRE74U4HU20110531

Richards, P. (2004) *No Peace, No War: An Anthropology of Contemporary Armed Conflicts* (Oxford: James Currey).

Richmond, O. (2009) 'Liberal Peace Transitions: A Rethink is Urgent', *OpenDemocracy*, 19 November, available online at https://www.opendemocracy.net/oliver-p-richmond/liberal-peace-transitions-rethink-is-urgent

Rivetti, P. (2015) 'Continuity and Change before and after the Arab Uprisings in Morocco, Tunisia and Egypt', *British Journal of Middle East Studies*, 42(1): 1–11.

Roberts, C., Elliott Armijo, L., and Katada, S. N. (forthcoming) *The BRICS and Collective Financial Statecraft* (Oxford: Oxford University Press).

Rodríguez-Garavito, C. (2010) 'Beyond the Courtroom: The Impact of Judicial Activism on Socioeconomic Rights in Latin America', *Texas Law Review*, 89(7): 1669–98.

Rodrik, D. (2011) *The Globalization Paradox: Democracy and the Future of the World Economy* (Oxford and New York: Oxford University Press).

Roett, R., and Paz, G. (eds) (2008) *China's Expansion into the Western Hemisphere: Implications for Latin America and the United States* (Washington, DC: Brookings Institute).

Rose-Ackerman, S. (2004) *The Challenge of Poor Governance and Corruption*, Copenhagen Consensus 2004, available online at http://www.copenhagenconsensus.com/sites/default/files/PP%2B-%2BCorruption1%2BFINISHED.pdf

Rose-Ackerman, S., and Truex, R. (2012) 'Corruption and Policy Reform', Yale Law & Economics Research Paper No. 444, available online at http://papers.ssrn.com/sol3/papers.cfm?abstract_id=2007152

Rosen, N. (2011) 'A Tale of Two Villages', *Al-Jazeera*, 24 October, available online at http://www.aljazeera.com/indepth/features/2011/10/2011102365913224161.html

Ross, M. L. (1999) 'The Political Economy of the Resource Curse', *World Politics*, 51(2): 297–322.

Ross, M. L. (2008) 'Oil, Islam and Women', *American Political Science Review*, 102(1): 107–23.

Rotberg, R. I. (ed.) (2004a) *When States Fail* (Princeton, NJ: Princeton University Press).

Rotberg, R. I. (2004b) 'Strengthening African Leadership: There is Another Way', *Foreign Affairs*, 83(4): 14–18.

Rothstein, B. (2011) *The Quality of Government. Corruption, Social Trust and Inequality in International Perspective* (Chicago, IL: Chicago University Press).

Rothstein, B., and Tannenberg, M. (2015) *Making Development Work: The Quality of Government Approach*, available online at http://openaid.se/app/uploads/2015/03/2015-07-Making-development-work-the-quality-of-government-approach.pdf

Rothstein, B., and Teorell, J. (2008) 'What is Quality of Government? A Theory of Impartial Government Institutions', *Governance*, 21(2): 165–90.

Rousseau, J. J. (1755) *Discourse on Inequality* (London: Everyman/Dent).

Rowden, R. (2011) 'India's Role in the New Farmland Grab', 19 August, available online at https://www.grain.org/bulletin_board/entries/4342-india-s-role-in-the-new-global-farmland-grab

Rubin, M. (2004) 'Iraq's Electoral System: A Misguided Strategy', *Arab Reform Bulletin*, 20 September, available online at http://carnegieendowment.org/2008/08/20/iraq-s-electoral-system-misguided-strategy/6fo4

Rudolph, L. I., and Rudolph, S. H. (1967) *The Modernity of Tradition: Political Development in India* (Chicago, IL: University of Chicago Press).

Rueschemeyer, D. (2004) 'Addressing Inequality', *Journal of Democracy*, 15(4): 76–90.

Rueschemeyer, D., Stephens, E. H., and Stephens, J. D. (1992) *Capitalist Democracy and Development* (Cambridge: Polity Press).

Ruhl, J. M. (2011) 'Political Corruption in Central America: Assessment and Explanation', *Latin American Politics and Society*, 53(1): 33–58.

Rustow, D. A. (1970) 'Transitions to Democracy', *Comparative Politics*, 2(3): 337–63.

Sachs, J. (1998) 'The IMF and the Asian Flu,' *The American Prospect*, March–April, available online at http://prospect.org/article/imf-and-asian-flu

Safa, H. I. (1990) 'Women's Social Movements in Latin America', *Gender and Society*, 4(3): 354–69.

Sahni, V. (2007) 'India's Foreign Policy: Key Drivers', *South African Journal of International Affairs*, 14(2): 21–35.

Said, E. W. (1993) *Culture and Imperialism* (London: Chatto & Windus).

Said, E. W. (1995 [1978]) *Orientalism* (Harmondsworth: Penguin).

Saideman, S. M. R., and Ayres, W. (2000) 'Determining the Causes of Irredentism: Logit Analyses of Minorities at Risk Data from the 1980s and 1990s', *The Journal of Politics*, 62(4): 1126–44.

Salehyan, I. (2007) 'Transnational Rebels: Neighboring States as Sanctuary for Rebel Groups', *World Politics*, 59(2): 217–42.

Samatar, A. I. (1999) *An African Miracle: State and Class Leadership and Colonial Legacy in Botswana's Development* (Portsmouth, NH: Heinemann).

Sambanis, N. (2001) 'Do Ethnic and non-Ethnic Civil Wars Have the Same Causes?', *Journal of Conflict Resolution*, 45(3): 259–82.

Sangmpan, S. N. (2007) 'Politics Rules: The False Primacy of Institutions in Developing Countries', *Political Studies*, 55(1): 201–24.

Sardenberg, C. M. B. (2007) 'Back to Women? Translations, Resignifications and Myths of Gender in Policy and Practice in Brazil', in A. Cornwall, E. Harrison, and A Whitehead (eds) *Feminism in Development: Contradictions, Contestations and Challenges* (London: Zed Books), 48–64.

Sardenberg, C. M. B., and Costa, A. A. A (2010) 'Contemporary Feminisms in Brazil: Achievements, Shortcomings and Challenges', in A. Basu (ed.) *Women's Movements in the Global Era* (Boulder, CO: Westview Press), 255–84.

Sartori, G. (1976) *Parties and Party Systems: A Framework for Analysis* (Cambridge: Cambridge University Press).

Satik, N. (2013) 'al-Hala al-Ta'ifiya fi al-Intifada al-Suriya [The Sectarian Dimension of the Syrian Uprising]', in Arab Centre for Research and Policy Studies (ed.) *Khilafiyat al-Thawra: Dirasat Suriya [Background to the Revolution: Syrian Studies]* (Doha: Arab Centre for Research and Policy Studies), 373–427.

Scarritt, J., and Mozaffar, S. (1999) 'The Specification of Ethnic Cleavages and Ethnopolitical Groups for the Analysis of Democratic Competition in Contemporary Africa', *Nationalism and Ethnic Politics*, 5(1): 82–117.

Scarritt, J., and Mozaffar, S. (2003) 'Why do Multi-Ethnic Parties Prevail in Africa and Ethnic Parties do Not?', unpublished paper.

Schedler, A. (1998) 'What is Democratic Consolidation?', *Journal of Democracy*, 9(2): 91–107.

Schedler, A. (2013) *The Politics of Uncertainty: Sustaining and Subverting Electoral Authoritarianism* (Oxford: Oxford University Press).

Schedler, A. (2014) 'The Criminal Subversion of Mexican Democracy', *Journal of Democracy*, 25(1): 5–18.

Schedler, A. (2015) *En la niebla de la guerra: Los ciudadanos ante la violencia criminal organizada* (Mexico City: CIDE).

Schedler, A., Diamond, L., and Plattner, M. (eds) (1999) *The Self-Restraining State* (Boulder, CO: Lynne Reinner).

Scheper-Hughes, N. (1992) *Death without Weeping: The Violence of Everyday Life in Brazil* (Berkeley, CA: University of California Press).

Schulte Nordholt, H., and van Klinken, G. (eds) (2007) *Renegotiating Boundaries: Local Politics in post-Suharto Indonesia* (The Hague: Nijhoff).

Selway, J. (2011) 'Cross-Cuttingness, Cleavage Structures and Civil War Onset', *British Journal of Political Science*, 41(1): 111–38.

Selznick, P. (1948) 'Foundations of the Theory of Organization', *American Sociological Review*, 13(1): 25–35.

Sen, A. (1992) *Inequality Re-examined* (Oxford: Oxford University Press).

Sen, A. (1999a) *Development as Freedom* (Oxford: Oxford University Press).

Sen, A. (1999b) 'Human Rights and Economic Achievements', in J. R. Bauer and D. A. Bell (eds) *The East Asian Challenge for Human Rights* (Cambridge: Cambridge University Press), 88–99.

Sen, A. (2006) *Identity and Violence: The Illusion of Destiny* (London: Allen Lane).

Shaffer, G., Nedumpara, J., and Sinha, A. (2015) 'State Transformation and the Role of Lawyers: The WTO, India, and Transnational Legal Ordering,' *Law and Society Review*, 49(3): 595–629.

Shaheed, F. (2007) 'The Women's Movement in Pakistan: Challenges and Achievements', in A. Basu (ed.) *Rethinking Global Women's Movements* (London: Routledge), 89–118.

Shaheed, F. (2010) 'Contested Identities: Gendered Politics, Gendered Religion in Pakistan', *Third World Quarterly*, 31(6): 851–67.

Sharkey, H. (2003) *Living with Colonialism: Nationalism and Culture in the Anglo-Egyptian Sudan* (Berkeley, CA: University of California Press).

Shin, K. (2008) 'A Development of the "Jinbo" Women's Movement in Korea since the 1980s', *Journal of Gender Studies*, 11: 107–24.

Shorter, E., and Tilly, C. (1974) *Strikes in France 1830–1968* (Cambridge: Cambridge University Press).

Shugart, M. S., and Carey, J. M. (1992) *Presidents and Assemblies* (New York: Cambridge University Press).

Sidahmed, A. (2013) 'Oil and Politics in Sudan', in G. Sørbø and G. A Ahmed (eds) *Sudan Divided: Continuing Conflict in a Contested State* (New York: Palgrave Macmillan), 103–20.

Silverman, S. F. (1977) 'Patronage and Community–Nation Relationships in Central Italy', in S. Schmidt, J. C. Scott, C. Landé, and L. Guasti (eds) *Friends, Followers and Factions: A Reader in Political Clientelism* (Berkeley, CA, and London: University of California Press).

Singh, S. K. (2007) 'India and West Africa: A Burgeoning Relationship', Chatham House Africa Programme Briefing Paper, available online at http://www.chathamhouse.org/publications/papers/view/108471

Sisk, T. D. (2013) *Statebuilding* (London: Polity Press).

Sklair, L. (1991) *Sociology of the Global System* (London: Prentice-Hall).

Skocpol, T. (1985) 'Bringing the State back in: Strategies of Analysis in Current Research', in P. Evans, D. Rueshmeyer, and T. Skocpol (eds) *Bringing the State back in* (Cambridge: Cambridge University Press), 3–38.

Slater, D. (2004) *Geopolitics and the Postcolonial: Rethinking North–South Relations* (Oxford: Blackwell).

Smith, A. D. (1991) *National Identity* (Harmondsworth: Penguin).

Smith, D. (1990) 'Limits of Religious Resurgence', in E. Sahliyeh (ed.) *Religious Resurgence and Politics in the Contemporary World* (Albany, NY: State University of New York Press), 33–44.

Snow, D. A., Soule, S. A., and Kriesi, H. (2004) *The Blackwell Companion to Social Movements* (Malden: Blackwell).

Snyder, J. (2000) *From Voting to Violence* (New York: W.W. Norton).

Snyder, R., and Durán-Martínez, A. (2009) 'Does Illegality Breed Violence? Drug Trafficking and State-Sponsored Protection Rackets', *Crime, Law, and Social Change*, 52(3): 253–73.

Sørbø, G., and Ahmed, G. A. (eds) (2013) *Sudan Divided: Continuing Conflict in a Contested State* (New York: Palgrave Macmillan).

State Council Information Office (2014) 'China's Foreign Aid (2014)', 20 July, available online at http://english.gov.cn/archive/white_paper/2014/08/23/content_281474982986592.htm

Stepan, A. (2000) 'Religion, Democracy, and the "Twin Tolerations"', *Journal of Democracy*, 11(4): 37–57.

Stewart, F. (ed.) (2008) *Horizontal Inequalities and Conflict: Understanding Group Violence in Multi-Ethnic Societies* (Basingstoke: Palgrave Macmillan).

Stiglitz, J. (1998) 'More Instruments and Broader Goals: Moving towards a Post-Washington Consensus', UNU-WIDER Annual Lecture, 7 January, Helsinki, Finland.

Stiglitz, J. (2002) *Globalization and its Discontents* (London: Allen Lane).

Stiglitz, J. (2012) *The Prices of Inequality* (London: Allen Lane).

Stiglitz, J. (2015) *The Great Divide* (London: Allen Lane).

Stockemer, D. (2011) 'The Successful Creation of Attac France: The Role of Structure and Agency', *French Politics*, 9(2): 120–38.

Stockholm International Peace Research Institute (SIPRI) (2015) *SIPRI Yearbook: World Armaments and Disarmament* (Oxford : Oxford University Press).

Stokes, S., Thad, D., Marcelo, N., and Valeria, B. (2013) *Brokers, Voters and Clientelism: The Puzzle of Distributive Politics* (New York: Cambridge University Press).

Suberu, R. J. (2008) 'The Supreme Court and Federalism in Nigeria', *Journal of Modern African Studies*, 46(3): 451–85.

Suh, D. (2011) 'Institutionalizing Social Movements: The Dual Strategy of the Korean Women's Movement', *The Sociological Quarterly*, 52(3): 442–71.

Suhrke, A. (2011) *When More is Less: The International Project in Afghanistan* (London and New York: Hurst & Co./Columbia University Press).

Sumner, A. (2010) 'Global Poverty and the New Bottom Billion: Three-Quarters of the World's Poor Live in Middle-Income Countries', IDS Working Paper No. 349, available online at http://www.ids.ac.uk/files/dmfile/Wp349.pdf

Sutton, P. (1991) 'Constancy, Change and Accommodation: The Distinct Tradition of the Commonwealth Caribbean', in J. Mayall and A. Payne (eds) *The Fallacies of Hope: The post-Colonial Record of the Commonwealth Third World* (Manchester: Manchester University Press), 106–17.

Swatuk, L. A., and Shaw, T. M. (1994) *The South at the End of the Twentieth Century* (New York: St Martin's Press).

Swedish International Development Cooperation Agency (SIDA) (2002) *Good Governance* (Stockholm: SIDA, Division for Democratic Governance).

Tan-Mullins, M., Mohan, G., and Power, M. (2010) 'Redefining "Aid" in the China–Africa Context', *Development and Change*, 41(5): 857–81.

Tarrow, S. (1998) *Power in Movement: Social Movements and Contentious Politics*, 2nd edn (Cambridge: Cambridge University Press).

Tawney, R. H. (1952) *Inequality* (London: Allen and Unwin).

Taylor, I. (2009a) *China's New Role in Africa* (Boulder, CO: Lynne Rienner).

Taylor, R. (2009b) *The State in Myanmar* (Honolulu, HI: University of Hawaii Press).

Teorell, J. (2010) *Determinants of Democratization: Explaining Regime Change in the World, 1972–2006* (Cambridge: Cambridge University Press).

Thelen, K. (2004) *How Institutions Evolve: The Political Economy of Skills in Germany, Britain, the United States and Japan* (New York: Cambridge University Press).

Thelen, K., and Steinmo, S. (1992) *Structuring Politics: Historical Institutionalism in Comparative Analysis* (New York: Cambridge University Press).

Therkildsen, O. (2004) 'The Autonomy of Revenue Authorities in sub-Saharan Africa: The Case of Uganda', *Forum for Development Studies*, 31(1): 59–88.

Thiong'o, N. (1986) *Decolonising the Mind: The Politics of Language in African Literature* (London: James Currey).

Thomas, C., and Wilkin, P. (2004) 'Still Waiting after All These Years: The Third World on the Periphery of International Relations', *British Journal of Politics and International Relations*, 6(2): 241–58.

Tilly, C. (ed.) (1975) *The Formation of National States in Western Europe* (Princeton, NJ: Princeton University Press).

Tilly, C. (1990) *Coercion, Capital and European States, AD 990–1990* (Oxford: Basil Blackwell).

Tilly, C. (2003) *The Politics of Collective Violence* (Cambridge, Cambridge University Press).

Toft, M. D. (2003) *The Geography of Ethnic Violence: Identity, Interests and the Indivisibility of Territory* (Princeton, NJ: Princeton University Press).

Tomlinson, B. R. (1993) *The New Cambridge History of India, III.3: The Economy of Modern India, 1860–1970* (Cambridge: Cambridge University Press).

Tomsa, D. (2008) *Party Politics and Democratization in Indonesia: Golkar in the post-Suharto Era* (London: Routledge).

Tomsa, D. (2009a) 'Electoral Democracy in a Divided Society: The 2008 Gubernatorial Election in Maluku, Indonesia', *South East Asia Research*, 17(2): 229–59.

Tomsa, D. (2009b) 'Uneven Party Institutionalization, Protracted Transition and the Remarkable Resilience of Golkar', in M. Bünte and A. Ufen (eds) *Democratisation in post-Suharto Indonesia* (London: Routledge), 176–98.

Tordoff, W. (1997) *Government and Politics in Africa* (London: Macmillan).

Törnquist, O. (2013) *Assessing Dynamics of Democratisation: Transformative Politics: New Institutions, and the Case of Indonesia* (New York: Palgrave MacMillan).

Transparency International (2005) *Global Corruption Report* (Cambridge: Cambridge University Press).

Transparency International (2012) 'Corruption Perceptions Index 2012', available online at http://www.transparency.org/cpi2012/results

Treisman, D. (2007) 'What Have We Learned about the Causes of Corruption from Ten Years of cross-National Empirical Research?', *Annual Review of Political Science*, 10: 211–44.

Tripp, A. M., Casimiro, I., Kwesiga, J., and Mungwa, M. (2009) *African Women's Movements: Changing Political Landscapes* (Cambridge: Cambridge University Press).

Tripp, C. (2002) *A History of Iraq* (Cambridge: Cambridge University Press).

Tsai, L. (2007) *Accountability without Democracy: Solidary Groups and Public Goods Provision in Rural China* (New York: Cambridge University Press).

Ufen, A. (2009) 'Political Parties and Democratization in Indonesia', in M. Bünte and A. Ufen (eds) *Democratization in post-Suharto Indonesia* (London: Routledge), 153–75.

United Nations (1992) *An Agenda for Peace: Preventive Diplomacy, Peacemaking and Peace-Keeping—Report of the Secretary-General pursuant to the statement adopted by the Summit Meeting of the Security Council on 31 January 1992*, UN Doc. A/47/277–S/24111, available online at http://www.un-documents.net/a47-277.htm

United Nations (2009) *Report of the Secretary-General on Peacebuilding in the Immediate Aftermath of Conflict* (New York: United Nations).

United Nations Conference on Trade and Development (UNCTAD) (2015a) *UNCTAD Handbook of Statistics* (New York and Geneva: United Nations).

United Nations Conference on Trade and Development (UNCTAD) (2015b) *State of Commodity Dependence 2014* (New York and Geneva: United Nations).

United Nations Department of Peacekeeping Operations (UN DPI) (2016) 'Peacekeeping Factsheet', available online at http://www.un.org/en/peacekeeping/resources/statistics/factsheet.shtml

United Nations Development Programme (Various years) *Human Development Reports* (New York and Oxford: Oxford University Press).

United Nations Development Programme (UNDP) (2013) *Humanity Divided: Confronting Inequality in Developing Countries* (New York: UNDP).

United Nations High Commissioner for Refugees (UNHCR) (2015) *World at War: UNHCR Global Trends—Forced Displacements in 2014* (Geneva: UNHCR).

United Nations Independent International Commission of Inquiry (2011) *Report of the Independent International Commission of Inquiry on the Syrian Arab Republic*, Human Rights Council, 17th special session, 23 November, available online at https://daccess-ods.un.org/TMP/5660051.70345306.html

United Nations Office for the Coordination of Humanitarian Affairs (UNOCHA) (2015) *Iraq, Crisis Situation Report No. 47*, 3–9 June, available online at https://www.humanitarianresponse.info/en/operations/iraq/document/ocha-iraq-crisis-situation-report-no-47-3-june-%E2%80%93-9-june-2015

United States Agency for International Development (USAID) (2005) 'Democracy and Governance', available online at http://www.usaid/gov/our_work/democracy_and_governance/

Van Cott, D. L. (2005) *From Movements to Parties in Latin America: The Evolution of Ethnic Politics* (New York: Cambridge University Press).

van Klinken, G. (2007) *Communal Violence and Democratization in Indonesia: Small Town War* (Leiden: KITLV).

van Klinken, G. (2010) 'Patronage Democracy in Provincial Indonesia', in J. Harriss, K. Stokke, and O. Törnquist (eds) *Rethinking Popular Representation* (Basingstoke: Palgrave Macmillan), 141–59.

van Klinken, G., and Barter, J. (eds) (2009) *State of Authority: State in Society in Indonesia* (Ithaca, NY: Cornell University Press).

Vanhanen, T. (2000) 'A New Dataset for Measuring Democracy, 1810–1998', *Journal of Peace Research*, 37(2): 251–65.

Vincent, L. (2004) 'Quotas for Women: Do the Numbers Count?', *Journal of Legislative Studies*, 10(1): 71–96.

Viswanathan, G. (1990) *Masks of Conquest: Literary Study and British Rule in India* (London: Faber & Faber).

Vogel, D. (1997) *Trading up: Consumer and Environmental Regulation in the Global Economy*, 2nd edn (Cambridge, MA: Harvard University Press).

Walker, A. (2012) 'What is Boko Haram?', US Institute of Peace Special Report No. 308, available online at http://www.usip.org/sites/default/files/SR308.pdf

Wallerstein, I. (1979) 'The Rise and Future Demise of the World Capitalist System: Concepts for Comparative Analysis', in I. Wallerstein (ed.) *The Capitalist World-Economy* (Cambridge: Cambridge University Press), 1–36.

Wallerstein, I. (2003) *The Decline of American Power* (New York: The New Press).

Warburg, G. (2003) *Islam, Sectarianism, and Politics in Sudan since the Mahdiyya* (London: Hurst & Co.).

Watt, C. (2011) 'Introduction: The Relevance and Complexity of Civilizing Missions c. 1800–2010', in C. Watt and M. Mann (eds) *Civilizing Missions in Colonial and Postcolonial South Asia: From Improvement to Development* (London: Anthem Press), 1–34.

Waylen, G. (1993) 'Women's Movements and Democratisation in Latin America', *Third World Quarterly*, 14(3): 573–87.

Waylen, G. (2007) *Engendering Transitions: Women's Mobilization, Institutions and Gender Outcomes* (Oxford: Oxford University Press).

Weber, M. (1948 [1919]) 'Politics as a Vocation', in H. Gerth and C.W. Mills (eds) *From Maz Weber: Essays in Sociology* (New York: Oxford University Press), 77–128.

Weber, M. (1970) *From Max Weber: Essays in Sociology*, ed. H. H. Gerth and C. Wright Mills (London: Routledge).

Weber, M. (1978) *Economy and Society: An Outline of Interpretive Sociology* (Berkeley, CA: University of California Press).

Weigel, G. (2005) *Witness to Hope: The Biography of Pope John Paul II, 1920–2005* (New York: HarperCollins).

Weigel, G. (2007) *Faith, Reason, and the War against Jihadism: A Call to Action* (New York: Doubleday).

Westad, O. A. (2005) *The Global Cold War: Third World Interventions and the Making of Our Times* (Cambridge: Cambridge University Press).

Wezeman, P. D., and Wezeman, S. T. (2015) 'Trends in International Arms Transfers, 2014', SIPRI Factsheet, available online at http://books.sipri.org/files/FS/SIPRIFS1503.pdf

Whatley, W. (2015) 'The Economic Legacies of the African Slave Trades', in C. Monga and J. Y. Lin (eds) *The Oxford Handbook of Africa and Economics, Vol. 1: Context and Concepts* (Oxford: Oxford University Press), 504–21.

White House (2002) *The National Security Strategy*, September, available online at http://georgewbush-whitehouse.archives.gov/nsc/nss/2002/

Wickramasinghe, N. (2006) *Sri Lanka in the Modern Age* (London: Hurst).

Wilkinson, S. (2004) *Votes and Violence* (New York: Cambridge University Press).

Williams, D., and Young, T. (2009) 'The International Politics of Social Transformation: Trusteeship and Intervention in Historical Perspective', in M. Duffield and V. Hewitt (eds) *Empire, Development and Colonialism. The Past in the Present* (Woodbridge: James Currey), 102–15.

Wilson, D., and Purushothaman, R. (2003) 'Dreaming with BRICS: The Path to 2050', Goldman Sachs

Global Economics Paper No. 99, available online at http://www.goldmansachs.com/our-thinking/archive/archive-pdfs/brics-dream.pdf

Wilson, D., and Stupnytska, A. (2007) 'The N-11: More than an Acronym', Goldman Sachs Global Economics Paper No. 153, available online at https://www.chicagobooth.edu/~/media/E60BDCEB6C5245E-59B7ADA7C6B1B6F2B.pdf

Wimmer, A. (2002) *Nationalist Exclusion and Ethnic Conflict: Shadows of Modernity* (New York: Cambridge University Press).

Wimmer A., Cederman, L.-E., and Min, B. (2009) 'Ethnic Politics and Armed Conflict. A Configurational Analysis of a New Global Dataset', *The American Sociological Review*, 74(2): 316–37.

Winters, J. A. (2011) *Oligarchy* (New York: Cambridge University Press).

Wolf-Phillips, L. (1979) 'Why Third World?', *Third World Quarterly*, 1(1): 105–13.

Wong, S. (2016) 'China Launches new AIIB Development Bank as Power Balance Shifts', *Reuters*, 17 January, available online at http://www.reuters.com/article/us-asia-aiib-investment-idUSKCN0UU03Y

Woo-Cummings, M. (ed.) (1999) *The Developmental State* (Ithaca, NY: Cornell University Press).

Wood, E. J. (2008) 'The Social Processes of Civil War', *Annual Review of Political Science*, 11(1): 539–61.

Woodberry, R. D. (2004) 'The Shadow of Empire: Christian Missions, Colonial Policy, and Democracy in Postcolonial Societies', Unpublished PhD dissertation, University of North Carolina at Chapel Hill.

Woods, N. (2008) 'Whose Aid? Whose Influence? China, Emerging Donors and the Silent Revolution in Development Assistance', *International Affairs*, 84(6): 1205–21.

Woodward, P. (1990) *Sudan 1898–1989: The Unstable Border* (Boulder, CO: Lynne Rienner).

World Bank (1994) *Adjustment in Africa: Reforms, Results and the Road Ahead* (Washington, DC: World Bank).

World Bank (1997) *World Development Report 1997: The State in a Changing World* (New York: Oxford University Press).

World Bank (2000) *Reforming Public Institutions and Strengthening Governance: A World Bank Strategy*,

available online at http://elibrary.worldbank.org/doi/abs/10.1596/0-8213-4875-2

World Bank (2001) *World Development Report 2001* (Washington, DC: World Bank).

World Bank (2009) *Guatemala: Poverty Assessment—Good Performance at Low Levels* (Washington, DC: World Bank).

World Bank (2011) *World Development Report 2011: Conflict, Security and Development* (Washington, DC: World Bank).

World Bank (2012) 'Iraq Country Report', available online at http://data.worldbank.org/country/iraq

World Bank (2015) 'Country at Glance: Korea', available online at http://www.worldbank.org/en/country/korea/overview

World Bank (2016) 'World Bank DataBank', available online at http://data.worldbank.org/products/wdi

World Economic Forum (WEF) (2015) *The Global Gender Gap Report 2015*, 10th anniversary edn, available online at http://www3.weforum.org/docs/GGGR2015/cover.pdf

World Trade Organization (WTO) (2015) 'Time Series Agricultural Data', available online at http://stat.wto.org/StatisticalProgram/WSDBStatProgramSeries.aspx?Language=E

Wrong, M. (2009) *It's Our Turn to Eat: A Story of a Kenyan Whistle Blower* (London: Fourth Estate).

Wucherpfennig, J., Metternich, N. W., Cederman, L. E., and Gleditsch, K. S. (2012) 'Ethnicity, the State and the Duration of Civil War', *World Politics*, 64(1): 79–115.

Yadav, Y. (1996) 'Reconfiguration in Indian Politics: State Assembly Elections, 1993–95', *Economic and Political Weekly*, 13–20 January: 95–104.

Young, C. (1976) *The Politics of Cultural Pluralism* (Madison, WI: University of Wisconsin Press).

Young, C. (1994) *The African Colonial State in Comparative Perspective* (New Haven, CT: Yale University Press).

Young, C. (1998) 'Country Report: The African Colonial State Revisited', *Governance: An International Journal of Policy and Administration*, 11(1): 101–20.

Young, C. (2001) 'Nationalism and Ethnic Conflict in Africa', in M. Guibernau and J. Hutchinson (eds) *Understanding Nationalism* (Cambridge: Polity Press), 164–81.

Young, C. (2012) *The Postcolonial State in Africa: Fifty Years of Independence, 1960–2010* (Madison, WI: University of Wisconsin Press).

Yuval-Davis, N. (1997) *Gender and Nation* (London: Sage).

XE (2016) 'Trading Basics You Should Know', available online at http://www.xe.com/currencytrading/basics.php

Zakaria, F. (1997) 'The Rise of Illiberal Democracy', *Foreign Affairs*, 76(6): 22–43.

Zaytuneh, R. (2009) 'Al-Islamiyun as-Suriyun wa Ghawayat "al-Jihad" fi al-"Iraq" [The Syrian Islamists and the Lure of "Jihad" in Iraq]', *Markaz al-Mesbar li al-Dirasat wa al-Buhuth*, available online at http://www.ikhwanwiki.com/index.php?title= (الحركة_وعنف_لطائفة_ممانعة_)_سوريا_في_المسلمون_الإخوان #.D8.AA.D9.82.D8.AF.D9.8A.D9.85

Zia, A. S. (2009) 'The Reinvention of Feminism in Pakistan', *Feminist Review*, 91(1): 29–46.

Zolberg, A., Suhrke, A., and Aguayo, S. (1989) *Escape from Violence: Conflict and the Refugee Crisis in the Developing World* (New York: Oxford University Press).

Index